Alex Lewis
Tom Pacyk
David Ross
Randy Wintle

Microsoft®
Lync® Server
2013

UNLEASHED

SAMS | 800 East 96th Street, Indianapolis, Indiana 46240 USA

Microsoft® Lync® Server 2013 Unleashed

ISBN-13: 978-0-672-33615-7
ISBN-10: 0-672-33615-4

Library of Congress Control Number: 2013935207

Printed in the United States of America

First Printing April 2013

Trademarks

All terms mentioned in this book that are known to be trademarks or service marks have been appropriately capitalized. Sams Publishing cannot attest to the accuracy of this information. Use of a term in this book should not be regarded as affecting the validity of any trademark or service mark.

Warning and Disclaimer

Every effort has been made to make this book as complete and as accurate as possible, but no warranty or fitness is implied. The information provided is on an "as is" basis. The authors and the publisher shall have neither liability nor responsibility to any person or entity with respect to any loss or damages arising from the information contained in this book.

Bulk Sales

Sams Publishing offers excellent discounts on this book when ordered in quantity for bulk purchases or special sales. For more information, please contact

U.S. Corporate and Government Sales
1-800-382-3419
corpsales@pearsontechgroup.com

For sales outside of the U.S., please contact

International Sales
international@pearsoned.com

Editor-in-Chief
Greg Wiegand

Executive Editor
Loretta Yates

Development Editor
Mark Renfrow

Managing Editor
Kristy Hart

Senior Project Editor
Lori Lyons

Copy Editor
Cheri Clark

Indexer
Tim Wright

Proofreader
Katherin Ruiz

Technical Editor
Mitch Steiner

Contributing Writers
Tom Arbuthnot
Chad McGreanor

Publishing Coordinator
Cindy Teeters

Book Designer
Gary Adair

Compositor
Nonie Ratcliff

Contents at a Glance

Table of Contents

Foreword

I once remarked, "Nothing sells itself, but Lync comes pretty darn close." The statement resonates because Microsoft Lync is one of those products that come along every once in a while that infuse the user with superhuman power to take *action*. Where so many products *can* do something, Lync *does* do something—right out-of-the-box—and this something is as fundamental as human-to-human communication and collaboration.

If this sounds lofty and grand, it's because it is. Businesses that adopt Lync measure their return on investment in months, not years. They also gain something entirely new: accessibility and fluidity in collaboration that didn't previously exist and can't easily be measured. Although user adoption is a critical component of any successful deployment, the challenge is easily surmountable because the Lync user interface is inviting and intuitive. Our contacts are identified by their photos, not phone numbers, and video calling lets us look each other in the eye when we're having a conversation. Presence enables us to be telepathic about our peer's availability, and the desktop sharing gives new meaning to the phrase "a picture is worth a thousand words." The technology churning just below the surface is implemented in such a way that the user never thinks about it. It just works, especially when a user is outside of the office, when connectedness is most critical.

I predict that 2013 is the year that Lync will become the de facto communications platform for the Enterprise. If Lync 2010 answered the question about whether Lync could be a credible PBX replacement, then Lync 2013 goes a step further and changes the questions. Companies that are running separate projects to deploy voice and video should seriously consider revising their RFP process and take a hard look at Lync.

Video and mobility are the truly exciting new features in Lync 2013. Lync 2013 supports 1080p HD resolution for video conferencing so participants have a sharp, clear display. Lync 2013 also uses standard video codecs like H.264 SVC to provide compatibility across a broader range of platforms and devices, which provides greater flexibility in terms of how video is delivered. Microsoft is also developing Lync Mobile apps for Windows Phone, iOS, and Android, so these communications modalities are available almost universally, a feature that we've all been waiting for with bated breath.

This is all very exciting, but the technology doesn't implement itself. Alex, Randy, Tom, Dave, and the other contributors involved in creating this book are all experts and educators in their field, drawing on years of experience designing, deploying, and supporting unified communications technologies. Organizations will need to make choices about how to design and deploy Lync 2013, and this book is an exceptional resource and reference for informing the individuals who need to make those choices.

John Lamb
Co-Founder, Modality Systems

About the Authors

Alex Lewis

Alex Lewis, MCITP, CISSP, has a mixed background in telecommunications, IT, and consulting, with more than 15 years of experience. He has worked with the Lync family of products since the Exchange 2000 instant messaging service and a number of other solutions, including Cisco, Avaya, Nortel, Shoretel, and NEC. He has worked with a wide range of environments from small organizations to large enterprises requiring complex or custom communications solutions, and he is responsible for architecting and implementing some of the largest Lync deployments in the world. Alex is a strong believer in the power of business and technology alignment using technological solutions to reduce costs and drive revenue and leveraging Communications Enabled Business Processes (CEBP) to accelerate business success. Including titles on Active Directory and Exchange, and two on Lync, Alex has participated in writing eight books from 2004 to present. He is currently principal consultant at Modality Systems, a boutique international consulting firm focused on Microsoft unified communications. He loves a challenge and brings a wealth of experience to each new engagement. In his spare time Alex enjoys scuba diving with sharks and beach volleyball.

Tom Pacyk

Tom Pacyk is one of only a few people worldwide to hold both the Microsoft Certified Master certification and the Microsoft Most Valuable Professional award for Lync Server. Tom works as a Principal Systems Architect at ExtraTeam and is currently based in Chicago, Illinois. He began his career as a systems administrator and has moved into working as a consultant for the past seven years, designing and implementing collaboration solutions for large and small customers. His Unified Communications work began with the original Exchange 2000 instant messaging service, and he has been involved with implementations of every version of the product up to Lync Server 2013. Outside of work Tom runs a blog related to Microsoft Lync and Exchange topics, and he enjoys writing thrilling nonfiction books such as this one.

David Ross

David Ross, MCITP, VCP, CCEA, CCSP, has over 14 years of experience in IT consulting, the majority of which has been spent playing the lead architect role on network design and implementation projects throughout the San Francisco Bay area. David is currently acting as a principal engineer for Convergent Computing, and he develops hybrid solutions involving multiple vendor technologies for organizations of all sizes. Specialties for David include Active Directory, Exchange, Lync, Citrix technologies, virtualization solutions using VMware vSphere and Microsoft Hyper-V, and Cisco routing, switching, and security technologies.

Randy Wintle

Randy is a Unified Communications Architect specializing in planning, architecture, and implementation of enterprise unified communications solutions. Randy has an exceptional track record for driving success on large enterprise deployments of Microsoft OCS and Lync Server 2010. He has successfully guided several large organizations in their development of strategies to enhance their business through Microsoft UC solutions. Randy is both a Microsoft Certified Master and a Microsoft MVP for Lync Server 2010, a rare combination and evidence of his technical prowess and recognition as an industry expert. Randy frequently participates in community and Microsoft-sponsored technical events. He helped develop the Microsoft training and certification programs for Lync and OCS. Randy has been previously published in the book *Microsoft Lync Server 2010 Resource Kit.* He has also contributed to many online white papers and has a very successful UC blog.

Dedications

Alex Lewis: *I couldn't have done it without you, Kate. You're the best, on so many levels! I know I promised you no more books, yet you still love me in spite of this book...and the inevitable next one.*

Tom Pacyk: *This book is dedicated to my daughter Madeline, who was born this past year. May this book forever serve as a bedtime story guaranteed to easily put you to sleep.*

David Ross: *I dedicate this book to Lisette, my soul mate, who continues to provide inspiration even after she is no longer with us. You always encouraged everyone around you to continue growing and reach their potential, and this project is another evidence of the positive effect this had on me. When the day arrives that we can see you again, how wonderful it will be to catch you up on all the memories that you missed, and then make new ones. The boys and I look forward to that day with great anticipation.*

Randy Wintle: *I dedicate this book to my father, Rod Wintle, who is both my personal and my professional mentor.*

Acknowledgments

Alex Lewis

First of all, thank you to the Sams team for all your patience and hard work to make this book a success. It wasn't always smooth, but I'm very proud of the end product we've all produced. A *big* thank-you to John Lamb and the Modality Systems team. After being friends for years, I'm honored to be working together. We make a great team, like Maverick and Goose. Just remember, I'm Maverick. Thank you to Rand Morimoto of CCO for your mentorship, guidance, and help in balancing my technical skills with business expertise.

To all my friends, thank you for your endless understanding of all the nights I couldn't go out, all the trips I couldn't join you for, and all the fun I missed. Although you sufficiently rubbed it in, I love you all and I couldn't ask for better friends. Finally, to Pugsley, you've been my best friend and companion through two books now. Every tired night, working till sunrise, you've been there by my side urging me to go on...or at least to not type too loudly and wake you up. You epitomize man's best friend; you're definitely mine!

Tom Pacyk

The folks at Sams deserve a huge thank-you for formatting and making sense of the raw technical jargon we delivered to them. There is a massive amount of behind-the-scenes work that goes into making this text look respectable, so thank you to everyone involved on that end! Thank you to all the coauthors and contributors who helped make this book a solid resource for readers.

And thanks to all my family and friends for being so understanding about the lost nights and weekends spent writing, editing, and editing again. (I swear I would have rather spent the time with you!).

David Ross

Crissy and Jason, thanks for being there. Your value obviously goes far beyond this book, but the fact is this project would not have been possible without your help. Big thanks also to my entire "personal army" of family and friends for all of your love and support, and just for being a part of our lives at such a critical time. Special shout-out to the Schoenwald and Parish clans for the continuous help with the boys; don't underestimate what a huge help you are. Finally, thanks to Alex for the opportunity to collaborate on this book, and to the good folks at Sams, thanks for your support throughout the project.

Randy Wintle

I'd first like to thank the entire team that worked on this amazing project with me, including the Sams team, Alex, Tom, Dave, and Mitch. This book was an adventure, and one that was well worth the effort everyone has put into it.

To my wife, Caryn, and my son, Rylan. Your love and support motivate me to do everything that I do. I am the luckiest father and husband in the world. To my parents, who over the years have provided me endless support which has led to many opportunities, without which I would not be in the position I am today. Also, to the entire Lync community—especially my fellow MVPs and MCMs. The Lync community is so full of talented individuals who never think twice to help each other out. Lastly, I would like to thank Chris Claudio: By providing me a starting point for my professional consulting career, you have made all of this possible, and I truly appreciate all of your support.

We Want to Hear from You!

As the reader of this book, *you* are our most important critic and commentator. We value your opinion and want to know what we're doing right, what we could do better, what areas you'd like to see us publish in, and any other words of wisdom you're willing to pass our way.

We welcome your comments. You can email or write to let us know what you did or didn't like about this book—as well as what we can do to make our books better.

Please note that we cannot help you with technical problems related to the topic of this book.

When you write, please be sure to include this book's title and author as well as your name and email address. We will carefully review your comments and share them with the author and editors who worked on the book.

E-mail: consumer@samspublishing.com

Mail: Sams Publishing
         ATTN: Reader Feedback
         800 East 96th Street
         Indianapolis, IN 46240 USA

Reader Services

Visit our website and register this book at informit.com/register for convenient access to any updates, downloads, or errata that might be available for this book.

Introduction

Lync 2013 is an evolutionary step forward for Unified Communications (UC). It takes the Gartner-rated leader in UC a step further and widens the gap between Microsoft and a number of other contenders.

The authors of this book have been working with Lync through many name changes and since the Live Communications Server 2003 days. I remember when it launched on December 29, 2003. Back then, Windows Messenger 5.0 was the main client used, and the terminology was completely different. Even then, however, TLS communication was supported, although most IT departments went with the more familiar TCP option instead. Needless to say, a lot has changed through the years. Most people I work with don't realize that Lync Server 2013 is a sixth-generation product! It is even older if you count the Exchange Instant Messenger Service that was included in Exchange Server 2000, which was pulled out to build the first version of Live Communications Server.

In the beginning, Live Communications Server 2003 was only an IM server. Lync Server 2010 brought the platform to a widely deployed PBX replacement, and Lync Server 2013 expands on this functionality with large strides in the emerging video conferencing space and a much more advanced client. Lync 2013 includes:

▶ Web and audio conferencing server with an advanced web client

▶ Unified Communications (UC) integration across many other platforms, such as Office, SharePoint, and Exchange

▶ Soft phone

▶ Video conferencing system

▶ PBX replacement and integration with numerous existing PBX platforms

Back in 2003, IM was perceived as a novelty. No one used it to conduct business or even imagined it as a gateway to multimodal communications. Starting with Office Communications Server 2007 R2 and continuing with Lync Server, Microsoft introduced the concept of Communications Enabled Business Processes (CEBP).

> **NOTE**
>
> It seems every vendor and analyst defines CEBP in a different way. For this book, however, we stick with a more generic definition. CEBP adds a communications medium to a business process with the intent of streamlining and automating the process, or with the intent of reducing human latency through real-time communications. This is discussed in more detail throughout the book starting in Chapter 4.

Chronology of Lync Server 2013

Let's go through some history and chronology to better understand why and how Lync Server 2013 came to be over the last 10 years.

▶ **Exchange Server 2000 Instant Messenger Service**—It's hard to believe so few people, even Exchange administrators, had heard of the Exchange 2000 IM service. However, it is not hard to believe that even fewer deployed it. It was a rudimentary service with little integration to Exchange or other Microsoft Server products. Later versions utilized special engines, whereas the Exchange 2000 IM service leveraged an in-house middleware platform called Exchange Interprocess Communication (EXIPC) to translate between IIS 5 and Exchange. The solution was essentially composed of two types of servers—home servers and routing servers.

Home servers handled IM communications similarly to a front end in Lync Server 2010. However, there was little Active Directory integration. That's where routing servers came in. If two users were homed to different home servers, they would need to jump through a bunch of hoops to talk with each other. The routing server acted as a bridge connecting any two home servers. It was a basic solution, especially at a time when public IM providers such as Yahoo and AOL offered significantly more in terms of functionality.

▶ **Live Communications Server 2003**—Instant messaging functions were taken out of Exchange and given their own platforms with the 2003 wave of Microsoft Server products. It was code named Greenwich and initially called Office Real-Time Communications Server 2003 before being renamed Live Communications Server 2003 just prior to release. It wasn't long before it was better known by its three-letter acronym LCS 2003. LCS 2003 was the first version to support certificates and offer TLS-encrypted communications as the recommended method. LCS 2003 was also the first version to support enterprise archival of IM communications, though it was rarely implemented because the compliance regulations in effect today simply didn't exist or include IM conversations in 2003.

▶ **Live Communications Server 2005**—Live Communications Server 2005, or LCS 2005 as it's more commonly known, was the first widely deployed version of the Microsoft real-time communications platform. It was code named Vienna. Although one might argue that LCS 2005 was Microsoft's first attempt at a unified communications platform, few organizations deployed functions beyond IM and presence. LCS 2005 added new functions, including a more advanced presence engine that would change a user's presence status based on information from a user's Exchange calendar and remote access through the access proxy role. LCS 2005 SP1 added the capability to communicate with Office Communications Server 2007 users and a number of other features. In today's Microsoft nomenclature, it would likely be called Live Communications Server 2005 R2.

▶ **Office Communications Server 2007**—Code named RTC12, this is when the creative codenames went the way of the dodo bird. Commonly known as OCS 2007, the platform made a huge jump in terms of functionality and acceptance. OCS 2007 added the following functions:

▶ **On-Premise Web Conferencing**—The return on investment (ROI) from bringing web conferencing in-house almost always justified the cost of implementing OCS; thus, it became an important feature. However, voice conferencing was PC-only or needed to be hosted through a third-party provider.

▶ **Multi-party IM**—It might seem insignificant to add more than one person to an IM conversation, but it became an important market differentiator compared to products like IBM SameTime and Cisco CUPS.

▶ **Enhanced presence**—Also known as "rich presence," it enabled users to expose additional information beyond the red, green, and yellow gumdrop that was standard at the time. This information included name, title, and detailed calendar information. It also included a multitiered access mechanism called levels of access to display different amounts of personal information to different tiers of users.

▶ **Improved federation**—Open federation and widespread adoption of OCS 2007 changed the landscape of intercompany communication. E-mail became secondary for partner communication as users could see real time availability data and collaborate immediately, removing the latency inherent to asynchronous methods of communication.

▶ **Enterprise Voice**—It's simply not possible to call your solution a unified communications solution without the inclusion of a voice platform. Although it was basic, it was a proactive step in the right direction because almost every other UC vendor would also roll out a combined IM, meeting, and voice platform around the same time or soon after.

▶ **Office Communications Server 2007 R2**—When combined with Exchange Unified Messaging, this was the first version that could realistically be considered a PBX replacement, though it still lacked many traditional PBX features. Code named Wave 13 or W13, OCS 2007 R2 added a bunch of collaboration and voice features as noted in the following:

  ▶ **Call Delegation**—Also known as the boss-secretary function, this enabled delegates to answer a call for another user. The primary user also notified the delegate answered the call. This function was designed to be used with the Communicator Attendant Console. Much like with delegates in Exchange, the assistant could be given the rights to do almost everything for the manager yet make it appear that the manager was doing the work. A full call delegation feature list follows:

    ▶ Call screening for audio, video, or IM

    ▶ Joining a voice conference on behalf of the manager

    ▶ Checking voicemail for the manager

    ▶ Initiating a person-to-person call on behalf of the manager

    ▶ Initiating conference calls on behalf of the manager

    ▶ Transferring calls to the manager

▶ **Team Call**—A simple workflow that enabled call forwarding to multiple people. The call could be forwarded to specific people in sequence or in parallel. This was often used for out-of-office or out-to-lunch functions.

▶ **Group Chat**—A separate server role that also required a separate client from Communicator. It allowed persistent chat similar to IRC.

▶ **Desktop sharing**—This included desktop sharing from the Communicator client and with anonymous users through the Communicator Web Access service.

▶ **Audio conferencing**—Much like web conferencing in OCS 2007, this is another great ROI story. Third-party audio conferencing services can be expensive; tens of thousands of dollars per month can be saved by bringing it in-house. Many companies deployed OCS 2007 R2 strictly for this functionality; everything else was just a bonus.

▶ **Response Group Service**—This is Microsoft's version of a simple IVR workflow. It's often used for small call centers or IT help desks.

▶ **SIP trunking**—SIP trunking is still new but seeing a growth in adoption. Essentially, it enabled OCS 2007 R2 to connect to a SIP trunking provider that handled all outbound call routing. Although the process can be a little complex to set up initially, it greatly eases call routing topology because everything goes to the cloud service provider.

▶ **Improved codecs**—Improved codecs for voice and video enable better voice quality and more tolerance for nonideal networks. They also enable HD-quality video between clients over reasonable network links.

▶ **Lync Server 2010**—Code named CS2010 and OCS W14, this was the first version that found widespread adoption as a PBX replacement. Lync 2010 added the following functions:

▶ **Unified client**—Gone are the separate clients for IM and conferencing. With Lync 2010, everything could be done from a single client.

▶ **Web Conferencing Web Client**—A web-based conferencing client for participants who did not have the Lync client.

▶ **Photo Display**—The ability for users to display custom photos or a photo from Active Directory.

▶ **Advanced Voice Routing**—This function is two-fold. Lync Server 2010 introduced advanced voice routing on the server side but also allowed users a number of complex voice routing options in the Lync client.

▶ **Integration with Room-based Video Systems**—Through partnerships with Polycom and LifeSize, Lync is able to interoperate with traditional video conference room systems.

How This Book Is Organized

Everything you want to know about new features for Lync Server 2013 is included in Chapters 1–4. These chapters describe new features and benefits.

You will find that the improvements Microsoft has made to Lync Server 2013 are not only evolutionary, but they represent a major step forward for Unified Communications. Lync Server 2013 solidifies Microsoft's role as market leader in the UC field.

> **CAUTION**
>
> This book covers all aspects of Lync Server 2013. However, the book does assume the reader has at least a cursory knowledge of the basics of Active Directory, DNS, and the associated infrastructure of each.

This book is organized into nine parts, each one made up of several chapters focusing on a different core area of Lync Server 2013.

▶ **Part I, "Lync Server 2013 Overview"**—This part provides an introduction to Lync Server not only from the perspective of a general technology overview, but also to note what's new in Lync Server and what has compelled organizations we've worked with to implement it during the beta phase.

▶ **Part II, "Microsoft Lync Server 2013 Server Roles"**—This part provides an in-depth discussion of all the Lync Server 2013 roles including a general overview, the installation process, configuration, administration, troubleshooting, and best practices. Each role is examined in detail with step-by-step installation instructions and valuable screenshots. There have been some major changes since Lync Server 2010!

▶ **Part III, "External Dependencies"**—Lync Server 2013 leverages many other technologies including Active Directory, DNS, certificates, and SQL Server. It also has specific prerequisites and requirements around network latency, bandwidth, and firewall and reverse proxies for external access and federation. Lync Server 2013 relies heavily on Active Directory for integration to other Microsoft Server components such as Microsoft Exchange and Microsoft SharePoint.

▶ **Part IV, "Administration and Management"**—This part covers common administration tasks and the Lync Server Management Shell, which is the heart of all administration tasks. It moves on to discuss monitoring Lync Server 2013 through Microsoft Systems Center Operations Manager and high-availability processes for all the Lync Server roles.

▶ **Part V, "Migrating from Older Versions"**— A green field deployment is easy; migrating users, response groups, and dial plans from a previous versions of Lync Server can cause headaches. A solid, tested migration strategy is important for minimizing downtime and ensuring a successful migration. The bad news is there is only one way to do it. The good news is that it is explained in great detail in Part 5.

▶ **Part VI, "Lync Voice, Video, and Integration"**— Lync 2010 established the platform as a legitimate PBX replacement and video conferencing solution. Lync 2013 extends both of these functions and rewrites the interoperability story on both fronts. This section discusses Lync as a standalone telephony solution and integrated with other voice solutions, Lync integration with various video platforms and various 3rd party solutions such as voice gateways, video gateways and cloud services.

▶ **Part VII, "Integration with Other Applications"**—Lync Server 2013 has unique communications and collaboration features when integrated with other applications. Presence can be brought into a SharePoint page or Exchange Outlook Web Application. The Exchange Unified Messaging server completes the Microsoft UC solution. New in Lync Server 2013 are the Unified Contact Store and the ability to upload pictures to a dedicated server instead of bloating Active Directory.

▶ **Part VIII, "Office 365 and Lync Online"**—Cloud services ring loud from every CIO summit in the world. Regardless of their actual merit, many organizations are at least piloting cloud solutions. This section includes the Microsoft Office 365 story and hybrid integration with Lync Online.

▶ **Part IX, "Lync Server 2013 Clients"**—From a user's perspective, the solution *is* the client. That's all a user sees. Lync 2013 offers much improved clients over the already outstanding Lync 2010 versions. A fully featured web client with audio and video is offered along with a more robust mobile client. Lync 2013 rolls out a whole new list of UC-certified endpoints. Finally, VDI is now fully supported and provides a unique solution for deployment.

▶ **Part X, "Planning for Deployment"**—Every good deployment starts with a good plan. This part can help you build a plan for your organization. It covers the full gamut of Lync deployment options from a basic deployment to virtualization to complex voice deployments. Although Lync Server 2013 expertise is required, many other skill sets are also important to plan a successful deployment. Lync Server 2013 touches many other areas including PBX/telecommunications, Active Directory, Exchange, and the enterprise network. Although bringing in an expert is always a good strategy, this part educates you with the basics for planning your deployment.

▶ **Part XI, "Endpoints"**—UC adoption can be viral, but only if the right tools are in place and end users have a quality experience. To users, Lync is reflected in the quality of their experience. The best way to ensure a great experience is with certified quality UC endpoints. UC endpoints encompass a wide range of devices, which we cover. You'll also learn best practices for choosing and deploying UC endpoints for various scenarios.

The real-world experience we have working with Lync Server 2013, our combined experience with the platform since its beginnings, and our field experience deploying Lync Server enable us to present this information to you. We made the mistakes, found the workarounds, and simply know what works and how to do it right. We know you will find this book valuable with the planning and deployment of your Lync Server 2013 infrastructure.

PART I

Lync Server 2013 Overview

IN THIS PART

CHAPTER 1

Getting Started with Microsoft Lync Server 2013

For more than 10 years, Microsoft has been focused on a vision of providing an integrated software suite that allows users to communicate and collaborate in new and innovative ways. Lync Server 2013 represents the latest iteration in the product line that has been designed to fulfill that vision. As an alternative to traditional voice-only systems such as Private Branch Exchanges (PBX), Lync Server instead offers a software-based infrastructure that combines voice, video, instant messaging, conferencing, and collaboration managed from a single interface. The end result is a unified communications system that can easily adapt to the changing needs of an organization, and can be extended to provide new functionality as it becomes available.

In this new world of unified communications, users are no longer tied to a single device as a communication endpoint. They can choose to use a traditional-style desk phone, a headset attached to a laptop, or a mobile device to place and receive calls. In addition, plenty of flexibility exists in how these devices are provisioned to users. For example, instead of being assigned a phone that is tied to a specific phone number, a user can simply log in to any supported phone with appropriate credentials, and make use of that device for communications. Incoming calls are then routed to this device, and can also be routed to any other device that the user is logged in to, either simultaneously or one device at a time, depending on preference. At the same time, Presence information is published to allow a user to determine whether another user is available even before the caller picks up the phone to call the other user.

Lync Server allows users to choose and change their forms of communications seamlessly as the situation demands, using a single interface. For example, Dave and Jason are collaborating on a project, and Dave has a question for Jason. Dave looks at his Lync client and sees that Jason is listed as available. Dave sends Jason an instant message asking whether he has a moment to answer a question. Jason replies, "Sure." After a few messages, Jason determines that the subject is a bit too complicated to be explained via IM, and suggests that they have a voice conversation. Dave then escalates the session to a voice call with a single click, and Dave and Jason are able to speak directly. After a few minutes, Dave determines that he would like to see a document that Jason has referred to, and asks whether Jason could show him the document. At this point, Dave adds video to the call, and Jason uses application sharing to display the document as he continues talking.

The communication session just described could as easily take place with the two individuals being at coffee shops or at the beach using Internet-connected laptops, as opposed to a traditional corporate setting. Lync Server doesn't require participants to reserve or schedule video conferencing resources ahead of time, nor does it require users to be in a specific location, or even to use specific hardware. Lync Server allows users to dynamically control their own communications and to be available almost anywhere they can get an Internet connection, at almost any time.

Lync Server Overview

Lync Server is an integrated suite of communication tools that enable point-to-point or point-to-multipoint communications across various mediums. Even the most basic Lync Server implementations include several core features that are useful for almost any organization. For example, all Lync Server deployments enable instant messaging between two or more users for simple text-based communications, as well as point-to-point voice and video chat between clients. Also included in this core set of features is full-featured web conferencing, combining audio, video, desktop sharing, remote control, and more.

An additional core functionality that exists with all Lync implementations is the concept of Presence, in which one can view the status of other users in real time. Although Presence is a feature that has been widely adopted for use with the majority of communications software on the market, Lync Server presents an advantage in that the Presence information published by Lync is extended into other popular Microsoft applications, such as Microsoft Office, Exchange, and SharePoint. As an example, it is possible to view a document created by a co-worker that is stored in SharePoint, then quickly determine the status of the document owner, and contact that document owner with a single click, leading to an IM conversation or a voice call.

Moving beyond the basic features of Lync Server, this functionality can be extended in various ways depending on the needs of an organization. For example, through the use of media gateways or a qualified PBX, Lync users can participate in voice conversations with users of other voice systems, including the Public Switched Telephone Network (PSTN). Lync Server also enables extended methods of conferencing, such as calling into a conference from a PBX or the PSTN (dial-in conferencing) and integration with dedicated video conferencing systems. For larger conferences, Lync Server has the ability to provide most, if not all of an enterprise's conferencing needs.

Instant Messaging and Presence

Although instant messaging (IM) and Presence are two different functions, together they form the most basic functionality available in Lync. In fact, it is not possible to deploy one without the other. IM describes the now-ubiquitous function of engaging in a conversation with another user using simple text-based messaging. In addition to enabling IM for users within an organization, Lync Server supports public IM connectivity (PIC) with several of the more popular IM providers, including AOL, Skype, and Google Talk. In addition, Lync Server allows organizations to federate with other organizations that are also using Lync, extending the IM capabilities beyond corporate borders.

Federation effectively sets up a connection between multiple implementations of Lync or Office Communications Server, allowing both sides to selectively share Presence information with one another, and use the core features of Lync for communication. This is an especially useful feature for business partners who are required to frequently and quickly contact one another. Rather than the inherent delays involved in sending single sentence or short emails to one another, federated partners can simply exchange instant messages in real time.

> **NOTE**
>
> Although this might seem like a small distinction in methods of communications, administrators who manage email systems are quite satisfied to offload communications to alternate methods such as IM. This is largely due to the realization that a large percentage of the data stored in mail systems consists of nonessential conversations along the lines of "Where do you want to meet for lunch?"

Although on the surface it might seem minor, being informed as to a user's availability and willingness to communicate can be useful for both parties. For example, often a user won't bother to call another individual if it is evident that the other person is not likely to answer the call. At other times, a user might choose to intentionally call someone who is listed as not available so that the user can simply leave a quick message and avoid a lengthy conversation. These examples are common uses of Presence and illustrate the usefulness of this feature.

These are some of the more commonly used Presence states within Lync:

- ▶ Available
- ▶ Offline
- ▶ Away
- ▶ Busy
- ▶ Do Not Disturb

Lync can update a user's Presence status based on information available in other applications. One of the most useful examples of this is the client-side integration between Lync and Microsoft Outlook. If Microsoft Outlook is installed on the same client workstation as the Lync client, Lync will automatically update the user's Presence status based on information in the user's Outlook calendar.

Peer-to-Peer Audio

Peer-to-peer audio is a core feature of all Lync Server deployments, and is very simple to configure and support, since it doesn't involve integration with any other systems. Much like IM, P2P audio involves a point-to-point conversation between Lync endpoints; however, in this case the network communications include audio codecs rather than simple text. This audio communication requires more bandwidth than IM and is also much more sensitive to network latency. However, P2P audio still generally requires relatively little in the way of system resources. Because P2P audio communications traverse the data network only, generally good quality can be expected even across a wide area network (WAN) or the Internet.

Web, Audio, and Video Conferencing

Lync Server 2013 includes a comprehensive set of conferencing capabilities as an important core feature of the product. Web conferencing provides users with document collaboration and application sharing, along with whiteboard, remote control, session recording, and other useful collaboration tools. These features, combined with audio and video conferencing, provide a powerful set of features, all of which are made available via the Lync client software. Meetings can be either scheduled or ad-hoc, and through automatic integration with Microsoft Outlook they can be scheduled using a single click. All the Lync conferencing capabilities can be leveraged seamlessly in an on-demand fashion without interrupting a meeting and without requiring separate software, resulting in a conferencing experience that is extremely user-friendly.

> **NOTE**
>
> Web, audio, and video conferencing features are available with all Lync deployments and do not require additional components beyond the Lync Front End Server. However, dial-in conferencing, which allows users to join a conference using a PSTN phone, requires a PSTN gateway along with the Lync Mediation Server role before it can be used.

Enterprise Voice

Enterprise Voice describes the set of features that allow Lync Server to be leveraged as a complete telephony solution for an organization. This includes connectivity to the PSTN, as well as PBX and IP-PBX systems using media gateways and Session Initiation Protocol (SIP) trunks. It also includes voice features that are common to many voice platforms, such as call forwarding, hold, transfer, call parking, enhanced 9-1-1, call admission control, branch office survivability, distinctive ringing, and many more. Traditional voice management functions are also included, such as dial plans, call authorization, and call detail records.

The Enterprise Voice features included with Lync Server are on par with and in many cases exceed the functionality provided by a traditional PBX system. For this very reason, Lync Server can be considered a viable replacement for PBX systems, which can be accomplished either through attrition or via a greenfield replacement.

> **NOTE**
>
> As was the case with previous versions of the product, in Lync Server 2013 remote call control (RCC) will continue to be supported as a coexistence option. RCC allows integration between Lync and a PBX, such that RCC-enabled users can use the Lync interface to control calls on their PBX phone. This can be a particularly attractive option for organizations that want to evaluate Lync Server while maintaining their existing telephony investment, or as an effective method of gradually introducing Lync into the environment while retiring an older voice platform.

For many organizations, an important benefit of using a VoIP system such as Lync Server is the ability to bypass long-distance toll charges through the use of call routing, which is also referred to as toll bypass. For example, if a company has offices in San Francisco and New York, and these two locations are connected via a WAN link, calls between the sites can be routed internally via Lync Server, which makes the call effectively free since the data network is being utilized.

If, on the other hand, a user in San Francisco needs to call an external user in New Jersey, there are two ways this call can be routed. Either the VoIP call from San Francisco can directly exit the local PSTN gateway to the long-distance provider, or the call can first traverse the WAN to the New York office and then exit the PSTN gateway at that location. This would likely result in a cost savings, since the toll charges for a call to New Jersey are likely lower from New York than from San Francisco. Through the use of effective dial plans and call routing, a Lync Server administrator can leverage toll bypass to ensure that the least expensive call path is used for a given scenario. These rules are typically configured based on area codes so that the number of required rules remains manageable.

Persistent Chat

Persistent Chat is a Lync feature that allows users to create chat rooms that contain persistent conversations based on specific topics and categories. In contrast, a Lync IM conversation between three or more users is considered an IM conference, however when all parties leave the conversation, the content of that conversation cannot be retrieved or reviewed. With Persistent Chat, conversations remain even after all users involved in a conversation leave the chat room. The persistent nature of the messages allows Lync users to view ongoing conversations at their leisure, and also search for information within the chat rooms. Many organizations find that ongoing persistent conversations provide a valuable and effective tool for collaboration that can be leveraged by teams of users.

> **NOTE**
>
> Persistent Chat was available as a server role with previous versions of the product, but was known as Group Chat. With Lync Server 2013, this feature will likely find more widespread adoption than ever before, primarily due to the architectural changes that have been introduced with this version. For example, it is now supported to collocate the Persistent Chat server role with a Lync 2013 Standard Edition Front End server, and the Persistent Chat databases can now be collocated on the same SQL server with the rest of the Lync databases. Another significant improvement is that the Persistent Chat features are now included in the base Lync client, and therefore no additional client software is required to leverage this feature.

Lync Server Terms and Acronyms

In the world of unified communications, there are many terms and acronyms that are routinely used that might be unfamiliar to those new to the Lync product line. This publication contains many references to these terms and acronyms; therefore, becoming familiar with the most common of these allows one to more quickly absorb the information in the remaining chapters. Following are some of the more common terms and acronyms that will be used throughout this publication:

▶ **Call Admission Control (CAC)**—A method of preventing oversubscription of VoIP networks. Unlike QoS tools, CAC is call-aware and acts as a preventive congestion control by attempting to route calls across other media before making a determination to block a call. Ultimately, the result of a properly implemented CAC configuration is that the quality of existing calls is preserved, even when bandwidth is scarce.

▶ **Call detail records (CDR)**—A record produced by a phone system containing details of calls that have passed through it. Each record includes information such as the number of the calling party, the number of the called party, the time of call initiation, the duration of the call, the route by which the call was routed, and any fault condition encountered. These records might be used for billing, for tracking of an employee's usage of the system, or for monitoring system uptime and issues.

▶ **Client Access License (CAL)**—A software license that entitles a user to access specific systems or specific features in a system. A CAL is typically offered in two flavors: Standard and Enterprise.

▶ **Common Intermediate Format (CIF)**—A format used to standardize the vertical and horizontal resolutions in video signals, often in video conferencing systems.

▶ **Direct Inward Dialing (DID)**—A service offered by phone carriers wherein a block of telephone numbers is provided to a customer for connection to the customer's internal phone system (including Lync Server or a traditional PBX). Incoming calls to the DID block are routed to internal destination numbers, which allows an organization to have significantly more internal lines than external lines.

1

▶ **Dual-Tone Multi-Frequency (DTMF)**—A method for providing telecommunication signaling over analog telephones lines in the voice frequency band. DTMF is also referred to as *touch tone*. This technology enables users to initiate events in the phone system by simply pressing a button on a keypad.

▶ **Extensible Markup Language (XML)**—A set of rules for encoding documents in a machine-readable format. The goal of XML is to be a simple and open standard for representing arbitrary data structures, and it is most often used in web services.

▶ **Extensible Messaging and Presence Protocol (XMPP)**—An open, XML-based protocol designed to provide near-real-time extensible IM and Presence information. XMPP has more recently expanded into VoIP and file transfer signaling.

▶ **Hardware Load Balancing (HLB)**—A method of distributing a workload across multiple computers to optimize resource utilization, increase throughput, and provide a level of redundancy through the use of an external hardware device.

▶ **Instant messaging (IM)**—A form of real-time, direct, text-based communication between multiple parties. IM is sometimes referred to as *online chat*.

▶ **Interactive Voice Response (IVR)**—A technology that enables a system to detect voice and dual-tone multifrequency inputs. IVR is often used in telecommunications as an input for automated decision trees. For example, IVR technology is used behind the scenes with voice menu prompts that are frequently heard, such as "press 1 for English."

▶ **Mean Opinion Score (MOS)**—In multimedia, MOS provides a numerical indication of the perceived quality of a call after compression and/or transmissions. MOS is expressed as a single number ranging from 1 to 5, with 1 being the lowest perceived audio quality and 5 being the highest perceived audio quality.

▶ **Network Address Translation (NAT)**—A method of modifying network address information when packets pass through a traffic routing device. NAT effectively remaps a packet from one IP space to another, and is common in home usage when there are multiple computers with a private IP addressing site behind a router or firewall that holds a publicly routable address. NAT maps a port back to the initiating internal host and reroutes responses back to the originating host.

▶ **Network Load Balancing (NLB)**—A method of distributing a workload across multiple computers to optimize resource utilization, increase throughput, and provide a level of redundancy through the use of software running in the Windows operating system.

▶ **Plain Old Telephone Service (POTS)**—Another term for PSTN.

▶ **Public Switched Telephone Network (PSTN)**—The global network consisting of the world's public circuit-switched telephone systems. The first company to provide PSTN services was Bell Telephone.

▶ **Private Branch Exchange (PBX)**—A telephone system that serves a particular business or office as opposed to a common carrier or a system for the general public. A PBX is what traditionally provides voice services to companies that are connected to a local exchange, and provides external connectivity to the PSTN for users in that organization.

▶ **Quality of Experience (QoE)**—A subjective measure of a customer's experiences with a vendor or service.

▶ **Quality of Service (QoS)**—A mechanism to control resource reservation in a system; typically, it is a method to prioritize various traffic types to ensure a minimum level of performance for a particular type of traffic.

▶ **Realtime Transport Protocol (RTP)**—A standardized format for delivering audio and video over the Internet. A noted advantage of RTP is its ability to handle large amounts of packet loss before the impact on the call becomes noticeable.

▶ **Remote Call Control (RCC)**—A method of utilizing a phone resource on one system with a resource on another. Typically, in the context of Lync Server, this is the capability to use a Lync client to place a call through a desk phone that is controlled by a PBX rather than by Lync Server.

▶ **Role-based access control (RBAC)**—An approach to restricting system access to authorized users by granting the rights based on the role served by the user. This normally results in granular permissions with the goal of granting the minimum level of rights needed to perform a task.

▶ **Session Initiation Protocol (SIP)**—An Internet Engineering Task Force (IETF) defined protocol used for controlling multimedia communications sessions. The goal of SIP is to provide a common signaling and call setup protocol for IP-based communications.

▶ **SIP for Instant Messaging and Presence Leveraging Extensions (SIMPLE)**—An open standard protocol suite that provides for the registration of Presence information and the receipt of Presence status notifications.

▶ **Survivable Branch Appliance (SBA)**—A physical appliance that combines the Lync Registrar, Mediation Server, and PSTN gateway services in one compact unit; it is designed to maintain most voice services for a branch site that has lost connectivity to the main Lync Server site.

▶ **Transmission Control Protocol (TCP)**—One of the core protocols of the Internet, TCP is a protocol that provides reliable ordered delivery of a stream of packets from one device to another. TCP has the advantage of sending an acknowledgment of receipt of a packet back to the sender, resulting in increased reliability. This acknowledgment, however, comes at a performance price and can therefore serve to limit the scalability of TCP.

▶ **Uniform Resource Identifier (URI)**—A string of characters used to identify a name or a resource on the Internet. This allows interaction with representations of the resource over a network, often the Internet, using various protocols.

▶ **User Datagram Protocol (UDP)**—Another one of the core protocols of the Internet, UDP delivers a stream of packets from one device to another, but does not attempt to order or verify delivery of packets. UDP also does not need to first initiate a conversation with a destination host via a handshake. This behavior makes it faster and more scalable than TCP, but ultimately it is less reliable.

▶ **Virtual Private Network (VPN)**—A method of passing packets across a public network in a secured and authenticated manner. VPNs enable users to access their private corporate networks through connections to the public Internet.

▶ **Voice over IP (VoIP)**—A generic term for transmission technologies that deliver voice communications over IP-based networks. VoIP is also referred to as *IP Telephony* or *Internet Telephony*.

Versions and Licensing

Like previous versions, Lync Server 2013 comes in two flavors: Standard Edition and Enterprise Edition. The two versions present a variety of deployment options for organizations of all sizes. A Lync server topology can be relatively simple, or as complex as needed to meet the requirements and budget of even the largest organizations. Features between the two editions are very similar, with Enterprise providing more scalability, along with high availability and disaster recovery options that aren't available in the Standard Edition. However, to leverage these additional options, Enterprise Edition represents a more significant investment and requires higher-end components than Standard Edition. For example, a dedicated backend SQL server is required for Enterprise Edition rather than a local installation of SQL Express, which is automatically used and required with Standard Edition.

Lync Server Standard Edition

The Standard Edition of Lync Server provides a relatively simple way for small- to medium-sized organizations to introduce unified communications into a network. It offers a relatively low cost of entry based on the fact that all internal components are hosted on a single server, with the option of adding an edge server to support external connectivity.

Standard Edition utilizes a local SQL Server Express Edition database to store Lync information, and the database is installed automatically by the deployment wizard. Although Standard Edition does not provide all the high-availability options that are available with the Enterprise Edition, with Lync Server 2013 new functionality has been added in the form of Front End Pool Pairing. This new feature allows Standard Edition pools to be designed for a level of resiliency, even across multiple sites. For this reason, many organizations, will find that installing multiple Standard Edition servers across several sites will result in an ideal combination of low cost, site resiliency, and a solid set of features. The primary disadvantage to Standard Edition is that it is designed to handle relatively low user loads, because the all-in-one nature of the system limits scalability in terms of performance. At the same time, the consolidated design of a Standard Edition server makes it simpler to deploy and maintain than an Enterprise Edition topology, and the performance characteristics will be more than adequate for many small-to-medium sized organizations.

A typical Standard Edition deployment would involve a single system acting as a Front End server, which might include additional collocated roles depending on the requirements, such as Mediation Server, Archiving Server, Monitoring Server, and Persistent Chat Server. To round out the deployment, a PSTN gateway can be used to enable Enterprise Voice, and an Edge Server can be installed to provide external connectivity. An additional system hosting the Director role can optionally be used to redirect incoming user requests to the Front End. This configuration is sufficient to provide IM, voice, and video services for a small- to medium-sized organization, as well as public IM connectivity, A/V conferencing, and more.

> **NOTE**
>
> Although Lync Server Standard Edition is typically used in small-to-medium sized deployments, it is also quite common for both editions to be used within the same architecture. For example, some larger organizations deploy Enterprise Edition Lync pools in primary data centers, and use Standard Edition pools to service smaller, regional offices. The Enterprise and Standard editions of Lync Server can easily be mixed and matched as needed within a network to accommodate different levels of service and budget for different locations.

Lync Server Enterprise Edition

The Enterprise Edition of Lync Server provides a scalability jump compared to Standard Edition, and provides additional high-availability options. The increase in scalability results from the separating of roles onto separate systems for better performance, and also the use of more robust components in certain areas. For example, whereas Standard Edition can use only a local SQL Express database, Enterprise Edition requires the use of a full SQL instance installed on a dedicated system. In this one area alone, scalability is improved not only by using a more robust database, but also by isolating the database load from other systems.

In terms of high availability, Enterprise Edition provides several advantages compared to Standard Edition. Although the Front End Pool Pairing feature is available with either edition, only Enterprise Edition allows for the failure of a Front End server with no resulting loss of functionality for the pool users. This is possible because Enterprise Edition allows the installation of separate Front End servers for the same pool within a particular site. An additional resiliency advantage is that Enterprise Edition requires a separate database for backend data storage, which presents the opportunity to leverage native SQL high availability for the Lync data. Lync Server 2013 supports SQL mirroring, which requires two backend SQL servers and uses data synchronization between the two systems.

Of course, the additional scalability and high availability provided by Enterprise Edition come at a higher cost, in terms of both additional systems and licensing. A typical Enterprise Edition deployment at a given site consists of at least two Front End servers (up to a maximum of 10 per pool), with hardware load balancers (or a combination of hardware load balancers and DNS load balancing) used to distribute the load between the systems. At least one SQL server system would be used to store the backend data, although two such systems with SQL mirroring would be recommended for redundancy. On the Front End systems, several other Lync server roles can be collocated, including Mediation Server, Monitoring Server, and Archiving Server. The Mediation Server role can also be installed separately from the Front End to increase performance. Other systems that can be added to provide increased functionality with an Enterprise Edition deployment include one or more PSTN gateways to enable Enterprise Voice features, Persistent Chat Server, and an Edge Server or Edge Server pool to support external connectivity.

> **NOTE**
>
> With previous versions of the product, the Monitoring Server and Archiving Server roles were always installed separately from the Front End Server, and the A/V Conferencing Server role could be installed separately if desired. In Lync Server 2013, each of these roles is collocated with the Front End Server with all deployments. The Persistent Chat Server can also be collocated with the Front End Server in a Standard Edition deployment, but must be installed separately from the Front End with an Enterprise Edition deployment. The Mediation Server role can either be collocated with the Front End Server or installed separately depending on the specific Enterprise Voice requirements of the deployment.

Client and Server Licensing

Microsoft licensing for Lync includes both client and server licensing. Whereas the server licensing is straightforward, the client licensing can be challenging to absorb. As noted in the previous sections, there are two editions of the server software: Standard Edition and Enterprise Edition. All Front End Servers installed in a Lync deployment fall into one category or the other, and must therefore be licensed appropriately.

> **NOTE**
>
> Whereas each Lync Front End Server must be licensed for either Standard Edition or Enterprise Edition, any other Lync servers in the environment are always licensed using Standard Edition. This includes any systems hosting the Edge Server role, as well as standalone systems hosting the Persistent Chat Server or Mediation Server roles.

As for client licensing, one Client Access License (CAL) is required for each user to access the services of a Lync server. However, there are three types of CALs available for Lync Server 2013:

- ▶ Lync Server 2013 Standard CAL
- ▶ Lync Server 2013 Enterprise CAL
- ▶ Lync Server 2013 Plus CAL

The Standard CAL is the base CAL, which is required for all users and grants access to a standard set of Lync features, including IM and Presence and peer-to-peer audio and video communications. The Enterprise and Plus CALs are additive CALs that grant access to additional Lync features. Whereas the Enterprise CAL grants access to audio, video, and web conferencing features, the Plus CAL includes Enterprise Voice features. To enable access to the entire feature set provided with Lync, a user must be licensed with all three CALs. Note that this is the case regardless of the server edition installed on the Lync servers that the user connects to.

The CAL types mentioned can all be purchased individually as part of a standalone Lync deployment, and the Lync Standard and Enterprise CALs in particular can also be purchased as part of a volume licensing arrangement. For example, the Lync Standard CAL can be purchased as part of the Microsoft Core CAL Suite (CCAL), and the Lync Standard or Enterprise CAL can be purchased as part of the Microsoft Enterprise CAL Suite (ECAL). Many organizations purchase Lync licensing as part of a larger volume licensing agreement in order to save on overall licensing costs. Note that the Plus CAL must be purchased standalone, because it is not included in either the CCAL or the ECAL volume license offerings. There is also a licensing requirement for the Lync client software. The client software can be purchased as a standalone application, or it is included as part of the Office Professional Plus 2013 suite.

Integration with Other Microsoft Applications

One of the primary advantages of Microsoft Lync over competing products in the unified communications arena is integration with other Microsoft applications. Not only do other Microsoft applications provide functionality within Lync, but Lync was also designed to create hooks into other popular Microsoft software. The end result is that information stored in other applications such as Exchange and SharePoint can be accessed within Lync, and on the other end rich Presence information stored within Lync can be shared with other applications. With Lync Server 2013, Microsoft is continuing to leverage integration points within their portfolio to provide additional value across the software stack.

Integration with Exchange

Lync Server 2013 will continue to provide the integrations with Exchange that existed in previous versions, and will introduce several additional integrations as well.

> **NOTE**
>
> All the new Exchange integration features offered with Lync 2013 also require Exchange 2013. Therefore, an organization must upgrade both products to the newest versions in order to use all the Exchange integration features.

Continuing in Lync 2013 is integration with Exchange Outlook Web App (OWA). Lync and OWA integration allows Presence and IM capabilities within an OWA session, and includes the following useful features:

- ▶ Presence for internal and federated Lync Server contacts

- ▶ The capability to start and maintain chat sessions directly from OWA

- ▶ Lync Server contact list integration, including adding and removing contacts and groups

- ▶ The capability to control Lync Presence states from OWA

As in previous versions, Lync Server integrates with the Unified Messaging role in Exchange, which allows Lync Server to use Exchange as a replacement for traditional voice mail systems. Voice messages stored in Exchange can then be retrieved from the Lync client as well as from the user's Exchange mailbox.

Lync Archiving Integration is a brand-new feature that integrates the Lync Archiving role with the Exchange In-Place Hold feature, resulting in a common repository of archival data that simplifies compliance and eDiscovery tasks across the two communications platforms.

An additional new integration feature between Lync 2013 and Exchange 2013 is the Unified Contact Store, which presents a common repository for user contacts that is shared between the Lync and Outlook clients. When enabled, the Lync client connects to Exchange Web Services (EWS) to read and maintain contacts instead of using SIP to connect the Lync Front End server for contacts, as in previous versions.

> **NOTE**
>
> Unified Contact Store requires both Lync 2013 and Exchange 2013, however, it is an optional feature that can be enabled or disabled, even if the 2013 versions of both products are deployed.

Rounding out the new integration features between Lync and Exchange is the storage and retrieval of high-resolution photos that are shared between the two platforms. Both Lync 2013 and Exchange 2013 support photos of up to 648×648 pixels, which are stored in Exchange 2013 and are added to contacts within the Lync and Outlook clients. The photos are stored as a hidden item in the root of a user's Exchange mailbox. Having the option to store these photos in Exchange is an improvement from previous Lync versions, since the photos were typically stored in Active Directory, which presented some limitations due to potential problems with replication.

Integration with SharePoint

Similar to Exchange, Lync Server 2013 continues to offer integrations with SharePoint that were available with previous versions of the two products, and provides some additional functionality that is available only with the latest versions of both. Whenever a contact is shown in a SharePoint page, Lync presents Presence information along with the associated contact card for the user, and Lync functions can be initiated via a simple click on the Presence icon.

An interesting SharePoint integration feature that was introduced with Lync 2010 and will continue to be supported in Lync 2013 is Skill Search. With Skill Search, the Lync client can be used to search SharePoint My Site pages to find individuals with a specific skill set. With SharePoint integration, users are also able to access their SharePoint My Site profile page from the Options dialog box within the Lync client.

New with Lync 2013 and SharePoint 2013 is the ability to use SharePoint to search Lync archives using an eDiscovery site collection. The Lync archive data must first be integrated with Exchange 2013 to form a common repository for archive data to allow this search functionality within SharePoint.

This type of bidirectional integration presents many options for organizations to allow productive and efficient communication for the user base. For example, it can be challenging for new employees in a large organization to find the right resource to handle a particular question. With Lync and SharePoint integration, that employee can use Skill Search to display a list of employees who have a particular expertise, quickly determine whether they are available to communicate, and then initiate the communication using various methods. All of this can be accomplished using a single interface, compared to searching a company intranet, looking for the appropriate department, digging up contact information for individuals with the right skill set, and then manually contacting each one until someone is available.

Integration with Microsoft Office

On the client side, integration between Lync and Microsoft Office has provided valuable features with previous versions of Lync, and that will continue to be the case with Lync Server 2013. Some of the more compelling features provided through the integration of Lync and Microsoft Office are the following:

▶ Lync automatically updates the user's Presence status based on information in the user's Outlook calendar.

▶ The Online Meeting Add-in for Lync allows users to create a Lync conference from the Outlook client and automatically schedule the meeting in the user's calendar, providing a single interface to service all meeting requirements.

▶ Presence information is automatically displayed wherever mail recipients are shown in Outlook.

▶ Lync IM conversations are recorded in the Conversation History folder in Outlook, and can be viewed and searched along with other Outlook data.

▶ The Office Sharing Add-in for Lync allows users to view Presence status, initiate a Lync IM, and initiate a collaborative document-sharing session from within Microsoft Word, PowerPoint, and Excel (versions 2007 and above are required).

▶ The Lync client can be used to record personal notes regarding a meeting that are stored in a OneNote 2013 notebook.

▶ The Lync client can be used to open a shared OneNote 2013 notebook and distribute a link to connect to the shared notebook for all meeting participants.

Summary

Microsoft Lync Server 2013 is the latest chapter in Microsoft's unified communications story, offering a powerful suite of communication and collaboration tools that can be leveraged using a single interface. The core features of IM, Presence, conferencing, and peer-to-peer audio and video are included in all deployments, and additional features such as Enterprise Voice, archiving, monitoring, external access, and federation can be added as necessary. Several editions and a number of topology options are available to scale a Lync deployment to meet the needs of even the largest organizations. Lync Server 2013 can be used for anything from a simple IM platform to a full PBX replacement, to a distributed VoIP implementation. Microsoft continues to enable integrations between Lync and other popular Microsoft products such as Exchange, SharePoint, and Office, which presents new ways for users to communicate and provides additional value for the investment. Microsoft Lync Server 2013 enables users to simplify communications and expand the ways in which they can collaborate.

CHAPTER 2

What's New in Microsoft Lync Server 2013

Microsoft Lync Server 2013 has introduced a number of significant improvements from its predecessor, Lync Server 2010, and made yet another compelling case for organizations to consider upgrading. Microsoft has invested a great deal of engineering effort in enhancing the conferencing experience with features such as the Gallery View, in which up to five concurrent video streams can be displayed, and making a codec change from RTVideo to the industry-standard H.264.

On the server-side, Lync has even greater redundancy possible by replicating contact lists and conferencing data between paired pool sets. Lync Server 2013 also has tighter integration with Exchange Server and can leverage the same archiving policies and store already defined for eDiscovery purposes. Some roles such as Monitoring and Archiving have been consolidated on to Front End servers, and the old Office Communications Server XMPP gateway has been natively integrated in to the Front End and Edge Servers.

This chapter covers the major changes and improvements most organizations try to leverage in their business case for upgrading servers.

Conferencing Improvements

The most noticeable improvements in Lync Server 2013 center around conferencing scenarios and the collaboration experience. This section covers the various enhancements.

Gallery View

Previous versions of Lync leveraged active-speaker video switching, which meant that users would see a video stream only for the current speaker, and Lync would dynamically switch the video feed to another user when it detected that someone else was speaking. This meant that all users received the exact same video stream from the A/V MCU and there was no control over the layout or appearance. The user who was currently speaking would continue to receive the video stream for the user previously considered active.

Lync 2013 has introduced the new Gallery View option, shown in Figure 2.1, which displays up to five concurrent video streams while in a conference. These streams are displayed in a single-row, side-by-side horizontal orientation within the conference window. Since some meetings will exceed five participants, Lync displays the photo for each additional user in a row below the gallery video streams. Similar to active-speaker switching, users will move in and out of the five video streams as they speak. A user can also "pin" another user's video stream to his gallery so that the pinned user's video stream will always be visible to him. If a user is not providing a video stream, a static photo is displayed in its place.

FIGURE 2.1   Gallery View.

Active-speaker switching hasn't been removed from the product, but Gallery View is instead a new option available to administrators and users. While in a conference, users can actually use the new Gallery View, or switch back to the traditional active-speaker switching mode, which Lync calls Speaker View. These changes are unique to each user so there can be a mix of users within the conference using both Gallery View and active-speaker switching.

Each user has a level of control and flexibility over the layout in addition to the type of video stream. In addition to switching between Gallery View and Speaker View, a conference participant can enable Presentation View to hide all video streams and view only the current shared content. This can be useful on small portable screens since the video streams have been moved into the same window as shared content instead of the old side-by-side view. The last option available to users is the Compact View, which simply displays the static photo tiles of each participant along with the meeting content.

The addition of Gallery View natively within the product is a huge advantage to organizations because this was a feature previously provided only by third-party partner MCU solutions.

HD Video Conferencing

Lync was historically very limited in terms of video resolution for peer-to-peer calls and especially within any conferences. Office Communications Server 2007 R2 was limited to CIF quality 352×288 resolution for conferencing, and Lync Server 2010 allowed only up to VGA quality 640×480 for any conferences. These resolutions were perfectly acceptable for meetings exclusively involving workstation webcams and small screens, but as screen sizes have grown and webcam quality has improved, these resolutions were inadequate in a full-screen mode. These low conference resolutions looked especially poor on large HD television screens used by room-based video systems.

Lync Server 2013 has thankfully added support for both 720p (1280×720) and 1080p (1920×1080) HD video conferencing within the A/V MCU. Again, businesses were previously forced to leverage expensive third-party MCU hardware or software to take advantage of these resolutions in older product versions, so this is a very welcome addition.

H.264 Codec

The capability to support HD video conferencing resolutions and multiple video streams within the Gallery View is driven by Microsoft switching from the proprietary RTVideo codec to the more commonly used H.264 video codec.

The H.264 codec used by Lync 2013 supports Scalable Video Coding (SVC), which allows the server to provide unique streams to endpoints depending on their capabilities. For example, based on the same source stream, the A/V MCU can deliver a lower-resolution stream to a small tablet, deliver a medium-quality stream to a desktop, and still provide a 1080p stream to a room system.

The shift also enables clients to leverage GPU hardware for encoding and decoding, which means the processor requirements for client workstations have also been reduced. Instead of requiring a quad-core processor to send HD video, clients now need only a dual-core processor to send HD and a single-core processor to receive HD video. This helps reduce strain on the A/V MCU, which had previously required a significant amount of processor resources to mix and distribute a single RTVideo stream to endpoints. H.264 can also deliver HD video streams at lower bandwidth levels than RTVideo required, so organizations can support more HD video calls.

Lync Web App Audio and Video

Another weakness in the previous versions of the product was the fact that a thick client was required for anonymous participants to join any audio or video on their endpoint to the meeting. This requirement often caused confusion for participants using Lync Web

App because content-sharing features were available, but audio required PSTN dial-in and video couldn't be shared. Users could optionally install the Lync Attendee client to use IP audio and video from their workstation, but this was an extra step and never proved to be as popular as the old Live Meeting client.

Lync Server 2013 has rectified this situation by providing IP audio and video within Lync Web App through a browser-based plugin. This change provides anonymous users with a single option for joining conferences with all the functionality that could possibly be used, including the new Gallery View for video conferencing.

The newly revamped Lync Web App no longer uses Microsoft Silverlight and is instead based on HTML and JavaScript standards, although it is not entirely HTML5. Audio, video, and screen sharing capabilities are provided through a small plugin installed while the user joins a meeting. The plugin requires no administrative privileges and works on both PCs and Mac platforms, but there is no support for Linux browsers today.

Smart Cropping

The streams displayed in Gallery View are all a square aspect ratio instead of any VGA or HD resolution provided by the user's webcam. Lync uses a new feature called Smart Cropping, which locates the user's face within the video stream and centers a square crop around the face, removing any extra space in the video around the actual person. This is to ensure that both streams have a similar size and resolution while they are viewed in the side-by-side Gallery View. The feature is dynamic so if a user shifts positions within her seat, the smart crop will follow the user's face and adjust to ensure that she is still centered in the video stream.

The original release of Lync 2013 always cropped the user in meetings, but a later update added the option for users to control the cropping behavior. Lync Server 2013 has logic to detect if the source device is a Polycom CX5000, previously known as the Microsoft Roundtable, and automatically use a widescreen format, but basic webcams don't provide this logic.

High-Availability and Disaster Recovery Changes

Each version of Lync has made incremental improvements to the high-availability and disaster recovery capabilities of the product, and Lync Server 2013 is no exception. The addition of SQL mirroring, the Brick Model, and the Lync Backup Service all contribute to making Lync Server 2013 a highly resilient product capable of providing excellent recovery options.

SQL Mirroring for Databases

The one weak spot in any Office Communications Server 2007 R2 or Lync Server 2010 deployment was the backend SQL database for each Front End pool. This was traditionally a SQL server cluster hosted by multiple nodes, but the storage for the database had to be a single SAN. Administrators were anxious to remove this single point of failure by leveraging a feature in SQL called database mirroring, in which the databases are kept in sync between two separate nodes each with their own storage. It was technically possible to configure SQL mirroring for the database, but there was no automated or easy way to fail over between the mirrored nodes. More importantly, it wasn't ever a scenario supported by Microsoft.

Lync Server 2013 has finally introduced support for SQL server mirroring of the backend database, which allows administrators to remove the dependency on a SAN. This helps reduce the complexity and overall cost of any highly available deployment since Windows and SQL server clustering is no longer required. The resiliency of the solution is also improved since there are now two unique copies of the user data within the backend database.

Automatic failover between the mirrored SQL server nodes can be enabled when a SQL server mirroring witness server is deployed. The witness server acts as the third vote for which node should actively serve the databases, similar to a quorum disk in a cluster or a file-share witness in an Exchange Database Availability Group (DAG). The Express Edition of SQL Server can be used for the witness server to save on licensing costs, but regardless of whether the full or the Express Edition is used, it must match the major product version used for the backend nodes.

Brick Model and User Data Replication

Another welcome change in Lync Server 2013 is the addition of the Brick Model within Front End pools. One of the investments made was to reduce the dependency on the backend SQL server database's availability so that users should be unaware if database issues are occurring. The Brick Model moves more functionality into each Front End Server, which now manages the user's presence states directly. Changes to the backend database are done only for persistent data and are considered lazy writes, so a temporary issue at the database doesn't have a high impact on users.

Users are now automatically partitioned into objects called UserGroups within a Front End pool, similar to how each user had a preferred server order for a Lync Server 2010 pool. Each UserGroup is then assigned up to three Front End Servers within a pool, so there are up to three copies of the user's data stored directly on the pool members. If a UserGroup's primary Front End Server fails, the secondary or tertiary can immediately begin servicing that UserGroup because they already have the data stored.

These Brick Model changes also allow pools to scale out to larger numbers. Twelve Front End Servers can be deployed within a single Lync Server 2013 pool, up from only 10 in Lync Server 2010. This still only allows a single pool to now support up to 80,000 concurrent users, but allows for full operating capacity even after two Front End server failures.

Conferencing Resiliency and Backup Service

Lync Server 2010 introduced resiliency for the voice platform through Survivable Branch Appliances/Servers and the concept of primary and backup registrars. This allowed users to retain basic voice services during an outage, but all contact list and conferencing capabilities were lost until an administrator intervened to forcefully move users and restore information. Lync Server 2013's focus around conferencing resiliency automates this process for administrators by replicating conference data between each Front End pool member for both the primary and the backup registrar.

This resiliency is achieved through a new Lync Backup Service that replicates user and conferencing data between paired Front End pools on a continuous basis. The advantage to this can be seen when an organization has two locations, each with an active pool paired to the opposite location. During a server outage, full conferencing functionality can be provided through the opposite site. Failover between the two pools is not automated and must be initiated by an administrator through a set of Lync Management Shell commands. The combination of SQL Mirroring and the Lync Backup Service allows organizations to achieve a new degree of local and remote resiliency, as shown in Figure 2.2.

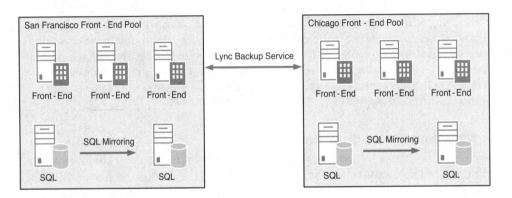

FIGURE 2.2   Local and remote resiliency.

One negative change from Lync Server 2010 is that Front End pools can be paired only with the same product version, meaning an Enterprise Edition pool is not recommended to be paired with a Standard Edition pool. Additionally, pool pairings are now a 1:1 ratio so multiple Front End pools can no longer be paired with a single disaster recovery site's Front End pool. A unique disaster recovery pool must be deployed for each primary pool, which means an even number of Front End pools are required for pairing.

Additionally, the conferencing resiliency benefits only users homed directly to the Front End pool. Users hosted on a Survivable Branch Appliance or Server still use a single Front End pool for voice resiliency, but do not gain resiliency for their conferencing.

Server Features

Administrators of Lync Server 2013 should be aware of the changes discussed in this section since they directly affect the architecture of a deployment.

Office Web Apps Server

A new dependency for any Front End pool in Lync Server 2013 is an Office Web Apps Server. This role is treated as an external dependency, similar to how a SQL Server or file share is leveraged by a Front End pool. For Lync Server 2013's purposes, the Office Web Apps server is exclusively used by rendering PowerPoint slide decks within the Lync client or Lync Web App. This is important because Microsoft Silverlight was used for rendering decks in Lync Server 2010, but the dependency on Silverlight has been removed to provide greater compatibility with web and mobile clients.

A single Office Web Apps Server, or farm of Office Web Apps servers, can be deployed to support Lync Server 2013, Exchange Server 2013, and SharePoint 2013 since all three platforms leverage the service for viewing or editing capabilities. The main advantage to Office Web Apps PowerPoint rendering is seen in improved support for animations and slide transitions, which Silverlight did not always render properly. This does, however, mean that organizations will need to deploy at least one additional server to support Front End pools.

Monitoring and Archiving Servers

The Monitoring and Archiving server roles have been removed as standalone servers in a Lync deployment. Instead, these services are now collocated on Front End Servers within a pool as a check-box option while the pool is being defined within Topology Builder. The data is still stored within a SQL server, which can be the same instance used by the Front End pool or a different instance. This reduces the number of servers an organization needs in order to deploy and manage so this is a welcome change.

Standalone A/V Conferencing Server

The option to deploy a standalone A/V conferencing server has been removed from Lync Server 2013. This role was geared toward supporting large A/V conferencing workloads, but the video conferencing codec change and performance improvements have negated the need to separate this role. The A/V conferencing role is now always installed on Front End servers within a pool, which helps to simplify deployments. Those migrating from older versions will notice the Front End servers taken on a much greater load.

Server-to-Server Authentication

New to Lync Server 2013 is the concept of server-to-server authentication, which allows for Lync to interact with Exchange Server 2013 and SharePoint Server 2013 on behalf of users. This authentication is done through a standard called Open Authorization (OAuth) where servers are granted a level of trust between each other via security tokens. There is no requirement to turn on this authentication feature, but it does enable a number of new features.

> **NOTE**
>
> Server-to-server authentication can be used only between Lync Server 2013, Exchange Server 2013, and SharePoint Server 2013. This means that users must already have Exchange Server 2013 mailboxes in order to take advantage of the following features.

Exchange Archiving

The first feature enabled through server-to-server authentication is the capability to target a user's Exchange mailbox as the archiving location. Lync Server 2013 still has the capability to store archived data in a SQL database, but using this feature instead directs the archive content to a hidden folder in the user's Exchange database.

The advantage to this is in the eDiscovery process because legal administrators can now run content searches against mailboxes and Lync data using just the Exchange Server tools. From a policy perspective it also allows a single archiving policy in Exchange to apply to both Lync and Exchange content, ensuring content is archived or purged on the same schedule. The Exchange Control Panel has a much more refined interface for searches than Lync has ever offered, so this should help simplify the eDiscovery process.

Unified Contact Store

The second feature enabled via server-to-server authentication is the Unified Contact Store (UCS), an option that nearly made it into Lync Server 2010, but was scrapped at the very end. Without UCS users maintain separate contact lists within Exchange and Lync, where information might not be in sync, and the data is stored independently. When the UCS feature is enabled for a user, the contact list is consolidated to Exchange and can no longer be directly edited with Lync, but users can now edit their contact lists without being signed in to a Lync endpoint.

The Lync servers maintain a cached, read-only copy of the contact list that users can still view when Exchange is offline, but any modifications are made to the copy that Exchange holds. When UCS is enabled, users see the same people card and favorites lists for contacts. The contacts are de-duped, and support for high-resolution Active Directory photos up to a 648×648 resolution is enabled.

Some of the drivers for this change were the fact that multiple contacts for the same user were returned in many Lync searches, potentially with different data, which often confused end users. Mobile clients also did not always have the same contact information stored locally, so this allows mobile users to see consistent data for a contact.

Skype Federation

Ever since Microsoft began the acquisition process of Skype, there have been questions and speculation about what type of integration would be made with Lync. In Lync Server 2013, federation to Skype has been added, and it looks similar to how federation with other public IM providers is achieved. For the initial release the integration will be for presence, IM, and audio only. Video support is still in the developmental stages and will likely be added during a future cumulative update package.

XMPP Gateway

The XMPP Gateway role was originally released for Office Communications Server 2007 R2 and had not received even as much as a name change when Lync Server 2010 came along. With Lync Server 2013 the XMPP gateway role has been moved into the Front End Server as a native service, and the Edge Server includes an XMPP proxy service to facilitate connections to remote XMPP partners.

The maddening limit of requiring one XMPP gateway per SIP domain has also been removed, and the gateway service can now handle XMPP connections for multiple SIP domains.

Persistent Chat

Group Chat has been rebranded as Persistent Chat starting with Lync Server 2013, and both the client and the server components have finally been integrated with the rest of Lync. The installation bits come on the same media, and the setup process for Persistent Chat has been moved into Topology Builder like any other role; also, the Lync Control Panel includes a section for room management. Persistent Chat has gained high-availability and disaster recovery capabilities similar to Front End Servers, and now scales to 15,000 endpoints per room. SQL Mirroring is used to provide high availability for the back end in a similar fashion to the Front End databases.

Hybrid and On-Premise Deployment Integration

Lync Server 2013 is the first release to offer integration with Office 365 in a hybrid mode. The only option available previously was to use a separate SIP domain for Office 365 cloud users and the on-premise users, but the hybrid model allows for the same namespace to be used in both sides.

Not only does a hybrid connection allow for IM and presence integration, but organizations can now connect their Office 365 hosted users with an on-premise telephony or video conferencing solution. This enables administrators to migrate some user accounts to the cloud, but maintain an on-premise phone number, as shown in Figure 2.3.

A strict requirement for Lync Hybrid scenarios is that an organization first deploy Active Directory Federation Services (ADFS) for single sign-on with Office 365. The Office 365 federated identity cannot be used.

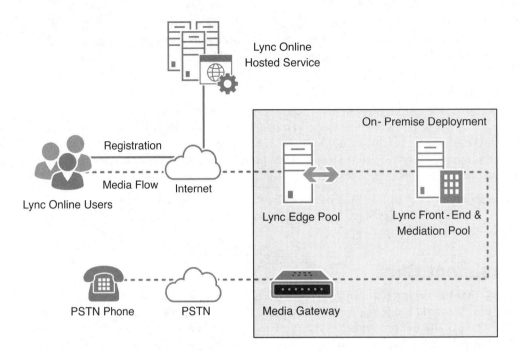

FIGURE 2.3   Hybrid voice topology.

Client Features

Lync Server 2013 also includes a new set of features users will immediately be able to enjoy. This section covers the enhancements made to the client applications.

High-Resolution Photos

Gone are the days of a small 96×96-pixel thumbnail photo representing each contact. In Lync 2013 the users can use high-resolution photos (648×648 pixels), which are displayed in various locations such as in contact cards and in the Gallery View. To be technically correct, high-resolution photos are actually stored in Exchange Server 2013 and are dependent on administrators configuring the server-to-server authentication required to support the feature.

Tabbed Conversations

For the Lync power users who regularly have many instant messaging windows simultaneously open, the new tabbed conversations view is a welcome addition to the product. In previous versions each IM window was a standalone entity, and as users reached the four-to-five-concurrent-conversations level, it became a desktop management annoyance to keep track of each conversation. Lync 2013 introduces a tabbed view, shown in Figure 2.4, in which a single window holds all conversations and users can click between different conversations tabs within the window. This feature is not enabled by default, but users can turn it on through their personal options.

FIGURE 2.4   Tabbed conversation window.

Presenting

A new presence status has been introduced to indicate when a user is currently presenting content during an Online Meeting. When Lync detects that a user is giving a presentation, it automatically changes the user's presence to "Presenting." Users have always had the ability to manually set presence to Do Not Disturb when they were giving a presentation, but the key difference is that this presence status is now set automatically. This helps prevent instant messages or calls from potentially interrupting a presentation, which is always embarrassing during a conference.

Mobile Client Audio and Video

A common misconception when the Lync 2010 mobile clients were released was that users could leverage a data connection for audio and video calls, which led to a feeling of disappointment when the users realized that the client was really geared toward IM and presence. The call via work feature helped bridge the gap by enabling the server to dial out to a user's mobile number over a cellular connection before placing a second call to the destination number, and the capability to join online meetings through the client without entering conference IDs, extensions, or PINs undoubtedly prevented an incredible number of car accidents. Microsoft even added the capability for iPads to view a PowerPoint presentation through a Cumulative Update package, but the user community still longed for media over the data connection.

Those users will be happy to hear that the new mobile clients will now support audio and video over the data connection. The Windows 8 client, displayed in Figure 2.5, has also been introduced; it uses the updated interface design found in other Windows 8 applications. These changes put the Lync mobile apps on par with products from competitors and provide a compelling way for remote workers to participate in conferences using small tablet devices.

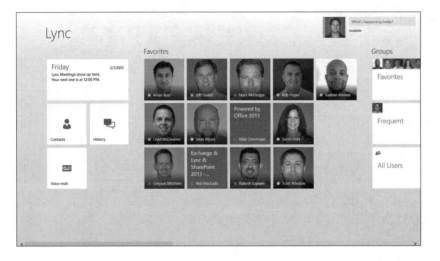

FIGURE 2.5   Windows 8 mobile client.

OneNote

Integration between conversations and Microsoft Office OneNote has existed since Office Communicator 2007 R2, but it was really a buried feature, accessible only via a submenu that most users were unaware even existed. Microsoft has made some great strides with the integration included with Lync 2013, and made the collaboration points much more obvious. While in a Lync Server 2013 conference, users can opt to start taking private notes about the meeting, at which point the meeting subject, date, and participant list are automatically populated within the new note.

The previously discussed feature is on par with the preceding version's features, although it is definitely more obviously accessible in Lync 2013. The new addition to OneNote integration is the concept of shared notes in a Lync conference. When a presenter uses shared notes from a notebook stored on SkyDrive or SharePoint, all participants can see and edit the OneNote note in real time during the conference. This eliminates the need for a single person to try to capture all the meeting notes, in which case some key pieces of information can be missed. Instead, each participant can contribute to the notebook simultaneously, ensuring that all relevant information has been recorded. A really nice touch here is that notes are displayed via OneNote Web App through the Office Web Apps Server if a user doesn't have the OneNote application installed. The OneNote integration during conferencing is shown in Figure 2.6.

The current disadvantage to this feature is that permissions to the shared notebook must be configured in advance and managed outside of Lync. Sharing the notebook within Lync does nothing to provision access to the notebook for each participant. Additionally, when a OneNote shared notebook is added to a meeting, all participants receive the sharing notification, but only those with access to the shared notebook can actually view and edit the notes. Users without access to the notebook will receive an error indicating that they do not have the appropriate permissions.

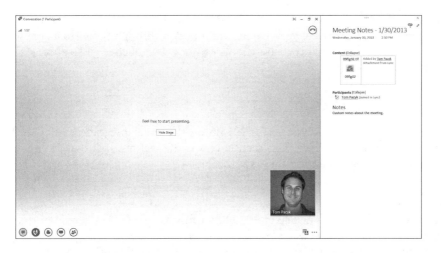

FIGURE 2.6   OneNote shared notes integration.

Audio Dial-Out

One of the key strategies in Lync voice implementations is the notion that organizations don't need to replace all the existing PBX phones and can instead leverage the Lync
dial-in conferencing features with the old phones during a lengthy migration. This worked
just fine for users who dialed *in* to the conferencing service, but there were some serious
caveats with the capability to support dial-out from the conferencing service to the PBX
phones. Although it was possible, there was no control over what numbers could be dialed
within Lync, so businesses had to turn to gateways or the old PBX to provide class of
restrictions or number manipulations. The last pain point was the fact that only a single
gateway would be targeted in this dial-out scenario, similar to the old 1:1 Mediation Server
to media gateway ratio in Office Communications Server 2007 R2.

Lync Server 2013 has added a feature to the conferencing policies to support audio dial-
out for non-Enterprise voice users. The end result is that users who are not enabled for
Enterprise Voice yet but have a Lync 2013 client can join a conference and have the
conferencing service call their desk phone. The user only needs to answer the call to
be placed in the conference. The primary advantage in Lync 2013 is that the dial out
numbers can now be controlled on a per-user basis with voice policies.

VDI

Lync Server 2010 supported a very limited number of workloads through a Virtual
Desktop Infrastructure (VDI) client and specifically excluded any kind of media sharing.
The only way to support audio for the VDI user was through USB redirection pairing of a
Lync Phone Edition client, so users had no ability to use headset or speakerphone audio
devices. There was also no capability to share video with a thin client user.

Lync 2013 has introduced a VDI plugin that is installed on the thin client and pairs with
the actual Lync 2013 application running on the remote desktop. The plugin allows the

end user to leverage devices local to the thin client for both audio and video so the media stream continues to be peer-to-peer between clients and not run through the virtualized remote desktop. The end result is that the thin clients can now be attached to local or built-in devices for audio and video.

Voice Enhancements

The final group of enhancements to Lync Server 2013 is on the voice integration when businesses use Lync for Enterprise Voice. This section covers the features that make Lync Server 2013 an even better voice solution for organizations.

Trunks and M:N Routing

As organizations began to expand Lync Server 2010 Enterprise Voice services, a common pain point was the fact that PSTN gateways could only be associated with a single Mediation server or pool. This was an improvement over the Office Communications Server 2007 R2 limitation in which each PSTN gateway required a separate Mediation server, but it still created some unnecessary headaches in trying to design a resilient solution.

For example, a common use case for a remote site was to place a Survivable Branch Appliance or Server in the site, and configure a gateway to interact with that server. For redundancy, though, it was desirable to create a separate connection between a Mediation server pool in the datacenter to make and receive calls using that gateway in case the Survivable Branch Appliance or Server was offline. This was possible only using tricks like creating a second "virtual" PSTN gateway object with a DNS name and associating the virtual PSTN gateway to the Mediation server pool in the datacenter. The disadvantage to this approach was that it usually required organizations to skip TLS security on the gateway due to certificate subject name mismatches, depending on which pool was interacting with the gateway.

Lync Server 2013 has again improved the SIP trunk experience and now defines trunks between PSTN gateways and Mediation server roles instead of directly assigning a PSTN gateway to a Mediation role. This allows the same gateway within the topology to be referenced by multiple trunks that are accessed in a prioritized order. Trunks are now based on the Mediation Server FQDN, a listening port on the Mediation Server, the PSTN gateway FQDN, and a listening port on the PSTN gateway. This change allows more flexibility on the Lync side and allows each Mediation Server to listen on multiple ports for incoming calls.

Inter-Trunk Routing

In previous versions of Lync Server 2010, all calls had to either start with or terminate on a Lync endpoint. There was no way to route calls through Lync Server between two IP PBXs or gateways. Inter-trunk routing in Lync Server 2013 allows for this scenario to take place, which might help organizations gradually move users to Enterprise Voice. Lync Server 2013 can be deployed as shown in Figure 2.7, such that it is "in front of" an existing PBX, and owns the core routing logic that allows calls to still reach users on a legacy PBX, or even allows calling between two existing PBX systems.

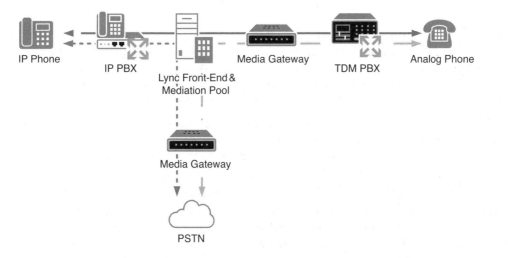

FIGURE 2.7   Inter-trunk routing.

Call control is achieved by assigning PSTN Usage objects directly to a trunk, which dictates how calls will be routed when they reach the Lync Mediation servers. This opens up new migration strategies, and requires fewer modifications to systems outside of Lync such as the IP PBX or media gateway.

Calling Party Manipulation

A really big pain point in Lync has been the lack of control over the calling party, or source, telephone number display in outbound calls. Trunk translation rules in Lync Server 2010 allowed modification of the called, or dialed, party, but had no support for the calling number. The best Lync could do was remove the leading + sign before sending the call to a PSTN gateway. The end result was that administrators had to manage translation rules both within Lync and at the media gateway, which undoubtedly led to inconsistencies and troubleshooting issues down the road.

Lync Server 2013 has introduced the capability to manipulate the calling party on trunk translation rules in addition to the called party. Administrators now have a single point of configuration for basic number manipulations, which should help simplify deployments. Media gateways can still be useful for advanced manipulations specific to a T1 or E1 circuit, but are no longer required for the outbound calling party.

Delegate Simultaneous Ringing

Lync Server 2010 offered some excellent delegation features to cover a boss/admin scenario, but one area where it fell short was if the admin user was not actually at a front desk or Lync endpoint. Even if the delegate had personally configured simultaneous ring to a mobile or additional phone, calls for the manager would ring only the delegate's Lync endpoints. In Lync Server 2013 the delegate receives calls for the manager's line on any number configured for simultaneous ring.

Voice Mail Escape

Many organizations have jumped to capitalize on the simultaneous-ring feature of Lync, which enables users to answer calls to their work phone number at a Lync endpoint, or on a mobile phone over their cellular connection. This flexibility enables workers to never miss an important call, even if they step away from their desk.

The downside to this feature was that if the user's mobile phone was turned off, or possibly was out of range for a cellular signal, the call would end up being answered by the user's cellular voice mail system. This created an inconsistency in the greetings heard by callers and in how users managed their voice mail messages because some work messages were now in their personal cellular store.

Lync Server 2013 now allows a parameter called `PSTNVoiceMailEscape` timer to be set on a voice policy that specifies the number of milliseconds for which Lync Server should ignore a call being answered by a simultaneous-ring target. The overall concept here is that administrators can dictate a time value that is probably too soon for a human to answer a call, which means the user's cellular voice mail probably answered. After this is detected, Lync Server 2013 ends the call to the simultaneous ring target, but continues to ring the user's Lync endpoints. If the call still goes unanswered, the call is routed to Exchange Unified Messaging for voice mail.

Response Group Managers

The Response Group Managers feature of Lync Server 2013 enables administrators to delegate control over Response Groups to specific users, which gives them access to the Lync Server Control Panel. Within the panel the Response Group Managers can see only Response Group workflows assigned to them, and can then manage the queues and groups belonging to that workflow.

This is a nice addition for small departments that would like control over their own workflows because it lets them manage agents, business hours, music on hold, and the entire workflow without opening a ticket with the Lync Server administrators.

Call Forwarding Restrictions

A common policy issue in previous versions of Lync Server was that numbers a user was allowed to call also dictated the numbers a user could configure as call forwarding or simultaneous ring destinations. This made it impossible for administrators to allow users to make calls to international locations, but only allow the users to simultaneously ring a national or local number. In practice many organizations just lived with this issue and would retroactively review call-detail reports to determine whether any user was incurring unusual charges.

Lync Server 2013 now enables administrators to configure separate call forwarding policies for each voice policy, and prevent call forwarding from leaving the organization or incurring toll charges.

IPv6 Support

Lync Server 2013 has added support for IPv6 addressing of all server roles, which can operate in a mixed IPv4 and IPv6 mode as organizations begin migrating internal networks to IPv6.

There is no support for down-level clients like Office Communicator 2007 R2 or Lync 2010 in a dual-stack site, so companies need to first migrate users to Lync Server 2013 in order to implement IPv6 support.

> **NOTE**
>
> Some of the advanced voice features such as Call Admission Control, E911, and Media Bypass do not fully support IPv6. The Lync Phone Edition software also does not support IPv6. Organizations requiring these features should plan on supporting a dual-stack approach for this release.

Summary

Lync Server 2013's new features make a compelling case for upgrades in organizations running Lync Server 2010, and especially for any businesses running prior versions of the products. The enhancements around video and conferencing are going to allow many businesses to leverage Lync as an end-to-end conferencing solution on multiple platforms without the need for third-party products. Additionally, the server-side and client features that now allow audio and video over data connections on mobile devices will help transform how users work with Lync.

CHAPTER 3

Feature Overview and Benefits of Microsoft Lync Server 2013

Lync Server is a difficult product to summarize in a single phrase, but it can be considered a secure, flexible, and extensible collaboration platform. From many people's perspective, it was simply considered Microsoft's instant messaging (IM) product since its inception. However, Lync Server has transformed into a complete Unified Communications (UC) solution for business that encompasses presence, IM, web conferencing, audio/video (A/V) conferencing, and complete Voice over IP (VoIP) services. Lync Server is the leading real-time collaboration platform available in the market today.

This chapter is a high-level overview of what Lync Server 2013 provides to an organization. Its features can be deployed together or in pieces, as determined by business requirements. It seamlessly integrates with other Microsoft products including Office, SharePoint, and Exchange. This flexibility is exactly what makes the product so compelling and beneficial to organizations. Because this chapter provides a complete overview covering topics both new and unchanged, if you're a Lync veteran you might find a bit of this redundant, but we also want to welcome our new Lync administrators to the fold!

Presence

Presence is the core feature of Lync Server and drives or enhances almost every other feature. In its simplest form, presence is defined as the combination of a person's availability and willingness to communicate at any given time. This presence is published to colleagues and peers.

It is what enables others to determine an appropriate time to contact a user and which communication modality makes the most sense at that time. A user has complete control over his presence state, which means he can choose when to appear available or unavailable to peers.

Without presence information, users tend to fall back on other communication methods such as sending email messages that say, "Are you free?" or, "Do you have time to talk now?" With presence information at their disposal, users have no need to send these types of messages. With a quick glance, users can see a contact's presence and make a determination about when it's appropriate to initiate a conversation. These conversations are not necessarily IM-based; they can be in the form of an IM, a phone call, or a video conference. However, the appropriate time and modality of communication are driven by the presence information. For instance, a user whose presence is currently Busy most likely isn't going to be receptive to a phone conversation, but might be willing to communicate through IM for a short period.

Enhanced Presence

Many presence engines have only a few presence states, such as Available or Away. These provide some insight into availability but traditionally require manual user management and offer little control over what information is actually published.

The presence engine Microsoft has developed behind Lync Server is referred to as Enhanced Presence, which is a combination of numerous presence states, access levels, interruption management, automated updates, application integration, location information, and multiple points of presence (MPOP). These features interconnect to provide a prolific amount of presence information that is simply not possible in many other systems.

Presence States

Lync Server presence consists of a presence icon and a status text string. A number of colors are associated with each presence class, operating on a scale similar to a stoplight from green to red. Although these colors provide a good indicator of presence, they are paired with a textual representation of the user's presence when published, providing even more insight into the current status. Some colors can take on separate text strings depending on the user's availability. For instance, the color red is displayed when a user manually sets her presence to Busy, but red can also be associated with the In a Call, In a Conference, and In a Meeting presence states. These are unique presence states, but they indicate a similar level of willingness to communicate at that moment. The core availability classes are listed in Table 3.1.

TABLE 3.1   Microsoft Lync Server Presence States

Presence Color	Presence Text String
Green	Available
Yellow	Away
	Out of Office
Red	Busy
	In a Call
	In a Conference
Dark Red	Do Not Disturb
	Urgent Interruptions Only
Empty Color	Offline

Access Levels and Privacy Relationships

Privacy relationships are the component of enhanced presence used to control the amount of information visible to contacts. In prior iterations of Communications Server, these were referred to as access levels, but they are now called privacy relationships in Lync Server. Instead of publishing the same presence to all subscribers, a user can control the flow of information based on differing privacy relationships assigned to contacts.

The enhanced presence model publishes more than just a user's presence name; it also includes email address, title, company, address, working hours, and a multitude of other attributes.

> **NOTE**
>
> A user might not want to expose all of this information to a user, so privacy relationships can be used to distribute only the necessary information to subscribers. A user can also adjust the relationship for each contact individually, giving the user complete control and flexibility for managing the information provided to contacts.

The privacy relationships available in Lync Server are as listed here:

▶ **Friends and Family**—Shares all contact information except for meeting subject and meeting location. This level is intended for personal contacts.

▶ **Workgroup**—Shares all contact information except for nonwork phone numbers. Contacts assigned to this relationship level can interrupt the user when his status is Do Not Disturb.

▶ **Colleagues**—Shares all contact information except for nonwork phone numbers, meeting subject, and meeting location. This is the default relationship assigned to contacts in the organization.

▶ **External Contacts**—Shares all information except for phone numbers, meeting subject, and meeting location.

▶ **Blocked Contacts**—Shows only the user's name and email address. Contacts assigned to this relationship cannot reach the user through Lync endpoints.

The functions allowed and information displayed for each privacy relationship are outlined in Table 3.2.

TABLE 3.2   Information Shared Based on Privacy Relationship

	Blocked	External	Colleagues	Workgroup	Friends and Family
Offline Presence	✓				
Presence State		✓	✓	✓	✓
Display Name	✓	✓	✓	✓	✓
Email Address	✓	✓	✓	✓	✓
Title		✓	✓	✓	✓
Work Phone			✓	✓	✓
Mobile Phone				✓	✓
Home Phone					✓
Other Phone					✓
Company		✓	✓	✓	✓
Office			✓	✓	✓
Work Address			✓	✓	✓
SharePoint Site			✓	✓	✓
Meeting Location				✓	
Meeting Subject				✓	
Free/Busy			✓	✓	✓
Working Hours			✓	✓	✓
Endpoint Location				✓	✓
Note			✓	✓	✓
Last Active				✓	✓

Interruption Management

Access levels control interruption management because they determine whether a contact can initiate a conversation with the user at a particular time. For example, a contact assigned to the Company access level cannot interrupt with a phone call or an IM message when the user's presence is set to Do Not Disturb, but someone assigned to the Team access level sees the status as Urgent Interruptions Only. This provides a visual cue to the team members that the user doesn't want to be disturbed, but can be interrupted for a critical issue. When a conversation is initiated, the receiver sees a pop-up notification called the toast in the lower-right corner of their screen.

> **TIP**
>
> Enhanced presence doesn't only help to suspend toast pop-ups or phone calls. Endpoints have the option to suspend audio sounds when a user's status is Busy or Do Not Disturb, and as an added bonus, they have the capability to pause Windows Media Player audio when an incoming audio or video call is detected. Although automatically pausing a media player might seem trivial, the value of not having to bring Windows Media Player to the foreground and fumble for a Pause button or Mute button before answering the phone call is significant. This speaks to the seamlessness of Lync Server and the productivity gains it can provide to end users.

Automated Status Updates

Presence is a great indicator of a user's willingness to communicate, but if left to the users to manually manage, it tends to be inaccurate. A user cannot always remember to change his presence to Busy when walking into a meeting or back to Available when returning to his desk, so Lync Server leverages a user's calendar and manages these kinds of updates on his behalf. If a user has an appointment on the calendar, his presence automatically changes to Busy during the appointment and then goes back to Available when the appointment concludes.

Endpoints also differentiate between personal calendar entries considered appointments and meetings with multiple attendees. In the preceding example, if the calendar entry is a meeting instead of an appointment, the status changes to In a Meeting instead of Busy, indicating that the user is most likely in the company of others and probably is engaged in conversation.

This calendar integration can be performed from Microsoft Office Outlook if installed, or if the user's mailbox is hosted by a Microsoft Exchange Server 2007 or later, endpoints can use Exchange Web Services to log in and pull the calendar data directly from the mailbox using Lync Server credentials.

In addition to the calendar integration, Lync Server keeps track of a user's activity at an endpoint and can automatically mark an endpoint as Inactive or Away after a certain period. This ensures that if a user has walked away from an endpoint without changing his presence, subscribers can see the last presence state with an Inactive designation as part of the status. Even though the user is still signed in, subscribers can tell they probably won't get a response when trying to initiate a conversation.

TIP

The integration points mentioned previously provide a way to keep presence information up to date automatically. However, the user has the option to manually override her presence to any state.

Multiple Points of Presence

Lync Server presence has the added flexibility of being read from multiple endpoints simultaneously. This enables a user to be signed in at multiple locations or endpoints that publish presence independently. The server then aggregates these endpoints and forms a single presence class that is published to subscribers.

For instance, a user can be signed in to Lync on a desktop, again on a roaming laptop, at home on a Mac, and also on a mobile device. Each of these endpoints publishes presence independently, and the server then forms the user's presence appropriately.

Having multiple clients signed in is generally considered a problem because how does a user know which endpoint to send a message to? Without multiple points of presence, there is a problem. However, when a user sends another user a message, the Lync Server determines which endpoint is currently most active for that user. For example, a user might be Away at three of the four endpoints, so the server sends the message only to the endpoint where the user is available.

If the server is unable to determine which state is most active, it sends the message to the endpoint it determines most likely active and waits to see whether the user acknowledges the toast at any location. If the user opens the toast at an endpoint, the server removes the message from the other endpoints. If an endpoint doesn't acknowledge the message, the server leaves the message at only one location, the most likely endpoint.

MPOP might not be perfect at all times, but it does enable a user to publish presence from multiple locations and still receive conversations at the most likely endpoint.

Extensible Presence

The built-in presence states provide an excellent array of options for users; but the Lync Server platform is extensible, and businesses can build on these choices using custom presence states. These custom presence states enable the user to select one of the standard presence classes and colors, but customizes the text displayed with the status. Although a subscriber might still see a green icon synonymous with availability, the user's presence can read "Catching Up on Email," which gives subscribers an additional piece of information to consider before initiating a conversation.

Some applications use the extensibility features to provide more information about an endpoint's capabilities. Mobile clients generally append a Mobile indicator to the presence status. This gives subscribers information that the user might be slow to respond because he is likely without a full keyboard or computer. Subscribers are aware that they likely won't be able to have a lengthy conversation but can have a short conversation.

This designation might also give users an idea that calling the user's mobile at that time is probably the quickest way to initiate a conversation.

Application Integration

Another component of Enhanced Presence is the automatic availability of presence in other Microsoft products. This means that although a Lync client runs in the background, users are able to see presence for those contacts in Outlook right next to their names. This presence can be seen directly in the context of the mail message, so there is no need to switch between applications to view a user's presence. Right from the email message or contact card, the user can see the presence and initiate an IM, email, or phone conversation with only one or two clicks of the mouse.

Lync Server can also integrate with Microsoft Exchange Server 2010 and 2013 Outlook Web App to provide presence and IM capabilities directly within the Outlook Web App interface. This allows users to see presence information within the context of email either from the full Outlook client or while using a web browser.

The same rich presence information is also available in Microsoft Office SharePoint, where users can view presence in the context of documents and files. The contact card displayed in other applications is the exact same card and interface displayed within Lync, ensuring that users have a consistent view of contacts and presence across any application.

With Lync any kind of telephone number displayed on a web page in Internet Explorer suddenly becomes a hyperlink and can be clicked to initiate a phone call. All of these integration points are not overwhelming by themselves, but collectively create an improved, unique end-user experience.

> **NOTE**
>
> The presence integration discussed previously is provided out-of-the-box with applications such as Outlook and SharePoint. However, presence can also be extended to other applications through the use of the published APIs. Companies can use these APIs to integrate presence into any existing applications or workflows of their own. Microsoft provides a software development kit with tools and documentation of the APIs to help businesses develop Lync and application integration.

Location

Another component of presence is the concept of publishing a user's physical location, which can be as vague as whether they are in the office or at home, or as exact as being on a particular floor of a building. Administrators can configure a Location Information Service (LIS) to integrate with Lync Server, which allows Lync Server endpoints to automatically identify what physical location they are connecting from and then publish that information with the user's presence. If the Location Information Service cannot identify the user's location, the user is prompted to enter one; the endpoint retains that information if the user returns to that location at any time so a user never has enter a location twice.

TIP

A user always has the option to block the publication of location if desired.

Instant Messaging

Collaboration through the use of IMs has been a part of Lync Server since the beginning along with presence. Although IMs are a simple mode of communication, they can be an excellent way to conduct a conversation in a quick manner without needing to resort to email or a phone call.

In Lync Server, IM is not unlike IM conversations that use other providers, but the main advantage to IM with Lync Server instead of a public solution is that by default all messaging is encrypted through TLS connections to the servers and an organization has complete control over how the system is used. This means that a rogue user on your network can't start a packet sniffer application and read messages sent between two other users.

NOTE

Although it might be an acceptable compromise on an internal network, this security in signaling extends to remote access scenarios too, ensuring that conversations that take place across the Internet are also encrypted.

The Lync Server endpoints support the same kind of features found in many other IM clients, such as rich text, emoticons, and saving messages. The end user and security features enable an organization to standardize on a single messaging client such as Lync instead of multiple clients and services.

NOTE

A long-standing issue with many IM applications is that users think the conversation is not captured unless conducted through email. Through integration with Microsoft Office Outlook, IM conversations can be saved automatically to the user's Microsoft Exchange mailbox. These conversations are then searchable in the same way that email messages are, so users can reference them at any time.

Web Conferencing

Lync Server gives users the ability to create or join virtual meetings referred to as web conferences, including attendees from inside the organization or guest users without an account in the Communications Server environment. Lync Server 2012 adds additional features to the Web Conferencing Web Client such as voice and video over IP from the browser. These capabilities are discussed in depth in Chapter 26, "Browser Client." Overall, many of the same features from the previous release exist, and some additional capabilities have been added. These new capabilities are discussed in Chapter 2, "What's New in Microsoft Lync Server 2013," and throughout Part IX, "Clients."

Audio and Video Conferencing

Organizations can leverage Lync Server to provide audio and video (A/V) conferencing services to their users without deploying additional clients or software. Deploying A/V conferencing enables users to perform peer-to-peer or multiparty conferences using high-fidelity audio and video conducted across the IP network. Users have a consistent experience because they can make and receive A/V calls through the same Lync client used for presence, IM, and web conferencing. Although A/V conferencing is sometimes linked to Enterprise Voice features, it can be deployed separately from any kind of telephony integration.

NOTE

It is important to note that although the term A/V is used, video is not a required component of these conversations. Users can conduct audio-only conversations using the Lync endpoint instead of a traditional phone call. These audio conversations are performed at a higher level of audio quality than a traditional PSTN call and are not subject to any long-distance or international charges like a regular call.

With video conversations, both peer-to-peer and multiparty video conversations can negotiate to use high-definition video quality using either Microsoft RTVideo or H.264 SVC/AVC.

Organizations have a wide variety of webcams to select what is compatible with Lync Server, and Microsoft provides a continuously updated list of certified devices. In Lync Server, video endpoints such as the Polycom CX5000 can be used in Lync to provide a full 360-degree panoramic view of the room.

Lastly, Lync Server video endpoints can be integrated with video conferencing systems from vendors such as Polycom, LifeSize, and Cisco.

Dial-In Conferencing

In addition to web or A/V conferencing, Lync Server can act as a conferencing bridge service for users. This enables individuals to schedule or launch an audio conference using a mix of Lync Server users and endpoints with users dialing in to a conference using traditional phone lines. Local numbers can be provided by region, or organizations can provide a toll-free number associated with one or many regions to external participants.

TIP

Instead of purchasing a third party on the premise or hosted, subscription-based audio conferencing service, Lync Server can be used to give each user in the organization a unique conference bridge through the existing infrastructure.

The dial-in conferencing service can be used as a standalone system or in conjunction with the web conferencing components of Lync Server to enable users to bridge PSTN audio with any web conference being conducted.

> **TIP**
>
> There isn't a dependency to deploy web conferencing or dial-in conferencing one before the other, but they offer the most beneficial feature set when deployed together.

Dial-in conferencing also has no dependency on Enterprise Voice services for users, meaning users do not need to be enabled for Enterprise Voice to use the audio conferencing service. A user can be enabled simply for IM and presence, but also to schedule and join dial-in conferences through the Lync client or PSTN. Enterprise Voice users can also use the conferencing service, but being enabled for Enterprise Voice does not provide additional audio conferencing features from a user perspective.

The Lync Server conference bridge has a number of added benefits over a traditional conferencing service, as covered in the following sections.

Permissions

Users can adjust the permissions for each conference to prevent specific types of attendees from participating. This gives end users the option to prevent meetings from being forwarded or from being accessed by anonymous participants on a per-meeting basis.

Flexible Conference IDs

When this is enabled for Lync Server, users are assigned a static, unique conference ID that is used for all of their meetings. A user's conference ID is persistent by default, but if a user has back-to-back meetings, it is beneficial to schedule the second meeting with a unique ID. End users can do this easily when creating a conference, and it helps to prevent attendees from the second meeting from joining the first meeting if it runs to the end of the time slot.

Lobby

The Lync Server lobby feature can be considered a type of waiting room where meeting attendees can be held before the meeting begins. As a presenter, the meeting can be configured to automatically admit all attendees from the lobby, admit only authenticated corporate users from the lobby, admit only authenticated corporate users invited specifically by the organizer, or admit no user from the lobby without manual acceptance. Attendees are allowed to join the meeting, but when held in the lobby, they are unable to hear the presenter or other users. The meeting organizer has the ability to allow or not allow attendees waiting in the lobby to attend the meeting.

As the organizer, participants are listed in the visual roster. Authenticated users show a display name, and users joining from the PSTN can display the phone number they dialed in from. Lync Attendee or Lync Web App users can enter a display name, which is shown in the roster, too.

Announcements

Typical conferencing services prompt a user to record his name, business name, or possi-bly location when dialing in to a meeting from the PSTN, and then the user can play that recorded greeting as he enters or leaves the conference. In Lync Server, where a visual roster is available to all participants, the need for this service is greatly diminished and can become a distraction to the actual meeting as attendees enter and leave.

Organizers can enable or disable the announcement service on a per-meeting basis, and it is disabled by default. Attendees who dial in from a PSTN telephone and want to hear a roster might use Dual-Tone Multi-Frequency (DTMF) tones to request a roll call, which is played only to the attendee. Additionally, the conferencing service aggregates announce-ments when batches of users enter or leave at the same time and make an announcement such as "Eight users are leaving" instead of announcing each user individually.

Languages

Administrators can define regions, and dial-in numbers for the regions can be associ-ated with specific language support. If multiple languages are associated with the region, users are presented with the option to select a language when joining via the PSTN. This enables users who speak different primary languages to participate in a single audio conference and hear menu or announcement recordings conducted in their selected language.

Enterprise Voice

Enabling a user for Enterprise Voice in Lync Server is a matter of associating a telephone number with the user's account, merging a user's audio conversations with the many functions Lync Server already provides. When telephony integration is in place, any calls to the user's telephone number ring at any Lync Server endpoints the user is signed into, and a user can place calls to the PSTN from a Lync Server endpoint.

Enterprise Voice users have a flexibility not found in most traditional PBX systems because the user has control over many functions that typically require a PBX administrator to configure, such as forwarding and simultaneous ringing. Enterprise Voice users also see visual call controls when in a call where they can mute, transfer, or end calls all with the click of a button, which can be an improvement over traditional key sequences on a phone to perform the same operations.

> **NOTE**
>
> An Enterprise Voice user has a wide array of endpoint choices from vendors that Microsoft has certified to use with Lync such as USB and Bluetooth handsets or headsets. These devices, which are designed to be plug-and-play, require no drivers and provide a high-quality experience to the end user. Some vendors also provide standalone IP phones that can log in to Lync Server directly through the Lync Phone Edition application.

Voice services are a large component of Lync Server and include some of the features mentioned in the following sections.

Call Forwarding

Call forwarding settings are available to Enterprise Voice users, and they give some flexibility not found in traditional PBX systems. Enterprise Voice users can control exactly what actions occur when an incoming phone call is received, such as ringing for a specified amount of time before being forwarded to an alternative number or to voice mail.

When an incoming call is received, users can have it ring their work number, mobile number, or home number, or simultaneously ring a combination of any of them. Furthermore, if the user doesn't answer any of these options, the call can be forwarded after a user-specified timeout, either to voice mail such as Microsoft Exchange Unified Messaging or until it rings an additional number.

Endpoints automatically use phone numbers published to Active Directory as options for the users, but individuals can add additional mobile or home phone numbers if necessary.

> **TIP**
>
> If a user works remotely—even for just a day—at a phone number not published in Active Directory, the user can configure Lync Server to forward calls to or simultaneously ring that number. These settings can also be configured based on working hours defined in Microsoft Office Outlook so that forwarding or simultaneous ringing occurs only during business hours.

The flexibility is the key component here because each user can configure settings individually to meet his own needs, and unlike with a traditional PBX, the changes require no effort from the administrator because the controls are part of Lync.

Delegation

Being enabled for Enterprise Voice enables users to define delegates to answer calls on their behalf, but the delegate functionality is slightly different from team-call, where a group of people are rung on behalf of a user. In the situation of a delegate and a boss, the boss might elect for calls to ring only the delegate first, allowing delegates to screen calls on behalf of the boss and transfer users if necessary.

Delegates have the option to use a blind or consultative transfer to send the caller to a boss. In a blind transfer, the caller is sent directly to the boss without notification, whereas in a consultative transfer, the delegate first calls the boss to check whether he wants to accept the call. Only if the boss desires to accept the call does the delegate transfer the caller.

Delegates can also perform safe transfers in which they remain on the line with the caller and principal to ensure that the two parties are connected before removing themselves from the conversation. A key advantage of Enterprise Voice delegation is that these options are performed using a graphical user interface, and users have no need to memorize phone keys and codes to perform these types of transfers.

Response Groups

Response Groups are a feature Lync Server provides to manage and direct inbound callers to agents. Workflows can be defined in which callers are prompted with specific questions and then directed to a queue of agents who consist of Enterprise Voice users. The callers' responses to any questions are converted from speech to text and displayed to the agent receiving the call.

Additionally, Response Group agents appear as anonymous to the caller. Administrators can define multiple workflows, queues, and algorithms for routing callers to the correct agents. Agents can also participate formally or informally, meaning they either can manually sign out of a Response Group or can be automatically included in a group that receives calls anytime they are signed in to Lync Server.

Call Park

Call Park features allow a Lync Server Enterprise Voice user to answer a call at one endpoint and then put the user on hold, or "park" the call temporarily. The user can then pick up that same call at some other location or endpoint.

Private Lines

An Enterprise Voice user can have a private telephone number hidden from address lists and contacts in addition to the primary telephone number, which is published to users. This additional line can be configured to ring with a different sound to differentiate calls to the private line from the regular number.

> **NOTE**
>
> Private lines do not ring delegates or team-call groups even when delegation is enabled for the user.

SIP Trunking

The concept of SIP trunking is a feature that has been supported in Communications Server since OCS 2007 R2. SIP trunking enables Lync Server to connect either to another IP-based PBX using SIP or to an Internet Telephony Service Provider (ITSP).

SIP trunking is generally used when integrating Lync Server directly with an existing IP-PBX from vendors such as Cisco or Avaya without the need for a media gateway device. Alternatively, it can be used to provide telephony service to Lync Server without the need for traditional PBX, media gateway, or wiring. Instead, an ITSP provides SIP trunking services across the Internet to allow Lync Server to make and receive phone calls using purely VoIP without a traditional phone infrastructure. It is also the method by which Lync Online users can leverage Lync for telephony functions.

E911

Enhanced 911 features are now provided in Enterprise Voice so users can dial 911 and have that call connected to an emergency routing service. Through the use of the location information discussed previously, the routing service is automatically provided with the endpoint location when dialed.

NOTE

It is important to note that Lync Server does not provide E911 capabilities, but can provide location information to an E911 routing service on behalf of the endpoints.

Remote Access

One of the strongest advantages of Lync Server is that it offers users a completely seamless and consistent user experience regardless of location. Users who travel and use a hotel's public Wi-Fi have access to the exact same features as users in an office that use the corporate network. This consistent experience is provided without a VPN connection or manual client configuration changes by the user, which allows all features to work from any location.

A Lync Server endpoint is aware whether it connects internally or externally by means of service (SRV) records in DNS, so users don't need to make any changes to their client configurations depending on their locations. When a user is remote, the signaling is performed over the standard HTTPS port 443, so it is secure and accessible from almost any remote network.

This feature is similar in function to the Outlook Anywhere feature, which has existed for Outlook users since Exchange 2003. Just as users have come to expect Outlook to function identically whether inside or outside the office, remote users have full access to the Lync Server feature set. They can view presence, exchange IMs, host or attend web conferences, share desktops, or perform A/V conversations. This even extends to Enterprise Voice users who can make and receive phone calls with their office numbers from anywhere in the world across the Internet.

Federation

Federation is a feature that enables organizations that have deployed Communications Server to communicate easily and securely across the public Internet. As long as both organizations have deployed an Access Edge Server, federation can be used to view presence and exchange IMs.

Organizations can also use federation to participate in web conferences with each other or have audio and video conversations with one another. Similar to the way email has become a standard means of communication, federation for rich collaboration capabilities has emerged as a standard way to conduct business across organizations.

> **NOTE**
>
> Federation is not limited to organizations with only Lync Server, but can also be used with IBM Sametime or Cisco Unified Presence Server for organizations that have not deployed Lync Server. Lync Server 2013 adds native federation with Skype to its impressive list of interoperability partners.

Public IM Connectivity

A special type of federation called public IM connectivity (PIC) enables MCS users to communicate with contacts using the various public IM networks. Although many organizations have deployed previous versions of a Communications Server and support federation, there are still needs to communicate with public IM contacts at times.

Lync Server supports the following public IM providers:

- ▶ AOL
- ▶ MSN
- ▶ Skype

Additionally, federation to Google Talk users can be provisioned through the XMPP Gateway Server role. PIC connectivity provides presence and peer-to-peer IM for all providers, but in Lync Server, peer-to-peer A/V conversations can also be used with Windows Live and Skype contacts.

Archiving

For organizations that have archiving or compliance needs, Lync Server provides the Archiving function, which captures IM traffic and web conferencing data. New for Lync 2013, this function is collocated on all the front-end servers in a pool. All archiving data is saved either to a Microsoft SQL Server database or to Exchange Server 2013, depending on the environment and administrator's choice.

Archiving can be enabled at the pool level to capture traffic for all users or it can be enabled on a per-user basis if archiving needs to be done only for a select group of users. If an organization has no need to capture internal traffic, archiving can also be configured to log only federated traffic.

Monitoring

A key factor in determining the success of an audio and video deployment is insight into how the system performs for the end users. Lync Server provides out-of-the-box monitoring capabilities with the Monitoring function. Like Lync Archiving, the Monitoring function is also now collocated on all the front-end servers for a pool. When deployed, endpoints submit reports when completing an audio or video call, which are then stored in SQL databases dedicated to call records and monitoring data.

Two types of reports are collected. One report, referred to as call detail records (CDR), contains information about when the call occurred and what endpoints were involved. The other is a Quality of Experience (QoE) report that contains comprehensive data, including the Mean Opinion Score (MOS) of various components, which indicates the call quality in both directions. These reports also identify which subnet the endpoints used so that administrators can quickly isolate any issues to a specific device or network segment.

> **NOTE**
>
> A SQL Server Report Pack is bundled with the installation media so administrators have immediate access to rich reports about how the system is used.

Lync Server also supports synthetic transactions that are PowerShell cmdlets an administrator can run, which simulate actions taken by users against the server. Examples of these transactions are a user signing in, two users sending IM messages to each other, and a test audio call between two endpoints. These synthetic transactions can be used to test user functionality systemwide on a recurring basis or in conjunction with the Microsoft System Center Operations Manager management pack for Lync Server, which includes support for the transactions.

Summary

All the features discussed in this chapter are compelling reasons to use Lync Server 2013 as an organization's UC solution, but users have come to expect a certain degree of reliability with communications, especially with a phone system. In Lync Server, all the features can be made redundant and resilient to a single server or site failures so that users can continue to operate in the event of a malfunction.

The methods of providing high-availability and disaster recovery for each server role vary and are outlined later, but steps have been taken to ensure that users can always hear a dial tone when they pick up a phone. Some key advancements include allowing a Mediation Server role to use multiple gateways, allowing inter-trunk routing that enables Lync to route between multiple PBXs, users receiving primary and backup pool information when signing in, and endpoints that don't depend on Active Directory during a network failure. These types of changes have made Lync Server 2013 a highly reliable, end-to-end UC solution for an organization.

CHAPTER 4

Business Cases for Lync Server 2013

In this chapter we will explore common business cases for Lync Server 2013. Before we understand the business cases for Lync Server 2013, it is important to understand some fundamentals about Unified Communications. The term "Unified Communications" has become quite a buzzword in the IT industry as of late. Unified Communications (UC) is defined as the integration of real-time communication services such as instant messaging, Presence, telephony, video conferencing, data sharing, call control, and Unified Messaging (integrated voice mail, email, and fax). The term is pretty self-explanatory. You are unifying your existing communication tools. A common approach to UC is to consolidate all communication tools into a single-vendor solution. This chapter outlines why many people believe that Microsoft Lync is the go-to product for Unified Communication, and it covers the following topics:

Why Unified Communications—Gives an overview of why UC is beneficial to all types of organizations.

Return on Investment—Describes how you define ROI, and how UC provides ROI.

Why Lync 2013 for Unified Communications—Explains why, based on what we know about UC, Lync 2013 is the ideal solution for UC.

Why Unified Communications

There are four key components to UC:

▶ Instant messaging and Presence

▶ Web, audio, and video conferencing

▶ Enterprise telephony (traditional PBX functionality)

▶ Unified Messaging

This section gives a brief description of each of the key UC components and explains why moving to a UC solution can be beneficial for organizations.

Instant Messaging and Presence

Instant messaging (IM) is the capability to communicate instantaneously between two or more people with text-based messages. Presence conveys the ability and willingness of a user to communicate. These two capabilities combine to be the most commonly used UC component in nearly every organization. Understanding how Enterprise IM and Presence evolved will help you understand why it is the core of any UC solution.

IM and Presence has been around since the 1990s. You might remember ICQ and AOL Instant Messenger (AIM). A lot of companies followed suit, and soon there was an explosion of consumer IM providers, all with different protocols and clients. Consumers started to use these consumer IM services for business communications, which was very risky for organizations. Business users were now using third-party tools that often were not secured in any form. Usage could not be tracked or controlled, and these tools were being used for day-to-day business on company PCs. When users were communicating through public networks, the exposure to malware increased, as well as the possibility of valuable company information leaving company PCs. Because of those risks, there was a need to develop an enterprise-grade solution that would allow business users to securely communicate the way they were used to communicating outside of work.

In 1998, IBM launched Lotus Sametime, the first enterprise instant messaging product. Shortly after that, Microsoft released Exchange Instant Messaging, which would later evolve into Live Communications Server, and would finally become what we know as Microsoft Lync. IM has evolved into a business-critical communications tool for most organizations. In fact, many organizations consider IM more critical than email, and some even more critical than dial tone.

Benefits of Instant Messaging and Presence

IM and Presence is the core of all UC solutions. These two features are often packaged together, and sometimes are simply referenced as only "instant messaging." IM is a feature most organizations will deploy on day one of a UC deployment. Presence is one of the major drivers for UC, because it is at the core of providing an increase in productivity to end users. Presence introduces the real-time availability of users, which allows organizations to see greatly increased productivity through more efficient communications. This benefit is best described in the scenario that follows.

Assume that Randy and Alex both work for CompanyABC. The company does not have a UC solution deployed today. Randy works in the Manhattan office and Alex works in the San Francisco office. If Randy wants to get in touch with Alex, he has two options: send Alex an email or call him on the telephone. The problem starts here: Randy does not know when Alex will respond to that email or whether Alex will be around to answer the phone when he calls. Most likely, time will be wasted with missed calls and emails while Randy is attempting to reach Alex. This type of inefficient communication impacts their overall business productivity.

Now, introduce a UC solution that leverages IM and Presence into this scenario. When Randy wants to communicate with Alex, he simply needs to look at his Presence indicator. If Alex shows as available, Randy can send an IM to Alex and ask whether he is available to talk. In some cases, an IM might be all that is needed to cover what Randy originally needed to talk to Alex about. If they need to communicate through voice, this is often a quick escalation in the same UI. If Alex is showing as not available, Randy will know what the most efficient way to communicate with him is. Randy could tag Alex's contact for status alerts, which would alert Randy when Alex becomes available. Randy could also communicate either through an email, or a phone call to voice mail, or Randy could simply wait until Alex is available to start an IM conversation.

The scenario just described clearly outlines why IM and Presence is a critical component for UC, and a major driver for organizations to introduce a UC solution to their environment.

Web, Audio, and Video Conferencing

Conferencing is not new to most organizations; however, a unified conferencing experience is new. Many organizations have web, audio, and video conferencing through three separate third-party providers. For web and audio conferencing, organizations are typically charged a monthly fee per user in addition to a per-minute fee for using these services. For video conferencing, some organizations have large deployments of video conferencing equipment on their network, whereas others might be using a third-party hosted solution.

The services available in each of these areas can vary greatly. Some audio conferencing solutions are simply PSTN dial-in bridges, in which all users in a conference will dial a PSTN phone number and be placed into a conference hosted by the provider. Some web conferencing solutions will provide a web browser application for conferencing functionality, whereas others require a desktop application to be installed. Which service options are available to organizations is not entirely important for this section; however, it is important that these services are usually not interoperable with each other. This leads to a disjoined conferencing experience, and organizations are not able to realize the true benefits of conferencing.

Benefits of Web, Audio, and Video Conferencing

When an organization deploys a Unified Communications solution that supplies all conferencing workloads as part of the solution, the most recognized benefit is a single vendor for your conferencing solutions. This often leads to a consistent user experience, and reduced costs to operate.

Providing users with a unified conferencing solution that is easy to use and that provides benefits to their productivity means that they are more likely to use it. Because end users are actually using this solution more often, the ROI is realized faster, and the organization benefits from increased productivity. In the ROI section we will explore these benefits in greater detail.

Enterprise Telephony

Enterprise telephony has evolved greatly over time. Most commonly this functionality is referenced using the term Private Branch Exchange (PBX). The term PBX was first used when switchboard operators were manually operating company switchboards, but it now is used to describe complex telephony switching systems of all types.

Enterprise telephony not only is the capability to make and receive audio calls between users, but also relates to complex features that many organizations demand of a PBX system. These can include the following:

▶ Auto Attendants

▶ Automatic Call Distribution (ACD)

▶ Call Accounting

▶ Call Forwarding

▶ Call Park

▶ Call Pickup

▶ Call Transfer

▶ Call Waiting

▶ Music on Hold

▶ Voice Mail

▶ Emergency Call Handling (911 and E911)

The features listed are commonly used to determine whether a modern telephony system is capable of performing PBX features. Many new systems are not marketed as PBXs. They are called PBX replacements with UC functionality instead (think Microsoft Lync [Enterprise Voice] or Cisco Call Manager [IPT]).

Understanding the Benefits of Enterprise Telephony as part of a UC Solution

Many UC solutions are designed to replace PBXs. Because of this, the benefits of introducing enterprise telephony as part of a UC solution is just that, to remove your PBXs. Many organizations have a PBX deployment with the following characteristics:

▶ There are many vendors across many locations.

▶ If the same vendor, there are many software versions.

▶ Each system has a separate maintenance contract.

▶ Each system has a local PSTN Ingress/Egress.

▶ Systems typically require specialized engineers to perform basic tasks.

When you introduce a UC solution like Microsoft Lync, you introduce the opportunity to remove such complexities. This results in hard cost savings in the organization. We will discuss how organizations can realize these benefits in the ROI section.

Unified Messaging

Unified Messaging (UM) is a term used to describe the integration of different messaging systems. This can include email, fax, SMS, and voice mail. This integration typically means that you can access all of these messages from the same interface and on different devices. The most common use of Unified Messaging is to combine voice mail and fax into an organization's email system.

Many organizations choose to use Microsoft Exchange Server as their UM solution. UM functionality was introduced in Exchange 2007 SP1. With Exchange UM you can connect your PBX and fax systems to Exchange Server and have voice mail, SMS, and fax delivered to the user's inbox. Many other solutions typically deliver voice mail and fax messages to a user's exchange email inbox as an email attachment, or through the use of an add-in. Modern UM systems offer functionality such as this:

▶ **Interactive Voice Response (IVR)**—The capability for the caller to interact with the UM system through voice commands.

▶ **Find Me, Follow Me**—The capability to ring other telephone numbers before leaving a voice mail.

▶ **Voice Mail Transcription**—The capability for the UM system to transcribe voice messages and present the text transcription in an email to the end user.

▶ **Secure Voice Messaging**—The ability for the UM system to encrypt voice messages and restrict the users who are able to listen to them.

▶ **Auto Attendants**—Often leveraging IVR, UM systems are able to act as a receptionist, receiving calls coming into the organization and directing callers to end users.

Understanding the Benefits of Unified Messaging as Part of a UC Solution

Deploying Unified Messaging as part of a UC solution has similar benefits to deploying enterprise telephony. Many organizations today have a separate voice mail system deployed with each PBX. Introducing a single UM solution can reduce costs, as well as increase user productivity by providing enhanced features in a single interface.

Unified Messaging is a key part of deploying UC in any organization. For many organizations, UM is considered "low hanging fruit." Exchange UM can often be deployed rather quickly and replace legacy voice mail systems, resulting in a quick ROI.

Return on Investment (ROI)

When organizations choose to deploy a new technology, there is always an investment that must be made. This investment is commonly referred to as a capital investment or capital expense.

Return on Investment is the performance measurement of how an organization will see a benefit on the investment made. When a UC solution is deployed, there are various types of cost savings, and these savings make up the ROI. This next section outlines what investments an organization must make when deploying a full UC solution, and the factors for realizing ROI.

UC Investments

Some organizations will have invested in UC prior to making the decision to move to a UC solution; however, it is still important to understand what these investments are, and ultimately how they can be paid for (ROI).

Consider the Capital Investments

The term *capital investment* in terms of UC is described as the cost to deploy the solution. When UC is being deployed, there are many components that can contribute to a capital investment. Some organizations will categorize certain purchases. For example, some organizations will spread purchases out over five or more years, resulting in a distributed capital investment, or amortization. Regardless of how an organization chooses to categorize its purchases, the following expenses are most commonly referred to as "capital expense" or "capex":

- ▶ Licensing

- ▶ Data center hardware (servers, storage, etc.)

- ▶ Media gateways (PSTN gateways, SBCS, etc.)

- ▶ End-user hardware (headsets, IP phones, cameras)

- ▶ Implementation costs (staff and professional consulting services)

- ▶ Network upgrade investments (hardware and other "setup" fees for network upgrades)

The capital investments will vary depending on the organization. Regardless of the size of the company, these investments will be significant.

Consider the Operating Expenses

In addition to capital expenses, organizations also have to consider an increase in certain operational expenses. Although UC solutions reduce operating expenses overall, it is common for organizations deploying UC to increase IT operating expenses.

When organizations consider capital and operating expenses for UC, there will be a common theme: an increase in network costs. Network investments tend to make up the most significant capital and operating investment for organizations that are deploying UC. In a worst-case scenario, existing enterprise telephony is not IP based, and because of this, organizations will not have any real-time voice running over their IP network. This results in a major investment in network expansion.

In an optimal scenario, the organization is already using an IP-based telephony system, and the new network investment must now account for increased usage like conferencing and video.

The first scenario often requires a complete network overhaul. MPLS circuits and Internet connections must be increased, and that often comes with upgraded hardware. The second scenario involves network optimization. This is a combination of increasing bandwidth and optimizing connections to provide priority to UC traffic (Quality of Service).

Consider the Committed or "Dual-Run" Costs

One factor in UC ROI that is often overlooked is committed costs. These costs can also be referred to as dual-running costs. In most scenarios, an organization cannot simply turn off a legacy system and immediately stop paying for it. Not only is there a transition period between systems, but there are often committed costs that are associated with a contract or lease. These committed costs can be attributed to hardware leases, as well as support and service contracts. Many organizations will also choose to amortize capital investments over any number of years. Hardware investments must be depreciated before they can leave the books. Organizations typically have the following committed costs when deploying a new UC solution:

▶ **Investment Depreciation**—Many organizations depreciate hardware over five years in order to spread out that capital investment.

▶ **Hardware Lease Costs**—Some organizations lease PBX hardware and PBX endpoints instead of purchasing them. These can have committed lease periods.

▶ **Dual-Running Solutions**—Costs to run legacy equipment, for example, if migrating off one UC solution to another.

▶ **Support Contracts**—Support contracts typically include a multiyear agreement between the organization and the support provider.

Before realizing return on investment, these costs must be accounted for.

In summary, a UC solution is not purely cost savings. There will always be a significant investment to successfully deploy UC. However, the benefits of a true UC solution lead to a rapid ROI, which ultimately makes UC worth the investment.

Realizing ROI with Audio Conferencing

It is common for many large organizations to spend millions of dollars a year on audio conferencing from a third-party provider. When deploying a UC solution that includes audio conferencing functionality, these organizations tend to see a significant cost savings. This cost savings is typically the largest UC ROI factor for businesses.

When deploying a UC solution like Lync, organizations can bring all of their audio conferencing to the internal UC system. Previously, organizations would pay per-minute audio conferencing charges for services that provided a dial-in conferencing bridge and audio conferencing. When this is brought in-house, those costs are reduced. The costs for audio conferencing are replaced by the costs to maintain the UC system and the inbound PSTN trunks for dial-in conferencing users. Many organizations are leveraging SIP Trunking for this functionality to even greater reduce costs. On average, organizations will reduce their dial-in conferencing usage by 85%. That 85% reduction accounts for users who are now leveraging a UC client to join a conference using IP Audio. The remaining 15% accounts for users who are still dialing in to the audio conference through the PSTN.

When the RIO of a UC solution is being evaluated, it is important to not completely remove audio conferencing costs from the total cost of ownership (TCO). A small portion of the costs that are removed are replaced by new costs. This can include PSTN trunks, PSTN gateways, bandwidth, and additional server hardware if needed. Additionally, many organizations require the use of a third-party audio bridge for advanced conferencing scenarios. This functionality is often referred to as managed conferencing. These scenarios include operator-assisted meetings, or very large audio conferences with more than 1,000 participants.

Realizing ROI with Centralized Telephony

As mentioned in earlier sections, most organizations have a distributed PBX system. When an organization is considering UC, one option is to replace the distributed PBX systems with a centralized UC Telephony platform. The centralization of the telephony platform can have many benefits.

Reduced Hardware Footprint

When an organization chooses to centralize its telephony platform, the hardware footprint is greatly reduced. This can provide ROI by reducing hardware purchase costs, hardware maintenance costs, and facility run costs.

Reduced Support Costs

Often when organizations move to a centralized telephony environment, the costs to support the environment are much smaller than the costs of a distributed system. UC telephony systems, although they are modern IP-based systems, are much less complex to manage than legacy systems. If support of the legacy telephony solution was outsourced before, the outsourcing contract might be reduced. If this was completely supported by internal staff, staffing can often be reduced, or allocated to other tasks.

SIP Trunking Opportunity

SIP Trunking is a relatively new trend in telephony. It is the capability to purchase PSTN services and have them delivered over IP connections rather than traditional T1/E1 PRI connections. Although SIP Trunking does not require a centralized deployment model, a centralized telephony deployment does introduce the opportunity to deploy SIP Trunking more easily. The combination of centralized telephony and SIP Trunking is ideal for realizing cost savings in PSTN Trunking.

Many organizations have a vast number of PRI connections delivering PSTN services. The problem with PRIs is that they come in only one size (23 voice channels per trunk in the U.S.). SIP Trunking allows organizations to have more control over how many channels are purchased. In simple terms, if you were a mid-size organization that needed 25 voice channels to support your call load, this would result in two PRIs. Those two PRIs would require two T1 connections. The end result is double the cost for a very small capacity increase.

These are the two ways in which SIP Trunking allows you to reduce your PSTN costs:

▶ **Reduction in the Number of Voice Channels**—Organizations that deploy SIP Trunking typically see a 40% reduction in the number of actual voice channels, because the capacity is much easier to predict and control. This reduction in voice channels also comes with a cheaper, more flexible delivery method: IP. Many times this is delivered through an MPLS connection from the provider directly to the organization's data center, but there are services that target small to mid-market customers that will also deliver these services over the Internet.

▶ **Shared Usage**—Organizations can reduce their voice channels even more in a centralized telephony model. When the PSTN trunks are centralized, they can be shared across all of your sites. This works very well in organizations spread across multiple time zones. In fact, SIP Trunking services can be tweaked based on time zones to provide capacity where it is needed, resulting in a large amount of cost savings.

▶ **Flexibility**—SIP Trunking introduces the ability to increase or decrease capacity as needs change. TDM connections would often require additional physical line configurations to accommodate capacity changes. With SIP Trunking, this simply becomes a matter of provisioning by the provider in many cases. SIP Trunking providers are also able to offer advanced functionality including failover routing, and multiple area codes and international numbers on the same connection, something that TDM trunks are simply not able to do.

The areas previously described are the most common areas in which organizations can realize cost savings and ROI from deploying a UC Telephony Solution. The level at which ROI is realized will depend on how willing the organization is to adopt the centralized and shared model for the telephony infrastructure.

Realizing ROI with Productivity Increases

When any UC solution is being introduced, an increase in productivity is one major selling point. How this increase in productivity influences ROI can be more difficult to calculate. Productivity increases are often referred to as soft costs, meaning that you cannot put a definitive dollar amount next to them. However, it is practical to make educated estimates based off of common scenarios that result in productivity increases. After the solution is deployed and used, it is possible to monitor usage and identify hard productivity cost savings.

A key scenario in which productivity increases can translate directly to dollar amounts is the task of checking voice mail. When you consider the process for listening to voice mail on a legacy voice mail system, it becomes clear how tedious this process is. Assume that you have a billable resource. This resource makes the company money at $300 per hour. If it takes that person three minutes per day to listen to his voice mail, it seems to be a small cost (under $2 per day). However, you must now multiply that number by all resources in your organization, say 10,000 users. That quickly turns into $20,000 dollars per day, or $100,000 per week.

When evaluating UC ROI, organizations should also consider time that is wasted for travel. Many organizations have resources that must travel to and from the office, as well as to and from clients. If you were to use similar logic as that used previously with a resource that can make the company $300 per hour, removing that travel time and replacing it with billable work will save the company money. Many organizations will charge customers travel time for such resources; however, if a business no longer has to charge for travel because moneymaking resources can work remotely with UC, that organization is now more attractive to do business with.

> **NOTE**
>
> Although I have referenced billable-type resources in my examples, in my experience organizations of all types typically associate a per-hour value with their workers; these same numbers can be used to predict productivity cost savings.

UC Presence makes it possible for users to spend less time on common tasks and allows users to increase productivity in many other areas. When users have the real-time availability for their peers, their communications are more efficient, less time is lost, and similar logic to that used previously can be applied to calculate soft cost savings.

Realizing ROI with Reduced Travel Costs

The preceding section mentions cost savings due to travel reduction. That section outlines the increased productivity and potential "billability" of users based on less travel. This next section explains how organizations can reduce their overall travel costs.

Many organizations with a global footprint spend millions of dollars per year on travel between their sites. Today, even completely U.S.-based organizations require their employees to travel between sites. In recent years, Telepresence video was introduced as a way to reduce those travel costs. However, the complexity and cost of Telepresence systems has resulted in many organizations not realizing travel cost savings. A new and more reliable trend for travel cost reduction is to deploy a common UC solution across the organization that targets each and every end user.

Not all in-person meetings can be replaced with a conference, even if HD video is involved, but the industry is realizing that the majority of these trips can be removed and replaced with a highly intuitive collaboration experience. When an organization empowers its end users with a tool that allows them to seamlessly collaborate with peers across the world, money is saved.

The process to calculate this savings varies across the different types of organizations. This is another cost that is hard to place a solid number on before the product is deployed and used for some time. However, as with the productivity increase, you can take estimates for common situations. Consider the travel expenses and the lost time associated with traveling for meetings, and estimate the savings when moved to a UC conference.

There are also many tools in the industry that allow organizations to monitor the usage of their UC system, and use that data to calculate estimated cost savings. Look for these tools to help you back up your original cost-saving estimates and show true contribution to the UC ROI.

Realizing ROI with Reduced Real Estate Costs

Another interesting trend in the industry is a cost reduction related to real estate. Many organizations are exploring the idea of a "modern work space." These modern work spaces typically contain less formal work spaces and more of a shared environment. The idea is that fewer users will actually be in the office, and therefore you can reduce the size of your offices, or remove some offices altogether. It is absolutely critical to have a true UC solution deployed to allow for this workspace transformation. Many organizations can save millions by moving to modern work spaces and reducing the real estate footprint.

This approach is not typically started with UC, but is driven by UC. In my experience, organizations that are exploring the benefits of this solution have already been working on this for quite some time. The amount of money that can be saved varies greatly across regions and business verticals.

Why Lync 2013 for Unified Communications

Now that we know what makes up a UC solution, and how UC can drive cost savings in an organization, let's talk about why you should choose Lync Server 2013 for a UC solution.

As you will read in this book, Lync Server 2013 enhances what was already a very powerful UC system in Lync Server 2010. With Lync 2013, organizations are given more deployment options, greater resiliency options, and enhanced voice, video, and web conferencing features. Lync 2013 introduces advanced UC features into a single platform, with a single piece of client software. This section outlines why Lync 2013 is the superior UC solution in the market.

Software-Based UC

The key to a true UC solution is software. Without intuitive, user-friendly software, a UC solution cannot be successfully deployed. When compared on paper, the UC solutions from companies such as Microsoft, Cisco, Avaya, and ShorTel have the same features. These solutions can perform the functionality that any organization needs for UC. The key difference between Microsoft and the competition is the software. If you look at the list of companies, which one is a software company and not a hardware company? Microsoft.

Hardware vendors are getting better at creating software, either through acquisition or through experience with development. However, these companies are playing catch-up with Microsoft. Since Microsoft Lync 2010, all UC functionality has been available in a single client UI. Even in the latest versions of Cisco's UC suite, functionality is spread across multiple applications. The complexity that this introduces to end users is a major deterrent to the successful deployment of UC.

For organizations to realize the full benefits of UC, there must be a high rate of adoption. Users are less likely to take advantage of a UC solution that is not user-friendly. Microsoft is the only company that can provide a truly unified communications experience and allow organizations to reach their full potential with UC.

Cisco is typically the biggest competitor of Microsoft Lync. The basic scenario that follows outlines the differences between Microsoft and other vendors' UC solutions, including Cisco. These differences can have a major impact on user productivity and overall user satisfaction. User satisfaction is critical to the success of UC deployments.

When you are using Microsoft Lync 2013, not only are all modalities (IM, Audio, Video, and Sharing) provided in a single application, but the conferencing experience for these modalities is in the same application. When you want to hold a conference, that conference is held in Lync. If you are in a peer-to-peer session and want to escalate to a conference, it will simply turn that call into a conference in Lync. Cisco, on the other hand, leverages two applications: Jabber for peer-to-peer functionality and WebEx for conferencing. This leads to two separate applications for end users to learn, and a disjointed experience when escalating between peer-to-peer and conference. When you want to turn a peer-to-peer session into a conference, a web page to the WebEx site must be opened. This is where the problem starts for end-user productivity.

In addition to the more intuitive user experience provided in Lync, the integration with Microsoft Office applications cannot be overlooked. Microsoft Office is the primary business application for many end users across the world. Having communication capabilities integrated into your business applications is a major factor for driving usage and enhancing productivity. Microsoft Lync integrates UC capabilities into Office applications, reducing the amount of effort required for end users to collaborate with their peers. Although other vendors can leverage APIs to show Presence and allow click-to-call capabilities from Outlook, they cannot integrate at a deeper level. Examples of this include the following:

▶ **SharePoint Skill Search**—The capability to search the SharePoint directory and view results based on skills and other user information, without leaving the Lync client.

▶ **Exchange Distribution List Expansion**—The capability to add Exchange Server distribution lists directly to the Lync client contact list as contact groups. These lists will query information directly from Exchange Server, so users do not have to worry about adding new contacts manually.

▶ **Exchange Integration**—The Lync client has the capability to display Out of Office messages that are configured by the user in the Outlook client, and stored in Exchange Server.

▶ **Conversation History Search in Outlook**—The Lync client has the capability to store conversation history in the user's Exchange mailbox. Users can also search this conversation history in the Lync client, and in Outlook or Outlook Web App with their mail.

The preceding examples show certain areas that competitors simply do not provide for integration. Office, SharePoint, and Exchange are deployed in nearly every organization, and that is why these features are important.

In addition to integrating with other Microsoft applications, Lync also allows for easy integration with other line-of-business applications. One major benefit to Lync is the development platform it is built on. The software API for the client and server are available to developers, and are currently heavily utilized for many custom solutions. The simplest form of this development is integrating functionality, such as Presence and click to call, to line-of-business applications. Many organizations have also taken advantage of the Lync Server APIs to build custom solutions that enhance business processes. This concept is known as Communications Enabled Business Processes (CEBP) and this is a major differentiator in the market. This ecosystem, which is open and partner-driven, has led many organizations to be more successful with UC than they ever could have imagined.

In summary, a UC deployment relies heavily on the software experience that is provided to users. Although UC includes telephony and IP phones are important to telephony, the true value of UC is seen through the software application providing anywhere access and collaboration. Microsoft Lync is a superior choice for UC because it is a software-based UC platform.

Lower Total Cost of Ownership (TCO)

The term TCO refers to total cost of ownership. Various solutions have components that are cheaper than others, but what is really important is TCO. Just because one software license is cheaper doesn't mean that the overall cost to purchase and run a solution is cheaper. For some time, Microsoft has claimed a lower TCO than the competition. At VoiceCon in 2010, Microsoft was able to provide some truth to this statement. VoiceCon held an RFP competition titled "Who Delivers the Goods?" This competition requested that all major UC vendors provide an RFP response. In the end, the responses were used to provide a TCO comparison between vendors. The results showed Microsoft being nearly 50% cheaper than all other vendors in the competition. Additionally, the Microsoft solution included the full UC stack, whereas other vendors' solutions were IP Telephony only.

As was mentioned before, TCO is the entire picture. In some of these cases and in my experience, Microsoft and the competition can be similar in costs when it comes to licensing. Microsoft licensing can even be more expensive depending on discount levels to the customer. However, Microsoft offers key advantages that contribute to a lower TCO:

▶ **Hardware Flexibility**—Lync allows organizations to choose the server platform as well as the endpoints to be used. This allows organizations to deploy whatever server hardware is right for them, at the right price. This includes the capability to virtualize across the different platforms available to organizations. Traditional "UC" systems will leverage IP phones as the primary endpoint. Not only does Microsoft offer an IP phone solution that is cheaper than the competition, but there are high-quality headsets available at low prices. Many Lync Optimized wired headsets are under $50, and that does not include a bulk purchase discount.

▶ **Leveraging Microsoft Investments**—In the RFP competition and in most organiza-tions, Active Directory and Exchange Server are deployed. Lync leverages Exchange for Unified Messaging features, which helps drive a lower cost. In addition to Exchange Server, many organizations are under enterprise agreements with Microsoft that include Lync core functionality (IM/Presence, Peer-to-Peer A/V and Sharing, and Conferencing Join). Because the Lync client also comes with Microsoft Office, organizations that have deployed Office benefit from their investment. This results in clients only needing to purchase conferencing and enterprise voice client access licenses, which is much cheaper than the total licensing cost from the competition.

▶ **Reduced Complexity**—Lync is based on other Microsoft technologies that IT Professionals are used to. This often results in a smaller learning curve for existing staff to ramp up on the solution. Additionally, the deployment and management of Lync is greatly simplified compared to other UC solutions in the industry. With this reduced complexity comes reduced maintenance and support costs when compared to other UC solutions.

▶ **Conferencing Cost Savings**—In my experience, no other UC solution in the indus-try is able to provide as great a level of cost savings on audio conferencing as Lync. When directly compared, the architecture and, sometimes, the additional licensing required will make Microsoft up to 50% cheaper than the competition in this area.

▶ **Rapid ROI**—Based on what was described earlier in this section, the Microsoft solution delivers a much more rapid ROI. The fact that Lync is a single system as opposed to multiple systems, providing all functionality to users, allows organiza-tions to realize ROI much faster than when deploying a competing UC solution.

The factors just described contribute to Lync having a lower TCO when compared to the competition.

NOTE

You can read more information on the VoiceCon 2010 RFP Competition at http://blogs.technet.com/b/uc/archive/2010/03/29/update-from-voicecon-orlando-2010.aspx.

Deployment Flexibility

I once had a customer make the following statement: "Give us speed where we need it." This proves to be a common theme among many organizations evaluating Lync and other UC solutions. Deployment flexibility is a key area in which Microsoft provides greater value than the competition through Lync:

▶ **Integration with Existing Systems**—Microsoft believes in integrating with existing systems and augmenting functionality, not ripping and replacing. This allows organizations to utilize their existing investments to their full potential, and then replace when necessary.

▶ **Hybrid Solutions**—Microsoft also allows organizations to leverage cloud solutions for hybrid deployments. Organizations can choose which deployment suits their needs best. For most conferencing scenarios, the cloud may be all that is needed for many organizations. When introducing true enterprise telephony, many organizations will look to move on-premises. With Lync 2013, the deployment and migration between on-premises and cloud is seamless for end users.

▶ **"Speed Where You Need It"**—Following up on the two previous statements, Microsoft allows organizations to choose at which speed they deploy their solution. If an organization has a desire to rapidly deploy the solution, it can easily be done. However, Microsoft does not force organizations to rip and replace, or upgrade scenarios. Many organizations will treat the core capabilities of UC as a more immediate need (IM, Peer-to-Peer A/V, Conferencing), and then choose opportunistic deployments for enterprise telephony. With the features and flexibility of the on-premises and Microsoft cloud solutions, organizations can truly move at whatever speed they need to, and can be successful with their UC deployment.

Remote Access and Federation

To provide the best UC ROI, organizations must be able to provide UC solutions to end users anywhere, on any connection, at any time. Some organizations have adopted the "living on the net" motto, meaning that their users must be able to do their job seamlessly from any Internet connection. Microsoft Lync is without a doubt the superior solution for remote access in the UC industry. Microsoft Lync was built with the Internet in mind. Not only does it provide users with all functionality over the Internet, securely, without a VPN, but the media codecs used by Lync Server 2013 were built for use on the Internet.

Many organizations can mistakenly discount the importance of choosing a UC solution that was developed for the Internet. Traditional IP telephony relied only on the LAN/WAN networks that were controlled by the organization. However, UC cannot be restricted to the same network conditions as traditional IP telephony. For UC to be successful in an organization, it must provide access to all functionality, from any connection, on any device. This is how organizations will see increased usage of the solution and, ultimately, rapid ROI.

Following on the remote access story, UC federation is a trend in UC technology. Microsoft Lync offers organizations the capability to "federate" and communicate seamlessly with other organizations that are running other versions of Microsoft LCS, OCS, or Lync, and public networks such as MSN, AOL, and Skype. Although competitors can provide IM and Presence federation to other organizations, no other solution allows for full audio, video, and conferencing federation like Microsoft Lync. The capability to seamlessly collaborate with business partners, customers, and now with Skype makes many organizations treat federation as a critical requirement. I have seen customers choose Microsoft Lync over the competition based on the federation capabilities alone.

CAUTION

When deciding between UC products, organizations should dig deeper than the "check box" for functionality. Federation is a good example: Cisco allows XMPP federation to other XMPP systems, with just IM and Presence available. An XMPP gateway is required on both ends to provide this federation. In Lync, XMPP and SIP federation is native to the Lync Edge Server, allowing organizations to federate with enhanced functionality to any other customer with an Edge Server deployed.

With the introduction of Skype federation in Lync 2013, these capabilities can now be expanded to the millions of current Skype users around the world. This includes both businesses and consumers. The flexibility this provides organizations for establishing communications with partners and customers is a feature that many users cannot live without. Some critics will discount the importance of UC federation over Internet connections. We are definitely not at the point where federation is going to replace the PSTN; however, many people do believe that this is the path the industry is going down. As of the writing of this book, a private, community-driven project called the "Lync Federation Directory" has verified that more than 11,000 organizations are using LCS, OCS, or Lync federation to communicate either openly or privately with other business partners. I am not alone in believing that the future is moving toward an Internet-centric communications platform.

Summary

This chapter covered in detail an overview of all UC functionality, and discussed why organizations would choose to deploy Unified Communications.

IM and Presence provides organizations with increased user productivity, and is the core to providing more efficient communications across organizations.

Web, audio, and video conferencing allows organizations to increase productivity, reduce costs, and provide users with a more immersive collaboration experience, no matter where they are in the world.

Enterprise telephony allows organizations to the break the molds of traditional, distributed telephony systems. Organizations can realize major cost savings by centralizing enterprise telephony.

Unified Messaging allows organizations to enhance the traditional messaging capabilities that users are stuck with. By introducing UM, organizations can reduce costs and increase user productivity.

Organizations that choose to invest in Unified Communications are able to achieve return on investment in five key areas:

Audio Conferencing—Many organizations are paying millions in audio conferencing fees per year. UC allows organizations to change their Audio Conferencing model and see significant cost savings.

Centralized Telephony—Organizations are able to reduce their telephony hardware footprint, reduce their support costs, and introduce the opportunity to deploy centralized SIP Trunking.

Productivity—UC introduces productivity increases that can be translated to real dollar amounts.

Travel Costs—UC functionality and UC conferencing allow organizations to reduce travel costs and become a more attractive business partner.

Real Estate—UC allows organizations to explore reducing real estate footprint through the use of modern workspaces.

Last, Microsoft Lync Server 2013 is considered by many to be the preferred UC solution for organizations large and small.

Software-Based UC—Microsoft is a software company that develops software targeted at end-user experience. End-user experience is absolutely critical for UC, and requires a truly software-based UC approach, which Microsoft Lync follows.

Lower TCO—Microsoft has proven to have a lower total cost of ownership than the major competitors in the industry.

Deployment Flexibility—Not only does Microsoft Lync integrate with an existing solution by adding value instead of replacing the system, but the combination of cloud and on-premises services allows organizations to choose at which pace they want to deploy UC.

Remote Access and Federation—The capability to communicate from anywhere, on any device, to nearly anyone in the world is thought by many to be one of the most important features of UC. Microsoft is the leading UC provider when it comes to remote access and federation.

PART II

Microsoft Lync Server 2013 Server Roles

IN THIS PART

Microsoft Lync Server 2013 Front End Server

Lync Server 2013 has various server roles. These can be combined in a number of ways to produce a myriad of architecture options. Even the collocation of services for a given role can be split out for added flexibility.

The Front End role in Lync Server 2013 is significantly changed from previous versions. There are three significant architecture changes related to the Front End Server role. First of all, the AV Conferencing role can no longer be split out as a separate role. It *always* exists on the Front End Server. Next, on a Standard Edition Server the Persistent Chat role can be collocated with the Front End Server. Finally, the Monitoring and Archiving roles, if deployed, are also now always collocated on the Front End Servers. This is true for Standard Edition Servers and Enterprise Edition Pools.

As in previous versions, a single Front End Server or multiple Front End Servers are organized into logical pools. A Standard Edition Server exists as the only server in a pool, whereas multiple Enterprise Edition Servers can exist in a pool to provide redundancy and scalability. HTTP traffic should still be load balanced by a hardware load balancer; however, other Lync services are often load balanced via DNS. This architecture moves complex traffic, SIP and media, off of hardware load balancers traditionally designed solely for HTTP traffic and simplifies the overall design.

NOTE

Assuming that all clients are Lync 2010 or higher, DNS load balancing is the preferred method, leaving only HTTP services to a hardware load balancer.

This chapter highlights the full life cycle of the Front End Server role. Because the Front End Server is deployed first, this chapter also reviews the steps necessary to prepare Active Directory. Then it moves on to the installation of the Standard and Enterprise Editions of the Front End Server role, followed by configuration and administration. Finally, the chapter concludes with troubleshooting and best practices.

Active Directory Preparation

Microsoft Lync Server 2013 heavily leverages Active Directory. This results in tight integration across the Microsoft stack, including Microsoft Exchange and Microsoft SharePoint Server. However, first Active Directory must be prepared before installation can begin. All the Active Directory preparation steps can be performed in either the Deployment Wizard GUI or the Lync Server Management Shell, a customized version of PowerShell. This chapter reviews both methods.

The first step is to ensure that your Active Directory environment meets the minimum requirements for Lync Server 2013. The requirements are outlined here:

▶ All domain controllers in the forest where Lync Server 2013 will be deployed must be Windows Server 2003 SP2 or higher.

▶ All domains where you deploy Lync Server 2013 must have a functional level of Windows 2003 native or higher.

▶ The functional level for the forest must be Windows 2003 native or higher.

After the Active Directory prerequisites have been met, the next step is to extend the Active Directory schema to support Lync Server 2013. The schema preparation process adds new classes and attributes to Active Directory that are required for Lync Server 2013. This process must be run as a user that is a member of the Schema Admins group and is a local administrator on the server that holds the Schema Master FSMO role.

NOTE

To run the preparation steps from another domain member server other than the Schema Master, ensure that the remote registry service is running and the appropriate registry key is set on the Schema Master. In addition, the Active Directory Remote Server Administration Tools (AD DS) feature must be installed on the server where the preparation steps will run.

To extend the Active Directory schema using the Lync Server Deployment Wizard, as shown in Figure 5.1, follow these steps:

1. From the Lync Server 2010 installation media, run `Setup.exe`.

2. Click Prepare Active Directory.

3. For Step 1: Prep Schema, click Run.

4. At the Prepare Schema screen, click Next. You'll see the Management Shell command that is being executed, as shown in Figure 5.2.

5. Ensure that the process was successful and click Finish to close the window.

6. Ensure that the information has replicated to all domain controllers before continuing to the next step.

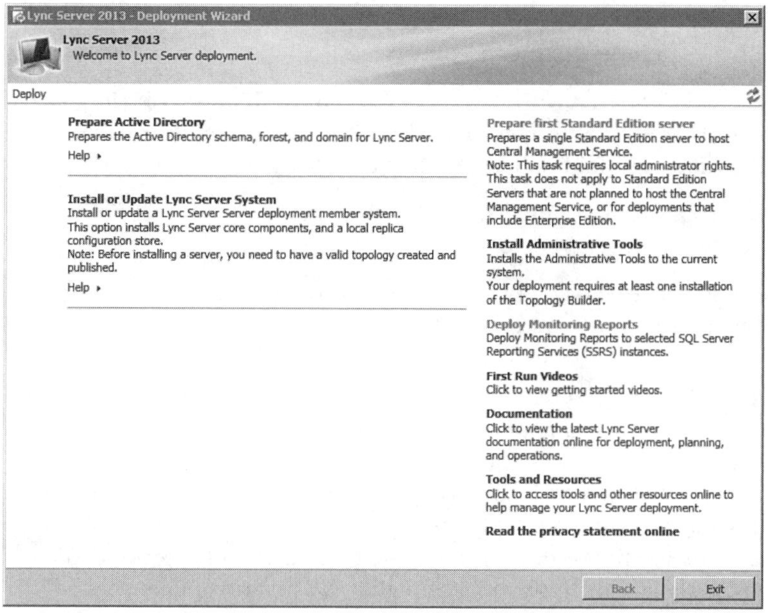

FIGURE 5.1   Lync Server 2013 Deployment Wizard.

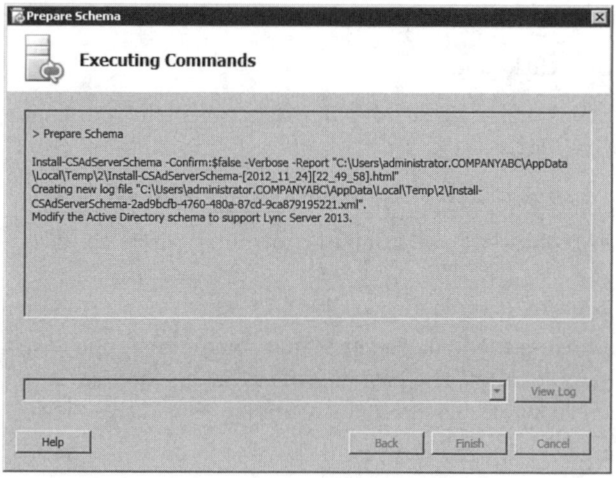

FIGURE 5.2   Prepare Schema command.

To prepare the Active Directory schema using the Lync Server Management Shell, open the shell and run the `Install-CsAdServerSchema` cmdlet. The proper syntax for the command is `Install-CsAdServerSchema -LDF <full directory path where the ldf files are located>`. For example

```
Install-CsAdServerSchema -LDF "C:\Program Files\Microsoft Lync Server
➥2013\Deployment\Setup"
```

The Lync Schema extension process adds the following attributes to Active Directory. The first two are flagged `MayContain` for every user account.

▶ **msExchUserHoldPolicies**—Shared with Exchange 2013 and will already be in place if the schema has already been extended for Exchange 2013. It is a multivalue attribute that holds identifiers for user hold policies applied to a given user account.

▶ **msRTCSIP-UserRoutingGroupId**—Defines the SIP routing group ID. The SIP routing group ID defines which Front End Server a user will register to.

▶ **msRTCSIP-MirrorBackEndServer**—Used to store the information for the mirrored SQL Server backend used by the front-end pool.

The next step is to prepare the Active Directory Forest. This process must be run by a user of the enterprise admins group or domain admins for the root domain. Forest preparation creates global objects and sets the appropriate permissions and groups to complete the installation process. Note that in a new deployment the global settings are automatically stored in the Configuration partition. If you are upgrading from an older version of Lync Server, you can still store the settings in the System container as was standard during previous versions' installation. However, although it is not a requirement, it is recommended to move the global settings container from the System partition to the Configuration partition as part of the Lync Server 2013 installation process.

The Deployment Wizard should still be up from the preceding step. If not, run `setup.exe` and it will pick up where you left off. Follow these steps to prepare the forest:

1. For Step 3: Prepare Current Forest, click Run.

2. At the Prepare Forest screen, click Next. You'll see the Management Shell command that is being executed, as shown in Figure 5.3.

3. Ensure that the process was successful and click Finish to close the window.

4. Ensure that the information has replicated to all domain controllers before continuing to the next step.

To prepare the Active Directory Forest using the Lync Server Management Shell, open the shell and run the `Enable-CsAdForest` cmdlet. The proper syntax for the command is `Enable-CsAdForest -GroupDomain <FQDN of the domain to create the universal groups>`. For example

```
Enable-CsAdForest -GroupDomain companyabc.com
```

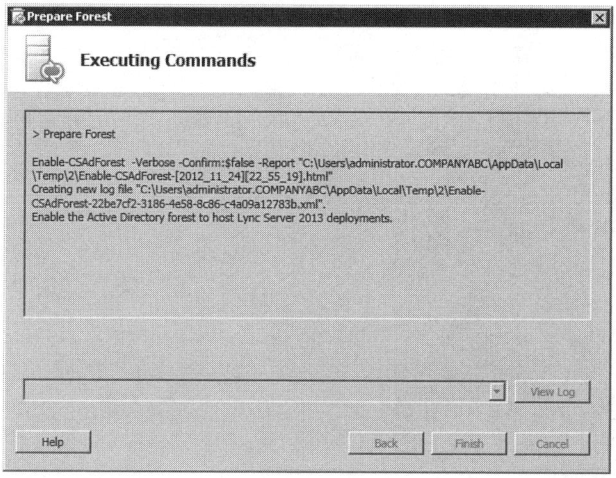

FIGURE 5.3   Prepare Forest command.

The final step is to prepare the active directory domain or domains. You'll need to run this in every domain where you plan to deploy Lync Server 2013. This step will add to universal groups the necessary ACEs (access control entries). As in the two previous steps, this can be done through the Lync Server Deployment Wizard or the Lync Server Management Shell.

Using the Deployment Wizard, perform the following steps. Note that if you closed the Deployment Wizard you'll need to run `setup.exe` again.

1. For Step 5: Prepare Current Domain, click Run.

2. At the Prepare Domain screen, click Next. You'll see the Management Shell command that is being executed, as shown in Figure 5.4.

3. Ensure that the process was successful and click Finish to close the window.

4. Ensure that the information has replicated to all domain controllers before continuing to the next step.

To prepare an Active Directory domain using the Lync Server Management Shell, open the shell and run the `Enable-CsAdDomain` cmdlet. The proper syntax for the command is `Enable-CsAdDomain -Domain <current domain FQDN> -GroupDomain <FQDN of the domain where the Universal groups were created>`. For example

`Enable-CsAdDomain -Domain companyabc.com -GroupDomain companyabc.com`

NOTE

Note that the PowerShell method is the only way to perform the domain preparation steps when only 32-bit domain controllers are available.

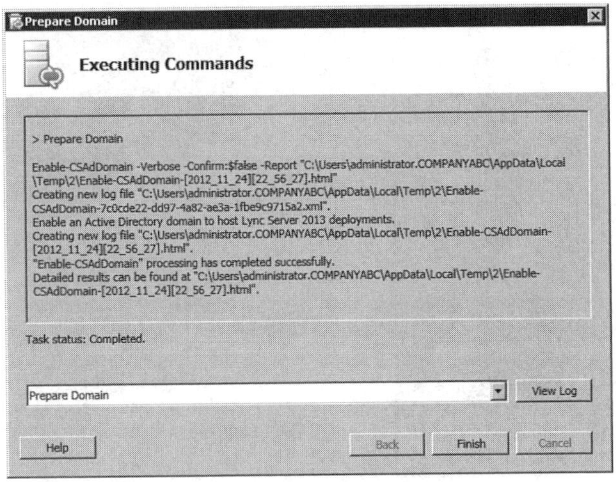

FIGURE 5.4   Prepare Domain command.

Following is a list of Active Directory Administration groups created by the preparation processes. They are referenced throughout the book and are good to be familiar with.

Service groups:

▶ RTCHSUniversalServices—Includes service accounts used to run Front End Server and allows servers read/write access to Lync Server global settings and Active Directory user objects.

▶ RTCComponentUniversalServices—Includes service accounts used to run conferencing servers, Web Services, Mediation Server, Archiving Server, and Monitoring Server.

▶ RTCProxyUniversalServices—Includes service accounts used to run Lync Server Edge Servers.

▶ RTCUniversalConfigReplicator—Includes Lync servers that participate in Central Management Store replication.

▶ RTCSBAUniversalServices—Grants read-only permission to Lync server settings and allows for the configuration of survival branch appliance devices.

Administration groups:

▶ RTCUniversalServerAdmins—Allows members to manage server and pool settings.

▶ RTCUniversalUserAdmins—Allows members to manage user settings and move users from one server or pool to another.

▶ RTCUniversalReadOnlyAdmins—Allows members to read server, pool, and user settings.

Infrastructure groups:

▶ `RTCUniversalGlobalWriteGroup`—Grants write access to global setting objects for Lync Server.

▶ `RTCUniversalGlobalReadOnlyGroup`—Grants read-only access to global setting objects for Lync Server.

▶ `RTCUniversalUserReadOnlyGroup`—Grants read-only access to Lync Server user settings.

▶ `RTCUniversalServerReadOnlyGroup`—Grants read-only access to Lync Server settings. This group does not have access to pool-level settings, only to settings specific to an individual server.

▶ `RTCUniversalSBATechnicians`—Grants read-only permission to the Lync Server configuration, and members of this group are placed in the local administrator group of the survivable branch appliance during installation.

Forest preparation then adds service and administration groups to the appropriate infrastructure groups, as described here:

▶ `RTCUniversalServerAdmins` is added to `RTCUniversalGlobalReadOnlyGroup`, `RTCUniversalGlobalWriteGroup`, `RTCUniversalServerReadOnlyGroup`, and `RTCUniversalUserReadOnlyGroup`.

▶ `RTCUniversalUserAdmins` is added as a member of `RTCUniversalGlobalReadOnlyGroup`, `RTCUniversalServerReadOnlyGroup`, and `RTCUniversalUserReadOnlyGroup`.

▶ `RTCHSUniversalServices`, `RTCComponentUniversalServices`, and `RTCUniversalReadOnlyAdmins` are added as members of `RTCUniversalGlobalReadOnlyGroup`, `RTCUniversalServerReadOnlyGroup`, and `RTCUniversalUserReadOnlyGroup`.

Forest preparation also creates the following role-based access control (RBAC) groups:

▶ `CSAdministrator`

▶ `CSArchivingAdministrator`

▶ `CSBranchOfficeTechnician`

▶ `CSHelpDesk`

▶ `CSLocationAdministrator`

▶ `CSResponseGroupAdministrator`

▶ `CSPersistentChatAdministrator`

▶ `CSServerAdministrator`

▶ `CSUserAdministrator`

▶ CSViewOnlyAdministrator

▶ CSVoiceAdministrator

▶ CSResponseGroupManager

Installation

This section outlines the steps for installing both the Standard and the Enterprise Edition of Lync Server 2013. Standard Edition is generally used for small deployments, whereas Enterprise Edition offers significant benefits for redundancy and a scalability. The largest difference between the Standard Edition and the Enterprise Edition of Lync Server 2013 is that the Standard Edition uses SQL Server Express, previously known as MSDE, whereas Enterprise Edition uses a full version of SQL 2008 or 2012. In addition, a Standard Edition Server can also host the Persistent Chat service whereas an Enterprise Edition front-end pool requires persistent chat to be hosted on a dedicated server.

Lync Server 2013 Topology Builder

After preparing Active Directory, the next step is install the Lync Server 2013 Topology Builder. This tool is new and very powerful. With a single tool it enables an administrator to design and validate a Lync Server 2013 topology and then publish it to Active Directory. This process is very similar to Lync 2010 but offers a bit more flexibility inline with the improved feature set of Lync 2013.

Installation of the Topology Builder does come with some prerequisites and requirements. First, the administrator must be a member of the Domain Admins account in Active Directory. The right to install the Topology Builder can be delegated, but only by a user that is a member of both the Domain Admins and RTCUniversalServerAdmin groups. The other requirements and prerequisites are outlined here:

▶ 64-bit edition of one of the following:

  ▶ Windows Server 2008 R2.

  ▶ Windows Server 2012.

  ▶ Windows 7.

  ▶ Window 8.

▶ .Net Framework 4.5.

▶ Microsoft Visual C++ 2008 Redistributable x64 11.0.50727.1. The Deployment Wizard will automatically install this package if it is not already installed.

▶ Windows PowerShell 3.0. This is already installed for Windows Server 2012. For Windows Server 2008 R2, it must be downloaded separately (Microsoft KB2506143).

▶ Windows Indentity Foundation (for Windows Server 2008 R2 only). This component must be downloaded separately (Microsoft KB974405). Note that this includes PowerShell 3.0.

After the prerequisites are installed, the actual installation of the Topology Builder tool can begin.

1. Run `setup.exe` from the installation media. It is located at `\setup\amd64\setup.exe`.

2. If the installer prompts you to install the Microsoft Visual C++ 2008 Redistributable, click Yes and follow the installation wizard.

3. Click Install Administrative Tools from the right-column menu of the Deployment Wizard. This installs all the tools, including Topology Builder.

4. After installation is complete, there should be a green check mark next to the Install Administrative Tools link, grayed out, as shown in Figure 5.5.

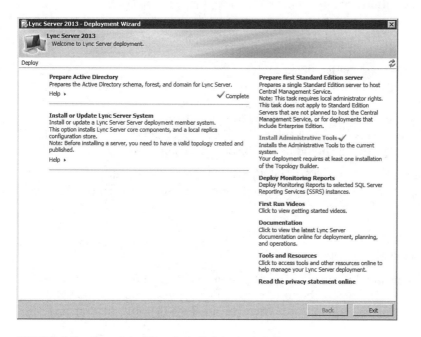

FIGURE 5.5   Completed Topology Builder installation.

The Topology Builder tool functions differently depending on your choice of Standard Edition or Enterprise Edition deployment. The process is outlined in each respective section that follows.

Standard Edition Installation

As noted previously, Lync Server 2013 Standard Edition is designed for smaller deployments. Standard Edition deployments can have only one server per pool and use SQL Server Express on the same server as the front end. This results in limited scalability and limited high-availability options. For this reason, Standard Edition is recommended only for small deployments. The first step for any Standard Edition deployment is to prepare the server as a Central Management Store and prepare the database:

1. From the main Deployment Wizard screen, click Prepare the first Standard Edition Server in the right-hand pane.

2. Click Next at the first screen.

3. The window displays the actions being performed to prepare the server as the first Standard Edition Server, including setting up the central management store. Wait as this process takes a few minutes to complete.

4. When it's done, ensure that it completed successfully and click Finish.

The next step is to define the topology with Topology Builder.

Topology Builder for Standard Edition Deployments

Lync Server 2013 uses the published topology to process traffic and maintain overall topology information. To ensure that the topology is valid, it is recommended to run the Topology Builder before your initial deployment and publish an updated topology after each topological change. This example shows a Standard Edition topology. Remember, if you change the topology later, it should be republished to ensure consistency.

When you first launch Lync Server 2013 Topology Builder, you'll see a fairly blank MMC screen, as shown in Figure 5.6. Compare that to the detailed result at the end of this example.

To begin using Topology Builder, follow these steps:

1. In the right-hand Action pane, click New.

2. Define the default SIP domain. In many deployments this is simply your domain name, as shown in Figure 5.7. In more complex deployments you can add SIP domains by clicking the Add button. When you are done defining SIP domains, click OK.

3. In the right-hand Action pane, click Define Site. Enter the appropriate information as shown in Figure 5.8, and click OK.

> **NOTE**
>
> Note that Lync Server sites have no relation to Active Directory sites. They are completely separate and unique to Lync Server.

FIGURE 5.6   Topology Builder with no topology defined.

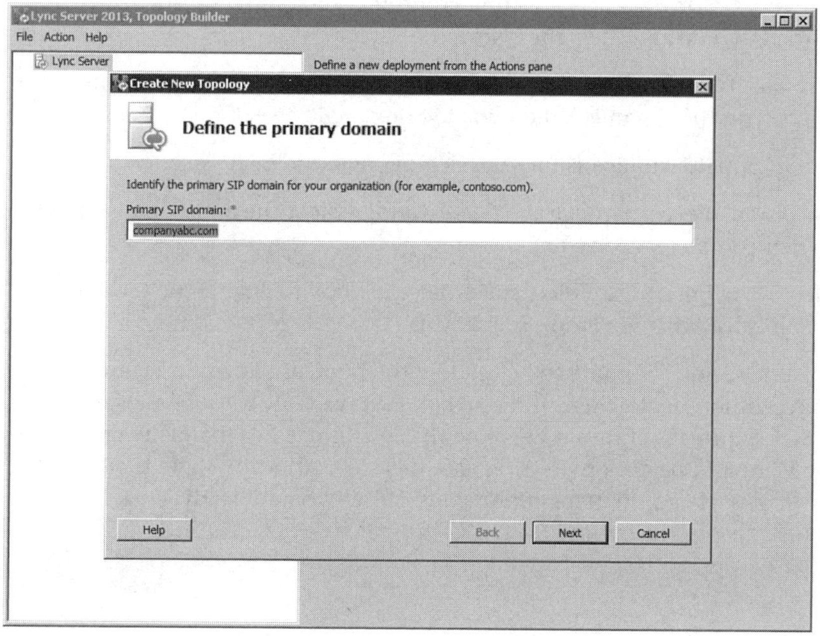

FIGURE 5.7   Define the default SIP domain.

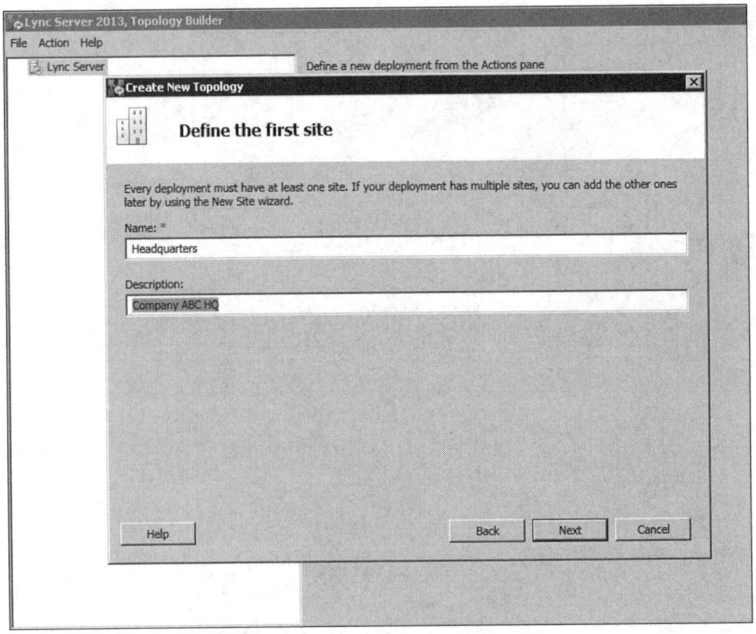

FIGURE 5.8   Define the site.

4. In the right-hand Action pane, click Define Front End Pool and click the radio button for Standard Edition; then click Next.

5. Define the System FQDN as shown in Figure 5.9. For a Standard Edition deployment this will also be your pool name. When you are done, click Next.

6. Choose the appropriate workloads for your deployment and click Next.

7. If you choose to enable archiving and/or monitoring, select the appropriate check box here. When complete, click Next.

8. If you are deploying Enterprise Voice, click the check box to enable the Mediation Server role collocated with the Front End Server.

9. Define the database and file share to be used by the pool, as shown in Figure 5.10. For a Standard Edition deployment the SQL box is grayed out because a local instance of SQL Express is always used. Note that you'll need to manually create the share on the front end before progressing past this step. After the share is created, Lync Server assigns the appropriate permissions. When you are ready, click Next.

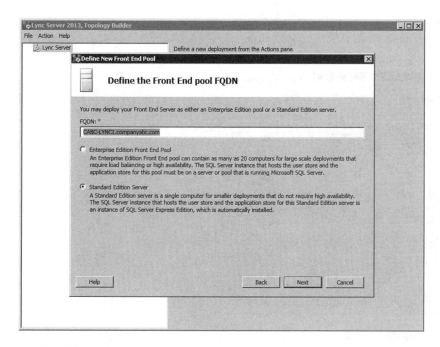

FIGURE 5.9   Define the front-end pool.

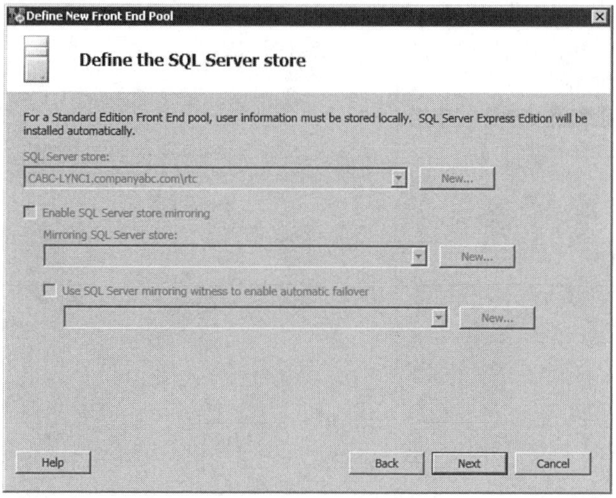

FIGURE 5.10   Define the SQL instance.

10. Define the file store as shown in Figure 5.11. In general, this is created on the Front End Server in a Standard Edition deployment.

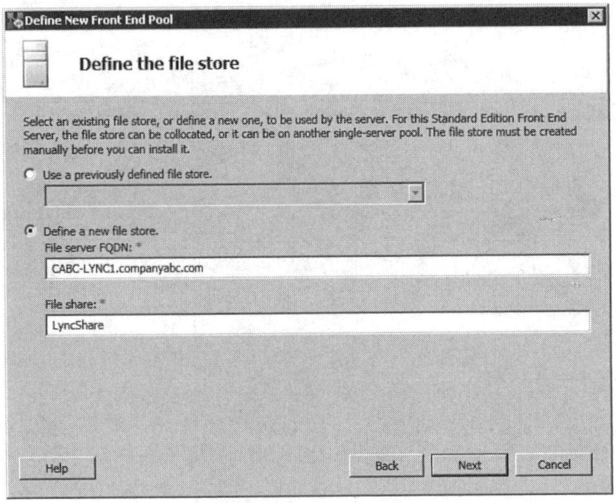

FIGURE 5.11   Define the file store.

11. Define the web services URLs for the pool. Often the internal and external URLs are different, as shown in Figure 5.12. They can be defined here. When complete, click Next.

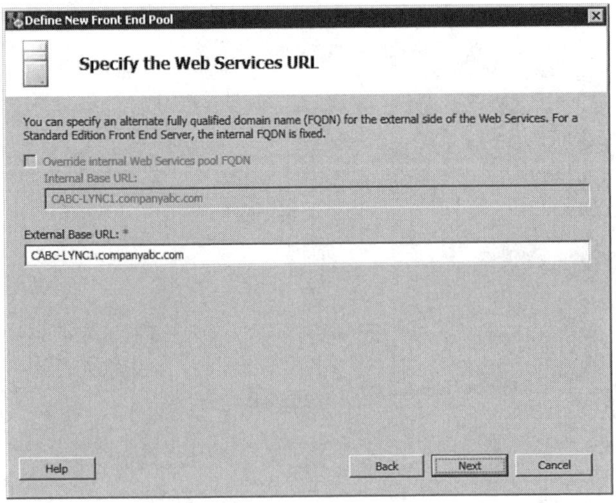

FIGURE 5.12   Web services URLs.

12. Define an Office Web Apps Server. Note that this server must be deployed in advance and pre-existing to define it here.

This completes the initial topology definition. However, there are additional steps to complete a fully functional topology. The next step is to define easy-to-remember URLs for common Lync Server 2013 functions:

1. From the main Topology Builder page, where your site name is highlighted, right-click and choose Properties. Select Simple URLs in the left pane, as shown in Figure 5.13, and enter your preferred simple URLs.

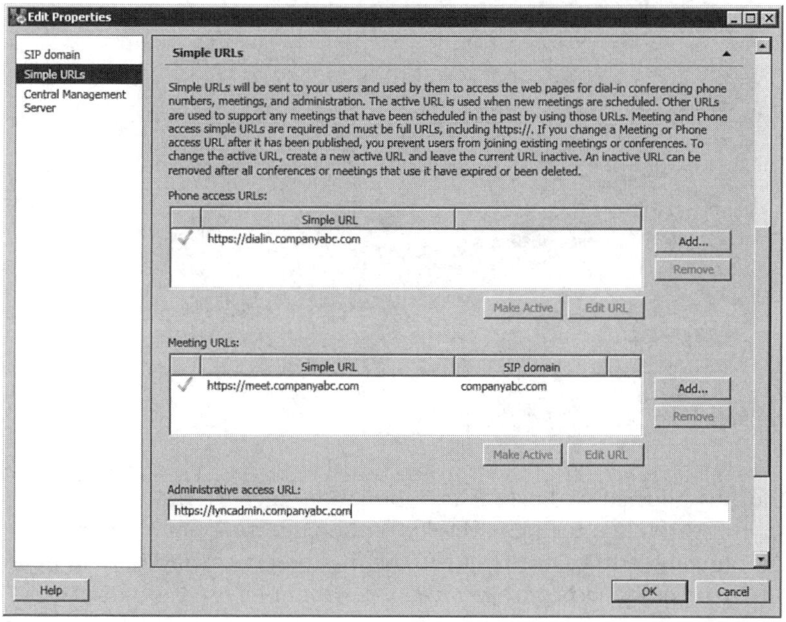

FIGURE 5.13   Expand the Simple URLs item.

> **TIP**
>
> It is recommended to leave the Phone Access and Meeting URLs at their default values. For the Administrative Access URL, define an easy-to-remember FQDN that is not already in use. Be sure to create this record in DNS pointing to the same IP address as the Web Services internal FQDN.

2. Enter easy-to-remember URLs for Phone Access Administrative Access, and Meeting services, as shown in Figure 5.14. Note that the following three examples are all valid for Lync Server Simple URLs:

▶ https://<function>.<domain _fqdn> - https://dialin.companyabc.com

▶ https://<sip_domain>/<function> - https://companyabc.com/dialin

▶ https://<External_WebPool_FQDN>/<function> - https://LyncWeb.
companyabc.com/dialin

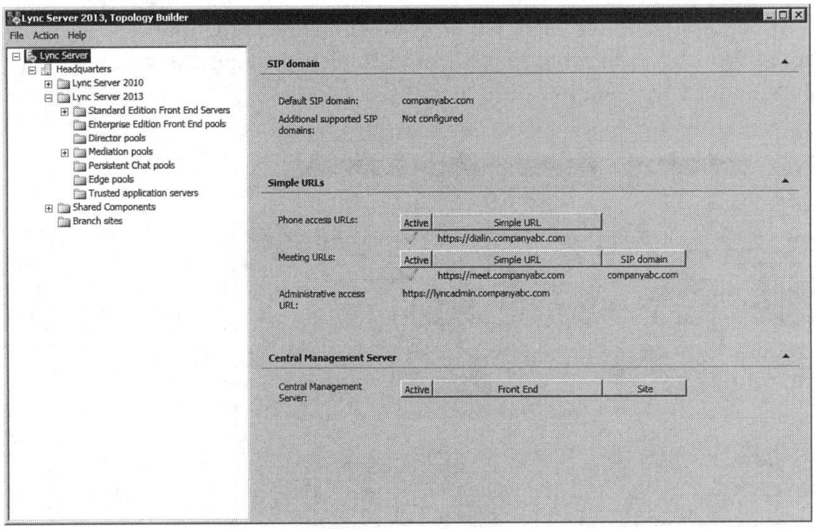

FIGURE 5.14   Configured Simple URLs.

Note that these are the only allowed syntaxes. Port information, such as https://dialin.
companyabc.com:443, is invalid. If you choose the first option, all the FQDNs will need
to be included as SANs on your certificates. If you choose the second or third option, note
that the following virtual directory names are reserved and cannot be used as part of a
Simple URL:

▶ ABS

▶ Conf

▶ LocationInformation

▶ RequestHandler

▶ AutoUpdate

▶ cscp

▶ OCSPowerShell

▶ RGSClients

▶ CertProv

▶ GetHealth

▶ ReachWeb

▶ RGSConfig

▶ CollabContent

▶ GroupExpansion

▶ RequestHandlerExt

▶ WebTicket

The final step is to publish the topology to the Central Management Store. In a Standard Edition deployment this is the first front end you define. Perform the following steps to publish your topology:

1. From the Topology Builder Tool, select the top-level menu item in the left-hand pane, Lync Server, as shown in Figure 5.15.

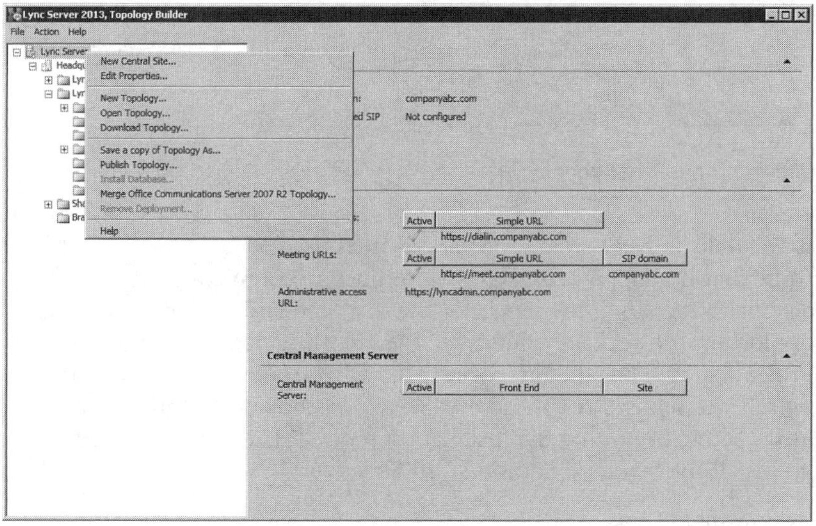

FIGURE 5.15   Publishing the Lync topology.

2. Expand the Central Management Server option in the main pane and click Edit.

3. Select Publish Topology, as shown in Figure 5.15.

4. At the opening screen, click Next.

5. Ensure that correct Central Management Store is selected and click Next. This starts the publishing process and overwrites any existing topologies.

6. Check the Create Other Databases box. Ensure that the account being used for installation has permission to perform this function. Click Next.

7. The Publish Topology window displays the actions being performed. Ensure that all steps say "Success" when it is finished, as shown in Figure 5.16, and then click Finish.

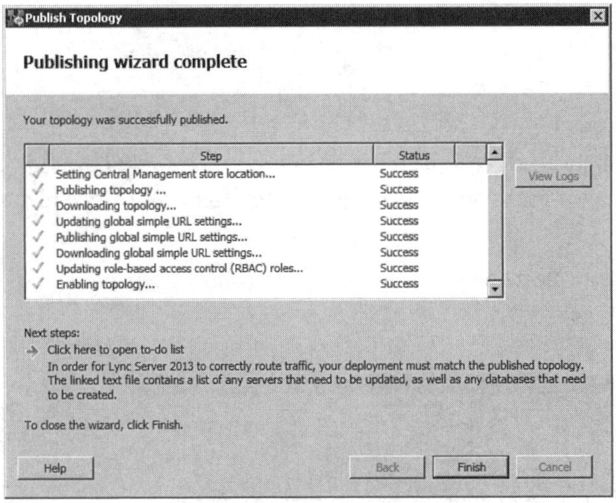

FIGURE 5.16   Successfully published topology.

Installing the Front End Role

It is important to note that if you jumped to this section before completing the preceding steps, you need to go back. Preparing the server for the first Standard Edition Server and building a valid topology in the Topology Builder tool are both prerequisites to installing the Front End role. It should be familiar if you've already installed Lync Server 2010. Administrators new to Lync Server 2013 are advised to review the new features, requirements, and prequisites before beginning the installation process. The following prerequisites are required to install the Standard Edition Front End role:

▶ IIS with the following options:

   ▶ Static Content

   ▶ Default Document

   ▶ Directory Browsing

   ▶ HTTP Errors

   ▶ HTTP Redirection

   ▶ ASP.NET (all)

- ▶ .NET Extensibility (all)

- ▶ Internet Server API (ISAPI) Extensions

- ▶ ISAPI Filters

- ▶ HTTP Logging

- ▶ Logging Tools

- ▶ Request Monitor

- ▶ Tracing

- ▶ Basic Authentication

- ▶ Windows Authentication

- ▶ Request Filtering

- ▶ Static Content Compression

- ▶ IIS Management Console

- ▶ IIS Management Scripts and Tools

▶ Message Queueing with Directory Service Integration

Note that this can also be done in PowerShell using the following commands. The first command, `Import-Module`, is not needed in Windows Server 2012.

```
Import-Module ServerManager
Add-WindowsFeature Web-Dyn-Compression,desktop-experience,RSAT-ADDS,Web-Server,Web-
Scripting-Tools,Web-Windows-Auth,Web-Asp-Net,Web-Log-Libraries,Web-Http-Tracing,
Web-Stat-Compression,Web-Default-Doc,Web-ISAPI-Ext,Web-ISAPI-Filter,Web-Http-
Errors,Web-Http-Logging,Web-Net-Ext,Web-Client-Auth, Web-Filtering,Web-Mgmt-
Console,Msmq-Server,Msmq-Directory
```

After you've completed the steps previously outlined, the server is ready to install the Front End role. From the main Lync Server 2013 Deployment Wizard screen click Install or Update Lync Server System from the main pane.

First click Install Local Configuration Store. Note that the local configuration store holds significantly more data in Lync 2013 than it did in Lync 2010. Follow these steps to complete the installation process:

1. For Step 2: Setup or Remove Lync Server Components, click Run.

2. At the screen that pops up, click Next.

3. The next screen shows the actions being performed, as shown in Figure 5.17. This process takes a few minutes to complete.

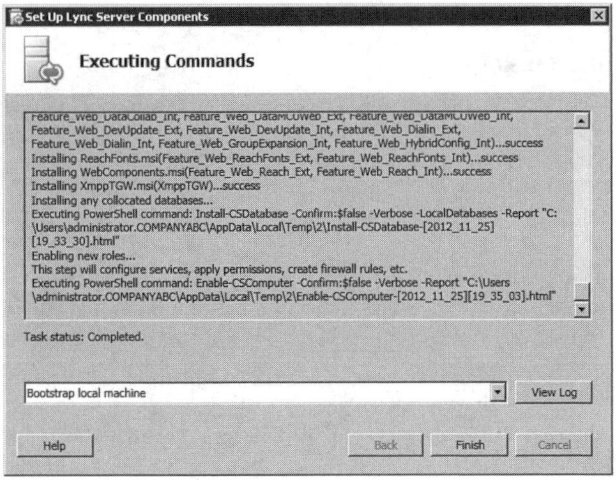

Set Up Lync Server Components

Executing Commands

```
Feature_Web_DataCollab_Int, Feature_Web_DataMCUWeb_Ext, Feature_Web_DataMCUWeb_Int,
Feature_Web_DevUpdate_Ext, Feature_Web_DevUpdate_Int, Feature_Web_Dialin_Ext,
Feature_Web_Dialin_Int, Feature_Web_GroupExpansion_Int, Feature_Web_HybridConfig_Int)...success
Installing ReachFonts.msi(Feature_Web_ReachFonts_Ext, Feature_Web_ReachFonts_Int)...success
Installing WebComponents.msi(Feature_Web_Reach_Ext, Feature_Web_Reach_Int)...success
Installing XmppTGW.msi(XmppTGW)...success
Installing any collocated databases...
Executing PowerShell command: Install-CSDatabase -Confirm:$false -Verbose -LocalDatabases -Report "C:
\Users\administrator.COMPANYABC\AppData\Local\Temp\2\Install-CSDatabase-[2012_11_25]
[19_33_30].html"
Enabling new roles...
This step will configure services, apply permissions, create firewall rules, etc.
Executing PowerShell command: Enable-CSComputer -Confirm:$false -Verbose -Report "C:\Users
\administrator.COMPANYABC\AppData\Local\Temp\2\Enable-CSComputer-[2012_11_25][19_35_03].html"
```

Task status: Completed.

Bootstrap local machine   ▼   View Log

Help   Back   Finish   Cancel

FIGURE 5.17   Installing the Front End role.

4. After the task completes, click Finish and you are brought back to the Deployment Wizard.

5. Review Step 3: Request, Install or Assign Certificates, and click Run.

6. At the next screen choose Default.

7. Click Request, as shown in Figure 5.18.

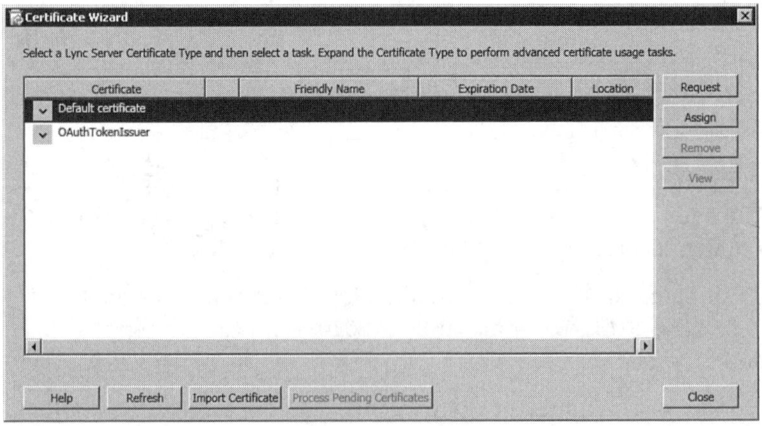

Certificate Wizard

Select a Lync Server Certificate Type and then select a task. Expand the Certificate Type to perform advanced certificate usage tasks.

Certificate	Friendly Name	Expiration Date	Location	
Default certificate				Request
OAuthTokenIssuer				Assign
				Remove
				View

Help   Refresh   Import Certificate   Process Pending Certificates   Close

FIGURE 5.18   Request the default certificate.

8. Assuming you are using an internal certificate authority (CA), choose Send the Request Immediately to an Online Certificate Authority, and click Next. This is the default option.

9. Select the appropriate certificate authority for your environment from the drop-down list, choose a friendly name and key length, and check the box for Mark the Certificate's Private Key as Exportable, as shown in Figure 5.19, and click Next.

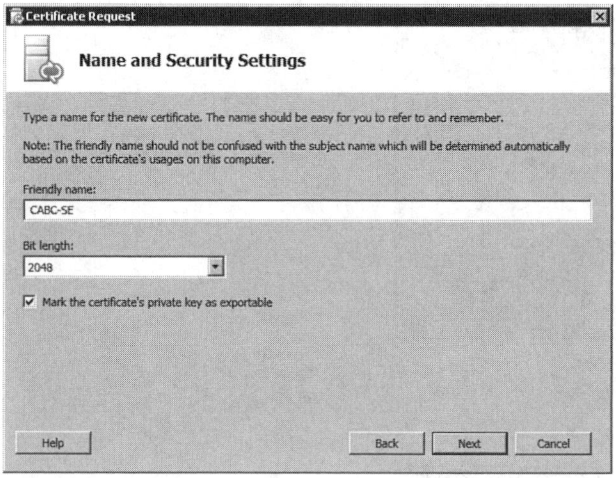

FIGURE 5.19   Certificate request settings.

10. Enter your Organization Name and Organizational Unit and then click Next.

11. Select your country from the drop-down menu and then enter your state/province and city/locality. Remember that full names must be entered; abbreviations are not considered valid for certificate requests. When complete, click Next.

12. The Deployment Wizard automatically adds the SANs required based on the published topology. Unless you have special requirements, select the option to Skip and click Next.

13. Review the information to ensure that it is correct and click Next. The following screen shows the commands to be executed, as shown in Figure 5.20.

14. Perform the same steps to request the OAuthTokenIssuer certificate.

15. Click Finish to go back to the Deployment Wizard screen.

16. Click Run again for Step 3 to assign the Default certificate.

17. On the first screen highlight Default Certificate and choose the option to assign.

18. Click Next.

19. Select the certificate you created earlier based on the friendly name assigned, as shown in Figure 5.21, and click Next.

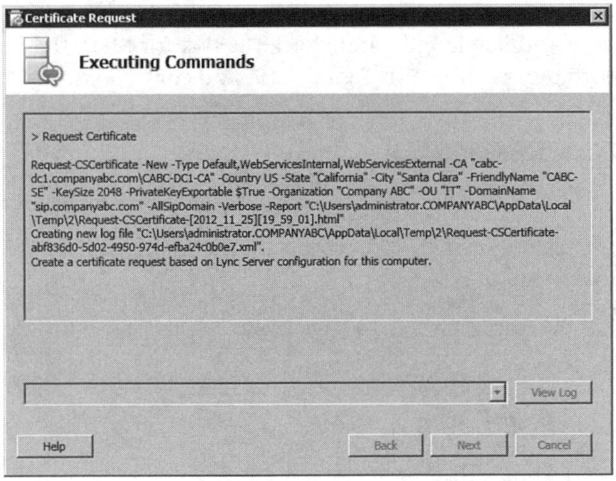

FIGURE 5.20   Certificate request process.

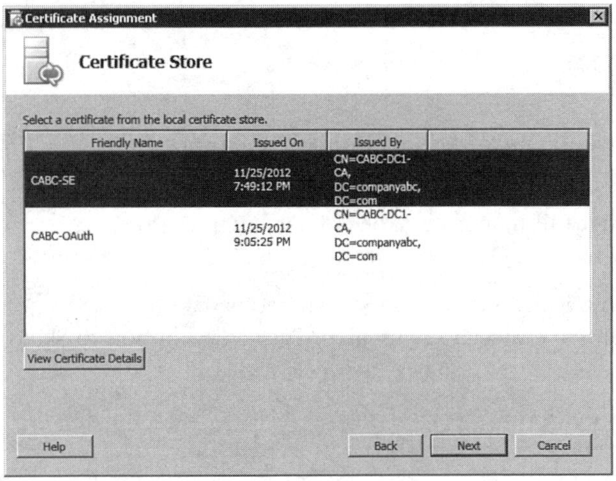

FIGURE 5.21   Choose the default certificate.

20. Ensure that the process completes successfully and click Finish.

21. Perform the same assign process for the OAuthTokenIssuer certificate.

22. After all the certificates have been assigned, there will be a green check mark by Step 3, as shown in Figure 5.22. If there is not a check mark, recheck your process because it's likely you skipped a step.

23. If the file store for the pool is located on this system, you'll need to reboot before continuing. After the reboot, restart the Deployment Wizard by launching Setup.exe.

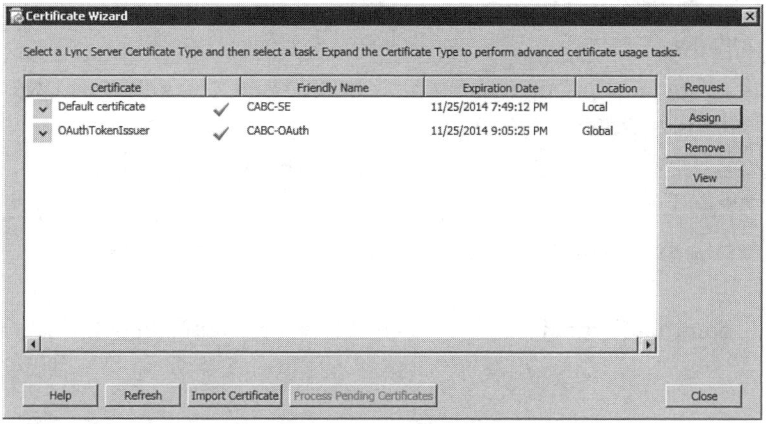

FIGURE 5.22   Certificate process completed.

24. Click Install or Update Lync Server System and then click Run for Step 4: Start Services.

25. Click Next.

26. Ensure the command finished successfully, as shown in Figure 5.23. You can also check the status of services in the Services MMC console found in the server administrative tools.

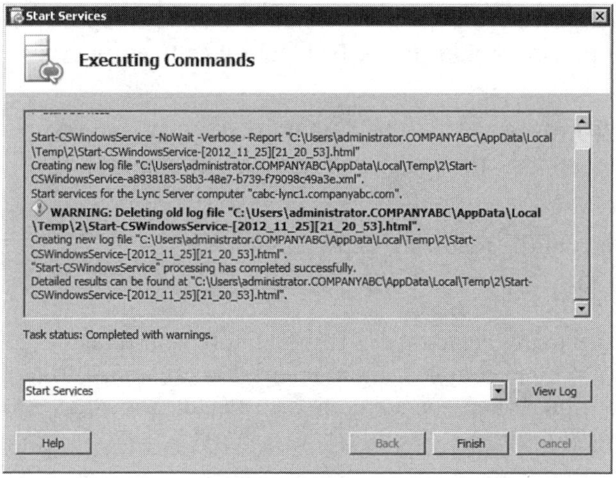

FIGURE 5.23   All services started.

27. Click Exit to leave the Deployment Wizard.

The Standard Edition front end is now installed and ready for further configuration using the Lync Server Control Panel.

Note that the client autoconfiguration requirements are still the same. The following DNS records are required for client autoconfiguration:

- ▶ SRV record of _sipinternaltls._tcp.<sip_Domain> for port 5061 pointing to the FQDN of your front-end pool or Director.

- ▶ sipinternal.<sip_Domain> pointing to the IP address assigned to your front-end pool or Director.

- ▶ sip.<sip_Domain> pointing to the IP address assigned to your front-end pool or Director.

Enterprise Edition Installation

Lync Server 2013 Enterprise Edition is designed for larger deployments or those that require high-availability or redundancy. Enterprise Edition allows for multiple Front End Servers in a pool and scales to support larger user counts with an outboard SQL database.

Topology Builder for Enterprise Edition Deployments

Lync Server 2013 uses the published topology to process traffic and maintain overall topology information. It is especially important to ensure that all information included in the Topology Builder is correct because it sets all the initial configuration information for deployed server roles. To ensure that the topology is valid, it is recommended that you run the Topology Builder before your initial deployment and publish an updated topology after each topological change. This example shows a Standard Edition topology. Remember, if you change the topology later, it should be republished to ensure consistency.

When you first launch Lync Server 2013 Topology Builder, you'll see a fairly blank MMC screen, as shown in Figure 5.24. Compare that to the detailed result at the end of this example.

To begin using Topology Builder, perform the following steps:

1. In the right-hand Action pane, click New.

2. Define the default SIP domain. In many deployments this is simply your domain name, as shown in Figure 5.25. In more complex deployments you can add SIP domains by clicking the Add button. When you are done defining SIP domains, click OK.

FIGURE 5.24   Topology Builder with no topology defined.

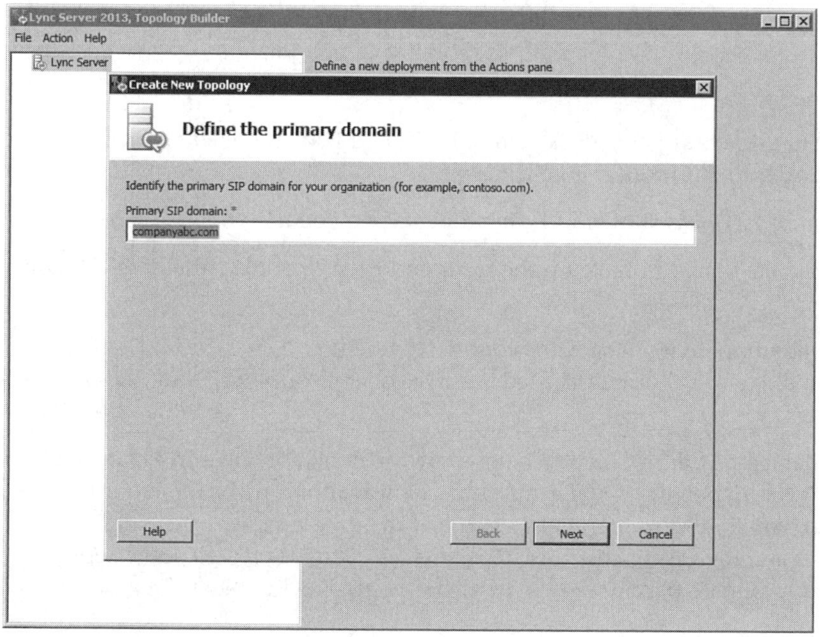

FIGURE 5.25   Define the default SIP domain.

3. In the right-hand Action pane, click Define Site. Enter the appropriate information, as shown in Figure 5.26, and click OK. Note that Lync Server sites have no relation to Active Directory sites. They are completely separate and unique to Lync Server.

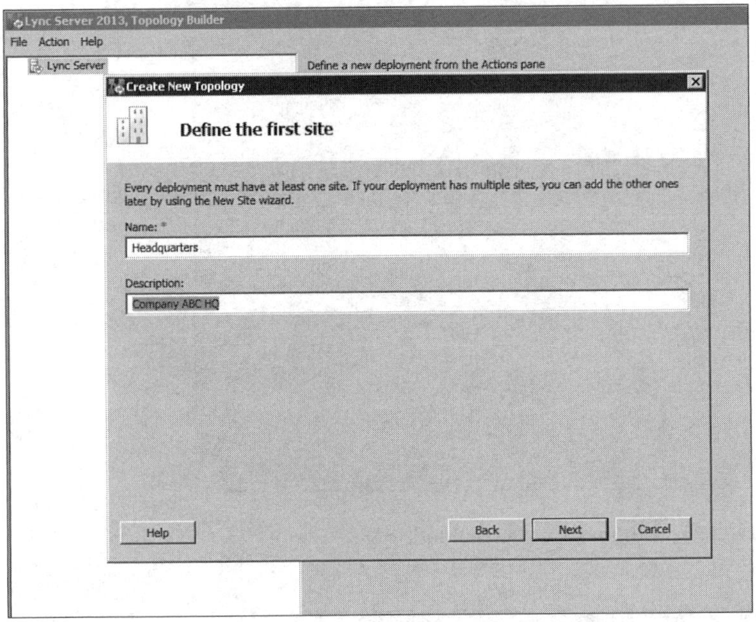

FIGURE 5.26   Define the site.

4. In the right-hand Action pane, click Define Front End Pool and click the radio button for Enterprise Edition; then click Next.

5. Define the pool FQDN as shown in Figure 5.27. When you are done, click Next.

6. Define the servers that will make up the front-end pool by adding their FQDNs and click Next.

7. Choose the appropriate workloads for your deployment and click Next. Then choose whether you'd like to collocate the Mediation Server role on your Front End Servers and click Next.

8. Define the database and file share to be used by the pool, as shown in Figure 5.28. For an Enterprise deployment SQL cannot be collocated on one of the Front End Servers. Also, you'll need to manually create the share on a server other than the front end before progressing past this step. After the share is created, Lync Server assigns the appropriate permissions. When you are ready, click Next.

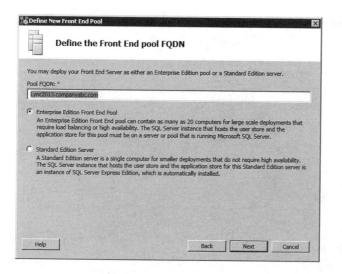

FIGURE 5.27   Define the front-end pool.

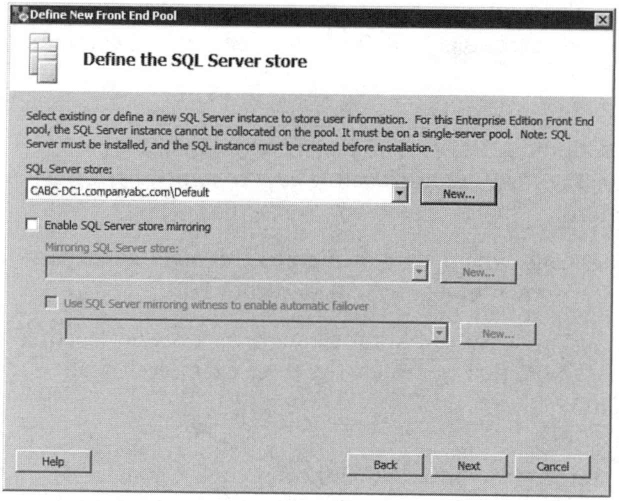

FIGURE 5.28   Define the SQL instance and file share for the front-end pool.

9. Specify the Lync Web Services URLs. Choose whether you want to override the default settings for the internal URL. This is useful when choosing DNS load balancing for the pool, as shown in Figure 5.29. Then click Next.

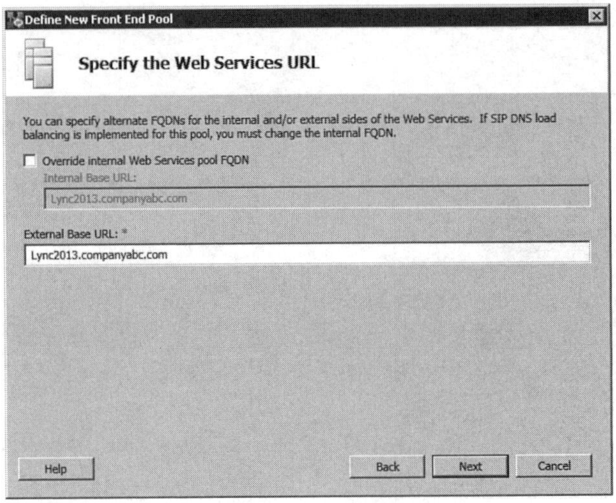

FIGURE 5.29   Web services URLs.

10. Decide whether this front-end pool will be associated with an Office Web Apps server/pool. You can choose an existing server or define a new one. When complete, click Finish.

This completes the initial topology definition. However, there are additional steps to complete a fully functional topology. The next step is to define easy-to-remember URLs for common Lync Server 2013 functions:

1. From the main Topology Builder page, where your site name is highlighted, expand Simple URLs in the main pane, as shown in Figure 5.30, and click Edit.

2. Enter easy-to-remember URLs for Phone Access, Administrative Access, and Meeting services, as shown in Figure 5.31. Note that the following three examples are all valid for Lync Server Simple URLs:

 ▶ https://<function>.<domain _fqdn> - https://dialin.companyabc.com

 ▶ https://<sip_domain>/<function> - https://companyabc.com/dialin

 ▶ https://<External_WebPool_FQDN>/<function> - https://cs2010.companyabc.com/dialin

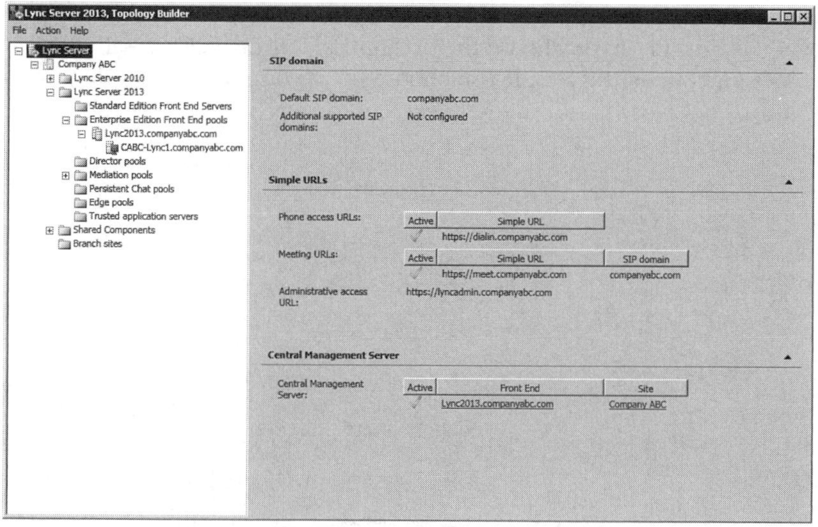

FIGURE 5.30 Expand the Simple URLs item.

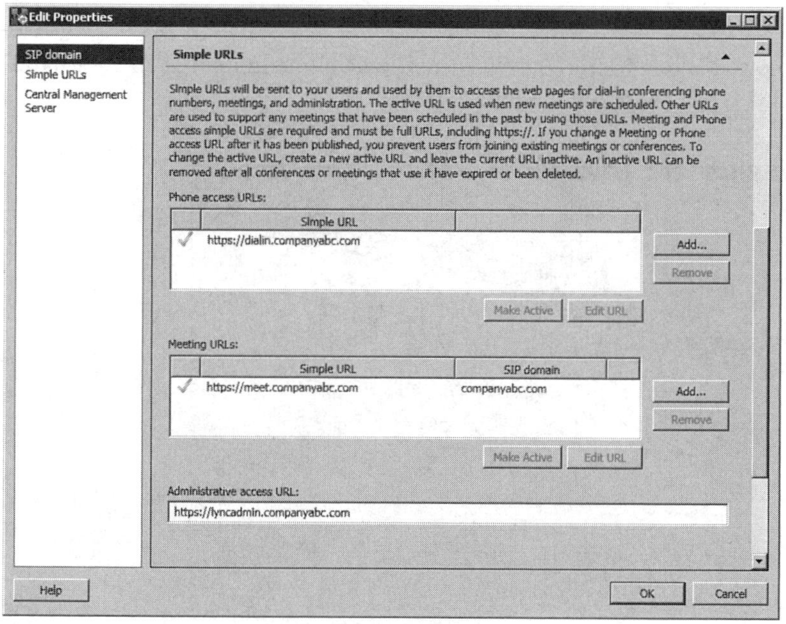

FIGURE 5.31 Configured Simple URLs.

Note that these are the only allowed syntaxes. Port information, such as https://dialin. companyabc.com:443, is invalid. If you choose the first option, all the FQDNs will need to be included as SANs on your certificates. If you choose the second or third option, note that the following virtual directory names are reserved and cannot be used as part of a Simple URL:

▶ ABS

▶ Conf

▶ LocationInformation

▶ RequestHandler

▶ AutoUpdate

▶ cscp

▶ OCSPowerShell

▶ RGSClients

▶ CertProv

▶ GetHealth

▶ ReachWeb

▶ RGSConfig

▶ CollabContent

▶ GroupExpansion

▶ RequestHandlerExt

▶ WebTicket

The final step is to publish the topology to the Central Management Store. In a Standard Edition deployment this is the first front end you define. Perform the following steps to publish your topology:

1. From the Topology Builder Tool, right-click the top-level menu item in the left-hand pane, Lync Server 2013, as shown in Figure 5.32.

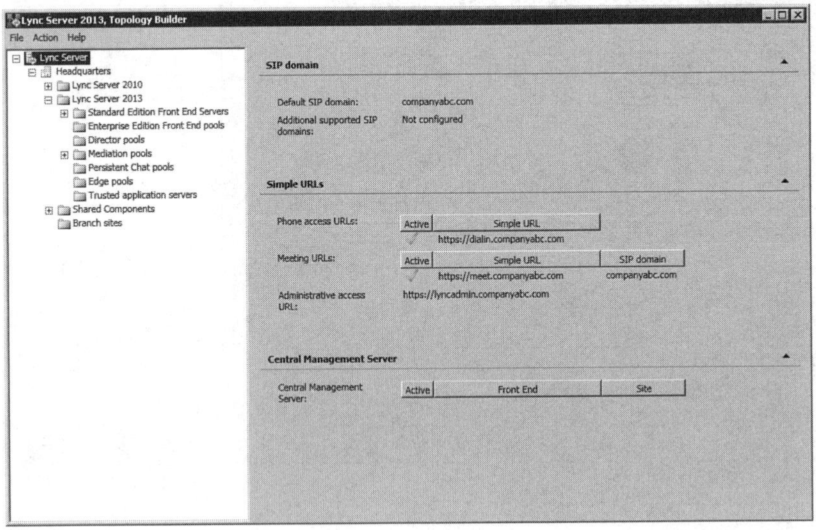

FIGURE 5.32   Top level of Topology Builder.

2. Click Publish Topology.

3. In the opening screen, click Next.

4. Select the front-end pool that will host the Central Management store and click Next.

5. Ensure that the database selections are correct and click Next. This begins the topology publishing process.

6. The Publish Topology window displays the actions being performed. Ensure that it completes successfully, as shown in Figure 5.33, and then click Finish.

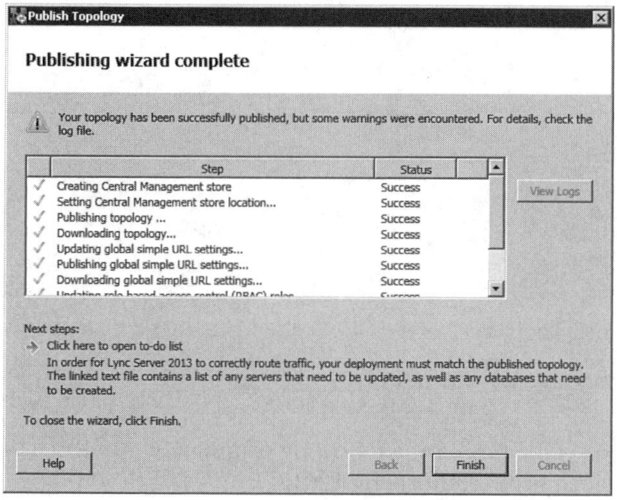

FIGURE 5.33   Successfully published topology.

Installing the Front End Role

It is important to note that if you jumped to this section before completing the preceding steps, you need to go back. Preparing the server for the first Standard Edition Server and building a valid topology in the Topology Builder tool are both prerequisites to installing the Front End role. It should be familiar if you've already installed Lync Server 2010. Administrators new to Lync Server 2013 are advised to review the new features, requirements, and prerequisites before beginning the installation process. The following prerequisites are required to install the Standard Edition Front End role:

▶ IIS with the following options:

  ▶ Static Content

  ▶ Default Document

  ▶ Directory Browsing

  ▶ HTTP Errors

- ▶ HTTP Redirection

- ▶ ASP.NET (all)

- ▶ .NET Extensibility (all)

- ▶ Internet Server API (ISAPI) Extensions

- ▶ ISAPI Filters

- ▶ HTTP Logging

- ▶ Logging Tools

- ▶ Request Monitor

- ▶ Tracing

- ▶ Basic Authentication

- ▶ Windows Authentication

- ▶ Request Filtering

- ▶ Static Content Compression

- ▶ IIS Management Console

- ▶ IIS Management Scripts and Tools

▶ Message Queueing with Directory Service Integration

Note that this can also be done in PowerShell using the following commands. The first command, `Import-Module`, is not needed in Windows Server 2012.

```
Import-Module ServerManager
Add-WindowsFeature Web-Dyn-Compression,desktop-experience,RSAT-ADDS,Web-Server,Web-
Scripting-Tools,Web-Windows-Auth,Web-Asp-Net,Web-Log-Libraries,Web-Http-Tracing,Web-
Stat-Compression,Web-Default-Doc,Web-ISAPI-Ext,Web-ISAPI-Filter,Web-Http-Errors,Web-
Http-Logging,Web-Net-Ext,Web-Client-Auth, Web-Filtering,Web-Mgmt-Console,Msmq-
Server,Msmq-Directory
```

After you've completed the steps previously outlined, the server is ready to install the Front End role. From the main Lync Server 2013 Deployment Wizard screen click Install or Update Lync Server System from the main pane.

First click Install Local Configuration Store. Note that the local configuration store holds significantly more data in Lync 2013 than it did in Lync 2010. Follow these steps to complete the installation process:

1. For Step 2: Setup or Remove Lync Server Components, click Run.

2. At the screen that pops up, click Next.

3. The next screen shows the actions being performed, as shown in Figure 5.34. This process takes a few minutes to complete.

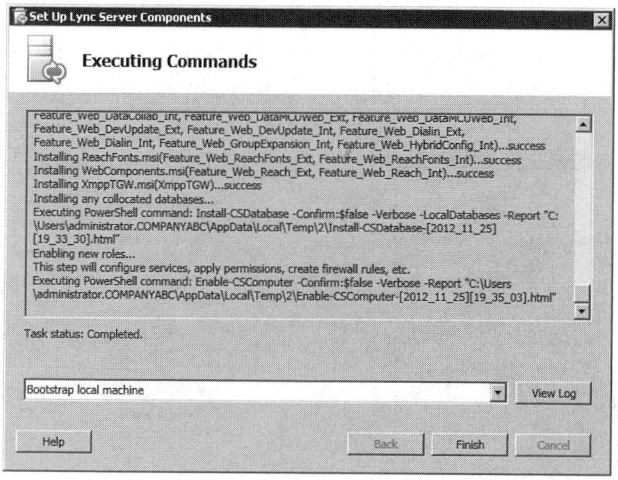

FIGURE 5.34 Installing the Front End role.

4. After the task completes, click Finish and you are brought back to the Deployment Wizard.

5. Review Step 3: Request, Install or Assign Certificates, and click Run.

6. At the next screen choose Default.

7. Select Request, as shown in Figure 5.35.

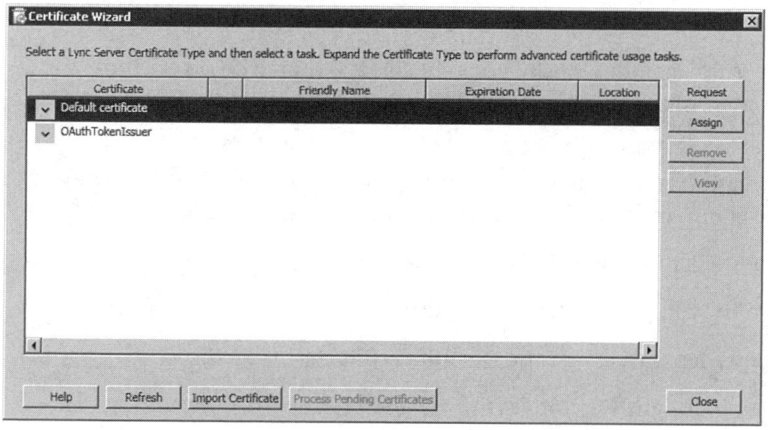

FIGURE 5.35 Request the default certificate.

8. Assuming you are using an internal certificate Authority (CA), choose Send the Request Immediately to an Online Certificate Authority, and click Next. This is the default option.

9. Select the appropriate certificate authority for your environment from the drop-down list, choose a friendly name and key length, and check the box for Mark the Certificate's Private Key as Exportable, as shown in Figure 5.36, and click Next.

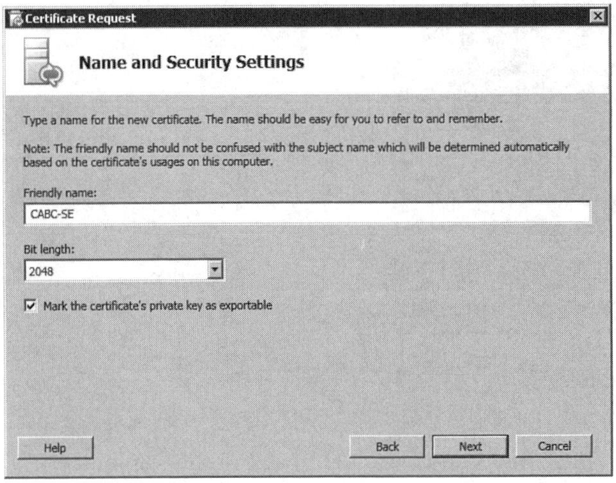

FIGURE 5.36   Certificate request settings.

10. Enter your Organization Name and Organizational Unit and then click Next.

11. Select your country from the drop-down menu and then enter your state/province and city/locality. Remember that full names must be entered; abbreviations are not considered valid for certificate requests. When complete, click Next.

12. The Deployment Wizard automatically adds the SANs required based on the published topology. Unless you have special requirements, select the option to Skip and click Next.

13. Review the information to ensure that it is correct and click Next. The following screen shows the commands to be executed, as shown in Figure 5.37.

14. Perform the same steps to request the OAuthTokenIssuer certificate.

15. Click Finish to go back to the Deployment Wizard screen.

16. Click Run again for Step 3 to assign the Default certificate.

17. On the first screen highlight Default Certificate and choose the option to Assign.

18. Click Next.

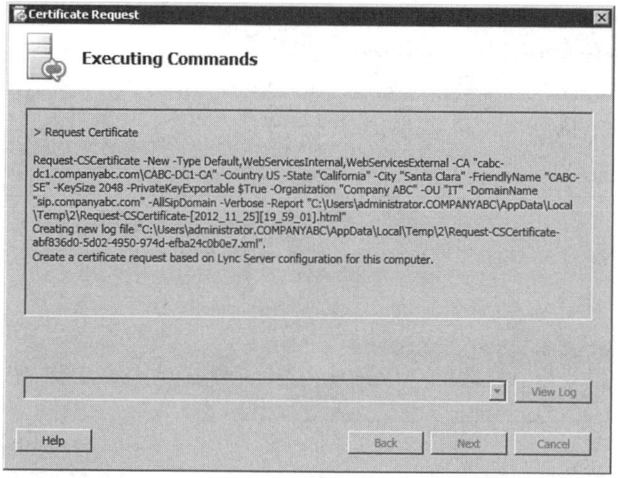

FIGURE 5.37   Certificate request process.

19. Select the certificate you created earlier based on the friendly name assigned, as shown in Figure 5.38, and click Next.

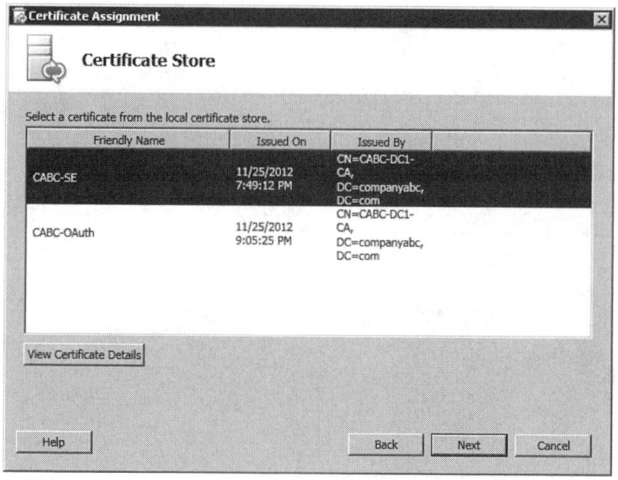

FIGURE 5.38   Choose the default certificate.

20. Ensure that the process completes successfully and click Finish.

21. Perform the same assign process for the OAuthTokenIssuer certificate.

22. After all the certificates have been assigned, there will be a green check mark by step 3, as shown in Figure 5.39. If there is not a check mark, recheck your process because it's likely you skipped a step.

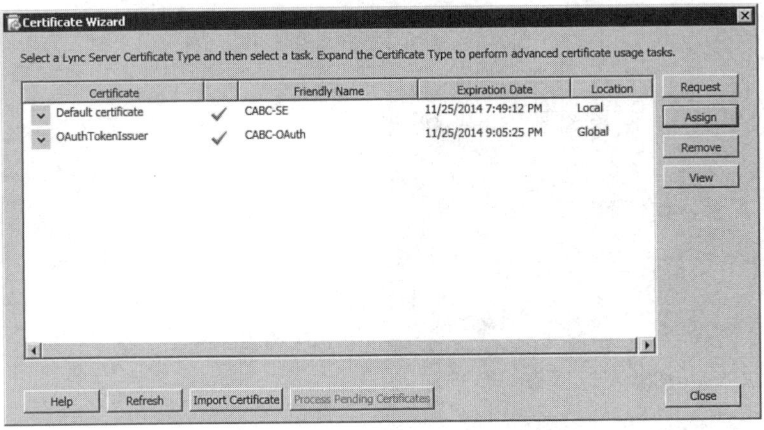

FIGURE 5.39   Certificate process completed.

23. If the file store for the pool is located on this system, you'll need to reboot before continuing. After the reboot, restart the Deployment Wizard by launching `Setup.exe`.

24. Click Install or Update Lync Server System and then click Run for Step 4: Start Services.

25. Click Next.

26. Ensure that all services were started, as shown in Figure 5.40.

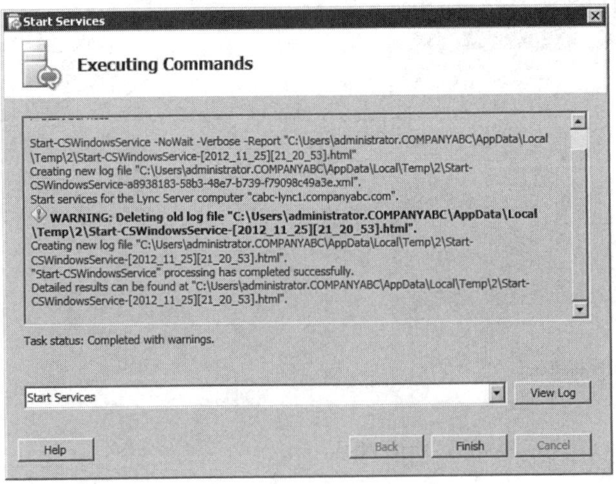

FIGURE 5.40   All services started.

27. Click Exit to leave the Deployment Wizard.

The Standard Edition front end is now installed and ready for further configuration using the Lync Server Control Panel.

Note that the client autoconfiguration requirements are still the same. The following DNS records are required for client autoconfiguration:

▶ SRV record of `_sipinternaltls._tcp.<sip_Domain>` for port 5061 pointing to the FQDN of your front-end pool or Director.

▶ `sipinternal.<sip_Domain>` pointing to the IP address assigned to your front-end pool or Director.

▶ `sip.<sip_Domain>` pointing to the IP address assigned to your front-end pool or Director.

Configuration and Administration Overview

The good news about Lync Server 2013 is that with the Topology Builder tool much of the configuration is done automatically. Although much of both configuration and administration can be done from the Silverlight web GUI, there are many tasks for which only the Lync Server Management Shell will suffice.

First, an introduction to the Lync Server Control Panel. This section reviews each of the tabs and options in the Silverlight Control Panel web application and cites Management Shell commands for functions that do not appear in the Control Panel.

Before opening the Control Panel for the first time, ensure that the server is included in the list of trusted sites on the server or your client. Without this setting, the Control Panel will fail to launch. To launch the Control Panel on a Lync Server 2013 server, select the Lync Server Control Panel link from the Start menu under the Microsoft Lync Server 2013 program group. To launch the Control Panel from another system, enter the Admin simple URL you entered during the initial installation or https://<poolFQDN>/cscp. In the example environment this would be either https://Lync2013.companyabc.com/admin or https://Lync2013.companyabc.com/cscp/. Either URL will bring you to the Control Panel.

When you first log in, you're brought to the Control Panel home page. The navigation bar is on the left and includes options for Home, Users, Topology, IM and Presence, Voice Routing, Voice Features, Response Groups, Conferencing, Clients, Federation and External Access, Monitoring and Archiving, Security, and finally Network Configuration.

On the Home page you'll see a link to a quick-start guide and other informational links in the center pane, and shortcuts to common tasks in the main pane. Explanations of these functions and more are covered in detail in Chapter 14, "Administration of Microsoft Lync Server 2013."

Troubleshooting

As with every version of Lync Server so far, there are two major gremlins with the Front End role, certificates, and DNS. The new Deployment Wizard takes most of the guesswork out of certificate generation by automatically filling the SAN fields with the appropriate FQDNs for a given deployment. However, in more complex environments manual configuration might be necessary. The added convenience of the Deployment Wizard doesn't lessen the importance of certificates. They are still core to all server and server-client communications. DNS, on the other hand, is not automated. For each pool created, the administrator will need to create an A record for each pool pointing to the load-balanced VIP for multiple server pools or to the front-end IP address for single server pools.

The Lync Server event log is also a good place to check for errors. From the Start menu select Administrative Tools and then select Event Viewer. Expand the Applications and Services Logs item and select Lync Server. All events related to Lync Server functions reside here. Often the error description is enough to identify the problem and make clear the resolution.

Lync Server 2013 now offers centralized logging as a feature. It is called the Centralized Logging Service, CLS. For anyone who has had to troubleshoot a large deployment this is a *very* useful function. Not only is logging for all servers centralized, but a base form of logging is always running by default. This means errors do not need to be manually reproduced; they are likely already captured in the logs.

Best Practices

The following are the best practices from this chapter:

▶ Use DNS load balancing for SIP traffic. A hardware load balancer is still required for web services such as the address book service.

▶ Explore the new failover functions of Lync Standard Edition before assuming that Lync Enterprise Edition is the right architecture. A full description of both is included in Chapter 30, "Planning for Basic Lync Services."

▶ Although the Lync Server 2013 Control Panel might seem more familiar at first, there are many functions that can be accomplished only in the Management Shell.

▶ Always install the SQL backward-compatibility pack to ensure that all cmdlets run correctly.

▶ Use the RBAC controls to delegate administration rights. Delegate only the minimum rights needed to accomplish the required tasks.

▶ Always publish a new topology before making changes or installing a new server role.

CHAPTER 6

Microsoft Lync Server 2013 Edge Server

The Lync Server Edge Server enables remote access to the internal Lync Server infrastructure. In addition to providing feature parity for external or remote users, the Edge Server can enhance a deployment by federating with partner organizations or public providers. These federation features help organizations use rich communication methods securely with each other across the Internet.

This chapter focuses on the Edge Server role installation and configuration. It covers how to deploy each of the Edge roles both in a standalone scenario and in a high-availability deployment where multiple Edge Servers are used.

Edge Server Overview

The Lync Edge Server in Lync Server 2013 is made up of four separate services: Access Edge Server, Web Conferencing Edge Server, A/V Edge Server, and the XMPP Gateway. Each service provides slightly different functionality, and depending on the organization's requirements, it might not be necessary to use all services. With Lync Server 2013, all services are deployed together on every edge server. Lync Server 2013 introduces the capability to deploy the XMPP Gateway Service directly on the Edge Server as opposed to a separate server role in previous product versions.

Unlike many of the internal roles, the Edge Server does not require database or file shares because it does not store data other than the Local Configuration Store replica from the Central Management Store. Because the Edge Server is designed to be deployed in a perimeter or DMZ network, it runs a limited set of services to make it as secure as possible. Edge Servers are also typically not joined to the internal Active Directory domain, but can be if necessary. The different Edge Server roles provide unique features, as shown in Figure 6.1.

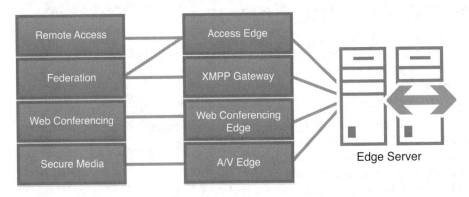

FIGURE 6.1   Edge Server Services.

In addition to the Lync Edge Server Services, a reverse proxy solution is required to publish web services, including Mobility. For more information on reverse proxy requirements, see Chapter 12, "Firewall and Security Requirements."

Access Edge Service

The Access Edge Service acts as a secure proxy for all remote Lync signaling traffic. Without the Access Edge Service deployed, all other edge roles would not be able to function. The Access Edge Service provides Remote Access, Federation, and Public Provider connectivity in Lync Server 2013.

Remote Access

One function of the Access Edge Server is to provide remote access capabilities to a Lync Server infrastructure. After an internal deployment of pools is complete, an Access Edge Server can be provisioned to enable users to sign in and use their endpoints across the Internet.

As long as the appropriate SRV records exist in DNS or the client is manually configured correctly, a user can travel in and out of the office without ever making a change to an endpoint. This enables users to have full access to their internal features regardless of location.

NOTE

Because 443 is a standard, well-known port, it is used for Remote Access by the Access Edge Service.

Federation

The Access Edge Server also provides the capability to federate with other organizations that have deployed Lync Server, meaning the two organizations can communicate with each other as if it were a single deployment.

Users have different feature sets available when using federation, depending on the version of Lync Server a partner has deployed. The feature set is the lowest common denominator between the two organizations. For example, if a partner runs Live Communications Server 2005, only IM and presence will be available. However, if a partner organization is running Office Communications Server 2007 R2, A/V and Desktop Sharing features can be used through federation. The largest feature set is available if both organizations are running Lync Server 2013.

Access Edge Servers use certificates and Mutual TLS (MTLS) to secure the SIP signaling used across the Internet with each other. This ensures that instant messaging and presence traffic is completely secure and is never transmitted in plain text.

> **NOTE**
>
> Organizations most often procure a certificate from a public certificate authority so that partners trust their server by default. However, it is possible to exchange certificate chains with a partner to support additional certificate authorities.

Public Provider Connectivity

A special form of federation is the capability to use Lync Server to communicate with contacts on the public IM networks, referred to as Public IM Connectivity (PIC). The Skype, AOL, and MSN networks are the native Public IM Connectivity providers to Lync Server. To communicate with these contacts, users simply need to add the address to a contact list.

Lync Server users can see presence and exchange instant messages with their contacts when Public IM Connectivity is provisioned. The conversations are limited to peer-to-peer, though, and they cannot include three or more participants as users are accustomed to within the organization or with federated contacts.

Audio and video support with the MSN or Windows Live networks was introduced in Lync Server 2010. In Lync Server 2013, Microsoft introduces audio federation to Skype as well. As of the writing of this book, Skype video federation is not available; however, it is on the road map for a future service. This functionality is included as part of the Lync Server Standard CAL; no additional licensing is required. Federation to other services including Google Talk and Jabber is available through the XMPP gateway service. The XMPP gateway service is covered in a later section.

Web Conferencing Edge Service

The Web Conferencing Edge Service enables remote users to participate in web conferences with internal users or other remote workers. The Web Conferencing Edge Service enables remote users to participate in collaboration sessions that involve whiteboards and polls. Any user who connects to the Web Conferencing Edge Service must authenticate with the Access Edge Service first.

Organizations can also elect to allow anonymous or unauthenticated users to join web conferences with their own users. Web conferencing uses Microsoft's Proprietary Shared Object Model (PSOM) protocol to facilitate the meetings and data. Like the Access Edge traffic, all Web Conferencing Edge traffic is conducted over HTTPS port 443, so it is secure and resilient to proxy servers. For more information on Web Conferencing functionality, see Chapter 19, "Lync Native Video and Data Conferencing."

A/V Edge Service

The A/V Edge Service is responsible for securely relaying audio and video media among internal, external, and federated contacts. The A/V Edge Service uses the Interactive Connectivity Establishment (ICE), Simple Traversal Utilities for NAT (STUN), and Traversal Using Relay NAT (TURN) methods to enable endpoints to communicate from nearly any network connection with Internet access.

When possible, endpoints attempt to use a peer-to-peer connection for media streams, but when an endpoint is behind a NAT device such as a home router, the A/V Edge role can act as a relay point between the endpoints to facilitate communication. The A/V Edge service uses a combination of HTTPS port 443 and UDP port 3478 to negotiate and provide the media stream.

To support media traffic between internal and external users, an additional service exists on the A/V Edge Server called the A/V Edge Authentication Service. This service is responsible for authenticating media requests from internal users to external contacts. When a user wants to initiate an external A/V conversation, the user is provided with a temporary media token that she uses to authenticate to this service before media is allowed to flow.

XMPP Gateway Service

Lync Server 2013 now integrates the XMPP proxy functionality into the Lync Edge Server. In previous versions, this was a dedicated server role. The XMPP Gateway is also deployed on Front End Servers for internal integration with XMPP Services. Organizations can deploy XMPP federation as an optional component. Deploying XMPP federation will allow users to perform Instant Messaging sessions with XMPP-based contacts such as Google's GTalk.

Collocation

The Edge Server roles cannot be collocated with any other role in Lync Server. Although many of the other roles depend on access to Active Directory, Edge Servers are typically placed in a perimeter network and might not even be joined to the corporate domain for security reasons.

In previous versions of Office Communications Server, it was possible to install only specific Edge roles. However, in Lync Server 2010, all Edge roles were consolidated on a single server. This change cut down on confusion of deployment models, which required knowing which Edge roles were safe to collocate together. This has carried through to Lync Server 2013; you must not collocate the Edge Server with any other Lync Server role, and all Lync Edge Services are installed together on a single server.

Edge Server Installation

The rest of this chapter focuses on the actual installation and configuration of the Edge Server. The next sections discuss the Edge Server hardware, operating system, and software prerequisites.

Hardware Requirements

The Lync Edge Server processor requirements are as follows:

▶ Dual processor, quad-core 2.0GHz or faster

▶ Four-way processor, dual-core 2.0GHz or faster

CAUTION

Lync Server is only a 64-bit application and requires a 64-bit-capable processor. This is generally not an issue with modern hardware, but be sure to verify that legacy hardware supports a 64-bit operating system before attempting to use it for an Edge Server.

The Lync Edge Server memory requirement is as follows:

▶ 12GB RAM

The Lync Edge Server disk requirement is as follows:

▶ Local storage, minimum 10K RPM or SSD, with at least 30GB of free space

The Lync Edge Server network requirement is as follows:

▶ Two interfaces, either one two-port 1Gbps network card, or two one-port 1Gbps network cards

---

TIP

When teaming multiple network adapters, use them only for fault tolerance. This means network adapters should be used for failover only and should not be combined for greater throughput.

Operation System Requirements

The Lync Edge Server supports the following operating systems:

▶ Windows Server 2008 R2 Standard or Enterprise Edition with SP1 64-bit version

▶ Windows Server 2012

Software Requirements

The Lync Edge Server requires the following software and updates to be installed:

▶ Microsoft .NET Framework 4.5 (must be installed before setup process)

▶ Windows Fabric (installed with setup process)

▶ Windows Identity Foundation (must be installed before setup process)

▶ Microsoft Visual C++ 11 Redistributable (installed with setup process)

Server Roles and Features

The Lync Edge Server requires the Application Server role to be installed on the Operating System.

Configure Networking

After the required components are installed, it is important to get the Edge Server networking configuration completed. An Edge Server must have at least two network adapters: one for external traffic and one for communicating with internal servers or clients. Figure 6.2 provides an overview of the Lync Edge Server network adapter configuration.

> **TIP**
>
> Make sure that necessary routing statements are entered on each Lync Edge Server so that the traffic for internal clients and servers uses the correct adapter. As shown in Figure 6.2, only the external facing adapter should have a default gateway assigned in the IP Network Settings to ensure consistent routing behavior. If your clients or internal servers are on a subnet separate from your Edge Server internal network interface, persistent routes must be added in Windows. Use the `Route Add -P` command for this configuration.

IPv6 Support

Lync Server 2013 now supports IPv6 addressing for all Edge Server services. If you have configured IPv6 addresses on your Windows Server, you can now configure the Lync Server Topology to use these IPv6 addresses. All services, including the XMPP gateway, support IPv6.

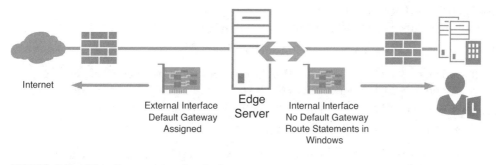

FIGURE 6.2   Edge Server network adapters.

> **TIP**
>
> To support IPv6, you must create DNS records for the IPv6 addresses. These host records are defined as AAAA records. The DNS records required is consistent between IPv4 and IPv6. For details on required DNS records, see Chapter 11, "Dependent Services and SQL."

Create the Edge Pool

After the server has been fully prepared for installation, the topology must be edited and published to reflect the new Edge Server pool. This involves editing the existing topology, if it exists, and then republishing the topology so that all other servers in the environment are aware of the new Edge Server pool.

Edit the Topology

The next step in deploying a Lync Edge Server is to edit the existing Lync Server topology. This task must be performed from a Lync Server on the internal network such as a Front End Server. To edit the topology, perform the following steps:

1. Open the Lync Server Topology Builder.

2. When prompted to download a topology from an existing deployment, click OK.

3. Save your topology file as appropriate.

4. Expand the Site node where the Edge Server will be deployed.

5. Expand the Lync Server 2013 node.

6. Right-click on the Edge Pools node, and select New Edge Pool.

7. Click Next to begin the wizard.

8. Enter the fully qualified name of the internal Edge Server Pool FQDN field.

9. Follow the appropriate following sections depending on whether a single Edge Server or a pool of load-balanced Edge Servers will be deployed.

Deploying a Single Edge Server Pool

If you are deploying a single Edge Server Pool, follow these steps:

1. Select Single Computer Pool, and click Next.

2. If a single public IP address will be used for the Access Edge, Web Conferencing Edge, and A/V Edge services, check the box Use a Single FQDN and IP Address. This requires using ports other than 443 for two of the services.

3. If federation will be used, check the Enable Federation box.

4. If XMPP federation will be used, check the Enable XMPP Federation box, and then click Next.

5. Check valid IP options as they relate to your deployment. If your deployment is using IPv6, check the IPv6 boxes for the internal and external interface. If not, ensure that only the IPv4 boxes are checked.

6. If the IP address used for the A/V Edge uses NAT, check the box The External IP Address of This Edge Pool Is Translated by NAT. Click Next when complete.

7. Under the Access Edge Service section, enter the external FQDN and port. Typically, this is similar to `sip.companyabc.com` and port 443.

> **NOTE**
>
> If you elected to use a single FQDN and IP address for your public edge services, you will be permitted to enter only a single FQDN, and the default ports will be set to 5061, 444, and 443.

8. Under the Web Conferencing Edge Service section, enter the external server FQDN and port. Typically, the name and port are similar to `webconf.companyabc.com` and port 443.

9. Under the A/V Edge Service section, enter the external server FQDN and port. Typically, the name and port are similar to `av.companyabc.com` and port 443. Click Next when complete.

> **NOTE**
>
> If you are using IPv6 in your environment, and have selected to enable IPv6 on the Edge Server, you will be required to enter the IPv6 and/or IPv4 address for each Edge Server.

10. Enter the internal-facing IP address for the Edge Server Pool and click Next.

11. Under the Access Edge Service section, enter the external IP address.

12. Under the Web Conferencing Edge Service section, enter the external IP address.

13. Under the A/V Edge Service section, enter the external IP address. When finished, click Next.

14. Select a next-hop pool to be used by the Edge Server pool and click Next. If a director is deployed, you should select the director as the next-hop.

15. Select any Front End Server pools or Mediation Server pools that will use this Edge Server pool for external media traffic. Click Finish to complete the wizard.

Deploying a Load-Balanced Edge Server Pool

To deploy a load balanced Edge Server Pool, follow these steps:

1. Select Multiple Computer Pool, and click Next.

2. If a single public IP address will be used for the Access Edge, Web Conferencing Edge, and A/V Edge services, check the box Use a Single FQDN and IP Address. This requires using ports other than 443 for two of the services.

3. If federation will be used, check the Enable Federation box.

4. If XMPP federation will be used, check the Enable XMPP Federation box, and then click Next.

5. Check valid IP options as they relate to your deployment. If your deployment is using IPv6, check the IPv6 boxes for the internal and external interface. If not, ensure that only the IPv4 boxes are checked.

6. If the IP address used for the A/V Edge uses NAT, check the box The External IP Address of This Edge Pool Is Translated by NAT. Click Next when complete.

7. Under the Access Edge Service section, enter the external FQDN and port. Typically, this is similar to `sip.companyabc.com` and port 443.

> **NOTE**
>
> If you elected to use a single FQDN and IP address for your public edge services, you will be permitted to enter only a single FQDN, and the default ports will be set to 5061, 444, and 443.

8. Under the Web Conferencing Edge Service section, enter the external server FQDN and port. Typically, the name and port are similar to `webconf.companyabc.com` and port 443.

9. Under the A/V Edge Service section, enter the external server FQDN and port. Typically, the name and port are similar to `av.companyabc.com` and port 443. Click Next when complete.

10. Define each server in the Edge Server Pool. Click Add.

11. Enter the internal IP Address of the Edge Server and the Internal Server FQDN, and click Next.

> **NOTE**
>
> Each member of the Edge Server pool must have a unique external IP address for each public service, as well as a unique internal IP address. Your load-balancing method will distribute traffic to each member on the designated IP addresses. In the wizard, make sure you are entering the IP addresses assigned to the pool member, not that of the pool.

12. Under the Access Edge Service section, enter the external IP address assigned to the Edge Server.

13. Under the Web Conferencing Edge Service section, enter the external IP address assigned to the Edge Server.

14. Under the A/V Edge Service section, enter the external IP address assigned to the Edge Server, and click Finish.

15. Repeat the previous steps for each pool member and then click Next.

16. Select a next-hop pool to be used by the Edge Server pool and click Next. If a director is deployed, you should select the director as the next-hop.

17. Select any Front End Server pools or Mediation Server pools that will use this Edge Server pool for external media traffic. Click Finish to complete the wizard.

Publish the Topology

After the topology is modified to include the Edge Server pool, the configuration can be published. This step publishes the changes to the Central Management Store, and all existing Lync Server servers will update their local configuration stores to match.

1. Ensure that the Lync Server Topology Builder is open and contains the Edge Server pool that was recently added.

2. Click the top node of the Topology Builder, Lync Server 2013.

3. Click the Action menu and select Publish Topology, or select Publish Topology from the Actions pane on the right side of the console.

4. Click Next to begin publishing the topology.

5. When the log indicates a successful update, click Finish to complete the wizard.

Installing the Edge Server

At this point, the target server should be fully prepared with all prerequisites outlined in the requirements sections earlier in this chapter.

Export Topology

The process for installing a local configuration store on an Edge Server varies depending on whether an Edge Server is part of the Active Directory domain and can access the configuration store directly. Typically, the Edge Server is isolated and requires a few extra manual steps to read the topology. These steps involve exporting the entire topology to a ZIP file and copying it to the Edge Server.

1. On an internal Lync Server, such as a Front End Server, open the Lync Server Management Shell.

2. Run the following command:

```
Export-CSConfiguration -FileName C:\LyncConfig.zip
```

3. Copy the exported file to the Edge Server before beginning the installation.

Installing a Local Configuration Store

To install any server role in Lync Server 2013, the target server must first have a local configuration store installed and populated with the topology information.

1. Insert the Lync Server media on the Edge Server and launch `Setup.exe`, found in the `Setup\amd64` folder.

2. Enter a location for the installation, and click Install.

> **NOTE**
>
> If you want to change the path for all Lync components that will be installed on this server, you must change it in this dialog box. For example, you might want to change the installation from the system drive to a separate data drive.

3. Click Install or Update Lync Server System.

4. Under Step 1: Install Location Configure Store, click Run.

5. Because the Edge Server is part of a workgroup and cannot access the Central Management Store, select Import from a File, and then click Browse. If the Edge Server is part of the same domain as your internal Lync Servers, it will be able to read the Central Management Store directly.

6. Select the ZIP file that was exported earlier, and then click Next.

7. Click Finish when the topology is imported successfully.

Installing the Lync Server Components

The following steps will have the server read topology information from the local configuration store, and then install any prerequisites and Lync Server roles for which the server is enabled.

1. Under Step 2: Setup or Remove Lync Server Components, click the Run button.

2. Click Next to begin the Edge Server installation.

3. When prompted to install the Microsoft Network service, click the Install button.

4. Click Finish when the installation completes.

Creating Certificates

Like all other roles in Lync Server, the Edge Server communicates to other servers in the organization using Mutual Transport Layer Security (MTLS). The Edge Server requires two certificates. At a minimum, the Edge Server always requires a certificate with its internal fully qualified domain name (FQDN) for communication to other servers, and a certificate for external services with all public FQDNs that are used. For internal certificates, the subject name should contain the Edge pool's internal FQDN.

The certificate used for Access Edge services should adhere to the following guidelines:

▶ The subject name should be the published name for Access Edge services.

▶ All supported SIP domains must be entered as a subject alternative name in the format `sip.<SIP domain>`.

The certificate used for Web Conferencing Edge services should adhere to the following guideline:

▶ The subject name should be the published name for Web Conferencing Edge services.

▶ The certificate used for A/V Authentication service has no specific guidelines. The certificate is used only to generate encryption keys, but the name used by the wizard matches the internal Edge pool FQDN.

See Chapter 11, "Dependent Services and SQL," for a more detailed explanation of certificate requirements.

> **NOTE**
>
> The Certificate Wizard in Lync Server automatically populates the subject name and required subject alternative names based on the published topology. This greatly simplifies certificate confusion created by prior versions. As long as the published topology is accurate, changing the certificate names or adding subject alternative names is unnecessary.

Use the following steps to request the necessary Edge Server certificates:

1. Under Step 3: Request, Install, or Assign Certificate, click the Run button.

2. Highlight the Edge Internal option and click the Request button.

3. Click Next to begin the wizard.

4. Select either Send the Request Immediately to an Online Certification Authority or Prepare the Request Now, but Send It Later (Offline Certificate Request), and click Next.

TIP

The option to send a certificate request immediately is usually reserved for internal servers. This requires communication between the Edge Server and an internal Domain Certificate Authority server. If your server has access, you can choose this option and enter the URL and credentials required. However, it is more common for offline requests to be generated, even for internal certificates.

5. Click the Browse button and select a file location for the certificate signing request (CSR) file to be saved, and click Next.

6. To use the standard WebServer template, click Next on the Specify Alternate Certificate Template page.

TIP

Many organizations with managed internal Certificate Authority deployments are not using the built-in WebServer templates. You should check with your CA administrator to verify the certificate temple that should be used for your Edge Server requests.

7. Enter a friendly name for the certificate such as Lync Server Internal. This is only a display name for the certificate.

8. Select a key bit length for your certificate: 2048 or 4096.

9. If the certificate should be exportable, select the Mark Certificate Private Key as Exportable check box, and click Next.

TIP

If this is the first server in a Lync Edge Server Pool, this certificate must be exportable. All Edge Servers in the Edge Server pool must share the same internal certificate. If this is not the first server in the pool, you should cancel the wizard and instead import the certificate from the first server, and follow the steps to Assign Certificates.

10. Through the next few steps, enter all organization information that applies to your organization. Click Next to continue.

11. Click Next after reviewing the automatically populated subject and subject alternative names.

12. For the internal certificate, you should not configure additional subject alternative names, because they are not needed. For the external certificate, it is possible to enter additional SAN entries if they are required. Click Next.

13. Click Next to complete the request, and then click Finish to complete the wizard.

After completing the wizard, it must be run one more time to generate a CSR for the External Edge Server certificate. Repeat all preceding steps, but choose the External Certificate as part of step 1.

Importing Offline Certificate Requests

After you have processed an offline certificate request from the certificate authority, you will be presented with a certificate file. The certificate file must be imported to your Edge Server, and the easiest way to do this is through the Lync Server Deployment Wizard.

1. Under Step 3: Request, Install, or Assign Certificate, click the Run button.

2. In the Certificate Wizard window, choose Import Certificate.

3. Choose the certificate file from your certificate authority and finish the import wizard.

4. This certificate should now be available to assign to Lync Services. See the next section for more information.

Assigning Certificates

After the necessary certificates have been created, the Edge Server services must have certificates assigned to them. This process binds each certificate to a specific Edge service. To assign a certificate, perform the following steps:

1. Under Step 3: Request, Install, or Assign Certificate, click the Run button.

2. Highlight Edge Internal and click the Assign button.

3. Click the Next button to begin the wizard.

4. Select Assign an Existing Certificate, and then click Next.

5. Select the correct certificate for this usage. Certificates will not appear here unless they can be verified to a Trusted Root Certification Authority and have a private key associated. Click Next.

6. Verify that the certificate is selected, and then click Next.

7. Click Finish when the process is complete.

Repeat the previous steps to assign the External Edge certificate.

Start Services

After the necessary certificates are requested and assigned, the Lync Server Edge Server services can be started.

1. Under Step 4: Start Services, click the Run button.

2. Click Next to start the Lync Server services.

3. Click Finish to complete the wizard.

At this point, the Edge Server installation is complete and functional.

Edge Server Configuration

This section outlines common configuration tasks for Edge Server pools. Major changes to the Edge Server configuration must be carried out using Lync Server Topology Builder. This includes changing IP addresses, changing DNS names, or changing pool associations. Any topology changes will require running the Lync Server Deployment Wizard again to ensure that the changes are reflected on the Edge Server.

Other configuration changes, such as enabling certain features or configuring federation, can be carried out in the Lync Server Control Panel, or the Lync Server Management Shell. Common configurations are outlined in this section, as well as the administration section.

Enabling Edge Server Features

To enable Edge Servers to process remote access and federation requests, the Access Edge configuration must be updated to enable these features. Figure 6.3 shows a sample policy configuration. Use the following steps to enable Access Edge features to the Lync Server infrastructure:

1. Open the Lync Server Control Panel.

2. Select Federation and External User Access in the navigation pane.

3. Click Access Edge Configuration.

4. Highlight the Global policy, and then click Edit and then Modify.

5. Check the Enable Federation and Public IM Connectivity box.

6. If DNS SRV lookups are allowed to discover federated partners, check the Enable Partner Domain Discovery box.

7. If an archiving disclaimer should be sent to federated contacts when initiating an IM conversation, check the Send Archiving Disclaimer to Federated Partners box.

8. Check the Enable Remote User Access box.

9. If the web conferencing service enables anonymous external participants, check the Enable Anonymous User Access to Conferences box.

10. Click Commit to accept the changes.

Alternatively, the Lync Server Management Shell can be used to configure the following setting:

```
Set-CSAccessEdgeConfiguration -AllowOutsideusers $true -AllowFederatedUsers $true -
➡EnablePartnerDiscovery $true -EnableArchivingDisclaimer $true
➡AllowAnonymousUsers $true
```

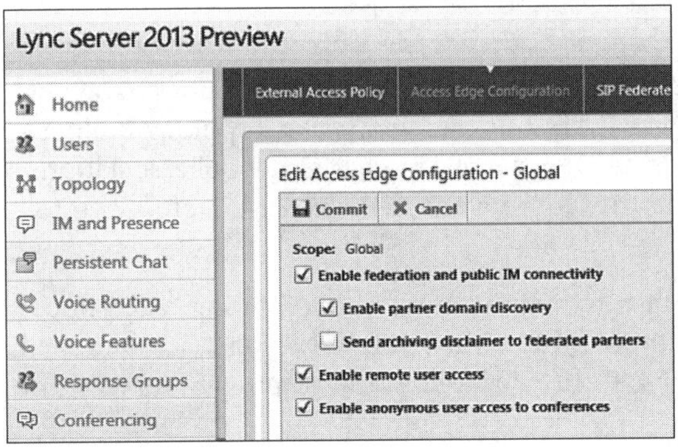

FIGURE 6.3   Access Edge configuration.

Some additional options are available for Access Edge Server configuration that are not exposed in the Lync Server Control Panel. The following parameters can also be used as part of the `Set-CSAccessEdgeConfiguration` cmdlet to configure external access:

▶ **BeClearingHouse**—This has a `true` or `false` value indicating whether the Access Edge Servers are directly connected to other organizations. A clearinghouse Access Edge Server can be used to support direct federation between multiple organizations. It can also be considered a federation gateway for multiple internal Lync Server deployments. Typically, this value is `false`.

▶ **CertificatesDeletedPercentage**—New to Lync Server 2013, this setting controls the percentage of Trusted Certificate entries that are deleted during certificate maintenance.

▶ **DefaultRouteFQDN**—This is used to override a default federation route. If it is required to proxy client connections through a specific server for federation, this parameter can be entered. This parameter must be used in conjunction with the `UseDefaultRouting` parameter.

▶ **EnableDiscoveredPartnerContactsLimit**—This has a `true` or `false` value. By default, any federated partners that are discovered automatically have a contact limit imposed. This setting can be used to disable that contact limit by default.

▶ **UseDefaultRouting**—This has a `true` or `false` value indicating whether the Access Edge Servers will use a manually entered default route FQDN. This value is `false` by default, which enables Access Edge Servers to use DNS SRV records for routing federation requests.

▶ **KeepCRLsUpToDateForPeers**—This has a `true` or `false` value indicating whether the Access Edge Servers will periodically check whether a partner's certificate is still valid based on the CRL. This parameter is `true` by default.

▶ **MarkSourceVerifiableOnOutgoingMessages**—This has a `true` or `false` value indicating whether the Access Edge Servers mark outgoing messages from a verified source.

This enables partners to assign a higher level of trust to messages they receive from an organization marking messages as verifiable. This parameter is `true` by default.

▶ `MaxAcceptedCertificatesStored`—New to Lync Server 2013, this setting allows administrators to control the maximum number of trusted certificates that are stored on each Edge Server. The default value is `1000`.

▶ `MaxContactsPerDiscoveredPartner`—By default, any federated partners that are discovered automatically have a contact limit of 1,000 imposed. This setting can be used to decrease or increase that limit.

▶ `OutgoingTLSCountForFederatedPartners`—This is a numeric value from 1 to 4 indicating the maximum number of connections that can be used for a federated partner. The default value is `4`, but if connections should be more limited, this value can be reduced.

▶ `VerificationLevel`—If you are using default routing, the `VerificationLevel` property is used to monitor and assess the verification level of incoming messages. These are the valid values:

> ▶ `AlwaysVerifiable`—All requests received on the default route are marked as verified. If a verification header is not present, it automatically is added to the message.

> ▶ `AlwaysUnverifiable`—Messages are passed only if the addressee (the user the message is intended for) has configured an Allow ACE (access control entry) for the person who sent the message.

> ▶ `UseSourceVerification`—Message verification is based on the verification level included with the message. If no verification header is present, the message is marked as unverified.

Managing A/V Edge Configuration

By default, an A/V Edge Server applies a global policy, which controls bandwidth limits for users and ports as well as the lifetime of media relay tokens. This setting is not exposed in the Lync Server Control Panel and must be managed with the Lync Server Management Shell.

First, use the `Get-CsAVEdgeConfiguration` cmdlet to view the Global defaults:

```
Identity:                   Global
MaxTokenLifetime:           08:00:00
MaxBandwidthPerUserKb:      10000
MaxBandwidthPerPortKb:      3000
```

Unless there is a need to limit the values, leave the Global policy in place. To create a new A/V Edge configuration, which applies at the SF site level, use the following command.

In this example, the `MaxTokenLifetime` is increased to 10 days, the bandwidth per user is decreased to 5000KB, and maximum bandwidth per port is decreased to 2000KB:

```
New-CsAVEdgeConfiguration "site:SF" -MaxTokenLifetime "10:00:00"
➥-MaxBandwidthPerUserKb 5000 -MaxBandwidthPerPortKb 2000
```

Introducing High-Availability

Redundancy for Edge Servers requires just adding more Edge Servers to a pool. There is no logical limit on the number of Edge Servers that can be part of an Edge Server Pool. Load balancing can be done either with DNS load-balancing requests or by using a hardware load balancer.

DNS load balancing is done by entering multiple host records for the Edge Server pool name within DNS. When clients or servers attempt to reach a server that is unavailable, they attempt to use an alternative server.

A hardware load balancer can still be used for Edge Servers in Lync Server, which adds greater load-balancing capabilities at the price of greater complexity. As in prior releases, the internal Access Edge and A/V Authentication Edge interfaces should be load balanced, but the Web Conferencing Edge internal ports should not be load balanced.

> **TIP**
>
> This method is best achieved using a single VIP for the internal-facing services. From an external perspective, all three services should be load balanced, but they should all use a separate VIP.

Adding Edge Servers to a Pool

Adding an Edge Server to a pool requires updating and publishing the topology to reflect the change. Use the following steps to add another pool member:

1. Expand the Edge Servers node.

2. Right-click the Edge Server pool name, and select New Server.

3. Enter the internal IP address and FQDN IP address of the Edge Server's internal interface. Click Next.

4. Enter the external IP addresses for the Edge Server's Access Edge, Web Conferencing Edge, and A/V Edge services. Click OK.

5. Click OK when complete.

Now, publish the topology again and proceed with the new Edge Server installation.

To complete installation of the Edge Server, follow the steps defined in the "Installing the Edge Server" section earlier in this chapter.

After installation, be sure to add the IP address to the pool in DNS, or in the Hardware Load Balancer configuration, so that clients can locate the new Edge Server.

Edge Server Administration

Administration of the Edge sever features is done through either the Lync Server Control Panel or Lync Server Management Shell. Much of the administration is configuring various external access and conferencing policies for the users.

Editing the Global External Access Policy

Even though the remote access services have been enabled on the Access Edge configuration, users must have their account enabled to use these features. This can be done at a global level so that it applies to all users, or it can be configured on a per-site or per-user basis. The following steps show how to enable the features for all users in the organization.

1. Open the Lync Server Control Panel.

2. Select Federation and External User Access in the navigation pane.

3. Click External Access Policy.

4. Highlight the Global policy, click Edit, and click Modify.

5. Check the Enable Communications with Federated Users box.

6. If XMPP federation is enabled, check the Enable Communications with XMPP Federated Users box.

7. Check the Enable Communications with Remote Users box.

8. Check the Enable Communications with Public Users box.

9. Click Commit when complete. A sample configuration is shown in Figure 6.4.

Alternatively, the Lync Server Management Shell can also be used to configure the following setting:

```
Set-CSExternalAccessPolicy Global -EnableOutsideAccess $true
➥-EnableFederationAccess $true -EnablePublicCloudAccess $true
➥-EnablePublicCloudAudioVideoAccess $true -EnableXMPPAccess $true
```

TIP

The `EnablePublicCloudAudioVideoAccess` parameter in the preceding example enables audio and video communication to Skype and MSN/Live.

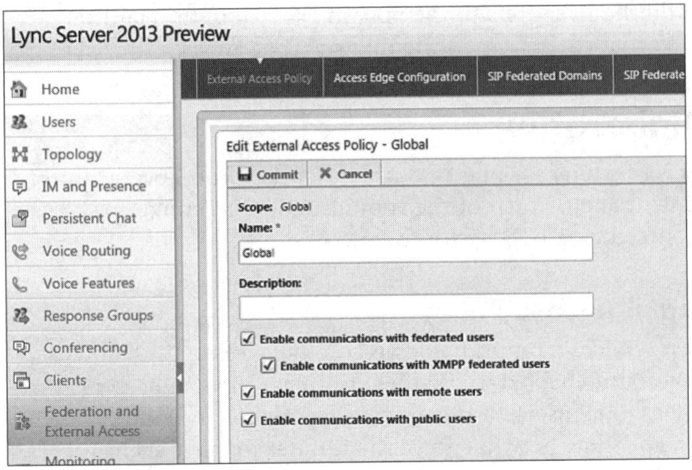

FIGURE 6.4   Edit the global External Access Policy.

Creating a New External Access Policy

In some scenarios, it is best to enable these features only for a select group of users or sites. Instead of remote access being enabled on the global policy, a new policy must be created and then assigned to a site or user accounts.

1. Open the Lync Server Control Panel.

2. Select Federation and External User Access in the navigation pane.

3. Click Access Edge Policy.

4. Click New and then select Site Policy or User Policy depending on what should be targeted.

NOTE

If a site policy is defined, all users associated with Front End pools in the site will automatically inherit the policy. This is used to automatically provision remote access features to some sites while not allowing it to others.

5. Check the Enable Communications with Federated Users box.

6. If XMPP federation is enabled, check the Enable Communications with XMPP Federated Users box.

7. Check the Enable Communications with Remote Users box.

8. Check the Enable Communications with Public Users box.

9. Click Commit when complete.

Alternatively, the Lync Server Management Shell can also be used to create the new policy:

```
New-CSExternalAccessPolicy -identity "Allow All Features"
➥-EnableOutsideAccess $true -EnableFederationAccess $true
➥-EnablePublicCloudAccess $true -EnablePublicCloudAudioVideoAccess $true
➥-EnableXMPPAccess $true
```

> **TIP**
>
> To create a policy with site scope using the Lync Server Management Shell, name the policy with a "site:" prefix followed by the site name. For instance, if a site called SF existed, the preceding sample policy should be named Site:SF to apply only to that site.

Assigning External Access Policies

After the new user policy is created, it must be assigned to a user account. If the external policy is created with a site scope, this step is not required.

1. Open the Lync Server Control Panel.

2. Select Users in the navigation pane.

3. Search for a user, highlight the account, click Modify, and click Assign Polices.

4. In the External Access Policy section, select the new external access policy, and click OK. An example of this configuration is shown in Figure 6.5.

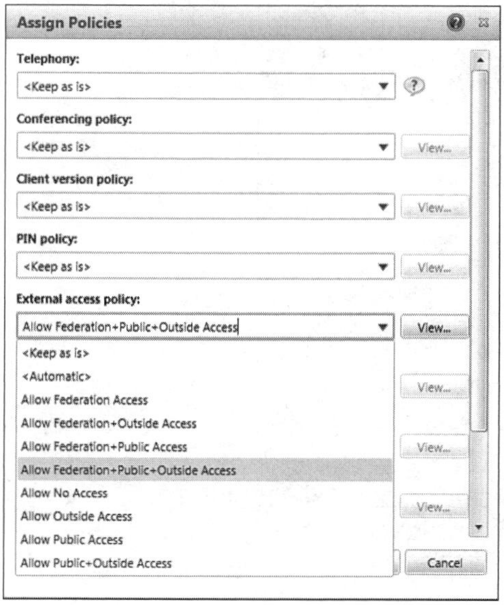

FIGURE 6.5   Assign an External Access Policy.

The Lync Server Management Shell can also be used to assign a policy to a user:

```
Grant-CSExternalAccessPolicy randy@companyabc.com -PolicyName "Allow all features"
```

Managing Federation

After enabling user accounts for federation, administrators can manage the organizations with which they want to federate through Lync Server. If partner discovery lookups are allowed on the Access Edge configuration, all domains are automatically allowed. Adding allowed domains can still be done to grant a higher level of trust to partners, but is not required. If partner discovery is not allowed, administrators must manually add all federated partners to the allow list.

Blocking a federated domain can be used to prevent internal users from communicating with specific partners. This is used in situations in which federation should be allowed globally, but blocked to only a few specific domain names. To allow or block a federated domain, use the following steps:

1. Open the Lync Server Control Panel.

2. Select Federation and External User Access in the navigation pane.

3. Click SIP Federated Domains.

4. Click New and then select either Allowed Domain or Blocked Domain.

5. Enter the SIP domain name of the federated domain allowed or blocked, as shown in Figure 6.6, and click OK.

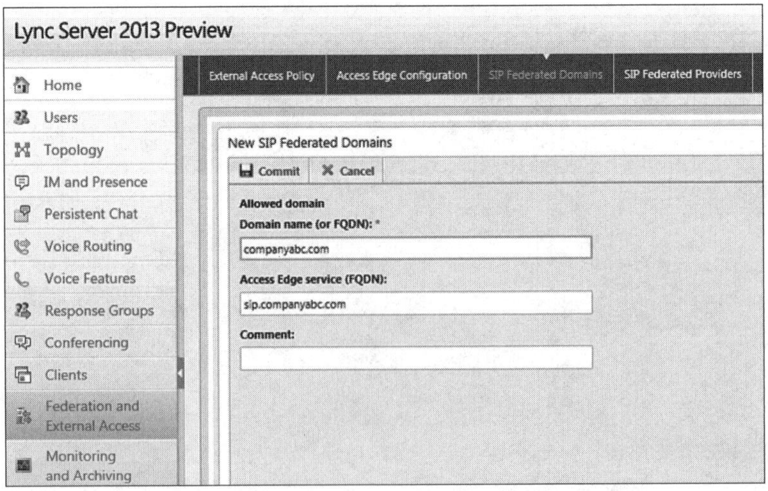

FIGURE 6.6   Adding an allowed domain for SIP federation.

CAUTION

When you are adding an allowed domain, the option exists to add the FQDN of the partner's Access Edge Server. This field is not required, but when it is used it grants a higher level of trust to the domain by allowing more requests per second from the domain. Be careful when using this field because if a partner changes its FQDN later, the name will no longer be valid.

The Lync Server Management Shell can also be used to perform these tasks. To allow a new domain, use the following command. The only required parameter is the domain name, but a comment and partner's Access Edge Server FQDN can also be specified. In addition, the `MarkForMonitoring` parameter can be set to enable quality monitoring to this domain by a Monitoring Server role.

```
New-CSAllowedDomain -Domain <SIP Domain Name> -Comment <Comment string>
↪-ProxyFQDN <Partner Access Edge FQDN> -MarkForMonitoring <True|False>
```

To block a domain from sending or receiving messages, use the following command:

```
New-CSBlockedDomain -Domain <SIP Domain Name>
```

Managing XMPP Federation

Lync Server 2013 now includes an XMPP gateway on the Edge Server and on the Front End Server or Front End Pool. To allow federated connections to XMPP solutions, you must add an XMPP allowed domain. To add an XMPP Domain, perform the following steps:

1. Open the Lync Server Control Panel.
2. Select Federation and External Access in the navigation pane.
3. Select XMPP Federated Partners.
4. To create a new configuration, click New.
5. Define a Primary Domain; this is the base domain of the XMPP partner.
6. Define a Description.
7. Define Additional Domains, if necessary. This can include any other domains that are available through this partner. You must do this for all available domains, including subdomains of the Primary Domain.
8. Select a Partner Type. You have the option of Federated, Public Verified, or Public Unverified. Many organizations will be using XMPP for public connections. The primary difference is that in a Public Verified configuration, the partner contact is allowed to invite your Lync users to conversations. In a Public Unverified configuration, your Lync users must add a contact to their contact list before any communications can occur.

NOTE

Google Talk is not a publicly verified XMPP service for Lync Server. GTalk users will not be able to add your Lync users as a contact unless your Lync users add them first.

9. You must identify security methods for connections to this partner. First, choose whether TLS Negotiation or SASL Negotiation is required.

CAUTION

Each XMPP configuration will have unique requirements for TLS and SASL. It is recommended to identify these requirements from the partner or public provider before configuring these settings.

10. Identify whether Dial-out Negotiation is enabled. The dial-out process uses DNS and an authoritative server to verify requests from an XMPP partner. This is another configuration that needs to be identified with the partner or provider before configuration.

11. Click Commit when completed. Figure 6.7 shows a sample configuration.

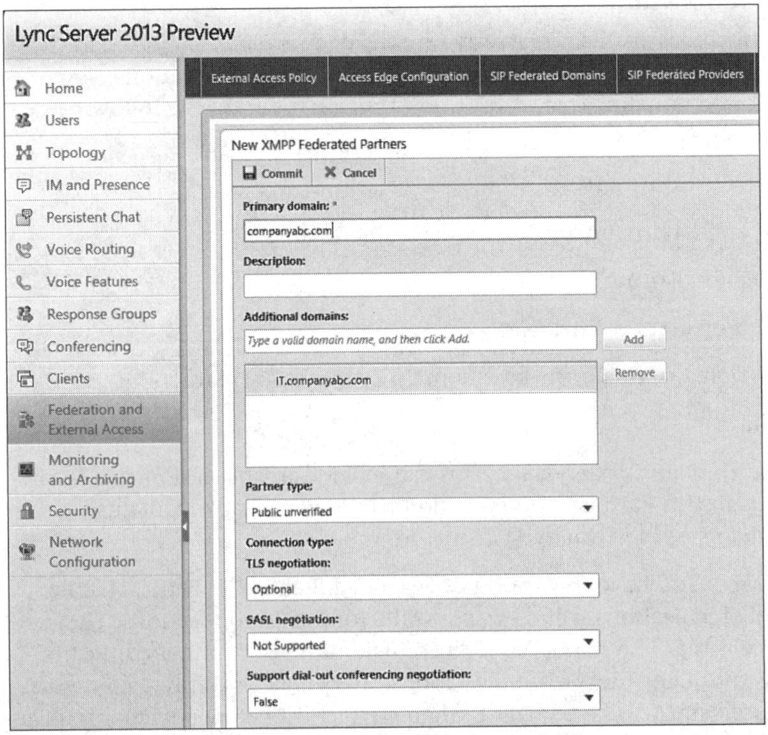

FIGURE 6.7 XMPP partner configuration.

Alternatively, the Lync Server Management shell can be used to configure XMPP domains. Use the following command:

```
New-CsXmppAllowedPartner companyabc.com -TlsNegotiation optional
➥-SaslNegotiation NotSupported -EnableKeepAlive $false
➥-SupportDialbackNegotiation $false
```

Managing Public Providers

Similar to managing federation, the Public IM providers can be allowed or blocked when configuring an Edge Server. By default, all the included providers are disabled and must be enabled before users can communicate with contacts in these domains.

The following additional options are available when dealing with the Public IM providers:

▶ **Allow Communications Only with Users Verified by This Provider**—This is the default setting and it means the Edge Server trusts the Public IM provider's determination of valid or invalid users trying to send messages to the Lync Server users.

▶ **Allow Communications Only with Users on Recipients' Contact Lists**—This setting limits communication only to users explicitly added to the contact list of a Lync Server user. If a contact who is not added tries to initiate a conversation with an internal user, the message is rejected by the Edge Server.

▶ **Allow All Communications with This Provider**—This setting enables all incoming communication from the provider regardless of whether the provider indicates that the message should be trusted.

To manage access to the public networks, use the following steps:

1. Open the Lync Server Control Panel.

2. Select Federation and External User Access in the navigation pane.

3. Click SIP Federated Providers.

4. Highlight one of the providers, click Edit, and click Show Details.

5. Check the Enable Communications with This Provider box, and click Commit.

6. Repeat for enabling additional providers.

Figure 6.8 displays the default Public IM configuration for a Lync Server 2013 deployment.

To perform these steps in the Lync Server Management Shell, use the following command:

```
Set-CSPublicProvider <Provider Name> -Enabled $true
```

To enable all three public IM providers in one step, use the following command:

```
Get-CSPublicProvider | Set-CSPublicProvider -Enabled $true
```

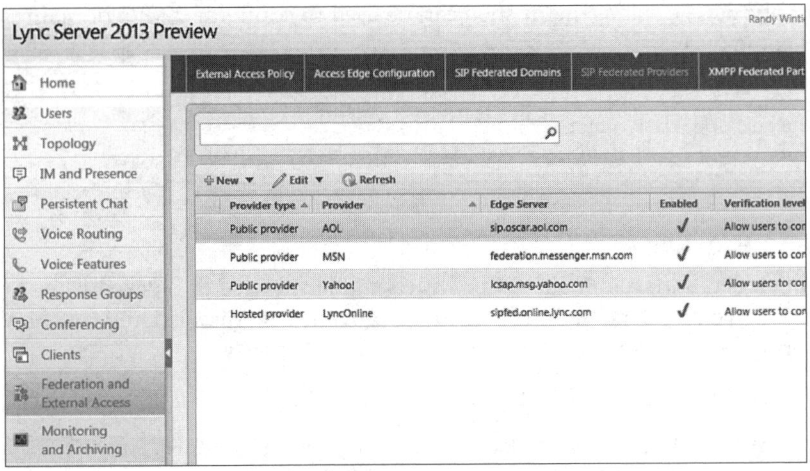

FIGURE 6.8 Configuring Public IM providers.

You can view the status of the public IM providers by running the `Get-CSPublicProvider` cmdlet. The following is the output is from the command:

```
Identity:              MSN

Name:                  MSN

ProxyFQDN:             federation.messenger.msn.com

VerificationLevel:     UseSourceVerification

Enabled:               True


Identity:              Yahoo!

Name:                  Yahoo!

ProxyFQDN:             lcsap.msg.yahoo.com

VerificationLevel:     UseSourceVerification

Enabled:               True


Identity:              AOL

Name:                  AOL

ProxyFQDN:             sip.oscar.aol.com

VerificationLevel:     UseSourceVerification

Enabled:               True
```

Managing External Web Conferencing Features

Enabling remote access to the web conferencing features of Lync Server is actually performed with the remote access policies. As long as a user is associated with a policy that enables remote access, the user has web conferencing capabilities through the Edge Server from the Global conferencing policy.

After deploying Edge services, the option exists to enable anonymous users to join web conferences hosted by the Lync Server infrastructure. Anonymous users are considered people who are not federated partners or users without a Lync Server enabled account. These users cannot authenticate with credentials, so they are considered anonymous to the pool users. Anonymous access to conferences can be enabled to allow authenticated users, federated users, and anonymous users to all collaborate.

To configure the external access rules and anonymous access, the conferencing policy must be edited:

1. Open the Lync Server Control Panel.

2. Select Conferencing in the navigation pane.

3. Highlight the Global policy, click Edit, and click Show Details.

4. Verify that the Allow Participants to Invite Anonymous Users check box is selected (see Figure 6.9).

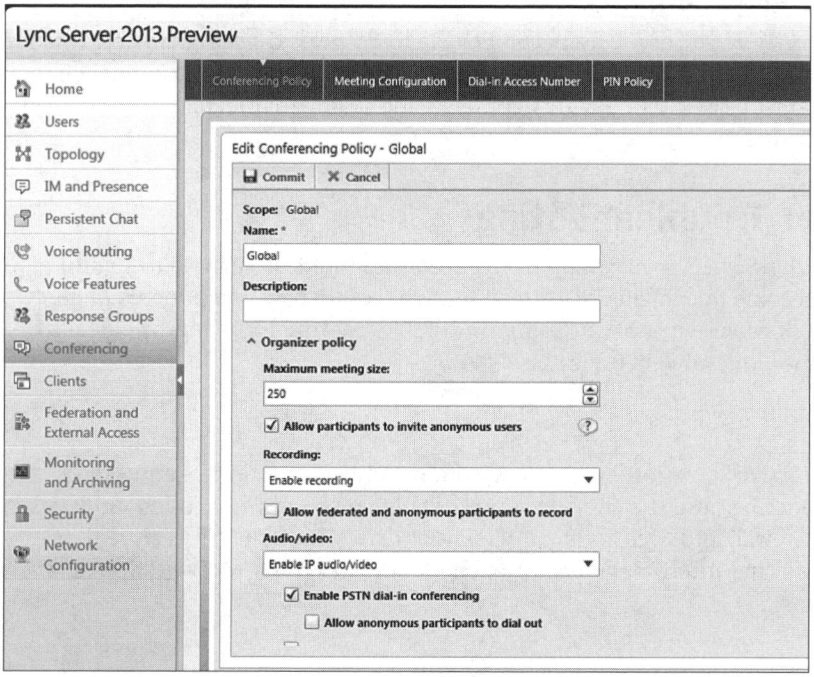

FIGURE 6.9   Editing web conferencing policies.

5. If external users should be allowed to control shared applications or desktops, ensure that the Allow External Users to Control Shared Applications check box is checked.

6. Click Commit.

To enable anonymous access and external sharing control for the Global policy through the Lync Server Management Shell, use the following command:

```
Set-CSConferencingPolicy Global –AllowAnonymousParticipantsInMeetings
➥$true –AllowExternalUserControl $true
```

> **NOTE**
>
> Selecting the Enable recording option in a meeting policy presents an additional check box, Allow External Users to Record Meeting, which lets an administrator control whether only internal users may record a meeting.

If enabling anonymous access and external user control features must be limited to specific locations or user groups, an additional conferencing policy should be created. As with the External Access Policy, a site policy automatically applies to an entire location, and user policies can be assigned to individual users.

Managing A/V Edge Features

After deploying an A/V Edge Server, users will be able to do peer-to-peer audio and video through the Edge Server without additional configuration. To support A/V conferencing features, the user must be associated with a conferencing policy that enables audio, video, and application sharing.

Edge Server Troubleshooting

Troubleshooting Edge Servers is necessary in the event that users are unable to sign in or some features become unavailable. This section discusses the key components of an Edge Server to check when issues arise. Common troubleshooting tools and tips are also provided, which should resolve many issues.

Firewall Ports

Connectivity to an Edge Server or reverse proxy can be limited by firewalls and can be tricky to troubleshoot because the connections generally cross a few network boundaries. See Chapter 12, "Firewall and Security Requirements." Check firewalls between remote clients, Edge Servers, and internal servers. Also, check whether the Windows Firewall is blocking connections.

Routing

Anytime a server has multiple network adapters, it can be problematic to make routing work correctly. Ensure that requests destined for the internal network are routed out the correct network adapter by using tools such as packet sniffers or traceroute. Packet capture tools have the capability to monitor a specific adapter, so it should be easy to determine whether traffic is flowing through an adapter. It is important to make sure you have properly configured Windows persistent routes. Use the ROUTE PRINT command to verify routes on each of your Edge Servers.

Certificates

Incorrectly issued certificates are a potential issue with Edge Server configuration. It is common for Intermediate and Root Certificates to be missing from Edge Server Deployments. This will cause intermittent, or even complete, failures on most connections to the Edge Server. Confirm that you have all required certificates installed from your public Certificate Authority. DigiCert offers a free certificate-checking utility online that can verify the proper installation of certificates. This tool can be found at http://www.digicert.com/help.

> **TIP**
>
> As a best practice, always use the built-in Certificate Wizards because they automatically generate the correct names for a server role. Only the Access Edge and Web Conferencing Edge certificates need to be issued by a public certificate authority. The internal Edge certificate and A/V Authentication certificates are used only by internal clients.

Follow the guidelines to rule out certificate issues.

- ▶ **Key Bit Length**—The certificate bit length must be 2048, or 4096, to be supported by Lync Server.

- ▶ **Template**—The template used to issue the certificate should be based on the web server template. If the Lync Server Certificate Wizard is used, the correct template is automatically applied.

- ▶ **Private Key**—The server certificate must have the private key associated to be used by Lync Server. In situations in which certificates are exported or copied between servers, export the private key with the certificate.

- ▶ **Certificate Chain**—The Edge Server must be able to verify each certificate up to a Trusted Root Certification Authority. Additionally, because the server presents the certificate to clients, it must contain each intermediate certificate in the certificate chain.

- ▶ **Certificate Store**—All certificates used by the Edge Server must be located in the Personal section of the local computer certificate store. A common mistake is to place certificates in the Personal section of the user account certificate store.

▶ **Certificate Trust**—Be sure that the clients and servers communicating with the Edge Server all contain a copy of the top-level certificate authority of the chain in their Trusted Root Certification Authority local computer store. When the certification authority is integrated with Active Directory, this generally is not an issue. When using an offline or nonintegrated certificate authority, install root certificates on clients and servers.

Additionally, each service has slightly different requirements for the subject and subject alternative names.

Edge Internal Certificate Names

The required name for the Internal Edge certificate is as detailed here:

▶ **Subject Name**—Ensure that the subject name matches the internal Edge pool FQDN entered in the Topology Builder.

▶ **Shared Certificate**—Remember that in a Load-Balanced Edge Server Pool, all servers in that pool must share the same internal certificate with the same private key.

Access Edge Certificate Names

The required names for an Access Edge Server certificate are as described here:

▶ **Subject Name**—Ensure that the subject name matches the Access Edge FQDN entered in the Topology Builder.

▶ **Subject Alternative Names**—The SAN field must contain all supported SIP domains in the `sip.<SIP Domain>` format.

Web Conferencing Edge Certificate Names

The required name for a Web Conferencing Edge Server certificate is as detailed here:

▶ **Subject Name**—Ensure that the subject name matches the Web Conferencing Edge FQDN entered in the Topology Builder.

A/V Authentication Certificate Names

The media relay certificate does not have any specific name requirements.

Wildcard Certificates

Some organizations attempt to use wildcard certificates or a single certificate with subject alternative names that attempt to cover all possible names. There are certainly some cases in which this configuration might work, but in the end the simplicity of following the actual name requirements tends to outweigh any small cost savings achieved by using fewer certificates. If you are attempting one of these configurations and experiencing issues, use the correct names to see whether that resolves the issue.

DNS Records

Successful sign-in to an Edge Server is heavily dependent on correctly configuring the DNS.

▶ The NSLookup tool can be used to verify that the necessary DNS records are in place as described in Chapter 11, "Dependent Services and SQL."

TIP

When troubleshooting any Edge Server issue, it is important to check that all necessary DNS records exist and are resolving to the correct IP addresses.

The following sample NSLookup sequence within a command prompt checks the host record of the pool:

```
nslookup
set type=a
lyncedgepool1.companyabc.com
```

A successful query returns a name and an IP address. Verify that the IP returned matches the IP addresses assigned to the Edge Servers or load balancer and that no extra, or surprise, IP addresses are returned.

To verify the SRV record required for automatic client sign-in externally, the syntax is slightly different. The following is another sample NSLookup sequence:

```
nslookup
set type=srv
_sip._tls.companyabc.com
```

A successful query returns a priority, weight, port, and server hostname. Verify that the server name matches the Edge pool Access Edge FQDN and that the correct port is returned.

Use the same steps to verify that the following services resolve correctly in public DNS:

▶ Access Edge FQDN

▶ Web Conferencing Edge FQDN

▶ A/V Edge FQDN

For internal DNS, verify that clients can resolve the following:

▶ Internal Edge pool FQDN

> **TIP**
>
> Ensure that the Edge Server can resolve internal DNS names of all Lync Servers. It must be able to properly resolve these DNS entries to communicate with internal servers and users.

Windows Event Logs

A good source of information when troubleshooting any server issue is the event logs. Lync Server creates a dedicated event log for informational activities, warnings, and errors within the standard Windows Server Event Viewer console. To view this event log, perform the following steps:

1. Open the Event Viewer Microsoft Management Console.

2. Expand the Applications and Services Logs folder.

3. Click the Lync Server log.

4. Examine the log for warning or error events, which might provide additional insight into issues.

Lync Centralized Logging

Lync Server 2013 introduced Centralized Logging. Each Lync Server runs a service that can receive commands from any other Lync Server to enable logging for troubleshooting scenarios. For Edge Servers, you must make sure that port 50001 to 50003 TCP is open from your Front End Servers to each server in the Edge Server Pool. These ports are used to communicate centralized logging commands. Windows Firewall is modified as part of the installation; however, these ports must be considered for any other firewalls in the environment. The following example uses centralized logging to collect data on an Edge Server Pool:

1. Open the Lync Server Management Shell.

2. Navigate to the CLS directory, which by default is `C:\Program Files\Common Files\Microsoft Lync Server 2013\ClsAgent`.

3. Type the following command to enable logging for the Instant Messaging and Presence scenario:

   ```
   Clscontroller.exe -start -scenario im -pools edgepool.companyabc.com
   ```

4. After the logging is enabled, reproduce the issue you are trying to troubleshoot.

5. From the same command prompt, run the following command to stop logging on the Edge Server Pool:

   ```
   Clscontroller.exe -stop -scenario -im -pools edgepool.companyabc.com
   ```

6. The next two commands must be executed to search and export any logs from the Edge Server Pool. If required, you can filter by specific components; however, this example will simply export data for all tracing components.

```
Clscontroller.exe -flush -pools edgepool.companyabc.com
Clscontroller.exe -search -pools edgepool.companyabc.com
➥-loglevel verbose > c:\EdgeLog.TXT
```

7. If you do not pipe the command to a text file, the log results will simply display in the command prompt. However, given the large amount of data in these log files, it is recommended to pipe to a text file.

8. At this point, you now have a readable log file from the Edge Server Pool. This file can be opened in Notepad or in Snooper.exe for viewing.

Lync Server Management Shell

The Lync Server Management Shell provides several cmdlets, which test various functions of a server. A useful cmdlet for verifying the overall health of a server is `Test-CSComputer` server, which verifies that all services are running, that the local computer group membership is correctly populated with the necessary Lync Server Active Directory groups, and that the required Windows Firewall ports are open.

The `Test-CSComputer` cmdlet must be run from the local computer and uses the following syntax:

```
Test-CSComputer -Report "C:\Test-CSComputer Results.xml"
```

After running the cmdlet, open the generated XML file to view a detailed analysis of each check.

Telnet

Telnet is a simple method of checking whether a specific TCP port is available from a client machine. From a machine that has trouble contacting an Edge Server, use the following steps to verify connectivity to the Access Edge or Web Conferencing services:

> **TIP**
>
> The Telnet client is not installed by default starting with Windows Vista and Server 2008. On a desktop operating system, it must be installed by using the Turn Windows Features On or Off option found in Programs and Features. On a server operating system, it can be installed through the Features section of Server Manager.

1. Open a command prompt.

2. Type the following command:

```
telnet <Access Edge FQDN> <443 or 5061>
```

3. For example:

```
telnet sip.companyabc.com 5061
```

If the window goes blank leaving a flashing cursor, the connection was successful and the port can be contacted without issue. If the connection fails, an error is returned. Check that the services are running on the Edge Server and that no firewalls are blocking the traffic.

Troubleshooting Lync Services

Basic troubleshooting begins with making sure that the Lync Server services are all running. When services are in a stopped state, users will notice many issues such as being unable to sign in or connect to the Edge Server. Verify that the following windows services are configured to start automatically and are running:

▶ Lync Server Access Edge

▶ Lync Server Audio/Video Authentication

▶ Lync Server Audio/Video Edge

▶ Lync Server Centralized Logging Service Agent

▶ Lync Server Replica Replicator Agent

▶ Lync Server Web Conferencing Edge

▶ Lync Server XMPP Translating Gateway Proxy (if installed)

▶ SQL Server (RTCLOCAL)

Edge Server Best Practices

The following are best practices from this chapter:

▶ Use Edge Servers to provide secure remote access for Lync Server.

▶ Place the Edge Servers in a perimeter or DMZ network.

▶ Use DNS load balancing or a hardware load balancer to provide high-availability for Edge Servers.

▶ Create external access policies with site-level scopes to apply automatically to users.

▶ Plan to use a reverse proxy server to publish external web services.

▶ Use DNS SRV records for routing federation requests to reduce management overhead with federation.

▶ Use certificates from a public certificate authority for the Access Edge and Web Conferencing Edge roles so that they are trusted automatically by remote clients and federated partners.

Summary

The Edge Server is a big part of why Lync Server is such a compelling product. The fact that users can be inside or outside the office with complete access to the same features drives productivity and collaboration. With the way the Edge services work regardless of location, users have no need to change their workflows whether they are in the office, at home, or traveling halfway around the world.

On the less glamorous side, the Edge Server is a safe and stable role designed to be a secure gateway to the Lync Server infrastructure. The granular external access and conferencing policies give administrators complete control over what features are deployed and who is allowed to use them.

The federation and public IM features enable an organization to extend the reach of their unified communications platform to partners or customers without additional products. Organizations considering Lync Server should include Edge services within the deployment to take full advantage of the features it offers.

CHAPTER 7

Microsoft Lync Server 2013 Monitoring and Archiving

Both the Monitoring role and the Archiving role have changed significantly since Lync Server 2010. The biggest change is that neither of them is a dedicated server role any longer. Although they remain logically separate, they are now collocated with the Lync Server 2013 Front End role. In fact, they are now simply listed as an option during the Front End Wizard in Topology Builder. As such, there won't be traditional "installation steps" as you'll find in the other chapters in this section. Instead, this chapter covers both roles at a high level and discusses how they apply to the Lync environment as a whole.

The Monitoring role in Lync Server 2013 has evolved from previous versions. For those new to Lync, the Monitoring role is actually an agent that lives on each Front End Server in a pool and collects and manages information from the Front End, Mediation, and other server roles and stores it in a database separate from the one used by the Front End. It leverages SQL Server Reporting Services to create reports related to call quality and metrics. These reports are often used for ROI (return on investment) justification. For example, if the legacy conferencing provider charged $.10 per minute and after conferencing was moved to OCS the current report showed 100,000 minutes of usage, then the company saved $10,000 in conferencing costs for that month. I've found that most companies can achieve 100% ROI in one to three months after deployment, even in large, highly redundant deployments.

The Archiving role in Lync Server 2013 primarily serves the purposes of legal compliance. That said, other companies might want to have a centrally searchable archive for other purposes because the Archive server role is able to archive communications across both IM and meetings. New to the 2013 generation of products, Lync archiving data can now be stored in a central repository with archived email in an Exchange 2013 environment; however, that is beyond the scope of this book. This chapter focuses on the native Lync Server 2013 tools as related to archiving.

The Archiving role scales well with the Front End collocated service capable of handling all the users hosted by the pool.

The Archiving Server role can archive the following content:

▶ Peer-to-peer instant messages

▶ Multiparty instant messages

▶ Web conferences, including uploaded content and events (for example, join, leave, upload)

▶ Audio/video for peer-to-peer instant messages and web conferences

▶ Web conferencing annotations and polls

Organizations should decide before the implementation of the Archiving role how archiving will be configured. Decisions around site and user-based archiving must be made. It is also critical to determine how archive data will be managed. The archiving database was not meant to be a long-term retention solution, and as such, Lync Server 2013 does not provide an e-discovery solution for archived data. Various third-party solutions, however, are optimized for e-discovery within archived Lync data. This data should optimally be moved to other storage or collocated with Exchange 2013.

> **TIP**
>
> When you're deciding how to configure the Archiving Server topology, the obvious question might be, "How much bandwidth does my Archive Server need?" The answer depends on your archiving configuration, policy, and user load. The user load should be monitored during your pilot implementation to get a feel for how much load it will generate.

Monitoring Components Installation

Although this section doesn't cover the simple "check box" to add the monitoring components to the Front End Server, it does cover the other items that are required for a fully functional Lync Monitoring deployment. The Monitoring role allows administrators to collect, trend, and review quantitative data related to audio calls, video calls, and IM messages. The Monitoring Server leverages Microsoft Message Queuing technology to collect information and deposit it in the monitoring database. Then it leverages SQL Server Reporting Services to display various canned and custom reports.

Installing Microsoft SQL Server 2012 Reporting Services

The Lync Server 2013 Monitoring server leverages Microsoft SQL Server Reporting Services to provide rich reports related to usage and quality of experience data. This section assumes you've already installed SQL and are familiar with the process. Small installations that chose to use the Enterprise edition of Lync Server 2013 can use the same SQL Server as the Front End pool; however, most larger deployments require a separate SQL Server and, in very large installations, a separate SQL Reporting Services server. In the steps that follow, you'll walk through the installation process and post-installation steps for SQL Reporting Services.

During the SQL Server 2012 Installation Wizard, ensure that the Reporting Services box is checked and continue through the wizard. Be sure to examine the scalability requirements for your environment to determine whether the reporting services role should be placed on the SQL database server or on a dedicated serve. The administrator must also decide where to install the Reporting Services database, either on an existing SQL server or on the Reporting Services server. In general, it is recommended to collocate the Reporting Services database on the Reporting Services Server. After the SQL Reporting Services role is installed, it needs to be configured before the Monitoring Server can use it.

From the Start Menu, navigate to All programs, Microsoft SQL Server 2012, Configuration tools and select Reporting Services Configuration Manager. Ensure that the appropriate server and instance are selected and click Connect. To finish installing the Monitoring Components, follow these steps:

1. Click the Server Account button in the left column and set the appropriate report server service account.

2. Click the Web Service URL button. Review the settings. Usually the default settings are acceptable. However, if you want to use SSL, you'll need to pick the certificate to be used. A certificate can be requested from the IIS console.

3. Click the Database button. Ensure that the proper database server is set. Ensure that the correct credentials are set to access the database.

4. Click the Report Manager URL button. Select the virtual directory to be used to access reports. By default, this is "Reports."

Now the SQL Reporting Services server is almost ready. After the Monitoring server is installed, you'll need to deploy the Monitoring Server Report Pack to the SQL Reporting Server as reviewed in the following text.

Monitoring Configuration

The good news about Lync Server 2013 is that with the Topology Builder tool much of the configuration is done automatically. Although both configuration and administration can be done from the Silverlight web GUI or the Lync Server Management Shell, the configuration section focuses on the former and the administration section focuses on the latter, to avoid duplication of concepts.

Open the Lync Server Control Panel. For reference, it can be found at the short URL you defined earlier, https://lyncadmin.companyabc.com/ in the sample environment, or https://<pool_FQDN>/Cscp/.

Scrolling down in the left bar, click on the Monitoring and Archiving button. This brings up the settings menus for the Monitoring and Achiving server roles. By default, there is only one Call Detail Recording policy. Select it and click Edit and then Modify. These are the available options:

▶ Name (the name of the policy)

▶ Enable Monitoring of Call Detail Records (CDRs)

▶ Enable Purging for Monitoring Servers

▶ Options for duration to keep CDRs and error reports

The next item across the top bar is the Quality of Experience (QoE) Data menu. Microsoft's approach to measuring the user experience is through QoE data that provides qualitative and quantitative analysis of every call. It also provides some metrics around instant messaging and network type (VPN versus LAN versus WAN) as well. This also comes with one policy by default. The only option is whether to enable purging and, if so, how long to keep QoE data. By default, this value is set to 60 days.

The next step is to deploy the Monitoring Server reports to the SQL Reporting Server. This step can be done using the Lync Server Management Shell or from the main screen of the deployment wizard. From any of the Lync Server 2013 servers, open the Lync Server Management Shell and run as administrator. Where D is the drive letter assigned to your CD/DVD drive where the Lync installation CD/DVD/ISO is mounted, run the `DeployReports.ps1` PowerShell script as this:

```
D:\setup\amd64\setup\reportingsetup\DeployReports.ps1 -storedUserName <domain\user>
➥-storePassword <password>
```

This is the most minimalist version of the command. The full syntax including optional items is outlined here:

```
DeployReports.ps1 -storedUserName <domain\user> -storedPassword <password>
-readOnlyGroupName <ReportReadOnlyGroupName> -reportServerSQLInstance
<ReportServerSQLInstance>
```

An explanation of each option is presented here:

▶ **storedUserName**—The username used to access the Monitoring Server store.

▶ **storedPassword**—The password for the value of storedUserName.

▶ **readOnlyGroupName**—The domain group that will be granted read-only access to the Monitoring Server reports. This group must already exist in Active Directory for the action to complete successfully.

▶ `reportServerSQLInstance`—The SQL instance that is hosting SQL Reporting Services. If this is left blank, the script assumes that it is the same server that holds the Monitoring Server databases.

Run the `get-CsService -MonitoringServer` cmdlet and pay special attention to the `ReportingURL` field. This is the URL where you'll access the Lync Server reports. For the sample environment it would be this: http://mcssql.companyabc.com/ReportServer?%2fM CSReports%2fMCS+Reports+Home+Page. The reports themselves are covered in detail in the following section.

Monitoring Administration

This section reviews common administration tasks for the Lync Server 2013 Monitoring role. In general, there isn't much day-to-day administration of the Lync Server 2013 Monitoring components. Instead, this section focuses on the reports generated by the Monitoring Server.

The most important page is the Dashboard. The Dashboard is broken up into four distinct areas or panes: System Usage, Per-User Call Diagnostics, Call Reliability Diagnostics, and Media Quality Diagnostics. By default, the Dashboard shows "this week" and a "6 week" view. However, a monthly view is also available via a link in the upper-right corner of the screen.

System Usage is the first section (see Table 7.1). Many of the fields are self-explanatory, and they are very useful for at-a-glance looks at the environment. For example, the total A/V Conference Minutes item is great for "back of the napkin" ROI on the savings Lync Server 2013 provides over outsourced conferencing services. Possibly even more important, it gives a snapshot of how your users are using Lync Server. Are they using Communicator as a softphone? How about for application sharing? Has overall collaboration time increased since Lync Server 2013 was implemented? This report isn't the end-all for these answers but it does provide an insightful view.

TABLE 7.1   The System Usage Section of the Dashboard

System Usage		
Registration		
Unique user logons	0	
Peer-to-Peer		
Total sessions	0	
IM sessions	0	
Audio sessions	0	
Video sessions	0	
Application sharing	0	
Total audio session minutes	0.00	
Avg. audio session minutes		

System Usage		
Conference		
Total conferences	0	
IM conferences	0	
A/V conferences	0	
Web conferences	0	
Total organizers	0	
Total A/V conference minutes	0.00	
Avg. A/V conference minutes		
Total PSTN conferences	0	
Total PSTN participants	0	
Total PSTN participant minutes	0.00	

The next section is Per-User Call Diagnostics (see Table 7.2). This is a great at-a-glance view for overall health of your voice deployment. It also makes for great bragging rights in a well-planned deployment.

TABLE 7.2   Per-User Call Diagnostics Section of the Dashboard

Per-User Call Diagnostics		
Users with Call Failures		
Total users with call failures	0	
Conference leaders with call failures	0	
Users with Poor-Quality Calls		
Total users with poor-quality calls	0	

The Call Reliability Diagnostics section (see Table 7.3) provides a deeper view into the health of your UC deployment and a window into the end-user experience. This is something new to Lync Server 2013 and is a very valuable resource to administrators.

TABLE 7.3   Call Reliability Diagnostics Section of the Dashboard

Call Reliability Diagnostics		
Peer-to-Peer		
Total failures	0	
Overall failure rate		
IM failure rate		
Audio failure rate		

Call Reliability Diagnostics

Conference

Total failures	0
Overall failure rate	
IM failure rate	
A/V failure rate	

Top 5 Servers by Failed Sessions

No server has failure reported.

The last section is Media Quality Diagnostics (see Table 7.4). This table gives information about quality of calls in terms of total poor-quality calls and percentage of poor-quality calls compared to the total number of calls. It also offers the same metrics for conferences.

TABLE 7.4   Media Quality Diagnostics Section of the Dashboard

Media Quality Diagnostics

Peer-to-Peer

Total poor-quality calls	0
Poor-quality call percentage	
PSTN calls with poor quality	0

Conference

Total poor-quality calls	0
Poor-quality call percentage	
PSTN calls with poor quality	0

Top Worst Servers by Poor-Quality Call Percentage

No server has media quality data based on current period.

From the main Monitoring Server reports page there are a plethora of reports to review. The next section summarizes each report in the order in which it is presented on the main page. Also, here is a full list of the available reports. You'll see that they are a deeper dive into the snapshots presented in the Monitoring Server reporting Dashboard.

▶ System Usage Reports

  ▶ User Registration Report

  ▶ Peer-to-Peer Activity Summary Report

  ▶ Conference Summary Report

  ▶ PSTN Conference Summary Report

▶ Response Group Service Usage Report

▶ IP Phone Inventory Report

▶ Per-User Diagnostics Reports

▶ User Activity Report

▶ Call Reliability Diagnostics Reports

▶ Call Reliability Summary Report

▶ Peer-to-Peer Activity Reliability Report

▶ Conference Reliability Report

▶ Top Failures Report

▶ Failure Distribution Report

▶ Media Quality Diagnostics Reports

▶ Media Quality Summary Report

▶ Server Performance Report

▶ Location Report

▶ Device Report

▶ User Registration Report—This report shows user registrations over time. This can be useful to determine peak login times and AD authentication requirements.

▶ Peer-to-Peer Activity Summary Report—This report shows peer-to-peer activity including IMs, application sharing, and file transfers.

▶ Conference Summary Report—The Conference Summary Report measures conference metrics including Communicator conferences and PSTN conferences, number of organizers, and total conference minutes.

▶ PSTN Conference Summary Report—This report contains data specific to PSTN Conferences in Lync Server.

▶ Response Group Service Usage Report—Metrics for Response Groups including agent response and number of calls answered by the response group.

▶ IP Phone Inventory Report—Statistics about the number and type of IP phones in the Lync Server deployment. Includes all Communicator Phone Edition devices.

▶ User Activity Report—This report reviews user-focused call failures for person-to-person calls and conferences. This report is useful for measuring the overall health of your conferencing deployment.

▶ Call Reliability Summary Report—This gives a high-level view of failed calls, total call minutes, and other call metrics.

▶ Peer-to-Peer Activity Reliability Report—This report contains information about failures in peer-to-peer activity including IMs and collaboration activity.

▶ Conference Reliability Report—This reports on failures during IM, peer-to-peer, and PSTN conferences.

▶ Top Failures Report—This report gives a snapshot view of the top failures in the organization. It can reveal systemic problems and configuration issues.

▶ Failure Distribution Report—This report provides statistics about the failures related to site or pool. It is a great troubleshooting tool for finding error conditions.

▶ Media Quality Summary Report—This report provides an overall high-level view of media quality across the whole environment. It should be referenced often to review the overall health of your voice deployment.

▶ Server Performance Report—This report breaks down media quality metrics by server. This is especially important in deployments that utilize separate mediation servers.

▶ Location Report—The Location Report reviews media quality statistics by location defined in Lync Server or by individual users.

▶ Device Report—Similar to the Location Report, the Device Report pivots media quality data by type of device used when a failure is experienced.

Although some of the reports might initially seem similar, they all examine the data from a different, unique angle. These reports are critical in proactively monitoring the health of your Lync Server environment. A wise administrator will leverage these reports along with a monitoring platform like Microsoft System Center Operations Manager.

Monitoring Troubleshooting

The Monitoring role is fairly straightforward; however, there are a few things that commonly go wrong during deployment. This section covers the common issues and areas to check should you find your Monitoring Server deployment not going smoothly.

Because a lot of server-to-server connections are involved in a Monitoring Server deployment, the most obvious problem area is in ensuring proper permissions. Also, ensure that usernames and passwords are typed correctly. When in doubt, reenter the usernames and passwords used for database access for the Monitoring Server and the Reporting Server. Also, ensure that the accounts aren't subject to password expiration in Active Directory. There's no "doh" feeling like having a service account's password expire 30 or 90 days into your deployment.

If you've chosen to use SSL for your Reporting Services URLs, ensure that the subject name (SN) of the certificate matches the site name you've chosen. Note that this might or might not be the same as the FQDN of your server, depending on your reporting server configuration.

The Lync Server event log is also a good place to check for errors. From the Start menu select Administrative Tools and then Event Viewer. Expand the Applications and Services Logs item and select Lync Server. All events related to Lync Server functions reside here. Often the error description is enough to identify the problem and determine the resolution.

Archiving Components Installation

The only component needed for Lync Server 2013 Archiving, outside of choosing to add it to all the Front End Servers during the Topology building process, is installation of SQL Server. SQL Server 2008 R2 and SQL Server 2012 are supported for Lync 2013. The SQL installation process is covered in detail in Chapter 11, "Dependent Services and SQL."

Archiving Configuration

With the Topology Builder tool, most of the configuration is done automatically. Although both configuration and administration can be done from the Silverlight web GUI or the Lync Server Management Shell, the configuration section focuses on the former and the administration section on the latter, to avoid duplication of concepts.

Open the Lync Server Control Panel, which can be found at https://<pool_FQDN>/Cscp/. Scroll down in the left bar, and click the Monitoring and Archiving button. This brings up the settings menus for the Monitoring and Achiving server roles. Because Call Detail Recording and Quality of Experience Data are Monitoring functions, skip directly to the Archiving Policy tab. Here, you see the default Global Policy. Select it and click Edit and then Show Details.

These are the available options:

▶ Name (the name of the policy)

▶ Description (your own notes to identify the policy)

▶ Archive Internal Communications check box

▶ Archive External Communications check box

Now move to the Archiving Configuration tab. Again, you see the default Global Policy. Select it and click Edit and then Show Details. The available options are as listed here:

▶ Name (the name of the policy)

▶ Archiving settings, including three options in the drop-down list:

  ▶ Disable Archiving

  ▶ Archive IM Sessions

  ▶ Archive IM and Web Conferencing Sessions

▶ Block Instant Messaging (IM) or Web Conferencing Sessions If Archiving Fails check box

▶ Enable Purging of Archiving Data check box

If purging is enabled, there are two radio button options:

▶ Purge Exported Archiving Data and Stored Archiving Data After Maximum Duration (Days)

▶ Purge Exported Archiving Data Only

If the "Days" option is selected, the administrator has the option to define how many days the archived data is stored.

Creating Site and User Policies

In addition to modifying the default Global policy, administrators can create additional policies. To create a site policy, follow these steps:

1. From the Monitoring and Archiving window, click the Archiving Policy tab and click New.

2. Choose either Site Policy or User Policy.

   A site policy can be associated with specific sites to allow their behaviors to be different from the default global policy. User policies are assigned directly to users and allow them to bypass the default global policy. This is useful when archiving is needed only for select users who are distributed across the environment.

3. For this example, choose a Site Policy. When prompted to select a site, choose it from the list and click OK.

4. Now, the policy is named after the site—this cannot be modified. Input a description and choose whether internal and external communications will be archived. Click Commit.

Administrators can also create user policies that can be assigned to individual users instead of at a site level. To create a user policy, follow these steps:

1. For a user policy, repeat steps 1 and 2 but choose User Policy.

2. Enter a name for the user policy.

3. Enter a description for the policy.

4. Choose whether internal and external communications will be archived. Click Commit.

This results in the creation of multiple policies that can be used to manage archiving.

To apply a user-based Archiving Policy to a user, perform the following steps:

1. From the Lync Server 2013 Control Panel, click Users in the left pane.

2. Click Find in the search area to view the list of enabled users.

3. Double-click the user you want to modify.

4. Scroll down to Archiving Policy and choose the policy you want to apply from the drop-down list.

> **NOTE**
>
> It is worth highlighting the Archiving Configuration option Block Instant Messaging (IM) or Web Conferencing Sessions If Archiving Fails. This is what Microsoft refers to as "critical mode." If archiving this content is deemed critical by an environment, usually due to regulatory compliance, this option prevents unarchived IMs or web conferences from occurring.

For administrators who prefer to do all their configuration tasks through PowerShell, Lync Server 2013 supports the capability to read and modify the archive policy and archive configuration through cmdlets:

```
Get-CsArchivingConfiguration
Identity                         :Global
EnableArchiving                  : ImAndWebConf
EnablePurging                    :True
PurgeExportedArchivesOnly        :False
BlockOnArchiveFailure            :True
KeepArchivingDataForDays         :120
```

Using Cmdlets for Configuration Tasks

As one might logically expect, the policies and configurations can also be created through cmdlets; for example:

```
New-CsArchivingConfiguration -Identity "site:Santa Clara" -EnableArchiving
➥ImAndWebConf -EnablePurging:$True -PurgeExportedArchivesOnly:$False
➥-BlockOnArchiveFailure:$False -KeepArchivingDataForDays:120
➥-ArchiveDuplicateMessages:$False
```

Notice the last argument set in this command: `ArchiveDuplicateMessages`. This is a good example of where there are options available through the cmdlets that aren't exposed to the GUI tools.

The power of using cmdlets to manage an application, such as Lync Server 2013, becomes readily evident when you are dealing with a large implementation. By scripting the configuration of the entire environment, you are able to eliminate the human error introduced by having a distributed group of people perform repetitive tasks. Similarly, the script written to perform the configuration immediately becomes the documentation of the configuration. If later changes need to occur, you can perform queries to find the objects and modify them at the same time. If you plan to manage the environment in this manner, it becomes helpful to put some thought into a logical naming convention for policies and configurations. This enables you to search on some common value in the policies and configurations to select them for modification.

In a similar manner, PowerShell-based cmdlets make it easy to pull configuration reports from a large implementation. For example, imagine that your company announced a policy that all IMs will be retained for at least 30 days. More than likely, someone will ask you to make sure that all your configurations retain messages for at least 30 days. Rather than scrolling through the GUI to find configurations with values under 30, you could simply run a cmdlet like the following to produce a report of all configurations in which the `CachePurgingInterval` is less than 30 days:

```
Get-CsArchivingConfiguration | Where {$_.CachePurgingInterval
➥-lt "30"} | select Identity
```

However, if you were going to do that, why not fix it all at once?

```
$Array=Get-CsArchivingConfiguration | Where {$_.CachePurgingInterval -lt "30"}
Foreach ($Name in $Array)
{
$Var = $Name.Identity
Set-CsArchivingConfiguration -Identity $var -CachePurgingInterval:30
}
```

This report searches all configurations in the topology and sets any that have a `CachePurgingInterval` of less than `30` to `30` without touching any that were already higher than `30`.

Archiving Administration

This section reviews common administration tasks for the Lync Server 2013 Archiving role, including Data Export and Purge Mode.

In general, there isn't much day-to-day administration of the Lync Server 2013 Archiving Server role. Instead, this section focuses on the management of data stored in the Archiving database.

One of the most common tasks you perform against the Archiving Server is exporting content from the Archive database. This is performed through the Lync Server Management Shell using the `Export-CsArchivingData` cmdlet as follows:

```
Export-CsArchivingData -DBInstance SQLSRV -StartDate 05/15/2012 -OutputFolder
"C:\Archiving" -UserUri Alex@Companyabc.com
```

This command exports all sessions pertaining to the `UserURI` defined in the cmdlet. The output is a series of `.eml` files that are created in the `OutputFolder` path.

Archiving Troubleshooting

The Archiving Server role is fairly straightforward; however, there are a few things that commonly go wrong during deployment. This section covers the common issues and areas to check if you find your Archiving Server deployment not going smoothly.

Because a lot of server-to-server connections are involved in an Archiving Server deployment, the most obvious problem area is in ensuring proper permissions. Also, ensure that usernames and passwords are typed correctly. When in doubt, reenter the usernames and passwords used for database access for the Archiving Server. Also, ensure that the accounts aren't subject to password expiration in Active Directory.

The Lync Server event log is also a good place to check for errors. From the Start menu, select Administrative Tools, and select Event Viewer. Expand the Applications and Services Logs item and select Lync Server. All events related to Lync Server 2013 functions reside here. Often the error description is enough to identify the problem and determine the resolution.

One common cause for Archiving to fail is that the Front End Server isn't able to install the Archiving agent properly due to a problem with the Message Queuing Service. You might see event ID 30517 in the Lync Server logs or you might see event ID 30509. Although the FE role requires Message Queuing Service, it doesn't require Message Queuing Directory Integration. However, the Archiving agent does require this. The fix is to simply install the additional feature on the FE servers that are targets for Archiving.

Best Practices

The following are the best practices from this chapter:

▶ Leverage the Monitoring reports to keep a close eye on the overall and ongoing health of your deployment and to troubleshoot user-experience quality issues.

▶ Although the Lync Server 2013 Control Panel might seem more familiar at first, there are many functions that can be accomplished only in the Management Shell.

▶ For larger deployments, use a dedicated SQL Reporting Services Server.

▶ Before running the `DeployReports.ps1` script, ensure that the group you specify for Read Only access already exists in Active Directory.

▶ Always publish a new topology before making changes or installing a new s erver role.

▶ Test your SQL Reporting Services deployment before loading the Monitoring Server Report Pack.

▶ New reports are often included in Lync cumulative updates. Be sure to redeploy the Monitoring reports following the same process as you did initially to add the new or updated reports.

▶ Leverage the Archiving Server to record messages for key employees.

▶ Be sure to understand compliance regulations around archiving that you might need to follow in Lync Server 2013.

▶ For some larger deployments, a dedicated Archiving Server per pool might be required.

▶ For larger deployments, use a dedicated SQL Archiving Server.

▶ When possible, perform your configurations through the Management Shell to simplify bulk tasks and keep a record of what changes were made.

▶ Make sure you have enough storage to maintain the Archive for the expected period.

▶ Be aware of any existing retention policies that might conflict with your plans for archiving in Lync Server 2013.

7

Mediation Server

The Microsoft Lync Server 2013 Mediation Server is a critical component for providing Enterprise Voice and Dial-In Conferencing services to users. The Mediation Server acts as a back-to-back user agent, translating signaling and media between your internal Lync infrastructure and the Public Switched Telephone Network (PSTN).

This chapter focuses on the Mediation Server role and how it interacts with other components of Lync Server 2013. An overview of how the Mediation Server provides connectivity to the PSTN is provided. Additionally, supported Mediation Server configurations are outlined.

This chapter also discusses the steps required to prepare a server for the Mediation Server role and how to actually install a Mediation Server in the environment. The components of a Mediation Server role are examined, and guidelines for troubleshooting common issues with a Mediation Server are provided for reference.

Mediation Server Overview

The Mediation Server in Microsoft Lync Server 2013 is a service that connects your Lync users and Lync Servers to the PSTN. This server role is required for any connections to the PSTN or a legacy PBX infrastructure. When organizations are planning to deploy Enterprise Voice or Dial-In Conferencing, a Mediation Server must be deployed and connected to a next-hop PBX or PSTN. There are various ways to connect to the PSTN, including a PSTN Gateway, an IP-PBX, as Session Border Controller (SBC), or directly to a SIP trunk. Details on planning and designing PSTN connectivity for your infrastructure can be found in Chapter 32, "Planning for Voice Deployment."

The Mediation Server is a back-to-back user agent (B2BUA). A B2BUA operates between both endpoints in a SIP call to facilitate communications. When routing calls to the PSTN, users are directed to a Mediation Server. The Mediation Server receives a PSTN call request directly from Lync clients and divides the call into two signaling and media sessions. The Mediation Server then initiates a call through the PSTN device it is connected to. During PSTN calls, all SIP signaling routes through the Mediation Server. Additionally, media can also route through the Mediation Server if Media Bypass has been disabled. Figure 8.1 outlines a sample call flow between a Lync client and the PSTN with the Mediation Server managing all signaling during the call.

FIGURE 8.1   Mediation Server signaling example.

All SIP signaling will traverse the Lync Mediation Server, but media can travel directly from Lync users and the PSTN gateway or IP-PBX. Lync Server 2010 introduced the Media Bypass feature, which allows Lync users to send media directly to supported gateways or PBXs using the G.711 media codec. This feature remains in Lync Server 2013 and provides improved call quality, and much larger capacity to the Mediation Server role. Figure 8.2 provides two examples of how media could flow in Lync Server 2013: with Media Bypass disabled and with it enabled.

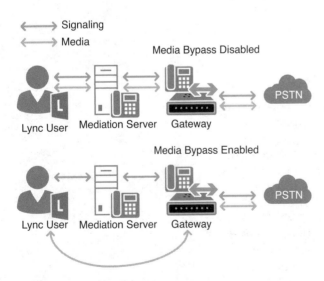

FIGURE 8.2   Mediation Server media flow example.

Media Bypass becomes more attractive in branch site scenarios. When a branch site is connected to a centralized Lync infrastructure and that branch site has its own PSTN connectivity, Media Bypass can allow Lync users in the branch site to communicate directly with the local media gateway, greatly reducing bandwidth requirements over the WAN. More details on design concepts for Media Bypass are discussed in Chapter 32.

The Mediation Server can also provide PSTN connectivity to remote users through the Lync Edge Server. When remote users make PSTN calls, they will be connected to a Mediation Server through the Edge Server, and the signaling and media flow will be handled as if the users were on the corporate network with the exception of Media Bypass, which is not enabled in Edge Server scenarios. As a summary, the Mediation Server is responsible for the following functions in Lync Server 2013:

▶ Encrypting and decrypting media from Lync users to a legacy PBX or the PSTN

▶ Maintaining SIP signaling sessions over TCP and/or TLS between Lync users and the PBX or PSTN

▶ Translating and/or transcoding media streams between Lync users and servers and the PBX or PSTN

Mediation Server Collocation

By default, the Mediation Server role is collocated with the Front End Server role. Microsoft supports collocation of the Mediation Server role with the Front End Server role, but no other server roles. Although it is supported, collocation should be carefully planned for based on the following:

▶ The number of gateway peers the Mediation Server will be connected to

▶ The amount of traffic through those gateways

▶ The percentage of calls that are enabled for Media Bypass

The Mediation Server can require heavy processing for media traversal and transcoding in some scenarios. Often, small organizations can collocate the Mediation Server role; however, many larger organizations will require dedicated Mediation Server roles for capacity purposes. Media Bypass also has a major impact on the number of calls a Mediation Server can support. Details on capacity planning for all roles including the Mediation Server can be found in Chapter 30, "Planning for Basic Lync Services." However, keep the capacity numbers included in Table 8.1 in mind when planning for Mediation Server collocation. Pay careful attention to the effects of media bypass being enabled.

TABLE 8.1   Mediation Server Collocated Capacity Numbers

Configuration	Maximum Calls
Collocated Mediation Server with Media Bypass disabled	150
Standalone Mediation Server with Media Bypass disabled	1100

Installing Mediation Server

Installing the Mediation Server role is similar to deploying any other role in Lync Server 2013. Much of the installation process is actually completing the prerequisite work, and installing the actual server can be done fairly quickly. A Mediation Server can be introduced into the environment at any time and does not necessarily need to be deployed from the start.

Prerequisites

A Mediation Server requires the same prerequisite software as all other Lync Server roles. The different hardware, operating system, and software prerequisites are discussed in this section.

Hardware Recommendations

This section gives the recommended minimum hardware recommendations for Lync Server 2013 servers.

These are the Lync Server 2013 Mediation Server processor recommendations:

▶ Dual processor, quad-core 2.0GHz or faster

▶ Four-way processor, dual-core 2.0GHz or faster

NOTE

Lync Server 2013 is only a 64-bit application and requires a 64-bit-capable processor. This is generally not an issue with any modern hardware, but be sure to verify that any legacy hardware supports a 64-bit operating system before attempting to use it for a Mediation Server.

This is the Lync Server 2013 Mediation Server memory recommendation:

▶ 16GB RAM

These are the Lync Server 2013 Mediation Server disk recommendations:

▶ 10K RPM HDD

▶ High-performance solid state drive (SSD) with performance equal to or better than 10K RPM HDD

▶ 2x RAID 10 (striped and mirrored) 15K RPM disks for database data files

These are the Lync Server 2013 Mediation Server network recommendations:

▶ Dual 1Gbps network adapters (recommended)

▶ Single 1Gbps network adapter (supported)

NOTE

When using multiple network adapters, it is recommended to use them only for fault tolerance. This means network adapters should be used for failover only and should not be combined for greater throughput.

Operating System Requirements

The Lync Server 2013 Mediation Server supports the following operating systems:

- ▶ Windows Server 2008 R2, Standard Edition with Service Pack 1

- ▶ Windows Server 2008 R2, Enterprise Edition with Service Pack 1

- ▶ Windows Server 2008 R2, Datacenter Edition with Service Pack 1

- ▶ Windows Server 2012, Standard Edition

- ▶ Windows Server 2012, Datacenter Edition

The Windows Server Core, Web, and High-Performance Computing Editions for any operating system version are not supported for deployment.

Software Requirements

The Lync Server 2013 Mediation Server requires the following components to be installed:

- ▶ Microsoft .NET Framework 4.5

- ▶ Windows Management Framework 3.0

- ▶ Windows Identity Foundation

- ▶ Visual C++ 11 Redistributable

Server Roles and Features

The Mediation Server does not require that any additional roles and services be deployed.

Create a Mediation Server Pool

After the server has been fully prepared for installation, the topology must be edited and published to reflect the new Mediation Server Pool. This involves both editing the existing topology and then republishing the updated topology so that the Mediation Server role can be installed on all servers in the pool.

Steps to Edit the Existing Topology

The next step in deploying a Mediation Server is to edit the existing Lync Server topology. To edit the topology follow these steps:

> **NOTE**
>
> If the Topology Builder is not already installed on the local computer or another computer in the environment, it can be installed from the Lync Server 2013 media.

1. Open the Lync Server Topology Builder.

2. When prompted to select the source topology, select Download Topology from Existing Deployment to retrieve the current topology.

3. Enter a location to which to save the temporary topology file.

4. Expand the Site node where the Mediation Server will be deployed.

5. Expand the Lync Server 2013 node.

6. Right-click on the Mediation Pools node and select New Mediation Pool.

7. If deploying a pool of servers, leave Multiple Computer Pool selected, enter the fully qualified name of the Mediation Server Pool in the Pool FQDN field. If you are deploying a single server, select Single Computer Pool and enter the FQDN of the server, and click Next.

8. Enter the fully qualified name of the Mediation Servers in the Computer FQDN field, click the Add button, and click Next.

9. Select a next hop server. This Front End Pool will be where the Mediation Server will route all inbound calls for lookup. Click Next.

10. Select an Edge Server Pool to be used for Media Relay, and click Finish.

Steps to Publish the Updated Topology

After the topology has been modified to include the Mediation Server Pool, the configuration can be published. This step publishes the changes to the Central Management Store, and all existing Lync Server 2013 servers will update their local configuration stores to match. Follow these steps to publish the updated topology.

1. Ensure that the Lync Server Topology Builder is still open and contains the Mediation Server Pool recently added.

2. Click the Action menu, select Topology, and then and select Publish.

3. Click Next to begin publishing the topology.

4. Review the Publishing Wizard log for any errors or warnings and remediate as necessary.

5. When the log indicates a successful update, click Finish to complete the wizard.

Install Lync Mediation Server Components

At this point the target server should be fully prepared and meet all prerequisites. Refer to earlier in this chapter for a full list of the Mediation Server requirements.

Cache Installation Files

The first step of the Lync installation process will be to cache the setup files locally on the server:

1. Insert the Lync Server 2013 media on the server to be used as a Mediation Server and launch `Setup.exe`, found in the `Setup\amd64` folder.

2. Enter a location for the installation files to be cached and click Install. The default location is `C:\Program Files\Microsoft Lync Server 2013`.

3. Select I Accept the Terms in the Licensing Agreement, and click OK.

NOTE

After you've browsed to the setup folder using Windows Explorer, the install window might appear behind the current Explorer window. It can be easy to miss this fact, so check the taskbar for the Lync install icon if some time has passed without any screen activity.

Install Local Configuration Store

To install any server role in Lync Server 2013, the target server must first have a local configuration store installed and populated with the topology information. The Lync Deployment Wizard will automatically open after the installation files have been cached on the system.

1. Click Install or Update Lync Server system.

2. Under Step 1: Install Local Configuration Store, click Run.

3. Select Retrieve Configuration Automatically from the Central Management Store, and click Next.

4. Click Finish after the local store is successfully created.

Install Lync Server Components

The following steps will allow the server to read the topology information from the local configuration store and then install the server roles matching its own FQDN:

1. Under Step 2: Setup or Remove Lync Server Components, click the Run button.

2. Click Next to begin the Mediation Server installation published in the topology.

3. Click Finish when the installation completes.

Create Certificates

Like all other roles in Lync Server, the Mediation Server communicates with other servers in the organization using Mutual Transport Layer Security (MTLS). To leverage MTLS, the Mediation Servers will need at least one certificate installed that meets a few requirements. A single certificate meeting these requirements can be used:

▶ The subject name should contain the pool's fully qualified domain name (FQDN).

▶ The server name should be included as a subject alternative name.

> **NOTE**
>
> The Certificate Wizard in Lync Server 2013 will automatically populate the subject name and any required subject alternative names based on the published topology, which greatly simplifies certificate confusion created by prior versions.

Follow these steps to request and assign the necessary certificates:

1. Under Step 3: Request, Install, or Assign Certificate, click the Run button.

2. Highlight the Default certificate and click the Request button to start the Certificate Request Wizard.

3. Click Next to continue.

4. Select either an online certificate request and certificate authority, or an offline certificate request and file path for the request. Click Next.

> **NOTE**
>
> The following steps here assume that an internal certificate authority is used to generate the request.

5. If user credentials other than the logged-on user are required to create the certificate request, check the box Specify Alternate Credentials for the Certification Authority. Enter a username and password and click Next. This is typically used in large environments where the Lync administrator does not have rights to request certificates.

6. If the default WebServer template will not be used, check the box Use Alternate Certificate Template for the Selected Certification Authority and enter the certificate template name. The template name, not the template display name, should be entered here. The template should already be published and available on the certificate authority issuing the certificate. In most cases the default WebServer template will be sufficient and there is no need to check this box.

7. Enter a friendly name for the certificate for identification purposes.

8. Select a key bit length of either 2048 or 4096.

9. If the certificate should be exportable, select the check box Mark Certificate Private Key as Exportable. This should be selected for Mediation Server Pools with multiple members, so the same certificate can be installed on each pool member.

10. Enter an organization name, typically the name of the business.

11. Enter an organizational name, typically the name of a division or department, and click Next.

12. Select a country, enter a state or province, enter a city or locality, and click Next.

13. Review the automatically populated subject name and subject alternative names. Click Next.

14. Review the certificate request summary screen for accuracy and when satisfied click Next.

15. The Lync Management Shell commands are displayed and the user can optionally review the certificate request log. Unless the request failed, this is not necessary. Click Next.

16. Leave the Assign This Certificate to Lync Server Certificate Usages check box selected to skip straight to the Certificate Assignment Wizard. Click Finish to complete the request process.

> **NOTE**
>
> It might not seem intuitive, but to process a response to an offline certificate request, use the Import Certificate button found at the bottom of the Certificate Wizard. If a request to an online certificate authority is in a pending state, the Process Pending Certificates button will be available to complete those requests.

Certificates issued from an online certificate authority will be installed automatically. If an offline request was performed, first copy the certificate authority response to the server. Then use the Import Certificate button found at the bottom of the wizard to complete the process. Follow these steps to import the completed request:

1. Click Browse and select the certificate authority response.

2. Uncheck the Certificate File Contains the Certificate's Private Key check box. Click Next.

3. Review the import certificate summary and click Next.

4. Click Finish to complete the process of associating the private key and certificate authority response.

Assign Certificates

After creating the necessary certificates, the Mediation Server services must have certificates assigned to them. To assign a certificate, follow these steps:

1. Under Step 3: Request, Install, or Assign Certificate, click the Run button.

2. Highlight the Default certificate and click the Assign button to start the Certificate Request Wizard.

3. Click Next to continue.

4. Select the certificate to be assigned and click Next. It's possible to view each certificate in more detail by highlighting it and clicking the View Certificate Details button.

> **NOTE**
>
> If a certificate is not available on this screen, that usually means a private key is not associated with the certificate. Be sure to complete any pending or offline requests before this step.

5. Click Next on the Certificate Assignment Summary screen.

6. The Lync Management Shell commands is displayed and the user can optionally review the certificate request log. Unless the request failed, this is not necessary. Click Next.

7. Click Finish to complete the wizard.

Start Services

After the necessary certificates have been requested and assigned, the Lync Server 2013 Mediation Server services can be started:

1. Beneath Step 4: Start Services, click the Run button.

2. Click Next to begin starting all the Lync Server services.

3. Click Finish to complete the wizard.

The wizard does not actually wait for the services to complete startup. Use the Services MMC to view the actual service state.

At this point the Mediation Server installation is complete and it should be functional.

Mediation Server Configuration

After a Mediation Server Pool has been installed, there generally is not much configuration left to do. This section discusses some of the configuration options available to a Mediation Server and addresses items that administrators should be aware of when configuring a Mediation Server.

Certificate Requirements

The Mediation Server role in Lync Server 2013 is much like any other role in that it uses certificates both for communication to other servers and for client services. A single certificate is required for each server in the Mediation Server Pool. This certificate is very basic, and has the following requirement:

▶ **Default**—The default certificate is used for MTLS communications between servers, and for securing SIP signaling in client communications. The certificate should contain the pool name in the Subject field, each Mediation Server's name as a subject alternative name.

High-Availability

Redundancy for the Mediation Server role is provided in a similar fashion as with Front End Servers and requires just adding more Mediation Servers to a pool. Load balancing is achieved via DNS load balancing, by providing multiple IP addresses that resolve to the pool name of the Mediation Servers. If one IP address is unavailable, the endpoint will attempt to connect to another IP address provided for the pool in DNS.

TIP

Plan for high-availability in the environment from the start, even if multiple Mediation Servers will not be deployed initially. Completing the planning and configuration for high-availability simplifies the deployment later and requires nearly no changes to the existing infrastructure. Adding high-availability to the environment later simply becomes a matter of adding a new server to the topology, and creating the DNS records.

Adding Mediation Servers to a Pool

Adding a Mediation Server to a pool is much like creating the initial pool. The topology must first be updated and published to reflect the change. Follow the steps described previously to import the existing topology in Topology Builder, and then follow these steps to add another pool member:

1. Expand the Mediation Pools node.

2. Right-click the Mediation Pool name and select New Server.

3. Enter the fully qualified domain name of the new Mediation Server.

4. Select either Use All Configured IP Addresses or Limit Service Usage to Selected IP Addresses and enter the IP addresses to be used by the Lync Server 2013 services.

5. Optionally, select the IPv6 check box if IPv6 is in use on the network.

6. Click OK when complete.

Now simply publish the topology again and proceed with the Mediation Server installation using the same steps defined in the "Installing Mediation Server" section earlier in this chapter. After installation, be sure to add the IP address to the pool in DNS so that clients can locate the new Mediation Server.

8

Mediation Server Administration

Administration of the Mediation Server role in Lync Server 2013 can be performed through a combination of the Lync Server Control Panel and the Lync Server Management Shell. This section discusses management of Mediation Server services.

Services

Installing a Mediation Server in Lync Server 2013 creates only a minimal number of Windows services. The following services will be visible within the Services MMC after the Mediation Server installation:

- ▶ Lync Server Centralized Logging Service
- ▶ Lync Server Mediation Server
- ▶ Lync Server Replica Replicator Agent
- ▶ SQL Server (RTCLOCAL)
- ▶ SQL Server Agent (RTCLOCAL)

> **NOTE**
>
> The SQL Server Agent services are installed, but set to disabled.

The Lync Management Shell can also be used to check the current service status. Open the Lync Management Shell and run the following command:

```
Get-CsWindowsService -ExcludeActivityLevel
```

Review the status report:

```
Status     Name
------     ----
Running    REPLICA
Running    RTCCLSAGT
Running    RTCMEDSRV
```

Lastly, the state of a Mediation Server can always be viewed through the Lync Server Control Panel. To check the status of a Mediation Server Pool, perform the following steps:

1. Open the Lync Server Control Panel.

2. Click Topology.

3. Highlight the server in question and click Properties.

4. Make sure that the green play button appears in the Service Status column. A red square indicates that a required service is not running.

Topology Status

A relatively easy method of checking the health status of a Mediation Server or pool exists through the Lync Server Control Panel. To check the status of a Mediation Server Pool, perform the following steps:

1. Open the Lync Server Control Panel.

2. Click Topology.

3. Highlight the server in question and view the Replication column. A green check mark indicates that the Mediation Server has an up-to-date copy of the topology. A red X indicates that it does not have the most recent topology change.

The Lync Management Shell can also be used to validate the topology status. Open the Lync Management Shell and run the following command:

```
Get-CsManagementStoreReplicationStatus -ReplicaFQDN MEDIATIONSERVER.companyabc.com
```

Check for the `UpToDate` parameter to report `true`:

```
UpToDate              : True
ReplicaFQDN           : MEDIATIONSERVER.companyabc.com
LastStatusReport      : 9/8/2012 3:34:09 PM
LastUpdateCreation    : 9/8/2012 3:34:06 PM
```

Services Management

Managing the Lync Server services is fortunately about the extent of administration involved with a Mediation Server after it's installed and configured. However, Enterprise Voice requires a fair bit more administration. The Mediation Server is just a supporting role of Enterprise Voice; for details on how to manage Enterprise Voice features, see Chapter 18, "Advanced Lync Voice Configuration."

Administrators can start, stop, or drain the Mediation Server services either from the Lync Server Control Panel or from the Lync Server Management Shell. Stopping the services ends all user sessions, but draining the services allows existing connections to continue but prevents new connections from being accepted. This enables an administrator to prepare a server for maintenance.

To manage the Lync Server services, perform the following steps:

1. Open the Lync Server Control Panel.

2. Click Topology.

3. Highlight the server to be modified.

4. Click Action and select one of the following: Start All Services, Stop All Services, or Prevent New Connections for All Services.

5. Alternatively, double-click the server to drill down further and manage the individual services.

Mediation Server Troubleshooting

Troubleshooting a Mediation Server might become necessary in the event that users are unable to make or receive calls to the PSTN. This section discusses the key components of a Mediation Server to check when issues arise. Common troubleshooting tools and tips are also provided that should resolve many issues.

Connectivity to Next-Hop Gateways

Given the Mediation Server's role of providing PSTN connectivity through a next-hop gateway, ensuring that connectivity to those next-hop services is healthy is important in all troubleshooting scenarios. Lync Server 2013 maintains health monitoring of these connections by default, and it does so in two ways:

- ▶ **SIP OPTIONS Requests**—The Mediation Server continuously communicates with the next-hop gateway through SIP OPTIONS requests. These exchanges are a method of validating a healthy connection between the two services. If these messages fail to be exchanged, Lync Server 2013 will alert administrators through the Lync Server Event Log. For information on checking this log, see the "Logs" section.

- ▶ **Routing Timeouts**—Lync Server 2013 identifies issues with a Mediation Server and next-hop gateway after a number of failed calls. If a Mediation Server is not able to route calls, it is marked as down. When this occurs, Lync Server routes calls through alternative routes if available; if not, users receive errors when making outbound calls and Event Logs are recorded identifying the error.

Whenever troubleshooting PSTN call issues, always ensure that a healthy connection between the Mediation Server and the Gateway is active. Look for the errors described previously, and also validate connectivity between the two servers utilizing tools such as Ping and Telnet.

Connectivity to Edge Servers

When Lync Edge Servers are deployed in the environment, the Mediation Server service requires constant communication with the Edge Server. The Mediation Server acts much like a Lync client in regard to Edge Server connectivity. When the Mediation Server is establishing any call, it must allocate Media Relay ports with the Edge Server in the event that a remote user might be involved. When the call is made from an internal user, this still happens, and although the actual call might not fail, a delay in call setup time can occur.

A common issue with call setup delays is connectivity between Mediation Servers and Edge Servers. Ensure that the Mediation Server can communicate with the Edge Server on port 3478 UDP and 443 TCP for port allocation. If that network connection is not available, a delay of several seconds might be incurred during call setup time. Additionally, if remote Lync users are not able to make calls to the PSTN, Edge Server connectivity is a key component to analyze.

DNS Records

Lync Server 2013 Mediation Server DNS requirements are fairly simple. However, because Mediation Server Pools rely on DNS load balancing, it is important to validate the DNS configuration. A Mediation Server Pool requires a DNS entry for each server in that pool. For every Mediation Server in the pool, ensure that there is an A record of the FQDN of the pool pointing to the IP of the server.

Logs

A good source of information in troubleshooting any server issue is the event logs. Lync Server 2013 creates a dedicated event log for informational activities, warnings, and errors within the standard Windows Server Event Viewer console. To view this event log, follow these steps:

1. Click Start.

2. Type `eventvwr.msc` and press Enter to open the Event Viewer Microsoft Management Console.

3. Expand the `Applications and Services Logs` folder.

4. Click the Lync Server log.

5. Examine the log for any warning or error events that might provide additional insight into any issues.

Lync Server Management Shell

The Lync Server 2013 Management Shell provides several cmdlets that can be used to test various functions of a server. A useful cmdlet for verifying the overall health of a server is `Test-CSComputer` which verifies that all services are running, that the local computer group membership is correctly populated with the necessary Lync Server Active Mediation Server groups, and that the required Windows Firewall ports have been opened. The `Test-CSComputer` cmdlet must be run from the local computer and it uses the following syntax:

```
Test-CSComputer -Report "C:\Test-CSComputer Results.xml"
```

After running the cmdlet, open the generated XML file to view a detailed analysis of each check.

Synthetic Transactions

A feature carried over from Lync Server 2010 is synthetic transactions, which are a set of PowerShell cmdlets used to simulate actions taken by servers or users in the environment. These synthetic transactions allow an administrator to conduct realistic tests against a service. In the case of a Mediation Server, the two most useful synthetic transactions are `Test-CSOutboundCall` and `Test-CSPSTNPeertoPeerCall`.

When `Test-CSOutboundCall` is run, a full outbound call is made to a phone number the administrator provides. This transaction tests the policies, and signaling and media connectivity to the PSTN. After the signaling path has been established, the transaction sends DTMF tones to validate media connectivity. Running this cmdlet requires a user account to authenticate and register to Lync Server 2013, as well as a valid destination phone number. The user credential parameter's username and password must be collected by an authentication dialog and saved to a variable, as seen in this command:

```
$Credential = Get-Credential "COMPANYABC\randy"
```

After the credentials have been collected, the cmdlet can be run with the user credential variable previously saved:

```
Test-CsPstnOutboundCall -TargetFqdn <Front End Pool FQDN>
➥-TargetPstnPhoneNumber "+15551234567" -UserSipAddress "sip:randy@companyabc.com"
➥-UserCredential $credential
```

Here's a `Test-CSPSTNOutboundCall` example:

```
TargetFQDN        : Lyncpool1.companyabc.com
Result            : Success
Latency           : 00:00:10.9506726
```

As seen in the output, the call was successful.

`Test-CSPSTNPeertoPeerCall` is very similar; however, it establishes a call between two Lync users over the PSTN. This transaction logs in two Lync users, dials through the PSTN gateway, and routes back in to Lync Server to connect to the second user. The call is established, and then terminates on its own after media connectivity has been validated. To run this cmdlet, you must provide two valid user accounts in Lync Server 2013. See the following text for an example.

The user credential parameter's username and password must be collected by an authentication dialog and saved to a variable, as seen in the following command:

```
$Credential1 = Get-Credential "COMPANYABC\randy"
$Credential2 = Get-Credential "COMPANYABC\alex"

Test-CsPstnPeerToPeerCall -TargetFqdn <FRONT END POOL FQDN>
➥-SenderSipAddress "sip:randy@companyabc.com" -SenderCredential $credential1
➥-ReceiverSipAddress "sip:alex@companyabc.com" -ReceiverCredential $credential2
```

Here's a `Test-CSPSTNPSTNPeertoPeerCall` example:

```
TargetFQDN        : Lyncpool1.companyabc.com
Result            : Success
Latency           : 00:00:10.9506726
```

As seen in the output, the call was successful.

Telnet

Telnet is a simple method of checking whether a specific TCP port is available from a client machine. From a machine that is having trouble contacting a Mediation Server, follow these steps to verify connectivity to the Mediation Server service:

> **TIP**
>
> The Telnet client is not installed by default in modern Windows operating systems. On a desktop operating system it must be installed by using the Turn Windows Features On or Off option found in Programs and Features. On a server operating system it can be installed through the Features section of Server Manager.

1. Open a command prompt.

2. Type the following command:

```
telnet <Mediation Server pool FQDN> 5061
```

If the window goes blank and only a flashing cursor is seen, it means the connection was successful and the port can be contacted without issue. If the connection fails, an error is returned. Check that the services are running on the Mediation Server and that no firewalls are blocking the traffic.

Time

A key component of any service running successfully in Lync Server 2013 is the computer time. Be sure to verify that the clocks on any Lync Server 2013 servers are correctly set and have the appropriate time zones configured. If the clocks between a server and a client are off by more than five minutes, Kerberos authentication will begin to fail, which will prevent users from authenticating successfully.

Summary

The Mediation Server in Lync Server 2013 remains a critical component for providing Enterprise Voice and Dial-In Conferencing to Lync users. Deploying Mediation Server Pools that are paired with next-hop gateways can provide organizations of any type with redundant and scalable voice connectivity.

The Mediation Server provides critical functionality that is required for interoperability with legacy PBXs, and should be deployed by any organization considering Lync Enterprise Voice.

The Mediation Server connects to many other Lync Server components including the Edge Server, the Front End Server, and Conferencing Servers, and because of this, troubleshooting Mediation Server issues often results in validating other components.

Best Practices

The following are best practices from this chapter:

- ▶ Mediation Servers are required for connectivity to the PSTN and Legacy PBXs.

- ▶ Deploy Mediation Server Pools for redundancy and scalability.

- ▶ Carefully consider collocating the Mediation Server with the Front End Server role. Often, unless Media Bypass is enabled, the Mediation Server should be a standalone server.

- ▶ When deploying Mediation Server roles, be sure to configure a DNS A record for each server in the pool for the pool FQDN.

- ▶ The Mediation Server must be able to connect to the Edge Server pool if deployed for all calls. This is required to allocate ports, and can result in call setup delays if not available.

CHAPTER 9

Director

The Microsoft Lync Server 2013 Director role has been a part of the Lync Server product ever since Live Lync Server 2005, Service Pack 1, but has typically been one of the least deployed server roles. Over the years the Director has typically been a recommended server role, but Microsoft has adjusted Lync Server 2013 so that the Director is now an optional role, and has removed it from the reference architecture with multiple pools.

This chapter focuses on the Director role and how it interacts with other components of Lync Server 2013. The benefits of a Director are explained both from an internal perspective and from an external viewpoint where it adds a degree of security and stability to the environment.

This chapter also discusses the steps required to prepare a server for the Director role and how to actually install a Director in the environment. The components of a Director role are examined, and guidelines for troubleshooting common issues with a Director are provided for reference.

Director Overview

The Director role in Microsoft Lync Server 2013 is a specialized subset of the Front End server, which simply provides authentication and redirection services. Unlike with a Front End server, it is not possible to home user accounts on a Director pool and it provides no user services to endpoints. The primary function is to authenticate endpoints and then "direct" users to the pool where their user account is actually homed.

When clients sign in to a Director, they are first authenticated and then informed of their primary and backup registrar pools. Directors are valuable in deployments where multiple pools exist because they provide a single point of authentication for the endpoints. When external access is used, a Director can also serve as the next hop server between Edge servers and the Front End pools. This extra hop between the Edge servers and Front End pools can provide an additional layer of protection against external attackers.

Dedicated Role

Just as in Lync Server 2010, the Director role is a standalone role that is defined and installed like any other server within the topology. For historical reference, during the Office Communications Server timeframe, installing the Director role was performed the same way as installing a Front End server and then was followed by a series of manual steps to deactivate most of the Front End services. These steps were well documented, but it was completely up to the administrator to follow them correctly and completely. There was also no way to prevent administrators or help desk users from homing new user accounts on a Director pool because they appeared just like any other Front End pool choice when enabling user accounts.

In Lync Server 2013 the Director is still a completely dedicated and specific role separate from a Front End server. It can be installed like any other role and requires none of the manual deactivation steps previously required. This separation not only improves the ease of deploying a Director, but increases the security and stability of the role by not installing unnecessary components and leaving deactivation to the administrator.

Benefits of a Director

The biggest challenge around planning for a Director is determining whether a business even needs to deploy the role. Historically, the Director has been an optional but recommended server to deploy. In Lync 2013 the "recommended" text has been removed and the role now appears to be optional, but that does not necessarily diminish the value of a Director. This section covers the reasons why organizations might still want to choose to deploy a Director for Lync 2013.

Internal Endpoint Sign-In Process

Before you review the benefits of a Director, it is important to first understand how an internal Lync client actually signs in. Clients default to searching DNS for service locator, or SRV, records based on the SIP address a user entered. Multiple SRV records can be returned, each with a different weight and priority so that a client can select the most preferred record. In the case of Lync 2013 the client will select the record with the lowest numeric priority and the highest numeric weight.

There is no logic in an endpoint to indicate that it is initially connecting to a Director pool and not a Front End server, meaning that the same DNS records, authentication methods, and signaling are used from the endpoint's perspective. The Director first authenticates the user and then simply provides the user's primary and backup registrar pools.

> **NOTE**
>
> The Registrar is a component of the Lync Front End service which runs on Front End pools and Director pools. This component is responsible for authenticating users and handling user sign-ins.

The client then attempts another sign-in to the primary registrar pool the Director provided, and if that pool does not respond it will attempt to register to the backup pool. The actual sign-in process looks like the following:

1. Endpoint requests DNS SRV records for automatic configuration.

2. Lowest-priority and highest-weight record returns the name of the Director pool.

3. Endpoint attempts to register to the Director pool.

4. The Director first attempts to verify the user's credentials via certificate authentication, Kerberos, or NTLM. If the credentials are invalid, the endpoint is not authenticated and the connection is closed.

5. If the credentials are verified successfully, the Director checks for the primary and backup registrar pools assigned to the user.

6. The primary and backup registrar pool information is provided to the user in the form of a 301 Redirect SIP message.

7. The Director closes the session with the endpoint.

8. The endpoint attempts to authenticate again to the primary registrar.

9. The endpoint attempts to authenticate again to the backup registrar if the primary registrar does not respond.

After a Director authenticates an endpoint and provides the registrar information, it will be removed from the communication path. An endpoint will communicate with its own Front End pool after receiving that information, as shown in Figure 9.1.

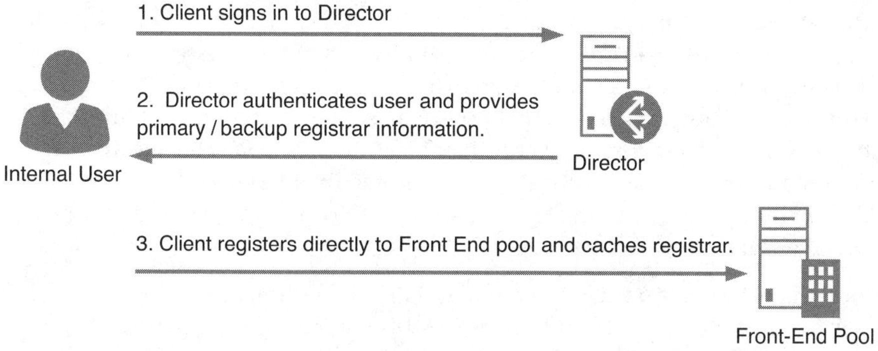

1. Client signs in to Director

2. Director authenticates user and provides primary / backup registrar information.

Internal User

Director

3. Client registers directly to Front End pool and caches registrar.

Front-End Pool

FIGURE 9.1   Director relation to internal pools.

The process shown in Figure 9.1 is true for clients as long as the DNS records for `lyncdiscover` and `lyncdiscoverinternal` are not published. These records are preferred by the Lync 2013 PC client over SRV records.

Centralized Sign-In

Based on the previously described sign-in process, administrators without a Director in a multiple Front End pool environment face a dilemma of determining which pool should handle the initial sign-in and authentication for all users. The Lync client applications use weighted DNS SRV record lookups to find a pool, and only one pool can be considered the most preferred. When a Director exists, these DNS records typically point at the Director, which then handles sending the user a SIP 301 Redirect message with the primary and backup registrar pool information. Without a Director, one of the Front End pools in the environment must be responsible for handling these tasks for all users.

Historically, the Director role played a much bigger part in the sign-in process every single day, and careful planning was required to ensure that there was enough processing capacity available to handle the bulk of sign-in and authentication traffic occurring during the morning hours in each region. The benefit of a dedicated Director from an internal perspective was that these initial authentication requests were offloaded from Front End servers.

However, since Office Communications Server 2007 R2, the client applications have maintained a file called `endpointconfiguration.cache` in the local settings folder of a user's PC. This file contains the user's primary pool and preferred server in a pool so that on subsequent sign-in attempts the client will actually attempt to first contact the server in the file before falling back to any DNS SRV record lookups and potentially leveraging a Director.

This means that although a Director can certainly offload authentication and sign-in traffic from a Front End pool for a user's first sign-in, it's of little benefit internally on later sign-in attempts. The clients are generally bypassing the Director altogether by leveraging their local cache information. Of course, if that cache is removed or fails at some point, the Director will be used again, but many organizations have begun to accept that temporary traffic increase to a Front End pool.

Optimized External Access Path

Another strong benefit of using a Director is its capability to serve as a barrier between internal pools and external traffic. To understand the benefit here, it is important to know that Edge servers do not authenticate external user requests across the Internet and merely pass this traffic to a next-hop internal server to handle authentication. This means that without a Director all external traffic is being authenticated by a Front End pool, or in other words, anonymous Internet traffic is being allowed to communicate with an internal domain member server.

Instead of allowing authentication requests from an Edge server to pass directly to a Front End pool, a Director can be placed in between this communication path and used to authenticate users before external traffic ever reaches a Front End server. This doesn't change the fact that an internal domain member is accepting unauthenticated traffic, but it does provide some protection for Front End pools because traffic will never get through the Director without being authenticated.

A Director can also help simplify the federation and remote access paths for SIP traffic within an organization. Instead of requiring firewall rules for SIP between all Front End pools, a Director pool can be specified as the outbound federation route. This means that all Front End pools send their remote traffic to the Director first, which then communicates with the Edge servers. This scenario is depicted in Figure 9.2 where the Director stays within the communication path at all times to ensure that the internal pools are protected. This topology also helps with troubleshooting efforts because the signaling path is more predictable, and reduces the number of firewall rules required.

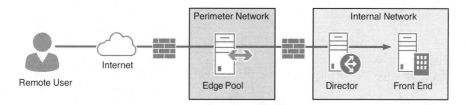

FIGURE 9.2   Director placement for Edge services.

Denial-of-Service Barrier

A compelling reason to deploy a Director is the fact that it provides some isolation for Front End pools from the Edge servers and Internet. If there was a denial-of-service attack against the Edge servers, only the Edge servers and the Director would be affected. This separation allows the Front End pools to continue operating as normal without being impacted by the attack. If a Director was not deployed as the next hop from an Edge server, an attack could potentially impact a Front End pool and cause a much larger disruption to user services.

Simple URL Entry Point

The final major benefit of a Director is to serve as a terminating point for the simple URLs in an environment, as shown in Figure 9.3. Simple URLs are web URLs defined within Topology Builder that handle redirects for meetings, dial-in access numbers, and, optionally, the Lync Server Control Panel admin page. Just as with SRV records for sign-in, these URLs each have a single namespace that can be shared globally throughout the organization. When anonymous users connect to one of these names with a valid request, they are provided a redirect to the correct web services URL for a Front End pool. As with user sign-in, any Front End pool can handle this functionality, but publishing the simple URLs through a Director could be attractive to organizations that don't allow anonymous remote users to access their Lync infrastructure.

As with the simple URLs in an environment, lyncdiscover.domain.com is a hard-coded DNS name that Lync mobile clients use to discover a connection point. Directors are a perfect target for this record because they also run the Autodiscover service within the internal and external IIS websites. Anonymous mobility requests reach the Director, the user is authenticated, and the user then receives a redirect to the web services URL for the primary registrar pool.

Director

DIRPOOL-SF-WEB.companyabc.com
MEET.companyabc.com
DIALIN.companyabc.com
LYNCDISCOVER.companyabc.com

Internal User

Front End

FEPOOL-SF-WEB.companyabc.com

FIGURE 9.3   Reverse proxy publishing of simple URLs to a Director.

Optional Role

Perhaps the biggest change for the Director in Lync Server 2013 is that Microsoft has declared it an optional role in the Lync topology. In prior years the documentation treated it as recommended, especially when deploying external services. Microsoft isn't trying to say that the Director isn't needed anymore; but many organizations have pushed for Lync Server 2013 to require less overall server count in the architecture, and Microsoft has responded to these requests by providing flexibility within the deployments based on business needs. This same initiative can be seen with the movement of the Archiving and Monitoring servers roles to services on the Front End pool, and organizations can further reduce server count by deciding not to deploy Director pools.

Why Deploy a Director?

The optional designation doesn't mean a Director should always be excluded from deployments—in fact, it still makes sense to deploy Directors in many cases. Organizations should review their own business requirements and consider the following points before making a decision on the Director pool deployment:

▶ Directors provide an additional layer of security from denial-of-service attacks at the Edge. Unauthenticated requests will never reach a Front End pool and affect internal users.

▶ Anonymous web traffic for Lync simple URLs such as meet, dialin, and admin can be terminated at the Director's web services.

▶ Directors provide centralized authentication and redirection for environments with multiple pools.

▶ Directors simplify the external federation and remote access signaling paths.

Placement

A Director pool should generally be placed in a location where the majority of the user base exists since it will be the initial point of sign-in for all users. It makes sense to place a Director in a datacenter with a Front End pool, and it's unnecessary to use a Director in branch office locations with small user counts. A backup Director pool with a slightly higher SRV record priority can be placed in a secondary datacenter. This ensures that internal clients can still locate a Director for sign-in even if the primary Director pool is unavailable due to a WAN or datacenter outage.

Another recommendation when planning for placement is to use a Director in any location where an Access Edge server role exists. This way, as unauthenticated traffic from the Internet is passed to the internal network, the Director is just a short hop away from the Edge server and can authenticate the traffic quickly. If the Director were in another physical location, that traffic from an Edge server would have to traverse a WAN connection before even being authenticated.

In remote locations where it might make sense to deploy an Edge server to support local media paths, it isn't necessary to deploy a Director. This is because the signaling traffic a Director sees is used only between the Access Edge server role and the Front End pools, unlike the media paths that flow between the endpoints shown in Figure 9.4.

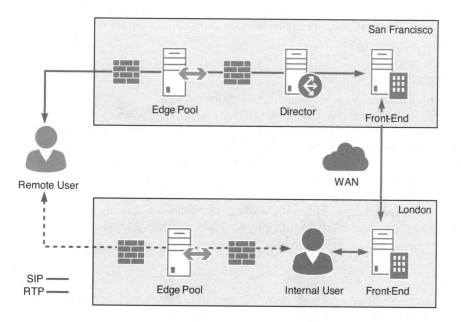

FIGURE 9.4   Signaling and media paths with a Director and Conferencing Edge server in an additional site.

Standard Edition Versus Enterprise Edition

For those migrating from Office Communications Server 2007 R2, the licensing situation around Directors and high-availability was always a confusing topic. In Office Communications Server 2007 an administrator had the option to deploy both Standard Edition and Enterprise Edition Directors, which caused some confusion around deployment methods and licensing. Back then, Directors could be deployed either as an array of multiple Standard Edition Front Ends, or as a pool of multiple Enterprise Edition servers with a dedicated back-end SQL server database. These options were simplified with Office Communications Server 2007 R2, and the only option for Director high-availability was a pool of Enterprise Edition servers. This simplified the options, but the model was problematic because a pool of Directors would create their own databases that matched the same name as the Front End pool. To alleviate this issue, an entirely separate SQL instance was required to separate the two.

In Lync Server 2010 this was again simplified and Directors no longer have a Standard Edition or Enterprise Edition designation. The deployment model now more closely resembles the array of Standard Edition servers option from Office Communications Server 2007, in which each server has a local database instance. This solves the duplicate database name issue and makes the deployment significantly easier because no SQL server setup is required. Nothing has changed from Lync Server 2010 in Lync Server 2013 as regards this model. Directors are still deployed as a single-computer pool or a multiple-computer pool for high-availability. The Director role also does not require a Standard or Enterprise Edition license in Lync Server 2013.

Back-End Database

In Lync Server 2013 each Director stores its information in a local SQL Express 2012 database instance. This change alleviates an issue found in previous releases in which a Director used the same back-end database name as the one for the Front End servers. With the Front Ends and Directors using the same database name, it became impossible to use the same SQL server instance for both functions, which meant that a new SQL server or SQL instance had to be provisioned exclusively for the Director pool. The other downside was that a Director has a relatively low usage of the SQL server, so providing an exclusive server or instance was generally considered a waste of resources. Continuing to use a local database instance in Lync Server 2013 will allow more businesses to include the Director role in their deployments.

Collocation

The Director role cannot be collocated with any other server role in Lync Server 2013. It must be installed on a server with no other roles to be fully supported by Microsoft.

Installing the Director Role

Installing the Director role is similar to deploying any other role in Lync Server 2013. Much of the installation process is actually spent completing the prerequisite work, and installing the actual server can be done fairly quickly. A Director can be introduced into the environment at any time and does not necessarily need to be deployed from the start. If Edge services are being deployed, it usually makes sense to deploy a Director at the same time.

Prerequisites

A Director requires the same prerequisite software as a Front End server because it is, after all, still a subset of the Front End role. The different hardware, operating system, and software prerequisites are discussed in this section.

Hardware Recommendations

This section discusses the minimum hardware recommendations for Lync Server 2013 servers.

The Lync Server 2013 Director processor recommendations are as listed here:

▶ Dual processor, quad-core 2.0 GHz or faster

▶ Four-way processor, dual-core 2.0 GHz or faster

> **NOTE**
>
> Lync Server 2013 is only a 64-bit application and requires a 64-bit capable processor. This is generally not an issue with any modern hardware, but be sure to verify any legacy hardware supports a 64-bit operating system before attempting to use it for a Director.

The Lync Server 2013 Director memory recommendation is as follows:

▶ 8GB RAM

The Lync Server 2013 Director disk recommendations are as shown here:

▶ 10K RPM HDD

▶ High-performance solid-state drive (SSD) with performance equal to or better than 10K RPM HDD

▶ 2x RAID 10 (striped and mirrored) 15K RPM disks for database data files

The Lync Server 2013 Director network recommendations are as listed here:

▶ Dual 1 gigabit per second (Gbps) network adapters (recommended)

▶ Single 1 gigabit per second (Gbps) network adapter (supported)

> **NOTE**
>
> When multiple network adapters are being used, it is recommended to use them only for fault tolerance. This means network adapters should be used for failover only and not be combined for greater throughput.

Operating System Requirements

The Lync Server 2013 Director supports the following operating systems:

▶ Windows Server 2008 R2, Standard Edition with Service Pack 1

▶ Windows Server 2008 R2, Enterprise Edition with Service Pack 1

▶ Windows Server 2008 R2, Datacenter Edition with Service Pack 1

▶ Windows Server 2012, Standard Edition

▶ Windows Server 2012, Datacenter Edition

The Windows Server Core, Web, and High Performance Computing editions for any operating system version are not supported for deployment.

Software Requirements

The Lync Server 2013 Director requires the following components to be installed:

▶ Microsoft .NET Framework 4.5

▶ Windows Management Framework 3.0

▶ Windows Identity Foundation

▶ Visual C++ 11 Redistributable

Server Roles and Features

In addition to the operating system and software requirements listed previously, a Director requires a number of Windows server roles, role services, and features to be installed. The IIS role services required for a Director installation are provided here:

▶ Static Content

▶ Default Document

▶ Directory Browsing

▶ HTTP Errors

▶ ASP.net

▶ .NET Extensibility

▶ ISAPI Extensions

▶ ISAPI Filters

▶ HTTP Logging

▶ Logging Tools

▶ Tracing

▶ Client Certificate Mapping Authentication

▶ Windows Authentication

▶ Request Filtering

▶ Static Content Compression

▶ Dynamic Content Compression

▶ IIS Management Console

▶ IIS Management Scripts and Tools

Installing Server Role Prerequisites

Windows PowerShell can be used to automate installation of the prerequisite roles and features instead of using the Windows Server Manager graphical interface. To use PowerShell for this purpose, use the following steps:

1. Log on to the server with an account that has administrative credentials.

2. Click Start and navigate to All Programs, Accessories, Windows PowerShell.

3. Right-click the Windows PowerShell shortcut and select Run as Administrator.

4. Click Yes when prompted by User Account Control.

5. Run the following command to make the server manager:

   ```
   Import-Module ServerManager
   ```

6. Run the following command to install the Windows features and IIS role services required:

   ```
   Add-WindowsFeature Telnet-Client,Web-Server,Web-Static-Content,
   Web-Default-Doc,Web-Http-Errors,Web-Asp-Net,Web-Net-Ext,Web-ISAPI-Ext,
   Web-ISAPI-Filter,Web-Http-Logging,Web-Log-Libraries,Web-Http-Tracing,
   Web-Windows-Auth,Web-Client-Auth,Web-Filtering,Web-Stat-Compression,
   Web-Dyn-Compression,Web-Mgmt-Console,Web-Scripting-Tools,Web-Dyn-Compression
   ```

7. Restart the server when complete.

Creating a Director Pool

After the server has been fully prepared for installation, the topology must be edited and published to reflect the new Director pool. This involves both editing the existing topology and then republishing the updated topology so that the Director role can be installed.

Edit Topology

The next step in deploying a Director is to edit the existing Lync Server topology. To edit the topology follow these steps:

1. Open the Lync Server Topology Builder.

2. When prompted to select the source topology, select Download Topology from Existing Deployment to retrieve the current topology.

3. Enter a location in which to save the temporary topology file.

4. Expand the Site node where the Director will be deployed.

5. Expand the Lync Server 2013 node.

6. Right-click on the Director pools node and select New Director Pool.

7. Leave Multiple Computer Pool selected, enter the fully qualified name of the Director pool in the Pool FQDN field, and click Next. Optionally, select Single Computer Pool if the Director pool will never have more than one server.

8. Enter the fully qualified name of the Director in the Computer FQDN field, click the Add button, and click Next.

9. Select the Monitoring check box if CDR and QoE metrics should be collected from the Director pool. Click Next.

10. Select a file store to be used by the pool. Enter a file server FQDN and file share if one does not exist, and click Next to continue.

11. If the pool will use DNS load balancing, check the box Override Internal Web Services Pool FQDN and enter an FQDN for the internal web services.

12. Confirm or modify the external base URL if necessary and click Next.

13. Select a Monitoring SQL Server store if the pool will collect CDR and QoE metrics. Click Finish to complete the wizard.

14. Review the Web Services URL and file share settings for the Director pool.

Publish Topology

After the Topology has been modified to include the Director pool, the configuration can be published. This step publishes the changes to the Central Management Store, and all existing Lync Server 2013 servers will update their local configuration stores to match.

1. Ensure that the Lync Server Topology Builder is still open and contains the Director pool recently added.

2. Click the Action menu, select Topology, and then and select Publish.

3. Click Next to begin publishing the topology.

4. Review the publishing wizard log for any errors or warnings and remediate as necessary.

NOTE

If a DFS share is used for the file store, a warning might be generated that the file share permissions cannot be read. This warning can be safely ignored as long as the DFS permissions were configured properly in advance.

---

5. When the log indicates a successful update, click Finish to complete the wizard.

Install Server

At this point the target server should be fully prepared and meet all prerequisites. Refer to the "Prerequisites" section, earlier in this chapter, for a full list of the Director requirements.

Cache Installation Files

The first step of the Lync installation process will be to cache the setup files locally on the server.

1. Insert the Lync Server 2013 media on the server to be used as a Director and launch `Setup.exe` found in the `Setup\amd64` folder.

2. Enter a location for the installation files to be cached and click Install. The default location is `C:\Program Files\Microsoft Lync Server 2013`.

3. Select I Accept the Terms in the licensing agreement and click OK.

NOTE

After you've browsed to the setup folder using Windows Explorer, the install window might appear behind the current Explorer window. It can be easy to miss this fact, so check the taskbar for the Lync install icon if some time has passed without any screen activity.

Install Local Configuration Store

To install any server role in Lync Server 2013, the target server must first have a local configuration store installed and populated with the topology information. The Lync Deployment Wizard will automatically open after the installation files have been cached on the system.

1. Click Install or Update Lync Server System.

2. Under Step 1: Install Local Configuration Store, click Run.

3. Select Retrieve Configuration Automatically from the Central Management Store, and click Next.

4. Click Finish after the local store is successfully created.

Install Lync Server Components

The following steps will allow the server to read the topology information from the local configuration store and then install the server roles matching its own FQDN.

1. Under Step 2: Setup or Remove Lync Server Components, click the Run button.

2. Click Next to begin the Director installation published in the topology.

3. Click Finish when the installation completes.

Create and Install Certificates

Like all other roles in Lync Server, the Director communicates to other servers in the organization using Mutual Transport Layer Security (MTLS). To leverage MTLS, the Director needs at least one certificate installed meeting a few requirements. A separate certificate can be used for each function, or a single certificate for MTLS and web services meeting the following requirements can be used:

▶ The subject name should contain the pool's fully qualified domain name (FQDN).

▶ The server name should be included as a subject alternative name.

▶ If the internal or external web services FQDN differs from the pool name, it should also be included as a subject alternative name.

▶ All supported SIP domains must be entered as a subject alternative name in the format sip.<SIP domain>.

▶ Any simple URLs that terminate at the Director should be included as a subject alternative name. These will typically be the `meet`, `dialin`, `lyncdiscover`, and `admin` URLs.

NOTE

The certificate wizard in Lync Server 2013 will automatically populate the subject name and any required subject alternative names based on the published topology, which greatly simplifies certificate confusion created by prior versions. If only one certificate will be used for the default, internal web services, and external web services, then the subject alternative names must be manually added when the wizard is run.

Use the following steps to request and assign the necessary certificates:

1. Under Step 3: Request, Install, or Assign Certificate, click the Run button.

2. Highlight the Default certificate and click the Request button to start the Certificate Request Wizard.

NOTE

It is possible to expand the Default certificate option and individually request the server default, web services internal, and web services external certificates. This is generally not required, and using a single certificate for all three functions is sufficient and saves on management overhead.

3. Click Next to continue.

4. Select either an online certificate request and certificate authority, or an offline certificate request and file path for the request. Click Next. The following steps here assume that an internal certificate authority is used to generate the request.

5. If user credentials other than the logged-on user are required to create the certificate request, check the box Specify Alternate Credentials for the Certification Authority. Enter a username and password and click Next. This is typically used in large environments where the Lync administrator does not have rights to request certificates.

6. If the default WebServer template will not be used, check the box Use Alternate Certificate Template for the Selected Certification Authority and enter the certificate template name. The template name, not the template display name, should be entered here. The template should already be published and available on the certificate authority issuing the certificate. In most cases the default WebServer template will be sufficient and there is no need to check this box.

7. Enter a friendly name for the certificate for identification purposes.

8. Select a key bit length of either 1024, 2048, or 4096.

9. If the certificate should be exportable, select the check box Mark Certificate Private Key as Exportable. This should be selected for Director pools with multiple members so that the same certificate can be installed on each pool member.

6

10. Enter an organization name, typically the name of the business.

11. Enter an organizational name, typically the name of a division or department, and click Next.

12. Select a country, enter a state or province, enter a city or locality, and click Next.

13. Review the automatically populated subject name and subject alternative names. Click Next.

14. Check the box for each configured SIP domain that will use the Director pool. Each selected SIP domain will add a subject alternative entry name for sip.<SIP Domain> to the certificate. Click Next.

15. Add additional subject alternative names if necessary; or if the pool configuration has been published, all required subject alternative names will be automatically added and the step can be skipped. Click Next.

16. Review the certificate request summary screen for accuracy and when satisfied click Next.

17. The Lync Management Shell commands will be displayed and the user can optionally review the certificate request log. Unless the request failed, this is not necessary. Click Next.

18. Leave the Assign This Certificate to Lync Server Certificate Usages check box selected to skip straight to the certificate assignment wizard. Click Finish to complete the request process.

NOTE

It might not seem intuitive, but to process a response to an offline certificate request, use the Import Certificate button found at the bottom of the Certificate Wizard. If a request to an online certificate authority is in a pending state, the Process Pending Certificates button will be available to complete those requests.

Certificates issued from an online certificate authority will be installed automatically. If an offline request was performed, first copy the certificate authority response to the server. Then use the Import Certificate button found at the bottom of the wizard to complete the process.

1. Click Browse and select the certificate authority response.

2. Uncheck the Certificate File Contains the Certificate's Private Key check box. Click Next.

3. Review the import certificate summary and click Next.

4. Click Finish to complete the process of associating the private key and certificate authority response.

Assign Certificates

After the necessary certificates have been created, the Director services must have certificates assigned to them. This process binds each certificate to either the Front End service or IIS websites, depending on selection. To assign a certificate use the following steps:

1. Under Step 3: Request, Install, or Assign Certificate, click the Run button.

2. Highlight the Default certificate and click the Assign button to start the Certificate Request Wizard.

3. Click Next to continue.

4. Select the certificate to be assigned and click Next. It's possible to view each certificate in more detail by highlighting and selecting the View Certificate Details button.

> **NOTE**
>
> If a certificate is not available on this screen, that usually means a private key is not associated with the certificate. Be sure to complete any pending or offline requests before this step.

5. Click Next on the Certificate Assignment Summary screen.

6. The Lync Management Shell commands are displayed and the user can optionally review the certificate request log. Unless the request failed, this is not necessary. Click Next.

7. Click Finish to complete the wizard.

If separate certificates were used for the WebServicesInternal and WebServicesExternal certificates, the preceding steps must be repeated for each use. Be sure to select the correct certificate for each function if unique certificates were generated.

> **NOTE**
>
> The Certificate Wizard also displays an OAuthTokenIssuer certificate option. If this has already been generated on another server in the environment, it should already be installed and assigned automatically. The location field will show Global as opposed to Local as with other certificates. Do not request another OAuthTokenIssuer certificate unless it needs to be replaced.

Start Services

After the necessary certificates have been requested and assigned, the Lync Server 2013 Director services can be started.

1. Under Step 4: Start Services, click the Run button.

2. Click Next to begin starting all the Lync Server services.

3. Click Finish to complete the wizard.

The wizard does not actually wait for the services to complete startup. Use the Services MMC to view the actual service state.

At this point the Director installation is complete and it should be functional. The Director pool will not be used automatically by internal clients, so the DNS SRV records for automatic client sign-in must be updated to point users to the new Director pool.

Configuring the Director

After a Director pool has been installed, there generally is not much configuration left to do. This section discusses some of the configuration options available to a Director and addresses items administrators should be aware of when configuring a Director.

Certificate Requirements

The Director role in Lync Server 2013 is much like any other role in that it uses certificates both for communication to other servers and for client services. There are three types of certificates a Lync Server 2013 Director requires, each with slightly different naming requirements. All three purposes and required names are usually combined on a single certificate, but can be broken out separately if required. These are the three types:

▶ **Default**—The default certificate is used for MTLS communications between servers, and for securing SIP signaling in client communications. The certificate should contain the pool name in the subject field, each Director's name as a subject alternative name, and any internally supported SIP domains as a subject alternative name in the sip.<SIP Domain> format.

▶ **WebServicesInternal**—The WebServicesInternal certificate is used to secure communication for internal clients to the web services. This certificate should contain the internal web services FQDN defined in the topology for the pool and any simple URLs such as `dialin`, `meet`, `lyncdiscover`, and `admin`. This certificate is bound to the internal web services website in IIS.

▶ **WebServicesExternal**—The WebServicesInternal certificate is used to secure communication for internal clients to the web services. This certificate should contain the external web services FQDN defined in the topology for the pool and any simple URLs such as `dialin`, `meet`, `lyncdiscover`, and `admin`. This certificate is bound to the external web services website in IIS.

SRV Records

The main point of a Director pool from an internal perspective is that it serves as the central point of sign-in and authentication in a deployment. After a Director is installed, clients will not automatically use it, so the SRV records for each SIP domain must be changed to point to the Director pool instead of a Front End pool. After the SRV records have been updated, any new client sign-ins will locate the Director, attempt sign-in, and ultimately be redirected to their primary registrar.

An issue with the architecture of Office Communications Server 2007 was that only a single DNS SRV record was used by clients. If a Director was in use, the SRV record would typically point to it to ensure that users signed in to a Director first and not directly to a Front End pool. On one hand, this provided the administrator with control over where users would initially authenticate to, but on the flip side this represented a single point of failure. If there was an issue with the Director or pool of Directors, no clients would ever be able to sign in. This dilemma was mitigated since Office Communications Server 2007 R2 supported the use of multiple weighted SRV records, although the feature wasn't actually documented until Lync Server 2010.

As in Lync Server 2010, Lync Server 2013 endpoints will now recognize multiple SRV records for automatic sign-in with different priorities, and if one pool or host is unavailable, they will move on and try the next host. This means organizations can deploy a Director with the lowest-priority SRV record, but also have the automatic sign-in backup be a Front End pool with a higher priority in case the Director pool is unavailable. There is also the potential option to use two Director pools with differing priorities, but using two Director pools in a single location would be necessary for only the most stringent of availability requirements. A more typical use-case would be to have two separate Director pools separated by major geographical boundaries.

> **NOTE**
>
> When resolving SRV records in DNS, clients will prefer the record with the lowest numerical priority and highest numerical weight. The terminology is a bit deceiving so be sure to always place a Director pool as the lowest priority to ensure that it is used before any other pool with a higher priority.

Web Services FQDN Overrides

When a Director pool is created in the Topology Builder, the web services FQDNs are automatically provisioned with an option to override the internal and external FQDNs. When a single Director is deployed, overriding the FQDN is unnecessary, but when multiple Directors are deployed, it might be necessary to change the URLs depending on load-balancing methods.

If a hardware load balancer is being used for the SIP, HTTP, and HTTPS traffic, it is perfectly acceptable to use the pool FQDN suggested by the Topology Builder. This works just fine because all the traffic is destined for the same virtual IP hosted by the load balancer.

As in Lync Server 2010, Lync Server 2013 has the option to use DNS load balancing for SIP traffic, but a hardware load balancer is still necessary for balancing HTTP and HTTPS traffic. This configuration means there is a split in the services, and one FQDN must resolve to the pool for SIP traffic and another FQDN is necessary for the web services traffic. These two FQDNs will resolve to different locations; the pool name will always resolve to Director pool member servers, and the web services FQDN will resolve to a load balancer virtual IP, as shown in Figure 9.5.

FIGURE 9.5   Using a combination of DNS and hardware load balancing for Director traffic.

The web services can also be configured differently for internal and external traffic depending on existing infrastructure. For example, an organization might use a combination of DNS load balancing and a hardware load balancer for all internal pools, so overriding the internal FQDN is required internally. The web services names will resolve to a load balancer VIP internally, and resolve to another load balancer VIP remotely through the reverse proxy.

Web Services Ports

When configuring the internal and external web services for a Director, options exist to define both the listening ports and the published ports. The differences between the two are outlined here:

▶ **Listening Ports**—Ports the IIS services will bind to on the Lync Server 2013 server.

▶ **Published Ports**—Ports used by clients to access the services. These can then be redirected by a load balancer, reverse proxy, or firewall to the listening port on a server.

In a default installation the internal web services are listening and published on ports 80 and 443, but because the external web services use a separate IIS site, they need to be running on an alternate port so as to not conflict with the internal web services. In a default scenario this means that the external web services will run on port 8080 for HTTP and 4443 for HTTPS.

Reverse Proxy

To support external access to the Director web services, it is recommended to use a reverse proxy as shown in Figure 9.6. Although this is technically possible, it is not supported by Microsoft to allow Internet traffic directly to the external web services ports. A reverse proxy helps to increase security by inspecting the HTTP and HTTPS traffic and filtering any malicious requests. Refer to Chapter 6, "Microsoft Lync Server 2013 Edge Server," for configuration of a reverse proxy such as Microsoft Forefront Threat Management Gateway.

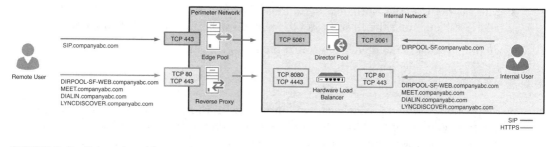

FIGURE 9.6   External and internal web services names.

> **WARNING**
>
> Performing a port translation at the firewall from TCP 4443 to TCP 443 is not a supported configuration. A reverse proxy offers additional inspection abilities and terminates the SSL stream from a remote user and initiates a new SSL connection to the Director.

High-Availability

Redundancy for the Director role is provided in a similar fashion as with Front End servers and requires just adding more Directors to a pool. Also as with a Front End pool, up to 12 servers can be defined in a Director pool. Load balancing is achieved via the same methods as Front End servers by providing multiple IP addresses that resolve to the pool name of the Directors. If one IP address is unavailable, the endpoint will attempt to log in to another IP address provided for the pool in DNS.

> **TIP**
>
> Plan for high-availability in the environment from the start even if multiple Directors will not be deployed initially. Completing the planning and configuration for high-availability simplifies the deployment later and requires nearly no changes to the existing infrastructure. Adding high-availability to the environment later simply becomes a matter of adding a new server to the topology, creating the DNS records, and potentially adding a pool member to a load balancer.

Adding Servers to an Existing Director Pool

Adding an additional Director to a pool is much like creating the initial pool. The topology must first be updated and published to reflect the change. Follow the steps described previously to import the existing topology in Topology Builder, and then use the following steps to add an additional pool member:

1. Expand the Directors node.

2. Right-click the Director pool name and select New Server.

3. Enter the fully qualified domain name of the new Director.

9

4. Select either Use All Configured IP Addresses or Limit Service Usage to Selected IP addresses, and enter the IP addresses to be used by the Lync Server 2013 services.

5. Optionally, select the IPv6 check box if IPv6 is in use on the network.

6. Click OK when complete.

Now simply publish the topology again and proceed with the Director installation using the same steps defined in the "Install Server" section earlier in this chapter. After installation, be sure to add the additional IP address to the pool in DNS so that clients can locate the new Director.

> **TIP**
>
> Unlike in Lync Server 2010, adding a new server to the pool requires a restart of each previously installed pool member.

Collecting Monitoring Data

When defining a Director pool within Topology Builder, an administrator is asked whether the pool should be associated with a Monitoring server for QoE and CDR statistics. This might seem puzzling at first since that type of data is traditionally considered related to the media streams and used to track down call quality issues. However, Directors can still report some data to the Monitoring store, so it is worth associating the Director pool if a Monitoring server already exists. Statistics such as user logons and client versions will be logged by the Director as it authenticates users and passes traffic. This type of data can be useful for trending analysis of sign-on volume and traffic spikes related to specific times of day for global organizations.

Administration of the Director Role

Administration of the Director role in Lync Server 2013 can be performed through a combination of the Lync Server Control Panel and the Lync Server Management Shell. This section discusses management of Director services and possible uses for the web services included in a Director installation.

Services

Installing a Director in Lync Server 2013 creates only a minimal number of Windows services. The following services will be visible within the Services MMC after the Director installation:

▶ Lync Server Centralized Logging Service

▶ Lync Server Front End

▶ Lync Server Replica Replicator Agent

- ▶ SQL Server (LYNCLOCAL)

- ▶ SQL Server (RTCLOCAL)

- ▶ SQL Server Agent (LYNCLOCAL)

- ▶ SQL Server Agent (RTCLOCAL)

TIP

The SQL Server Agent services are installed, but set to disabled.

Additionally, the IIS World Wide Web Publishing Service will also be installed and running as part of the prerequisite installations.

The Lync Management Shell can also be used to check the current service status. Open the Lync Management Shell and run the following command:

```
Get-CsWindowsService
```

Review the status report:

```
Status     Name
------     ----
Running    W3SVC
Running    REPLICA
Running    RTCCLSAGT
Running    RTCSRV
```

Lastly, the state of a Director can always be viewed through the Lync Server Control Panel. To check the status of a Director pool, perform the following steps:

1. Open the Lync Server Control Panel.

2. Click Topology.

3. Highlight the server in question and click Properties.

4. Validate that the Service status column reports the green play button. A red square as shown in Figure 9.7 indicates that a required service is not running.

Ports

It can be fairly interesting to view what kind of services and ports are actively listening for connections on a server role. Table 9.1 shows which ports are specific to Lync and active after installation of a Director.

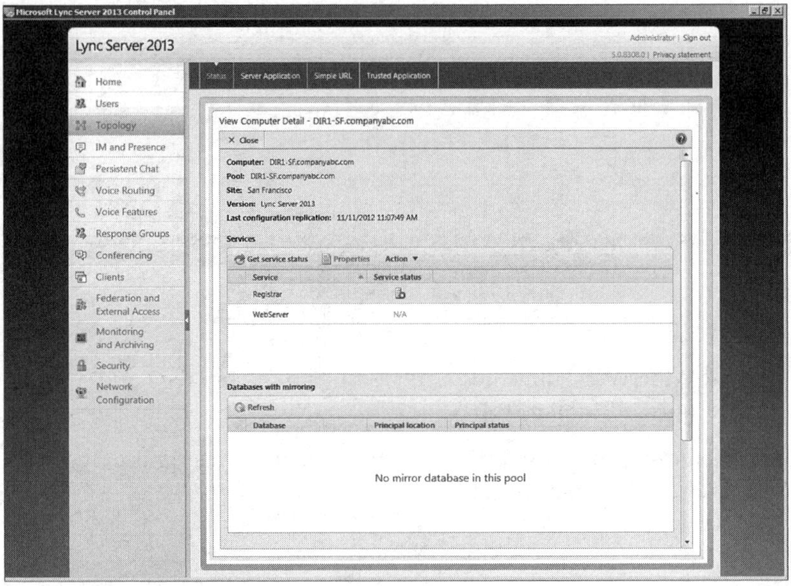

FIGURE 9.7   A Director with the Registrar service stopped.

TABLE 9.1   Director Ports

Port	Process	Function
TCP 80	w3wp.exe	Internal Web Services
TCP 135	RpcSS.exe	DCOM and RPC
TCP 443	w3wp.exe	Internal Web Services
TCP 444	w3wp.exe	Inter-Server Communication
TCP 445	System	CMS Replication
TCP 4443	w3wp.exe	External Web Services
TCP 5061	RTCSrv.exe	Front End Service
TCP 5077	LysSvc.exe	Storage Service
TCP 5090	Fabric.exe	Windows Fabric Federation
TCP 5091	Fabric.exe	Windows Fabric Lease Agent
TCP 5092	Fabric.exe	Windows Fabric Client Connections
TCP 5093	Fabric.exe	Windows Fabric Inter-Process Communication
TCP 5094	Fabric.exe	Windows Fabric Replication
TCP 50001	ClsAgent.exe	Centralized Logging
TCP 50002	ClsAgent.exe	Centralized Logging
TCP 50003	ClsAgent.exe	Centralized Logging
TCP 8080	w3wp.exe	External Web Services
UDP 1434	Sqlbrowser.exe	SQL Browser

> **TIP**
>
> If the ports for `ClsAgent.exe` do not appear to be listening, try restarting the Lync Centralized Logging Service on the affected server.

Firewall Rules

Installation of a Director role creates the necessary Windows firewall rules automatically, which are a combination of port-based and process-based rules. Table 9.2 describes each of the rules and port exceptions created during installation.

TABLE 9.2   Director Windows Firewall Rules

Name	Port	Process	Function
CS LYSS	All	`Lyssvc.exe`	Storage Service
CS Replica	All	`ReplicaReplicator Agent.exe`	CMS Replication
CS RTCCLSAGT	All	`ClsAgent.exe`	Centralized Logging
CS RTCHOST	All	`rtchost.exe`	Front End Application Host
CS RTVSRV	All	`RTCsrv.exe`	Front End Service
CS TCP13457	TCP 13457	All	Kerberos password configuration for web services
CS TCP135	TCP 135	All	DCOM and RPC
CS TCP443	TCP 443	All	Internal Web Services
CS TCP444	TCP 444	All	Inter-Server Communication
CS TCP4443	TCP 4443	All	External Web Services
CS TCP445	TCP 445	All	CMS Replication
CS TCP50001	TCP 50001	All	Centralized Logging
CS TCP50002	TCP 50002	All	Centralized Logging
CS TCP50003	TCP 50003	All	Centralized Logging
CS TCP5086	TCP 5086	All	Mobility Service
CS TCP5088	TCP 5088	All	UC Web API Service
CS TCP5090	TCP 5090	All	Windows Fabric Federation
CS TCP5091	TCP 5091	All	Windows Fabric Lease Agent
CS TCP5092	TCP 5092	All	Windows Fabric Client Connections
CS TCP5093	TCP 5093	All	Windows Fabric Inter-Process Communication
CS TCP5094	TCP 5094	All	Windows Fabric Replication
CS TCP80	TCP 80	All	Internal Web Services

9

Name	Port	Process	Function
CS TCP8060	TCP 8060	All	Reach Internal PSOM
CS TCP8061	TCP 8061	All	Reach External PSOM
CS TCP8080	TCP 8080	All	External Web Services

Topology Status

A relatively easy method of checking the health status of a Director server or pool exists through the Lync Server Control Panel. To check the status of a Director pool, perform the following steps:

1. Open the Lync Server Control Panel.

2. Click Topology.

3. Highlight the server in question and view the Replication column. A green check mark indicates that the Director has an up-to-date copy of the topology. A red X like the one shown in Figure 9.8 indicates that it does not have the most recent topology change.

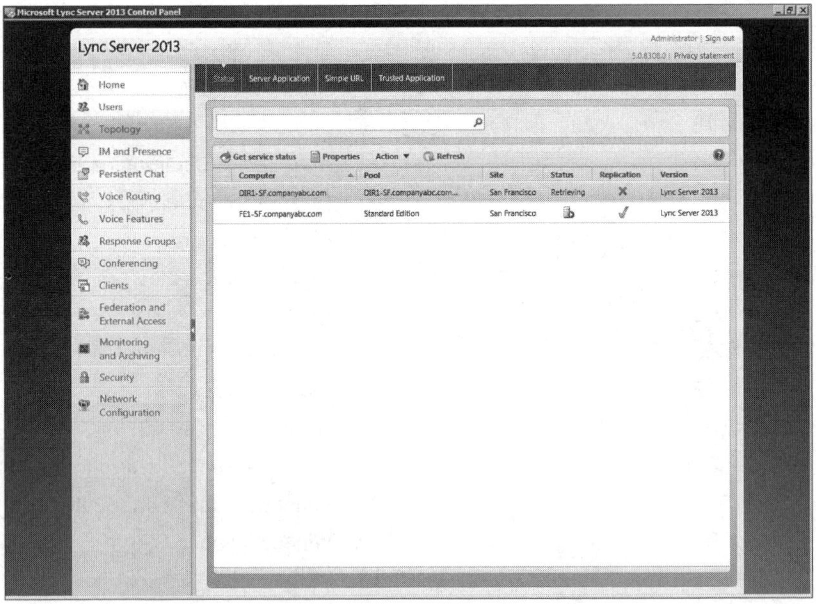

FIGURE 9.8   Lync Server Control Panel topology status example.

The Lync Management Shell can also be used to validate the topology status. Open the Lync Management Shell and run the following command:

```
Get-CsManagementStoreReplicationStatus –ReplicaFQDN DIR1-SF.companyabc.com
```

Check for the `UpToDate` parameter to report `true`:

```
UpToDate              : True
ReplicaFQDN           : DIR1-SF.companyabc.com
LastStatusReport      : 9/8/2012 3:34:09 PM
LastUpdateCreation    : 9/8/2012 3:34:06 PM
```

Services Management

Managing the Lync Server services is fortunately about the extent of administration involved with a Director after it has been installed and configured. Administrators can start, stop, or drain the Director servers from either the Lync Server Control Panel or the Lync Server Management Shell. Stopping the services will end all user sessions, but draining the services will allow existing connections to continue but stop accepting new connections. This allows an administrator to prepare a server for maintenance.

To manage the Lync Server services, perform the following steps:

1. Open the Lync Server Control Panel.

2. Click Topology.

3. Highlight the server to be modified.

4. Click Action and select one of the following: Start All Services, Stop All Services, or Prevent New Connections for All Services.

5. Alternatively, double-click the server to drill down further and manage the individual services.

Load Balancer Drain

Draining a hardware load balancer's connections to a pool server is a task that should be done in conjunction with the Prevent New Connections for All Services option in the Lync Server Control Panel. The Lync Server services have no method of managing a hardware load balancer, so if one is being used for the web services traffic, it must be started, stopped, and drained independently. Failure to perform this step will result in the server receiving connections to the IIS web service, but can potentially generate errors for the client.

Client Version Filter

One potential use case for a Director is to control the client versions connecting to the Lync Server infrastructure. Since the Director is an initial sign-in point for any client, it makes sense to perform a filter check at the sign-in point. To manage which types of clients can connect to a Director, use the following steps:

1. Open the Lync Server Control Panel.

2. Click Clients.

3. Ensure that Client Version Policy is highlighted, click New, and select Pool Policy.

> **NOTE**
>
> If a policy is edited at the Service level as in this previous example, it will apply only to the selected service and pool. The example only enforces the client version filter at the Director, meaning that an endpoint could sign in to a Front End pool directly without a client check. Be sure to edit the global policy if the client filtering should be performed on all pools.

4. Highlight the Director pool name and click OK.

5. Highlight a client application such as OC and click Modify.

6. Note the Action at the end of the screen. This can be modified to block or allow, with the option to present a URL to the user, or even upgrade the application at sign-in. Click OK to save any changes.

7. Add, modify, or remove any specific client applications and versions the Director pool should check as shown in Figure 9.9, and click Commit.

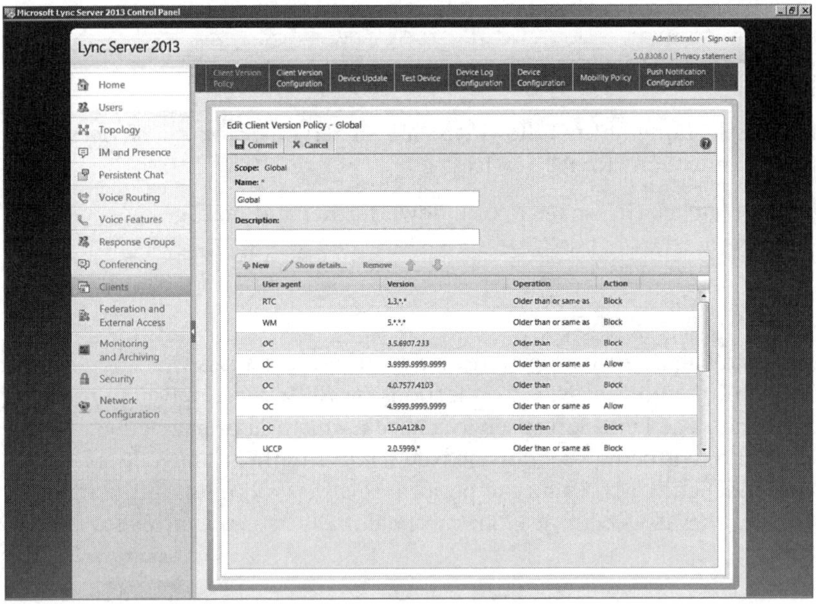

FIGURE 9.9   The client version filter in Lync Server 2013.

8. Click the Client Version Configuration menu option.

9. Highlight the Global Policy, click Edit, and then click Modify.

10. The default action here applies to any client application not listed within the Client Version Policy. By default, any client application not listed in the Client Version Policy will be allowed to sign in.

Director Troubleshooting

Troubleshooting a Director might become necessary in the event that users are unable to sign in or servers become unable to communicate with a Director pool. This section discusses the key components of a Director to check when issues arise. Common troubleshooting tools and tips are also provided, which should resolve many issues.

Redirects

The main advantage to a Director for internal users is to provide the user's primary and backup registrar information. This way, a client knows exactly which server to contact next if it is unable to contact the primary server. This information can be viewed within the SipStack traces of a sign-in. After the client authenticates, the Director responds with a 301 Redirect message, and informs the client of the primary and backup registrar. This first sample sign-in shows a user attempting a registration to the Director:

```
Start-Line: SIP/2.0 301 Redirect request to Home Server
From: <sip:tom@companyabc.com>;tag=45a7e6cf7b;epid=9671160f70
To: <sip:tom@companyabc.com>;tag=CED5D09DABBD634B55450D19A37449C4
CSeq: 2 REGISTER
Call-ID: e126d3d70dc44b81a5c41a610abd273f
Proxy-Authentication-Info: Kerberos qop="auth", opaque="7D22174B", srand="4F219DA8",
➥snum="1", rspauth="040401ffffffffff0000000000000000f3ad4a4a3e15044bcae0f914",
➥targetname="sip/DIR1-SF.companyabc.com", realm="SIP Communications Service",
➥version=4
Via: SIP/2.0/TLS 192.168.1.100:50350;ms-received-port=50350;ms-received-cid=400
Contact: <sip:SBS1-NY.companyabc.com:5061;transport=TLS>;q=0.7
Contact: <sip:FEPOOL-SF.companyabc.com:5061;transport=TLS>;q=0.3
```

Notice how the Contact field within the SIP message is used to relay the primary and backup registrar. The q= values indicate the preferred weight of the server, so in this case SBS1-NY.companyabc.com is considered the primary registrar and FEPOOL-SF.companyabc.com is the backup.

> **NOTE**
>
> It's possible to have SRV records that point directly to a Front End server, but keep in mind that backup registrar information is not passed to clients if they sign in directly to their own primary registrar. This doesn't prevent a client from finding another server through the use of weighted SRV records, but it might take longer to fail over when the primary registrar is offline.

Certificates

Incorrectly issued certificates are a potential problem with Director configuration. Be sure to follow the guidelines outlined here to rule out any certificate issues:

▶ **Subject Name**—Ensure that the subject name matches the fully qualified name of the pool.

▶ **Subject Alternative Names**—A Director's SAN field must contain the server name, and any supported SIP domains in the sip.<SIP Domain> format. Additionally, it must include the simple URLs for `dialin`, `meet`, `lyncdiscover`, and `admin`.

▶ **Key Bit Length**—The certificate bit length must be 1024, 2048, or 4096 to be supported by Lync Server 2013.

▶ **Template**—The template used to issue the certificate should be based on the web server template. If the Lync Server 2013 certificate wizard is used, the correct template will automatically be applied.

▶ **Private Key**—The server certificate must have the private key associated to be used by Lync Server 2013. In situations where certificates are exported or copied between servers, be sure to export the private key with the certificate.

▶ **Certificate Chain**—The Director must be able to verify each certificate up to a Trusted Root Certification Authority. Additionally, because the server is presenting the certificate to clients, it must contain each intermediate certificate in the certificate chain.

▶ **Certificate Store**—All certificates used by the Director must be in the Personal section of the local computer certificate store. A common mistake is to place certificates in the Personal section of the user account certificate store.

▶ **Certificate Trust**—Be sure that the clients and servers communicating with the Director all contain a copy of the top-level certificate authority of the chain in their Trusted Root Certification Authority local computer store. When the certification authority is integrated with Active Directory, this is generally not an issue, but when an offline or nonintegrated certificate authority is used, it might be necessary to install root certificates on clients and servers.

DNS Records

Successful sign-in to a Director pool is heavily dependent on DNS being correctly configured. The NSLookup tool can be used to verify that the necessary DNS records are in place as described in Chapter 10, "Persistent Chat." It is important to check that all necessary DNS records exist and resolve to the correct locations.

A sample `nslookup` sequence within a command prompt to check the host record of the pool is presented here:

```
nslookup
set type=a
dirpool-sf.companyabc.com
```

A successful query will return a name and IP address. Verify that any IP returned matches the IP addresses assigned to the Directors or load balancer and that no extra, or incorrect, IP addresses are returned.

To verify the SRV record required for automatic client sign-in on internal networks the syntax is slightly different. Another sample nslookup sequence is presented here:

```
nslookup
set type=srv
_sipinternaltls._tcp.companyabc.com
```

A successful query will return a priority, weight, port, and server hostname. Verify that the server name matches the Director pool and the correct port is returned.

Logs

A good source of information in troubleshooting any server issue is the event log. Lync Server 2013 creates a dedicated event log for informational activities, warnings, and errors within the standard Windows Server Event Viewer console. To view this event log, use the following steps:

1. Click Start.

2. Type `eventvwr.msc` and press Enter to open the Event Viewer Microsoft Management Console.

3. Expand the Applications and Services Logs folder.

4. Click the Lync Server log.

5. Examine the log like shown in Figure 9.10 for any warning or error events that might provide additional insight into any issues.

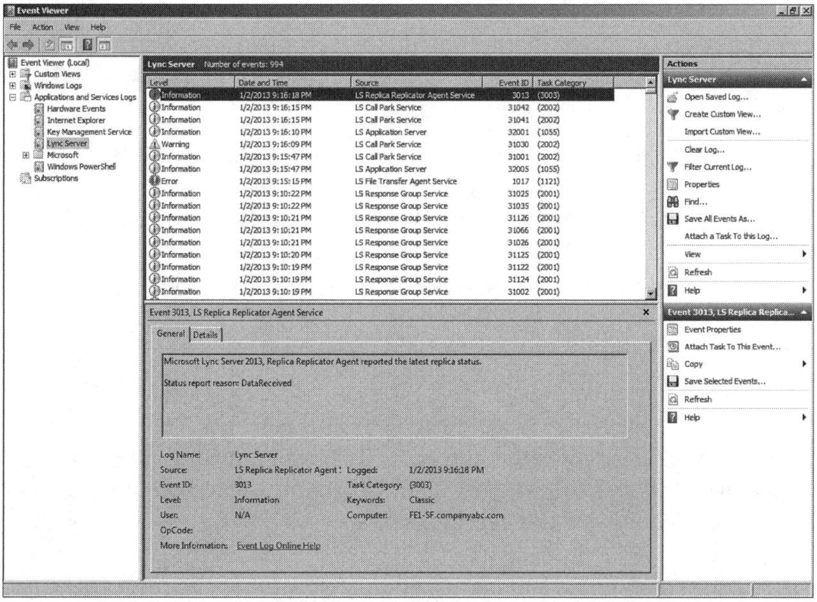

FIGURE 9.10   The Lync Server 2013 application log.

Lync Server Management Shell

The Lync Server 2013 Management Shell provides a number of cmdlets that can be used to test various functions of a server. A useful cmdlet for verifying the overall health of a server is `Test-CSComputer server`, which verifies that all services are running, that the local computer group membership is correctly populated with the necessary Lync Server Active Directory groups, and that the required Windows Firewall ports have been opened. The `Test-CSComputer` cmdlet must be run from the local computer and uses the following syntax:

```
Test-CSComputer -Report "C:\Test-CSComputer Results.xml"
```

After running the cmdlet, open the generated XML file to view a detailed analysis of each check.

Synthetic Transactions

A feature carried over from Lync Server 2010 are synthetic transactions that are a set of PowerShell cmdlets used to simulate actions taken by servers or users in the environment. These synthetic transactions allow an administrator to conduct realistic tests against a service. In the case of a Director, the most useful synthetic transaction is the Test-CSRegistration cmdlet, which simulates a user signing in to the specified server.

Running the Test-CSRegistration cmdlet requires providing a target server, user credential, and SIP address. A registrar port can optionally be included. The user credential parameter's username and password must be collected by an authentication dialog and saved to a variable, as seen in this command:

```
$Credential = Get-Credential "COMPANYABC\tom"
```

After the credentials have been collected, the cmdlet can be run with the user credential variable previously saved.

```
Test-CSRegistration -TargetFQDN DIR1-SF.companyabc.com -UserCredential $Credential -
➥UserSipAddress sip:tom@companyabc.com -RegistrarPort 5061 -Verbose
TargetFQDN     : DIR1-SF.companyabc.com
Result         : Success
Latency        : 00:00:10.9506726
```

As seen in the output, the registration test was successful.

Telnet

Telnet is a simple method of checking whether a specific TCP port is available from a client machine. From a machine that is having trouble contacting a Director, use the following steps to verify connectivity to the Registrar service:

> **TIP**
>
> The Telnet client is not installed by default in modern Windows operating systems. On a desktop operating system it must be installed by using the Turn Windows Features On or Off option found in Programs and Features. On a server operating system it can be installed through the Features section of Server Manager.

1. Open a command prompt.

2. Type the following command:

```
telnet <Director pool FQDN> 5061
```

If the window goes blank and only a flashing cursor is seen, the connection was successful and the port can be contacted without issue. If the connection fails, an error will be returned. Check that the services are running on the Director and that no firewalls are blocking the traffic.

Time

A key component of any service running successfully in Lync Server 2013 is the computer time. Be sure to verify that the clocks on any Lync Server 2013 servers are correctly set and have the appropriate time zones configured. If the clocks between a server and a client are off by more than five minutes, Kerberos authentication will begin to fail, which will prevent users from authenticating successfully.

Summary

The Director in Lync Server 2013 hasn't changed much from Lync Server 2010 other than being slightly deemphasized by Microsoft. There are still some clear advantages to deploying a Director, but there is no absolute recommendation for every deployment. Each organization will need to make that decision based on its business requirements.

Organizations are most likely to deploy a Director in their Lync Server 2013 environment when they fully understand the benefits of the role. For organizations with multiple internal pools, a Director can improve the environment by acting as a single point of initial authentication and offload that responsibility from the Front End pools. Other businesses might be more inclined to deploy a Director because of the security benefits from an external perspective where it acts as a barrier between the Front End pools and Edge servers.

Either way, deployments including a Director had already been declining in Lync Server 2010, and it's likely that even fewer new deployments will still include the role.

Best Practices

The following are best practices from this chapter:

▶ Use a Director as the next hop in any location with an Edge server. This provides a degree of separation from the Front End pools and protects the internal infrastructure from any kind of attack. Users are also authenticated at the Director when logging in remotely, so a Front End server does not have to handle authentication requests.

▶ Order SRV records such that a Director pool has the lowest priority and highest weight.

▶ Use Directors as an entry point for the simple URLs.

▶ Be sure to publish the Director external web service URLs through a reverse proxy for remote users.

▶ Plan for adding high-availability in the environment. Completing the planning work up front makes adding high-availability at a later time much simpler.

▶ Use multiple Directors within a pool to provide high-availability.

▶ Spend time carefully planning certificate names to match pool and web service URL requirements.

CHAPTER 10

Persistent Chat

For many organizations, the primary focus of a new Lync deployment is the adoption of IM and presence. This is understandable because the brief and simple nature of IM, along with the dynamic nature of presence information, makes for an efficient and flexible means of communication. However, organizations are also increasingly finding that ongoing, persistent communication provides valuable benefits as well, particularly for teams of users who collaborate on projects and share knowledge on specific topics. Lync Server 2013 provides for this form of communication as well, in the form of the Persistent Chat server role.

Persistent Chat Overview

Persistent Chat is a Lync server role that enables administrators and/or users to create chat rooms containing persistent conversations based on specific topics and categories. The persistent nature of the messages enables Lync users to view ongoing conversations at their leisure, and also search for information within the chat rooms. The benefits of Persistent Chat become evident when there is a need to share information with multiple people on a specific topic, and that data needs to be available at a later time and be easily searchable. Although this can be accomplished to some degree using other forms of communication, none of these other forms is as effective as Persistent Chat for these specific requirements. Some of the primary uses for Persistent Chat are project communications, group discussions, meetings, and knowledge bases.

NOTE

Persistent Chat was available as a third-party trusted application with previous versions of Lync, and was known as Group Chat. With Lync Server 2013, Persistent Chat is now being included as part of the Lync topology along with other Lync server roles for the first time. For this reason, along with other important architectural changes, Persistent Chat will likely find more widespread adoption than ever before with Lync Server 2013.

Like several other Lync server roles, Persistent Chat consists of a front-end component as well as a back-end SQL database component. As further detailed in later text, these components can in some cases be collocated with other Lync 2013 server roles depending on the Lync topology and the requirements for Persistent Chat.

Persistent Chat Deployment

Since Persistent Chat is now included as part of the Lync topology for the first time, the deployment process is very streamlined compared to that of previous versions. This section provides the details on installation of the Persistent Chat server role into an existing Lync 2013 environment.

Topology Options and Scaling

Several topology options are available with Persistent Chat, and these are dependent on the overall Lync deployment. Similar to the Lync Front End Services, an instance of Persistent Chat is referred to as a pool, even if just a single server is used. As with other Lync server roles, both front-end and back-end components are included in a Persistent Chat pool. The front-end components include the Persistent Chat service and the Compliance service. Back-end databases for Persistent Chat include the Persistent Chat Store and the Persistent Chat Compliance Store.

With a Standard Edition deployment, the Persistent Chat Server role can be collocated with the Front End Server. The single-server deployment can support up to 20,000 users. However, since all Lync services are hosted using a single system with this topology, Persistent Chat performance will be entirely dependent on the resource usage requirements for all Lync services. With an Enterprise Edition deployment, Persistent Chat cannot be collocated with the Lync Front End Services, and therefore dedicated systems are required. However, the Persistent Chat databases can be collocated on the same SQL Server, or even the same SQL instance, as the Lync Back End databases. Hosting the Persistent Chat Stores on a dedicated SQL Server is of course also an option, and is recommended particularly for larger Lync implementations to ensure the best performance.

NOTE

The requirement to install Persistent Chat on dedicated systems with an Enterprise Edition deployment is better understood when considering the differences in how resiliency is handled between a Persistent Chat pool and a Front End pool. When Enterprise Edition Front End pools are configured for Front End Pool Pairing, the Lync Server Backup Service replicates the databases between the pools for high-availability. In contrast, to achieve high-availability with Persistent Chat a single pool is stretched across two locations, and SQL log shipping is used to replicate database information between SQL systems at the two locations.

Persistent Chat also includes support for multiple-server topologies, with several high-availability and disaster recovery options. Up to eight Persistent Chat Servers can be installed into a single pool, and these servers can be installed across multiple locations for site resiliency. Up to four Persistent Chat Servers in a pool can be active at any time, and each active server can support up to 20,000 concurrent connected endpoints, for a total of 80,000 users. The load is automatically distributed evenly across the active servers, and in the event of a server failure, users are automatically transferred to a remaining active server. When multiple Persistent Chat Servers are used, the file stores and databases are shared among the servers, and the servers freely communicate with each other as needed to form a cohesive Persistent Chat system. The end result is that all chat history is available to any of the servers in the pool, and users connected to different Persistent Chat Servers can freely chat with each other.

> **TIP**
>
> It is not possible to add additional servers to a Persistent Chat pool if the first Persistent Chat Server is collocated with a Standard Edition Front End Server. If there is any question as to whether multiple servers will eventually be needed for Persistent Chat, it is recommended to install the first server as a standalone instance to allow the pool to grow accordingly.

Intra-site high-availability can be achieved with the installation of multiple SQL Servers in a datacenter and using SQL mirroring to replicate the data between them. For cross-site disaster recovery, at least one set of Persistent Chat Front End Servers and dedicated Back End database servers must be installed at each location. SQL log shipping is then used to replicate Persistent Chat database information between the two locations. For more detailed information regarding high-availability and disaster recovery options with Persistent Chat, see Chapter 15, "High-Availability and Disaster Recovery."

Prerequisites

The infrastructure requirements for a Persistent Chat pool are very similar to the requirements for a Front End pool. For example, the Active Directory requirements are identical with one small exception: At least one AD global catalog server must exist in the forest root domain for Persistent Chat to be installed in that forest. Also similar to the Front End pool, a file store must be defined for use with Persistent Chat, which serves as a repository for files that are uploaded using the chat rooms. With a single-server deployment, the file store can be defined as a local file path on the Persistent Chat Server. For multiple server deployments, a UNC path location must be specified. If desired, the same UNC path location can be used as a file store for both the Front End pool and the Persistent Chat pool.

The system requirements for a Persistent Chat Server are summarized here:

▶ Windows Server 2008 R2 with SP1 and Windows Server 2012 are supported operating system platforms (Standard, Enterprise, or Datacenter Editions).

▶ .NET Framework 4.5 (included with Windows Server 2012).

▶ Windows PowerShell 3.0 (included with Windows Server 2012).

▶ Windows Identity Foundation (included with Windows Server 2012).

▶ The Message Queuing feature (including Directory Service Integration) included with Windows Server is required if the Persistent Chat Compliance service is enabled.

▶ Microsoft Visual C++ 11 x64 redistributable (automatically installed from the Lync media if not present when starting the Lync installation).

▶ One standard SSL certificate is required, from either a third party or an internal certificate authority (no subject alternative names are required).

Hardware guidelines for a Persistent Chat Server are the same as for other Lync Server roles and are summarized here:

▶ Quad-core 64-bit dual processor (2.0GHz or higher), or dual-core four-way processor (2.0GHz or higher)

▶ 16GB RAM

▶ Two 10,000 RPM hard disk drives with at least 72GB of free space, or RAID 1 or RAID 10 volume on a storage area network

▶ One network adapter, 1Gbps or higher (NIC teaming with a single MAC and single IP address are supported)

> **NOTE**
>
> Microsoft's listed hardware guidelines are based on a user pool of 80,000 users, and can therefore be scaled back appropriately as needed.

For the Persistent Chat database server, SQL Server 2008 R2 and SQL Server 2012 are the only supported database platforms. The hardware guidelines for a Persistent Chat database server are the same as for other Lync database servers, and are summarized here:

▶ Quad-core 64-bit dual processor (2.0GHz or higher) or dual-core four-way processor (2.0GHz or higher)

▶ 32GB RAM

▶ Eight or more 10,000 RPM hard disk drives with at least 72GB of free space, or RAID 1 or RAID 10 storage area network with four dedicated LUNs

▶ One network adapter, 1Gbps or higher (NIC teaming with a single MAC and single IP address are supported)

Topology Update

As with all Lync Server roles, the Topology Builder must be updated to include Persistent Chat before the server role is installed. Follow these steps to update the Lync topology to include Persistent Chat:

1. Log on to a system where the Lync Server 2013 administrative tools are installed using an account that is a member of the `Domain Admins` and `CsAdministrator` groups, and open the Lync Server Topology Builder.

2. At the prompt, select Download Topology from Existing Deployment to retrieve the current topology from the Central Management Store.

3. At the Save Topology As prompt, select a name and location for the Topology Builder file and click Save.

4. In the left pane, expand the Lync site where Persistent Chat will be installed, expand Lync Server 2013, and then right-click on the Persistent Chat pools node and select New Persistent Chat Pool.

5. At the Define the fully qualified domain name (FQDN) screen, enter the FQDN that will be used for the Persistent Chat pool. If Persistent Chat will be collocated with a Standard Edition Front End, the FQDN entered here must be the FQDN of the Front End Server. If Persistent Chat will be deployed using separate servers, the FQDN entered will be new to the topology. After the FQDN is entered, choose either the Multiple computer pool or Single computer pool option, and click Next.

> **TIP**
>
> Although a new FQDN is created in the topology for Persistent Chat pools that are deployed on separate hardware, it is not necessary to enter the FQDN of the Persistent Chat pool as an internal DNS record. The Front End Server handles all the routing for Persistent Chat without requiring DNS queries.

6. If the Multiple computer pool option was selected on the preceding screen, the Define the computers in this pool screen appears. Enter the FQDN of each system that will be added as a Persistent Chat Server, and click Add to add each to the pool. When finished, click Next.

> **NOTE**
>
> If the Single computer pool option was selected, the Standard Edition Front End Server is automatically chosen as the Persistent Chat Server, since this is the only option.

7. At the Define properties of the Persistent Chat pool screen, enter a display name for the pool, and keep the default Persistent Chat port number of 5041. Select from among the listed options to enable compliance, or to define this pool as the default for the Lync site. If the Multiple computer pool option was selected earlier, the option to enable disaster recovery is also presented. After the desired options are selected, click Next.

8. At the Define the SQL Server Store screen, several SQL options are presented, as shown in Figure 10.1. To use a SQL Server that is not currently part of the topology, click New, enter the FQDN of the new SQL Server, enter the instance name if the default instance is not being used, and the SQL mirroring option if high-availability will be used. To use a SQL Server that is already part of the topology, use the drop-down menu to select the SQL Server that will be used. If SQL mirroring will be used for high-availability with this server, select this option and then click New to enter the information for a new SQL store for this purpose, or use the drop-down menu to select one that is already part of the topology. If automatic failover will be used requiring a SQL Server mirroring witness, enable this option as well, and click New to enter the information for a new system to act as a SQL witness, or use the drop-down menu to select one that is already part of the topology. After the SQL Server Store options have been selected, click Next.

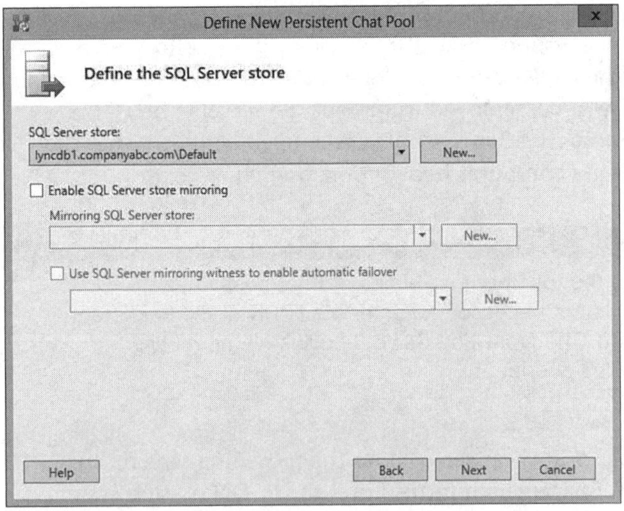

FIGURE 10.1   Persistent Chat SQL Server Store options.

9. If the compliance option was enabled on an earlier screen, the Define the Compliance SQL Server Store screen appears, and presents the same SQL options for the compliance store that were presented for the Persistent Chat Store. To use a SQL Server for compliance that is not currently part of the topology, click New, enter the FQDN of the new SQL Server, enter the instance name if the default instance is not being used, and the SQL mirroring option if high-availability will be used. To use a

SQL Server for compliance that is already part of the topology, use the drop-down menu to select the SQL Server that will be used. If SQL mirroring will be used for high-availability with this server, select this option and click New to enter the information for a new SQL store for this purpose, or use the drop-down menu to select one that is already part of the topology. If automatic failover will be used requiring a SQL Server mirroring witness, enable this option as well, and click New to enter the information for a new system to act as a SQL witness, or use the drop-down menu to select one that is already part of the topology. After the compliance SQL Server store options have been selected, click Next.

10. The Define the File Store screen appears, as shown in Figure 10.2. If using a file store that is already part of the topology, use the drop-down menu to select the existing file store. If a new file store will be defined, select Define a new file store and enter the fully qualified name of the file server as well as the file share name. When finished, click Next.

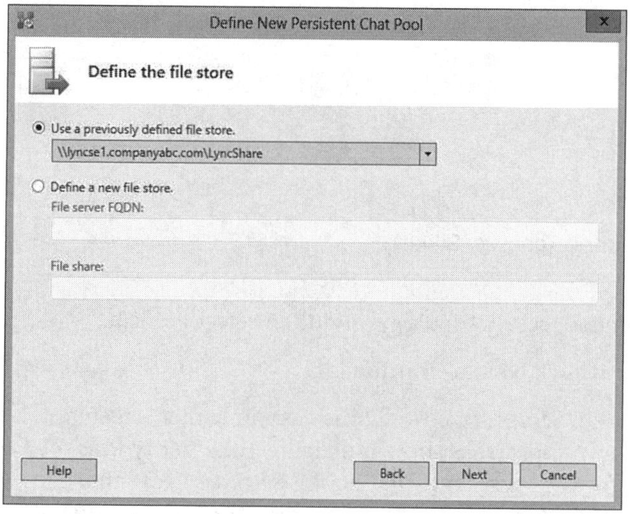

FIGURE 10.2   Persistent Chat file store options.

TIP

When using a new file store for Persistent Chat, the file store does not need to be created before it is defined in Topology Builder. However, it must be created before the topology is published.

11. If the option to install the chat pool using separate servers was chosen on an earlier screen, the Select the Next Hop Server screen will appear. Use the drop-down menu to select the next hop pool for traffic sent from this Persistent Chat pool, and then click Finish to complete the wizard and return to the Topology Builder.

12. The Persistent Chat pool details are now displayed in Topology Builder, as shown in Figure 10.3.

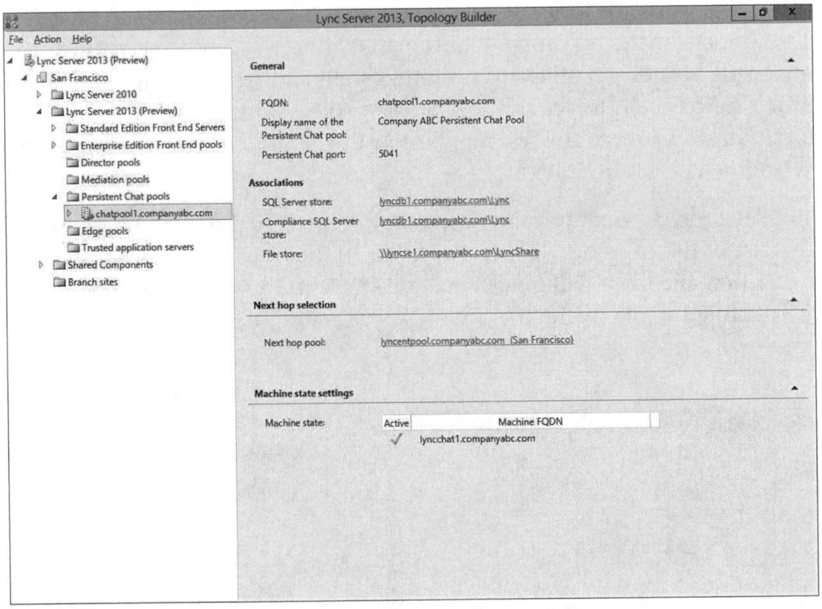

FIGURE 10.3   Persistent Chat pool in the Topology Builder.

13. From the Action drop-down menu, select Topology, and then select Publish.

14. At the Publish Topology screen, click Next to continue.

15. If the option to define a new SQL Server store was chosen on an earlier screen, The Create Databases screen now appears, as shown in Figure 10.4. Verify that the correct target database server for the Persistent Chat pool is selected. Note that the wizard defaults to the option of automatically determining the file locations for the Persistent Chat database. If alternative database paths are needed, for example, if dedicated volumes have been created on the target SQL Server for database and log files, then select the target store in the wizard and click the Advanced button. The Select Database File Location dialog is then presented. To specify alternative paths for the database files, select the option for Use These Paths on Target SQL Server; then enter the specific paths to the database files and the log files on the target server, and click OK. Click Next to continue.

16. The topology updates are now published, and the new Persistent Chat databases are created on the target SQL server. When the topology has been successfully published, click Finish to complete the topology update for Persistent Chat.

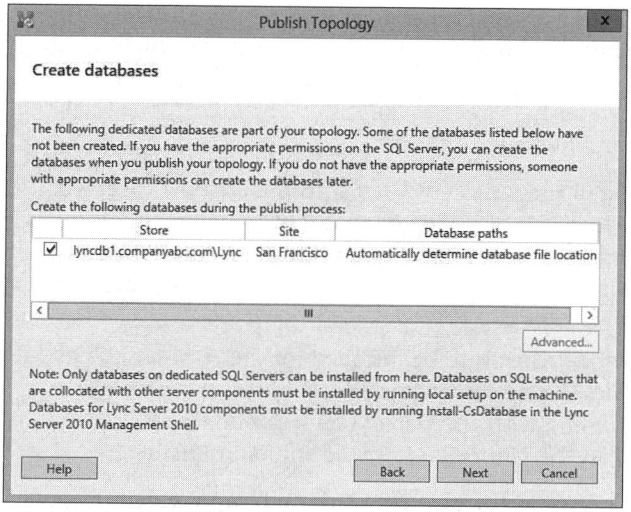

FIGURE 10.4   Topology Builder database options.

Installing the Persistent Chat Server Role

After the Lync topology has been updated to include the Persistent Chat pool, the Lync Server role installation can be run on each Persistent Chat server that has been added to the topology. The following procedure is used to install Persistent Chat on one of the servers that has been defined in the topology:

1. Log on to the server using an account that has local administrative rights on the system, and execute the `setup.exe` file from the Lync media.

2. If it's not already installed, a prompt appears regarding the installation of Microsoft Visual C++ X64 Minimum Runtime as a prerequisite. Click Yes to install the software.

3. When the wizard displays, either browse to your intended installation location or accept the default location, and then click Install.

4. When prompted, read the software license terms, click the I Accept the Terms in the License Agreement option if you agree to the terms, and click OK.

5. The core components of Lync Server 2013 are now installed, which includes the Lync Management Shell and the Lync Deployment Wizard. After the Deployment Wizard launches, click Install or Update Lync Server System.

6. The wizard now determines the current state of the local system and provides links to various installation options as needed. At Step 1: Install Local Configuration Store, click Run.

7. At the Configure Local Replica of Central Management Store screen, keep the default option of Retrieve Directly from the Central Management Store, and click Next.

10

8. The commands required to install a local configuration store are executed. After the installation is complete, click Finish to return to the Deployment Wizard.

9. At Step 2: Setup or Remove Lync Server Components, click Run.

10. At the Set Up Lync Server Components screen, click Next.

11. The commands required to install the Persistent Chat software are now executed. After the installation is complete, click View Log to determine whether any errors occurred during the software installation process. When finished, click Finish to return to the Deployment Wizard.

After the software is installed, a certificate needs to be installed for the Persistent Chat Server. As with other Lync Server roles, Persistent Chat supports certificates issued by a third party or an internal CA. Continuing with the Deployment Wizard, the following steps are used to request and assign an SSL certificate from an online internal CA:

1. At Step 3: Request, Install or Assign Certificates, click Run to begin the certificate request.

2. When the Certificate Wizard screen appears, a single certificate type is displayed for the Default certificate. Click Request.

3. The Certificate Request Wizard now launches. Click Next.

4. At the Delayed or Immediate Requests screen, online and offline request options are presented. Since this request will be sent to an internal CA, select Send the Request Immediately to an Online Certificate Authority, and then click Next.

5. At the Choose a Certification Authority (CA) screen, the online certificate authority systems that have been detected by the wizard are listed, as shown in Figure 10.5. Keep the default option of Select a CA from the List Detected in Your Environment, and then use the drop-down menu to select the target CA for this certificate. When finished, click Next to send the request.

6. At the Certificate Authority Account screen, the option to specify alternative credentials for the certificate request is presented. If the user account of the installer does not have sufficient permissions to request a certificate from the CA, then the option for alternative credentials should be selected, and the credentials of a user account that does have the required permissions can be entered. If the installer account has the required permissions, simply click Next.

7. By default, the wizard creates the certificate request using the WebServer (SSL) template. If a different certificate template is planned, select the option for Use Alternate Certificate Template for the Selected Certification Authority, and then enter the name of the template into the Certificate Template Name field. When finished, click Next.

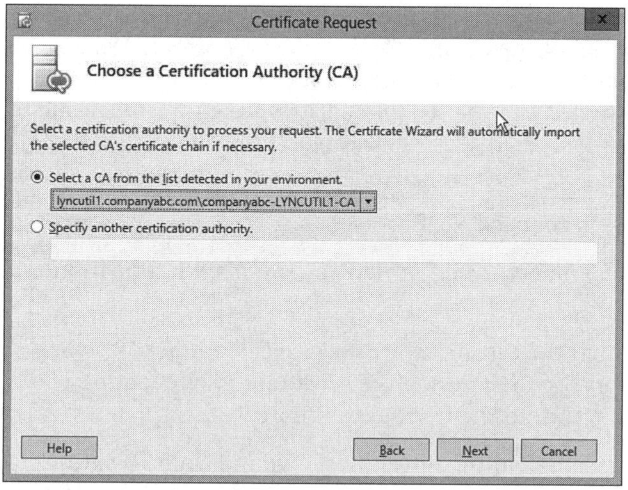

FIGURE 10.5   Internal certificate authorities detected.

8. At the Name and Security Settings screen, enter a friendly name for the certificate, which makes it easier to identify later. Also, choose a bit length for the certificate. If the private key will need to be exported later, select the option for Mark the Certificate's Private Key as Exportable. Click Next.

9. At the Organization Information screen, enter the name of the organization and organizational unit into the corresponding fields, and then click Next.

10. At the Geographical Information screen, select the country from the drop-down menu, and then enter the information into the State/Province and City/Locality fields. Click Next.

11. The names that are automatically populated into the certificate by the Wizard are now displayed. Click Next.

12. The opportunity to enter additional Subject Alternate Names outside those automatically determined by the wizard is presented. For a Persistent Chat Server, typically no additional names are needed. Click Next.

13. At the Certificate Request Summary screen, review the values for accuracy, and then click Next.

14. The commands required to generate the certificate request file are now executed. Click View Log to determine whether any errors occurred during the certificate request process. When finished, click Next.

15. At the Online Certificate Request Status screen, the results of the certificate request are shown. To view the properties of the certificate, click View Certificate Details. At this point, the certificate has been installed to the local certificate store on the system, but it has not been assigned to Lync. To immediately assign the certificate to Lync, keep the default selection of Assign This Certificate to Lync Server Certificate Usages, and click Finish.

16. At the Certificate Assignment screen, click Next.

17. At the Certificate Assignment Summary screen, review the summary information, and then click Next.

18. The commands required to assign the certificate are now executed. Click View Log to determine whether any errors occurred during the certificate assignment process. When finished, click Finish to return to the Certificate Wizard.

19. The default certificate is now assigned to the server, as shown in Figure 10.6. Click Close to exit the Certificate Wizard.

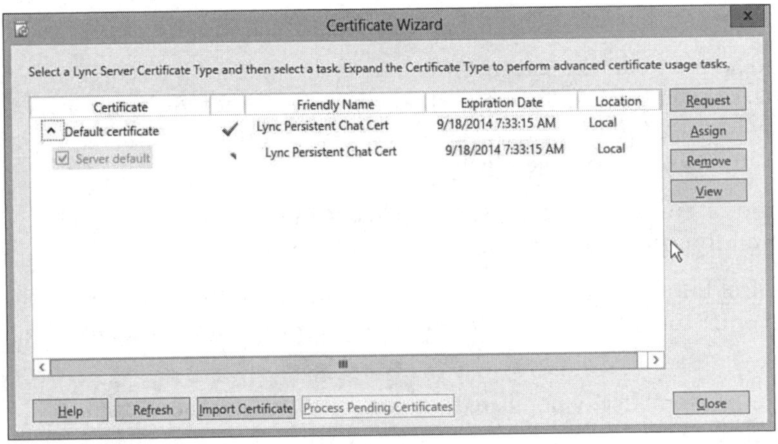

FIGURE 10.6   Viewing the assigned certificate.

Now that the software has been installed and the certificate has been assigned, the final step is to start the Persistent Chat services for the first time. Continuing with the Deployment Wizard, the Persistent Chat services are started as shown here:

1. At Step 4: Start Services, click Run.

2. At the Start Services screen, click Next.

3. The commands required to start the Persistent Chat services are now executed. Click View Log to determine whether any errors occurred during the process of starting the services. When finished, click Finish to return to the Deployment Wizard.

4. Click Exit to close the Deployment Wizard.

Configuring Persistent Chat

With Lync Server 2013, Persistent Chat configuration is performed using the standard Lync Server administration tools, greatly simplifying the entire process of configuring and maintaining the Persistent Chat environment. Both the Lync Server Control Panel and the Lync Server Management Shell can be used to perform Persistent Chat configuration tasks. The following sections provide details on the primary tasks that are necessary for a Persistent Chat deployment.

Administrative Access

The first task in configuring the Persistent Chat environment is granting administrative permissions to the accounts that will be managing the environment. With all Lync Server roles, RBAC (role-based access control) is used to grant privileges by assigning users to predefined Lync Server administrative roles represented by Active Directory security groups, and this includes Persistent Chat. One such group is provided specifically for the administration of the Persistent Chat environment, the `CsPersistentChatAdministrator` group. This security group, along with the rest of the predefined Lync security groups, is located by default in the top-level Users container in the forest root AD domain. Members of the `CsPersistentChatAdministrator` group are granted access to the Lync Persistent Chat cmdlets, which can be executed using either the Lync Management Shell or the Lync Server Control Panel.

> **NOTE**
>
> While the `CsPersistentChatAdministrator` group grants specific access to the Persistent Chat portion of the Lync environment, two other groups also have administrative access to much of the Persistent Chat configuration as part of their broader administrative scope: `CsAdministrator` and `CsUserAdministrator`. Therefore, in smaller organizations where one group of administrators manages the entire Lync environment including Persistent Chat, it might not be necessary to populate the `CsPersistentChatAdministrator` group.

By default, there are no members of the `CsPersistentChatAdministrator` group, and therefore the group must be populated with user accounts to delegate administrative rights to the Persistent Chat configuration.

Persistent Chat Policies

Persistent Chat policies are used to determine which Lync users are enabled for Persistent Chat. There are four levels of policies that can be used: global, pool, site, and user. There is only one global policy, which is automatically created when Persistent Chat is deployed, and is simply named Global. This default Global policy does not need to be used, but it cannot be deleted.

Only one Persistent Chat pool policy can be created per Lync pool, and it affects all users within that pool. Similarly, one Persistent Chat site policy can be created per Lync site, and it affects all users in that site. On the other hand, multiple Persistent Chat user policies can be created, and applied on a user-by-user basis as needed. Pool and site policies override the global policy, and user policies override the pool and site policies.

TIP

Only a single setting exists in a Persistent Chat policy; it simply allows users that are assigned to the policy to be enabled for Persistent Chat. For this reason, at most only a few Persistent Chat polices are typically needed. If it is determined that all users in the environment will be enabled for Persistent Chat, this can be accomplished using just the global policy. If, on the other hand, Persistent Chat will be assigned to specific users, then the pool, site, or user policies will be useful.

The following example shows the steps for creating a user policy and then assigning the policy to a user:

1. Log on to a system where the Lync administrative tools are installed using an account that is a member of the CsAdministrator or CsPersistentChatAdministrator security groups, and open the Lync Server Control Panel.

2. In the left pane, select Persistent Chat, and then click the Persistent Chat Policy tab at the top.

3. From the New drop-down menu, select User Policy.

4. At the New Persistent Chat Policy screen, enter a name and description for the policy, and then select the Enable Persistent Chat setting, as shown in Figure 10.7.

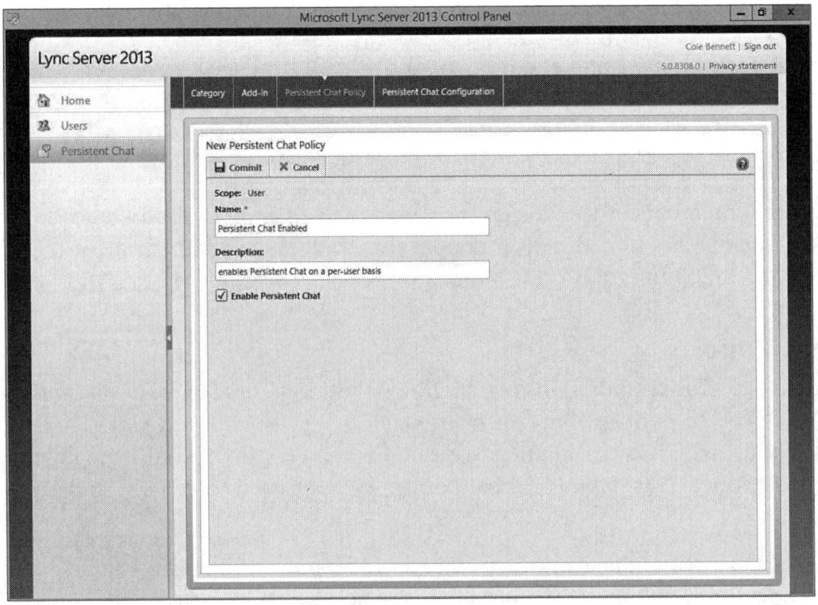

FIGURE 10.7   Creating a Persistent Chat user policy.

5. Click Commit to save the policy.

6. In the left pane, select Users.

7. Type a portion of the target user's name in the search field at the top of the screen, and then click Find to list all users that meet the search criteria.

8. Select the target user account in the bottom pane, and then from the Edit drop-down menu click Show Details.

9. Scroll down to the bottom of the user properties, and then use the Persistent Chat Policy drop-down menu to select the user policy created previously.

10. Click Commit to save the setting.

Persistent Chat Server Options

Lync Server 2013 provides the capability to create a set of server options that can be applied globally to all Persistent Chat pools, or alternatively these same server options can be applied to a specific site or pool. There is only one global configuration, which is automatically created when Persistent Chat is deployed, and is simply named Global. This default Global configuration contains default settings that can be changed as needed, but the configuration itself cannot be deleted. A configuration that is applied at the pool or site level overrides the same settings that are configured at the global level. Persistent Chat server option settings include the following:

▶ **Default Chat History**—The number of chat messages that are immediately available for each chat room upon first request (the global default is 30 chat messages).

▶ **Maximum File Size (KB)**—The maximum size of a file that can be uploaded to or downloaded from a room (the global default is 20MB).

> **NOTE**
>
> The Maximum file size setting applies only in environments that include legacy Group Chat clients, since these are the only clients that can post files to a chat room. The Lync Server 2013 Persistent Chat client does not have file upload/download capability, and therefore this setting does not have any effect on a native Lync Server 2013 environment.

▶ **Participant Update Limit**—The maximum number of participants in a given room for which Persistent Chat will send roster updates (the global default is 75). Roster updates are used to inform connected clients about who is present in the chat room.

▶ **Room Management URL**—The URL used for custom chat room management. This is an optional setting that allows the use of a custom room management solution. For example, an organization can develop their own web application used to manage Lync chat rooms. If the URL for the custom web application is specified as the room management URL within the Persistent Chat options, then users will be redirected to the custom room management site when they create or manage a chat room using the Lync client.

10

Use the following steps for creating and applying server options to a specific Persistent Chat pool:

1. Log on to a system where the Lync administrative tools are installed using an account that is a member of the CsAdministrator or CsPersistentChatAdministrator security groups, and open the Lync Server Control Panel.

2. In the left pane, select Persistent Chat, and then click the Persistent Chat Configuration tab at the top.

3. From the New drop-down menu, select Pool Configuration.

4. At the Select a Service dialog box, select the Persistent Chat service from the list and click OK.

5. The New Persistent Chat Configuration screen now appears. The name for the configuration is automatically chosen based on the name of the Persistent Chat pool, as shown in Figure 10.8.

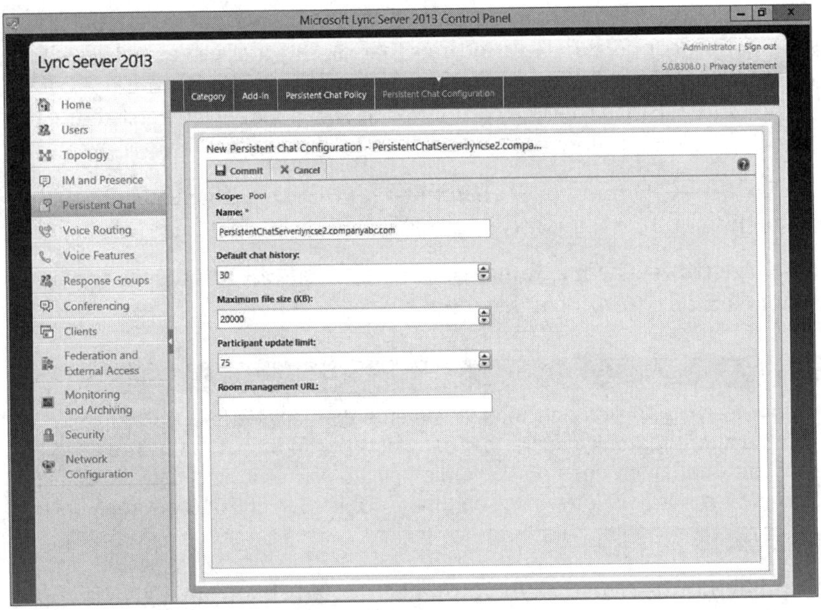

FIGURE 10.8   Creating a new Persistent Chat configuration.

6. The Default chat history, Maximum file size, and Participant update limit fields are automatically populated with the same default values used in the Global policy. Enter new values for these fields to meet the Persistent Chat requirements of the pool.

7. If a custom room management site will be used, enter the URL for the site in the Room management URL field.

8. When finished, click Commit to save the configuration.

Chat Room Categories

Chat room categories are used to develop a logical structure for the organization of chat rooms, and also serve as a mechanism for controlling which users and groups are permitted to create or join the chat rooms within those categories. Each category also contains properties that determine the options available for the chat rooms within that category.

Each chat room has only one parent category. For each category created, Persistent Chat administrators can allow or deny membership to rooms that belong to that category, and can also assign users to be creators for the category. A user who is assigned as a creator for a category has permissions to create chat rooms, assign members, and assign managers for the chat rooms within that category. Assigning creator rights at the category level is therefore an effective means for Persistent Chat administrators to delegate chat room management to responsible users, typically department heads or power users. Users who have creator rights can then in turn assign other users to be managers of individual chat rooms. Chat room managers can configure many aspects of the chat rooms for which they have been assigned as a manager, including chat room membership.

Categories that are well-designed result in an effective chat room structure that meets the needs of the users, and at the same time simplifies delegated administration of the Persistent Chat environment. Figure 10.9 shows an example of a category and chat room structure that might be used to model an organization's departmental structure.

Following are the options that are available for configuration with each category:

▶ **Invitations**—Controls whether chat rooms within the category will support invitations, which are used to notify users when they have been added as chat room members.

▶ **File Upload**—Determines whether file uploads are permitted for chat rooms within the category.

NOTE

The File Upload setting applies only in environments that include legacy Group Chat clients, since these are the only clients that can post files to a chat room. The Lync Server 2013 Persistent Chat client does not have file upload/download capability; therefore, this setting does not have any effect on a native Lync Server 2013 environment.

10

▶ **Chat History**—Determines whether chat history will be maintained for chat rooms within the category. Disabling chat history at the category level effectively makes chat nonpersistent for all chat rooms in that category.

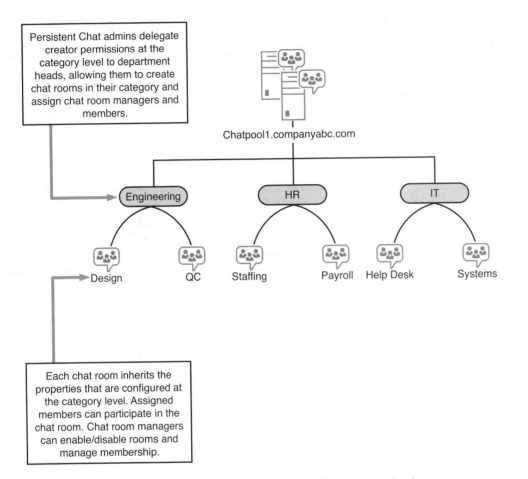

Persistent Chat admins delegate creator permissions at the category level to department heads, allowing them to create chat rooms in their category and assign chat room managers and members.

Chatpool1.companyabc.com

Engineering   HR   IT

Design   QC   Staffing   Payroll   Help Desk   Systems

Each chat room inherits the properties that are configured at the category level. Assigned members can participate in the chat room. Chat room managers can enable/disable rooms and manage membership.

FIGURE 10.9   Example of a Persistent Chat category and chat room structure.

▶ **Allowed Membership**—Determines which users are allowed to be members of chat rooms in the category.

TIP

Adding Active Directory objects to the allowed membership at the category level does not automatically cause the affected users to become members of any chat room. It simply allows those users to be added as members to the chat rooms in that category, which is configured at the chat room level. Users who are denied at the category level cannot be members of any chat room in that category.

The following steps would be used to create one of the Persistent Chat categories shown earlier in Figure 10.9:

1. Log on to a system where the Lync administrative tools are installed using an account that is a member of the CsAdministrator or CsPersistentChatAdministrator security groups, and open the Lync Server Control Panel.

2. In the left pane, select Persistent Chat, and then click the Category tab at the top.

3. Click New; then, at the Select a Service dialog box, select the Persistent Chat pool that will be associated with this category, and click OK.

> **NOTE**
>
> The Select a Service dialog box determines the Persistent Chat pool that will be used by Lync clients to identify which pool a particular category belongs to. After it has been created, a category can belong to only one pool, and cannot be moved to a different pool.

4. At the New Category screen, enter the name for the category, and optionally enter a description.

5. Select the chat room options that will be enabled for the chat rooms in this category: invitations, file upload, and chat history (see previous description).

6. In the Allowed Members section, click Add.

7. The Select Allowed Members dialog box now appears, which allows the option to search for four types of Active Directory objects that can be added as allowed members: organizational units, distribution groups, domains, and individual user accounts. Enter the name of an AD object to search and click Find.

8. After the object appears in the list, select the object and click OK.

9. The New Category screen now shows the AD object as an allowed member for the category, as shown in Figure 10.10. Repeat steps 6 through 8 as needed to add additional allowed members.

10. Scroll down farther in the New Category screen to bring the Denied Members and Creators sections into view.

11. In the Denied Members section, click Add.

12. The Select Denied Members dialog box now appears, which allows the option to search for Active Directory objects that can be added as denied members. Enter the name of an organizational unit, a distribution group, a domain, or an individual user account and click Find.

13. After the object appears in the list, select the object and click OK.

14. Repeat steps 11 through 13 as needed to add additional denied members.

15. In the Creators section, click Add.

10

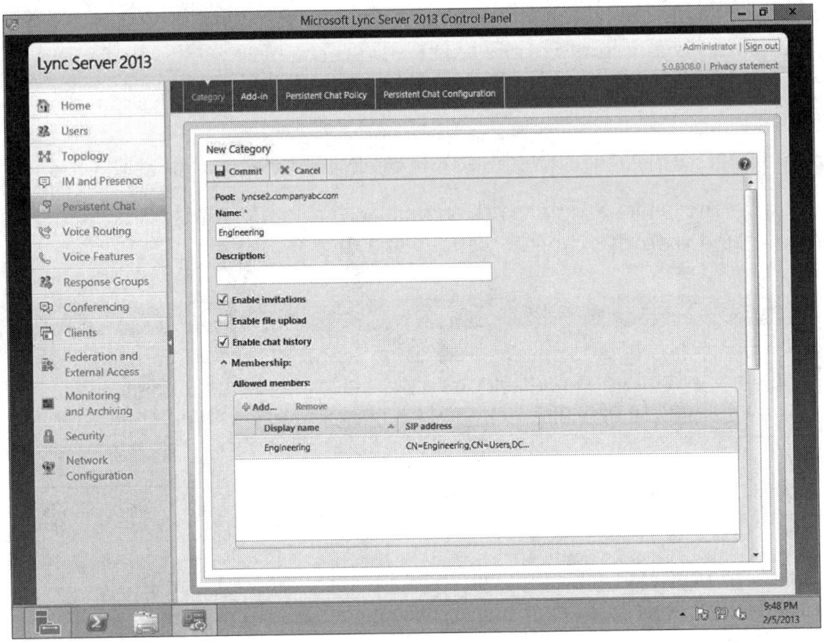

FIGURE 10.10   New Persistent Chat category.

16. The Select Creators dialog box now appears, which allows the option to search for Active Directory objects that can be added as creators. Enter the name of an organizational unit, a distribution group, a domain, or individual user account and click Find.

> **NOTE**
>
> Each user who is added as a creator must first be added to the allowed member list for the category, either explicitly or via membership in an organizational unit or a distribution group. Also, a user must not be a member of the denied member list for the category to be added as a creator.

17. After the object appears in the list, select the object and click OK.

18. Repeat steps 15 through 17 as needed to add additional creators.

19. When finished, click Commit to save the new category.

Chat Room Add-ins

Chat room add-ins are used to extend the Persistent Chat user experience by associating customized websites with chat rooms. When add-ins are registered by the Lync administrator and associated with chat rooms, the content of the specified websites is embedded in the conversation extensibility pane of the Lync 2013 client. A good example of how an add-in might be used would be embedding a Microsoft OneNote URL within a chat room dedicated to a particular department, where the site provides information that would be of interest to the department members.

The following steps would be used to create a chat room add-in:

1. Log on to a system where the Lync administrative tools are installed using an account that is a member of the CsAdministrator or CsPersistentChatAdministrator security groups, and open the Lync Server Control Panel.

2. In the left pane, select Persistent Chat, and then click the Add-in tab at the top.

3. Click New; then, at the Select a Service dialog box, select the Persistent Chat pool that will be associated with this add-in, and click OK.

4. At the New Add-in screen, enter a name for the add-in, enter the URL that will be associated with the add-in, and then click Commit to save the configuration.

After an add-in has been registered, it is associated with a chat room using the Lync Server Management Shell. The following procedure would be used to associate an add-in named Engineering Design Add-in with the Engineering chat room shown earlier in Figure 10.9:

1. Log on to a system where the Lync administrative tools are installed using an account that is a member of the CsAdministrator or CsPersistentChat Administrator group and the RTC Local Administrators group on the Persistent Chat Server, and that has administrative rights on the local system.

2. Open the Lync Server Management Shell, and execute the following cmdlet:

```
Set-CsPersistentChatRoom -Identity chatpool1.companyabc.com
➥-Add-in Engineering Design Add-in
```

Chat Rooms

After categories have been created, chat rooms can be created within those categories, and they will inherit the options that have been configured at the category level. Chat rooms can be created either by a Persistent Chat administrator, or by another user who has been assigned as a creator for one or more categories. Unlike the other Persistent Chat configuration tasks described previously, the creation and configuration of chat rooms is not performed using the Lync Server Control Panel. There are two ways to create a chat room: using the Lync Server Management Shell, or using the Lync 2013 client. Both methods are described next.

Creating a Chat Room Using the Lync Server Management Shell

The first method that can be used to create a chat room is using the Lync Server Management Shell, which would typically be used by Lync administrators or other IT personnel who have been delegated administrative permissions to the Persistent Chat deployment. To execute Persistent Chat PowerShell cmdlets remotely, a user must be a member of the CsAdministrator or CsPersistentChatAdministrator groups, must be explicitly listed as a member of the RTC Local Administrators group on the Persistent Chat Server, and must also have local administrative rights on the system where the Management Shell is used.

Following is the procedure for using the Lync Server Management Shell to create one of the chat rooms shown earlier in Figure 10.9:

1. Log on to a system where the Lync administrative tools are installed using an account that is a member of the CsAdministrator or CsPersistentChatAdministrator groups in AD, and the RTC Local Administrators group on the Persistent Chat Server, and has administrative rights on the local system.

2. Open the Lync Server Management Shell, and execute the following cmdlet to create a chat room named Design within the Engineering category:

```
New-CsPersistentChatRoom -Name Design -PersistentChatPoolFqdn
➥chatpool1.companyabc.com -Category chatpool1.companyabc.com\Engineering.
```

3. If the command is successful, the chat room is created and the properties of the new chat room are displayed, as shown in Figure 10.11.

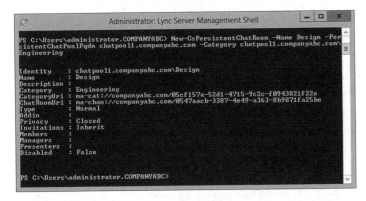

FIGURE 10.11   Creating a chat room using the Management Shell.

Note from Figure 10.11 that when the room is initially created, there is no membership. Additional commands can then be used to configure various properties of the room, including room type, membership, managers, and more. For details on the configuration of chat rooms, see the "Persistent Chat Administration" section later in this chapter.

Creating a Chat Room Using the Lync 2013 Client

The second method that can be used to create a chat room is using the Lync 2013 client, which would typically be used by a user who has been assigned creator permissions to one or more categories. To create a chat room using the Lync 2013 client, a user must first be enabled for Persistent Chat via a Persistent Chat policy, in addition to being assigned as a creator.

Following is the procedure for using the Lync 2013 client to create one of the chat rooms shown earlier in Figure 10.9:

1. Log on to the Lync 2013 client using an account that has been enabled for Persistent Chat, and has been assigned as a creator in a Persistent Chat category.

2. If the user has been enabled for Persistent Chat, the Chat Rooms icon automatically appears as the second icon from the left, as shown in Figure 10.12. Click on the Chat Rooms icon to display the Chat Rooms section of the Lync client.

FIGURE 10.12   Chat Rooms section of the Lync 2013 client.

3. On the right side of the window, click on the plus symbol, and then from the list of options that appears, click Create a Chat Room.

4. At the prompt, enter the credentials of the user with creator rights.

5. The My Rooms page now displays. Click on Create a New Room.

6. The Create a Room page now appears, as shown in Figure 10.13. Begin by entering a name, and optionally a description for the new chat room.

10

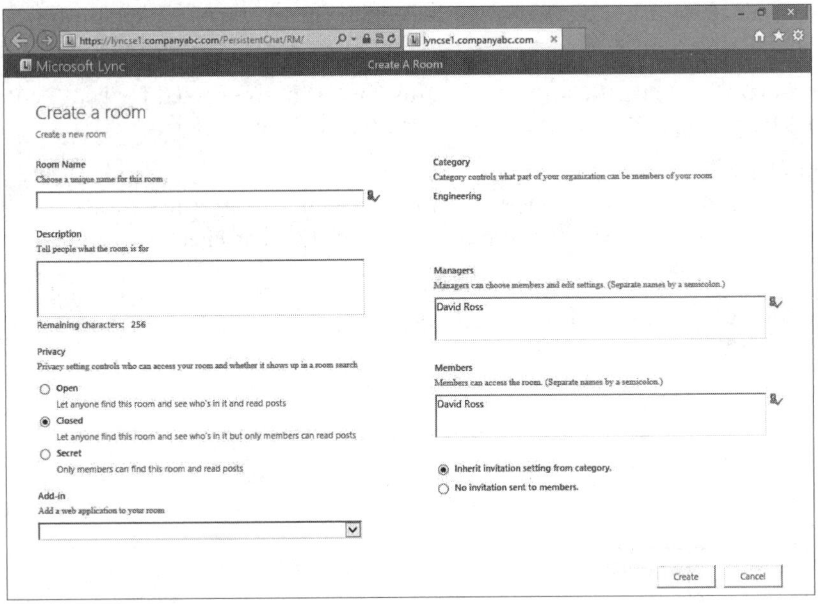

FIGURE 10.13   Creating a chat room using the Lync 2013 client.

7. Additional properties that can be configured when the chat room is created include the following:

   ▶ **Privacy**—Select Open, Closed, or Secret. Open rooms can be searched and accessed by anyone. Closed rooms can be searched by anyone, but can be accessed only by members. Secret rooms can be searched and accessed only by members of the room.

   ▶ **Add-in**—Use the drop-down menu to associate an add-in with the chat room, which allows URL content to be viewed by members while participating. Add-ins must be previously approved by a Persistent Chat administrator in order to appear in this list.

   ▶ **Managers**—The creator of the chat room is listed by default as the initial chat room manager; however, this can be changed as needed. If a different user will be assigned as the manager, or if additional chat room managers will be assigned, enter one or more names within the Managers box, with multiple names separated by a semicolon. The check mark icon at the right of the Managers box can be used to verify the accuracy of the manager names entered.

   ▶ **Members**—If the chat room privacy setting is configured as Closed or Secret, individual names can be entered within the Members box, with multiple names separated by a semicolon. The check mark icon at the right of the Members box can be used to verify the accuracy of the member names entered.

▶ **Invitations**—If the chat room privacy setting is configured as Closed or Secret, the invitations setting can be configured to either inherit the invitation setting from the parent category, or disable invitations for the chat room. Invitations are used to notify users when they have been added as chat room members.

8. When finished, click Create to create the new chat room.

Compliance Configuration

Persistent Chat compliance allows Lync administrators to maintain an archive of Persistent Chat messages as well as activities. For example, the activities that can be recorded and archived through compliance include new messages, new events such as a user entering a chat room, and searches that are performed against chat history. The compliance information can then be retrieved from the Compliance SQL database as needed.

After the Persistent Chat compliance feature has been enabled using the Topology Builder, it can then be configured using the Lync Server Management Shell. The cmdlet used to configure Persistent Chat compliance is Set-CsPersistentChatComplianceConfiguration. The parameters that can be set using this command include the following:

▶ AdapterType—An adapter is a third-party product that converts the data in the compliance database to a specific format. Adapter types include Akonix, Assentor, Facetime, and XML (the default).

▶ OneChatRoomPerOutputFile—This parameter allows separate reports to be created for each chat room.

▶ AddChatRoomDetails—When enabled, this records additional details about each chat room in the database. This setting can greatly increase the size of the database, and therefore is disabled by default.

▶ AddUserDetails—When enabled, this records additional details about each chat room user in the database. This setting can greatly increase the size of the database, and therefore is disabled by default.

▶ RunInterval—This parameter dictates the amount of time before the server outputs the next compliance output file (the default is 15 minutes).

▶ Identity—This setting allows compliance settings to be scoped for a particular collection, including the global, site, and service levels. If no identity is specified, the settings will apply to the global collection.

Additional parameters are also available and you can view them by executing the following command in the Management Shell:

```
Get-Help Set-CsPersistentChatComplianceConfiguration -Detailed
```

The following example sets the compliance properties for the global collection, specifying that separate reports be created for each chat room, and reducing the run interval to 10 minutes:

```
Set-CsPersistentChatComplianceConfiguration -OneChatRoomPerOutputFile $true
➡-RunInterval 00:10:00
```

Persistent Chat Administration

Administration of the Persistent Chat environment is largely focused on managing the individual chat rooms. From the Lync administrator's perspective, chat room management is performed using the Lync Server Management Shell. However, management of chat rooms can also be delegated to responsible users, for example, department heads or other personnel. Chat room management by end users is typically handled simply by use of the Lync 2013 client. This section provides details on some of the more common administrative tasks that are required to maintain the Persistent Chat environment.

Chat Room Management by Administrators

The basic procedure for creating a chat room using the Lync Server Management Shell was covered earlier in the "Configuring Persistent Chat" section. Although it is possible to configure some chat room parameters when the room is created using the New-CsPersistentChatRoom cmdlet, these same parameters and more can be configured after the chat room is created using the Set-CsPersistentChatRoom cmdlet. Parameters that can be configured using this cmdlet include the following:

▶ **Disabled**—Allows the status of the chat room to be disabled or enabled using the $true or $false values.

▶ **Type**—Allows a chat room to be specified as either a normal chat room, which accepts messages posted by any member, or an auditorium chat room, which allows only the presenter to post messages that other members can only read.

▶ **Addin**—Associates a previously configured add-in with a chat room, which allows URL content to be viewed by members while participating.

▶ **Privacy**—Allows a chat room to be configured as Open, Secret, or Closed. Open rooms can be searched and accessed by anyone. Secret rooms can be searched and accessed only by members of the room. Closed rooms can be searched by anyone, but can be accessed only by members. By default, each new room is initially configured as Closed.

▶ **Invitations**—Allows enabling or disabling of chat room invitations, which are used to notify users when they have been added as chat room members. The default setting for invitations is inherit, which causes the chat room to adopt the invitation setting configured on the category it belongs to. Configuring the invitations setting to false at the chat room level allows the category setting to be overridden.

▶ **Members**—Configures membership for the chat room. You can add or remove either individual or multiple members using a single cmdlet by specifying the SIP address of the users. To allow users to be added in bulk, Active Directory organizational units or distribution groups can also be specified.

▶ **Managers**—Allows managers to be assigned to the chat room. Managers have the permissions to define membership of a chat room along with other settings.

▶ **Presenters**—Allows presenters to be assigned to an auditorium chat room.

Using one of the sample chat rooms shown earlier in Figure 10.9, the following command would be used to temporarily disable the chat room:

```
Set-CsPersistentChatRoom -Identity chatpool1.companyabc.com\Staffing
➥-Disabled $true
```

The following command would be used to change the privacy setting to Secret, assign members using a distribution group, and assign an individual as a manager:

```
Set-CsPersistentChatRoom -Identity chatpool1.companyabc.com\Staffing
➥-Privacy secret -members @{Add="CN=HR Staff,OU=Groups,DC=companyabc,DC=com"}
➥-Managers @{Add="sip:HRlead@companyabc.com"}
```

If the command is successful, the updated parameters for the chat room are listed, as shown in Figure 10.14.

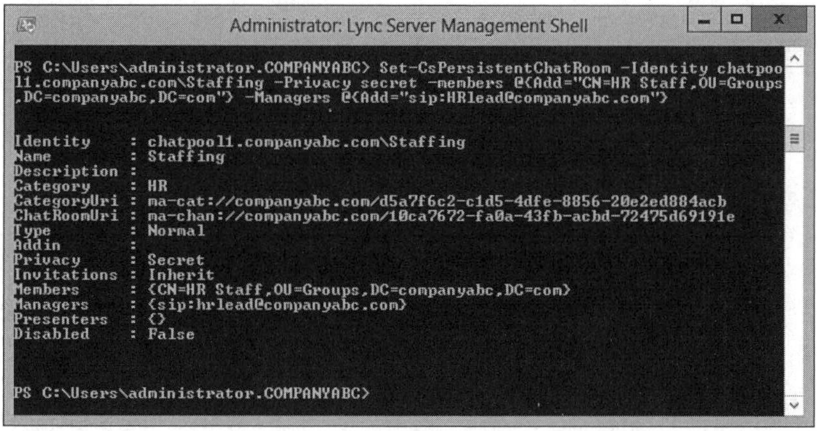

FIGURE 10.14   Adjusting chat room parameters using the command line.

You can view the complete syntax of the `Set-CsPersistentChatRoom` cmdlet along with helpful examples by executing the following command using the Management Shell: `Get-Help Set-CsPersistentChatRoom -Detailed`. It is also simple to view the parameters for an existing chat room by executing the `Get-CsPersistentChatRoom` cmdlet, specifying the identity of the room.

After a user has been assigned as a member of a chat room, the room automatically appears in the Lync client, as shown in Figure 10.12. From here, participation in a room is simply a matter of double-clicking on one of the listed rooms to view existing chat messages and adding new messages.

> **NOTE**
>
> The message history initially presented to the user when viewing a chat room is based on the Default Chat History setting configured by the administrator, as described earlier in the "Persistent Chat Server Options" section. However, this does not prevent a user from searching the chat room for additional messages that are maintained within the chat history for the room.

After chat rooms become available within the Lync client, the user can configure topic feeds, notifications, and more. For details on the client-side aspects of Persistent Chat, see Chapter 25, "Windows Client."

From time to time, it might be necessary for a Lync administrator to clear messages from a room, which can be accomplished with the `Clear-CsPersistentChatRoom` cmdlet. The clearing of messages from a room always starts with the oldest messages, but it is possible to specify an end date to provide a range of messages to be cleared. For example, the following command would be used to clear all of the messages from a chat room that are older than a specific end date:

```
Clear-CsPersistentChatRoom -Identity chatpool1.companyabc.com\Staffing
➡-EndDate "9/28/2012"
```

On occasion it might also be necessary for an administrator to remove individual messages from a chat room, perhaps because they are deemed inappropriate. This can be accomplished via the `Remove-CsPersistentChatMessage` cmdlet. To assist in finding messages to be removed, multiple keywords can be specified in the cmdlet as search criteria. For example, the following command would be used to search the Payroll chat room and remove any messages that contain both of the words "executive" and "salaries":

```
Remove-CsPersistentChatMessage -Identity chatpool1.companyabc.com\Payroll
➡-Filter "executive salaries" -MatchClause And
```

If one or more matches are found, the removed messages are replaced with a notification that the message has been removed by a Persistent Chat administrator, as shown in Figure 10.15.

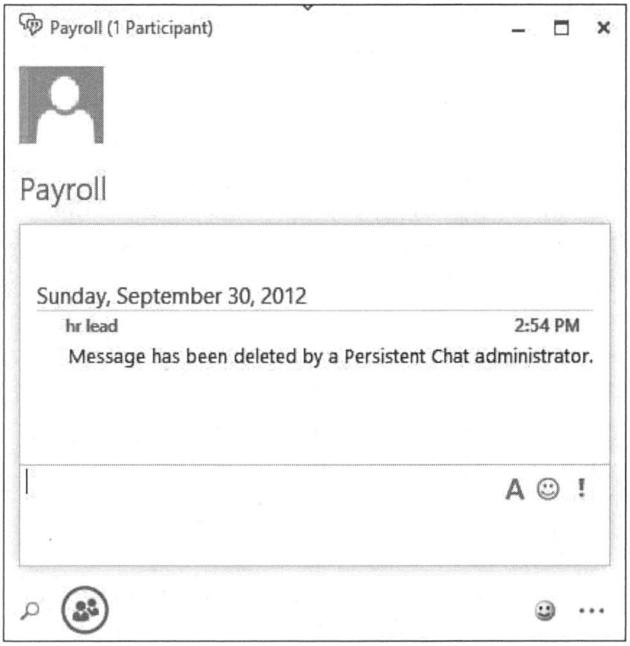

FIGURE 10.15   Chat message removed by an administrator.

TIP

Unless otherwise specified, removed messages are replaced with the default text shown in Figure 10.15. However, it is also possible to specify different replacement text using the `-ReplaceMessage` parameter. Additional parameters are also available, including date ranges for the search. You can find further details by executing the following command in the Management Shell: `Get-Help Remove-CsPersistentChatMessage -Detailed`.

Chat Room Management by End Users

As noted previously, chat room management can be handled not only by Lync adminis-trators, but also by end users who are delegated low-level administrative permissions to the chat room configuration. This level of administration can be performed simply by using the Lync 2013 client. End users can be delegated permissions to manage various aspects of the chat room configuration by being assigned the following roles:

▶ **Creator**—Users who are assigned as creators for a category can create new chat rooms within that category, and can change all the properties of the chat rooms they create, with the exception of the chat room category.

10

▶ **Chat Room Manager**—Users who are assigned as chat room managers can change all the properties of the chat rooms they manage, with the exception of the chat room category. This includes adding and removing members from a room, adding and removing managers, and disabling (but not deleting) a room.

The management activities handled by creators and chat room managers are performed using the Lync client, which initiates a connection to the chat room management web pages that are included as part of the Lync web components on the Front End Server. The following procedure is used to manage a chat room using the Lync client:

1. Log on to the Lync 2013 client using an account that has been enabled for Persistent Chat, and has been assigned as either a creator in a Persistent Chat category or a manager of one or more chat rooms.

2. If the user has been enabled for Persistent Chat, the Chat Rooms icon automatically appears as the second icon from the left, as shown earlier in Figure 10.12. Click on the Chat Rooms icon to display the Chat Rooms section of the Lync client.

3. Double-click on one of the rooms from the list to open it.

4. Click on the (...) symbol at the lower-right corner of the window, and from the list of options that appear, click Manage This Room.

5. At the prompt, enter the credentials of the user with creator or chat room manager rights.

6. The Edit a Room page now appears, as shown in Figure 10.16. Adjust the properties of the room as needed (see description for each property in the "Creating a Chat Room Using the Lync 2013 Client" section earlier in this chapter).

7. When finished, click Finish to save the changes to the chat room.

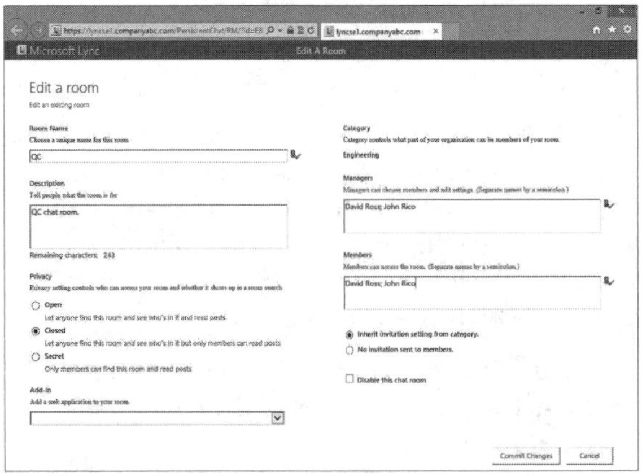

FIGURE 10.16   Editing a chat room using the Lync 2013 client.

Persistent Chat Troubleshooting

Troubleshooting for Persistent Chat starts with the basics, which consists of the Event Viewer and the Services console on the Persistent Chat Server. Error messages that are logged for Persistent Chat appear in the Lync Server portion of the Event Log under the Applications and Services log heading, and this is typically the first place to look when you are experiencing problems with Persistent Chat. There are also several Windows services installed as part of the role installation on each Persistent Chat Server. Two of these services are specifically related to Persistent Chat: the Lync Server Persistent Chat service, and the Lync Server Persistent Chat Compliance service. Both of these services are set to start up automatically when the system is turned on, and need to remain started continually for the Persistent Chat service to function. Additional information about the Persistent Chat environment can also be quickly retrieved by executing the following command using the Lync Server Management Shell: `Get-CsService -PersistentChat`.

If the Persistent Chat services are started and the Event Log does not provide helpful clues as to the cause of an issue, an additional useful tool for troubleshooting a Persistent Chat problem is synthetic transactions. Synthetic transactions can be used to test sending and receiving messages in a chat room between two users. You can initiate a synthetic transaction using the Lync Server Management Shell by executing the `Test-CsPersistentChatMessage` cmdlet. Sender and receiver credentials are supplied as parameters, and you obtain these by first using the `Get-Credential` cmdlet to store the credentials in variables that are referenced within the `Test-CsPersistentChatMessage` cmdlet.

The following example shows the commands used to execute a synthetic transaction, testing the sending of chat room messages between two users who are members of the chat pool named Design:

```
$cred1 = Get-Credential "companyabc\david"
$cred2 = Get-Credential "companyabc\kevin"
Test-CsPersistentChatMessage -TargetFqdn lyncentpool.companyabc.com
➥-ChatRoomName Design -SenderSipAddress "sip:david@companyabc.com"
➥-SenderCredential $cred1 -ReceiverSipAddress "sip:kevin@companyabc.com"
➥-ReceiverCredential $cred2.
```

The first and second commands cause interactive prompts for the password of the sender and receiver users, respectively. After these credentials are entered, they are stored in the variables that are referenced in the third command. The end result is then displayed as either Success or Failure, as shown in Figure 10.17. If the transaction fails, an error message is displayed to assist in further diagnosing the cause of the issue.

10

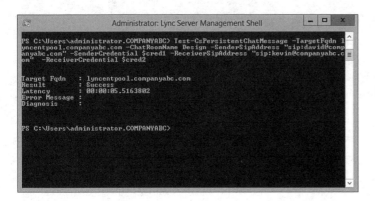

FIGURE 10.17   Persistent Chat synthetic transaction used for troubleshooting.

Best Practices

Following are some best practices from this chapter:

▶ If there is any question as to whether multiple Persistent Chat servers will be needed, install the first server as a standalone instance. If the first Persistent Chat server is collocated with a Standard Edition Front End, no additional servers can be added to the pool.

▶ If ethical walls are required to prevent conflict of interest in the organization, configure Persistent Chat categories to meet these requirements, where the allowed members for each category are limited to specific groups of users.

▶ In smaller businesses or when no ethical walls are required, a single category can be used for all chat rooms. The allowed members of the category would include all users, and then membership lists can be used to grant or restrict access to the chat rooms.

▶ If a central support team such as the help desk will be used to create new rooms, assign the members of this team as creators on each category using a distribution group or an organizational unit containing all the members. This will make it easy to maintain the appropriate permissions when members of the team change.

▶ The category names are not visible to the end users; only the chat room names are. With that in mind, choose category names that are meaningful to the administrators, whereas the chat room names need to be meaningful to the users. A description can also be assigned to each chat room for further clarity if needed.

▶ Assign appropriate add-ins to chat rooms to enhance the overall Persistent Chat experience for end users. If the organization maintains websites that provide useful business data to specific teams, these can be assigned as approved add-ins by the administrator, which will allow chat room creators and managers to associate these with chat rooms under their control.

▶ If there is a requirement for an "announcement style" chat room that is read-only for the majority of users, create a chat room with auditorium as the type. Assign one or more users as presenters for the room so that these users can post announcements and other information to be read by the members.

Summary

With Persistent Chat now being included in the Lync topology for the first time, this technology will likely get much more exposure with Lync 2013 than ever before. No doubt many organizations will find that having the combination of ongoing, persistent communication alongside IM and presence will provide valuable benefits to the various teams of users that share knowledge on specific topics. With the added architectural changes that Microsoft has introduced with this version, Lync administrators will also find Persistent Chat to be relatively easy to deploy and manage, and Lync users will appreciate the capability to use a single client to access all features of Lync 2013, including Persistent Chat.

PART III

External Dependencies

IN THIS PART

Dependent Services and SQL

Lync Server 2013, like many other Microsoft applications, depends on a number of infrastructure services to function properly. Lync Server integrates with Active Directory to store configuration information on user objects, and DNS is required for name resolution services. Server certificates are used to secure connections between the various components of Lync. There are also a number of network dependencies that have an impact on both the performance and the functionality of Lync. A new requirement for Lync Server 2013 is the Office Web Apps Server. Finally, SQL Server is used as the database platform to store Lync information. This chapter provides details on these dependencies and helps Lync Server administrators understand and configure these items to ensure a healthy Lync environment.

Active Directory

Like many other Microsoft applications, Lync Server has a high level of dependency on Active Directory (AD). Lync Server must be installed in an Active Directory environment, and there are certain attributes that must be available in the AD schema for Lync to install. For these reasons, Microsoft includes a set of wizards with the Lync media that assist administrators with preparing Active Directory to support Lync Server. Using these AD preparation wizards in the appropriate order makes this aspect of the Lync installation quite simple. However, since the health of the Lync environment is highly dependent on the health of Active Directory, it makes sense for administrators to perform a basic health check of AD prior to using the Lync AD preparation wizards.

Active Directory requirements for Lync include the following:

▶ All domain controllers in the forest must run Windows Server 2003 or higher.

▶ The domain functional level for domains where Lync Server is deployed must be Windows Server 2003 native or higher (not Windows Server 2003 mixed).

▶ The forest functional level for the forest must be Windows Server 2003 native or higher (not Windows Server 2003 mixed).

Schema Extensions

To provide the necessary attributes used by Lync Server, it is necessary to extend the AD schema. This process is typically easiest to run on a system that is planned as a Lync Front End Server, and must be run by a user that is currently a member of the Schema Admins group. If an installer user account is temporarily added to the Schema Admins group in preparation for installing Lync Server, it will be necessary to log off of the system and then log back on to reflect the group membership change. Before extending the schema, the following components must first be installed on the system:

▶ Remote Server Administration Tools, AD DS and AD LDS tools only (available as integrated Windows Features)

▶ Microsoft Visual C++ 11 x64 redistributable (automatically installed from the Lync media if not present when starting the Lync installation)

From the Lync Server installation media, follow these steps:

1. Launch `Setup.exe`.

2. When the wizard displays, either browse to your intended installation location or accept the default location, and then click Install.

3. When prompted, read the software license terms; then click the I Accept the Terms in the License Agreement option if you agree to the terms, and click OK.

4. The core components of Lync Server 2013 are now installed, which includes the Lync Management Shell and the Lync Deployment Wizard. When the Deployment Wizard launches, it determines the current state of the environment and provides links to various installation options as needed. In the case of a fresh installation, the option to prepare Active Directory is presented. Click Prepare Active Directory, as shown in Figure 11.1.

NOTE

To avoid permissions issues, be sure that the domain controller hosting the Schema Master role is online, and that the installer account has Schema Admin credentials, before using the Deployment Wizard.

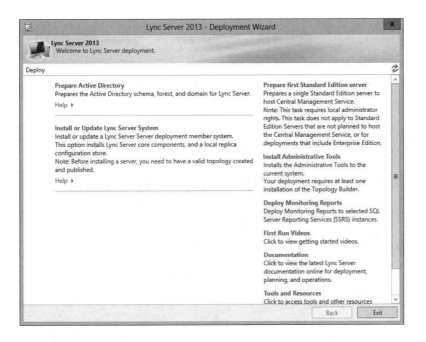

FIGURE 11.1   Running the Deployment Wizard.

5. If all the prerequisites are met, click Run on Step 1: Prepare Schema, which launches the wizard shown in Figure 11.2.

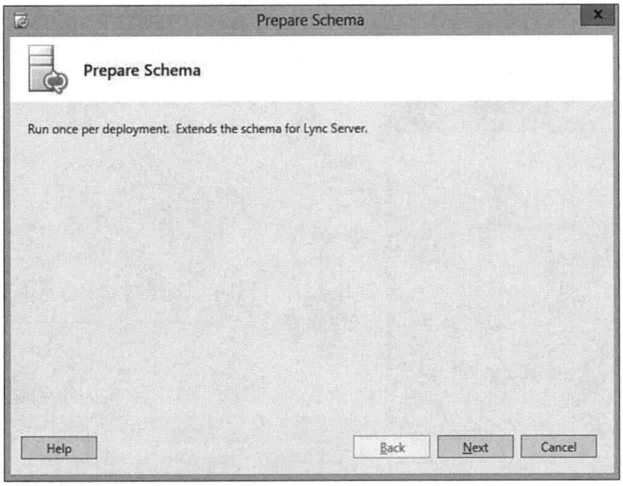

FIGURE 11.2   Preparing the schema.

6. Click Next. This action invokes the `Install-CSAdServerSchema` PowerShell command, which loads the AD schema files required for Lync Server 2013.

7. When the command has finished executing, click View Log to review the log file and ensure that no errors or warnings were generated during the schema extension process.

8. When finished, click Finish to complete the procedure and return to the Deployment Wizard.

TIP

Particularly in larger network environments, after the AD schema is extended, some time will be needed to allow the schema changes to replicate throughout the forest before moving on to the forest prep stage. To verify that replication has completed, the ADSI Edit utility can be used to verify the values associated with the `ms-RTC-SIP-SchemaVersion` object. If the value of the `rangeUpper` attribute is `1150` and the value of the `rangeLower` attribute is `3`, then the schema was successfully updated and replication has completed.

Forest Prep

After the schema has been updated, the Deployment Wizard enables the remaining AD preparation steps. The next step is to prepare the forest for the Lync Server installation, which creates global configuration settings and universal security groups required for the Lync deployment. The forest prep step must be performed by a user that is currently a member of the Enterprise Admins group. Continuing with the Deployment Wizard, the following steps are used to prepare the forest:

1. Click Run on Step 3: Prepare Current Forest. The Prepare Forest task launches, as shown in Figure 11.3. Click Next.

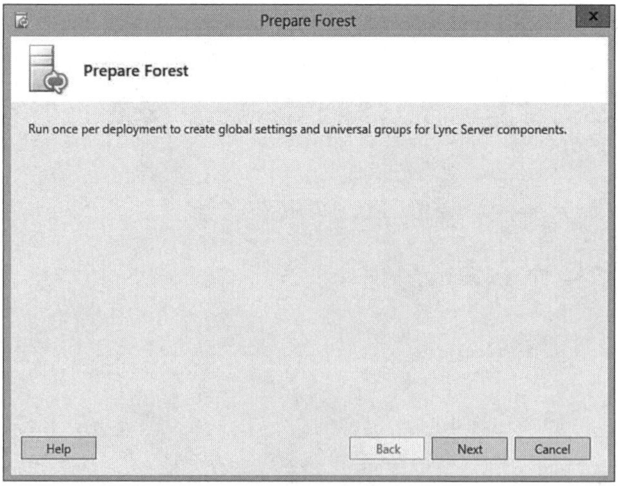

FIGURE 11.3   Preparing the forest.

2. At the Universal Group Location screen, the option is presented to create the Lync security groups in another domain in the forest. Either choose the Domain FQDN option and enter the fully qualified name of another domain, or keep the default setting to create the groups in the local domain. When finished, click Next. This action invokes the `Install-CSAdForest` PowerShell command, which creates the global configuration settings and universal security groups required by Lync.

TIP

By default, the Lync installer will create the Lync universal security groups in the domain where the wizard is being run. However, for some organizations it may make sense to select an alternate domain to host these groups. For example, some organizations use an empty placeholder domain as the AD forest root domain. In this situation, one of the child domains would likely be selected to host the Lync security groups to maintain organizational policy.

---

3. When the command has finished executing, click View Log to review the log file and ensure that no errors or warnings were generated during forest preparation.

4. When finished, click Finish to complete the procedure and return to the Deployment Wizard.

5. Verify that the changes introduced during Forest Prep have replicated throughout the AD forest before continuing with the next step.

TIP

Replication of the forest prep changes can be verified by simply using the Active Directory Users and Computers console to determine whether the Lync security groups have been created. In the Users container at the root of the domain chosen in step 2, 11 new groups named with the "CS" prefix should be present, for example, CSAdministrator.

Domain Prep

After the forest is prepared, the final AD preparation task is to prepare the domain for Lync Server. Unlike the previous two steps, domain prep must be performed on every domain that will host either Lync servers or Lync users. The domain prep step configures the permissions required for the universal security groups created in the previous step, and must be performed by a user that is currently a member of the Domain Admins group for the domain that the tool is run against. Continuing with the Deployment Wizard, the following steps are used to prepare the domain:

1. Click Run on Step 5: Prepare Current Domain.

2. Click Next. This action will invoke the `Install-CSAdDomain` PowerShell command, which creates the security group access control entries required by Lync.

3. When the command has finished executing, click View Log to review the log file and ensure that no errors or warnings were generated during domain preparation.

4. When finished, click Finish to complete the procedure and return to the Deployment Wizard.

5. Verify that the changes introduced during domain prep have replicated throughout the AD forest before installing the first Lync Server into the environment.

TIP

Replication of the domain prep changes can be verified using the Lync Server Management Shell, using the following command: `Get-CsAdDomain`. If the domain prep changes have replicated successfully, the cmdlet returns a value of `LC_DOMAIN_SETTINGS_STATE_READY`.

Lync Server 2013 Security Groups

After the Active Directory preparation steps previously described have been completed, a number of new AD security groups are introduced. The groups can be divided into four primary categories: service groups, administration groups, infrastructure groups, and role-based access control (RBAC) groups. The purpose of each security group is described next.

Lync Server 2013 service groups include the following:

▶ **RTCHSUniversalServices**—Includes service accounts that can be used to run the Front End services and grants Lync servers read/write access to Lync Server global settings and Active Directory user objects.

▶ **RTCComponentUniversalServices**—Includes service accounts that can be used to run Lync conferencing and web components services.

▶ **RTCProxyUniversalServices**—Includes service accounts that can be used to run a Lync proxy service.

▶ **RTCSBAUniversalServices**—Grants read access to the Lync deployment for survivable branch appliance installation.

Lync Server 2013 administration groups include the following:

▶ **RTCUniversalServerAdmins**—Allows members to manage server and pool settings.

▶ **RTCUniversalUserAdmins**—Allows members to manage user settings and move users from one server or pool to another.

▶ **RTCUniversalReadOnlyAdmins**—Allows members to read server, pool, and user settings.

▶ **RTCUniversalSBATechnicians**—Grants read access to the Lync deployment, as well as local administrative access to a survivable branch appliance during installation.

Lync Server 2013 infrastructure groups include the following:

▶ **RTCUniversalConfigReplicator**—Allows Lync servers to participate in replication of the Lync configuration.

▶ **RTCUniversalGlobalWriteGroup**—Grants write access to global settings for Lync Server.

▶ **RTCUniversalGlobalReadOnlyGroup**—Grants read-only access to global settings for Lync Server.

▶ **RTCUniversalUserReadOnlyGroup**—Grants read-only access to Lync Server user settings.

▶ **RTCUniversalServerReadOnlyGroup**—Grants read-only access to individual Lync Server settings.

Lync Server 2013 RBAC groups include the following:

▶ **CSAdministrator**—Grants full administrative access to the Lync Server 2013 environment.

▶ **CSArchivingAdministrator**—Grants access to the archiving-related Lync settings and policies.

▶ **CSHelpDesk**—Grants read-only access to Lync user properties and policies, along with access to specific troubleshooting functions.

▶ **CSLocationAdministrator**—Grants access to the E911 management functions of Lync.

▶ **CSPersistentChatAdministrator**—Grants access to the Lync Persistent Chat admin cmdlets.

▶ **CSResponseGroupAdministrator**—Grants access to configure the Response Group application within Lync.

▶ **CSResponseGroupManager**—Grants access to manage limited configuration of Lync Response Groups that have been assigned.

▶ **CSServerAdministrator**—Grants access to manage, monitor, and troubleshoot Lync servers and services.

▶ **CSUserAdministrator**—Grants access to enable, disable, and move Lync users, as well as assign existing policies.

▶ **CSViewOnlyAdministrator**—Grants read-only access to the Lync deployment for monitoring purposes.

▶ **CSVoiceAdministrator**—Grants access to create, configure, and manage voice-related Lync settings and policies.

Domain Name System

Lync Server heavily relies on domain name system (DNS) for name resolution and service lookups. Since Lync is always installed in an Active Directory environment, which also requires DNS, this service is typically already in production before the installation of Lync, and therefore simply needs to be configured to meet Lync requirements.

Lync Server utilizes DNS for several purposes. First, there is the requirement for hostname–to–IP address lookups, which is the typical use of DNS. However, Lync Server also uses specialized DNS records to identify particular services. Lync Server is also able to leverage DNS round robin functionality to provide load balancing for specific Lync functions. The DNS record types that are primarily used by Lync are the following:

▶ A, or host records

▶ SRV, or service location records

A very basic Lync deployment involving only the core services requires only a few DNS records. However, as additional Lync features and services are deployed in the environment, quite a few additional DNS records might be required. For this reason, the DNS requirements for each Lync feature will be detailed in the various chapters of this publication corresponding to that particular feature. For example, edge services, the Device Update Web service, and Lync Mobility all have specific DNS requirements. In this section, the DNS records required to allow basic Lync functionality are covered.

Lync Server requires registration of the hostname for each Lync server as an internal A record. For Standard Edition, a DNS A record that resolves the fully qualified name of the pool to the IP address of the Front End server is also needed. For Enterprise Edition Front End pools involving a hardware load balancer, a DNS A record that resolves the fully qualified name of the pool to virtual IP address of the load balancer is needed.

DNS Load Balancing

Lync Server 2013 provides the option to employ DNS load balancing in combination with hardware load balancing to split the incoming Lync server traffic across the two load-balancing mechanisms for an Enterprise pool. With this configuration, the HTTP traffic is load balanced using a hardware load balancer, whereas the SIP and media traffic is load balanced using DNS. To enable this functionality, a very specific DNS configuration is required. First, two DNS A records are used to resolve the fully qualified name of the pool to the IP address of each of the Front End servers. An additional DNS A record is then used to resolve the fully qualified name of the pool web components service to the virtual IP address of the load balancer. The following is a sample DNS configuration that leverages both DNS load balancing and hardware load balancing for an Enterprise pool:

```
EntFE1.companyabc.com    A   10.1.1.2   Standard host record
EntFE2.companyabc.com    A   10.1.1.3   Standard host record
LyncPool.companyabc.com  A   10.1.1.2   DNS load balancing for SIP and media traffic
LyncPool.companyabc.com  A   10.1.1.3   DNS load balancing for SIP and media traffic
LyncWeb.companyabc.com   A   10.1.1.4   Hardware load balancing for HTTP traffic
```

Automatic Client Sign-in

Although the sample DNS configurations just shown can be used to meet the minimum requirements for Lync, many organizations rely on the Lync client's capability to automatically find the Lync pool and sign in the user, an optional but very useful feature. To provide automatic client sign-in, an SRV record is required for `_sipinternaltls._tcp.<domain>` over port 5061 that maps to the fully qualified name of the pool. For example, Figure 11.4 shows the configuration of the SRV record that would be added to the sample DNS configuration shown previously to provide automatic client sign-in for the `companyabc.com` Lync deployment.

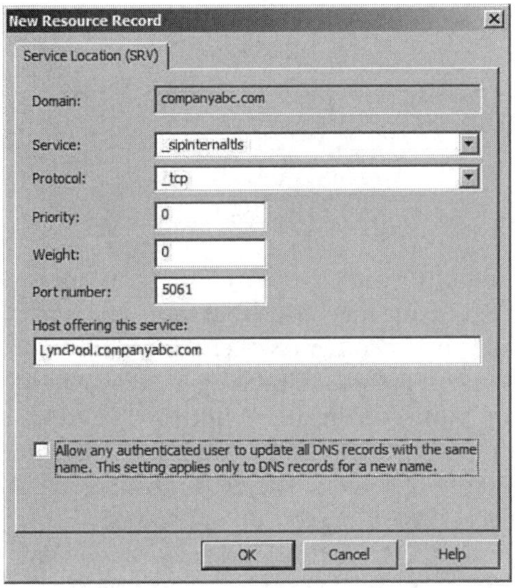

FIGURE 11.4   SRV record used for automatic client sign-in.

Note that SRV records hold information that is not used with other types of DNS records, such as priority, weight, and port number. In addition to specifying the location of the service, this information provides a means to influence how the incoming traffic load will be shared or directed.

TIP

For Lync deployments that use several SIP domains, one SRV record is required for each domain to support automatic client sign-in.

Simple URLs

An additional Lync feature that affects the DNS configuration is simple URLs. Simple URLs are used to provide access to common Lync services using names that are easy to remember. Lync Server 2013 provides the capability to configure simple URLs for three services: web conferencing, dial-in conferencing, and administrative access to the Lync Server Control Panel. Several options are available for the configuration of simple URLs, and each requires the configuration of at least one DNS A record for the simple URL to function. For the majority of Lync deployments, the option to use a separate base URL for each simple URL is used, because this configuration results in a naming convention that is typically the easiest for users to remember. For this configuration, each of the simple URLs requires one DNS A record that resolves the URL to either the Front End server (for Standard Edition) or the virtual IP address of the hardware load balancer (for Enterprise Edition). The following is an example of a DNS configuration that might be used to add simple URLs for the `companyabc.com` Lync deployment:

```
meet.companyabc.com       A  10.1.1.4   Simple URL for web conferencing
dialin.companyabc.com     A  10.1.1.4   Simple URL for dial-in access to meetings
lyncadmin.companyabc.com  A  10.1.1.4   Simple URL for access to the Lync Server
                                        Control Panel
```

Server Certificates

In recent years, Microsoft has adopted a "secure out of the box" approach for both operating system and application releases. Lync Server 2013 continues with that same approach, requiring SSL certificates to protect communications between Lync servers, as well as between client and server. In addition, a second type of certificate is being introduced with Lync Server 2013, the Open Authentication (OAuth) certificate. While the SSL certificates will continue to be used to encrypt communications, the OAuth certificates will be used to establish trust across the Office 2013 family of servers. The OAuth certificates allow the exchange of security tokens that grant access to resources for a period of time. Server-to-server authentication and authorization using OAuth is supported between Lync 2013 servers, as well as among Lync 2013, Exchange 2013, and SharePoint 2013 servers for integration scenarios.

The certificates applied to Lync Server systems can be either public certificates issued by a third party certificate authority (CA), or internal certificates issued using a self-managed public key infrastructure (PKI). The most ideal scenario for most organizations is to use a mix of both public and internal certificates for the Lync deployment, with third-party certificates being used for services that are public-facing (such as Edge services), and internal certificates being used for services that are strictly internal (such as communication between Lync Front End Servers). Although this hybrid approach serves to meet the certificate requirements of Lync and reduce the cost of the certificates, it does require that an internal PKI be deployed before the installation of the Lync environment. Since an internal PKI deployment is a project unto itself, organizations that do not already manage an internal PKI deployment will likely need to procure server certificates from a third-party CA for Lync services. The one exception to this is the OAuth certificate, since this can be a self-signed certificate generated internally.

The topic of how to plan and manage an internal PKI goes well beyond the scope of this chapter. However, the specifics of what types of certificates are required for Lync are included here to allow for this aspect of a Lync deployment to be planned appropriately.

Lync Server Certificate Requirements

Following are the primary uses for certificates within Lync:

▶ Communication between Lync clients and Lync servers is encrypted using TLS.

▶ Authentication between Lync 2013 servers, as well as authentication among Lync 2013 servers, Exchange 2013 servers, and SharePoint 2013 servers, uses server-to-server OAuth certificates.

▶ Communications between Lync servers is encrypted using MTLS.

▶ Automatic DNS discovery of partners for federation uses certificates for authentication.

▶ Remote or external user access for any Lync functionality is encrypted, including IM, audio/video (A/V) sessions, application sharing, and conferencing.

▶ A mobile request using automatic discovery of Web Services is encrypted.

Following are the common requirements that apply to the SSL certificates issued for use with Lync Server:

▶ All server certificates must support server authorization (Server EKU).

▶ All server certificates must contain a CRL Distribution Point (CDP).

▶ Auto-enrollment is supported for internal Lync servers, but is not supported for Lync Edge Servers.

▶ Key lengths of 1024, 2048, and 4096 are supported.

▶ Supported hash algorithms include RSA (the default), ECDH_P256, ECDH_P384, and ECDH_P521.

▶ All certificates are standard web server certificates, and must include the private key.

Following are the requirements that apply to the OAuth certificates issued for use with Lync Server:

▶ The certificate issued for OAuth must be the same across all Lync servers in the environment, and therefore the private key must be exportable for the certificate.

▶ A Web Server certificate that has the name of the SIP domain as subject can be used as an OAuth certificate.

▶ Generally, any Lync Server SSL certificate can also be used as an OAuth certificate, provided that all other requirements are met. However, if the default Lync Server certificate is used for both SSL and OAuth, it must be assigned twice, once for each certificate usage.

NOTE

Distribution of the OAuth certificate between Lync Server 2013 Front End Servers is handled automatically via Central Management Store replication.

Installing Lync Certificates

The number of certificates required for a Lync deployment and the configuration of those certificates vary greatly depending on the topology chosen and the Lync features that are installed. The internal Lync server roles that require certificates include Front End Server, Mediation Server, Director, and Persistent Chat Server. For external user access, a combination of public and internal certificates is used on the Edge Server, and a public certificate is also required for the reverse HTTP proxy system.

Lync Server 2013 provides a wizard for requesting, installing, and assigning certificates. For example, the following procedure is used to create an offline SSL certificate request to be sent to a third-party CA for a Front End Server:

1. Log on to the Front End Server, and launch the Lync Server Deployment Wizard.

2. At the opening screen, click Install or Update Lync Server System.

3. The Deployment Wizard determines the current state of the environment and provides links to various installation options as needed. Assuming that the Local Configuration Store is installed and at least one Lync Server component has been installed, the link to run Step 3: Request, Install or Assign Certificates will be available. Click Run on Step 3 to begin the certificate request.

4. When the Certificate Wizard screen appears, expand the arrow to the left of Default Certificate to display the certificate usage options. As shown in Figure 11.5, by default the certificate requested will be used as the default Lync server certificate, and will also be used for both the internal and the external web services. If a separate certificate is planned for any of these, that usage can be deselected here. When finished, click Request.

5. The Certificate Request Wizard now launches. Click Next.

6. For a certificate request that will be sent to a third-party CA, choose Prepare the Request Now, but Send It Later (offline certificate request). If the request will be sent to an internal CA, it is possible to instead select Send the Request Immediately to an Online Certificate Authority.

7. If offline certificate request was chosen in the previous step, the Certificate Request File screen appears. Browse to a location where the certificate request file will be stored, such as a local subdirectory on the server, and enter a name for the certificate request file. After the location is selected, click Next.

8. By default, the wizard creates the certificate request using the WebServer (SSL) template. If a different certificate template is planned, select the option Use

Alternate Certificate Template for the Selected Certification Authority, and then enter the name of the template into the Certificate Template Name field. When finished, click Next.

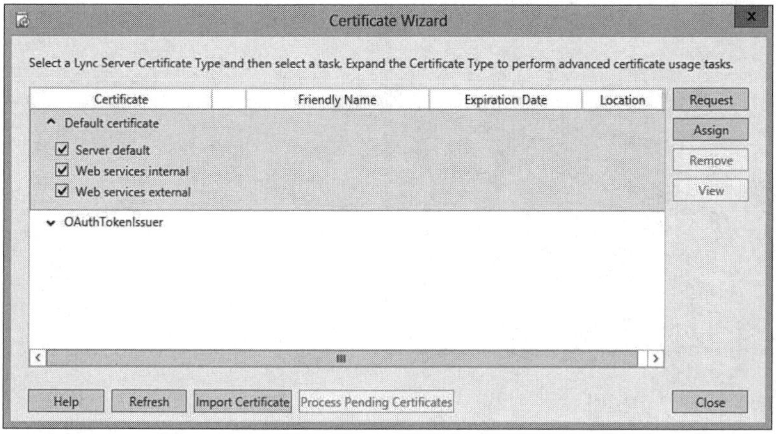

FIGURE 11.5   Lync certificate usages.

9. At the Name and Security Settings screen, enter a friendly name for the certificate, which makes it easier to identify later. Also, choose a bit length for the certificate. If the private key will need to be exported later, which is typically the case when a SAN cert is imported onto multiple computers, select the option for Mark the Certificate's Private Key as Exportable. Click Next.

10. At the Organization Information screen, enter the name of the organization and organizational unit into the corresponding fields, and then click Next.

11. At the Geographical Information screen, select the country from the drop-down menu, and then enter the information into the State/Province and City/Locality fields. Click Next.

TIP

With an external CA, typically the values for the organizational and geographical information have already been defined as naming constraints, in which case the information entered on these screens must match the values already defined with the certificate provider.

12. Review the names that are populated into the certificate as shown in Figure 11.6, and then click Next.

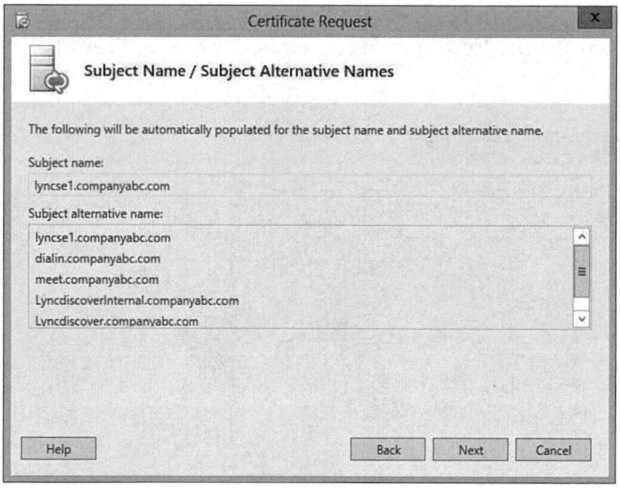

FIGURE 11.6   Certificate names.

TIP

Figure 11.6 shows that the wizard has automatically populated several subject alternative names that are required for specific Lync functions. These include the Simple URLs described in the "Domain Name System" section earlier in this chapter, as well as several SAN entries that are required for Lync Mobility (`LyncdiscoverInternal` and `Lyncdiscover`).

13. For each SIP domain, if automatic sign-in will be used without DNS SRV entries, if strict domain matching will be used, or if Lync Phone edition devices will be used, the check box shown in Figure 11.7 should be selected for that domain to provide an additional required SAN. When finished, click Next.

TIP

For each SIP domain selected on the previous screen, the wizard will add a subject alternative name of `sip.<domain>`, which is required for the scenarios that are mentioned. Using the example in Figure 11.7, a SAN of `sip.companyabc.com` will be added.

14. The opportunity to enter additional subject alternate names outside those automatically determined by the wizard is presented. Enter each additional SAN that will be used, and then click Next.

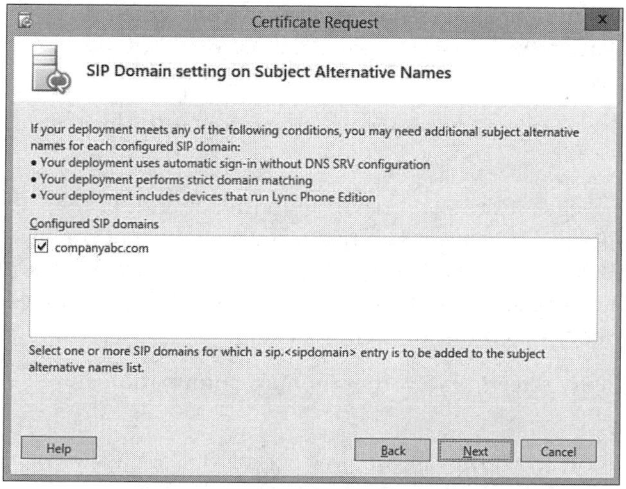

FIGURE 11.7   Configuring SANs per SIP domain.

TIP

The screen described in step 14 provides an opportunity for the Lync administrator to "future proof" a public certificate that will be purchased for use with Lync. For example, there may be Lync services that are planned for a future phase of the Lync deployment. Adding the names that will be used for those services now will both save time and prevent any additional certificate costs.

---

15. At the Certificate Request Summary screen, review the values for accuracy, and then click Next.

16. The commands required to generate the certificate request file are now executed. Click View Log to determine whether any errors occurred during the certificate request process. When finished, click Next.

17. At the Certificate Request File screen, the opportunity is presented to view the resulting certificate request text file. With most third-party certificate providers, it is typically necessary to copy and paste this text into the provider's web portal when requesting the certificate. If so, click View and use the resulting Notepad file to copy the text to the Windows clipboard. When finished, close the Notepad file and click Finish.

After the certificate has been issued by the vendor, the Lync Server Deployment Wizard is used to import the certificate and assign it, as described here:

1. Log on to the Front End Server, and launch the Lync Server Deployment Wizard.

2. At the opening screen, click Install or Update Lync Server System.

3. The Deployment Wizard determines the current state of the environment and provides links to various installation options as needed. Click Run on Step 3 to install and assign the certificate.

4. At the Certificate Wizard screen, click the Import Certificate button at the bottom of the screen.

5. At the Import Certificate screen, click Browse and navigate to the location of the certificate issued by the third-party CA. If there is a private key contained in the file (for example, if it was exported from another Lync server), select the Certificate File Contains Certificate's Private Key check box and enter the password that was applied to the export in the field provided. When finished, click Next.

6. At the Import Certificate Summary screen, review the summary information and click Next.

7. The commands required to import the certificate are now executed. Click View Log to determine whether any errors occurred during the certificate import process. When finished, click Finish to return to the Certificate Wizard.

8. At the Certificate Wizard screen, click Assign.

9. At the Certificate Assignment screen, click Next.

10. The certificates that are available in the local certificate store of the server are now displayed, as shown in Figure 11.8. Select the certificate that will be assigned to Lync, and then click Next.

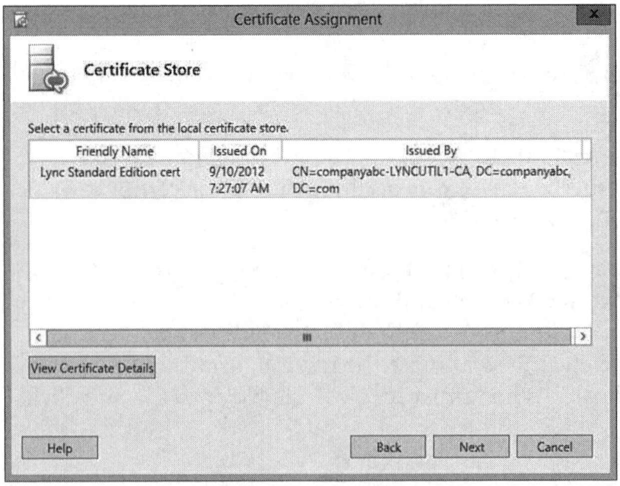

FIGURE 11.8   Assigning a certificate to Lync.

> **TIP**
>
> If there are several certificates in the local certificate store of the server, at first glance it might be difficult to differentiate between these in order to make the right selection. If so, click the View Certificate Details button at the bottom of the screen. Typically, the Friendly Name or the Subject Alternative Name fields will make it evident as to which certificate is intended for Lync.

11. At the Certificate Assignment Summary screen, review the summary information, and then click Next.

12. The commands required to assign the certificate are now executed. Click View Log to determine whether any errors occurred during the certificate assignment process. When finished, click Finish to return to the Certificate Wizard.

13. The default certificate is now assigned to the server, as shown in Figure 11.9. Click Close to exit the Certificate Wizard.

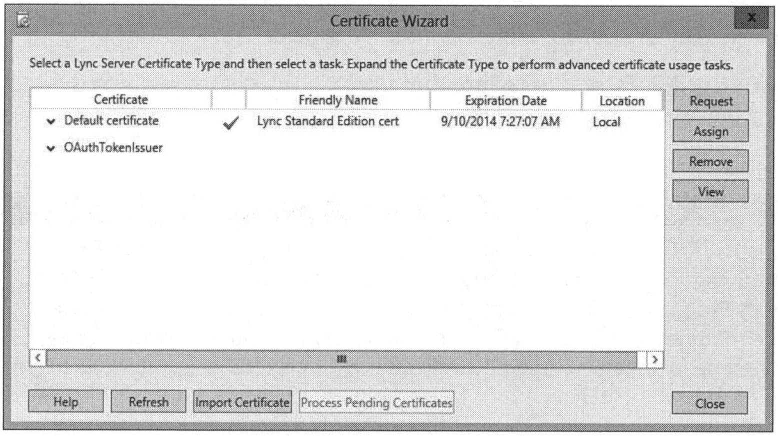

FIGURE 11.9   Viewing the assigned certificate.

Network Dependencies

Lync Server 2013, like any unified communications product, depends heavily on the network it is installed on to deliver needed functionality. Whereas some network dependencies are obvious, such as connectivity and sufficient bandwidth, other dependencies might not be so evident, such as DHCP requirements, network site definitions, and configuration of specific features on network switches.

Supporting Lync Phone Edition with DHCP

Whereas Lync software clients inherit network connectivity from the host they are installed on, networking for specialized devices such as VoIP desk phones is typically managed centrally. Traditionally, these devices are configured via dynamic host configuration protocol (DHCP), not only for IP addressing assignments but also as a centralized method of informing the devices that updated firmware is available. To allow centralized management of Lync Phone Edition devices, specific DHCP requirements must be met.

Standard enterprise DHCP services, such as the DHCP server role integrated with Windows Server operating systems, can be used to meet Lync DHCP requirements. However, there are unique DHCP options that are used to support Lync Phone Edition devices, including the following:

▶ **Option 43**—A specialized DHCP option that consists of a series of sub-options. With Lync Server, these sub-options are used to specify the Lync Pool Certificate Provisioning Service URL in the form of https://WebPoolDFQDN:443/CertProv/CertProvisioningService.svc.

▶ **Option 120**—Specifies the list of SIP servers that can handle authentication requests for the device.

▶ **Option 55**—Supplies the values of DHCP options 43 and 120 to the DHCP client.

▶ **Option 60**—Specifies the vendor for which option 43 provides sub-options.

▶ **Option 4**—Specifies an NTP server to ensure that time on the device remains in sync with other systems on the network.

> **NOTE**
>
> Additional DHCP options might also be required for Lync depending on the network. For example, the preferred method of configuring phone devices with a dedicated voice VLAN is Link Layer Discovery Protocol-Media Endpoint Discovery (LLDP-MED), but not all Ethernet switches support this feature. Where LLDP-MED is not supported, additional DHCP vendor classes and associated options can instead be configured to supply the voice VLAN ID to the device.

Although several of the DHCP options previously listed are very straightforward for anyone familiar with DHCP, option 43 in particular can be challenging to configure correctly, due to the fact that numerous sub-options are used, each involving hex-encoded binary strings. Thankfully, Microsoft provides the DHCPUtil utility along with an associated script, which together can be used to generate and then apply the correct values for options 43 and 120 to a Microsoft DHCP server. For environments where a non-Microsoft DHCP server is used, these values will need to be configured manually in order to support Lync Phone Edition devices.

> **NOTE**
>
> Each Lync Front End Server also includes a built-in DHCP component, which is disabled by default. The built-in Lync DHCP service cannot provide IP address leases, and is simply used to provide the values for DHCP options 43 and 120 for very small Lync environments where IP addressing is handled manually.

The following procedure is used to configure DHCP options 43 and 120 using DHCPUtil:

1. Copy the `DHCPUtil.exe` and `DHCPConfigScript.bat` files from the following location on a Lync Front End Server to a local subdirectory on the DHCP server: `C:\Program Files\Common Files\Microsoft Lync Server 2013`.

2. If it is not already installed, install the Microsoft Visual C++ Redistributable Package on the DHCP server as a prerequisite for running `DHCPUtil.exe` (located in the `Setup\amd64` directory on the Lync media with a filename of `vcredist_x64`).

3. On the DHCP server, open an elevated command prompt. Navigate to the subdirectory where the files were copied previously in step 1, and execute the following command, in which the fully qualified name of the Lync pool is used as `<PoolName>`: `DHCPUtil.exe -SipServer <PoolName> -RunConfigScript`. A series of netsh commands executes, configuring the appropriate values for DHCP options 43 and 120 within the local DHCP instance.

TIP

Only a 64-bit version of `DHCPUtil.exe` is supplied with Lync Server 2013, and this cannot be used to configure a 32-bit DHCP server. In this situation, the next best option is to run `DHCPUtil.exe` directly on the Lync Front End Server, and then use the output from the command to manually supply the values that will be used with the `DHCPConfigScript.bat` script on the DHCP server.

Segregation of Traffic

To ensure the best experience for users, it is highly recommended that administrators separate VoIP traffic from other network traffic by placing voice devices on a VLAN that is dedicated to voice functions. Also, users with USB-based devices should connect to a wired network rather than a wireless network whenever possible. Using a segregated VLAN for phone devices makes it much easier to leverage important network features such as Quality of Service (QoS) to ensure the best possible voice quality for end users. This configuration also serves to simplify monitoring, because endpoint devices are logically grouped at the network level.

Ethernet Switch Considerations

All Lync Phone Edition devices have two important features that have an impact on the choice of Ethernet switch: LLDP-MED and PoE (Power over Ethernet). To leverage these features, the connected Ethernet switch ports must support these same features. Specifically, LLDP-MED requires support for the IEEE802.1AB and ANSI/TIA-1057 standards. To utilize PoE, the switch ports must support one of two PoE standards, either 802.3AF or 802.3at.

The configuration of LLDP-MED is specific to the Ethernet switch model. Often, this feature needs to be enabled globally within the switch, and typically the voice VLAN must be specified for use with LLDP-MED within the switch configuration.

Defining Network Sites

Lync Server sites are used to organize resources according to geography and bandwidth. IP subnets are then associated with the sites so that the Lync Servers can identify the locations where endpoints are located. A correctly configured Lync site topology allows Front End Servers to determine how call setup and routing should be handled; therefore, this is an important aspect of the Lync configuration. All subnets in a network should be defined and associated with a Lync site. Although this can be configured using the Lync Server Control Panel, in an enterprise network it could take a considerable amount of time to input all IP subnets into the configuration. For larger networks, this task is more easily handled using a simple comma-separated value (CSV) file and the Lync Management Shell. For example, a CSV file can be created including separate fields for network address, subnet mask bits, description, and Lync site ID, as shown here:

```
IPAddress, mask, description, NetworkSiteID
10.0.0.0, 24, "NA:SF subnet", SF
10.1.0.0, 24, "EMEA:Dublin subnet", Dublin
10.2.0.0, 24, "EMEA:London subnet", London
```

Using a sample CSV filename of subnet.csv, these values can then be easily imported into the Lync Server network configuration by using the Lync Management Shell to execute the following command:

```
import-csv subnet.csv | foreach {New-CSNCSSubnet $_.IPAddress -MaskBits
➥$_.mask -Description $_.description -NetworkSiteID $_.NetworkSiteID}
```

This command can then be scheduled to run regularly as a script, such that whenever new sites or subnets are added to the network, the CSV file is adjusted to reflect these and the script maintains the most current network topology.

> **NOTE**
>
> Although somewhat similar in purpose, Lync Server sites are not related to Active Directory sites. Both the Active Directory and the Lync site configurations allow resources to be grouped by geography and bandwidth such that related network traffic is routed appropriately; therefore, it is common to see a similar pattern of site definitions and associated subnets between these two technologies.

Office Web Apps Server

Although not a Lync Server role in itself, a new server product that is very much a dependency for conferencing in Lync Server 2013 is the Office Web Apps Server. The purpose of the Office Web Apps Server is to deliver browser-based versions of Microsoft Office applications. The service is designed to work with products that support Web Application Open Platform Interface protocol (WOPI). Lync Server 2013 is among the first Microsoft applications to leverage the Office Web Apps Server, along with SharePoint 2013 and Exchange

2013. A single Office Web Apps Server instance or farm can provide browser-based file viewing and editing of Office documents for all of these applications.

For Lync Server 2013 specifically, one Office Web Apps Server is required for any deployment in which conferencing is enabled, and is used to deliver enhanced PowerPoint presentations that are streamed to the Front End Server. This provides several advantages over previous versions of Lync for such conferencing scenarios. For example, higher-resolution displays are now available, and a wider range of mobile devices are supported.

> **NOTE**
>
> With previous versions of Lync, PowerPoint presentations could be viewed by using either the embedded PowerPoint Viewer or dynamic HTML and Silverlight, depending on the client used. These methods presented several limitations; for example, the embedded PowerPoint viewer is available only for Windows, and Silverlight is not supported with many popular mobile devices. The Office Web Apps Server overcomes these limitations, and also supports newer PowerPoint features, such as slide transitions and embedded video.

System Requirements

Office Web Apps Server must be installed on a separate system in the environment, because it cannot be collocated with any of the Lync Server roles. High-availability is also supported for Office Web Apps Server and can be implemented via the installation of multiple servers and use of a hardware or software load-balancing solution. Whether a single system or multiple systems are deployed, each installation is referred to as an Office Web Apps Server farm. The following requirements and guidelines apply for systems used to host Office Web Apps Server:

- ▶ Supported operating systems are Windows Server 2008 R2 SP1 and Windows Server 2012.

- ▶ Minimum hardware requirements are 4 x 64-bit cores, 8GB RAM, 80GB system hard drive.

- ▶ Server virtualization is supported.

- ▶ No other applications can be installed on the system, including any Lync roles, SQL, and Microsoft Office.

- ▶ For multiple server farms, any software or hardware load-balancing solution can be used.

A server certificate is also required in order to use Lync Server 2013 with Office Web Apps Server. The following requirements apply to the certificate that will be used:

- ▶ The certificate must be issued by a trusted CA (either internal or third-party).

- ▶ For single-server installations, the FQDN of the Office Web Apps Server must be included in the SAN (subject alternative name) field of the certificate.

▶ For load-balanced server farms, the certificate must be imported into the load balancer.

▶ The certificate must have an exportable private key.

▶ The Friendly name applied to the certificate must be unique within the Trusted Root Certificate Authorities store on the system running Office Web Apps Server, as this allows the cmdlet to determine which certificate is being targeted.

NOTE

Standard procedures can be used to request and install the certificate used for the Office Web Apps Server using the IIS Management Console, Certificate Authority Web Enrollment, or another method. However, the certificate binding should not be performed using the IIS Management Console. Rather, the certificate binding for Office Web Apps Server is performed using the same PowerShell command used to create the farm (`New-OfficeWebAppsFarm`), as detailed later.

Browser support for Office Web Apps Server includes Internet Explorer 6 through 9, as well as the latest public release versions of Google Chrome, Mozilla Firefox, and Apple Safari. There are also language packs available for English, Japanese, and Spanish, which must be installed on the Lync Front End Server as well as the Office Web Apps Server to be used.

The following are prerequisites for the installation of Office Web Apps Server:

▶ .NET Framework 4.5 (included with Windows Server 2012)

▶ Windows PowerShell 3.0 (included with Windows Server 2012)

▶ Windows Update KB2592525 (Windows Server 2008 R2 only)

▶ The Web Server (IIS) server role, along with the following role services:

   Static Content

   Default Document

   ASP.NET (Windows Server 2008 R2) or ASP.NET 4.5 (Windows Server 2012)

   .NET Extensibility (Windows Server 2008 R2) or .NET Extensibility 4.5 (Windows Server 2012)

   ISAPI Extensions

   ISAPI Filters

   Server Side Includes

Windows Authentication

Request Filtering

IIS Management Console

Static Content Compression (recommended)

Dynamic Content Compression (recommended)

▶ The Ink and Handwriting Services feature

Office Web Apps Server Installation

The Office Web Apps Server software can be downloaded directly from the Microsoft site. After the prerequisite software has been installed along with the server certificate, the following procedure is used to install and then configure the Office Web Apps Server:

1. From the Office Web App Server media, double-click on the `setup.exe` file.

2. Read the licensing terms. If you agree, select I Accept the Terms of This Agreement and then click Continue.

3. At the File Location screen, either keep the default location for file installation on the C: volume, or enter an alternative path if desired. When finished, click Install Now.

4. After the file installation is complete, click Close.

5. Open Windows PowerShell, and execute the following command to import the Office Web Apps application into PowerShell: `Import-Module OfficeWebApps`.

6. Execute the following PowerShell command to create a single-server Office Web Apps Server farm, with the fully qualified name of the Office Web Apps Server used as the `<servername>` value, and the friendly name of the certificate used as the `<CertFriendlyName>` value:

```
New-OfficeWebAppsFarm -InternalURL https://<servername> -CertificateName
"<CertFriendlyName>"
```

If the farm is successfully created, the attributes of the new farm are automatically displayed in PowerShell, as shown in Figure 11.10.

7. Verify that the Office Web Apps Server is installed and configured correctly by using a web browser to connect to the discovery URL at the following address, with the fully qualified name of the Office Web Apps Server used as the `<servername>` value: `https://<servername>/hosting/discovery`. If the installation is successful, a WOPI discovery XML file is displayed in the browser.

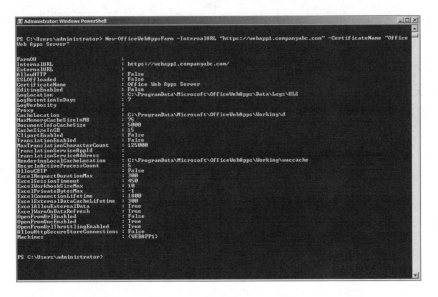

FIGURE 11.10   New Office Web Apps Server farm.

SQL Server Dependencies

Lync Server, like many other Microsoft applications, depends on SQL as a Back End storage platform. With Lync Server 2013, SQL databases are used for topology, configuration, and application information. One of the primary differences between the Standard and Enterprise Editions of Lync is the Back End database configuration. With Standard Edition, a local SQL Server Express Edition database is automatically installed by the deployment wizard as part of the Lync installation. Enterprise Edition, on the other hand, requires a dedicated Back End SQL system. This section covers installation of SQL as it pertains to a Lync Server Enterprise Edition deployment, and introduces Lync Server administrators to some basic SQL management tasks.

Lync Database Requirements

The first SQL database required for a new Lync installation is the Central Management Store (CMS), which is used to store the configuration data that is replicated to all the Lync servers in the environment. Beyond the CMS, the Front End Servers also require databases for persistent and dynamic user data, and address book information. Additional databases are also used depending on specific optional features that might be deployed, such as the Response Group and Call Park services. Collectively, these databases are referred to as the Lync Back End databases, and the two database platforms that can be used for these are SQL 2008 R2 and SQL 2012.

TIP

Either the Enterprise or Standard Editions of both SQL 2008 R2 and SQL 2012 can be used for the Lync Back End databases. Both editions also support SQL mirroring, which is the recommended high-availability solution for the Lync 2013 Back End databases.

Depending on the topology, it is also possible to collocate databases that are used by other Lync server roles with Lync Back End databases. For example, the Archiving and Monitoring Server roles both have their own databases, and both can be installed on the same SQL instance as the Lync Back End databases. The Persistent Chat databases can also be installed on the same SQL system with the Lync Back End databases. The decision as to whether to collocate these databases on the same SQL system with each other or with the Lync Back End databases is largely a matter of whether performance requirements can be met. With that in mind, these configuration decisions need to be considered on a case-by-case basis. All the database collocation possibilities mentioned previously are applicable to Enterprise Edition pools only. This is because the Standard Edition uses SQL Express, which does not meet the database requirements for any of the other Lync server roles.

NOTE

Microsoft supports installation of the Back End, Monitoring, Archiving, and Persistent Chat databases on the same SQL Server, and these can use either the same SQL instance or separate instances. However, only one of each type of database is supported on any given SQL Server. For many Lync deployments, only one of each type of database is actually required, however there are circumstances in which more than one of a certain database might be needed. For example, the Monitoring Server role can only be associated with a single Front End pool. In a Lync environment with multiple pools, this means that several Monitoring Server databases, and therefore several SQL Server systems, would be needed to provide monitoring for the entire environment.

Installing SQL Server for Lync

As noted earlier, for an Enterprise Edition pool, SQL Server 2008 R2 and SQL Server 2012 are the supported Back End database platforms. Since it is the most recent database release, this section provides step-by-step procedures for installing SQL 2012 in preparation for hosting the Lync Server 2013 Back End databases. However, installation of SQL 2008 R2 for Lync involves very similar steps. To install SQL Server 2012 in preparation for Lync Enterprise Edition, perform the following steps:

1. Double-click `setup.exe` on the SQL 2012 DVD.

2. If the .NET Framework is not already present, an installation prompt appears. Click OK to enable installation of the .NET Framework Core.

3. When the SQL Server Installation Center displays, as shown in Figure 11.11, click Installation in the left pane, and then click New SQL Server Stand-Alone Installation or Add Features to an Existing Installation.

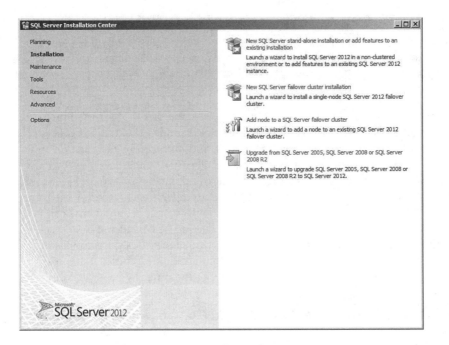

FIGURE 11.11   SQL Server Installation Center.

4. A first round of setup support rule checks now runs automatically, identifying any problems that might need to be corrected before the installation continues. If any failures occur, click the status for additional information and follow the recommended steps to remediate the problem. After all rule checks pass successfully, click OK.

5. At this point the setup files are installed, followed by a second set of setup support rule checks. If any failures occur, click the status for additional information and follow the recommended steps to remediate the problem. After all rule checks pass successfully, click Next.

6. At the Product Key screen, enter your product key and click Next.

7. Read the licensing terms. If you agree, select I Accept the License Terms and then click Next.

8. When the Setup Role screen appears, choose SQL Server Feature Installation and click Next.

9. The Feature Selection screen now appears, as shown in Figure 11.12. For a Lync Enterprise Edition installation, Database Engine Services is the only feature that is required. However, Management Tools - Basic is recommended for maintenance and troubleshooting purposes, and SQL Server Replication should be installed if SQL mirroring will be used for high-availability. Other features can be installed if desired.

After selecting the features to be installed, either keep the default installation paths for SQL shared features or enter an alternative path for these files, and click Next.

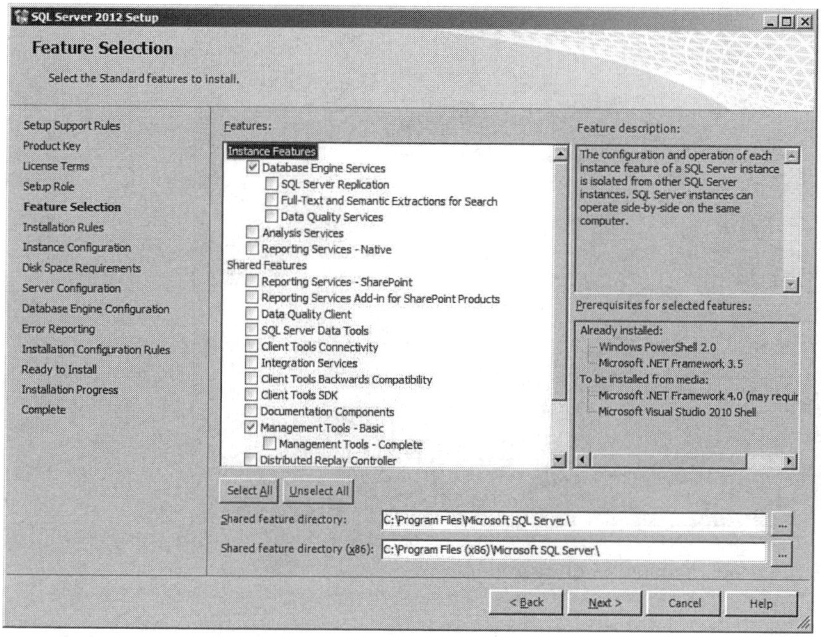

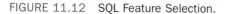

FIGURE 11.12   SQL Feature Selection.

10. Installation rules are now checked to identify any problems that block installation. If any failures occur, click the status for additional information and follow the recommended steps to remediate the problem. After all rule checks pass successfully, click Next.

11. At the Instance Configuration screen, select the option for Default Instance, and keep the default settings for Instance ID and Instance root directory. Click Next.

12. At the Disk Space Requirements screen, review the disk space usage summary and click Next.

13. The Server Configuration screen now appears, as shown in Figure 11.13. For Lync, the default configuration of using built-in service accounts will suffice; however, dedicated domain-based accounts can be chosen if these have been configured. If dedicated accounts will be used, enter the account names and passwords for each service. Leave the startup types at their default values, and click Next.

14. At the Database Engine Configuration screen, select the Authentication Mode for the server, either the default setting of Windows Authentication Mode or Mixed Mode, which allows both SQL and Windows accounts to be used. If Mixed Mode is selected, enter the initial password for the SQL system administrator (sa) account.

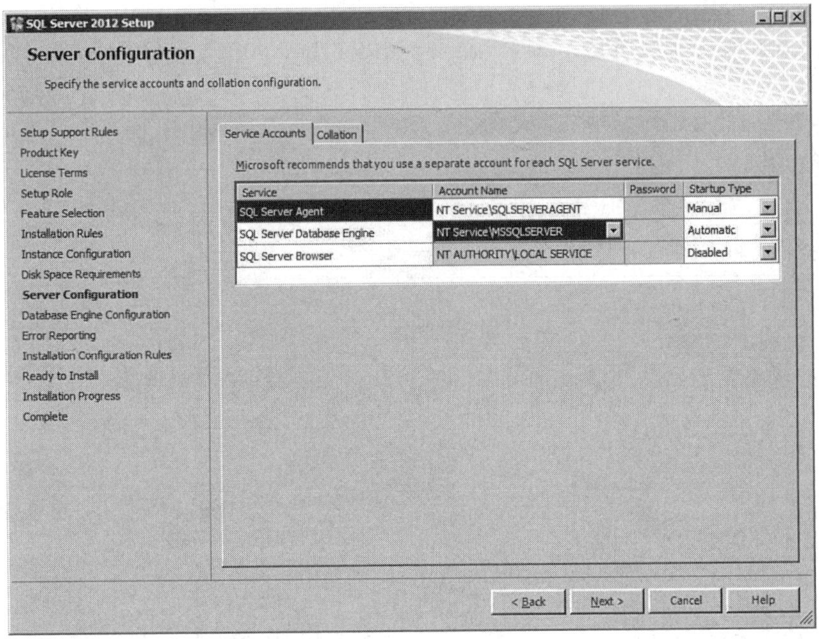

FIGURE 11.13   SQL service accounts configuration.

TIP

Windows authentication is generally considered to be the more secure authentication method for SQL. However, mixed mode does provide an additional method of connecting to SQL in the event that there are problems communicating with Active Directory, which can be useful for troubleshooting purposes. The decision of which authentication mode to use should therefore be made based on the security policy of the organization.

15. Still on the Database Engine Configuration screen, at the bottom of the screen click Add, and then use the object picker to select the administrative groups and users that will be granted unrestricted access to the database engine. For many organizations, the built-in Administrators group on the local server will be added here, as shown in Figure 11.14. click Next.

16. Still on the Database Engine Configuration screen, click the Data Directories tab to view the default locations for the data root directory, user database directory, temp database directory, backup directory, and the user and temp database log file directories. Either keep the default locations on the C: volume for each of these, or, if dedicated volumes have been created in advance, edit the locations to reflect these alternative locations. When finished, click Next.

17. At the Error Reporting screen, select whether Windows and SQL Server Error Reports will be sent to Microsoft, and then click Next.

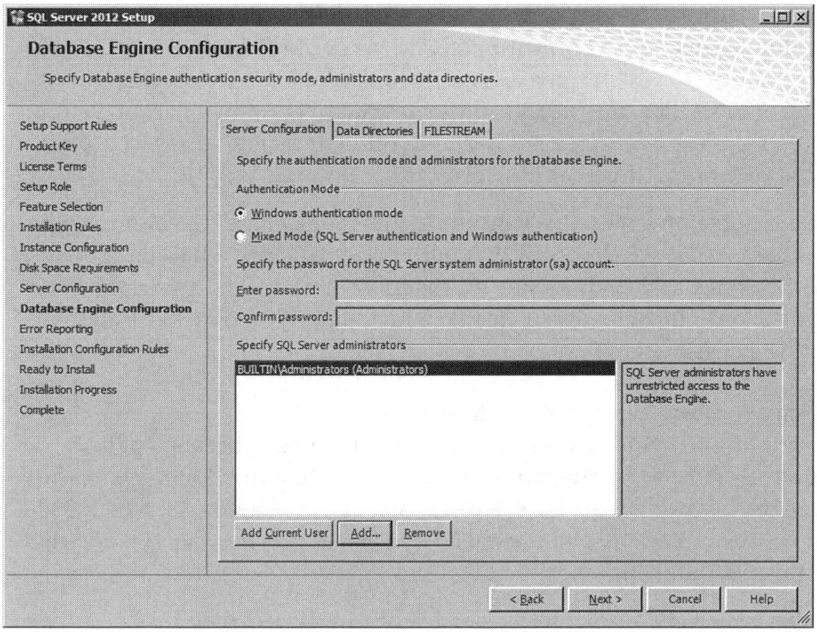

FIGURE 11.14   SQL authentication and administrator accounts configuration.

18. Installation configuration rules are now checked to identify any problems that block installation. If any failures occur, click the status for additional information and follow the recommended steps to remediate the problem. After all rule checks have passed successfully, click Next.

19. At the Ready to Install screen, review the configuration summary to verify that the correct selections have been made. When finished, click Install to proceed with the installation.

20. When the installation is completed, click Close.

TIP

After the SQL installation is complete, use Windows Update to search for SQL-related updates.

SQL Backup Procedures

The new high-availability features of Lync Server 2013 present new considerations for the backup of Lync Server data as well. For example, the Front End Pool Pairing feature includes the Lync Server Backup Service, which synchronizes the Lync Back End databases between two Front End pools, including the Central Management Store. For this reason, with some Lync Server 2013 topologies individual backups of SQL databases can be diminished in importance in comparison with previous versions of the product. However, there are still circumstances in which it makes sense to perform a manual backup of the Lync SQL databases. For example, it is always recommended to perform a backup before performing major configuration changes. With that in mind, it makes sense to be familiar with the options for performing this type of backup.

There are actually a number of ways to back up the Lync SQL databases, including native Windows Server backup, SQL-based backups that output the data into a flat file, and third-party backup solutions that support SQL. In the following sections, two methods of backing up the Lync Back End databases are detailed, including Windows Server native backup and SQL 2012 native backup.

Backing Up SQL Using Windows Server Native Backup

Windows Server 2008 R2 and Windows Server 2012 contain a native backup application called Windows Server Backup. The sample backup procedure that follows is based on Windows Server 2012; however, the steps are very similar for Windows Server 2008 R2. Because Windows Server Backup is not installed by default, it is necessary to add this feature by performing the following steps:

1. From the Server Manager console, select Local Server in the left pane.

2. From the Manage drop-down menu, click Add Roles and Features.

3. At the Select Installation Type screen, keep the default option of Role-Based or Feature-Based Installation, and click Next.

4. At the Select destination server screen, keep the default option of Select a Server from the Server Pool, and verify that the Lync database server is selected in the Server Pool list at the bottom of the screen. Click Next.

5. At the Select Server Roles screen, click Next.

6. At the Select Features screen, scroll down to the bottom of the list of features and select Windows Server Backup, as shown in Figure 11.15. Click Next.

7. At the Confirm Installation Selections screen, click Install.

8. When the installation has completed, click Close.

Now that the Windows Server Backup feature is installed, it can be used to back up SQL using the following procedure:

1. From the Server Manager console, select Local Server in the left pane.

2. From the Tools drop-down menu, click Windows Server Backup.

3. In the Action pane at the far right, click Backup Once.

4. In the Backup Options Wizard, either select Scheduled Backup Options to use previously configured backup settings, or select Different Options to make a backup with new options. Click Next.

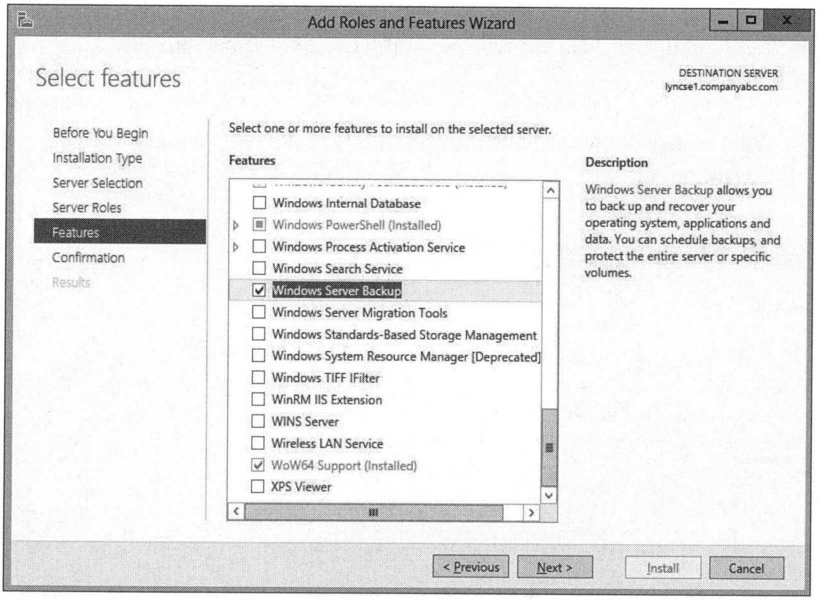

FIGURE 11.15   Adding the Windows Server Backup feature.

> **NOTE**
>
> If this is the first time that Windows Server Backup is being used, the Scheduled Backup Options selection will not be available.

---

5. At the Select Backup Configuration screen, choose either Full Server or Custom Backup. If Custom Backup is selected, be sure that all volumes containing SQL program files and data are included in the backup item selections. For Lync Server SQL backup purposes, Full Server backup is typically the best choice. After the selection is made, click Next.

6. At the Specify Destination Type screen, select either Local Drives to store the backup file locally, or Remote Shared Folder to store the backup file on the network. Click Next.

> **NOTE**
>
> Windows Server Backup will only allow backups to be targeted to drive volumes that are not selected as part of the backup job. Therefore, unless an external disk is attached to the system that can be used as a target, the Remote Shared Folder option is typically the best choice for destination type.

---

7. Depending on the selection made on the preceding screen, either the Select Backup Destination screen or the Specify Remote Folder screen is presented. For a local

backup destination, choose an available drive volume from the drop-down menu and select whether backup verification will be enabled after the backup file is written. For a remote folder, specify the remote location using the UNC path format, as shown in Figure 11.16; then in the Access Control section select whether access to the backup file will require credentials. When finished, click Next, which will validate the backup destination.

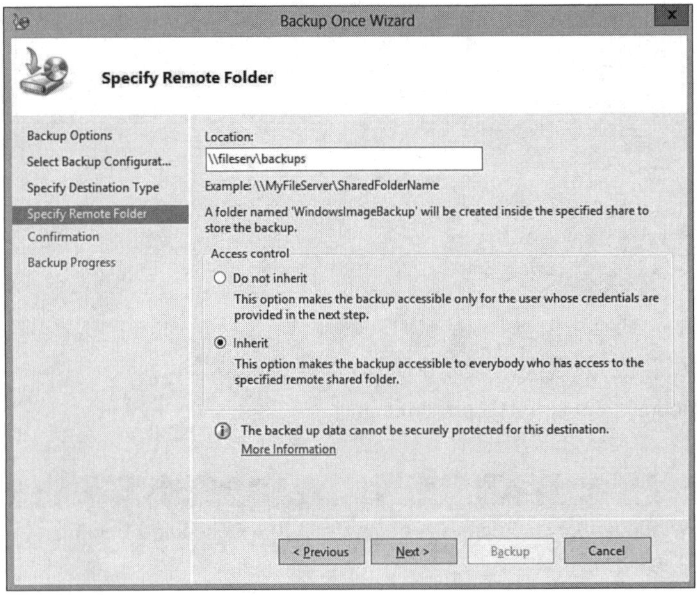

FIGURE 11.16   Remote folder backup settings.

8. After the backup destination is validated, review the backup job settings listed on the Confirmation screen, and then click Backup to begin the backup job.

9. After the backup job completes, click Close.

Backing Up SQL Using SQL Server Management Studio

Another way to back up SQL is by using the native backup function of SQL to create a flat file backup, which can then become the target for a separate backup application if necessary. This method is especially useful if an environment already has a centralized backup infrastructure that doesn't support SQL natively. The sample backup procedure that follows is based on SQL Server 2012; however, the steps are very similar for SQL Server 2008 R2.

To back up SQL through the SQL Server Management Studio, perform the following steps:

1. Log on to the server where Lync Back End databases are installed using an account with SQL administrative rights, and open SQL Server Management Studio.

2. At the Connect to Server prompt, keep the default options of connecting to the local server with Windows Authentication, and click Connect.

3. Expand Databases in the left pane.

4. Right-click on the database you want to back up, select Tasks, and click Back Up.

5. At the Back Up Database screen, the first set of options for the backup job appears, as shown in Figure 11.17. In the Source section, select a backup type of either Full or Differential, and select the Copy-Only Backup option if desired. In the Backup Set section, either keep the default name for the backup set or enter an alternative name, along with a description if desired. Also, you can choose a backup set expiration date if necessary. In the Destination section, either keep the default backup destination, which is the standard SQL Backup directory on the local system, or click Add and specify an alternative destination.

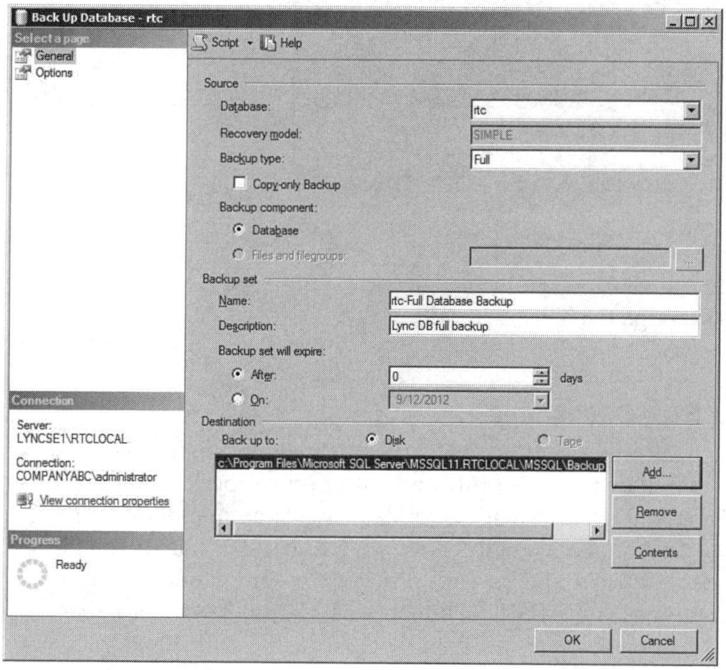

FIGURE 11.17   SQL backup options.

6. Click Options in the left pane to view a second set of options for the backup job, as shown in Figure 11.18. In the Overwrite Media section, several media set options are available, which will determine whether the backup data will append to or overwrite an existing backup set, or create a new media set. In the Reliability section, options for backup verification, checksums, and error handling are available. In the Compression section, one of several compression options can be selected. After making the desired selections, click OK to start the backup job.

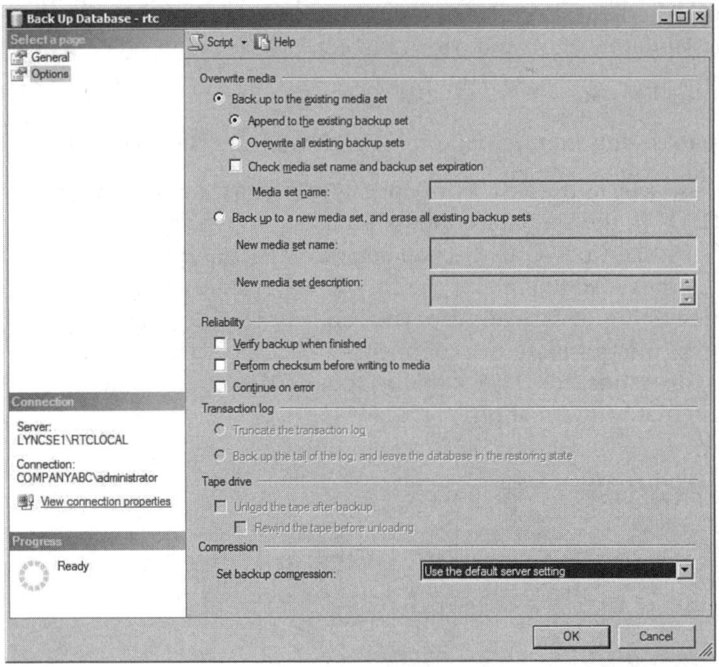

FIGURE 11.18   Additional SQL backup options.

7. When the backup has completed, click OK.

Maintaining the Lync SQL Databases

An important aspect of the health of any Lync deployment is maintaining the Lync SQL databases. To keep Lync Server operating smoothly and with optimal performance, regular maintenance should be performed on each SQL Server database. Such maintenance tasks include rebuilding indexes, checking database integrity, updating index statistics, and performing internal consistency checks and backups. Database maintenance tasks can be performed either by executing Transact-SQL commands or by running the Database Maintenance Wizard.

This section provides information and recommendations for maintaining the databases that store Lync Server data and configurations. Also, details are provided on how to automate and schedule the major maintenance tasks by creating database maintenance plans through SQL Server Database Maintenance Wizard.

Checking and Repairing Database Integrity

DBCC CHECKDB is a Transact-SQL command that is frequently used for checking the logical and physical integrity of databases. Essentially, DBCC CHECKDB is a superset command that actually runs three checks (CHECKALLOC, CHECKTABLE, and CHECKCATALOG) by issuing a single command.

The following are some recommendations for using DBCC CHECKDB to check and repair SQL database integrity:

▶ Always ensure that recent backups are on hand before running the command.

▶ Generally it is better to run the DBCC CHECKDB superset command than to execute the individual operations, because this will serve to identify the majority of the errors and is generally safe to run in a production environment.

▶ After DBCC CHECKDB has been run, the command can be run again with the REPAIR argument to repair reported errors. However, consideration should also be given to restoring the database from backup instead, because the REPAIR options should be considered a last resort.

▶ DBCC CHECKDB can require a considerable amount of time to run against large databases, and it performs schema locks that prevent metadata changes. Therefore, it is highly recommended to run the command during nonproduction hours.

▶ For large databases, the command can be run with the PHYSICAL_ONLY option, which will limit checking to the integrity of the physical structure of the page and record headers, along with the allocation consistency of the database. For these larger databases, it is therefore recommended to run the command with the PHYSICAL_ONLY option on a more frequent basis, and perform a full run of DBCC CHECKDB only on a periodic basis.

Monitoring and Reducing Fragmentation

Although indexes can speed up the execution of queries, there is also some overhead associated with them. Indexes consume extra disk space and require some time to be updated whenever any data is updated, deleted, or inserted in a table. When indexes are first built, little or no fragmentation is present. Over time, as data is inserted, updated, and deleted, fragmentation levels on the underlying indexes can begin to increase.

When a data page is completely full and further data must be added to it, a page split occurs. To make room for the new data, SQL Server creates another data page somewhere else in the database (not necessarily in a contiguous location) and moves some of the data from the full page to the newly created one.

The effect of this is that the blocks of data are logically linear but physically fragmented. Therefore, when searching for data, the database engine is forced to jump from one page to somewhere else in the database looking for the next page it needs, instead of just sequentially moving to the next physical page. The end result is performance degradation and inefficient space utilization.

The fragmentation level of an index is the percentage of blocks that are logically linear and physically nonlinear. In SQL Server versions starting with SQL Server 2005, the sys.dm_db_index_physical_stats transact-SQL command can be used to monitor this, with the avg_fragmentation_in_percent column showing the fragmentation level. The value for avg_fragmentation_in_percent should be as close to zero as possible for maximum performance. However, up to 10% might be acceptable without noticeable degradation.

Shrinking Data Files

In SQL Server 2005 and above, free space can be reclaimed from the end of data files to remove unused pages and recover disk space. However, shrinking data files is not recommended unless the database has lost at least half of its data. This typically occurs after an activity has been performed that creates whitespace in the database, such as moving a large amount of data from one database to another, or deleting a large amount of data. Shrinking Lync Server databases is generally not recommended, since there are typically not enough deletions to cause a significant amount of free space.

Creating SQL Server Maintenance Plans

Maintaining the Lync Server Back End databases is important to the overall health and performance of a Lync deployment. Yet this is an aspect that frequently gets overlooked, primarily because Lync administrators are kept busy caring for other aspects of the Lync environment.

Fortunately, Microsoft has provided maintenance plans as a way to automate the tasks required to maintain SQL database health. A maintenance plan performs a comprehensive set of SQL Server jobs that run at scheduled intervals. For example, a maintenance plan can include tasks that ensure that databases are performing optimally, are regularly backed up, and are checked for anomalies.

> **TIP**
>
> SQL maintenance plans should be scheduled to run during off-peak hours to minimize the performance impact.

The example SQL Server maintenance plan configuration below is based on SQL Server 2012, however the steps are very similar for SQL Server 2008 R2. The following steps are used to configure a SQL Server database maintenance plan:

1. Log on to the server where Lync Back End databases are installed using an account with SQL administrative rights, and open SQL Server Management Studio.

2. At the Connect to server prompt, keep the default options of connecting to the local server with Windows Authentication, and click Connect.

3. In the Object Explorer, expand Management, and then right-click on Maintenance Plans and select Maintenance Plan Wizard.

> **TIP**
>
> If the Maintenance Plan Wizard is initiated on a new instance of SQL Server, an error might occur stating that the command cannot be executed due to the security configuration for the server. If this is the case, the SQL Server Agent extended stored procedures need to be enabled. You can do this by executing the following statements in the SQL Query window:

```
sp_configure 'show advanced options', 1;
GO
RECONFIGURE;
GO
sp_configure 'Agent XPs', 1;
GO
RECONFIGURE
GO
```

4. At the SQL Maintenance Plan Wizard screen, click Next to begin the configuration.

5. At the Select Plan Properties screen, enter a name and description for the maintenance plan. Several options are also presented for the scheduling of the maintenance plan. To configure separate schedules for individual tasks within a single maintenance plan, select Separate Schedules for Each Task. To configure a single schedule for the entire plan, select Single Schedule for the Entire Plan or No Schedule. If this option is selected, the Change button is available to configure the scheduling for the plan.

6. Click Change to display the New Job Schedule dialog box, shown in Figure 11.19. Select from the available scheduling options to configure the frequency and timing of the plan. When finished, click OK to save the schedule, and click Next to continue with the Maintenance Plan Wizard.

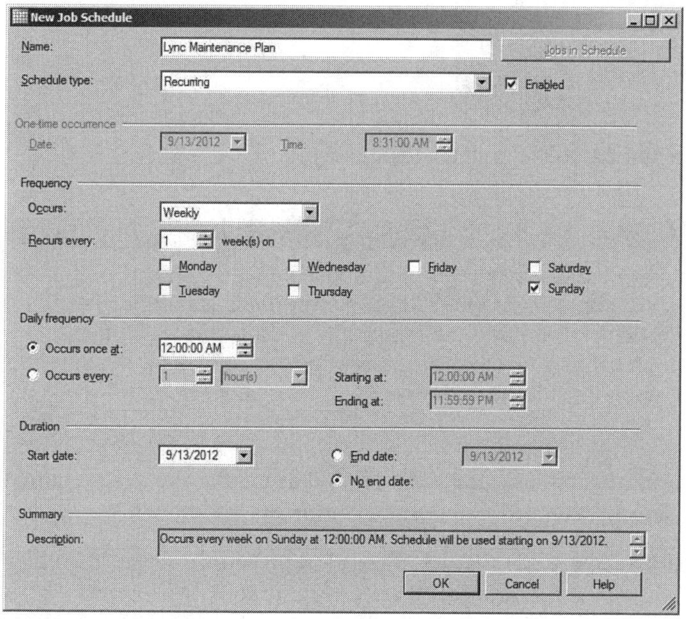

FIGURE 11.19   SQL maintenance plan scheduling.

7. On the Select Maintenance Tasks screen, select the maintenance tasks to include in the plan, and then click Next to continue.

8. At the Select Maintenance Task Order page, review the order in which the tasks will be executed. If necessary, change the order by selecting a task and then clicking either Move Up or Move Down as needed. When finished, click Next.

9. The wizard now provides options for each task that was selected. For example, Figure 11.20 shows the configuration options for the Database Check Integrity task. Using this example, the All Databases option has been selected for integrity checking.

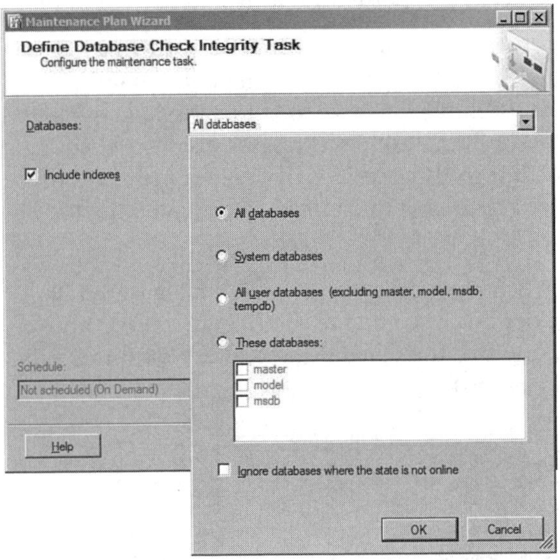

FIGURE 11.20   Configuration of the Database Check Integrity task.

TIP

From the list of available maintenance tasks, the Check Database Integrity and Maintenance Cleanup tasks should be selected for all Lync Server databases. It is also recommended to *not* select the Shrink Database task, primarily because the automatic shrinking of databases on a routine basis leads to excessive fragmentation as well as excessive I/O, which can negatively impact the performance of Lync Server.

10. Continue the configuration of each task that was selected as part of the maintenance plan on each successive screen, selecting the desired options.

11. At the Select Report Options page, keep the default option of Write a Report to a Text File, and change the report file location if necessary. If an email report is desired, select this option and enter the target email address. When finished, click Next.

12. At the Complete the Wizard screen, review the listed options for accuracy and then click Finish to complete the Wizard.

Summary

As with any Unified Communications product, Lync Server 2013 depends on a number of external systems to provide needed functionality. Active Directory and DNS provide vital infrastructure services, and server certificates are used to secure communications between systems. There are various network dependencies that come into play depending on Lync components and topology. The Office Web Apps Server is a new dependency that provides an enhanced conferencing experience. SQL is also an important part of the Lync ecosystem. Proper maintenance of the Lync SQL databases will help ensure smooth operation for the Lync Server 2013 environment.

CHAPTER 12

Firewall and Security Requirements

Most companies deploy Lync Server 2013 so that they can support IM and conferencing services with users that connect outside the corporate network. To properly protect the Lync Server 2013 systems from attack, apply a layered approach to security. In the case of Lync Server 2013, this means a combination of local firewalls, network firewalls, reverse proxies, and a responsible methodology for provisioning access to shares and services.

This chapter lays out approaches for applying layers of security onto the Lync Server 2013 systems. Although securing a system and configuring accounts for least privilege can be a fair amount of effort, the benefits reaped in terms of security greatly outweigh the efforts.

Firewall Requirements Overview

Wikipedia defines a *firewall* as a part of a computer system or network that is designed to block unauthorized access while permitting authorized communications. It is a device or set of devices configured to permit or deny computer applications based on a set of rules and other criteria.

There are several types of firewall techniques, including these:

▶ **Packet Filtering**—Packet filtering inspects packets as they are passed through the network and rejects or accepts these packets based on defined rules. Typically, these rules will specify a source and destination address, a port, and either an allow or deny statement to define the behavior of the packet-filtering rule. Packet-filtering firewalls are generally fast but can be difficult to configure for applications that dynamically choose ports for communications after an initial handshake.

▶ **Application Gateway**—Application gateways apply security enforcement to specific applications. In other words, the gateway understands the applications and can recognize their packets. It makes its decisions based on which applications are allowed to pass through the firewall. Application gateways can be relatively easy to configure but are generally processor intensive and thus cannot handle as much throughput as a packet-filtering firewall.

▶ **Proxy/Reverse Proxy Server**—A proxy server intercepts all messages entering and leaving the network. It inspects the packets and then continues the conversation on behalf of the protected system. In this way, packets never go directly from the source to the protected destination or from the protected source directly to the uncontrolled destination. Not unlike applications gateways, proxy servers are processor intensive.

Network-Based Firewalls

Most implementations of Lync Server involve some form of a network-based firewall, usually in the DMZ (demilitarized zone). The purpose of this device is to ensure that only the necessary services on the Lync Server systems are made available externally.

To maximize security, it is fairly common to configure the external services of Lync Server so that not only is there a firewall between the Internet and the Lync Server servers, but there also is a firewall between the internal network and the Lync Server servers. This can be accomplished either with dual firewalls or by placing the Lync Server servers into a DMZ on a three-or-more-legged firewall. Dual firewalls are technically more secure because if an attacker compromised the firewall that was exposed externally, he would still have to compromise a second firewall before having access to the internal hosts.

The first step in implementing this type of firewall for Lync Server is to understand what services you plan to make available from outside the network and then to determine exactly which ports and protocols need to be opened on the firewall.

Ports Required for Internal and External Access

The specific ports needed to open on a firewall vary somewhat depending on what services are placed into the DMZ and which services need to be accessible from the Internet. This section summarizes commonly deployed DMZ roles and the ports necessary to support them. The description calls out the port, traffic type, type of firewall it applies to (internal or external), and purpose for the opening. Table 12.1 describes, in detail, the port requirements for Lync Server 2013.

TABLE 12.1   Edge Server Port Requirements

Service	Protocol	Port	Direction	Description
A/V Edge	TCP	50000-59999	Inbound	These ports are required to be opened inbound only if federating with OCS 2007 for A/V.
A/V Edge	TCP	50000-59999	Outbound	These ports should be opened outbound for federation, as well as for ensuring the optimal media path for internal to external communications for Desktop Sharing.
A/V Edge	UDP	50000-59999	Inbound/Outbound	These ports are required only if federating with OCS 2007 for A/V.
A/V Edge	UDP	3478	Inbound/Outbound	You must open this port for media to flow among all internal and external participants, including federation.
A/V Edge	TCP	443	Inbound	You must open this port for media to flow among all internal and external participants, including federation.
Access Edge	TCP	80	Outbound	You must allow Certificate Revocation List check requests outbound from the Edge Server for federation.
Access Edge	TCP/UDP	53	Outbound	The Edge Server must be able to query external DNS.
Access Edge	TCP	443	Inbound	You must allow external users to connect to the Access Edge Service over 443 using TLS.
Access Edge	TCP	5061	Inbound/Outbound	This port must be opened inbound and outbound to allow for federation. These connections will use TLS.
Web Conferencing Edge	TCP	443	Inbound	This port must be open to allow for web conferencing traffic.
XMPP Service	TCP	5269	Inbound/Outbound	If XMPP federation is enabled, you must allow this port for XMPP federation to work.
Internal Edge Service	TCP	5061	Inbound/Outbound	You must open this port between the internal servers (Director, Front End, etc.) and the Internal Edge interface.
Internal Edge Service	TCP	8057	Inbound	All Front End Servers must be able to communicate with the Edge Server on 8057 for Web Conferencing Media traffic.

12

Service	Protocol	Port	Direction	Description
Internal Edge Service	UDP	3478	Inbound	You must open this port to allow internal clients to communicate with the Edge Internal Service for media traversal.
Internal Edge Service	TCP	443	Inbound	You must open this port to allow internal clients to communicate with the Edge Internal Service for media traversal.
Internal Edge Service	TCP	5062	Inbound	You must open this port to allow all Front End Servers to communicate with the A/V Authentication service that lives on the Internal Edge Service.
Internal Edge Service	TCP	4443	Inbound	This port must be opened to the Edge Server to allow for CMS replication.

NOTE

"Inbound" and "Outbound" refer to the direction between the Internet or internal network and the specified Access Edge Service. For example, if the service is A/V Edge, and it says "Inbound," you must open the port with the destination address of the A/V Edge Service IP Address.

Using Operating System Firewalls

In Windows Server 2003 SP1, Microsoft introduced an integrated firewall into the Windows operating system. As with most Microsoft products, it has improved with each iteration. Flash-forward to Windows Server 2012 and you find that the integrated firewall is quite good. Lync Server does an excellent job of integrating into the Windows Server Firewall at the time of installation.

Layering an operating system layer firewall with a network layer firewall is an excellent way to improve overall security of a system with minimal expense. With these two layered together, if the network firewall becomes compromised, the attacker has to pierce the OS layer firewall to compromise the systems. Similarly, given that many attack vectors can come from within the company itself, the OS layer firewall offers protection from trusted systems that might become compromised.

Configuring the Windows Server Firewall for Lync Server

If the Windows Firewall is enabled and started at the time of installation of Lync Server components, the necessary exceptions are created automatically.

CAUTION

Although many administrators are tempted to disable the Windows Firewall, it is certainly worth leaving it in place with the necessary rules configured. If you are convinced you don't want to use the Windows Firewall, and you don't plan to use a third-party operating system layer firewall, leave the Windows Firewall service running, but configure the rules to allow all traffic to pass unhindered. This prevents possible problems in interacting with the Windows Filtering Platform.

TIP

If Windows Firewall was off during the first installation, you can simply turn on Windows Firewall and run the Lync Server Deployment Wizard to configure Lync Server 2013 Windows Firewall Rules.

Using Network Address Translation (NAT) with Lync Server

If a single Edge Server is placed behind a firewall, it is acceptable to enable NAT. NAT effectively takes packets bound for the firewall and forwards them to hosts inside the firewall based on port rules. This enables a company with limited numbers of routable IP addresses to support multiple services with fewer IP addresses. It also provides a layer of security by requiring the firewall to process the packet first before it reaches the eventual destination. In addition, it enables protected systems to hide their IP information because they never appear to be a source of a packet to a system on the Internet; the firewall always appears to be the source.

TIP

If you enable NAT for the external firewall, configure firewall filters that are used for traffic from the Internet to the Edge Server with Destination Network Address Translation (DNAT). Similarly, configure and filter for traffic going from the Edge Server to the Internet with Source Network Address Translation (SNAT). Important to note is that the inbound and outbound filters for this purpose must use the same internal and external addresses. If externally, the Edge is 11.22.33.44 and is mapped to an Edge Server at 10.1.1.44. The mapping for the Edge to talk to the Internet needs traffic from 10.1.1.44 to come from 11.22.33.44. Although this might seem obvious, there are many situations in which all internal hosts appear to come from the same IP address. This is called PAT, or port address translation, or is sometimes called NAT overload.

CAUTION

If multiple Edge Servers are deployed in a load-balanced fashion, the external firewall cannot be configured for NAT. Regardless of whether load balancers are used, an internal firewall used to protect Edge Servers cannot be NAT enabled for the internal IP address of an Edge Server.

Reverse Proxy Requirements

Reverse proxies, such as ISA 2006 SP1 or Forefront Threat Management Gateway (TMG), are excellent ways to securely publish applications, such as Lync Server, to users on the Internet. By controlling specific ports to pass traffic and limiting destination URLs to only the desired paths, you can safely pass traffic from the Internet to Lync Server roles. The following sections discuss how to configure reverse proxies to work with Lync Server.

Why a Reverse Proxy Is Required

It is important to understand why a reverse proxy solution is required for Lync Server 2013. In Lync Server 2013, a reverse proxy is required to publish Lync Web Services to external users. These services are responsible for the following:

▶ **Simple URL Publishing**—This is required for users to join a Lync Online Meeting.

▶ **Web Conferencing Content**—Users will download PowerPoint, Whiteboard, and Poll data through the Lync Web Services when in a meeting.

▶ **Address Book and Distribution List (DL) Expansion**—This is required for users to download the Lync Address Book and perform DL expansion.

▶ **User Certificates**—Lync Server utilizes client certificate authentication for many purposes; external users must connect to the Lync Web Services to obtain certificates.

▶ **Device Updates**—Lync Phone Edition devices require access to the Lync Web Services to obtain software updates.

▶ **Mobility**—Lync Mobile clients on Windows Phone, Android, and Apple IOS connect through the Lync Web Services.

Deploying a Reverse Proxy solution with Lync Server 2013 is absolutely critical in order to enable external user access. This book provides a configuration guide for Microsoft Forefront Threat Management Gateway 2010; many other solutions are available to securely publish these services. To deploy Lync Web Services, the reverse proxy solution must meet the following requirements:

▶ **HTTP and HTTPS Publishing**—Devices must be capable of securely publishing application content. Devices that support this functionality will specifically call this out as a feature.

▶ **SSL Bridging**—Lync Server 2013 requires the reverse proxy server to listen for connections on TCP port 443, but to bridge these connections to the Front End Server Pool on TCP port 4443. This is required because the Lync Web Services contain separate virtual web directories for security purposes. The external Lync Web Services directory listens on port 4443, and should be used when publishing to the Internet.

▶ **Authentication Bypass**—The proxy solution should allow for authentication to occur at the Lync Servers, not at the proxy itself.

CAUTION

It is not supported by Microsoft, and it is not recommended to deploy external web services without a reverse proxy solution. Do not use NAT as a replacement for a reverse proxy solution.

Certificate Requirements

Chapter 11, "Dependent Services and SQL," covers all certificate requirements in detail. In general, the reverse proxy certificate requires a public certificate with the following entries:

- ▶ **Lync Web Services External FQDN**—This is defined in the topology and should be configured as the Subject Name of your certificate.

- ▶ **Simple URL Entries**—There should be a certificate entry in the SAN field for every meeting and dial-in simple URL. There is typically a single dial-in FQDN, and there will be a meeting FQDN for each SIP domain in the environment.

- ▶ **LyncDiscover**—Lync Mobile devices are hard-coded to look for the DNS entry `lyncdiscover.<sipdomain>`. This should terminate at the reverse proxy, as such a certificate entry is required for each SIP domain in your environment.

Reverse Proxy Configuration

This section outlines tasks for configuring a reverse proxy solution or Lync Server 2013.

Create DNS Records for Lync Server Reverse Proxy

To enable clients on the Internet to find Lync Server services, add an Address (A) record to an external DNS that is authoritative for the DNS domain that services Lync Server externally. This includes (A) or (SRV) records, as described in Chapter 11.

NOTE

The procedure for creating records depends on the DNS server used. In the case of an externally hosted DNS, it might be as simple as calling your service provider and requesting the records.

Keep in mind that it might take several minutes to as much as a few hours for the new records to propagate to an external DNS server and become available to clients.

On most reverse proxy solutions, it is possible to have all external Lync Web Services DNS records point to the same IP Address.

Verifying Access to the Lync Web Services

Before making Lync Server available externally, the administrator should verify that the environment is working correctly through the reverse proxy. Assuming that the firewall rules are in place and that the necessary DNS records are available externally, the following procedure helps administrators determine whether their environment is configured correctly:

1. From an externally connected computer, open a web browser and type `https://externalwebfarmFQDN/abs/`, where `externalwebfarmFQDN` is the external FQDN of the web farm that hosts the Address Book Service. If the URL returns an HTTP challenge, the site is configured correctly. You receive this challenge because the Address Book Server folder is configured to use Microsoft Windows Integrated Authentication.

2. From an externally connected computer, open a web browser and type `https://externalwebfarmFQDN/conf/Tshoot.html`, where `externalwebfarmFQDN` is the external FQDN of the web farm that hosts meeting content. This URL should display the troubleshooting page for web conferencing if it is configured correctly.

3. From an externally connected computer, open a web browser and type `https://externalwebfarmFQDN/GroupExpansion/ext/service.asmx`, where `externalwebfarmFQDN` is the external FQDN of the web farm that hosts Group Expansion. If the URL returns an HTTP challenge, the site is configured correctly. You receive this challenge because the Address Book Server folder is configured to use Microsoft Windows Integrated Authentication.

4. From an externally connected computer, open a web browser and type `https://lyncdiscover.<sipdomain>` where `<sipdomain>` is the external SIP domain defined for the users. This URL should prompt your web browser to download a file; if you open this file with notepad, it should contain the external web farm FQDN URL.

Configuring Microsoft Threat Management Gateway (TMG) for Lync Server

Forefront TMG is the logical successor of ISA 2006 SP1 and a common choice for use as a reverse proxy with Lync Server.

Assuming that TMG 2010 is already installed and network cards are already configured, the following steps outline how to publish the Lync Web Services through TMG:

1. Configure a web farm FQDN.

2. Request and configure SSL certificates.

3. Create a web server publishing rule.

4. Configure authentication and certification on IIS virtual directories.

5. Create an external DNS entry.

6. Verify access.

Configure Web Farm FQDN

During the setup of Enterprise pools and Standard Edition servers, there is an option to configure an external web farm fully qualified domain name (FQDN) on the web farm FQDN's page during the Create Pool Wizard (or the Deploy Server Wizard). If a URL was not chosen during this process, it is necessary to configure the settings using the following procedure:

1. Open the Lync Server Topology Builder.

2. Choose Download Topology from Existing Deployment and click OK.

3. In Topology Builder, in the console tree, navigate to your Enterprise or Standard pool, and right-click the name of the pool.

4. Click Edit Properties.

5. In the middle of the Edit Properties screen, there is a field under external web services titled FQDN. Enter the FQDN to be used for Web Services and click OK.

6. In the left pane right-click Lync Server, and then click Publish topology.

7. Click Next.

8. Select the database where the topology will live, and click Next.

9. Click Finish.

Request and Configure SSL Certificates

Before configuring your Web Publishing Rules in TMG 2010, the certificate that will be used on your Lync Server rules must be installed correctly with the private key. Instructions for installing this certificate can typically be obtained from the provider of the certificate.

> **TIP**
>
> If your Public Certificate Authority provides a package of certificates, it is recommended to install all certificates they provide. This can include root and intermediate certificates. If these certificates are not installed on your servers, it can often cause issues with external clients.

Configuring Web Publishing Rules

Web publishing rules are used by Forefront TMG Server to securely publish internal resources over the Internet. In addition to providing web service URLs for the various Lync Server virtual IIS directories, it is also necessary to create publishing rules for simple URLs and the LyncDiscover service. For each simple URL, it is necessary to create an individual rule on the reverse proxy that references that URL. The following procedures can be used to create web publishing rules:

1. Log on to the Forefront TMG Server.

2. Click Start, All Programs, Microsoft Forefront TMG, and Forefront TMG Management.

3. In the left pane, expand the name of the TMG Server.

4. Right-click Firewall Policy, click New, and click Web Site Publishing Rule, as shown in Figure 12.1.

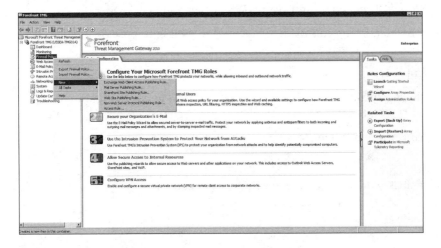

FIGURE 12.1   Creating a new website publishing rule.

5. On the Welcome to the New Web Publishing Rule page, enter a name for the publishing rule that will be easy to reference in the future. Click Next.

6. On the Select Rule Action page, choose Allow. Click Next.

7. On the Publishing Type page, select Publish a Single Web Site or Load Balancer and click Next.

8. On the Server Connection Security page, choose Use SSL to Connect to the Published Web Server or Server Farm. Click Next.

9. On the internal Publishing Details page, enter the FQDN of the internal web farm where meeting content and the Address Book are hosted in the Internal Site name box.

NOTE

The TMG Server must be able to resolve the FQDN entered in step 9. If the TMG Server will not be able to reach a DNS server that can resolve the FQDN, select Use a Computer Name or IP Address to Connect to the Published Server, and then enter the IP address in the Computer Name or IP Address box, as shown in Figure 12.2.

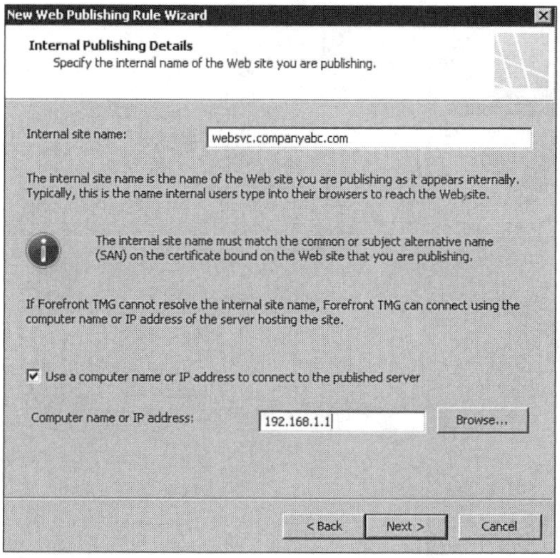

FIGURE 12.2   Connecting to an IP address.

10. On the internal Publishing Details page, enter /* as the path of the published folder. Click Next.

11. On the Publish Name Details page, verify that This Domain Name is selected under Accept Requests For. Type the FQDN of the external web farm into the Public Name box. Click Next.

12. On the Select Web Listener page, click New.

13. On the Welcome to the New Web Listener Wizard page, enter a name for the new web listener in the Web Listener Name box. Click Next.

14. On the Client Connection Security page, choose Require SSL Secured Connections with Clients. Click Next.

15. On the Web Listener IP address page, select External, and click Select IP Addresses.

16. On the external Listener IP selection page, select Specified IP Address on the TMG Server Computer in the Selected Network, select an IP address, and click Add. Click Next.

17. On the Listener SSL Certificates page, click Assign a Certificate for Each IP Address, and select the IP address that was added in step 16. Click Select Certificate.

18. On the Select Certificate page, select the certificate matching the public name selected in step 11, as shown in Figure 12.3, and click Select. Click Next.

19. On the Authentication Settings page, select No Authentication. Click Next.

20. On the Single Sign On Settings page, click Next.

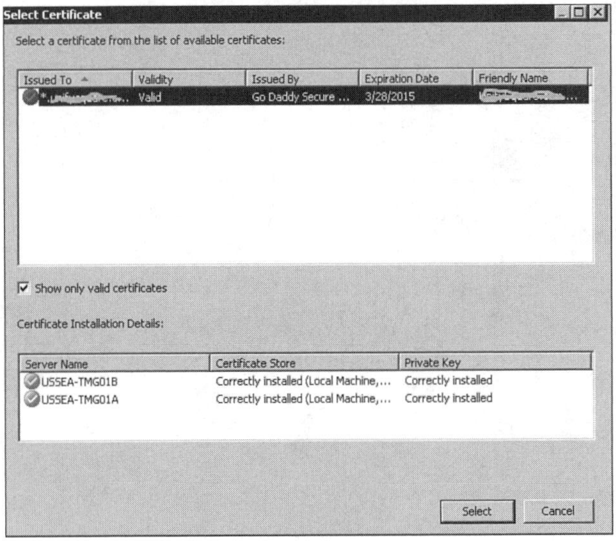

FIGURE 12.3   Selecting the certificate.

21. On the Complete the New Web Listener Wizard page, click Finish.

22. Returning to the Select Web Listener page, select the listener that was just created and click Next.

23. On the Authentication Delegation page, select No Delegation but the Client May Authenticate Directly. Click Next.

24. On the User Sets page, click Next.

25. On the Completing the New Web Publishing Rule Wizard page, verify the rule settings and click Finish.

26. Click Apply to save the changes, as shown in Figure 12.4, and update the configuration.

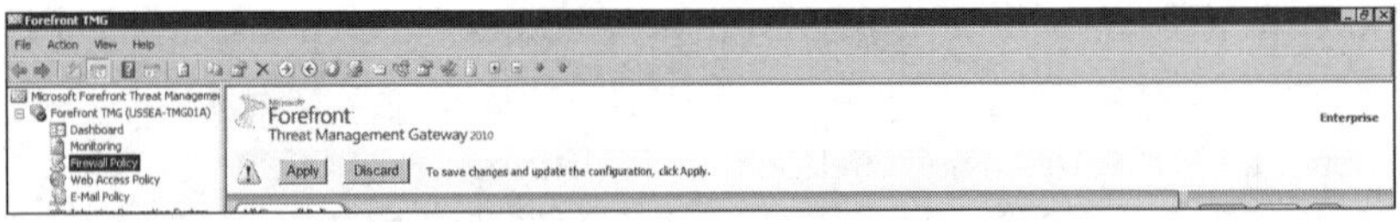

FIGURE 12.4   Applying the firewall policy.

Configuring Authentication and Certification on IIS Virtual Directories

To correctly pass SSL encrypted packets through the reverse proxy into the IIS directories on the Lync Server servers, make sure that certification is properly configured on IIS. This task can be performed with the following steps:

1. Log in to the Lync Server that is being published through the reverse proxy.

2. Click Start, All Programs, Administrative Tools, and select Internet Information Services (IIS) Manager.

3. In the IIS manager, expand the ServerName, and expand Sites.

4. Click Lync Server external Web Site.

5. In the Actions pane, click Bindings. Verify that the HTTPS is associated with port 4443, as shown in Figure 12.5, and click HTTPS.

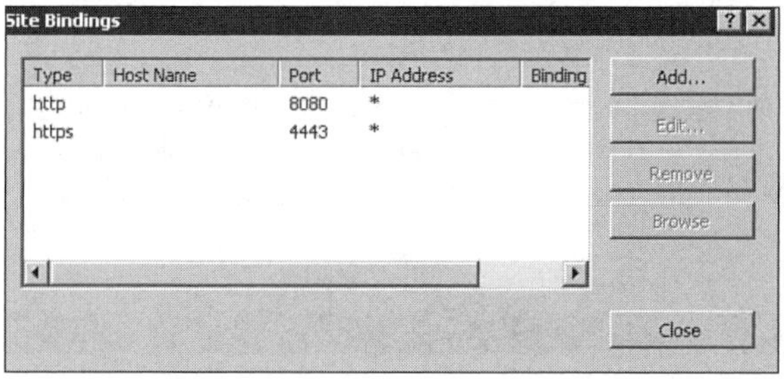

FIGURE 12.5   Verifying the HTTPS port.

6. In the Edit Site Binding dialog box, verify that the correct certificate is associated, as shown in Figure 12.6. This should be the certificate used in the previous TMG Listener configuration.

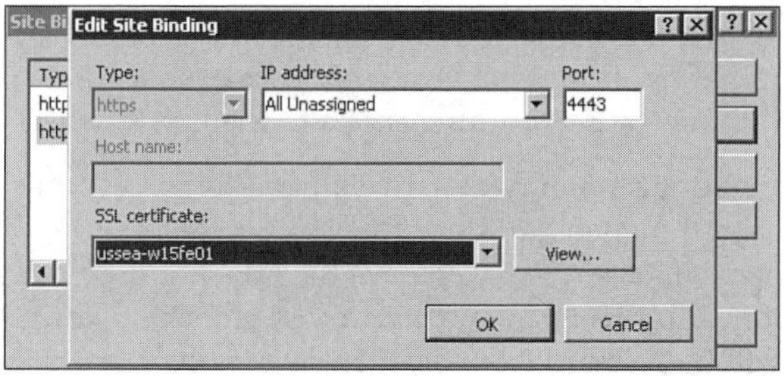

FIGURE 12.6   Verifying the SSL certificate.

7. On the Directory Security tab, click Server Certificate, located under Secure Communications.

8. On the Welcome to the Web Server Certificate Wizard page, click Next.

9. On the Server Certificate page, click Assign an Existing Certificate, and click Next.

10. On the SSL Port page, verify that the value is set to 4443 in the SSL Port this Web Site Should Use box and click Next.

11. On the Certificate Summary page, verify the settings, and click Next.

12. Click Finish.

13. Click OK to close the Default Web Site Properties dialog box.

File Share Permissions

Lync Server 2013 utilizes a file share for each pool for many scenarios. This includes conferencing, configuration replication, address book, and many other critical tasks. These file shares have strict permission requirements, and Lync Server 2013 will assign permissions to these file shares during the deployment of your Topology.

When deploying any Lync Server 2013 topology changes, the administrator must make sure that they have read/write access to the file shares in the topology. When the administrator publishes a topology change, the topology publisher will validate permissions on the file shares.

> **TIP**
>
> If the file-share permissions are ever changed by accident, simply publish the Lync Server topology again and these permissions will be re-created.

Summary

As shown in this chapter, properly securing a Lync Server 2013 implementation is a valuable process because it protects the servers from potential exploitation. By utilizing existing technologies such as firewalls and proxies, one can greatly reduce the attack surface of Lync Server 2013. Through the use of limited rights and managed service accounts, one can greatly reduce the possibility of unauthorized users gaining access to the new system.

Configuring protective features in the operating system is a relatively painless process that can go a long way toward securing the overall implementation. Tasks as simple as limiting rights to shares and controlling services will also serve to reduce the attack surface of a Lync Server 2013 deployment. As mentioned in this chapter, this process of locking down systems is especially important if hosts will be accessed from outside the organization or if sensitive information will be communicated within Lync Server 2013.

PART IV

Administration and Management

IN THIS PART

Monitoring Lync Server 2013

Organizations deploying Lync Server 2013 all have unique requirements for monitoring the health, performance, and usage of the environment. At a minimum, all organizations should be concerned with the health and performance of the environment, and organizations in certain verticals will be required to retain usage data for regulatory purposes. Lync Server 2013 includes many tools that enable organizations to meet monitoring and archiving needs of all types. In addition to built-in tools, a rich ecosystem exists with many third-party vendors catering to the needs of all organizations.

This chapter provides an understanding of key areas to monitor in Lync, as well as of the features and tools available to perform such monitoring.

Understanding Key Areas to Monitor in Your Deployment

When you are deploying Lync Server 2013, it is important to identify all monitoring and archiving requirements for the organization that is deploying the solution. Every organization deploying Lync Server 2013 should be encouraged to monitor the health and performance of the environment. Additionally, many organizations require communication data retention for legal compliance purposes.

Clearly, outlining requirements and strategies for monitoring and archiving will go a long way in ensuring a successful Lync Server 2013 deployment. The sections that follow provide a definition of each common requirement and common examples of where they would apply.

Health and Performance Requirements

Monitoring the health and performance of the environment should be a top priority for any Lync Server deployment. Without the proper tools in place, guaranteeing service availability and troubleshooting service quality issues are nearly impossible. Lync Server 2013 spans many different IT systems in order to provide services to end users. Monitoring the Lync solution from end to end enables administrators to confidently support all Lync modalities. At the same time, solutions that monitor the entire Lync solution enable upper management to have insight into the health of the environment, and to have confidence in the system deployed.

Monitoring the health of the Lync environment can be accomplished in various ways. The details of how to use these tools for health monitoring are described in later sections but they include the following:

▶ Windows event logs

▶ Lync synthetic transactions

▶ System Center Operations Manager (SCOM)

▶ Third-party (non-Microsoft) monitoring solutions

In addition to monitoring the overall health of the environment, the performance of the system should be carefully monitored. When Lync is being deployed, careful planning will ensure that capacity requirements are met. However, it is important to identify performance baselines and to monitor system performance for issues. There are many instances in which systems can malfunction, or usage has simply increased, which can result in service degradation. Although performance is a contributing factor to the health of the environment, it is important to identify performance baseline establishment and ongoing monitoring as a separate task in the deployment and post-deployment phases.

Performance can be monitored using various tools. This chapter outlines how to use these tools in later sections, but they include the following:

▶ Windows Performance Monitor (Perfmon)

▶ SCOM

▶ Third-party network monitoring tools

When planning to establish performance baselines and performance monitoring, do not forget the supporting infrastructure such as the network, SQL Server, and, if virtualization is used, the virtual infrastructure.

Usage, Adoption, and Archiving Requirements

Nearly every organization is required to retain communications data for compliance purposes. Organizations across all common verticals must follow strict regulations, and these regulations will carry over to the Lync infrastructure to retain data such as instant messaging conversations and web conferencing content. Additionally, some organizations require audio recordings of all calls for certain users. There are many ways to meet these requirements, including Lync Server 2013 built-in functionality, as well as third-party solutions.

It is also important to track the usage and adoption of the Lync system. Monitoring the usage and overall adoption of a Lync service is critical in the deployment and post-deployment stages. During the deployment, identifying how users are adopting the solution will provide key metrics for success of the project, as well as the return on investment (ROI) of the solution. Post-deployment, identifying how users are utilizing the system can provide insight into cost analysis, as well as performance tweaking metrics. These are just some examples of why it is important to monitor the usage and adoption of the Lync system. Many organizations have key performance indicators (KPIs) for their Lync deployment, and monitoring these areas is critical in reporting on the status of those KPIs.

Monitoring the Health and Performance of Lync Server 2013

For any Lync deployment to be successful, a robust set of solutions should be deployed to monitor the health and performance of the service. Any organization that has designated an SLA to their Lync system will require monitoring all components of Lync to ensure availability of the environment. The end goal should be to provide the highest level of availability, and the highest level of insight on the environment, with the least amount of effort for administrators. A combination of solutions can be utilized to enable administrators and management with the necessary confidence in the health of their Lync Server deployment, and this section outlines common examples and considerations for deployment.

Using Performance Monitor to Establish Performance Baselines

The Windows operating system has included a performance monitoring utility for many releases. Over the years, this tool has become more powerful, and applications continue to allow critical performance monitoring through this tool. The tool, Performance Monitor (sometimes called Perfmon), enables administrators to view numerous metrics about the hardware and software on a Windows machine. In relation to Lync, key performance metrics related to CPU, disk, memory, and network can be monitored as part of the default OS configuration. Additionally, Lync Server 2013 includes a vast library of counters that can be tracked in the Performance Monitor utility.

It is best practice to establish a performance baseline when first enabling a Lync Server deployment. A performance baseline enables administrators to have a record of how one or many Lync Server systems are performing during normal operations. This baseline can then be referenced when issues are reported.

Establishing a performance baseline also enables administrators to confirm proper sizing of the deployed environment. Microsoft provides recommended topologies based on standard use cases and environmental variables. If an organization does not match all conditions of the Microsoft use cases, Performance Monitor can be used to validate sufficient system resources and load distribution for various Lync services.

NOTE

When establishing a performance baseline, be sure to capture a sufficient amount of data. At least one week of data should be collected to identify all peak-hour and off-hour usage for all Lync Services.

If major changes to the Lync service occur, such as adding users or functionality, or adding or removing servers, a new baseline should be established.

Important Performance Monitor Counters

The Windows Operating System and Lync Server 2013 enable administrators to monitor a very large number of counters in Performance Monitor. This section outlines key Performance Monitor counters for a performance baseline with Lync Server 2013. It is recommended to explore the Performance Monitor counters available on your servers to become familiar with the tools you will have available in any troubleshooting situation.

To explore the Performance Monitor counters available for Lync Server 2013, do the following:

1. Open the Performance Monitor tool, located in the Administrative Tools on a Windows Server.

2. Select Performance Monitor, and then click the green plus sign to add a new counter. See Figure 13.1 for an example.

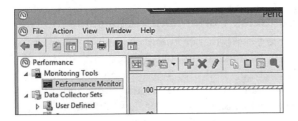

FIGURE 13.1   Add a performance counter.

3. All Lync Server 2013 counters will start with "LS:"; check the box for Show Description and each counter will display a description to help with identifying the counters. Figure 13.2 shows an example of the initial set of LS counters in Performance Monitor.

After you've explored the available performance counters for Lync Server 2013, it should be evident that there are many different aspects of Lync Server 2013 available for monitoring. However, establishing a performance baseline on your servers should involve only a few key counters. Use the sections that follow as a guide for counters to choose when establishing a performance baseline.

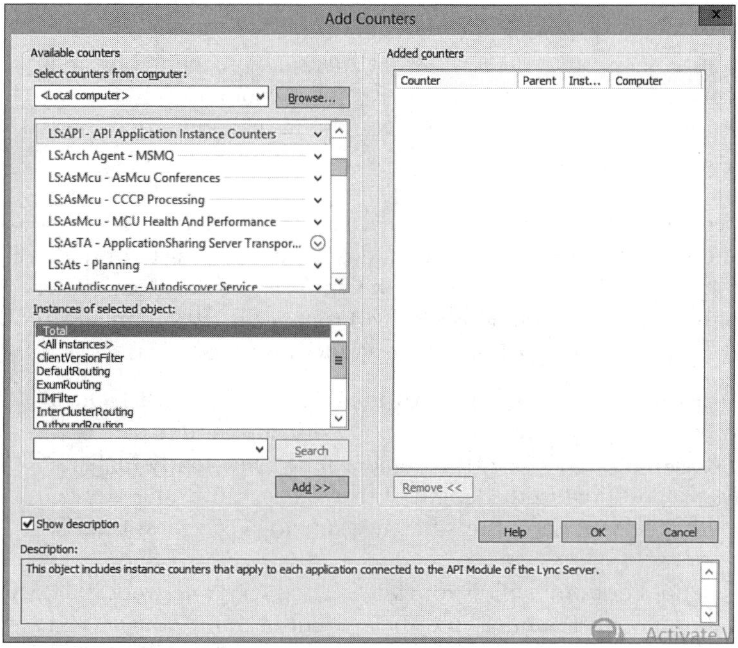

FIGURE 13.2   Lync Server 2013 performance counters.

CPU   Lync Server 2013 media processing can apply a large CPU load on any server. Depending on how the Lync deployment was designed, servers can have varying CPU utilization. Use the following counter to ensure that CPU usage is not too great on your Lync Servers.

Processor\% Processor Time: This counter is the percentage of time elapsed that the processor spends to execute a non-idle thread. This is the primary indicator of processor activity, and it displays the average percentage of busy time observed during the sample interval. If this value is above 80% consistently, a machine might be overutilized.

Memory   Lync Server services are heavy in memory utilization, especially conferencing servers. Use the following counters to ensure that memory utilization is not too high on your Lync Servers.

Memory\Available Mbytes: This counter simply keeps track of the available memory to the system. When this value is low, it is a sign of memory utilization being too high. This will also help with understanding the scaling impact that additional features and users have on your Lync Server systems.

Memory\Pages/sec: Pages/sec is the rate at which pages are read from or written to disk to resolve hard page faults. This counter is a primary indicator of the kinds of faults that cause systemwide delays. It is the sum of Memory\Pages Input/sec and Memory\Pages Output/sec. It is counted in numbers of pages, so it can be compared to other counts of pages, such as Memory\Page Faults/sec, without conversion. It includes pages that are retrieved to satisfy faults in the file-system cache and that are usually requested by applications using mapped memory files. A high rate for the Pages/sec counter could indicate excessive paging. Monitor the Memory\Page Faults/sec counter to make sure that the disk activity is not caused by paging.

Disk   Lync Server 2013 performs a large amount of disk activity on the Front End and Back End servers. Front End servers maintain presence and other dynamic data in the local SQL database, and Back End servers are responsible for all Lync user information, conference information, and configuration information. Disk performance is critical on all Lync Servers. Use the following counters to keep track of disk performance.

Physical Disk\Current Disk Queue Length (select All Instances): Current Disk Queue length represents the number of requests outstanding on the disk at the time data is collected. If a disk is overloaded, it is likely that this value will be consistently high. Requests experience delays proportional to the length of this queue, minus the number of spindles on the disks. For good performance, the difference should average less than 2.

Network   Modern hardware does not often allow for overutilizing server network interface cards (NICs). However, it is important to understand the amount of traffic your servers are sending and receiving for baseline performance. In some instances, this network traffic might increase without notice, and it might help identify issues.

Network Interface\Bytes Total/sec: Bytes Total/sec is the rate at which bytes are sent and received over each network adapter, including framing characters. Network Interface\Bytes Total/sec is a sum of Network Interface\Bytes Received/sec and Network Interface\Bytes Sent/sec. This counter should be lower than the maximum bandwidth that the current network link provides.

Lync Server   Lync Server 2013 includes many counters that monitor the service activity, health, and performance. The following counters are important for baseline performance monitoring, as well as ongoing monitoring and troubleshooting.

LS:SIP - Peers\TLS Connections Active: The number of established TLS connections that are currently active. A TLS connection is considered established when the peer certificate and the hostname are verified for a trust relationship. Having a baseline of this counter will allow administrators to identify problem areas in troubleshooting scenarios.

LS:SIP - Peers\Incoming Requests/sec: This counter represents the per-second rate of received SIP requests. Having a baseline of this counter enables administrators to identify problem areas in troubleshooting scenarios.

LS:SIP - Responses\Local 503 Responses/sec: This counter represents the per-second rate of 503 SIP responses that are generated by the server. A SIP 503 response indicates a service failure.

LS:SIP - Load Management\Average Holding Time for Incoming Messages: This counter represents the average time that a server held incoming messages before processing. A healthy Lync Server system should have a holding time of less than 3 seconds.

LS:USrv - REGDBStore\Queue Depth: This counter represents the number of requests waiting to be run by the Lync Registrar Service. A healthy Lync Front End Server should show a queue depth of less than 500.

LS:USrv - REGDBStore\Queue Latency (msec): This counter represents the time a request spends in a Lync Server queue waiting to be serviced by the SQL Server Service. A healthy Lync Server and SQL Server connection should show a value of less than 5000 msec.

LS:USrv - REGDBStore\SProc Latency (msec): This counter represents the time it takes for the SQL Server Service to service requests from the Lync Server. This value should have an average of less than 80 msec during normal operations. A high value for this counter is a clear sign of SQL Server performance issues.

LS:USrv - DBStore\Queue Depth: This counter represents the number of requests waiting to be run by the Lync Server User Services to the SQL Server Service. A healthy Lync Front End Server should show a queue depth of less than 1000.

LS:USrv - DBStore\Queue Latency (msec): This counter represents the time a request spends in a Lync Server queue waiting to be serviced by the SQL Server Service. A healthy Lync Server and SQL Server connection should show a value of less than 5000 msec.

LS:USrv - DBStore\SProc Latency (msec): This counter represents the time it takes for the SQL Server Service to service requests from the Lync Server. This value should have an average of less than 80 msec during normal operations. A high value for this counter is a clear sign of SQL Server performance issues.

LS:USrv - Directory Search\Search Latency (ms): This counter represents the average time it takes to perform LDAP searches. This counter can be used to identify delays in queries to Global Catalog servers in AD.

LS:USrv - Pool Conference Statistics\Active Conference Count: This counter represents the number of active conferences of all types in the Front End Server Pool. This can be used to show the true maximum concurrency of any Conferencing Pool. This can also be referenced when changes are made to the environment to see the effect those changes have had on usage.

LS:USrv - Pool Conference Statistics\Active Participant Count: This counter represents the number of active conferencing participants of all types in the Front End Server Pool. This can be used to show the true maximum user concurrency of any Conferencing Pool. This can also be referenced when changes are made to the environment to see the effect those changes have had on usage.

13

LS: MEDIA - Operations\Global Health: This counter represents the overall health of the different Lync Server Media components installed on a server. This can include the Application Sharing MCU (ASMCU), the A/V MCU (AVMCU), Call Park Service, Conferencing Announcement Service, Conferencing Attendant, Response Group Service, Reach Server (Web App), and the Mediation Server Service. Every media component provides a numeric health indicator, the values of which follow:

0 Disabled

1 Normal

2 Light Load

3 Heavy Load

4 Overload

LS:MEDIA - Planning\Number of Conferences with NORMAL Health State: This counter represents the number of currently active conferences across all media components. It provides an overview of what media or conferences are currently active, and how many are in a healthy state. This can include the ASMCU, the AVMCU, Call Park Service, Conferencing Announcement Service, Conferencing Attendant, Response Group Service, Reach Server (Web App), and the Mediation Server Service.

LS:MEDIA - Planning\Number of Conferences with OVERLOADED Health State: This counter represents the number of currently active conferences across all media components. It provides an overview of what media or conferences are currently in an unhealthy state. This can include the ASMCU, the AVMCU, Call Park Service, Conferencing Announcement Service, Conferencing Attendant, Response Group Service, Reach Server (Web App), and the Mediation Server Service.

Collecting and Analyzing Performance Monitor Data

The Performance Monitor utility enables administrators to collect data and view it in real time, or to collect data over a period and report on that data when collection has been stopped. For collecting a performance baseline, the latter approach is more appropriate. This feature, called Data Collection Sets, allows a number of counters and various other settings to be combined into a single collection activity. To create a data collector set for Lync Server 2013, perform the following steps:

1. Open the Performance Monitor utility, located in the Administrative Tools on a Windows Server.

2. Expand Data Collector Sets and select User Defined. Right-click and choose New, and then Data Collector Set. See Figure 13.3 for an example.

3. On the Create New Data Collector Set screen, enter a name such as Lync Server Baseline, and select the option for Create Manually (Advanced). Figure 13.4 shows an example of this process. Click Next to continue.

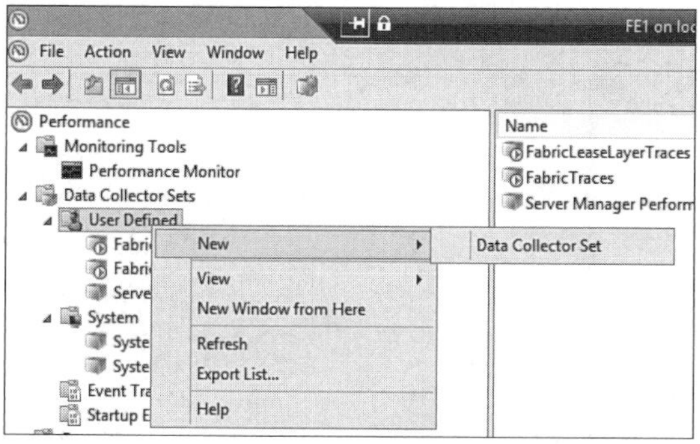

FIGURE 13.3   Creating a new data collector set.

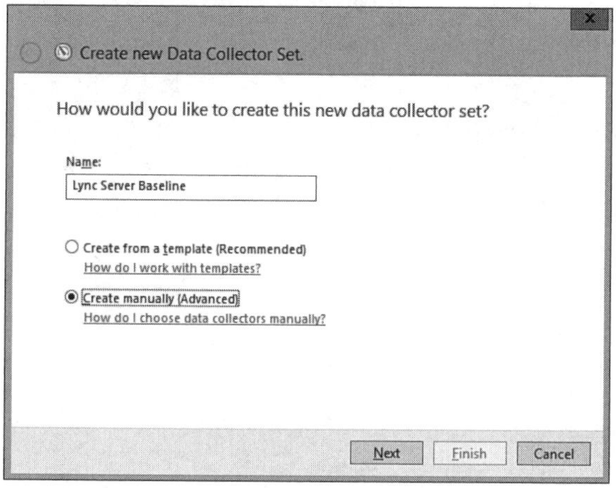

FIGURE 13.4   Name the data collector set.

4. Choose the option to Create Data Logs and check the box for Performance Counter. Click Next to continue.

5. Add the performance counters outlined in the preceding section to the list, and choose a sample interval. Keep in mind, the smaller the sample interval, the larger the data logs will be. When you are finished, the list should look similar to that shown in Figure 13.5. Click Next to continue.

6. On the next page, enter a path to save the data files. By default, these are stored on the system drive in a `PerfLogs` folder. If you have a separate disk to store these on, it is important to define this here. Click Finish to complete the wizard.

7. The new data collector set now shows in the user-defined list. If you want to apply other settings such as a schedule, or stop conditions based on disk space or duration, right-click on the collector set and choose Properties.

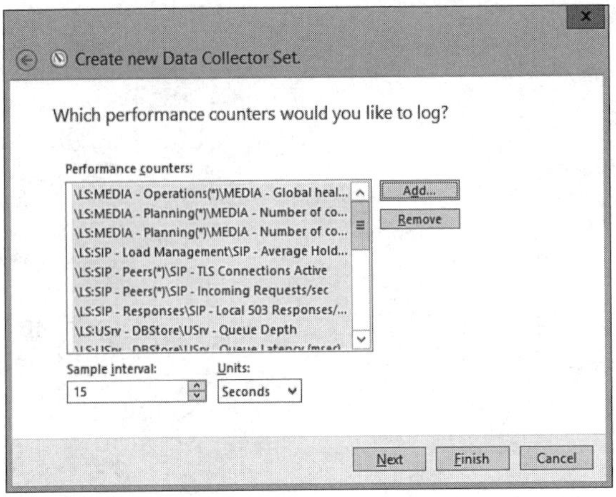

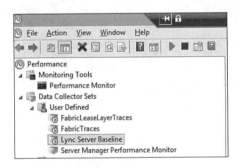

FIGURE 13.5   Data collection set counters selected.

8. When you are ready to begin collecting data, right-click on the data collector set and choose Start. When the set is running, it displays a running symbol over the icon (which is green), as shown in Figure 13.6.

FIGURE 13.6   Example of a data collection set running.

Analyzing Performance Monitor Data Logs

Perform the following steps to analyze Performance Monitor data logs collected using the data collection set created in the preceding section.

1. Right-click on the data collection set and choose Stop.

2. Right-click on the data collection set and choose Latest Report. The report should automatically appear, enabling you to analyze the data collected. Use this screen to view a graph, or a numeric representation of each value. When you select each value, you are presented with the Last, Average, Minimum, and Maximum values for each counter. Compare these numbers with the acceptable values described in earlier sections to determine the health of your environment. See Figure 13.7 for a sample report.

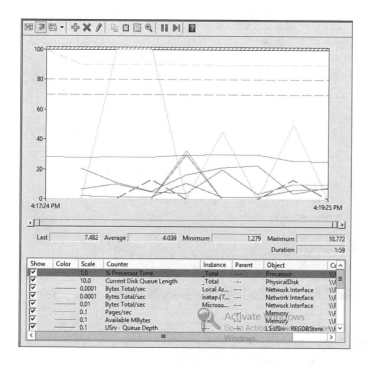

FIGURE 13.7   Example of a Performance Monitor report.

In addition to the reports built into Performance Monitor, a community tool is available to analyze Performance Monitor data logs and provide feedback based on known thresholds. The tool, named Performance Analysis of Logs (PAL), reads performance logs generated by Performance Monitor, analyzes them, and then outputs an HTML report that attempts to call out critical areas based on known thresholds. Although this is not built specifically for Lync Server 2013, it does understand basic thresholds from Office Communications Server 2007 R2, as well as the Windows operating system thresholds. The goal of PAL is to automate the analysis work, and provide administrators with a clear definition of counters that show a problem with a system. Also, you can edit and add threshold files for models that PAL does not support. To download PAL, see the following link: http://pal.codeplex.com/.

Performance Monitor is a powerful tool. Lync administrators should be familiar with the counters available to them. Not only will this be helpful for planning purposes, but it has produced great results in troubleshooting scenarios as well.

Features Available in Lync Server 2013 for Health Monitoring and Troubleshooting

In addition to identifying performance baselines, and monitoring the performance of Lync Servers, there are many other critical components of Lync Server 2013 that should actively be monitored to determine the health of the service. Lync Server 2013 allows for various ways to monitor and test the health of the system, all of which are familiar to administrators of the Windows operating system. This section provides an overview of how to use the Windows Event Viewer and synthetic transactions to monitor and troubleshoot the health of Lync services.

Using Windows Event Logs to Identify Health Issues

Windows event logs are a critical resource for any administrator of a Windows-based application. In addition to the operating system writing all activity in these logs, many applications, including Lync, write activity to the Windows event logs. Lync Server logs important informational, warning, and critical events to the Windows event log. These logs can be found in Event Viewer under Applications and Services Logs, under Lync Server. Figure 13.8 shows an example of these logs on a Lync Server.

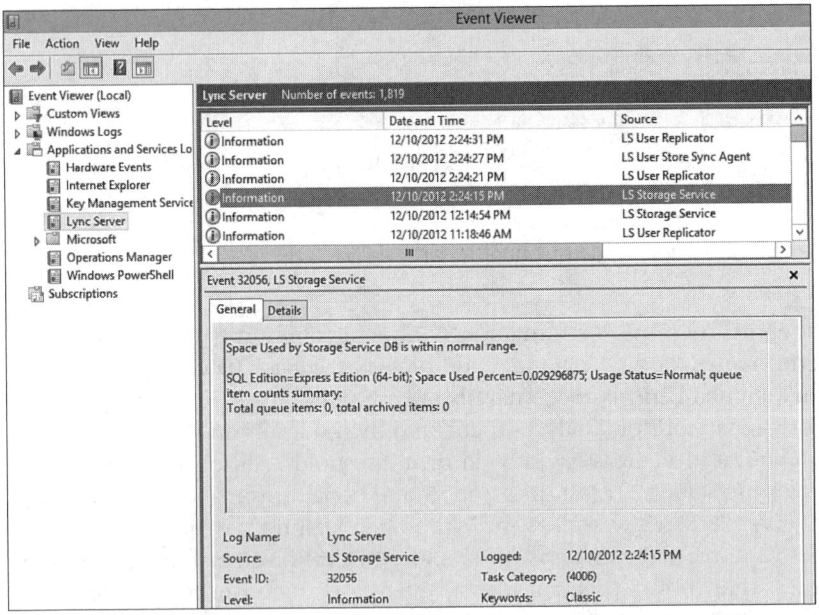

FIGURE 13.8   Lync Server event logs in Event Viewer.

Because event logs are written in the order in which they occur, they often should be the first place to look when you are troubleshooting issues. Lync Server 2013 writes all service activity, as well as critical failures in the application such as conference join failures, or outbound call routing failures.

In Lync Server 2013 deployments of all sizes, collecting event logs for each server can become a daunting task. In order to help with this it is recommended to configure a server to receive event logs for all machines. This functionality requires the following:

▶ Windows Remote Management (WinRM) enabled on all Lync servers

▶ Visual C++ 2012 Redistribution Package on the receiving server

▶ Lync Server 2013 core components on the receiving server

The Lync Server 2013 core components allow the receiving machine to understand Lync Server logs without any additional work from the administrator.

Perform the following tasks to create an Event Collector for Lync Server 2013 event logs:

1. Open Event Viewer, located in the Administrative Tools on Windows Server.

2. Right-click on the Subscriptions folder, and choose Create Subscription.

3. When in the Subscription Wizard, you should set a Subscription Name and choose the Computers and Events you will be collecting. Figure 13.9 shows an example of the basic subscription properties configuration.

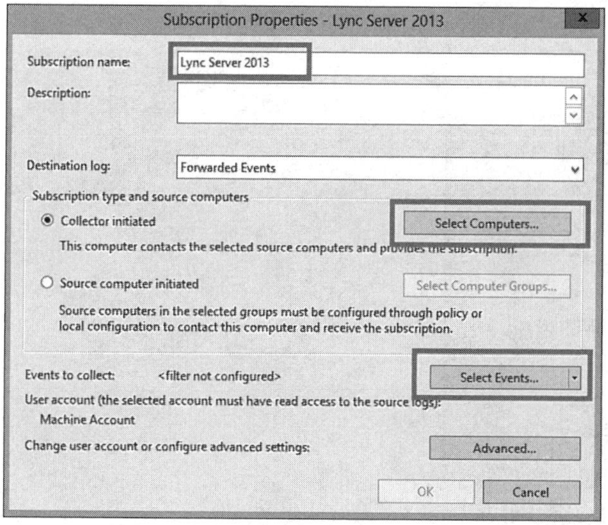

FIGURE 13.9   Lync Server 2013 event subscription.

4. Choose Select Computers and add the appropriate servers for your environment. Figure 13.10 shows an example of a Persistent Chat and SQL Server being selected for the subscription.

5. Next, choose Select Events. This box enables you to filter the events you want to receive. Figure 13.11 shows an example of just Lync Server events being selected for the subscription.

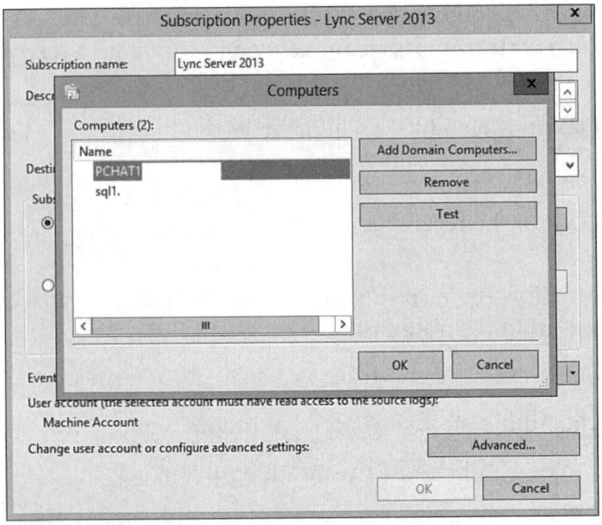

FIGURE 13.10   Adding Lync Servers to an event subscription.

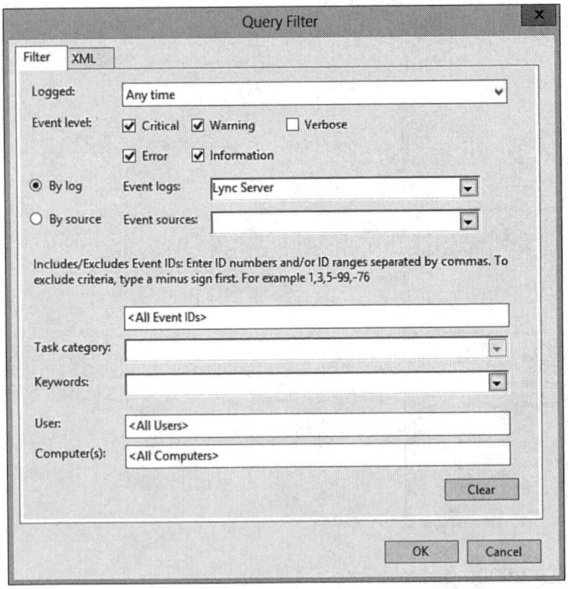

FIGURE 13.11   Choosing events for an event subscription.

6. Click OK to close the Select Events box. Then click OK to close the Subscription Wizard.

7. Events from this subscription now show under the Windows Logs\Forwarded Events folder in Event Viewer.

Windows Event Viewer can also be used on client machines to diagnose issues. By default, logging on Lync 2013 clients is not enabled. However, enabling this feature is recommended and provides a great source of information in troubleshooting specific end-user scenarios. When this is turned on, the Application event log on client machines is populated with Lync client event logs. This can be used to troubleshoot sign-in and other critical issues. Turning on this feature can be done in two ways: on the Lync 2013 client and through a Lync Client Policy, controlled by the administrator.

To enable event logging in the Lync Client Policy, do the following:

1. Open the Lync Server Management Shell (PowerShell).

2. Run the following command. The command shown here enables the global client policy with event logging; if you have separate client policies, substitute the `Identity` value.

```
Set-CSClientPolicy -Identity Global -EnableEventLogging $True
```

To enable event logging on the Lync 2013 client, do the following:

1. Open the Lync Options menu by clicking on the Options Wheel in the upper-right corner of the Lync 2013 client. See Figure 13.12 for an example.

FIGURE 13.12   Opening the Lync Options menu.

2. When in the General options window, check the box for Also Turn On Windows Event Logging for Lync to Collect Troubleshooting Info. See Figure 13.13 for an example.

Windows event logs are a powerful resource for many reasons. Utilize this tool to troubleshoot and monitor the health of your Lync Server 2013 environment.

Using Synthetic Transactions to Identify Health Issues

Synthetic transactions were introduced in Lync Server 2010 and are a powerful way for administrators to validate the health of the environment. Lync Server synthetic transactions allow many different scenarios to be tested, all through PowerShell. These tasks are able to validate end-to-end scenarios such as making a call or joining a Lync conference. This section provides an understanding of how synthetic transactions work and common transactions that can be used to identify health issues.

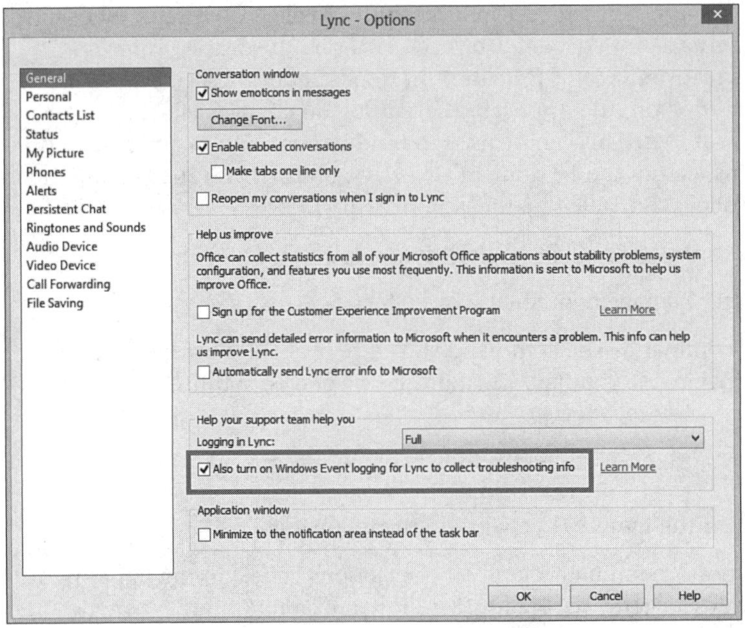

FIGURE 13.13   Enabling Lync client event logging.

Creating Lync Test Accounts for Synthetic Transactions   Test user accounts are required for synthetic transactions to validate user functionality. Although it is possible to run synthetic transactions by providing the credentials for valid user accounts, it is not recommended. The New-CSHealthMonitoringConfiguration cmdlet is used to define test accounts for each pool. When administrators specify two valid test accounts for each pool, it makes running synthetic transactions much easier because administrators are not required to provide credentials for each test. Before running this command, you should create two test accounts and enable the accounts for Lync Server. Also, be sure to assign any appropriate policies to account for scenarios you want to test. If you want to test PSTN calling, make sure that these users are enabled for Enterprise Voice and configured properly.

The command shown next creates a new health-monitoring configuration for NYPOOL01. COMPANYABC.COM. This pool will use test1@companaybc.com and test2@companyabc.com for synthetic transaction test accounts.

```
New-CSHealthMonitoringConfiguration -Identity NYPOOL01.companyabc.com -
➥FirstTestUserSIPUri "sip:test1@companyabc.com"sip:test1@contoso.com -
➥SecondTestUserSipURI sip:test2@companyabc.com
```

Using Synthetic Transactions   After test accounts have been created, services can be tested using synthetic transactions. When performing synthetic transactions using preconfigured health accounts, the Lync Server machine account will be used to impersonate those users.

As such, the use of synthetic transactions can become very simple; see the following text for examples.

To test that a user can sign on to the pool, essentially proving that the Front End Server is healthy for registration, use this:

```
Test-CSRegistration -TargetFQDN nypool01.companyabc.com
```

If it's successful, the output should look similar to this:

```
Target Fqdn     : nypool01.companyabc.com
Result          : Success
Latency         : 00:00:07.6614315
Error Message   :
Diagnosis       :
```

To test that a user can make an outbound PSTN call, including testing registration, the dial plans, and routing policies assigned, as well as the signaling and media path to the PSTN endpoint, use this:

```
Test-CSPSTNOutboundCall -TargetPSTNPhoneNumber 6000
➥-TargetFQDN nypool01.companyabc.com
```

If successful, the output should look similar to this:

```
Target Fqdn     : nypool01.companyabc.com
Result          : Success
Latency         : 00:00:10.5099552
Error Message   :
Diagnosis       :
```

> **TIP**
>
> All Lync synthetic transactions are PowerShell cmdlets that begin with `Test-`. To identify a full list of cmdlets available, you can type `Get-Command *test-*` into a PowerShell window, which will return a list of available cmdlets.

The previous examples are just a small taste of what is available as part of Lync synthetic transactions. For a full list of synthetic transactions, navigate to the following URL, and explore all cmdlets with `Test-CS` in the name: http://technet.microsoft.com/en-us/library/gg398867.aspx.

Enabling Rich Logging for Synthetic Transactions   In Lync Server 2010, synthetic transactions were a great utility for identifying service issues. However, the information reported by a failed transaction test was often not enough to help users identify where the failure was occurring. At best, the verbose output of the cmdlets would provide a record of each step tested and it might enable an administrator to narrow down the source of the issue.

Lync Server 2013 introduces rich-logging capabilities in synthetic transactions. Each time a transaction is run, the following information is generated:

▶ The time started

▶ The time finished

▶ The action that was performed

▶ Messages generated by the activity (informational, verbose, warning, or error)

▶ SIP registration messages

▶ Exception records or diagnostic codes generated when the activity ran

▶ The result of the activity

Although this information is generated each time, a parameter must be added to a manually run synthetic transaction to output to a log file. This parameter is `OutLoggerVariable`. Use the following example to test logging in to Lync Server 2013 using `Test-CSRegistration`, and then to export the logging data to an HTML file for review.

Run the `Test-CSRegistration` cmdlet with the output parameter:

```
Test-CSRegistration -TargetFQDN Nypool01.companyabc.com -OutLoggerVariable
➥TestRegistration
```

The logging data is then stored in the variable `$TestRegistration` as defined in the preceding cmdlet. Use the following command to export this data to HTML format:

```
$TestRegistration.ToHTML() | Out-File C:\logs\TestRegistration.Html
```

The report can then be opened in Internet Explorer to view the sequence of events, and any errors as appropriate. The example in Figure 13.14 shows a successful registration test.

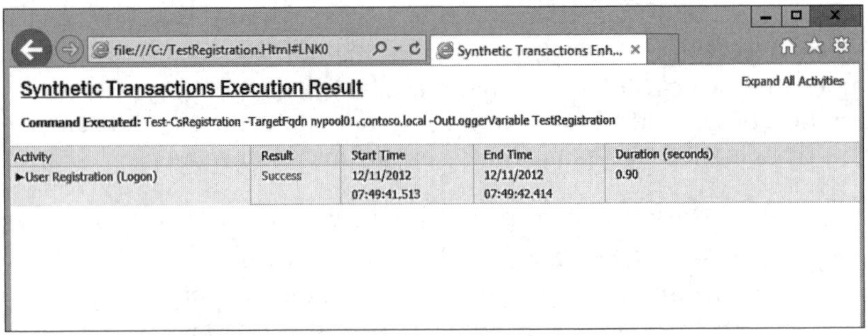

FIGURE 13.14   Viewing a synthetic transaction rich logging report.

Synthetic transactions should be a primary tool for administrators of all Lync Server 2013 environments. With this utility administrators have the ability to test and troubleshoot end-to-end user scenarios without requirements for end-user intervention.

Capabilities and Benefits of System Center Operations Manager with Lync Server

System Center Operations Manager is a comprehensive monitoring solution by Microsoft. SCOM is deployed at many organizations to monitor servers and networking equipment. SCOM operates on a model of Management Packs, which are a collection of monitors, rules, and configuration criteria that define how to monitor a service. SCOM includes Windows Server and network equipment monitoring by default. Many organizations also use SCOM to monitor applications such as Exchange Server, Active Directory, SQL Server, and other third-party applications.

Microsoft also provides a management pack for Lync Server 2013. When deploying the Lync Server 2013 Management Pack for SCOM, organizations can proactively monitor the end-to-end Lync Server environment. Essentially, all topics discussed previously in this chapter, including Performance Monitor, event logs, and synthetic transactions, are wrapped into a monitoring package with the Lync Server 2013 Management Packs for SCOM. The benefits of using SCOM for Lync Server 2013 monitoring are as listed here:

- ▶ **Scenario Availability Using Synthetic Transactions**—The Lync Server 2013 Management Pack allows synthetic transactions to automatically be run for a number of scenarios. SCOM also supports running synthetic transactions from outside the corporate network to test Edge Server scenarios.

- ▶ **Rich Transaction Logging**—The rich logging available with synthetic transactions is available in SCOM as well. Administrators can access the HTML logs to determine why the transaction failed.

- ▶ **Call Reliability Monitoring**—SCOM monitors the data from the Lync Monitoring server to monitor and alert on the real-time call quality for users. In Lync Server 2013 this also includes IM and conferencing scenarios.

- ▶ **Monitoring Downstream Components**—The health of Lync Server relies on many different components, even inside the Windows OS. The Lync Server 2013 Management Pack for SCOM checks several critical dependencies and alerts administrators on their impact as it relates to Lync.

- ▶ **Historical Reporting**—All data that is collected by SCOM can provide historical reports that help administrators with scenario availability, capacity planning, and the overall health of the environment.

SCOM combines the detailed Windows OS performance and health monitoring with enhanced Lync functionality such as synthetic transactions, call reliability alerts, media quality alerts, service and component health, and dependency health. Figure 13.15 shows an example of a monitoring view in SCOM, monitoring the critical services for Lync Server 2013.

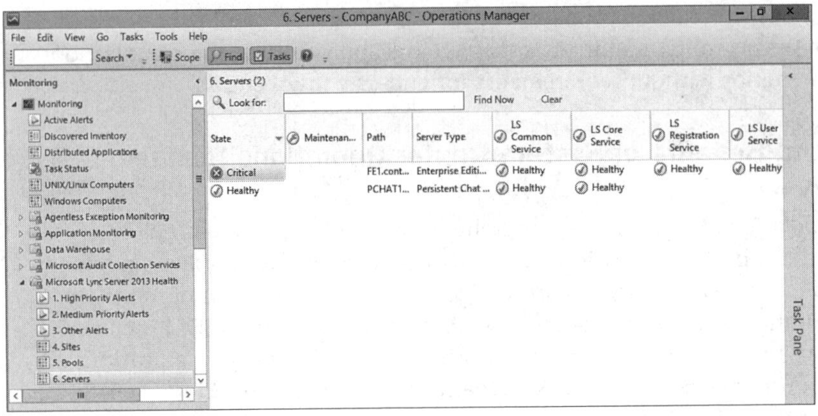

FIGURE 13.15   Example of the SCOM monitoring console for Lync Server 2013.

Monitoring the Health of Lync Server 2013 with SCOM

Deploying SCOM to monitor Lync Server 2013 is a relatively simple task. The model of importing preconfigured managed packs allows administrators to enable Lync Server 2013 monitoring with little effort. Lync Server 2013 has two management pack offerings for SCOM:

▶ **Component and User Management Pack**—This management pack is responsible for tracking event logs, performance counters, and CDR/QoE data. This allows for an out-of-the-box monitoring experience for the service health and performance of Lync Server 2013.

▶ **Active Monitoring Pack**—This management pack is responsible for running synthetic transactions through SCOM. This allows for a greater level of monitoring, but requires additional configuration.

Both management packs can be downloaded from the following URL: http://www.microsoft.com/en-us/download/details.aspx?id=35842&WT.mc_id=rss_alldownloads_all.

The sections that follow outline basic configuration tasks required to monitor Lync Server 2013 with SCOM.

Configure Component Monitoring by Importing the Component and User Management

Pack   The following tasks assume that a SCOM server has been deployed already. Additionally, all Lync Servers in the environment should already have a SCOM agent deployed to them.

1. Open the SCOM Operations Console, and navigate to the Administration pane.

2. Right-click on Management Packs and choose Import Management Pack.

3. In the Import Management Packs Wizard, choose Add and then Add from Disk.

4. Navigate to the location where you downloaded your Lync Server 2013 management packs; by default this location is `%SystemDrive%\Program Files\Microsoft Lync Server 2013\Management Packs\Management Packs.` Choose the `Microsoft.LS.2013.Monitoring.ComponentAndUser.mp` and `Microsoft.LS.2013.Monitoring.ActiveMonitoring.mp` files and click Open.

5. Click Install and wait for the import to be completed.

6. Every Lync Server must be configured as a System Center Agent Proxy. To do this, in the Administration panel click on the Agent Managed section.

7. Right-click on each Lync Server computer and choose Properties.

8. Under the Security tab, check the box for Allow This Agent to Act as a Proxy and Discover Managed Objects on Other Computers. See Figure 13.16 for an example.

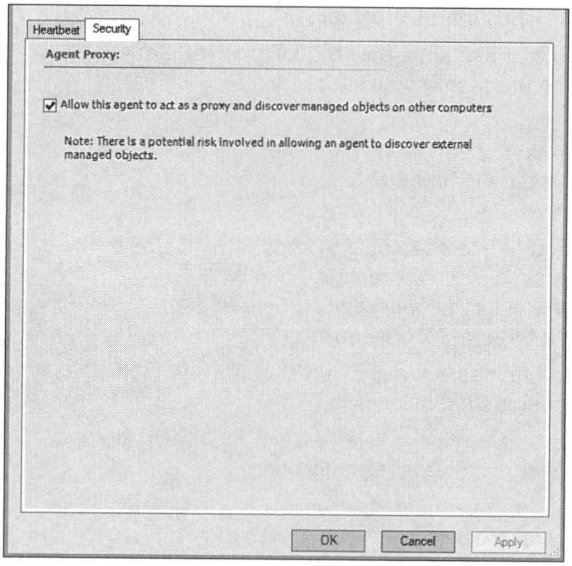

FIGURE 13.16   Agent proxy configuration.

The discovery process will happen over a random period. To validate proper discovery of your environment, expand the Microsoft Lync Server 2013 folder under the Monitoring Pane, and validate that Lync Server 2013 computers show under the Servers tab, and that services are monitored.

It is recommended to monitor the frequency of events in your environment to establish a proper notification configuration. Before configuring email alerts, consider analyzing the active alerts in the environment over a set period. After the environment has been stabilized and cleaned up, it is then appropriate to configure email alerting for critical issues in the environment.

Deploying Synthetic Transaction Monitoring with SCOM   SCOM also allows for synthetic transactions to be automated through the SCOM service. Enabling this functionality requires the deployment of a watcher node. The watcher node acts as a trusted Lync Server 2013 computer that is running synthetic transactions on behalf of test users. This watcher node reports statuses to SCOM servers, resulting in real-time monitoring and alerting on real user scenarios.

The synthetic transactions available in the Lync Server 2013 Management Pack test the scenarios given in Table 13.1.

TABLE 13.1   Synthetic Transactions Available in SCOM

Test Name	Scenario	Default/ Nondefault
Test-CsAddressBookService (ABS)	Confirms that users are able to look up users who aren't in their contact list.	Default
Test-CsAddressBookWebQuery (ABWQ)	Confirms that users are able to look up users who aren't in their contact list via HTTP.	Default
Test-CsAVConference (AvConference)	Confirms that users are able to create and participate in an audio/video conference.	Default
Test-CsGroupIM (IM Conferencing)	Confirms that users are able to send instant messages in conferences and participate in instant message conversations with three or more people.	Default
Test-CsIM (P2P IM)	Confirms that users are able to send peer-to-peer instant messages.	Default
Test-CsP2PAV (P2PAV)	Confirms that users are able to place peer-to-peer audio calls (signaling only).	Default
Test-CsPresence (Presence)	Confirms that users are able to view other users' presence.	Default
Test-CsRegistration (Registration)	Confirms that users are able sign in to Lync.	Default
Test-CsPstnPeerToPeerCall (PSTN)	Confirms that users are able to place and receive calls with people outside of the enterprise (PSTN numbers).	Nondefault, Extended
Test-CsAVEdgeConnectivity	Confirms that the Audio Video Edge servers are able to accept connections for peer-to-peer calls and conference calls.	Nondefault
Test-CsDataConference (DataConference)	Confirms that users can participate in a data collaboration conference (an online meeting that includes activities such as whiteboards and polls).	Nondefault

Test Name	Scenario	Default/ Nondefault
`Test-CsExumConnectivity` (ExumConnectivity)	Confirms that a user can connect to Exchange Unified Messaging (UM).	Nondefault
`Test-CsGroupIM` `-TestJoinLauncher` (JoinLauncher)	Confirms that users are able to create and join scheduled meetings (by a web address link).	Nondefault
`Test-CsMCXP2PIM` (MCXP2PIM)	Confirms that mobile device users are able to register and send instant messages.	Nondefault
`Test-` `CsPersistentChatMessage` (PersistentChatMessage)	Confirms that users can exchange messages by using the Persistent Chat service.	Nondefault
`Test-CsUnifiedContactStore` (UnifiedContactStore)	Confirms that a user's contacts can be accessed through the unified contact store. The unified contact store provides a way for users to maintain a single set of contacts that can be accessed by using Lync 2013, Microsoft Outlook messaging and collaboration client, and/ or Microsoft Outlook Web Access.	Nondefault
`Test-CsXmppIM` (XmppIM)	Confirms that an instant message can be sent across the Extensible Messaging and Presence Protocol (XMPP) gateway.	Nondefault

Transactions in Table 13.1 marked as Default are transactions that are turned on by default when you configure a watcher node in SCOM. Transactions marked as Nondefault are not run by default, but can easily be enabled on the watcher node. Transactions marked as Extended are nondefault transactions that can also be run multiple times during each pass. Extended transactions are targeted at scenarios such as multiple voice routes for a pool.

The watcher node used for Lync Server 2013 monitoring should be a dedicated server. Synthetic transactions can generate a large amount of traffic, as such an existing production server should not be used. A server that will act as a watcher node must meet the following requirements:

▶ All Lync Server 2013 prerequisites

▶ Full version of .NET Framework 4.5

▶ Windows Identity Foundation

▶ Windows PowerShell 3.0

13

The high-level steps required for deploying a watcher node are as listed here:

1. Install the Lync Server 2013 core files on the watcher node computer. You can do this by running the Lync Deployment Wizard and choosing to install administrative tools.

2. Install the SCOM agent files by deploying an agent to the watcher node computer using the SCOM console.

3. Run the `watchernode.msi` file included as part of the Lync Server 2013 Management Pack on the watcher node computer.

4. Configure the watcher node settings in Lync Server 2013 using Lync Management Shell and `New-CSWatcherNodeConfiguration`.

A watcher node computer can authenticate with Lync Server 2013 in two ways to run synthetic transactions. The authentication method will decide configuration steps that are required. See Table 13.2 for an overview of these authentication methods.

TABLE 13.2   Authentication Methods Available to Watcher Nodes

Authentication Method	Description	Location Supported
Trusted Server	Uses a certificate to authenticate as a Lync server and bypass user authentication challenges. This is the recommended configuration and requires the least amount of operational overhead.	Inside the corporate network. The watcher node must be in the same domain as the servers being monitored.
Credential Authentication	Stores usernames and passwords securely in the Windows Credential Manager on the watcher node. This requires more operational overhead to manage passwords.	Outside the corporate network. Inside the corporate network.

If the watcher node will be used inside the corporate network, it should be deployed as a trusted server. To configure the watcher node computer as a trusted server, perform the following steps:

1. Open Lync Server Management Shell (PowerShell).

2. Run a command similar to the following. This example shows creating `watcher.companyabc.com` as a watcher node:

```
New-CSTrustedApplicationPool -identity watcher.companyabc.com -Registrar
➥NYPOOL01.companyabc.com -ThrottleAsServer $True -TreatAsAuthenticated $True -
➥OutboundOnly $false -RequiresReplication $True -ComputerFQDN
➥watcher.companyabc.com -site "New York"
```

3. After creating the trusted application pool, a trusted application identity must be created. Run the following command:

```
New-CSTrustedApplication -ApplicationID STWatcherNode
➡-TrustedApplicationPoolFQDN watcher.companyabc.com -Port 5061
```

4. Next, run `Enable-CSTopology` in the Lync Management Shell. When it has completed, restart the watcher node computer.

After the watcher node computer has been configured as a trusted application server, run the Lync Server Deployment Wizard and install a certificate using the Request, Install or Assign Certificate Wizard.

After the previous steps are completed, the `watchernode.msi` file must be run on the watcher node computer. Perform the following steps on the watcher node computer:

1. Open a command prompt as Administrator.

2. Navigate to the folder where `watchernode.msi` is located.

3. Run the following command:

```
watchernode.msi Authentication=TrustedServer
```

TIP

The `watchernode.msi` syntax is case-sensitive. `TrustedServer` must be entered exactly as shown or the install will fail.

After the watcher node computer has had all files installed, the watcher node must be configured to run synthetic transactions. Before enabling synthetic transactions, health testing accounts should be created. For information on how to create test accounts, see the section "Creating Lync Test Accounts for Synthetic Transactions," earlier in this chapter. To test all scenarios, you must enable three test accounts for use with the watcher node.

When test accounts have been created, perform the following steps to enable a new watcher node to run synthetic transactions:

1. Open the Lync Server Management Shell (PowerShell).

2. Run the following command to deploy the default synthetic transactions:

```
New-CSWatcherNodeConfiguration -TargetFQDN nypool01.companaybc.com
➡-PortNumber 5061 -TestUsers
➡@{add="sip:test1@companyabc.com","sip:test2@companyabc.com",
➡"sip:test3@companyabc.com"}
```

This command will create a new watcher node using default settings. The target Front End Pool will be NYpool01.companaybc.com. The watcher node will use the test accounts test1@companyabc.com, test2@companyabc.com, and test3@companyabc.com.

At this point, the environment will be configured with basic activity monitoring. To validate the configuration of the watcher nodes in the environment, run the cmdlet Test-CSWatcherNodeConfiguration.

This section has provided a summary of the benefits of monitoring Lync Server 2013 with SCOM and how to enable this functionality in a Lync Server 2013 environment. This monitoring solution includes many more features than described here, and it is recommended that you explore all the available configuration options and capabilities of SCOM monitoring. For a complete guide on monitoring Lync with SCOM, see the TechNet library located at http://technet.microsoft.com/en-us/library/jj205188.aspx.

Summary

Lync Server 2013 is a complex service that spans multiple technologies. A major key to success in deploying Lync at any organization is establishing a proper monitoring plan. Identifying all components to be monitored, and implementing a solution that seamlessly monitors each solution, will move organizations one step closer to the goal of a successful Lync deployment.

The Windows operating system includes tools available to monitor Lync including Performance Monitor and event logs. Additionally, Lync Server 2013 can provide end-user scenario testing and health validation using synthetic transactions. System Center Operations Manager is a utility that can be used to automate all monitoring tools available to Lync under a single management interface. SCOM enables organizations to successfully monitor the availability and quality of the Lync service deployed in their environment.

CHAPTER 14

Administration of Microsoft Lync Server 2013

Administration of Lync Server 2013 is a welcome relief for those who ever spent time managing a Live Communications Server or Office Communications Server deployment. The older products were based on a Microsoft Management Console snap-in that was not intuitive and often required many clicks to perform simple tasks. This chapter covers some of the improvements found in Lync Server 2013, such as the Lync Server Control Panel and the Lync Server Management Shell.

The addition of the Lync Server Management Shell follows the precedent set by the Microsoft Exchange Server team, and the Lync team has taken another cue by including role-based access control (RBAC) in this release. The Lync RBAC differs slightly from Exchange RBAC and is compared in this chapter.

Also discussed is the new topology model in which all server planning and configuration are performed centrally. Building a topology using the Topology Builder and storing the configuration in the new Central Management Store (CMS) are explained in this chapter. The new scope-based policies are covered as well.

Common management tasks, such as draining servers or configuring Quality of Service settings, are detailed in this chapter. Finally, common troubleshooting steps are described with examples, and how to use the new Centralized Logging Service (CLS) is covered.

Administration Overview

The life of a Lync Server administrator varies depending on the role within the organization, and Lync Server 2013 accommodates many different scenarios and administrator use cases. Instead of resorting to a complex and difficult management console or Visual Basic script files, Lync Server 2013 continues with an improved user interface backed by a management shell based on Windows PowerShell just as in Exchange Server since 2007. Combined with the role-based access control, administrators can tackle delegated specific tasks either in the Lync Server Control Panel or via the Lync Server Management Shell command-line interface.

Lync Server Control Panel

A fairly drastic shift that started with Lync Server 2010 was the initiative to completely remove the emphasis on managing servers using the Microsoft Management Console (MMC). As in Lync Server 2010, the MMC is replaced with the Lync Server Control Panel (LSCP), which is a web-based management interface that uses the Microsoft Silverlight runtime for management tasks. Figure 14.1 shows the layout of the new interface.

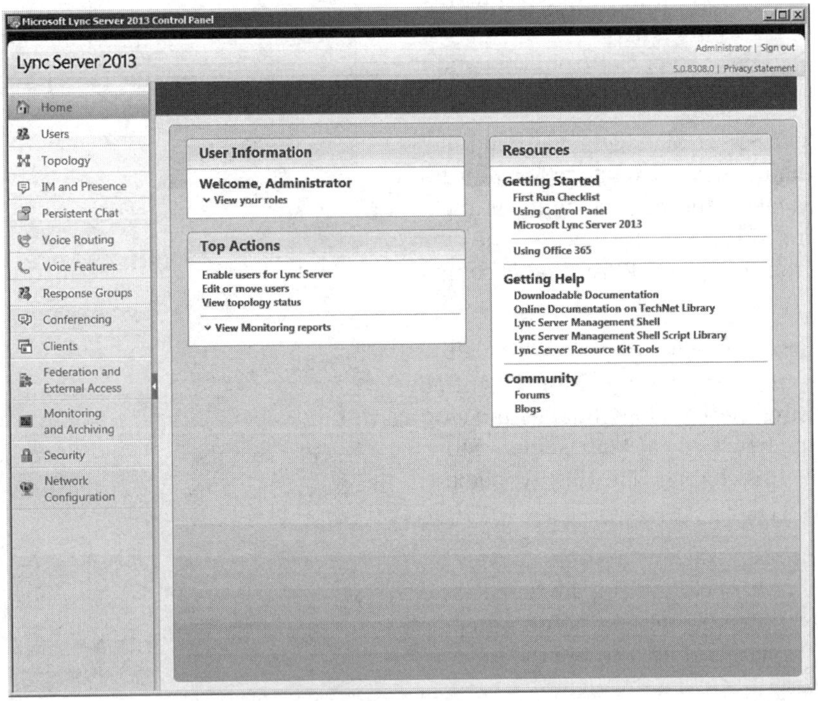

FIGURE 14.1   Lync Server Control Panel interface.

This change has several benefits that are immediately visible to administrators familiar with installing the old management tools on a separate workstation. Installation of the administrative tools took manually going through four to five different installation package prerequisites before the OCS administrative tools could be installed. Instead, the requirement now is that the end user must have the latest Silverlight plugin for the web browser.

From within the Lync Server Control Panel, administrators have a centralized dashboard for all management activities. This includes managing user accounts and policies that control what features are available to users.

> **NOTE**
>
> Opening the Lync Server Control Panel is similar to opening a web browser to the administrative web page. By default, Internet Explorer does not pass credentials to a site unless specifically allowed, so administrators are prompted for credentials each time. To prevent the prompt for credentials, add the Lync administrative URL to the Local Intranet Zone in Internet Explorer. By default, this is https://<Pool FQDN or admin simple URL>.

The Lync Server Control Panel is divided into several sections, and each section has subsections for specific actions or policies. An overview of the options available within each section is given in the following:

▶ **Users**—Enables or disables users for Lync services, assigns policies to users, and moves users between pools.

▶ **Topology**—Provides a health overview of the deployment and reports on the status of all services. The different server applications and trusted applications are also displayed in this section.

▶ **IM and Presence**—Provides the file transfer, and intelligent IM filter settings.

▶ **Persistent Chat**—Sets the configuration for persistent chat categories, policies, and global configuration.

▶ **Voice Routing**—Contains settings for dial plans, voice policies, routes, trunk configuration, and PSTN usages. This section also contains test cases for assessing whether dial plans and routing are working as expected.

▶ **Voice Features**—Contains settings for the voice applications such as call park and unassigned number routing.

▶ **Response Groups**—Provides links to the management interface for Response Group configuration. Queues and groups can be added or modified in this section as well.

▶ **Conferencing**—Configures conferencing policies, meeting configuration, dial-in access numbers, and PIN policies.

▶ **Clients**—Controls Lync client versioning and updates. Firmware updates for Lync Phone Edition phones are also managed in this section.

▶ **Federation and External Access**—Contains external access policies controlling federation and public IM connectivity. Federated domains and allowed public IM networks are configured within this section.

▶ **Monitoring and Archiving**—Configures settings for Call Detail Records, Quality of Experience monitoring, and instant message archiving.

▶ **Security**—Controls authentication methods for clients and PIN policies for Lync Phone Edition devices.

▶ **Network Configuration**—Configures the topology used for Call Admission Control, Media Bypass, and E-911.

NOTE

Although the Lync Server Control Panel has its advantages over MMC management tasks, there are also some downsides, such as the fact that no right-click functionality is available. This might be an adjustment that helps drive more administrators to learn the Lync Server Management Shell instead.

Lync Server Management Shell

A big change first introduced in Lync Server 2010, and now carried into Lync Server 2013, is the addition of the Lync Server Management Shell (LSMS). The LSMS is built on Microsoft's PowerShell command and scripting environment and is really the core of what drives Lync Server 2013 management. Many administrators will use the Lync Server Control Panel by default because they are more familiar with a graphical user interface, but as time goes on, it should become apparent that much of Lync server management can be done in a more efficient manner through the LSMS.

Many organizations that use Microsoft Exchange Server are already familiar with how the Management Shell operates. When Microsoft first introduced the Exchange Management Shell as part of Exchange Server 2007, many administrators were frustrated and even intimidated by having some functionality available only in a command-line interface. The same is now true with the LSMS for previous administrators of LCS and OCS. Often, the same team within an organization who manages Exchange is responsible for managing Lync. If administrators have experience with the Exchange Management Shell, the change might not seem quite as drastic. For those entirely new to a command-line interface, it might take some time to feel comfortable.

Benefits of the Management Shell

For administrators primarily familiar with using graphical user interface (GUI) tools to manage systems, the LSMS might seem a bit intimidating at first, but Lync Server administrators new to PowerShell should spend some time getting acquainted with the new command-line-based toolset for several reasons. One reason for using LSMS is that some tasks and actions simply do not exist within the LSCP, so for these types of features, administrators must resort to using the LSMS. For example, in Live Communications

Server and Office Communications Server, changing the port that a Front End Server used for SIP communication involved just a few check boxes within the management console. With Lync Server 2010, the only way to modify the port or add a port is to use the LSMS.

Another major benefit of the LSMS is that bulk tasks are much easier to accomplish. With the older products, a task such as moving users between pools or modifying assigned policies was typically done through the management consoles and involved running through multiple pages of a wizard. Selecting the correct users to modify was also somewhat difficult because there was no breakdown of groups or divisions within the GUI. In the end, it was apparent that performing bulk tasks needed some attention from the product group. With the LSMS, administrators have an incredible degree of flexibility in how to perform certain tasks. It is easy for administrators to select a group of users based on an attribute and modify all policies or move users quickly.

> **CAUTION**
>
> Although bulk changes are easy to make with the LSMS, that also means it can be easy to make a mistake and have it affect many user accounts. Be sure to always test bulk changes on a smaller subset of users. If possible, have a test or development environment where bulk changes can be verified before they run against the production systems.

Some organizations familiar with PowerShell use custom scripts to provision new user accounts. Scripting these kinds of operations greatly reduces the chance for a human error to affect the account creation.

Just imagine how many times the wrong dial plan, voice policy, or conferencing policy can be applied to a new account when left as a manual process. For small organizations this isn't typically an issue, but for larger companies having a standardized, automated method is a necessity.

This kind of PowerShell-based provisioning has been fairly typical for Exchange mailboxes since Exchange 2007. Because OCS did not have any native PowerShell support, organizations were forced to continue using VBScript or some other method to automatically enable new accounts for OCS. With the LSMS, an entire workflow script can be used to create new accounts. When a new user joins the company, a PowerShell script is used to automatically create the new user account, place it in the correct organizational unit, provision a home folder, create an Exchange mailbox on the correct database, enable the user for Lync, and assign the correct voice and conferencing policies. Not only is the chance for error reduced, but consider how much time is saved by not requiring extra work.

Management Shell Basics

Tasks are performed in PowerShell through commands called cmdlets. Cmdlets each have a specific function and their names begin with a verb, such as Get or Set, indicating what action will be taken. The remainder of the cmdlet name determines what specific object will be viewed or acted on. The Lync Server Management Shell is built on top of the Windows PowerShell engine, meaning that everything you can do within Windows

PowerShell can also be done within the Lync Server Management Shell. The opposite, however, is not true.

When the Lync Server Management Shell is loading, an extensive list of more than 500 custom cmdlets is loaded on top of the base PowerShell cmdlets available. These new cmdlets are specific to Lync Server and enable administrators to manage Lync components through the Management Shell.

Most of the cmdlets within the Lync Server Management Shell are consistent in their naming approach because they follow a format consisting of a verb, a hyphen, the letters "Cs," and, lastly, an item.

NOTE

All the cmdlets in Lync Server 2013 include the `Cs` designator, which stands for Communications Server. The history here is that the actual name change from Communications Server 2010 to Lync Server 2010 happened fairly late in the product life cycle, and the cmdlet naming was never, and probably never will be, updated.

This might seem long, but it makes sense when you view the actual cmdlets. Commands to view the configuration or properties of an item all begin with `Get`, and when changing or assigning new properties, the cmdlet begins with `Set`. For example, to view the properties of a particular Lync user account, the cmdlet `Get-CsUser` can be used. To set one of the properties for a user account, such as a phone number, the `Set-CsUser` cmdlet can be used.

The first parameter in any cmdlet is referred to as the identity, which signifies what object will be acted on. Not all `Get` cmdlets require an identity to be provided, and when it is omitted, a list of all the matching objects is returned. For example, running `Get-CsUser -Identity sip:tom@companyabc.com` returns the properties of only a single user, but simply running `Get-CsUser` with no identity specified returns a list of all users and their properties.

When a `Set` command is used, though, an identity must be specified so that the Management Shell knows which object should be modified. Additionally, the attribute of the object being modified must be specified. Only the attribute being changed must be included, so if other attributes are staying the same there is no need to include them. For example, if a user needs to be enabled for Enterprise Voice and assigned a Line URI, the command looks like the following string:

```
Set-CsUser -Identity sip:tom@companyabc.com -EnterpriseVoiceEnabled $true
➥-LineUri tel:+12223334444
```

Commands can also be strung together, or "piped" to one another. When piped to another cmdlet, the object passed from the first cmdlet is assumed to be the identity in the second cmdlet. Continuing the preceding example, an equivalent command to the `Set-CsUser` example is the following string:

```
Get-CsUser -Identity sip:tom@companyabc.com | Set-CsUser -EnterpriseVoiceEnabled
➥$true -LineUri tel:+12223334444
```

This might not seem beneficial when a single user is involved, but when multiple objects are piped to another cmdlet, they will each run through the destination cmdlet. Consider a scenario in which an organization wants to enable all users who have a display name starting with the letter T for Enterprise Voice. First, the Get-CsUser cmdlet is used, but to return only the users whose display name begins with T, a Filter parameter is used. For those familiar with filtering using the Where-Object cmdlet, the Filter parameter uses the same syntax and operators. The Where-Object cmdlet can also be used here, but the built-in Filter parameter is more straightforward:

```
Get-CsUser -Filter {DisplayName -like "T*"}
```

This can be built on even further by piping the results to a Set-CsUser cmdlet where the users can be enabled for Enterprise Voice:

```
Get-CsUser -Filter {DisplayName -like "T*"} | Set-CsUser
➥-EnterpriseVoiceEnabled $true
```

This short string of cmdlets can enable thousands of users for Enterprise Voice in a much faster method than using the Lync Server Control Panel.

Tips and Tricks

There are quite a few shortcuts and tricks that can be used within the Lync Server Management Shell to save time. This section discusses a few tips that might make using the Management Shell a bit easier and more efficient.

Use the Tab Key

Instead of typing a full cmdlet name, begin typing the first few letters after the action verb and press the Tab key. The Management Shell automatically cycles through the cmdlets that match the string already entered. For example, typing Get-CsP and then pressing Tab automatically changes the string to Get-CsPinPolicy. Pressing Tab again changes it to Get-CsPool. Use Tab to go forward through the list and press Shift+Tab to cycle backward. The Tab key can also autocomplete parameters inside the cmdlet, so it is handy when recalling the exact parameter name. If the tab complete feature is not working it probably means the command is already misspelled and no match can be found.

Skip the Identity

Although the identity specifies an object and is a required parameter when changing an object, it's not required to type the entire identity parameter. If the identity is not explicitly referenced, the first string after the cmdlet is assumed to be the identity. For example, the following two commands are equivalent in functionality, but one requires fewer characters:

```
Get-CsVoicePolicy -Identity Executives
Get-CsVoicePolicy Executives
```

Surround Spaces with Quotation Marks

When referencing objects or names that have spaces or special characters, make sure that the entire text string is enclosed in quotation marks or single quotation marks. When PowerShell detects a space, it assumes that the next character will be the beginning of a new parameter. When the text string is not within quotation marks, commands might fail. Both single and double quotation marks are acceptable. For example, when trying to retrieve the user Tom Pacyk, this command generates an error:

```
Get-CsUser Tom Pacyk
```

To successfully return the correct user, use the following command:

```
Get-CsUser "Tom Pacyk"
```

Leverage `Get-Help`

Included within all the Lync Server Management Shell cmdlets is a built-in help reference. To retrieve assistance with any cmdlet, simply type `Get-Help` followed by the name of the cmdlet. For example, to get assistance with the `Set-CsDialPlan` cmdlet, type

```
Get-Help Set-CsDialPlan
```

This help request returns a description of the cmdlet's purpose, the full syntax and parameters available in the cmdlet, and a summary of what the cmdlet does. More information can also be requested using the `-Examples`, `-Detailed`, and `-Full` flags at the end of the command. `-Examples` returns sample commands with the correct syntax, `-Detailed` returns a description of each parameter, and `-Full` returns the complete documentation available.

Having this help reference available without manually searching through documentation is incredibly useful. It can also come in handy when you're having trouble remembering a specific cmdlet name. In these cases, wildcards can be used to search through the documentation for a match. For example, the following command returns a list that displays `Set-CsBandwidthPolicyServiceConfiguration` and `Set-CsBlockedDomain`:

```
Get-Help Set-CsB*
```

Role-Based Access Control

As originally introduced in Lync Server 2010, Lync Server 2013 has the concept of role-based access control. RBAC allows for a degree of flexibility in management of the infrastructure simply not possible with a traditional approach to administration control. In prior versions of the product, an administrator typically had full control of the environment and was able to modify any part of a deployment. With RBAC, permissions can be defined in a more granular method so that different levels of administrators can be delegated specific settings to manage.

Lync Versus Exchange RBAC

The basis for role-based access control is to provide a specific set of permissions and actions allowed to a group. For those familiar with Exchange RBAC, it should be apparent that the Lync version is not nearly as flexible. Exchange 2010 administrators can define the exact cmdlets and attributes allowed for each management role. With Lync Server 2013, administrators can only base new roles on an existing template. Individual cmdlets cannot be added or removed. Assignment of a management role can be done only by placing user accounts within a security group.

Default Roles

Lync Server 2013 ships with several predefined RBAC roles. These roles exist in any deployment after the preparation steps have been completed and have a global scope. The default RBAC roles in Lync Server 2013 include the following:

▶ `CsAdministrator`—This is the equivalent of RTCUniversalServerAdmins from OCS 2007. Users assigned this role have complete control over any part of the system. They can modify the topology, manage user accounts, and create additional RBAC roles. The CS Administrators group in Active Directory is assigned this role.

▶ `CsArchivingAdministrator`—Allows for modifying the archiving policies and configuration within the organization. This role is intended for compliance or legal department users who are responsible for archiving policies. The CS Archiving Administrators group in Active Directory is assigned to this role.

▶ `CsHelpDesk`—This role is slightly more advanced than `CsViewOnlyAdministrator` and includes the capability to perform basic troubleshooting. This role cannot modify any user properties or assign policies as `CsUserAdministrator` can. The CS Help Desk group in Active Directory is assigned to this role.

▶ `CsLocationAdministrator`—This role has the capability to modify and associate the locations and network subnets involved in E-911. The CS Location Administrators group in Active Directory is assigned to this role.

▶ `CsPersistentChatAdministrator`—This role has the capability to manage the Persistent Chat global settings, categories, and chat rooms. The CS Persistent Chat Administrators group in Active Directory is assigned to this role.

▶ `CsResponseGroupAdministrator`—This role permits modification of Response Group queues, agent groups, and workflows. It is intended for users who are responsible for a small call center or the Interactive Voice Response (IVR) systems in the organization. The CS Response Group Administrators in Active Directory is assigned to this role.

▶ `CsUserAdministrator`—This role relates to the RTCUniversalUserAdmins group from OCS 2007. This role is geared toward help desk administrators and allows for enabling or disabling users for Lync. This role can also move users between pools and assign policies to accounts. The CS User Administrators group in Active Directory is assigned this role.

14

▶ **CsServerAdministrator**—This role can manage individual Lync servers. It is geared toward users who manage, monitor, and troubleshoot Lync servers. It is slightly a step below the `CsAdministrator` role because no changes that globally affect the deployment, such as topology modifications, are permitted. This role typically is assigned to users who are responsible for day-to-day operations and management of Lync servers. The CS Server Administrators group in Active Directory is assigned to this role.

▶ **CsViewOnlyAdministrator**—Permits read-only access to the Lync Server deployment. This includes topology, pool, server, and user configuration, but no changes can be made. The CS View-Only Administrators group in Active Directory is assigned to this role.

▶ **CsVoiceAdministrator**—Users assigned to this role can manage any of the voice features found in Lync Server 2030. This includes creation and modification of dial plans, routes, voice policies, and PSTN usages. Typically this is assigned to telephony or voice team users. The CS Voice Administrators group in Active Directory is assigned to this role.

NOTE

You cannot modify the default RBAC roles. Instead, create new roles to suit the needs of each organization.

Creating New Roles

Organizations can build on the default RBAC roles by creating their own custom roles. To create a new role, use the following steps:

1. Create a security group with the same name as what the role will be named.

2. Identify a preexisting RBAC role that contains most of the cmdlets required for the new role. It will serve as a template for the new role.

3. Decide on a Lync server scope for the new role. This can be a global site, a single site, or multiple sites.

4. (Optional) Decide on an organization scope for the new role. A role can be limited to affect only user accounts within a specific OU in Active Directory.

To create a new RBAC role, use the following syntax within the Lync Management Shell:

```
New-CsAdminRole -Identity <AD Security Group Name> -Template <Preexisting Role Name>
➥-ConfigScopes <Lync Configuration Scope> -UserScopes <Organizational Units>
```

For example, to create a new role called `SanFranciscoUserAdmins` scoped to the SF site and the SF OU, use the following syntax:

```
New-CsAdminRole -Identity SanFranciscoUserAdmins -Template CsUserAdministrators
➥-ConfigScopes "site:SF"
➥-UserScopes "OU=SF Users,OU=Company ABC,DC=companyabc,DC=com"
```

> **NOTE**
>
> Users logged on locally to a Lync Server and executing the commands in the Lync Management Shell are not affected by RBAC. RBAC roles are enforced only when using the Lync Server Control Panel or PowerShell Remoting.

Using the Lync Topology Model

Starting with Lync Server 2010, some significant changes to how the deployment is managed have been made. Instead of individually installing and configuring servers, the deployment is managed centrally through a tool called Topology Builder. This shift in management helps make administration easier for organizations and limits the potential for mistakes.

For those familiar with Office Communications Server 2007 R2, administrators had to log on to each server in the topology and manually configure options such as next hops, monitoring associations, and service ports. With Lync Server 2013, the configuration is completed in advance and then published to the Central Management Store (CMS).

When a server is deployed, it installs SQL Server Express. A local copy of the CMS is then replicated to this SQL instance so that the server can reference the entire topology. When the administrator begins installation, the server reads the topology and installs any roles within the topology that match the fully qualified domain name of itself.

> **NOTE**
>
> The only configuration required to link or associate servers with each other is performed automatically during the installation process. This helps reduce the chance for incorrect settings that cause unpredictable or problematic behavior for the servers.

To review, the deployment model with Lync Server follows the following high-level steps:

1. The administrator creates the topology by defining all sites, servers, and gateways in the deployment.

2. The topology is then published to the Central Management Store.

3. A Lync server installs the SQL Express engine and creates a local replica of the CMS.

4. The Lync server reads the local CMS replica and installs the roles matching its FQDN.

14

Central Management Store

The preceding section referenced the Central Management Store. To understand the responsibility of the CMS, it is important to understand how prior versions of the product operated such that server and service configuration was stored within Active Directory. Live Communications Server and Office Communications Server both stored configuration information within the System partition of the forest root domain. In many cases, this was acceptable, but it caused performance problems in scenarios in which a remote office had poor connectivity to a domain controller in the forest root domain.

This was because the System container is not replicated to all domain controllers in the forest, so servers could be required to leverage WAN links to read settings even if a domain controller existed locally.

To mitigate these problems, Office Communications Server 2007 R2 recommended migrating the settings to the Configuration container instead, which is replicated to all domain controllers in the forest. This solved the problem, but organizations had a confusing manual migration path to move settings to the new container and often skipped this step. Furthermore, organizations could not move the settings after installing OCS 2007 R2, so they were stuck in this state with performance problems.

With Lync Server 2010 and 2013, the settings for the deployment have moved from Active Directory to the CMS, which is just an additional SQL database. The CMS must be populated before the first pool is created, and this is done automatically if the first pool is a Standard Edition server. The CMS can be stored on the same SQL server and instance acting as a Back End Server for a pool, and after installation the CMS can be moved to another server at any time.

As indicated earlier, when a server is prepared for a Lync Server installation, the first action it takes is to install a local replica of the CMS. As changes occur in the CMS, these changes are synchronized out to all members of the topology, which removes the need for servers to maintain a constant connection to a centralized configuration store. Servers synchronize the changes regularly and use the information stored locally instead of contacting a central point for settings, which improves performance and stability.

Topology Builder

Included with Lync Server 2013 is the Topology Builder application, shown in Figure 14.2. The Topology Builder is a centralized configuration point for adding servers to the deployment or changing configuration. All naming, IP addressing, and association of servers are performed through the Topology Builder so that administrators do not need to individually configure servers. This helps reduce the number of errors made during configuration of pools with multiple members.

Each server site is defined within the Topology Builder, and then each specific server role is defined and associated with a site. When completed, administrators can publish the topology to the CMS, where it can be read by servers.

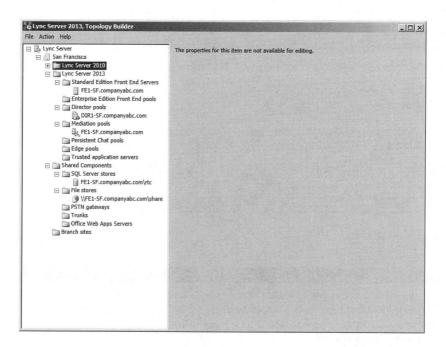

FIGURE 14.2   The Topology Builder tool.

Scopes

Scopes in Lync Server 2013 are available to help define the boundary of a policy. Scopes are applied based on the topology built within the Topology Builder. The highest level that exists is the Global level. Within the Global level are sites, which represent physical locations where pools exist. Sites typically are data centers where the Front End pool servers reside. Each site then contains the pools that make up the deployment. A site can have one pool or multiple pools. This arrangement is depicted in Figure 14.3.

After the topology is defined, default policies for many aspects of Lync Server 2013 are created. For example, global policies are created for Voice Policies, Conferencing Policies, and External Access Policies.

Global policies apply to all sites, pools, and users by default. Additional policies can be created at any of the other scopes as well, giving flexibility on overriding the defaults. The benefit of applying policies to a site or pool scope is that the additional task of assigning a policy directly to the users is no longer required. Instead, policies defined at a higher level are automatically applied to all scopes below as long as the lower scope does not have a policy already defined.

Administrators can still create new policies and assign them directly to a user account to override any global or site policies. This might be necessary to grant executives or VIP users a higher level of access than the default for everyone else in the site.

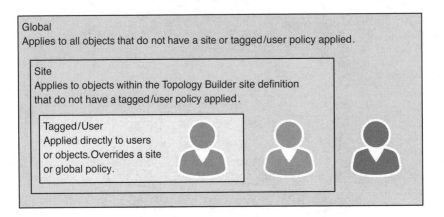

Global
Applies to all objects that do not have a site or tagged/user policy applied.

Site
Applies to objects within the Topology Builder site definition
that do not have a tagged/user policy applied.

Tagged/User
Applied directly to users
or objects. Overrides a site
or global policy.

FIGURE 14.3   Scope priority.

NOTE

In terms of priority, the policy assigned closest to the user account takes precedence. User policies override pool policies, pool policies override site policies, and site policies override the global policy. Policies automatically trickle down from the global level unless a policy exists closer to the user.

Managing Servers and Users

There are some tasks that any administrator of Lync Server 2013 will manage at some point. This section covers some of these items that don't occur on a daily basis but might be required at some point.

Lync Server Logging Tool

When all else fails and the problem cannot be diagnosed, perform a diagnostic trace of the server traffic. Logging in Lync Server 2013 has changed quite a bit from prior versions in which a GUI logging tool was available to collect traces. Logging in Lync Server 2013 now uses the Centralized Logging Service, which is collecting logs by default, and is intended to give a single management point for retrieving necessary traces. In older versions of Lync, an administrator had to enable logging individually on every single server in a pool, even multiple pools if the issue involved a few hops. This was a very tedious process and made it very difficult to locate a particular message flow.

The CLS is constantly logging by default, so administrators no longer need to reproduce an issue after enabling the traces in order to capture basic traffic. Now, when users report an issue, the Lync administrators can easily conduct a search across all servers involved in a user's message and see that traffic centrally.

NOTE

Traditional tools like Microsoft Network Monitor or Wireshark are unable to display Lync traffic by default because it is TLS-encrypted. Although it is possible to decrypt the traffic after loading certificates and private keys, it is far easier to use the native tools and CLS to Lync SIP traffic.

The `ClsController.exe` tool is now used manage the logging and searches. It can be found on any system with the Lync administration tools installed in `C:\Program Files\Common Files\Microsoft Lync Server 2013\ClsAgent`, but it is actually managed using PowerShell cmdlets native to Lync. Another change is that the tool now logs based on specific scenarios instead of requiring an administrator to select specific trace components.

You can retrieve the current logging configuration using

```
Get-CsCsClsConfiguration
```

The logs are stored on each server in the `%TEMP%\Tracing` folder by default, and will allow only up to 80% of available disk space.

Searching the Log Files

Since most cases will be covered by the default AlwaysOn scenario, administrators can begin troubleshooting by searching for a specific pool or user with the `Search-CsLogging` cmdlet.

For example, to search for a specific user's traffic on a single pool during a known time frame, use this:

```
Search-CsClsLogging -Pools LYNCPOOL1.companyabc.com -Uri "tom@companyabc.com"
➥-StartTime "12/9/2012 10:00AM" -EndTime "12/9/2012 1:00 PM" -MatchAll
```

By default, any parameter included in the search is considered an acceptable match. That is to say that the `-MatchAny` parameter is always assumed unless the administrator specifies `-MatchAll` within the search. The preceding example would have returned all traffic on `LYNCPOOL1.companyabc.com`, all traffic from the user `tom@companyabc.com`, and all traffic in the organization between 10:00 a.m. and 1:00 p.m. on 12/9/2012 if `-MatchAll` had not been specified.

Alternatively, use the following syntax to search for a single user's traffic across all pools in the organization, which is the really powerful part of the new service:

```
Search-CsClsLogging -Uri "tom@companyabc.com"
```

Viewing Log Files

`Search-CsClsLogging` generates log files that can be read using the same Snooper tool found in the Resource Kit download package. Open the resulting file in Snooper to inspect the traffic.

A message-by-message view of the conversation is located on the left side. Clicking any of the lines changes the view in the right-side pane to display the entire SIP message selected. Error messages are highlighted in red for easy identification. A search bar, where keywords such as a username or phone number are entered, is located at the top of the window. After you've entered a search string and pressed Enter, the view is filtered to display only messages with that string. This kind of filtering can be useful when searching for problems with a single user because it removes all the other traffic through the server.

Figure 14.4 displays a sample SIP trace using the Snooper tool.

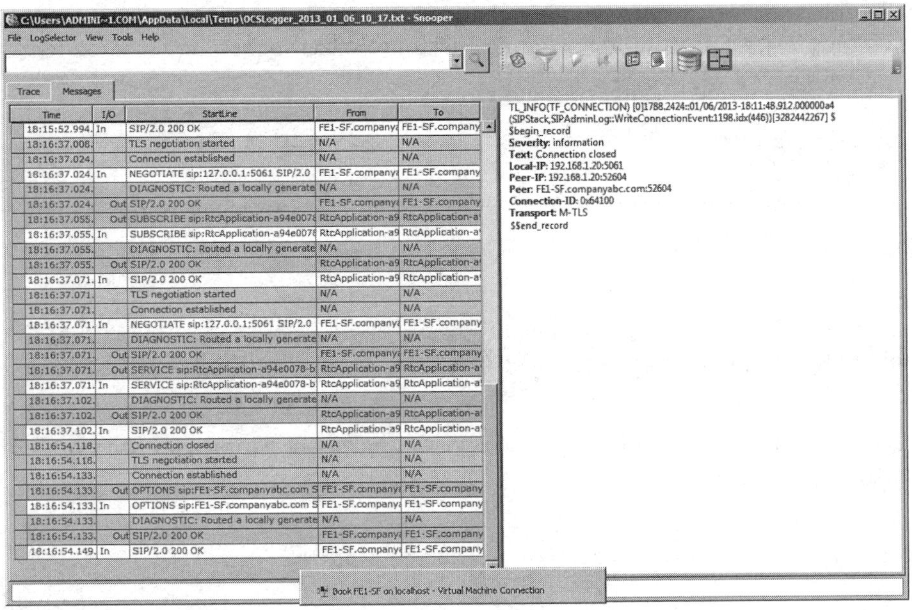

FIGURE 14.4   Using Snooper to view a SIP trace.

Starting and Stopping Logging

As mentioned previously, most scenarios are going to be covered by AlwaysOn being enabled by default. If administrators do need to log on different components, the following syntax can be used with a specific scenario:

```
Start-CsClsLogging -Scenario <Scenario Name> -Duration <Time in Days:Hours:Minutes>
➥-Pools <Comma-Separated List of Pool Names>
```

Use the Stop-CsClsLogging cmdlet to manually stop a scenario, but keep in mind that any started logging scenarios will stop automatically after the specified duration expires. The different scenarios available include those in Table 14.1.

TABLE 14.1   Available Centralized Logging Scenarios

Scenario	Description
AlwaysOn	Default
AddressBook	Address book generation and distribution group expansion
ApplicationSharing	Desktop and application sharing
AudioVideoConferencingIssue	Audio and video conferencing
CAA	Conferencing Auto Attendant
CLS	Centralized Logging Service
CPS	Call Park Service
DeviceUpdate	Device update service
IMAndPresence	Instant messaging and presence
IncomingAndOutgoingCall	Call routing
HostedMigration	Hosted migration
HybridVoice	Office 365 hybrid voice
LILRLegacy	Log retention
LILRLYSS	Log retention for Lync Storage Service
LYSSaAndUCS	Lync Storage Service
MediaConnectivity	Media connections
MeetingJoin	Meeting join experience
MonitoringAndArchiving	Monitoring and archiving service
RGS	Response Group Service
SP	Support Portal
UserReplicator	User Replicator Service
VoiceMail	Exchange voice mail integration
WAC	Office Web Apps integration
XMPP	XMPP Service

Server Draining

A useful feature in Lync Server 2013 is the concept of draining a server when preparing it for maintenance. This enables an administrator to prepare a server for maintenance without immediately affecting users. Existing sessions on the server are ended immediately and users are transferred to a different server within the pool.

To prepare a server for maintenance, follow these steps:

1. Open the Lync Server Control Panel.

2. Click Topology.

3. Highlight the server to be modified.

4. Click Action and select Prevent New Connections for All Services.

5. Alternatively, double-click the server to drill down further and manage the individual services.

> **NOTE**
>
> Preventing new connections is a feature that only works with DNS load balancing and has no effect on whether a hardware load balancer continues to send traffic to a server. If using a hardware load balancer, perform the draining steps there instead.

This feature also does not cover load balancing of the web component services. The hardware load balancer used to distribute traffic to these services must also be drained to prevent new connections to the server prepared for maintenance.

Database Import/Export

A tool familiar to many LCS, OCS, and Lync Server 2010 administrators is the database import/export tool called `dmbimpexp.exe`. This tool enables administrators to import or export user contact lists using XML files. Typically a SQL server backup captures the rtc database that contains the user contact lists, but having the XML version available can be useful when restoring from a backup that is slow or unavailable.

Starting with Lync Server 2013, this tool has been removed and replaced with a series of native cmdlets providing similar functionality. The `Export-CsUserData`, `Import-CsUserData`, `Update-CsUserData`, and `Convert-CsUserData` cmdlets provide these same features and offer a solution native to the Lync Server Management Shell.

There are many options when running dbimpexp, but the basic functionality is fairly straightforward. For a full list of the options available, see the `dbimpexp-readme.html` file included in the same folder as the executable.

To export all user contact lists from an Enterprise or Standard Edition pool, the same syntax can now be used:

```
Export-CsUserData -PoolFQDN "<Pool FQDN>" -FileName "<Path and Filename>.zip"
```

After the contact lists are exported to XML and safe, they can be applied back to the users at any time. A scheduled task can easily perform this action on a nightly or weekly basis. Importing the contact lists is just as simple as the export procedure. By default, the contents of the XML file are merged with a user's existing contacts, but the `/delete` option can be used to empty the contact list before an import is performed.

To import all user contact lists from an Enterprise or Standard Edition pool, use the following syntax:

```
Import-CsUserData -PoolFQDN "<Pool FQDN>" -FileName "<Path and Filename>.zip"
```

> **CAUTION**
>
> In prior versions of the product, these imports would take effect immediately. In Lync Server 2013 the Front End Service must be restarted on all pool members before the imports are visible. Use the `Update-CsUserData` cmdlet instead to skip the restart requirement.

These cmdlets are very powerful tools and can have a visible impact on user accounts if used incorrectly, so run some test scenarios before doing these changes in bulk. The export and import procedures can be targeted to only a single user via the `-UserFilter` parameter.

Configuring Quality of Service

Quality of Service (QoS) can be used in networks where the media traffic used by Lync Server 2030 servers and clients should have a higher priority than other traffic using the same infrastructure. This is done by having the Lync servers and endpoints tag their media traffic packets with a specific Differentiated Services Code Point (DSCP) value. Routers within the network are then configured to prioritize traffic based on the DSCP values included with packets.

DSCP marking in Lync Server 2013 is done by using the policy-based QoS first introduced with Windows Server 2008 and Windows Vista. These policies are controlled through Windows Group Policy and can mark traffic with DSCP codes based on application names and port ranges. Because these policies can be centrally managed and controlled by the organization, it should be acceptable to trust the markings sent from client endpoints. Using a separate port range for each type of traffic enables the policy-based QoS to tag the traffic appropriately. For example, audio traffic using one port range can be assigned a DSCP code with higher priority than the port range used for video or application sharing.

> **CAUTION**
>
> Network equipment is typically configured to ignore or not trust DSCP markings from computers on the regular data network. Because Lync is a softphone and operates using the same VLAN as PCs, the markings from machines on the data VLAN must be trusted to use QoS with Lync.

Server Configuration

Lync servers operate similarly to clients and tag media traffic through the use of policy-based QoS in Group Policy. Each media type has one of the following default port ranges assigned:

- ▶ Audio (49,152–57,500)

- ▶ Video (57,501–65,535)

- ▶ Application sharing (49,152–65,535)

These port ranges can then be matched through policy-based QoS and assigned a DSCP marking. The default port range for application sharing overlaps with both audio and video. If application sharing is tagged differently than either traffic, a separate port range must be configured. Port ranges for each media type can be configured using the `Set-CsConferenceServer` and `Set-CsMediationServer` cmdlets.

Unfortunately, the Lync product team uses overlapping port ranges by default, so administrators cannot determine whether traffic is application sharing or audio or video. To effectively implement QoS, the port ranges should be nonoverlapping. For example, to separate application sharing into its own port range, run the following command:

```
Set-CsConferenceServer -AppSharingPortStart 40803
```

This changes application sharing to use ports 40,803–57,185 while keeping the same number of ports available. The latest Lync documentation actually recommends also adjusting the `AppSharingPortCount` to 8348 as part of the QoS configuration.

Using the same port ranges on each conferencing, application, and Mediation server will help simplify configuration. Use the `Set-CsConferenceServer`, `Set-CsApplicationServer`, and `Set-CsMediationServer` cmdlets to configure these ranges.

Client Configuration

QoS tagging of the media is performed by the Lync client itself, so it must be provisioned in a way that it understands what ports to use for each type of traffic. By default, no tagging is done and all traffic uses the port range 5350–5389. The Lync client supports using different port ranges for the following types of traffic and recommends using a minimum of 20 ports per modality. This roughly translates to 20 concurrent calls per modality, which should be more than enough for any single endpoint.

First, to enable separate port ranges for each media type, run the following command:

```
Set-CsConferencingConfiguration -ClientMediaPortRangeEnabled $true
```

Next, define a unique port range for each type of traffic. As an example, the ports used on the client side can be the same as those on the server. The sample numbers used here are well beyond the minimum number of ports required and are used only to show how the default port ranges can be moved. The port ranges used should be limited to the recommended sizes for ease of management and troubleshooting.

```
Set-CsConferencingConfiguration -ClientAudioPort 500020 -ClientAudioPortRange 20
➥-ClientVideoPort 58000-58019 -ClientVideoPortRange 20 -ClientAppSharingPort 40803
➥-ClientAppSharingPortRange 20 -ClientFileTransferPort 40783
➥-ClientFileTransferPortRange 20
```

NOTE

The suggested port range from TechNet as of this writing uses overlapping ranges for application sharing and file transfer. The preceding example breaks File Transfer into a separate range so it is not accidentally tagged as application-sharing traffic.

Creating a Client QoS Policy

After modifying the Lync clients and servers to use specific port ranges, QoS policies must be created for the servers and clients to add the appropriate DSCP value to traffic originating from each port range. The steps required to use policy-based QoS through Group Policy are similar, but the port ranges used for servers and clients will likely differ. Create at least two separate policies: one for servers and one for clients. To create a new policy, perform the following steps:

1. Open a new Group Policy object.

2. Expand Computer Configuration, Windows Settings, and then click Policy-Based QoS.

3. Right-click Policy-Based QoS and select Create New Policy.

4. Enter a name for the policy, such as `Lync Audio`.

5. Enter a DSCP value, such as `46`, and click Next.

6. For the client policy, limit the tagging only to Lync clients by selecting Only Applications with This Executable Name, and enter `lync.exe`. Do not specify an executable for the server policies. Click Next.

7. Allow the policy to apply to Any Source IP Address and Any Destination IP Address.

8. In the Select the Protocol This QoS Policy Applies To area, select TCP and UDP.

9. In the Specify the Source Port Number section, select From This Source Port Number or Range, and enter the range used for audio traffic, such as `50020:50039`.

10. Click Finish to complete the policy.

11. Repeat these steps for each type of media using a unique port range, which should be tagged differently. Figure 14.5 demonstrates what a policy with separate audio and video settings looks like.

NOTE

The A/V Edge Service behaves a bit differently. First, because it typically is not part of the domain, it might be necessary to create the policies locally on each server. Second, the port range used to define each service should be specified as a *destination* port instead of source port. This ensures that traffic passed between the Edge Server and the Front End pool is marked correctly. The defined port range used for the Front End or clients will always be a destination port range from the Edge Server's perspective.

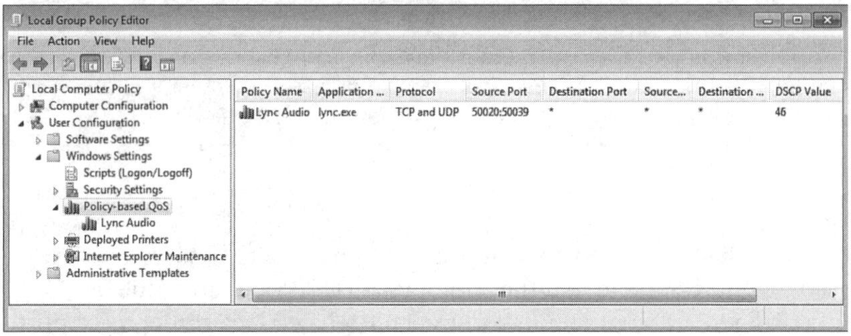

FIGURE 14.5   Policy-based QoS.

Non-Windows-Based Devices

Because QoS policies can be created only on Windows Vista or later operating systems, the process for enabling QoS on third-party devices is slightly different. These devices receive instructions to enable QoS through the following command:

```
Set-CsMediaConfiguration Global -EnableQoS $true
```

Lync Phone Edition QoS

The final client type that can use QoS settings is the Lync Phone Edition client, which can run on third-party partner hardware. Lync Phone Edition settings are determined through in-band signaling to the devices. In addition to a DSCP value for audio traffic, the Lync Phone Edition clients also support 802.1p.

To set the Lync Phone Edition QoS settings, use the following command on a Lync server:

```
Set-CsUcPhoneConfiguration -VoiceDiffServTag 46
```

Set-CsUcPhoneConfiguration still includes the Voice8021p parameter used to define a 802.1p class, but it has no effect on devices in Lync Server 2013. Instead, use DSCP values for providing QoS markings.

Troubleshooting

Troubleshooting a Lync Server installation might become necessary in the event that users are unable to sign in or features seem to not work correctly. This section discusses the key components to check when issues arise. Common troubleshooting tools and tips are also provided, which should resolve many issues.

Certificates

Incorrectly issued certificates were a common issue in Office Communications Server deployments, but these issues should mostly be mitigated with the new Lync Server wizards. The option to manually request and modify the certificate still exists, which might lead to some problems.

Follow these guidelines to rule out any certificate issues:

▶ **Subject and subject alternative names**—Ensure that the required subject name and subject alternative names have been entered for each role. The guidance for each role varies, so verify the names required when deploying a new server. Always use the certificate wizard suggested names if possible. Wildcard certificates are still technically supported for certain scenarios, but the recommendation is still to avoid these due to a number of caveats.

▶ **Key bit length**—The certificate bit length must be 1024, 2048, or 4096 to be supported by Lync Server 2013.

▶ **Template**—The template used to issue the certificate should be based on the web server template. If the Lync Server 2013 certificate wizard is used, the correct template will automatically be applied.

▶ **Private key**—The server certificate must have the private key associated to be used by Lync Server 2013. In situations in which certificates are exported or copied between servers, export the private key with the certificate.

▶ **Certificate chain**—The server must be able to verify each certificate up to a Trusted Root Certification Authority. Additionally, because the server is presenting the certificate to clients, it must contain each intermediate certificate in the certificate chain.

▶ **Certificate store**—All certificates used by a server must be located in the Personal section of the local computer certificate store. A common mistake is to place certificates in the Personal section of the user account certificate store.

▶ **Certificate trust**—Be sure that the clients and servers communicating with the server all contain a copy of the top-level certificate authority of the chain in their Trusted Root Certification Authority local computer store. When the certification authority is integrated with Active Directory, this is generally not an issue, but when an offline or nonintegrated certificate authority is used, it might be necessary to install root certificates on clients and servers.

DNS Records

Successful operation of Lync servers is heavily dependent on correctly configuring DNS. All necessary DNS records should exist and resolve to the correct locations. Verify that all servers have a host record configured in DNS. Separate web component URLs and simple URLs are not automatically entered and must be manually created by an administrator.

Use the following sample nslookup sequence within a command prompt to check the host record of the pool:

```
nslookup
set type=a
lyncpool1.companyabc.com
```

A successful query returns a name and an IP address. Verify that the IP returned matches the IP addresses assigned to the servers or load balancer and that no extra, or surprise, IP addresses are returned.

To verify the SRV record required for automatic client sign-in internally, the syntax is slightly different. The following is another sample nslookup sequence:

```
nslookup
set type=srv
_sipinternaltls._tcp.companyabc.com
```

A successful query returns a priority, weight, port, and server hostname. Verify that the server name matches the pool name and that the correct port is returned.

Event Logs

A good source of information in troubleshooting any server issue is the event logs. Lync Server 2013 creates a dedicated event log for informational activities, warnings, and errors within the standard Windows Server Event Viewer console. To view this event log, following these steps:

1. Click Start.

2. Type `eventvwr.msc` and click OK to open the Event Viewer Microsoft Management Console.

3. Expand the `Applications and Services Logs` folder.

4. Click the Lync Server log.

5. Examine the log for warning or error events, which might provide additional insight into any issues.

Lync Server Management Shell

The Lync Server 2013 Management Shell provides several cmdlets, which are used to test various functions of a server. A useful cmdlet for verifying the overall health of a server is `Test-CSComputer` which verifies that all services are running, the local computer group membership is correctly populated with the necessary Lync Server Active Directory groups, and the required Windows Firewall ports have been opened. The `Test-CSComputer` cmdlet must run from the local computer and uses the following syntax:

```
Test-CSComputer -Report "C:\Test-CSComputer Results.xml"
```

After running the cmdlet, open the generated XML file to view a detailed analysis of each check.

Synthetic Transactions

A new feature in Lync Server 2013 is the introduction of synthetic transactions, which are a set of PowerShell cmdlets used to simulate actions taken by servers or users in the environment. These synthetic transactions enable an administrator to conduct realistic tests against a service. In the case of a Director, the most useful synthetic transaction is the `Test-CSRegistration` cmdlet, which simulates a user signing into the specified server.

The `Test-CSRegistration` cmdlet requires providing a target server, user credential, and SIP address. A registrar port can optionally be included. The user credential parameter's username and password must be collected by an authentication dialog and saved to a variable as in the following command:

```
$Credential = Get-Credential "COMPANYABC\tom"
```

After the credentials are collected, the cmdlet can be run with the user credential variable previously saved:

```
Test-CSRegistration -TargetFQDN lyncpool1.companyabc.com -UserCredential $Credential
➥-UserSipAddress "sip:tom@companyabc.com" -RegistrarPort 5061 -Verbose
```

also

```
TargetFQDN    : lyncpool1.companyabc.com
Result        : Success
Latency        : 00:00:10.9506726
Error         :
Diagnosis     :
```

As seen in the output, the registration test was successful.

Telnet

Telnet is a simple method of checking whether a specific TCP port is available from a client machine. From a machine that is having trouble contacting a server, use the following steps to verify connectivity to the Registrar service:

1. Open a command prompt.

2. Type the following command:

   ```
   telnet <Director pool FQDN> 5061
   ```

If the window goes blank and only a flashing cursor is seen, it means the connection was successful and the port can be contacted without issue. If the connection fails, an error is returned. Check that the services are running on the Director and that no firewalls are blocking the traffic.

TIP

The Telnet client has not installed by default since Windows Vista and Windows Server 2008. On a desktop operating system, it must be installed using the Turn Windows Features On or Off option found in Programs and Features. On a server operating system, it can be installed through the Features section of Server Manager.

Time

A key component of any service running successfully in Lync Server 2013 is the computer time. Verify that the clocks on the Lync Server 2013 servers are correctly set and have the appropriate time zones configured. If the clocks between a server and a client are off by more than five minutes, authentication will begin to fail, which might prevent users from logging on successfully.

Services

Basic troubleshooting always begins with making sure that the Lync Server services are all running. When services are in a stopped state, users will see many issues such as being unable to sign in or connect to the server. Verify that the following services are configured to start automatically and are running. Verification of the services can be done either through the traditional Services MMC or through the Lync Server Management Shell.

To verify that the services are running, open the Lync Server Management Shell and run the Get-CsWindowsService cmdlet. As shown here, this cmdlet returns both the service status and how many active connections exist, which can be valuable information when a server is being drained for maintenance.

```
PS C:\> Get-CsWindowsService
Status Name            Activity Level
Running W3SVC
Running REPLICA
Running RTCCLSAGT
Running RTCSRV          Incoming requests per second=0
Running RTCCAA          Concurrent Calls=0
Running RTCCAS          Concurrent Conferences=0
Running RTCRGS          Current Active Calls=0
Running RTCCPS          Total Parked Calls=0
Running RTCATS          Current Active Calls=0
Running RTCIMMCU        Active Conferences=0
Running RTCDATAMCU      Active Conferences=0
Running RTCAVMCU        Number of Conferences=0
Running RTCASMCU        Active Conferences=0
Running RTCMEDSRV       Current Outbound Calls=0
```

The following command quickly identifies nonrunning services by skipping the activity check:

```
Get-CsWindowsService -ExcludeActivityLevel | Where-Object {$_.Status -ne "Running"}
```

Best Practices

The following are best practices from this chapter:

▶ Use the new Lync Server Management Shell for bulk administration tasks or to perform tasks more quickly than possible within the Lync Server Control Panel.

▶ Create RBAC roles, which are scoped appropriately for administrators within the organization. Different sets of users can be managed by different administrators easily with this new flexibility.

▶ Use Quality of Service on Lync servers and clients to help improve media quality on unreliable or oversaturated networks.

▶ Use synthetic transactions to test Lync Server services easily. These PowerShell cmdlets do not require a test workstation, but can simulate user activities against the server.

▶ Become familiar with the Lync Server Logging Tool and how to diagnose issues with SIP tracing. This greatly improves the speed and accuracy in resolving problems.

Summary

It should be apparent that the new changes to the administration model are going to make lives easier within many organizations. Although the Lync Server Control Panel certainly has its nuances, such as no right-click functionality, the layout and organization are welcome changes. For the tasks that are tedious to perform in a user interface, administrators now have the full power of the Lync Server Management Shell at their disposal. This automates batch tasks or enables organizations to develop scripts to create new users based on PowerShell.

The topology model also helps to reduce the number of errors or anomalies created by requiring administrators to configure servers individually in prior versions. This centralized approach to setup ensures that all pool members are identical and that the topology should work before ever being placed into production. Scope-based policies enable organizations to standardize on global or site policies easily, ensuring that users are not assigned different policies.

A good portion of any Lync Server administrator's life includes some troubleshooting, so becoming familiar with the most common issues and tools is highly recommended. The new synthetic transactions can help administrators stay on top of problems before they become major issues, and the Lync Server Logging Tool is a valuable resource for diagnosing errors.

CHAPTER 15

High-Availability and Disaster Recovery

Planning for availability and recovery of business-critical applications is a process that must be carried out in every IT organization. As organizations shift real-time communications to Lync Server 2013, there are many important considerations for ensuring Service Level Agreement (SLA). This chapter provides best practices for deploying Lync Server 2013 as a highly available, business-critical application in any organization.

Defining Business Requirements for High-Availability and Disaster Recovery

For a Lync Server 2013 deployment of any type to be successful, the person deploying the technology must first understand the business requirements for the solution. Not only is this important for defining functional requirements, but the business must also be consulted on the SLA requirements for the environment. Organizations must plan and document the availability requirements of the Lync infrastructure, as well as the disaster recovery requirements. For disaster recovery, there are two key requirements that must be identified, recovery point objective (RPO) and recovery time objective (RTO). This section should help you understand what is required to properly identify what level of availability is required, as well as identify the RPO and RTO for organizations.

Identifying Availability Requirements

Many organizations have predefined service levels for IT applications and services. Lync Server 2013 often falls into many different service-level definitions, depending on the workloads deployed. Table 15.1 provides an example of service levels in a typical enterprise organization.

TABLE 15.1   Lync Service Levels

Lync Functionality	Service Level	Description
IM and Presence	Medium	IM and Presence is often classified as requiring medium or even high service levels at organizations. Many businesses rely on IM and Presence for business-critical communications.
Conferencing	High	When conferencing is moved to Lync Server 2013 from a previous provider, the service level should be considered high. This functionality is critical for internal and external collaboration and communications. Audio bridges are often used as the primary tool for communicating with customers and partners.
Enterprise Voice	High	When Lync Server is being used to replace a legacy telephony system, the Lync service is classified as a high service level.

The service levels described in Table 15.1 represent a generic overview of common Lync service levels. These levels also translate to detailed requirements for availability. Availability is presented based on the percentage of downtime throughout the entire year. Services with a high service level are often targeting 99.999% availability. However, it is important to understand what those percentages actually translate to in order to guide businesses down the right path for a highly available Lync Server system.

What Do Service Levels Really Mean?

Availability is defined as the level of redundancy applied to a system for ensuring an absolute degree of operational continuity during planned and unplanned outages. Many organizations will require that Lync Server systems are available without service interruption at all times. However, many people forget to consider the impact that regular maintenance on the Lync systems, as well as contributing components such as the network and directory services, can have on the availability of Lync. When an organization states that they want to have "five 9's" of availability for Lync, it would mean that the Lync service can have no more than 5.256 minutes of downtime for the entire year! SLA percentages are often misunderstood, and they can have a major impact on the design of the infrastructure a well as the surrounding operations. Table 15.2 outlines the most common SLA definitions and the associated downtime.

TABLE 15.2   SLA Definitions and Associated Downtime

Nines	Availability	Downtime Per Year
One nine	90%	36.5 days
Three nines	99.9%	8.76 hours
Four nines	99.99%	52.56 minutes
Five nines	99.999%	5.256 minutes
Six nines	99.9999%	31.536 seconds

It is important to be familiar with common SLA definitions when you are defining business requirements for any organization. Because planned outages such as maintenance and upgrades are often counted toward the overall downtime of a system, it is critical to design the Lync system to accommodate that requirement. A Lync system with the SLA of four nines would allow only 52.56 minutes of downtime for the entire year. This will require maintenance to happen without any service interruption to end users.

Understanding the Business Impact of High-Availability and Disaster Recovery

The availability required of a Lync Server system can have a major financial impact. It is important to work with the business owners to understand the appropriate balance of availability and cost. As the availability of a system is increased, cost rises in the areas covered in the following subsections.

Server Hardware and Software

The most obvious area where an organization will see increased costs is in server costs. When a Lync service is being scaled to match high service levels, additional servers as well as software for those servers are required. In a typical case, each server can come with additional costs, such as these:

- ▶ Physical hardware

- ▶ Hardware warranty/service

- ▶ Datacenter space (if physical)

- ▶ Windows Operating System license

- ▶ SQL Server license (if backend or witness for failover)

- ▶ Lync Server license

- ▶ Antivirus license

- ▶ System management software license (such as SCCM or other management software)

As can be seen in the preceding list, adding more systems to the environment can introduce lots of new costs. In many organizations, the cost to deploy additional servers is worth the investment for providing service availability. However, it is important to consider these costs when designing for availability.

Networking   Major network investments must be made to support any highly available Unified Communications (UC) service. In addition to often having to increase bandwidth, and deploy additional circuits for redundancy, the network configuration will become much more complex. Consider the following areas when planning for network costs related to availability:

- ▶ Network bandwidth

- ▶ Additional network circuits

- ▶ Network hardware (routers, switches, firewalls, hardware load balancers, and so on)

- ▶ Licensing for advanced features (many systems require additional licensing to support high-availability scenarios)

The network often requires a major investment when deploying UC. A major portion of the network investment might be related to capacity and quality increases to support usage, but a large portion should also be considered for supporting the availability of the entire UC service.

System Operations Complexity   To support the additional servers and network equipment and configurations that are deployed, highly skilled engineers are required to follow very well-defined procedures. Keep in mind that in order to ensure that the service availability for Lync Server, end-to-end management of the infrastructure must be streamlined. This includes everything from server management, client deployment, and support, to network management and facilities management.

The processes deployed to support a highly available service increase the complexity of the environment, and as a result the service is more expensive to run. This cost is associated with the staff to manage the environment. Consider the time that must be spent supporting the complex systems, as well as following procedures to ensure proper availability. This will result in additional head count, as well as more advanced resources. In some instances, this will also result in third-party support contracts. Although a third-party support service might be required to ensure service availability, it often is not accounted for in initial financial planning.

Designing for High-Availability

With an understanding of the business requirements for high-availability, you can now properly design for providing that level of service availability. This section outlines how to properly design for high-availability. It also provides detailed high-availability options for Lync Server 2013 components.

Understanding High-Availability

Availability describes the redundancy that has been applied to Lync Server 2013 to keep the service up and running for users. The secondary focus of high-availability is to reduce the end-user impact in the event of a system failure. To make a Lync Server system highly available, it often means deploying redundant quantities of every component. The simplest example of this is to deploy at least two of each server type; in theory, this provides the system with high-availability. However, that simple concept is much more complicated. Lync Server 2013 has many components, as well as shared systems, that must be accounted for.

High-Availability Options in Lync Server 2013

Lync Server 2013 was designed by Microsoft to enable organizations to support even the most stringent of high-availability service requirements. The next sections outline how each system component can be made highly available.

Table 15.3 outlines the failure scenarios, and the capabilities to provide high-availability in earlier versions of Lync, and Lync Server 2013.

TABLE 15.3   Lync Server High-Availability Capabilities

Scenario	OCS 2007 R2	Lync 2010	Lync 2013
Server Failure	Server pool via hardware load balancing	Server pool via HLB and DNS load balancing	Same as Lync Server 2010
Backend (SQL) Failure	SQL Backup and Restore	SQL clustering and SAN-based shared storage	SQL mirroring without the need for shared storage Support for auto failover and failback with a witness Integrated configuration with Planning Tool, Topology Builder, and Control Panel

What Services Are Supported for Lync High-Availability?

First, let's cover what services are able to be made highly available. Table 15.4 outlines the highly available components in Lync Server 2013.

TABLE 15.4   Features Supported for High-Availability

Feature	Supports HA
Peer-to-peer (all modalities)	Yes
Presence	Yes
Conferencing (all modalities)	Yes
UC Web App	Yes
Archiving	Yes
CDR/QOE	Yes
Federation	Yes
PIC federation	Yes

Feature	Supports HA
Unified Contact Store	Yes
Topology Builder	Yes
Lync Server Control Panel	Yes
Persistent Chat	Yes
Planning Tool	Yes
PSTN Voice	Yes
Voice applications (CAA,CAS,PVA,GVA)	Yes
RGS, Call Park, E911	Yes
Call Admission Control	Yes
XMPP	Yes

As shown in Table 15.4, Lync Server 2013 allows all components to be made highly available.

SQL Server Backend High-Availability

Lync Server relies on a SQL Server backend to support the environment. In previous versions, a SQL Enterprise Cluster was required to provide high-availability to SQL. However, Lync Server 2013 introduces support for SQL Server mirroring, and SQL Clustering is no longer supported. SQL mirroring introduces a primary and secondary model for the backend database. Essentially, the primary publish (SQL Server 1) will copy all databases to the secondary subscriber (SQL Server 2). This happens after every SQL transaction has been completed. Each transaction is then committed to the mirror, resulting in an always-up-to-date copy of the information.

In the event of a SQL Server failure, the mirror server takes over. This failover can be invoked by an administrator, or can happen automatically. For the failover to happen automatically, a third server must be deployed as a witness. The witness will monitor the availability of the SQL Servers, and in the event of a failure, it will invoke the failover to the mirror.

To deploy this functionality, the minimum supported SQL version is SQL Server 2008 R2; you must also deploy all SQL Servers in the mirroring configuration on the same SQL version.

> **NOTE**
>
> It is possible to deploy the primary and mirror with one SQL version, and deploy the witness with a separate SQL version. However, best practice is to keep the versions the same across the board.

For SQL best practices in terms of which SQL versions are supported for a witness role, see "Database Mirroring Witness" in the MSDN Library at http://go.microsoft.com/fwlink/?LinkId=247345.

The actual configuration of SQL mirroring is covered in the "Configuring SQL Server Mirroring" section. For an overview of how SQL Mirroring provides high-availability, see Figure 15.1.

Witness

SQL 1

SQL 2

Transaction Replication

Front End Pool

FIGURE 15.1   SQL Server mirroring in Lync Server 2013.

RTO and RPO for SQL Mirroring   Microsoft has tested and designed for a 5-minute RTO and 5-minute RPO for SQL Server mirroring. This means that the service can be brought back online within 5 minutes, and only up to 5 minutes of data could be lost.

User Impact During Failover   In the event of a SQL Server failure, very little use impact is expected. If a witness is configured, the failover will happen so quickly that users are not likely to notice the system disconnect. However, the Lync client will reregister in the event of a SQL mirror failover. If no witness is configured, users will enter resiliency mode. This will provide a notification that the system is down, and some features will not be available to the users until the administrator has initiated the failover.

File Share High-Availability
Microsoft recommends deploying file servers configured with Distributed File System (DFS) to provide high-availability of Lync Server file shares. DFS has been tested to support failover between file servers in the same datacenter. Although DFS itself can support

replication across multiple sites, for Lync it is recommended that DFS be used only for redundancy in the site.

RTO and RPO for File Share DFS   DFS is considered best-effort for file replication. Because of this, there is no published RTO objective or RPO commitment. The failover tends to happen quickly, but data replication can prevent a seamless transition. The Lync file share is used for address-book data, as well as conferencing data that is uploaded. Therefore, many organizations are not as concerned with the RPO of the system, but it is important that the file share be active for general user experience.

It is recommended to back up the DFS file shares frequently. This will prevent data loss if replication has not completed in the time frame of a server failure. For an overview of how DFS can be used to provide high-availability, see Figure 15.2.

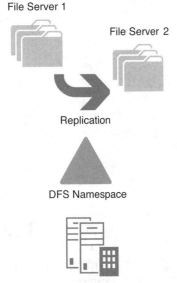

File Server 1

File Server 2

Replication

DFS Namespace

Front End Pool

FIGURE 15.2   DFS for Lync Server 2013 file share.

Lync Front End Server High-Availability

Providing high-availability to Lync Front End Servers is the core of a Lync high-availability design. Front End Servers run nearly every critical service in a Lync deployment, and without access to a Front End Server, users cannot even sign in. Lync Front End Servers can be configured in the topology as pools. These pools can contain up to 20 servers, allowing for increased scale and redundancy.

Lync Server 2013 allows for load balancing Front End Server pools using two methods, DNS load balancing and hardware load balancing.

DNS Load Balancing   DNS load balancing is the primary, and preferred, method for providing high-availability to Lync Front End Server pools. DNS load balancing leverages DNS round robin functionality to provide users the IP addresses of all Front End Servers in the Front End Server Pool. DNS Load Balancing in Lync Server 2013 is a combination of DNS round robin and application level load balancing intelligence that is built in to Lync Server 2013 that is used to dynamically manage registration and conferencing load on the Front End Servers. DNS load balancing provides the simplest method of providing high-availability to Front End pools. However, even when using DNS load balancing, a hardware load balancer (HLB) is still required for providing high-availability to Lync Web Services. Configuration of DNS load balancing is covered in Chapter 11, "Dependent Services and SQL."

Hardware Load Balancing (HLB)   Hardware load balancing has been around for some time. However, these devices were originally used to distribute web traffic to web servers. As applications have evolved, HLBs have evolved to support more advanced traffic such as SIP traffic. HLBs are used to provide high-availability to Lync Front End Server pools by providing a virtual IP (VIP) for the Lync Web Services, and directing traffic to available Front End Servers in that pool. HLBs can also be used to distribute SIP traffic across Front End Server pools. However, these configurations are often complex, and if possible it is suggested to use DNS load balancing for SIP traffic.

Lync Edge Server High-Availability
The Lync Edge Server provides remote access and federation functionality to users. The Edge Server allows for the same high-availability configurations as Front End Servers. Lync Edge Servers can be configured as a pool of servers in the topology, and be load balanced through DNS load balancing or a hardware load balancer.

Unlike Lync Front End Servers, Edge Servers do not have web services that must be load balanced. In many organizations, this allows for a simple DNS load-balancing configuration to provide redundancy to Edge Server pools. However, it is important to note that OCS 2007 R2 and earlier do not support connecting to servers using DNS load balancing. This becomes important when you are federating with partners running OCS 2007 R2 and earlier versions. If your organization will be federated with these earlier server versions, it is important to plan your redundancy approach appropriately.

Lync Mediation Server High-Availability
Lync Mediation Servers provide connectivity to the PSTN and legacy telephony systems. Mediation Servers can also be configured as a pool in Topology Builder. Mediation Server pools are load balanced using DNS load balancing for inbound calls, and for outbound calls Lync Server dynamically routes calls to maintain an even load across servers.

Persistent Chat High-Availability
Lync Server Persistent Chat contains two key components, a backend and a front end. The backend component is SQL based, and follows the same rules for redundancy as described in the "SQL Server Backend High-Availability" section. When deploying Persistent Chat, you can use the same SQL Servers used for your Front End pools, or deploy new SQL Servers for Persistent Chat.

Persistent Chat Front End Servers act much like Lync Front End Servers. These servers can be configured in a pool, with up to eight servers in each pool. However, only four servers may ever be active in a pool at a time. DNS load balancing is used to distribute traffic among the four active servers. Hardware load balancing is not supported for distributing traffic to Persistent Chat servers.

Stretched Persistent Chat pools are covered in the "Persistent Chat Disaster Recovery" section later in this chapter.

Shared Components High-Availability

Lync Server relies on many commonly shared services to provide Lync services. This includes Active Directory, Office Web Apps Server, Exchange Server, and various network components such as firewalls and hardware load balancers.

Active Directory   It is important to ensure that Active Directory is configured in a redundant fashion. Active Directory topologies vary across every organization; however, a general rule of thumb is to make sure that each site where Active Directory components are deployed always contains a redundant server configuration. It is more important to take Active Directory availability into consideration when planning for availability of your Lync infrastructure, and to identify any gaps in redundancy before deployment.

Office Web Apps Server   In the context of providing high-availability to Office Web Apps Server, it is best to be classified as a simple web application. Office Web Apps Server can be configured as a farm with multiple servers in the farm. Office Web Apps Server supports using a hardware load balancer to distribute traffic to all servers in the farm, providing redundancy and increased scale.

Exchange Server   Exchange Server redundancy probably has many books of its own, and is not outlined in detail here. However, much as with Active Directory, it is important to consider the availability of Exchange Server in your Lync service availability planning. Remember, the availability of your Lync solution is only as high as the weakest link; if voice mail goes down, your SLA will not be honored.

Network Equipment, Firewalls, Reverse Proxies and Hardware Load Balancers   Network switches, routers, firewalls, reverse proxies and hardware load balancers of all types support redundant configurations. In many cases, these devices support being configured as a redundant pool or pair. This allows for a seamless failover of one node while retaining services on the failover node. Regardless of how the devices are configured for redundancy, it is important to make sure that all equipment supporting your Lync users and servers is deployed with high-availability in mind.

Designing for Disaster Recovery

The preceding section discussed how to provide redundancy and high-availability to Lync Server components. This section outlines how to design for disaster recovery, and explains why that sometimes differs from high-availability.

Defining Disaster Recovery

By definition, recovery is the restoration or continuation of a technology infrastructure critical to an organization after a natural or human-induced disaster. Disaster recovery assumes that a major event has occurred, resulting in the loss of an entire site or a large section of infrastructure.

Disaster recovery is measured on recovery point objective and recovery time objective, two measurements that were discussed earlier in this chapter. Designing for disaster recovery differs from that of high-availability because the two goals, though they might seem relatively similar, are actually different. Designing for disaster recovery requires planning for redundant resources end to end, even across multiple sites. Additionally, disaster recovery planning involves defining a recovery playbook, which outlines exact steps for performing a recovery in the event of a disaster.

In its simplest form, disaster recovery for Lync implies deploying a secondary infrastructure that can support users in the event that the primary infrastructure is not available. However, the operational considerations for the recovery procedure often become much more complicated.

As the RPO and RTO objectives get closer to zero, the cost of the infrastructure and the operations will become much more expensive. This is why disaster recovery should be considered outside of the scope of high-availability and redundancy. High-availability should refer to the level of redundancy inside the pool of servers, or inside the Lync site. Disaster recovery should refer to how users will be provided services in the event of a total pool or total site loss.

Disaster Recovery Options in Lync Server 2013

Lync Server 2013 has come a long way in providing disaster recovery options in a simplified manner. In Lync Server 2010, there were three options for disaster recovery:

▶ **Backup Registrar**—Backup registrar functionality was introduced in Lync Server 2010. This feature allowed pools to be configured as a backup for the registrar service only. In the event of a pool failure, users would register against the backup pool in limited functionality mode, essentially enabling users to make and receive calls. This was critical in providing the level of availability required for Enterprise Voice.

▶ **Metropolitan Site Resiliency**—This solution split pools between two physical servers. Geographically dispersed clusters were deployed to support SQL and file servers. Synchronous data replication was then deployed between the geographically dispersed clusters. This solution introduced unnecessary complexity to environments, requiring high-speed, high-latency WAN connectivity across physical sites using stretched VLANs. Although this solution worked for a unique set of enterprise customers, it did not provide an acceptable disaster recovery solution for the general population.

▶ **Forced Failover**—This solution resulted in deploying a secondary pool, and all supporting servers in the second physical site. The administrator would configure backups of all primary data and copy that data to the secondary site. In the event of a disaster, the data could be restored using `DBIMPEXP.EXE`, and users could be force-moved to the secondary site. This solution was the better of the two options, although it did result in a high RTO. Importing data and moving a large number of users could often take hours and had a heavy dependency on custom scripts and resource kit tools.

Lync Server 2013 combines the best of Forced Failover and Metropolitan Site Resiliency functionality in to an integrated disaster recovery model. Backup Registrar functionality remains in Lync Server 2013 and is unchanged. Lync Server 2013 introduces the concept of pool pairing, which allows for Lync Server 2013 to constantly replicate critical data across multiple server pools. Exactly how pool pairing works is described in a later section.

Lync Server 2013 pool pairing is the only supported disaster recovery method; previous methods are not supported, and are not recommended.

Table 15.5 outlines the disaster recovery capabilities in earlier versions of Lync as well as Lync Server 2013.

TABLE 15.5   Lync Server Disaster Recovery Capabilities

Scenario	OCS 2007 R2	Lync 2010	Lync 2013
Pool Failure	SQL Backup and Restore	Voice resiliency through backup registrar Metropolitan site stretched pool for presence and conferencing resiliency	Maintain voice resiliency in Lync 2010 PSTN trunks can be configured for auto failover and failback Support presence and conferencing resiliency via pool pairing through manual failover and failback Integrate with Planning Tool, Topology Builder, and Control Panel Does not cover RGS/CPS/E911/CAC
Site Failure	SQL Backup and Restore	Metropolitan site stretched pool	Same as above

What Services Are Supported for Lync Disaster Recovery?

First, let's cover what services are available in a disaster recovery scenario. Table 15.6 provides an outline of these services.

TABLE 15.6   Lync Services Available During Disaster Recovery

Feature	Supports Disaster Recovery
Peer-to-peer (all modalities)	Yes
Presence	Yes
Conferencing (all modalities)	Yes
UC Web App	Yes
Archiving	Yes
CDR/QOE	No
Federation	Yes
PIC federation	Yes
Unified Contact Store	Yes
Topology Builder	Yes
Lync Server Control Panel	Yes
Persistent Chat	Yes
Planning Tool	Yes
PSTN Voice	Yes
Voice Applications (CAA,CAS,PVA,GVA)	Yes
RGS, Call Park, E911	No
Call Admission Control	No
XMPP	Yes

As shown in Table 15.6, applications that often have a unique site configuration such as E911, Call Park, Response Group, and Call Admission Control are not supported in a disaster recovery scenario. In the event of a disaster, this functionality will not be available to users until connectivity to the primary pool is restored. Additionally, CDR and QOE information will not be submitted from users who are in recovery mode.

SQL Server Backend Disaster Recovery

Providing disaster recovery to the SQL backend services in Lync Server 2013 does not require admin intervention. Data that is stored in the SQL Server database will instead be replicated through the Lync pool pairing functionality, and imported to the secondary site SQL database.

SQL mirroring should be deployed only in a single site, and should not be considered for cross-site configurations to provide some level of disaster recovery.

Lync Front End Server Disaster Recovery

Lync Front End Server disaster recovery is at the core of disaster recovery in Lync Server 2013. As mentioned earlier, Lync Front End Servers provide disaster recovery first through backup registrar functionality. This enables users to immediately fail over to a secondary pool for basic registration and inbound and outbound voice routing.

15

In the event of a prolonged outage, administrators can leverage pool pairing to provide presence and conferencing services to users. Lync Server pool pairing uses Windows Fabric to synchronize data across multiple Lync Front End pools. In the event of a failure, the administrator can invoke a pool failover, which will result in the import of presence and conferencing data to the secondary pool database.

Backup Registrar Relationship Details

Lync Server 2013 backup registrar relationships must always be a 1:1 configuration and will always be reciprocal. This means that if Pool 1 is the backup for Pool 2, then Pool 2 must be the backup for Pool 1. Additionally, neither can be the backup for any other Front End pool. The exception to this rule is that each Front End pool can also be the backup registrar for any number of Survivable Branch Appliances, or Survivable Branch Servers.

Pool Pairing Relationship Details   When planning for pool pairing, the following items should be considered:

▶ **Consider the distance between the datacenters**—Although there is no limit on the distance between two datacenters that contain paired pools, keep in mind that depending on the connectivity between sites, data replication might take longer, resulting in a longer RPO. Additionally, it is important to not have two datacenters in close proximity to each other in the event of a natural disaster.

▶ **Pool types must match**—Enterprise Edition pools can be paired only with other Enterprise Edition pools. Similarly, Standard Edition pools must be paired only with other Standard Edition pools.

▶ **Physical and virtual must match**—Physical pools can be paired only with other physical pools. Similarly, virtual pools can be paired only with other virtual pools.

▶ **Consider capacity**—Each pool in the pair should have the capacity to serve all users from both pools in the event of a disaster. This is very important when planning server capacity in a multisite scenario.

These best practices are recommended to avoid providing an insufficient disaster recovery design.

NOTE

Topology Builder will not prevent an administrator from configuring two pools in an unsupported matter. However, it is absolutely critical to deploy solutions in a supported configuration, and as such, Microsoft's recommendations should always be followed.

RTO and RPO for Lync Pool Pairing   Microsoft has engineered Lync pool pairing to provide a recovery time objective of 15 minutes. Administrators must manually initiate the failover as part of a disaster recovery procedure. Fifteen minutes is the time it takes for the procedure to complete—it does not account for the time it takes to identify the disaster and make a decision for failover. When an administrator initiates a pool failover, the data must be imported to the new pool. The time it takes for the failover to complete results in the engineered RTO of 15 minutes.

For Lync pool pairing, the recovery point objective is also 15 minutes. This means that up to 15 minutes' worth of data could be lost due to replication latency of the Lync Backup Service.

The RTO and RPO numbers are based off of a pool with 40,000 concurrent users, and 200,000 users enabled on the pool.

Central Management Store Recovery   The Central Management Store (CMS) is responsible for all configuration data in the Lync Server 2013 environment. The CMS runs on one active Front End pool in the environment, and subsequently one active SQL backend. When pool pairing is configured on a pool that is hosting the CMS, a backup CMS database is configured on the backup pool, and the CMS services are also installed on that pool. CMS data is also replicated by the Lync Backup Service to the standby pool. When initiating a pool failover involving the CMS, the administrator must first execute a CMS failover.

The engineering target for RPO and RTO of the CMS is 5 minutes. CMS data is not as large as presence and conferencing data; as such, the replication latency and import time are reduced when compared to Front End pool RPO/RTO.

Lync Edge Server Disaster Recovery

Lync Server 2013 Edge Servers do not provide a native disaster recovery solution. In the event of a disaster scenario, manual steps must be taken to direct services through the secondary Edge Server pool. However, proper planning can reduce the amount of effort required for these tasks. When planning for Edge Server disaster recovery, consider the strategies discussed in the following subsections.

Weighted DNS Records for Access Edge Services   It is possible to deploy the DNS SRV records required for Lync remote access and federation with a priority and weight. This configuration essentially allows for a primary and secondary DNS A record to be configured. Clients will always use the DNS record with the lowest-numbered priority value first and fall back to other records if the connection to the host fails. The weight value on SRV records should be used only for providing load balancing between services.

Example for Access Edge sign-on services:

```
_sip._tls.companyabc.com 86400 IN SRV 10 10 443 sip.companyabc.com
_sip._tls.companyabc.com 86400 IN SRV 20 10 443 sip2.companyabc.com
```

In the preceding configuration, the first record has a priority of 10, and as a result, clients would attempt to connect to the server `sip.companyabc.com`. If the client cannot connect to that server, the second record, with a priority of 20, would be used, and users would attempt to connect to `sip2.companyabc.com`.

This configuration can provide an automatic failover for inbound Access Edge services. However, failover will not be immediate. Keep in mind that the Lync client will cache records of servers to connect to, and will first attempt to connect to servers in that cache first. This can result in a slight sign-on delay in disaster scenarios while the client discovers the secondary DNS record.

Example for Access Edge federation services:

```
_sipfederationtls._tcp.companyabc.com 86400 IN SRV 10 10 5061 sip.companyabc.com
_sipfederationtls._tcp.companyabc.com 86400 IN SRV 20 10 5061 sip2.companyabc.com
```

In the preceding configuration, the first record has a priority of 10, and as a result, federated partner Edge Servers would attempt to connect to the server `sip.companyabc.com`. If the server cannot connect to `sip.companyabc.com`, the second record, with a priority of 20, would be used, and the server would attempt to connect to `sip2.companyabc.com`.

This configuration can provide an automatic failover for inbound federation requests; however, it does not account for enhanced federation configurations. Enhanced federation is when organizations define Access Edge server records for a federated partner. In this configuration, federation requests do not query the SRV record for connectivity options. If your organization is deploying enhanced federation, keep this in mind.

Outbound Federation Route Every Lync Server Topology may have only a single outbound federation route defined. These routes may be defined per site; however, they are defined to a single Edge Server pool. In the event of a failure, this configuration must be manually updated to point to the secondary pool. The steps to perform this are covered in the "Executing Disaster Recovery Procedures" section.

A/V Edge Failover The A/V Edge services on each Edge Server are statically associated with a Front End pool. No intervention is required in the event of a failure. When users are connected to the secondary pool, they will use the Edge Server pool in the secondary site for media traversal capabilities.

Lync Mediation Server Disaster Recovery

Providing disaster recovery to Lync Mediation Servers is not done through a Mediation Server configuration. Instead, voice routes should be configured to contain multiple Mediation Server pools for failover purposes. When you are planning for voice resiliency, it is important to identify all inbound and outbound routing policies, and to make sure that cross-pool policies are configured where necessary. Pool 1 users should be able to route calls through the Pool 2 Mediation Servers to the PSTN as a last resort. Additionally, inbound PSTN should be configured to have redundancy to Pool 2 in the event that Pool 1 is not available. The details of designing Lync Enterprise Voice, including resiliency, are given in Chapter 32, "Planning for Voice Deployment."

Persistent Chat Disaster Recovery

With Lync Server 2013, the disaster recovery mechanism for Persistent Chat has become more in line with the rest of the product when compared to Lync Server 2010. Unlike

Lync Server Front End pools, Persistent Chat pools cannot be paired to provide disaster recovery. Persistent Chat pools require introducing a stretched pool configuration to provide disaster recovery.

Providing disaster recovery to Persistent Chat pools will require the following configurations:

▶ **Primary SQL Servers**—Persistent Chat will rely on a stretched pool configuration. SQL Servers should be located in the same physical datacenter as the Persistent Chat Front Ends to provide normal operations. For high-availability purposes, it is recommended that this be a SQL mirror, with a third SQL Server configured as a witness for automatic failover.

▶ **SQL Log Shipping**—Providing disaster recovery to the Persistent Chat backend is done through SQL log shipping. This must be manually configured by administrators, and will perform transaction backups to the secondary datacenter.

▶ **Primary File Share**—SQL Log Shipping requires a file share to be created and designated for SQL transaction logs. The share must have read and write privileges to all SQL Server services that are running Persistent Chat services in both datacenters.

▶ **Secondary File Share**—A secondary file share must be designated to receive SQL transaction logs. This can be located on the secondary SQL Server.

▶ **Secondary SQL Server**—In the datacenter designated for disaster recovery, a secondary SQL Server should be designated. SQL log shipping will be used to back up all SQL data to the secondary datacenter.

The configuration options covered in the following subsections are available when Persistent Chat is being deployed with disaster recovery available.

Stretched Persistent Chat Pool in Low-Bandwidth and High-Latency Scenarios Persistent Chat pools can contain up to eight servers. However, only four servers can be active at once. In a scenario in which the connectivity between two datacenters is not efficient, placing four servers in each datacenter in an active/standby configuration is ideal. The requirements outlined in the preceding section, "Persistent Chat Disaster Recovery," outline the resources required to complete this configuration. See Figure 15.3 for an example of this design.

The following statements are true in this configuration:

▶ Site A and Site B both contain a Front End Server pool, servicing a subset of users. Each site shares Persistent Chat Pool A for Persistent Chat.

▶ Site A contains four active Persistent Chat servers; all users in Site A and Site B will connect to those servers for access to Persistent Chat Pool A.

▶ SQL Log Shipping is configured between SQL1 and SQL3. Every transaction will be shipped to SQL3, and in the event of a disaster, data can be restored.

15

▶ Site B contains four standby Persistent Chat servers. In the event of a disaster, these servers can be marked as active and serve users from Site A and Site B.

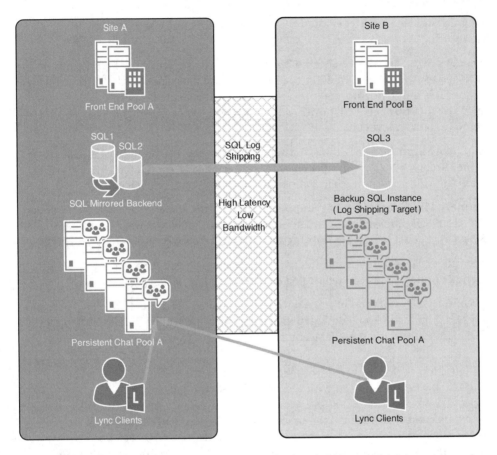

FIGURE 15.3   Stretched Persistent Chat pool in low-bandwidth and high-latency scenarios.

Stretched Persistent Chat Pool in High-Bandwidth and Low-Latency Scenarios   When bandwidth and latency are efficient, it is possible to split the Persistent Chat pool in an active/active configuration across two datacenters. Requirements discussed in earlier sections apply. However, in this configuration two servers in each datacenter are designated as active. See Figure 15.4 for an example of this design.

The following statements are true in this configuration:

▶ Site A and Site B both contain a Front End Server pool, servicing a subset of users. Each site shares Persistent Chat Pool A for Persistent Chat.

▶ Site A and Site B both contain two active Persistent Chat Front End Servers. DNS load balancing will be used to distribute traffic across the pool to all four active servers. Users in Site A and Site B will connect to any active server, including in the other datacenter.

► SQL Log Shipping is configured between SQL1 and SQL3. Every transaction will be shipped to SQL3, and in the event of a disaster, data can be restored.

► Site A and Site B will contain two standby Persistent Chat Servers each. In the event of a disaster, the standby servers can be activated to maintain capacity. All users will connect to the active datacenter in that scenario.

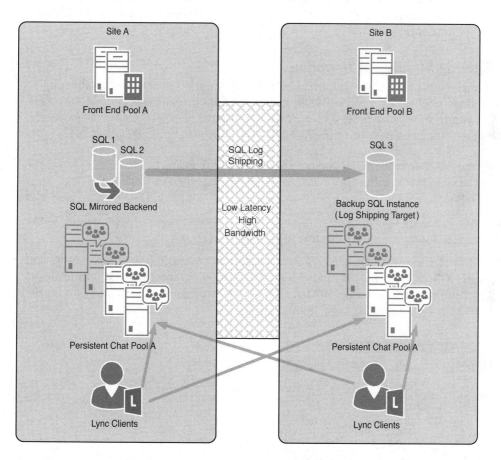

FIGURE 15.4   Stretched Persistent Chat pool in high-bandwidth and low-latency scenarios.

The process for configuring Persistent Chat disaster recovery, as well as initiating a failover, are covered in the "Executing Disaster Recovery Procedures" section.

Shared Components Disaster Recovery

Lync Server 2013 relies on several shared services to provide various functionality. It is important when planning for disaster recovery scenarios that all shared components are accounted for. This includes Active Directory, Exchange Server, Office Web Apps Server, and Network Equipment. It is critical to ensure a seamless transition to the second datacenter in a disaster scenario. When developing a disaster recovery strategy, make certain to document all dependencies and ensure that those dependencies will be available in the secondary environment.

Configuring Lync Server for High-Availability

This section acts as a guide for configuring Lync Server for high-availability. Step-by-step instructions for configuring SQL, Lync Servers, and other shared components for high-availability are covered.

Configuring SQL Server Mirroring

In Lync Server 2013, Microsoft has included the configuration of SQL Server mirroring as part of the deployment process. When deploying a Front End Server pool in Topology Builder, administrators have the option of configuring the SQL Server Store for mirroring. Follow the steps given next to configure SQL Server mirroring for Lync Server 2013.

Configuring SQL Server Mirroring During Pool Creation in Topology Builder
Follow the steps below to configure SQL Server Mirroring when deploying a Lync Server Pool.

1. With Topology Builder open, and as part of the pool creation process, on the Define the SQL Store page click New next to the SQL Store box.

2. On the Define New SQL Server Store page, specify the primary SQL Server Store and select This SQL Instance Is in Mirroring Relation. Then, specify the SQL mirroring port number (the default is 5022), and click OK. See Figure 15.5 for an example of this configuration in Topology Builder.

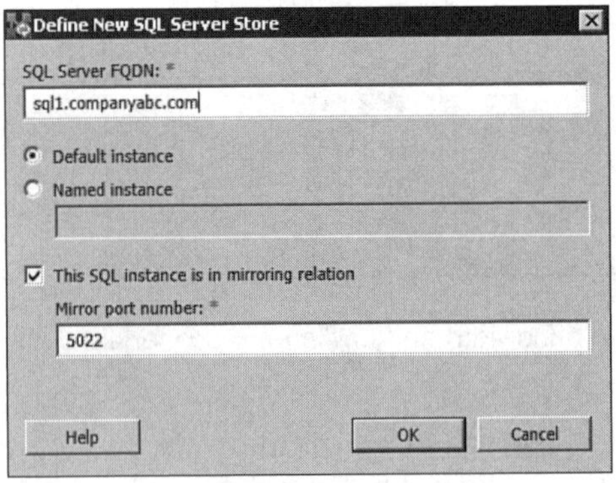

FIGURE 15.5   Defining a new SQL Server Store.

3. Back on the Define the SQL Store page, select Enable SQL Store Mirroring and select New to define a new SQL Server.

4. On the Define New SQL Server Store page, specify the secondary SQL Server Store and select This SQL Instance Is in Mirroring Relation. Then, specify the SQL mirroring port number (the default is 5022), and click OK.

5. If you want to enable automatic failover, a witness is required. To define a witness, select Use SQL Server Mirroring Witness to Enable Automatic Failover, and then either select New to define a new SQL Server or select an existing server from the drop-down list.

6. On the Define New SQL Server Store page, specify the witness SQL Server Store and define a witness port number (the default is 7022). Figure 15.6 provides an overview of how this configuration would look in Topology Builder.

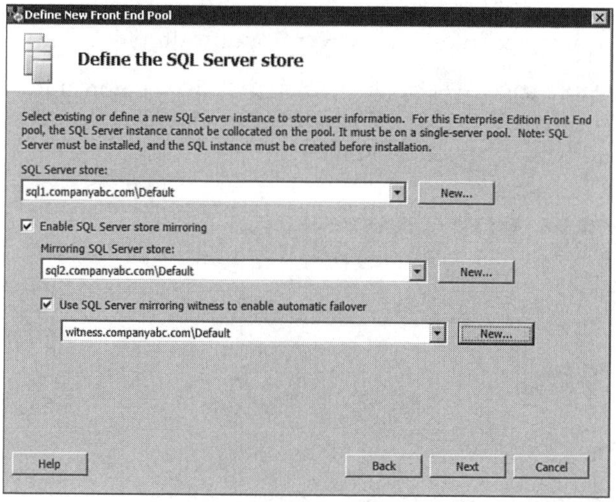

FIGURE 15.6   Results of defining a SQL mirror with automatic witness failover.

7. Complete the rest of the Pool Configuration Wizard in the Topology Builder.

8. Use Topology Builder to publish the topology. When you are publishing the topology, you will see an option to create both the primary and the mirror SQL databases.

9. Click Settings. You must define a path to use as the file share for the mirroring backup. This is used only when creating the initial mirror to copy files between SQL Servers.

10. Click OK and then Next. This process creates the databases and publishes the topology. This process also configures all SQL mirroring configurations. Any errors are reported in the final report.

Configuring SQL Server Mirroring on Existing Front End Server Pools

Perform the following steps to configure SQL Server Mirroring for an existing Front End Server Pool.

1. To add SLQ mirroring to an existing pool, open Topology Builder.

2. While in Topology Builder, right-click on the Enterprise Edition pool and click Edit Properties.

3. Scroll down to Associations, Select Enable SQL Store Mirroring, and select New to define a new SQL Server.

4. On the Define New SQL Server Store page, specify the secondary SQL Server Store, and select This SQL Instance Is in Mirroring Relation. Then, specify the SQL mirroring port number (the default is 5022), and click OK.

5. If you want to enable automatic failover, a witness is required. To define a witness, select Use SQL Mirroring Witness to Enable Automatic Failover; then, either select New to define a new SQL Server or select an existing server from the drop-down list.

6. On the Define New SQL Server Store page, specify the witness SQL Server Store and define a witness port number (the default is 7022). Figure 15.7 provides an overview of how this configuration should look in Topology Builder.

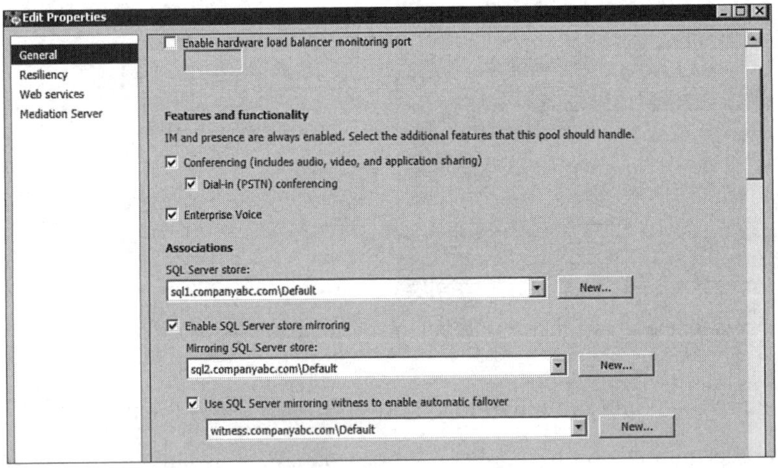

FIGURE 15.7   Results of adding SQL Server mirroring to an existing pool.

7. Click OK to close the Pool Properties page.

8. Use Topology Builder to publish the topology. When you are publishing the topology, you will see an option to create both the primary and the mirror SQL databases.

9. Click Settings. You must define a path to use as the file share for the mirroring backup. This is used only when creating the initial mirror to copy files between SQL Servers.

10. Click OK and then Next. This process creates the databases and publishes the topology. This process also configures all SQL mirroring configurations. Any errors are reported in the final report.

As mentioned earlier, configuring SQL mirroring is tightly integrated into the deployment process for Lync Server 2013. If you want to confirm that mirroring was successfully deployed, open the SQL Server Management Studio on a SQL Server that is part of the mirroring relationship. While in SQL Server Management Studio, expand the Databases section, and all Lync Server databases that have been configured for mirroring should say "Synchronized" next to them. See Figure 15.8 for an example.

```
⊞  cpsdyn (Principal, Synchronized)
⊞  LcsCDR (Principal, Synchronized)
⊞  LcsLog (Principal, Synchronized)
⊞  mgc (Principal, Synchronized)
⊞  QoEMetrics (Principal, Synchronized)
⊞  ReportServer
⊞  ReportServerTempDB
⊞  rgsconfig (Principal, Synchronized)
⊞  rgsdyn (Principal, Synchronized)
⊞  rtcab (Principal, Synchronized)
⊞  rtcshared (Principal, Synchronized)
⊞  rtcxds (Principal, Synchronized)
```

FIGURE 15.8   SQL mirroring synchronization in SQL Management Studio.

Failing Over a Failed SQL Store to the SQL Server Mirror

In the event of a SQL Server failure, automatic failover to the secondary SQL Server is possible if a witness has been deployed. However, if no witness has been configured, manual steps must be taken. Follow these steps to initiate a SQL mirror failover to a secondary server:

1. Before initiating the failover, confirm which server is acting as the Primary and which is acting as the Secondary by running the following command in Lync Management Shell:

```
Get-CSDatabaseMirrorState -PoolFQDN <Pool FQDN with failed SQL Server>
➥-DatabaseType User
```

2. The command executed above will return a **Principal** and a **Mirror** value. To perform the failover, run the following command to fail over to the mirror server:

```
Invoke-CSDatabaseFailover -PoolFQDN <Pool FQDN with failed SQL Server>
➥-DatabaseType User -NewPrincipal <FQDN of the Mirror SQL Server> -Verbose
```

3. When the command completes, the mirror SQL Server should now be servicing the pool with backend services.

Configuring Front End Server Pools

Providing Lync Server Front Ends with high-availability involves creating a pool of servers that will service all users assigned to that pool. The following section outlines how to configure a pool of servers in the Topology Builder, as well as how to configure DNS load balancing for proper availability.

Configuring a Front End Server Enterprise Edition Pool

Enterprise Edition pools can contain up to 20 Front End Servers to provide scaling and high-availability to Lync services. The steps that follow outline how to configure these pools in Topology Builder:

1. Open Lync Topology Builder.

2. Download the Topology from the existing deployment, or create a new topology if this is a brand-new infrastructure.

3. Expand Lync Server 2013, expand the site where this pool will be located, and expand Lync Server 2013.

4. Right-click on Enterprise Edition Front End Pools, and select New Front End Pool.

5. Click Next and continue with the Define New Front End Pool wizard (see Figure 15.9). Specify a Pool FQDN such as `Lyncpool.companyabc.com` and click Next.

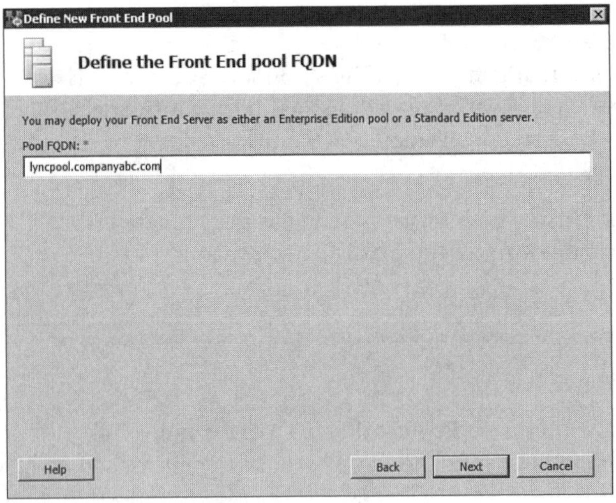

FIGURE 15.9   Specify a pool FQDN.

6. Next, you must define the computers in the pool. These names should be the computer FQDN of all Lync Front End Servers currently part of this pool. Specify the Computer FQDN and click Add for each server in the pool. When finished, click Next. Figure 15.10 provides an example of how the pool members configuration should look in Topology Builder.

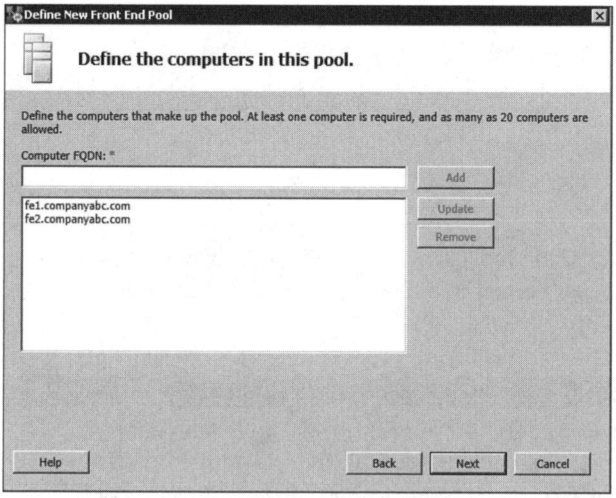

FIGURE 15.10   Defining pool members.

7. Specify the services the pool will offer. This can include Conferencing, PSTN Conferencing, Enterprise Voice, Call Admission Control (only one pool per site is allowed to be enabled for CAC), Archiving, and Monitoring. Select all boxes that apply to this pool and click Next.

8. Complete the remaining wizard tasks to deploy your Enterprise Edition pool. For complete details on this process, see Chapter 5, "Microsoft Lync Server 2013 Front End Server."

Configuring DNS Load Balancing for Enterprise Edition Pools

DNS load balancing is the preferred load-balancing method for all Lync Server components, excluding the Lync Web Services, which still require a Hardware Load Balancer (HLB). Table 15.7 outlines the DNS records that would be required to provide DNS load balancing for a single Enterprise Edition pool.

TABLE 15.7   DNS Records for DNS Load Balancing a Front End Server Pool

Hostname	IP Address	Description
Fe1.companyabc.com	192.168.1.10	Front End Server #1
FE2.companyabc.com	192.168.1.11	Front End Server #2
LYNCPOOL.companyabc.com	192.168.1.10	Lync Pool FQDN Entry #1
LYNCPOOL.companyabc.com	192.168.1.11	Lync Pool FQDN Entry #2
LYNCPOOLWEBSVC.companyabc.com	192.168.1.12	Web Services FQDN, should point to HLB VIP

The important takeaway from this table is that you should ensure that DNS entries for your Enterprise Edition pool FQDN are properly defined. A record for the pool FQDN should be entered for each Front End Server in the pool. This results in DNS Round Robin requests to each Front End Server in the pool. Lync Server's built-in distribution logic handles the load distribution after users connect.

Configuring File Shares

File share high-availability can be provided via Distributed File System (DFS). For a step-by-step configuration guide for Windows Server 2008 DFS, see http://technet.microsoft.com/en-us/library/cc732863(WS.10).aspx.

TIP

When Lync components are being deployed to the file share, Topology Builder requires that the administrator that is deploying the topology have full Administrator access to the file share. The Lync Topology Builder uses NTFS file permissions to provide ACLs to the folders. Make sure that the account being used to deploy the topology has these permissions.

Configuring Persistent Chat Server Pools

When Persistent Chat is being configured for high-availability or disaster recovery, a single pool is created regardless of the physical location of the servers. Defining a Persistent Chat pool is a simple process, and is completed in the Topology Builder. These are the steps to follow:

1. While in Topology Builder, expand Lync Server 2013. Right-click on the Persistent Chat Pools node and choose New Persistent Chat Pool.

2. Select Multiple Computer Pool and specify the pool FQDN, such as `chatpool.companyabc.com`. Click Next. See Figure 15.11 for an example of how this configuration should look in Topology Builder.

3. On the Define the Computers in This Pool page, specify the FQDN of each computer in the pool and click Add. Click Next. Figure 15.12 provides an example of how the defining members configuration should look in Topology Builder.

4. On the Define Properties of the Persistent Chat Pool page, specify a Display Name. This name can be anything, and is mainly used for administrative purposes.

5. Specify a Persistent Chat Port (the default is 5041). There should be no reason to change this port number.

6. If compliance is required, check the box to Enable Compliance on the pool.

7. If you plan to provide disaster recovery through a backup SQL Server store using SQL Log Shipping, check the box Use Backup SQL Server Stores to Enable Disaster Recovery.

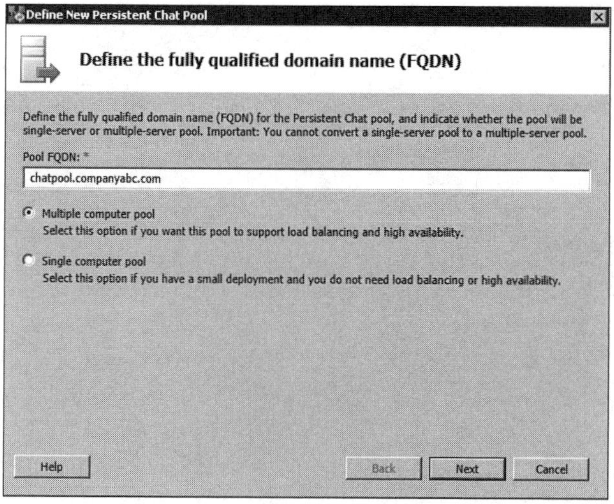

FIGURE 15.11   Defining a new Persistent Chat pool.

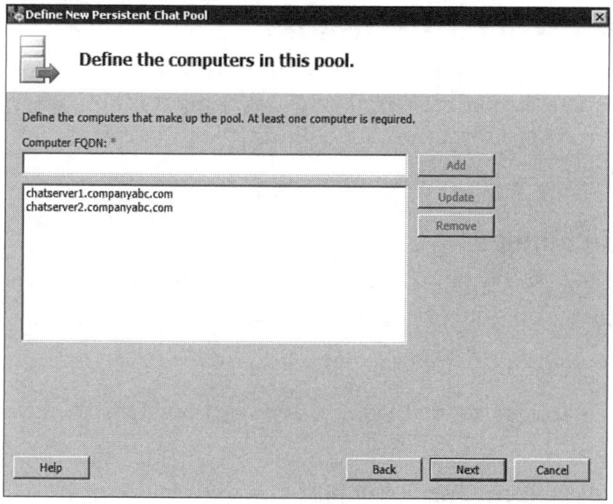

FIGURE 15.12   Defining computers in a Persistent Chat pool.

8. If you want to make this Persistent Chat pool the default for any or all sites, check the remaining boxes as they apply. Figure 15.13 provides an overview of the Persistent Chat properties configuration in Topology Builder.

9. Complete the remaining steps for the Persistent Chat pool and publish the topology. For complete details on this process, see Chapter 10, "Persistent Chat."

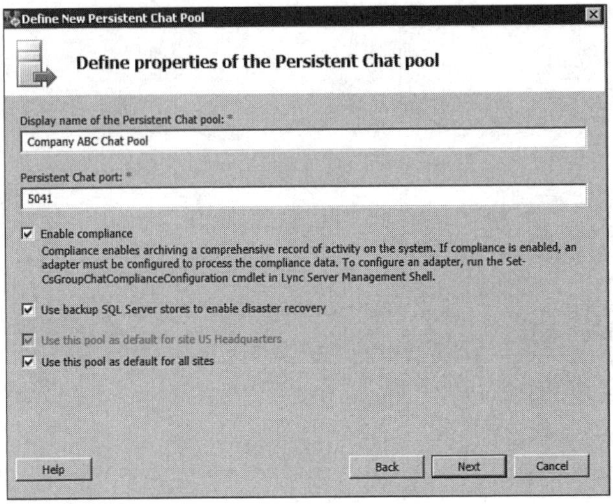

FIGURE 15.13   Summary of Persistent Chat properties.

Executing Disaster Recovery Procedures

A detailed document should be developed to outline all procedures in the event of a disaster recovery scenario. Think of this as the disaster recovery "playbook," and it is absolutely critical to being successful in disaster recovery scenarios. The following section covers common disaster recovery procedures.

Configuring Front End Server Pairing

To provide disaster recovery to Front End Server pools, each pool must be paired for failover. Follow these steps to configure Front End Server pool pairing:

1. Open the Topology Builder.

2. If the two pools you want to pair are not yet defined, use Topology Builder to create these pools.

3. In Topology Builder, navigate to the Front End Server pool you want to configure pairing on. Right-click on one of the two pools, and choose Edit Properties.

4. Select Resiliency, and then select the check box Associated Backup Pool.

5. Specify the pool you want to configure as a pair. This is for voice resiliency and for pool failover. Figure 15.14 provides an example of how this configuration should look in Topology Builder.

6. If you want to provide automatic failover for voice services (this is recommended), check the box Automatic Failover and Failback for Voice.

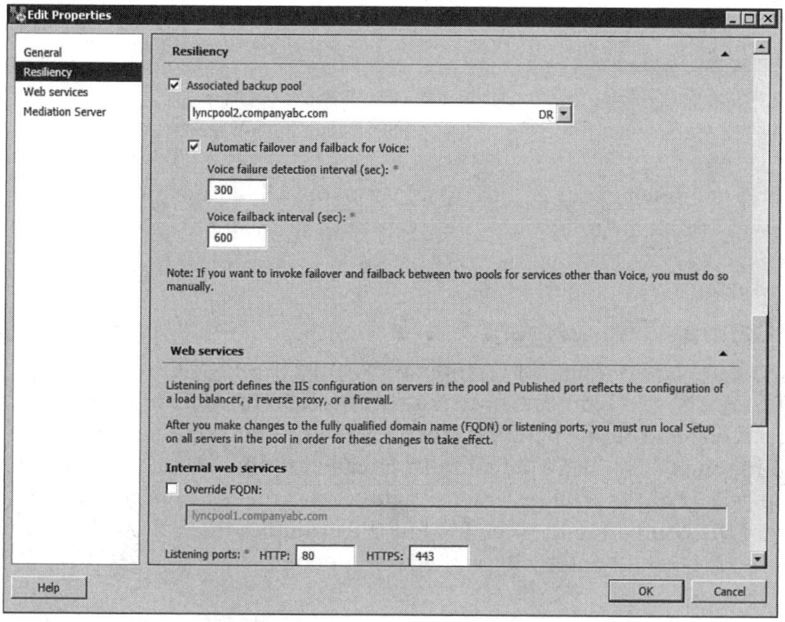

FIGURE 15.14   Specifying a backup Front End Server pool.

TIP

Consider the timing for your failover and failback intervals. Be sure not to set these values too low; however, you should note that by default failure detection is 300 seconds, or 5 minutes. If you want to provide failover more quickly than that, adjust that timer. Setting these values too low can result in failover and failback occurring too quickly in scenarios in which a pool is going up and down for whatever reason.

---

7. This configuration will set resiliency options on the other pool as well. When you are finished, use Topology Builder to publish the topology.

8. The Lync Server 2013 Deployment Wizard must now be run on all Front End Servers in the pools where you configured pairing. This is required to install the Lync Backup Service, which will be responsible for backing up pool data.

9. After running the Deployment Wizard on each server, run the following command in the Lync Management Shell on each server to start the Lync Backup Service:

```
Start-CSWindowsService -Name LyncBackup
```

10. After the service has been installed and started on all servers, you can now force a synchronization of the pool data. To do this, run the following commands on Lync Management Shell from any server in the pools (you need to run this only once):

```
Invoke-CSBackupServiceSync -PoolFQDN <FQDN of the First Lync Pool>
Invoke-CSBackupServiceSync -PoolFQDN <FQDN of the Second Lync Pool>
```

11. To check on the status of the synchronization, run the following commands in Lync Management Shell:

```
Get-CSBackupServiceStatus -PoolFQDN <FQDN of the First Lync Pool>
Get-CSBackupServiceStatus -PoolFQDN <FQDN of the Second Lync Pool>
```

When synchronization is complete, your Front End Server pools will automatically maintain synchronization without any administrator intervention. At this point, your pools are configured for disaster recovery.

Failing Over the Central Management Store

In the event of a pool or site failure, the first consideration must be of the Central Management Store (CMS). The CMS must be functional in order to provide failover of any other services. If a Front End Server pool has failed, or the site hosting that pool has failed and it was running the CMS, the CMS first must be failed to the secondary pool. The CMS is backed up as part of the pool pairing configured in earlier steps. Figure 15.15 provides an overview of the configuration to be used in the examples that follow. Pool A is currently running the CMS, and Pool A will be the failing pool.

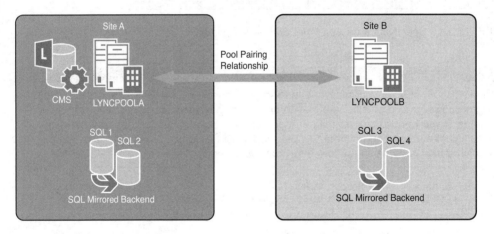

FIGURE 15.15   Lync Server 2013 disaster recovery example.

1. To find out which pool is hosting the CMS, run the following command from the Lync Management Shell:

```
Invoke-CSManagementServerFailover -WhatIf
```

2. The following example assumes the CMS is hosted on LYNCPOOLA. Next, identify the backup pool relationship for Pool A. You can complete this by opening Topology Builder and reviewing resiliency settings, or by running the following command:

```
Get-CSBackupRelationship -PoolFQDN LYNCPOOLA.COMPANYABC.COM
```

3. Before initiating the CMS failover, ensure that the secondary pool has been config-ured to host the CMS in the event of a failover. To do this, check the database state for the existence of a CMS mirror. Run the following command (the secondary pool in this example is LYNCPOOLB.COMPANYABC.COM):

```
Get-CSDatabaseMirrorState -DatabaseType CentralMgt -PoolFQDN
➥lyncpoolb.companyabc.com
```

4. This command displays the SQL Server FQDN that is currently acting as the primary for the secondary pool. If the SQL Server Store for Pool B is in a mirrored configura-tion, it is possible that there could be a primary or a mirror running the database, depending on the current health status. Assuming that the primary server is listed, run the following command to invoke the CMS failover. In this example, the primary will be SQL3.COMPANYABC.COM.

```
Invoke-CSManagementServerFailover -BackupSQLServerFQDN SQL3.COMPANYABC.COM
```

5. When this command has completed, you can validate that the CMS has failed over by running the following command. The ActiveMasterFQDN and ActiveFileTransferAgents attributes should point to the FQDN of Pool B.

```
Get-CSManagementStoreReplicationStatus -CentralManagementStoreStatus
```

6. After you have validated that the secondary pool is now hosting the CMS, run the following command to validate CMS replication across all servers. When all replicas have a value of True, you can continue with your disaster recovery procedures.

```
Get-CSManagementStoreReplicationStatus
```

At this point, the CMS should now be hosted on Pool B. The next section outlines how to initiate a pool failover.

Initiating a Pool Failover

The following procedures can be used to initiate a pool failover for full feature recovery. Voice resiliency will automatically failover and provide users with basic registration and voice routing. The following tasks are required to failover functionality that relies on the SQL back end to the secondary pool such as contact lists, presence, and conferencing. Figure 15.15 provides an overview of the sample configuration used in this scenario.

> **CAUTION**
>
> Before failing over your Front End pool, check whether the Edge Server is still active in that site. If only the Front End pool is down, but the Edge Server is up and accept-ing requests, you should adjust the next-hop destination for that Edge Server. Adjust this setting in Topology Builder and publish the topology, or run the Set-CSEdgeServer command in Lync Management Shell.

15

1. Failing over a Front End Server pool can be done only via the Lync Management Shell and is done using a single command. Run the following command to failover Pool A to Pool B:

   ```
   Invoke-CSPoolFailover -PoolFQDN lyncpoolA.companyabc.com -DisasterMode -Verbose
   ```

2. When Pool A has been restored, initiating a pool failback is also completed in Lync Management Shell using a single command. Run the following command to fail back Pool A:

   ```
   Invoke-CSPoolFailback -PoolFQDN lyncpoolA.companyabc.com -Verbose
   ```

Initiating Persistent Chat Failover

Persistent Chat failover for disaster recovery relies on SQL Log Shipping as well as setting active Persistent Chat servers. Reference the earlier section "Persistent Chat Disaster Recovery" for possible scenarios. This section outlines the steps required to fail over the Persistent Chat database to the secondary server using SQL Log Shipping, as well as how to configure active Persistent Chat servers for the stretched pool.

The following procedures must be completed from the secondary Persistent Chat Server database. This server will have been the destination for Log Shipping.

1. First, disable SQL Log Shipping. Open SQL Server Management Studio and connect to the database instance where the secondary Persistent Chat server database is located.

2. Open a SQL query window on the Master database and use the following command to disable log shipping:

   ```
   exec sp_delete_log_shipping_secondary_database mgc
   ```

3. Next, bring the backup Persistent Chat database (MGC is the database name) back online. In the same SQL query window that was used before, run the following command:

   ```
   \restore database MGC with recovery
   ```

   If there are existing connections on the MGC database, you must end these connections by running the following command:

   ```
   \exec sp_who2
   ```

   Based on the connections previously identified, run the following command to end the connection:

   ```
   \kill <SPID of Connectino>
   ```

4. At this point, the SQL configuration is complete and the database will be brought online with the latest data available.

5. Now, Lync Server must be configured to recognize the SQL Server change for failover. On a Lync Server, run the following command in Lync Management Shell:

```
Set-CSPersistentChatState service:<Persistent Chat Pool FQDN>
➥-PoolState FailedOver
```

This command allows Lync to use the backup SQL Server as the SQL database for Persistent Chat.

6. Lastly, because Persistent Chat relies on stretched pools, and these pools will have a subset of servers that are not active, a failover scenario requires activating these servers for Persistent Chat service. Reference the disaster recovery design in place, and use the Set-CSPersistentChatActiveServer command to set these servers online. The example that follows assumes a stretched Persistent Chat pool with four active and four passive servers. CHAT1 and CHAT2 are located in Site A, which is the failed site, and CHAT3 and CHAT4 are located in Site B, which is the secondary site being activated.

```
Set-CSPersistentChatActiveServer -Identity
➥<Persistent Chat Pool Display Name or FQDN> -ActiveServers $null
Set-CSPersistentChatActiveServer -Identity
➥<Persistent Chat Pool Display Name or FQDN> -ActiveServers
➥@{Add="CHAT3.COMPANYABC.COM","CHAT4.COMPANYABC.COM"}
```

The first command will remove all active servers from the configuration; this is the quickest way to adjust those servers in a failover scenario. The second command will add CHAT3 and CHAT4 to the active server configuration.

At this point, the failover for Persistent Chat is complete.

Summary

Lync Server 2013 introduces many more efficient ways to provide high-availability and disaster recovery to organizations deploying Lync. Proper planning is critical for the success of a Lync Server deployment. Before the Lync infrastructure is designed, the business requirements must be understood first. Business requirements for recovery and availability will drive key decisions in the Lync Server design. After all requirements have been identified, a clear path to a final Lync Server design will be available.

As part of the high-availability and disaster recovery design, it is critical to establish clear documentation with step-by-step instructions on executing all related tasks. These tasks, which were outlined in this chapter, have been simplified in Lync Server 2013, but still require detailed documentation to be successful.

15

PART V

Migrating from Older Versions

IN THIS PART

CHAPTER 16

Migrating from Lync Server 2010

Much as with Microsoft Exchange, there's only one way to do an upgrade or a migration to Lync Server 2013. The upgrade process is a migration in the sense that Lync must be built on separate servers in parallel to the existing deployment. This is commonly referred to as a side-by-side migration. The process is fairly straightforward with only a few challenging areas. The lack of options can be a blessing in the sense that there is less to go wrong when there is only one "right" way to do it. Keep in mind that in most migration scenarios there will be a period of coexistence with Lync Server 2010.

If your organization is still using Live Communications Server 2003 or 2005, you'll need to crawl out from under that rock and upgrade to Office Communications Server 2007 R2 as an interim step before moving on to Lync Server 2013.

Assuming that Lync Server 2010 is already in place, the Lync Architect will want to plan the architecture, starting with deploying a Lync Server 2013 pool, and then Edge Server. The Lync 2013 Edge Server can proxy connections for users in both Lync Server 2013 pools and Lync Server 2010 pools. This means there is no need to maintain separate Edge Servers during the coexistence period. This chapter goes into more detail in the "Edge Migration to Lync Server 2013" section coming up. If you have completed a migration from Office Communications Server 2007 to Lync Server 2010, the process will be very familiar to you.

This chapter highlights the full life cycle of the migration process. The migration sequence is always site-by-site and side-by-side, starting with the first site deploying the

Lync 2013 pool, Edge, and Director (if required), and then migrating the pools side-by-side. Where the "migration" is a simple rip-and-replace, such as the archiving server role and monitoring server role, the topic isn't covered in great detail. Finally, the chapter concludes with troubleshooting and best practices.

Front End and User Migration to Lync Server 2013

The Front End Server migration is where you will start your migration process to Lync Server 2013. The first step is to prepare Active Directory for Lync Server 2013. In fact, all the necessary steps to build a Lync Server 2013 Front End are covered in Chapter 5, "Microsoft Lync Server 2013 Front End Server."

> **NOTE**
>
> After a Lync Server 2013 pilot pool is deployed, you cannot use Lync Server 2010 Topology Builder or Lync Server 2010 Control Panel to manage any Lync Server 2013 resources. You must use Lync Server 2013 tools to manage Lync Server 2013 and Lync Server 2010 resources. In general, you must use the administrative tools that correspond to the server version you want to manage. Lync Server 2010 and Lync Server 2013 administrative tools cannot be installed together on the same computer.

Before you begin the migration process, it is important to ensure that you have the latest Lync Server 2010 updates applied to the environment. As with any major migration, it is also prudent to back up the Lync Server 2010 environment. You should back up the SQL databases, export user configuration, and content using the `dbimpexp.exe` tool, and the CMS from the Lync Server 2010 pool. Configuration of the Lync Server 2010 clients should be considered as well. It is recommended that a Client Version Filter to only allow clients with the most current updates to connect. The Client Version Filter is found in the Lync Control Panel under the main heading "Clients" and the subheading "Client Version Policy."

Any experienced Architect will understand that if the existing environment is having problems, those problems should be resolved before migration. A migration is not going to fix things that were not working correctly to begin with. Here is a high-level overview of items to check:

▶ Verify that the Lync Server 2010 services are started.

▶ Verify the federation and Edge Server settings.

▶ Verify XMPP services and federated partners.

After the forest and domain have been prepared, you need to download the existing topology using the Lync Server 2013 Topology Builder from the Lync Server 2010 homed Central Management Server (CMS). After this has been completed, you will be able to define the new Lync Server 2013 servers. This is shown in Figure 16.1.

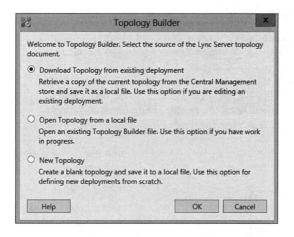

FIGURE 16.1   Download the topology from an existing Lync Server 2010 environment.

The Central Management Server was introduced in Lync Server 2010 to hold important configuration information related to the entire Lync environment. Since Lync Server 2013 also uses the Central Management Server architecture, there is no need to import any configuration from the Lync Server 2010 environment. When you open Topology Builder, you will see your Lync 2010 environment and right below you will see the Lync 2013 node, as shown in Figure 16.2. You add servers to the topology the same way you did with the legacy Lync 2010 Topology Builder.

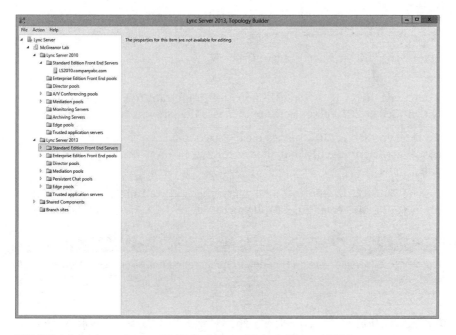

FIGURE 16.2   Lync Server 2013 topology with Lync Server 2010.

NOTE

You might see references to the Central Management Server and Central Management Store. The main difference is that the Central Management Server is the Front End responsible for the read/write copy of the Central Management Store, which is the actual data in the database. The master database location is referenced by a service connection point (SCP) in Active Directory Domain Services (AD DS). Connect to the correct context, whether Configuration or System. Below I am showing the configuration context. Expand CN=Services, CN=RTC Service, CN=Topology Settings. The location in Active Directory is shown in Figure 16.3.

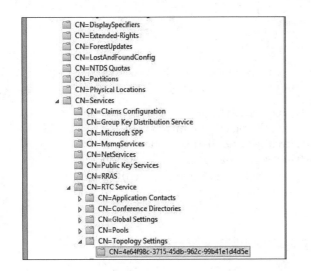

FIGURE 16.3   Lync Server SCP location in Active Directory.

After you have deployed the Lync Server 2013 pool, it is important to verify coexistence with the legacy Lync Server 2010 pool. Here are the tasks that should be completed:

▶ Verify that the Lync Server 2013 servers have started, navigate to the Administrative Tools\Services applet, and verify that all services that begin with "Lync Server" are in the started state.

▶ Open the Lync Server 2013 Control Panel. Open the Control Panel from the Front End Server in your Lync Server 2013 deployment. Select the Lync Server 2013 pool.

NOTE

On Lync Server 2013, Silverlight version 5 needs to be installed before the Lync Server Control Panel is used.

▶ In the topology section of the Lync Server 2013 Control Panel, the Topology now includes the Lync Server 2010 and Lync Server 2013 roles.

After a successful Lync Server 2013 pool installation, the next step is to set the Lync Server 2013 pool to use the legacy Lync Server 2010 Edge Server. This allows a period of coexistence, which is necessary so that you can maintain full external functionality while you are in coexistence mode. Later you will transition to the Lync Server 2013 Edge for external connectivity. To finish this process, you need to complete the following steps:

1. Open Topology Builder and select your site, which is directly below the Lync Server node.

2. Under the Actions menu, select Edit Properties.

3. In the left pane, select Federation Route.

4. Under Site Federation Route Assignment, select Enable SIP Federation, as shown in Figure 16.4, and then select the Lync Server 2010 Edge Server (this can be a Lync Server 2010 Director if a Director exists in the legacy environment).

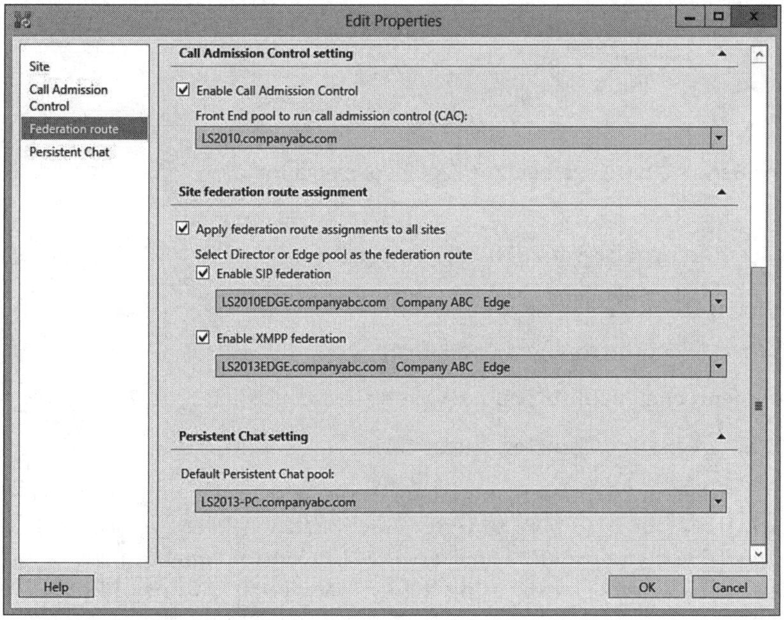

FIGURE 16.4   Site federation route assignment association.

5. Click OK to close the Edit Properties page.

6. In Topology Builder, under the Lync Server 2013 node, navigate to the Standard Edition server or Enterprise Edition Front End pools, right-click the pool, and then click Edit Properties.

7. Under Associations, select the check box next to Associate Edge Pool (For Media Components). This is shown in Figure 16.5.

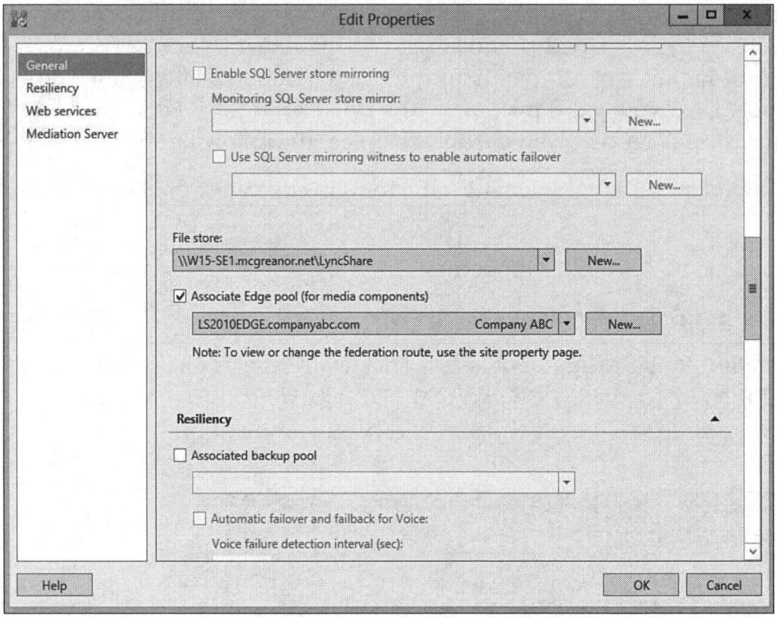

FIGURE 16.5   Set Lync Server 2010 Edge pool for Edge pool media route.

8. From the list, select the Lync Server 2010 Edge Server.

9. Click OK to close the Edit Properties page.

10. In Topology Builder, select the topmost node, Lync Server.

11. From the Action menu click Publish Topology, and then click Next.

12. When the Publishing Wizard completes, click Finish.

Now that you have a Lync Server 2013 pool, and a Lync Server 2010 pool, you can move pilot users to the new Lync Server 2013 pool to verify functionality between pools. To move a user between pools, you can use the Lync Server 2013 Control Panel or Lync Server 2013 Management Shell. Let's go over using the Lync Server 2013 Control Panel first.

1. From the Lync Server 2013 Front End, open the Lync Server 2013 Control Panel. Click on Users, click Search, then click Find.

2. Select a user that you want to move to Lync Server 2013.

3. On the Action menu, select Move Selected Users to Pool.

4. From the drop-down list, select the Lync Server 2013 pool. Click OK.

A Force option is present in the Move Users dialog box. Force should be used only in a failure scenario. Never use the Force option unless you are confident you know you should.

Verify that the Registrar Pool column for the user now contains the Lync Server 2013 pool. If you see the Lync Server 2013 pool, the move was successful.

Now that you know how to move a user in the Lync Server 2013 Control Panel, let's take a look at moving a user using the Lync Server 2013 Management Shell. Use the following commands to move a user using the Lync Management Shell:

1. Open the Lync Server 2013 Management Shell.

2. At the command line, type the following:

```
Move-CsUser -Identity "Chad McGreanor" -Target "pool02.companyabc.com"
```

3. Next, to verify that the move was successful, type the following:

```
Get-CsUser -Identity "Chad McGreanor"
```

4. The `RegistrarPool` identity now points to the Lync Server 2013 pool.

At this point in the migration process, you are in a coexistence configuration. You have a Lync Server 2010 pool and a Lync Server 2013 pool configured. For external Edge services you are using the legacy Lync Server 2010 Edge Server. In the next section you will complete the migration process to Lync Server 2013 for the Edge services.

It is recommended that you test functionality between users in both the Lync Server 2010 pool and the Lync Server 2013 pool before moving all users and services Run the following tests:

▶ Users from at least one federated domain, an internal user on Lync Server 2013, and a user on Lync Server 2010. Test instant messaging (IM), presence, audio/video (A/V), and desktop sharing.

▶ Users of each public IM service provider that your organization supports (and for which provisioning has been completed) communicating with a user on Lync Server 2013 and a user on Lync Server 2010.

▶ Verify that anonymous users are able to join conferences.

▶ A user hosted on Lync Server 2010 using remote user access (logging in to Lync Server 2010 from outside the intranet but without VPN) with a user on Lync Server 2013, and a user on Lync Server 2010. Test IM, presence, A/V, and desktop sharing.

▶ A user hosted on Lync Server 2013 using remote user access (logging in to Lync Server 2013 from outside the intranet but without VPN) with a user on Lync Server 2013, and a user on Lync Server 2010. Test IM, presence, A/V, and desktop sharing.

So that's it for the Front End pool. The next section covers Lync Server 2010 Edge to Lync Server 2013 Edge migration.

Edge Migration to Lync Server 2013

The Edge Server migration process is actually the easiest part of the overall migration process; it's a direct replacement. A Lync 2013 Edge Server can proxy connections for Lync Server 2010 Front End pools, meaning there is no need to run both versions of Edge in parallel during the coexistence period. This section covers the migration aspect of the Lync Server 2013 Edge Server; a full review of the Edge Server design process is covered in Chapter 31, "Planning to Deploy External Services." In addition, the Edge Server build process is covered in detail in Chapter 6, "Microsoft Lync Server 2013 Edge Server." This section covers the changes that need to be made for migrating from the Lync Server 2010 Edge Server to a Lync 2013 Edge Server.

This section covers adding a Lync Server 2013 Edge Server to the Lync Server 2013 pool and migrating Lync Server 2010 external Edge functions to the Lync Server 2013 Edge Server.

The first step in the Edge Server migration process is to update the federation routes. The Federation Route needs to be updated to use the Lync Server 2013 Edge Server. Federation is a trust relationship between two or more SIP domains that permits users in separate organizations to communicate across network boundaries. At this point in the migration, you are using the Lync Server 2010 Edge Server as your Federation Route for the Lync Server 2013 pool. You need to update this configuration so that you can begin to move Lync Edge functions from the legacy Lync Server 2010 Edge Server to the new Lync Server 2013 Edge Server.

Finally, the administrator must repoint the appropriate DNS records to the new Edge Server, that is, `sip.companyabc.com`. In addition to the new DNS records listed in Chapter 6, the existing SRV records need to be modified as well. Here are the SRV records required and what they should be changed to:

▶ For Remote User Access

▶ `_sip._tls.companyabc.com` points to port 443 for the FQDN of the Access Edge Service on the Edge Server.

▶ For Federation

▶ `_sipfederationtls._tcp.companyabc.com` points to port 5061 for the FQDN of the Access Edge Service on the Edge Server.

▶ `_xmpp-server._tcp.companyabc.com` points to port 5269 for the FQDN of the Access Edge Service on the Edge Server.

> **NOTE**
>
> If your organization has any partners who do not use open federation, they will need to update their Edge Server federation settings with the name of the new Lync Edge Server.

> **NOTE**
>
> Changing the federation and media traffic route requires that you schedule maintenance downtime for the Lync Server 2013 and Lync Server 2010 Edge Servers. During the transition, federated access will be unavailable for the duration of the outage. There are several reasons why downtime is required. You might have decided to use new IP addresses on the Lync Server 2013 Edge Server. This means that external DNS entries would need to be updated to reflect the new IP addresses. DNS propagation can take a while depending on TTL values and other external DNS servers updating records. Downtime can also be caused by the decision to use the same IP addresses on the Lync Server 2013 Edge Server that were used on the Lync Server 2010 Edge Server. In that case, you will have to be really quick and swap an Ethernet cable (I still picture an engineer in the datacenter, hand on the Ethernet cable, waiting for the word "GO!" and then quickly moving the cable to the new server hoping there is no outage), or disable the NIC on the legacy Lync Server 2010 Edge Server and enable the NIC on the Lync Server 2013 Edge Server. That of course would mean that you had preconfigured the NIC(s) on the Lync Server 2013 Edge Server before the downtime.

To transition the federation and media route from the Lync Server 2010 Edge Server to the Lync Server 2013 Edge Server, there are a few configuration changes that need to take place. First you need to remove the legacy federation association from Lync Server 2013 sites. To do that, you must complete the following steps:

1. Open Topology Builder on the Lync Server 2013 Front End Server.

2. In the left pane, navigate to the site node, which is located directly below Lync Server.

3. Right-click the site and then click Edit Properties.

4. In the left pane, select Federation Route.

5. Under Site Federation Route Assignment, clear the Enable SIP Federation check box to disable the federation route through the legacy Lync Server 2010 environment, as shown in Figure 16.6.

6. Click OK to close the Edit Properties page.

7. From Topology Builder, select the top node, Lync Server.

8. From the Action Menu, click Publish Topology.

9. Click Next to complete the publish process and then click Finish.

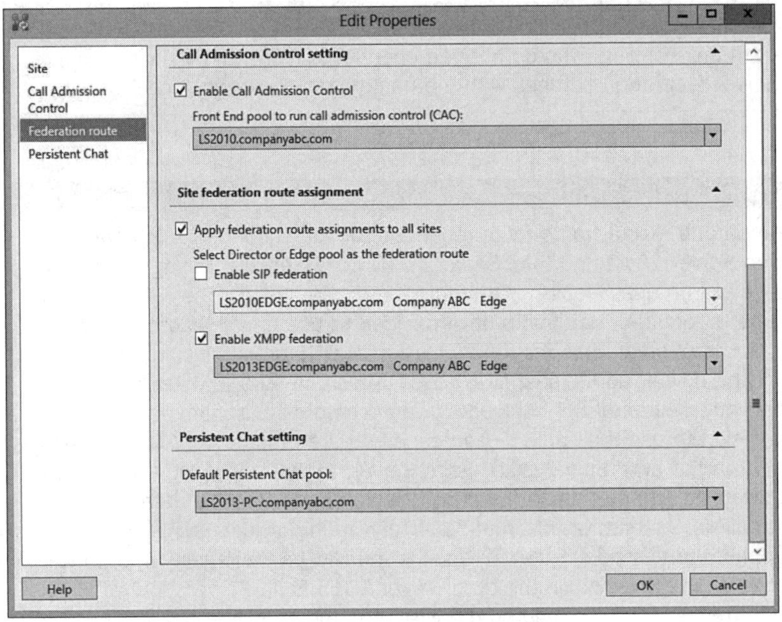

FIGURE 16.6   Federation disabled at the site level.

The next step is to configure the legacy Lync Server 2010 Edge Server as a nonfederating Edge Server. This is in preparation for the Lync Server 2013 Edge Server to take over this function. Here are the steps to follow:

1. In the left pane, navigate to the Lync Server 2010 node and then to the Edge Pools node.

2. Right-click the Edge Server, and then click Edit Properties.

3. Select General in the left pane.

4. Clear the Enable Federation for This Edge Pool (Port 5061) check box entry, as shown in Figure 16.7, and click OK to close the page.

5. From the Action menu, select Publish Topology, and then click Next.

6. When the Publishing Wizard completes, click Finish to close the wizard.

7. Verify that federation for the legacy Edge Server is disabled in the legacy end server properties.

You now need to enable federation on the Lync Server 2013 Edge Server, and change the Lync Server 2010 federation route to use the Lync Server 2013 Edge Server.

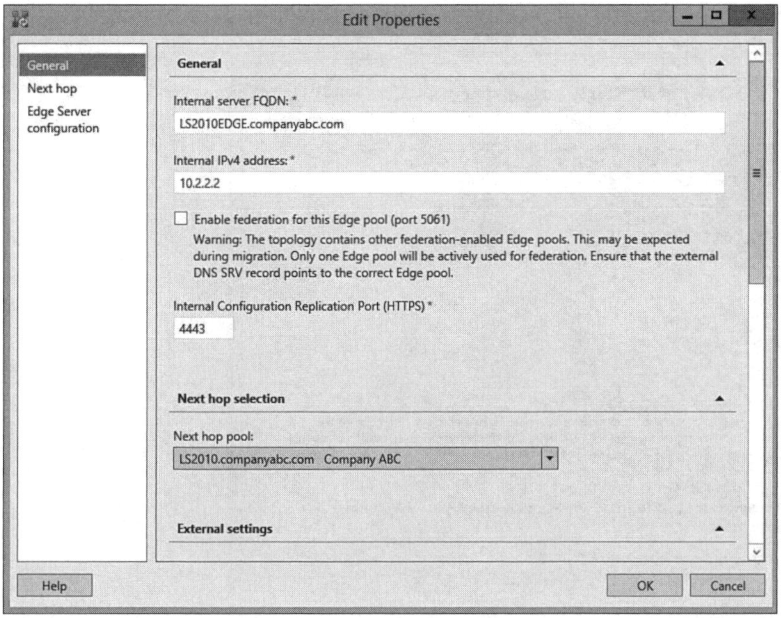

FIGURE 16.7   Federation disabled at the Edge pool level.

> **NOTE**
>
> At this point it is important to remind you of the certificate requirements of the Lync Server 2013 Edge. It is assumed that the Lync Server 2013 Edge Server has all the correct IP addresses assigned and external SSL Certificates assigned to the Access Edge Service, Web Conferencing Edge Service, and A/V Edge External service (also referred to as the A/V Authentication Service). It is also important in an Edge pool configuration where there are multiple Lync Server Edge Servers that the same SSL certificate with private key be assigned to the A/V Edge Service (A/V Authentication Service) of each Edge Server in the pool.

Here are the steps to complete:

1. From Topology Builder, in the left pane, navigate to the Lync Server 2013 node and then to the Edge Pools node.

2. Right-click the Edge Server, and then click Edit Properties.

3. Select General in the left pane.

4. Select the check box for Enable Federation for This Edge Pool (Port 5061) and then click OK to close the page.

5. From the Action menu, select Publish Topology, and then click Next.

6. When the Publishing Wizard completes, click Finish to close the wizard.

7. Verify that Federation (Port 5061) is set to Enabled, as shown in Figure 16.8.

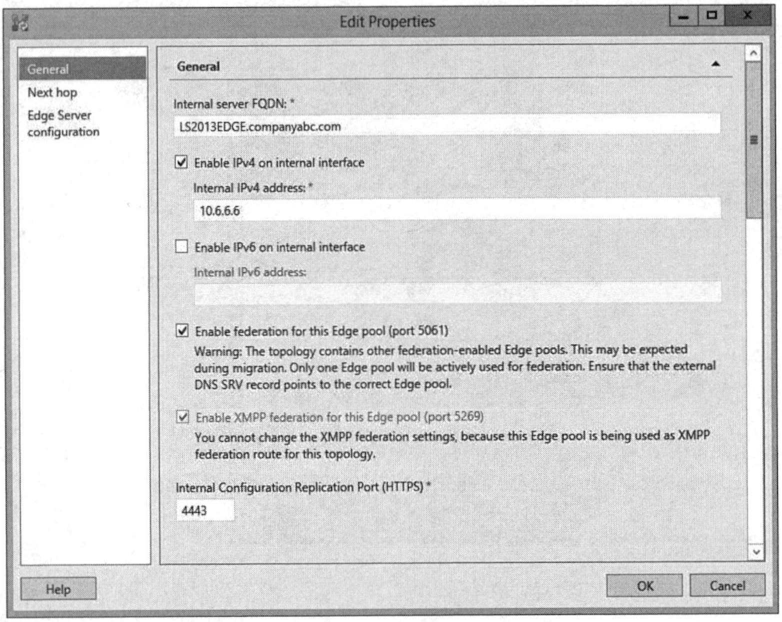

FIGURE 16.8   Federation enabled at the site level.

Next you need to configure the Lync Server 2013 Edge Server next hop to point to the Lync Server 2013 pool:

1. From Topology Builder, in the left pane, navigate to the Lync Server 2013 node and then to the Edge Pools node.

2. Expand the node, right-click the Edge Server listed, and then click Edit Properties.

3. On the General page, under Next Hop Selection, select the Lync Server 2013 pool from the drop-down list as shown in Figure 16.9.

4. Click OK to close the Edit Properties page.

5. From Topology Builder, select the top node Lync Server.

6. From the Action menu, click Publish Topology and complete the wizard.

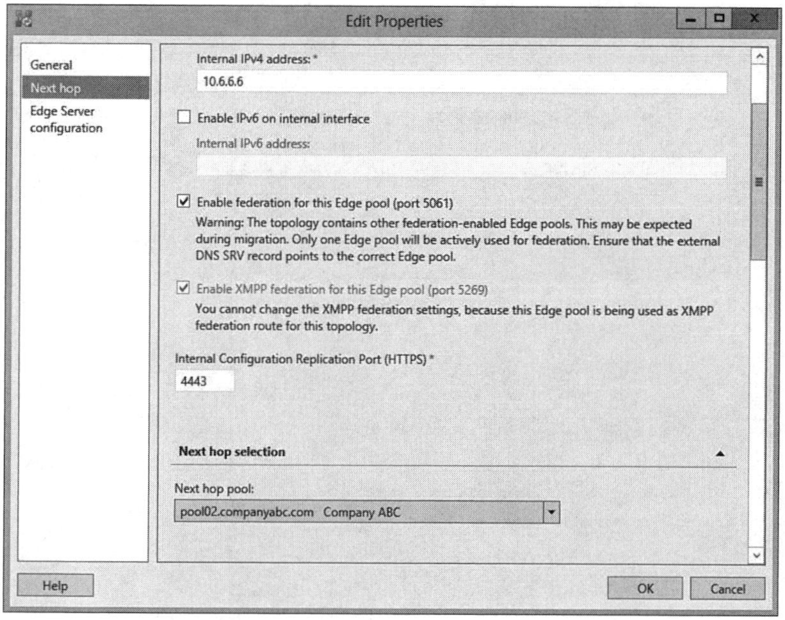

FIGURE 16.9   Edge pool federation enabled.

Next you need to configure the Lync Server 2013 pool to use the Lync Server 2013 Edge Server as the outbound media path:

1. From Topology Builder, in the left pane, navigate to the Lync Server 2013 node and then to the pool below Standard Edition Front End Servers or Enterprise Edition Front End pools.

2. Right-click the pool, and then click Edit Properties.

3. In the Associations section, select the Associate Edge Pool (For Media Components) check box.

4. From the drop-down box, select the Lync Server 2013 Edge Server, as shown in Figure 16.10.

5. Click OK to close the Edit Properties page.

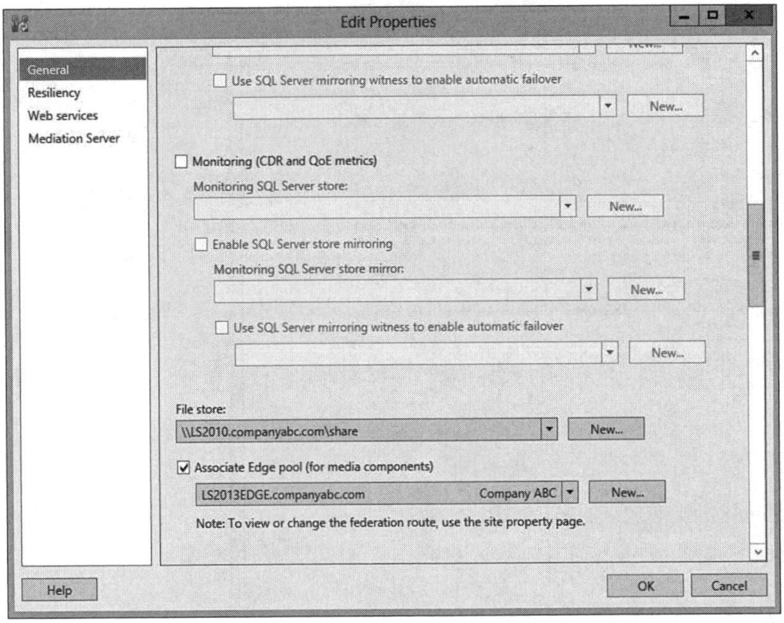

FIGURE 16.10   Lync Server 2013 Edge Server associated for media.

To enable the Lync Server 2013 Edge Server for federation, follow these steps:

1. From Topology Builder, in the left pane, navigate to the Lync Server 2013 node and then to the Edge Pools node.

2. Expand the node, right-click the Edge Server listed, and then click Edit Properties.

3. On the General page, verify that the Enable Federation for This Edge Pool (Port 5061) setting is checked.

4. Click OK to close the Edit Properties page.

5. Next, navigate to the site node.

6. Right-click the site, and then click Edit Properties.

7. In the left pane, click Federation Route.

8. Under Site Federation Route Assignment, select Enable SIP Federation, and then from the list select the Lync Server 2013 Edge Server listed as shown in Figure 16.11.

9. Click OK to close the Edit Properties page.

For multisite deployments, complete this procedure at each site.

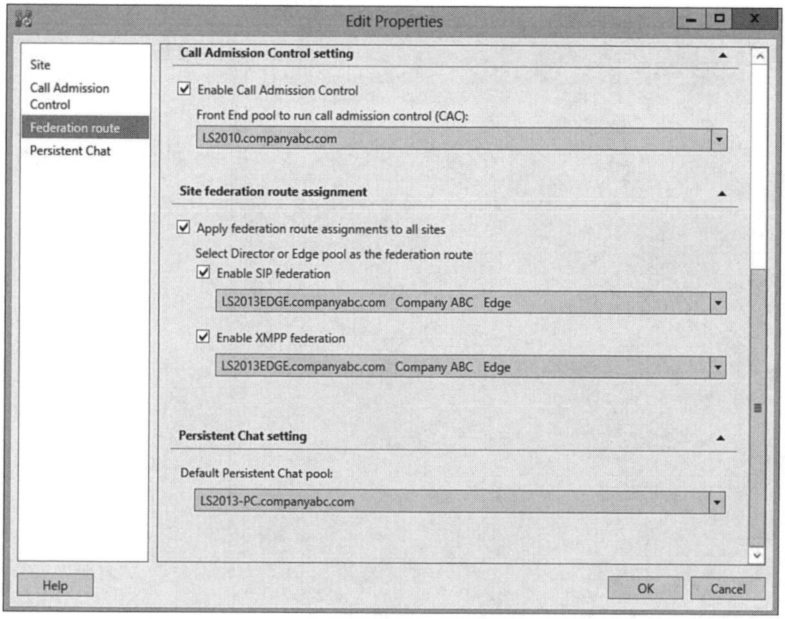

FIGURE 16.11   Lync Server 2013 Edge pool enabled for federation route.

Next you need to configure the Lync Server 2010 pool to use the Lync Server 2013 Edge Server for outbound media. This is required so that the users that are homed on the Lync Server 2010 pool will be able to use the Lync Server 2013 Edge Server for external Edge features. If all users and services have been moved to Lync Server 2013, this step is not required.

1. From Topology Builder, in the left pane, navigate to the Lync Server 2010 node and then to the pool below Standard Edition Front End Servers or Enterprise Edition Front End pools.

2. Right-click the pool, and then click Edit Properties.

3. In the Associations section, select the Associate Edge Pool (For Media Components) check box.

4. From the drop-down box, select the Lync Server 2013 Edge Server as shown in Figure 16.12.

5. Click OK to close the Edit Properties page.

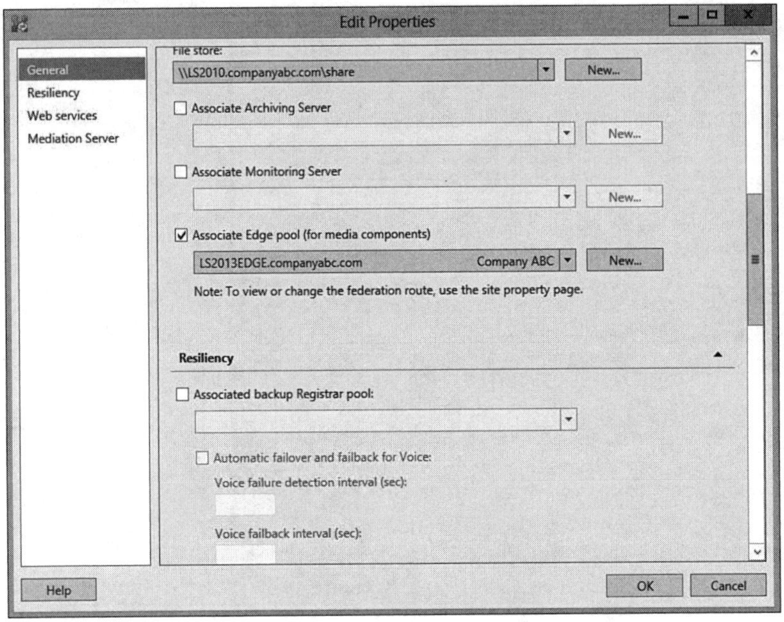

FIGURE 16.12   Lync Server 2013 Edge pool associated for media.

The last step is to publish the Edge Server configuration changes:

1. From Topology Builder, select the top node, Lync Server.

2. From the Action menu, select Publish Topology and complete the wizard.

3. Wait for Active Directory replication to occur in all pools in the deployment.

NOTE

You might see the following message:

Warning: The topology contains more than one Federated Edge Server. This can occur during migration to a more recent version of the product. In that case, only one Edge Server would be actively used for federation. Verify that the external DNS SRV record points to the correct Edge Server. If you want to deploy multiple federation Edge Servers to be active concurrently (that is, not a migration scenario), verify that all federated partners are using Lync Server. Verify that the external DNS SRV record lists all federation-enabled Edge Servers.

This warning is expected and can be safely ignored. This is because there is more than one Edge Server pool defined in the topology enabled for federation, and only one pool can be used for the federation route.

Simple URLs were introduced in Lync Server 2010. There are three simple URLs:

▶ Meet is used as the base URL for all conferences in the site or organization.

▶ Dial-in enables access to the Dial-in Conferencing Settings web page.

▶ Admin (optional) enables quick access to the Lync Server Control Panel.

It is important that after migrating to Lync Server 2013 you are aware of the impacts to DNS records and certificates for simple URLs. After you have migrated all services from the Lync Server 2010 environment, the simple URLs DNS records need to be updated to point to the reverse proxy that is publishing web services to the Lync Server 2013 web service.

Completing the Migration to Lync Server 2013

So let's recap where you are at this point. You have deployed a Lync Server 2013 pool in an existing Lync Server 2010 environment. You added a Lync Server 2013 Edge Server and moved all Edge functionality to the new Lync Server 2013 Edge Server. There are only a few items left to finish before the migration process is complete.

At this point the remaining users on Lync Server 2010 should be moved to the Lync Server 2013 pool. This is completed in a similar way as the process that was discussed earlier when we moved a single user using the Lync Server 2013 Control Panel, and Lync Server 2013 Management Shell. The only difference is that instead of selecting a single user in the Lync Server 2013 Control Panel you would select multiple users by pressing Control or Shift on the keyboard while selecting the users you would like to move to the Lync Server 2013 pool.

If you are completing this process in the Lync Server 2013 Management Shell the process would be as follows:

1. Open the Lync Server 2013 Management Shell.

2. At the command line, type the following:

```
Move-CsUser --OnLyncServer | Move-CsUser -Target "pool02.companyabc.com"
```

> **CAUTION**
>
> This command will move ALL users who were previously homed on the legacy Lync 2010 environment.

3. To verify that the move was successful, use the following command. It should not return any users.

```
Get-CsLegacyUser
```

4. The `RegistrarPool` identity now points to the Lync Server 2013 pool.

> **CAUTION**
>
> In addition to migrating users, there are several other items that need to be migrated, as detailed in the subsections that follow.

Dial-In Access Numbers

Dial-in access numbers need to be migrated from Lync Server 2010 to Lync Server 2013 before the legacy pool is decommissioned.

> **NOTE**
>
> Dial-in access numbers that you created in Lync Server 2010 but moved to Lync Server 2013 or that you created in Lync Server 2013 before, during, or after migration have the following characteristics:
>
> ▶ Do not appear on Office Communications Server 2007 R2 meeting invitations and the dial-in access number page
>
> ▶ Appear on Lync Server 2010 meeting invitations and the dial-in access number page
>
> ▶ Appear on Lync Server 2013 meeting invitations and the dial-in access number page
>
> ▶ Cannot be viewed or modified in the Office Communications Server 2007 R2 administrative tool
>
> ▶ Can be viewed and modified in the Lync Server 2010 Control Panel and in Lync Server 2010 Management Shell
>
> ▶ Can be viewed and modified in the Lync Server 2013 Control Panel and in Lync Server 2013 Management Shell
>
> ▶ Can be resequenced within the region by using the `Set-CsDialinConferencing AccessNumber` cmdlet with the `Priority` parameter

To identify and move dial-in access numbers, complete the following steps:

1. Start the Lync Server Management Shell: Click Start, All Programs, Microsoft Lync Server 2013, and then select Lync Server Management Shell. To identify the existing dial in access numbers run the following command:

   ```
   Get-CsDialInConferencingAccessNumber
   ```

2. To move each dial-in access number to a pool hosted on Lync Server 2013, from the command line run this:

   ```
   Move-CsApplicationEndpoint -Identity "+14255551212@companyabc.com" -Target
   "pool02.companyabc.com"
   ```

3. Open Lync Server Control Panel.

4. In the left navigation bar, click Conferencing.

5. Select the Dial-in Access Number tab.

6. Verify that no dial-in access numbers remain for the Lync Server 2010 pool from which you are migrating.

Call Park Application Settings

The Call Park configuration includes Call Park orbit range, the pickup timeout threshold, the maximum call pickup attempts, the timeout request, and music-on-hold files. It is important to note that the process of configuring the Call Park application does not move the configuration or music-on-hold files that the service might be using. Those files are stored on the Lync Server 2010 pool filestore. A file copy utility like Xcopy would need to be used to copy the files from the Lync Server 2010 pool filestore to the Lync Server 2013 filestore. An example of an Xcopy command is shown here:

```
Xcopy "<Lync Server 2010 Filestore Path>\OcsFileStore\coX-ApplicationServer-
➥X\AppServerFiles\CPS\"  "<Lync Server 2013 Filestore Path>\OcsFileStore\
➥coX-ApplicationServer-X\AppServerFiles\CPS\"
```

To reconfigure the Call Park service settings, you need to follow the procedure listed here:

> **NOTE**
>
> You are just configuring the Call Park service for the Lync Server 2013 pool at this point. All the values being entered would be obtained by referencing the Lync Server 2010 Call Park configuration.

1. From the Lync Server 2013 Front End Server, open the Lync Server Management Shell.

2. At the command line, type the following:

```
Set-CsCpsConfiguration -Identity "<LS2013 Call Park Service ID>"
➥-CallPickupTimeoutThreshold
"<LS2010 CPS TimeSpan>" -EnableMusicOnHold "<LS2010 CPS value>"
➥-MaxCallPickupAttempts "<LS2010
CPS pickup attempts>" -OnTimeoutURI "<LS2010 CPS timeout URI>"
```

The next step would be to reassign all Call Park orbit ranges from Lync Server 2010 pool to the Lync Server 2013 pool. This can be completed in either the Lync Server 2013 Control Panel or the Lync Server 2013 Management Shell. Let's go through the Lync Server 2010 Control Panel first:

1. Open Lync Server Control Panel.

2. In the left pane, select Voice Features.

3. Select the Call Park tab.

16

4. For each Call Park orbit range assigned to a Lync Server 2010 pool, edit the FQDN of the destination server setting and select the Lync Server 2013 pool that will process the Call Park requests.

5. Click Commit to save the changes.

To reassign all Call Park Orbit Ranges using Lync Server Management Shell, follow this process:

1. Open Lync Server Management Shell.

2. At the command line, type the following:

```
Get-CsCallParkOrbit
```

This cmdlet lists all the Call Park orbit ranges in the deployment. All Call Park orbits that have the `CallParkServiceId` and `CallParkServerFqdn` parameters set as the Lync Server 2010 pool must be reassigned.

To reassign the Lync Server 2010 Call Park orbit ranges to the Lync Server 2013 pool, at the command line, type the following:

```
Set-CsCallParkOrbit -Identity "<Call Park Orbit Identity>" -CallParkService
"service:ApplicationServer:<Lync Server 2013 Pool FQDN>"
```

Response Groups

The Response Group move process is an all-or-nothing procedure. You can move either all the Lync Server 2010 Response Group configuration or none at all. It is also a 1:1 move process between pools. You cannot move unique Response Groups from one pool between different pools. To move the Response Group applications, complete the following:

1. Log on to the computer with an account that is a member of the `RTCUniversalServerAdmins` group or has equivalent administrator rights and permissions.

2. Start the Lync Server Management Shell: Click Start, All Programs, Microsoft Lync Server 2013, and then select Lync Server Management Shell.

3. Run the following:

```
Move-CsRgsConfiguration -Source pool01.companyabc.com -Destination
➥ pool02.companyabc.com
```

4. After you migrate response groups and agents to the Lync Server 2013 pool, the URL that agents use to sign in and sign out is a Lync Server 2013 URL and is available from the Tools menu. Remind agents to update any references, such as bookmarks, to the new URL.

Address Book

The Address Book can be an important item that most of the time is left to be forgotten on the Lync Server 2010 pool. This file is important if there are any customized rules for the organization, such as normalizing Active Directory telephone numbers, or normalizing telephone numbers in RCC environments. It is important to replicate this configuration in the Lync Server 2013 environment. Here are the steps to take:

1. Find the `Company_Phone_Number_Normalization_Rules.txt` file in the root of the Address Book shared folder, and copy it to the root of the Address Book shared folder in your Lync Server 2013 pilot pool.

> **NOTE**
>
> The sample Address Book normalization rules have been installed in your ABS Web component file directory. The path is `$installedDriveLetter:\Program Files\ Microsoft Lync Server 2013\Web Components\Address Book Files\Files\ Sample_Company_Phone_Number_Normalization_Rules.txt`. This file can be copied and renamed as `Company_Phone_Number_Normalization_Rules.txt` to the Address Book shared folder's root directory. For example, for the Address Book shared in `$serverX`, the path will be similar to `\\$serverX \LyncFileShare\2-WebServices-1\ABFiles`.

2. Use a text editor, such as Notepad, to open the `Company_Phone_Number_ Normalization_Rules.txt` file.

3. Certain types of entries will not work correctly in Lync Server 2013. Look through the file for the types of entries described in this step, edit them as necessary, and save the changes to the Address Book shared folder in your pilot pool.

Strings that include required whitespace or punctuation cause normalization rules to fail because these characters are stripped out of the string that is input to the normalization rules. If you have strings that include required whitespace or punctuation, you need to modify the strings.

For example, the following string *would* cause the normalization rule to fail:

`\s*\(\s*\d\d\d\s*\)\s*\-\s*\d\d\d\s*\-\s*\d\d\d\d`

The following string *would not* cause the normalization rule to fail:

`\s*\(?\s*\d\d\d\s*\)?\s*\-?\s*\d\d\d\s*\-?\s*\d\d\d\d`

Common Area Phones

Common Area Phones have a contact object that is associated with the pool they were created for. In a migration scenario it is important to move all Common Area Phone contact objects to the Lync Server 2013 pool. Here is the process:

1. From the Lync Server 2013 Front End Server, open Lync Server Management Shell.

2. From the command line, type the following:

```
Get-CsCommonAreaPhone -Filter {RegistrarPool -eq "pool01.companyabc.com"} |
Move-CsCommonAreaPhone -Target pool02.companyabc.com
```

3. To verify that all contact objects have been moved to the Lync Server 2013 pool, from the Lync Server Management Shell type the following:

```
Get-CsCommonAreaPhone -Filter {RegistrarPool -eq "pool02.companyabc.com"}
```

Analog Devices

Analog Devices are very similar to Common Area Phones in the sense that they are also contact objects associated with the Lync Server 2010 pool. These objects need to be moved. The process is pretty much the same as moving Common Area Phones, but using a slightly different command:

1. Start the Lync Server Management Shell: Click Start, All Programs, Microsoft Lync Server 2013, and then select Lync Server Management Shell.

2. At the command line, type this:

```
Get-CsAnalogDevice -Filter {RegistrarPool -eq "pool01.companyabc.com"} |
Move-CsAnalogDevice -Target pool02.companyabc.com
```

3. Verify that all contact objects have been moved to the Lync Server 2013 pool. At the command line, type this:

```
Get-CsAnalogDevice -Filter {RegistrarPool -eq "pool02.companyabc.com"}
```

Voice Routing

Voice routes and how they are impacted during a migration to Lync Server 2013 is an important item to cover. When you are in a period of coexistence with a Lync Server 2010 pool that includes Lync Server 2010 mediation servers, you probably have gateways and/or SBCs associated with Lync Server 2010 mediation server or Mediation Server pool. Voice routing interoperability between Lync Server 2010 and Lync Server 2013 is fully supported, meaning that you can have users homed on Lync Server 2010 and use a Lync Server 2010 or a Lync Server 2013 mediation server/pool, or have users homed on Lync Server 2013 and use a Lync Server 2013 or Lync Server 2010 mediation server/pool. The point here is that before decommissioning the Lync Server 2010 environment, you will need to configure Lync Server 2013 Mediation Servers or Pools with the gateways and/or SBCs and also configure the Voice over IP gateways and/or SBCs to direct inbound traffic to the Lync Server 2013 Mediation Servers.

Another important note here is that a Lync Server 2013 SBA (Survivable Branch Appliance) is not supported in a Lync Server 2010 pool.

Before you decommission the Lync Server 2010 environment, there are a few configuration changes that need to be made before you can call the migration task complete. This first is to update internal DNS SRV records for every SIP domain that is supported by your environment. The process that follows describes how to complete this task. Complete this task from a server that has the DNS administrative tools installed:

1. On the DNS server, click Start, Administrative Tools, DNS.

2. In the console tree for your SIP domain, expand Forward Lookup Zones, expand the SIP domain in which Lync Server 2013 is installed, and navigate to the _tcp setting.

3. In the right pane, right-click _sipinternaltls and select Properties.

4. In Host Offering This Service, update the host FQDN to point to the Lync Server 2013 pool (if the pool is a Standard Edition Server, enter the server FQDN). This is shown in Figure 16.13.

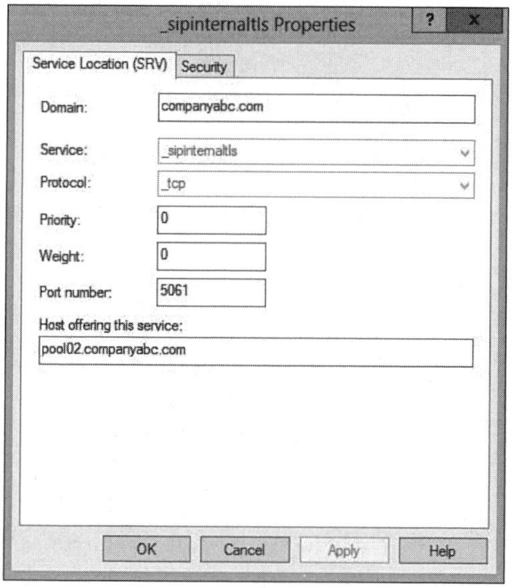

FIGURE 16.13   Update SRV record for all SIP domains supported.

5. Click OK.

Earlier you read about the Central Management Server. If you recall, the Central Management Server is still associated with the Lync Server 2010 pool. You need to move the Central Management Server to the Lync Server 2013 pool. This process is outlined next.

If you deployed Lync Server 2013 Standard Edition, here are the steps for preparing the environment:

1. On the Lync Server 2013 Standard Edition Front End Server where you want to relocate the Central Management Server: Log on to the computer where the Lync Server Management Shell is installed, as a member of the RTCUniversalServerAdmins group.

2. Open the Lync Server Deployment Wizard.

3. In the wizard, click Prepare First Standard Edition Server.

4. On the Executing Commands page, SQL Server Express is installed as the Central Management Server. Necessary firewall rules are created. When the installation of the database and prerequisite software is completed, click Finish.

5. To create the Central Management Store, you need to complete this process from the Lync Server 2013 Management Shell. Type the following:

```
Install-CsDatabase -CentralManagementDatabase -SQLServerFQDN "lync.companyabc.
com" -SQLInstanceName RTC
```

6. Confirm that the status of the Lync Server Front End service is Started.

If you deployed Lync Server 2013 in a Enterprise Pool configuration, here are the steps for preparing the environment:

1. On the Lync Server 2013 Standard Edition Front End Server where you want to relocate the Central Management Server: Log on to the computer where the Lync Server Management Shell is installed, as a member of the RTCUniversalServerAdmins group.

2. Open the Lync Server 2013 Management Shell.

3. To create the new Central Management store in the Lync Server 2013 SQL Server database, in the Lync Server Management Shell, type this:

```
Install-CsDatabase -CentralManagementDatabase -SQLServerFQDN
➥"SQL01.companyabc.com"-SQLInstanceName LYNC
```

4. Confirm that the status of the Lync Server Front End service is Started.

Now that you have prepared the environment and created a blank XDS and LIS database, you can move the Central Management Server to the Lync Server 2013 pool. To do that, you have a few more commands to run:

1. On the Lync Server 2013 server that will be the Central Management Server: Log on to the computer where the Lync Server Management Shell is installed, as a member of the RTCUniversalServerAdmins group. You must also have the SQL Server database administrator user rights and permissions.

2. Open Lync Server Management Shell.

3. In the Lync Server Management Shell, type this:

```
Enable-CsTopology
```

4. On the Lync Server 2013 Front End Server or from one of the Front End pool servers in an Enterprise pool, in the Lync Server Management Shell, type this:

```
Move-CsManagementServer
```

5. Lync Server Management Shell displays the servers, filestores, database stores, and service connection points of the Current State and the Proposed State. Read the information carefully and confirm that this is the intended source and destination. Type Y to continue, or N to stop the move.

6. Review any warnings or errors generated by the `Move-CsManagementServer` command and resolve them.

7. On the Lync Server 2013 server, open the Lync Server Deployment Wizard.

8. In the wizard, click Install or Update Lync Server System, click Step 2: Setup or Remove Lync Server Components, click Next, review the summary, and then click Finish.

9. On the Lync Server 2010 server, open the Lync Server Deployment Wizard.

10. In the wizard, click Install or Update Lync Server System, click Step 2: Setup or Remove Lync Server Components, click Next, review the summary, and then click Finish.

11. To confirm that replication with the new Central Management store is occurring. In the Lync Server Management Shell, type this:

```
Get-CsManagementStoreReplicationStatus
```

> **NOTE**
>
> The replication may take some time to update all replicas.

If you had Lync Server 2010 Archiving or Monitoring roles installed and associated with the Lync Server 2010 pool, those associations will need to be removed before the decommissioning of the Lync Server 2010 environment. Details on that process are not given here.

Okay, you are on the home stretch. Migration from Lync Server 2010 to Lync Server 2013 involves quite a few components, as you might have been able to tell. You have a few more items left, and then you can go grab a cup of coffee!

Call Admission Control (CAC) has a component called PDP (Policy Decision Point). This component is responsible for making CAC decisions and adhering to the policies defined.

That service is hosted on a single pool in each site. You need to move this configuration to the Lync Server 2013 environment. Following is the process:

1. Open Topology Builder.

2. Right-click the site node, and then click Edit Properties.

3. Under Call Admission Control setting, make sure that Enable Call Admission Control is selected.

4. Under Front End Pool to Run Call Admission Control (CAC), select the Lync Server 2013 pool that is to host CAC, as shown in Figure 16.14. Click OK.

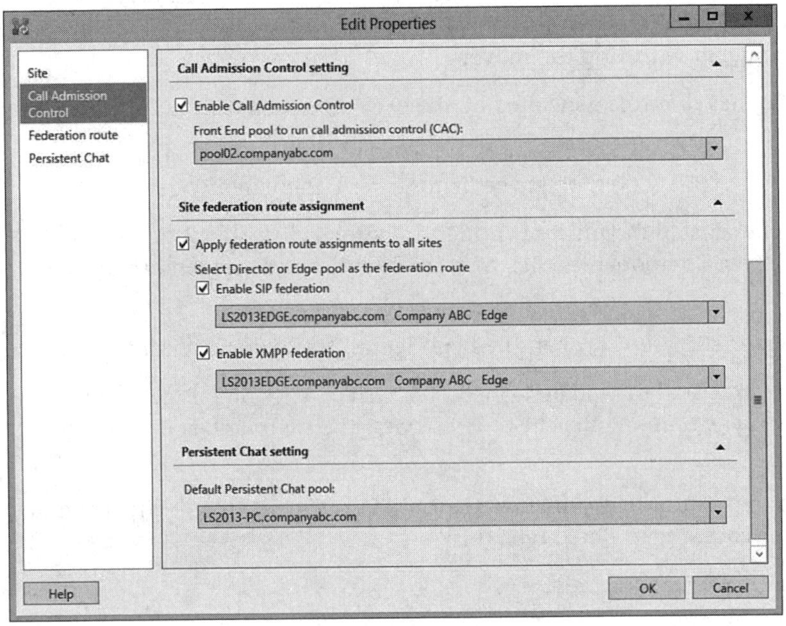

FIGURE 16.14   Update PDP, Call Admission Control configuration.

5. Publish the topology.

After the topology has been published, it is important to update the Lync Server 2010 and Lync Server 2013 pools so that the CAC Services are removed and added correctly. To do that, complete the following steps on each pool:

1. In Lync Server Deployment Wizard, click Install or Update Lync Server System, click Step 2: Setup or Remove Lync Server Components, click Next, review the summary, and then click Finish.

2. On the Lync Server 2010 server, open the Lync Server Deployment Wizard.

3. In the wizard, click Install or Update Lync Server System, click Step 2: Setup or Remove Lync Server Components, click Next, review the summary, and then click Finish.

Now that all dependent services have been moved to the Lync Server 2013 environment, it is time to remove the Lync Server 2010 configuration.

The first thing you need to do is stop services and prevent new sessions to the Lync Server 2010 pool:

1. From each server in the pool, run the following command:

```
Stop-CsWindowsService
```

Lync Server 2010 Enterprise Edition does not exist as a stand-alone computer. At least from a Lync Server Topology perspective, you always need to define a pool, and in the pool you define the Enterprise Edition Servers. The process the follows guides you through removing an individual Front End Server from an existing environment:

1. Open the Lync Server 2013 Front End Server, and open Topology Builder.

2. Navigate to the Lync Server 2010 node.

3. Expand Enterprise Edition Front End Pools, expand the Front End pool with the Front End Server that you want to remove, right-click the Front End Server that you want to remove, and then click Delete.

The final step is removing the actual Lync Server 2010 Standard Edition or Enterprise Edition pools from the topology.

To remove an Enterprise Edition Front End Server pool, follow this procedure:

1. Open Topology Builder.

2. Navigate to the Lync Server 2010 node.

3. Expand Enterprise Edition Front End pools, expand the Front End pool, right-click the Front End pool that you want to remove, and then click Delete.

4. Publish the topology, check the replication status, and then run the Lync Server Deployment Wizard as needed.

To remove a Standard Edition Front End Server, follow this procedure:

1. Open Topology Builder.

2. Navigate to the Lync Server 2010 node.

3. Expand Standard Edition Front End Servers, right-click the Front End Server that you want to remove, and then click Delete.

16

4. Expand SQL stores, right-click the SQL Server database that is associated with the Standard Edition Front End Server, and then click Delete.

> **NOTE**
>
> You must remove the collocated SQL Server databases from the Standard Edition Front End Server.

5. Publish the topology, check the replication status, and then run the Lync Server Deployment Wizard as needed.

So that's it—if you are reading this, you survived a Lync Server 2010 to Lync Server 2013 migration. If you followed the steps in this chapter you should have great success with your migration efforts.

Troubleshooting

As with any migration, there's a lot that can go wrong regardless of how well you've planned. The biggest item to check is ensuring that Active Directory is healthy and functioning properly. A close second is ensuring that all the required manual DNS changes have been made and that DNS is working flawlessly. Of course, there are the firewall ACLs that need to be in place for the new Lync Server 2013 Edge Server as well. The added convenience of the Deployment Wizard doesn't lessen the importance of certificates. They are still core to all server and server-client communications.

Be sure to check the various log files that are created. It's great news that nearly every action, whether done in the Lync Control Panel or the Lync Management Shell, creates a detailed XML log file in the Windows `temp` directory. Administrators should review these files regularly to gain insight into their deployment and understand any errors that occur. The Lync Server event log is also a good place to check for errors. From the Start menu select Administrative Tools and then Event Viewer. Expand the Applications and Services Logs item and select Lync Server. All events related to Lync Server functions reside here. Often the error description is enough to identify the problem and make clear the resolution.

Best Practices

The following are the best practices from this chapter:

▶ Perform an Active Directory Health Check before beginning the upgrade and migration process. Resolve any issues before starting the process.

▶ Although the Lync Server 2013 Control Panel might seem more familiar at first, there are many functions that can be accomplished only in the Lync Server Management Shell.

▶ Publish the topology often and after each significant configuration change.

▶ Ensure that all users and other objects, such as Exchange Unified Messaging (UM) Autoattendant accounts, are migrated to Lync Server before beginning the Lync Server 2010 decomission process.

16

PART VI

Lync Voice, Video, and Integration

IN THIS PART

Lync Telephony and Voice Integration

In the days of Office Communications Server 2007 when Microsoft first dipped into the voice integration features, there was a lot of discussion about whether it could actually function as a real PBX replacement. Over the next few years there was a lot of back-and-forth debate comparing its shortcomings to more mature systems, but since Lync Server 2010 and now with Lync Server 2013, Microsoft has an incredibly strong story with the product. It's no longer considered an add-on or supplemental service to existing PBXs—Lync Server 2013 functions well on its own and can provide complete voice services for many organizations.

This chapter is intended to provide a foundation for some of the concepts found in later chapters covering Enterprise Voice and Planning for Voice services. A high-level overview of telephony concepts is discussed to provide a starting point of reference. Afterward, the various integration methods used to provide coexistence or migration paths to Lync Server 2013 are covered, and the same is done from the perspective of an end user in each of those scenarios.

Analog device connectivity for phones and fax machines was introduced in Lync Server 2010 and remains unchanged in Lync Server 2013, but the overall call-flow concepts are reviewed. The final section of this chapter is an absolute must-read for any Lync voice administrator; it covers each of the components used within Lync voice routing, and provides examples of how they interact to allow users to place a phone call.

Understanding Telephony Fundamentals

To understand the options for integrating Lync Server with an existing voice infrastructure, it is important to understand some fundamentals of telephony. This section discusses some basic concepts in telephony and how they apply to Lync Server.

Public Switched Telephone Network (PSTN)

The Public Switched Telephone Network is the common network of telephony systems across the world. For those with more of a systems administration background, consider it similar to the Internet, like a cloud through which phone systems (as opposed to computers) are connected. The PSTN is composed of circuit switched analog lines, digital trunks such as T1s or E1s, cellular connections, and satellite transmissions, all of which can call each other through connected switching centers around the world. There is an incredible number of varying protocols and standards between different vendors and regions of the world to the point where it's remarkable how well the system works. Figure 17.1 shows a logical representation of the PSTN.

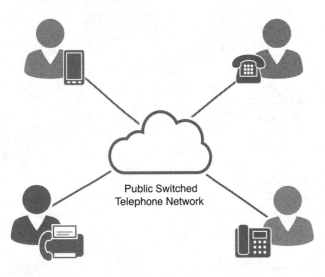

FIGURE 17.1   The Public Switched Telephone Network.

Private Branch Exchange

A Private Branch Exchange (PBX) is a device that organizations install in their environment which enables internal connectivity for phones or fax machines. PBXs were historically expensive to purchase or required long lease agreements, but were considered an investment that could be utilized for a period as long as 10 to 30 years.

The PBX on-premise allows for users within the organization to call each other without traversing the PSTN and incurring any charges. A PBX also usually has trunk lines that connect to the PSTN so that internal users can make and receive calls with other PSTN users outside of the office, as shown in Figure 17.2.

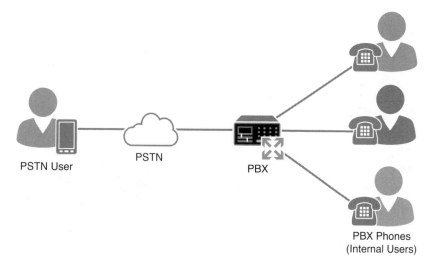

PSTN User   PSTN   PBX

PBX Phones
(Internal Users)

FIGURE 17.2   A Private Branch Exchange (PBX).

As telephony has evolved over the years, different types of PBXs have been used by companies. Usually they fall into one of three categories:

▶ **Traditional PBX**—A traditional PBX is one that does not have any IP capabilities. These are generally older or low-end systems with limited feature sets. These systems are usually entirely based on analog or digital handsets for end users.

▶ **IP PBX**—An IP PBX is a system that is entirely based on Voice over IP (VoIP). It does not support any analog devices natively and all endpoints are IP-based network devices.

▶ **Hybrid PBX**—Many PBXs have the capability to function both as a traditional PBX with analog endpoints and as an IP PBX through the purchase of expansion modules and software upgrades, like shown in Figure 17.3. These PBXs offer the most flexibility for an organization because they can connect many types of devices as the business transitions to IP telephony.

Signaling

In the world of telephony, some information must be exchanged between the PBX and the end users, such as the phone number of the caller and the phone number of the callee, in order to place a call. This is referred to as the signaling information, and it usually contains much more than just phone numbers; for the sake of this section, however, it can be considered what controls the calls. The signaling information is how a call is placed, transferred, or ended. The actual voice traffic, or the audio a user speaks and hears, is considered the media. So in any call there is signaling information to control the call, and a media stream that is the actual audio heard. Keep in mind that the path taken by these two items does not have to be identical.

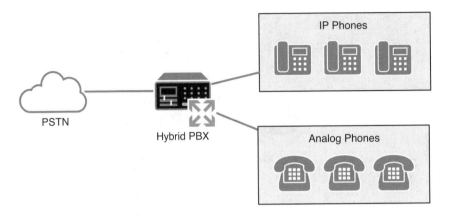

FIGURE 17.3   Hybrid PBX connecting analog and IP phones.

Signaling information can come in the form of in-band or out-of-band. In-band means the information shares the same channel or line as the media. The most common form of in-band signaling is Dual-Tone Multi-Frequency signaling (DTMF), which is what is sent when pressing keys on a phone. Each key transmits a unique tone, indicating a different piece of information to the PBX.

Signaling can also be carried out-of-band, which is typical for PBX trunk lines to the PSTN or when connecting directly to another PBX. Out-of-band signaling usually uses a dedicated channel for the signaling information while the media or actual voice traffic is carried in different channels. Take a North American T1 connection as an example; there are 24 channels each with 64Kbps of bandwidth available. For a primary rate interface (PRI), the first 23 channels will each carry voice traffic, so with one call per channel 23 simultaneous calls are supported. The 24th channel carries the signaling information for all the first 23 channels concurrently. This is considered out-of-band because the signaling and media are in separate channels on the connection. An example of this is shown in Figure 17.4.

Voice over IP (VoIP)

As internal networks began to grow, it paved the way for Voice over IP (VoIP) based PBXs to emerge. Instead of using traditional analog lines to provide connections between internal users, the VoIP handsets connected to the PBX over the IP protocol, just like a computer or any other device on the network. This allowed voice and data traffic to share a common infrastructure, which cuts down on wiring and management overhead. The disadvantage to VoIP in early implementations was that it relied on shared networks where there were few controls in place and no QoS deployed for the voice traffic. As networks and IP PBX systems matured in later years, more businesses attracted by the lower total cost of ownership and advanced feature sets offered by IP PBX systems began to migrate away from legacy PBXs.

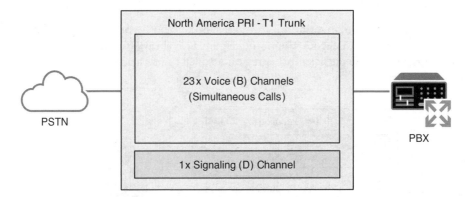

North America PRI - T1 Trunk

23 x Voice (B) Channels
(Simultaneous Calls)

PSTN

1 x Signaling (D) Channel

PBX

FIGURE 17.4   Out-of-band signaling.

Just as with traditional PBXs, VoIP requires some form of signaling to control the calls. An early form of signaling used for VoIP was H.323, and the Media Gateway Control Protocol (MGCP) also has gained widespread adoption.

The Session Initiation Protocol, or SIP, has also emerged as a standard that many IP PBXs use for signaling, including Lync Server. Lync 2013 and all previous versions of the product use SIP for the internal signaling and for integrations with other PBX vendors because it provides a common framework for controlling calls. Vendors can also implement extensions on top of SIP to provide additional signaling capabilities. That's not to say that because two systems both use SIP they will be compatible. Often there are differences in the SIP message flow, protocols used, or extensions used that prevent systems from direct integration. Still, the basic concepts of SIP messaging should be understood by any Lync administrator.

Media and Codecs

Although SIP meets the needs for signaling information in calls, VoIP PBXs still require a method to transmit the actual media stream, whether it is audio or video. The Real-Time Transport Protocol (RTP) is used in almost every VoIP implementation and was developed specifically for transmitting audio and video traffic across networks. Encryption of the media traffic was later added in the form of Secure Real-Time Transport Protocol (SRTP), which is what Lync Server 2013 uses by default to ensure that the media cannot be intercepted and played back.

It's important to note that RTP and SRTP only provide a standard for carrying the media traffic which can be composed of various media codecs. Think of the RTP stream as a wrapper around the actual audio, which could be encoded by any type of codec. Media

17

codecs are a way of translating audio and video data into bits that can be transmitted across a network. A codec analyzes an analog audio waveform and determines the best way to represent that audio stream as digital bits of 0s and 1s. That process is called encoding, and the reverse, decoding, is what the receiving end does in order to reconstruct the audio waveform for playback.

For two users to have an audio conversation, the codec used by both parties must match in order to correctly encode and decode the traffic. Figure 17.5 shows that while SRTP carries the real-time media, the parties must agree on a codec to use in order to actually have a conversation.

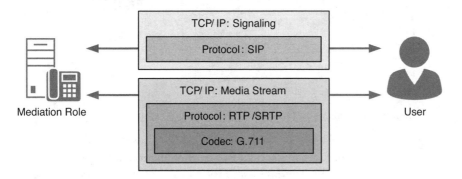

FIGURE 17.5   SIP signaling and SRTP media.

Lync Audio Codecs

Lync endpoints use various codecs within the RTP streams but select the appropriate one for each situation. This codec selection is mostly based on the type of call being placed, but endpoint type, server policies, or Call Admission Control settings can force alternative behaviors. These are the types of codecs used:

▶ **RTAudio Wideband**—The default codec used between two Lync endpoints in a peer-to-peer call. It produces a high-fidelity audio call using minimal bandwidth.

▶ **RTAudio Narrowband**—Used between a Lync endpoint and a Mediation Server when a PSTN call is placed. The PSTN user cannot hear the wideband audio fidelity so there is no need to send a higher-quality stream between the Lync endpoint and the Mediation Server. This can also be used in peer-to-peer Lync calls when bandwidth is restricted.

▶ **G.711**—Used between the Mediation Server and a media gateway. The Mediation Server transcodes a Lync endpoint's RTAudio Narrowband stream and sends it as G.711 to the gateway. If the Media Bypass feature is enabled, a Lync endpoint can send G.711 audio directly to the media gateway, bypassing the Mediation Server transcoding operation.

▶ **G.722**—Used for conference calls when the round-trip latency to the A/V conferencing server is less than 25ms. This is a high-quality wideband audio codec.

▶ **Siren**—Used for conference calls when the round-trip latency to the A/V conferencing server exceeds 25ms. It is typically used by users joining a conference across a WAN connection or through the A/V Edge server.

The main RTAudio codecs are Microsoft proprietary technology, which means they can be used only by endpoints which license the technology. IP PBX and media gateway vendors typically do not want to incur this additional cost or complexity, so they instead support more common codecs such as G.711. This is why the Mediation Server role exists; it handles the conversion, or transcoding, process by translating an RTAudio stream to G.711 and vice versa, allowing for integration through the media gateways covered in the next section. Another unique feature of the Microsoft media stack is the ability to switch between many of these codecs on the fly.

Integration Methods

There are various ways to integrate Lync Server 2013 with an existing PBX, whether it is a legacy or IP PBX. The methods discussed in this section can be used to support a period of coexistence with the existing telephony infrastructure, which allows businesses to evaluate and test Lync Enterprise Voice without performing a full migration. A brand-new Greenfield deployment is rare to come across, so many deployments will require this coexistence situation for some time. The following methods allow for a coexistence period during which the feature sets of Lync are evaluated and users are gradually migrated.

Direct SIP

The easiest and generally most cost-effective way of integrating Lync Server 2013 with an existing PBX is if the PBX supports SIP trunking. Many IP PBXs support this functionality natively, and many other hybrid PBXs support SIP trunking through minor hardware or software upgrades. This type of integration requires no hardware because the link between systems is purely a logical trunk that exists between two IP endpoints.

In Direct SIP scenarios the Mediation Server role serves as the conversion point between the two systems. The signaling on both sides of a SIP trunk is SIP, but the Mediation role translates the media stream between G.711 on the PBX side and RTAudio on the Lync Server side, as shown in Figure 17.6.

Direct SIP integration allows for various end-user scenarios, which are discussed later in this chapter. Generally, specific extensions, or a range of extensions, will be configured to be "owned" by Lync Server instead of the PBX. These extensions will be then configured on the old PBX to route across the SIP trunk to let Lync handle the call. It is the PBX's way of saying it is not responsible for those numbers, but it knows where they can be reached. This type of routing is similar to tie-lines or trunks that can exist between multiple legacy PBXs.

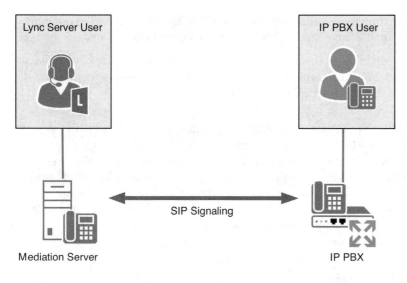

FIGURE 17.6   Direct SIP integration.

A very compelling new feature in Lync Server 2013 is the ability to route calls between two SIP trunks associated with Lync Mediation Servers with inter-trunk routing. Prior to Lync Server 2013, all calls had to either start or end with a Lync endpoint, but the voice routing can now be configured to send calls between two different trunks that are potentially attached to two different PBXs. This allows an organization to place the Lync servers "in front" of legacy systems, and handle the core routing logic within Lync, which can help simplify a migration.

Media Gateways

If Direct SIP is not an option because the PBX does not support the feature or has no IP PBX capabilities, a third-party device called a media gateway can be used to complete the integration. Media gateways act as an intermediary between the PBX and Lync Server to help translate traditional PBX protocols to SIP traffic that Lync Server 2013 can understand. In some cases it may be preferable to use a media gateway instead of Direct SIP to handle additional number translation of transcoding features. Media gateways are produced by many vendors today and provide a wide array of integration options for businesses looking to implement the voice features of Lync Server 2013. They typically have traditional telephony ports for T1/E1 digital trunks or FXS/FXO ports, along with network adapters to communicate with Lync Server. Media gateways can be used to provide interoperability with an existing PBX, or connect directly to the PSTN. Figure 17.7 shows a logical layout of how a media gateway fits in the topology.

Also like when a Direct SIP trunk link is being configured, some configuration of the PBX is necessary so that it knows to route calls for specific extensions to the media gateway, which will then deliver the calls to Lync Server. An additional layer of complexity is involved because the media gateway must also be configured to route calls appropriately, but on the other hand, the media gateway provides a degree of flexibility in call manipulation that sometimes is not possible natively with a PBX or Lync Server.

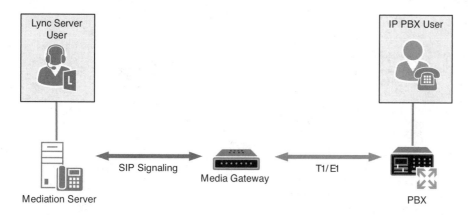

FIGURE 17.7   PBX Integration with media gateway.

Depending on the media gateway and business requirements, it might make sense to terminate existing trunks at the media gateway and place it in front of an old PBX, as shown in Figure 17.8. This could potentially have a bigger impact on the organization, but can greatly simplify some of the routing configuration during a large migration. Some gateway vendors have software that can detect whether a user's extension is Enterprise Voice or whether they have a legacy phone by reading specific Active Directory attributes. This might not seem like a big advantage up front during a pilot phase, but as users are migrated to Enterprise Voice it becomes advantageous not to have to constantly change routing rules on the PBX itself to indicate where an extension exists.

Regardless of the media gateway placement, it can provide a great deal of flexibility for organizations looking to move to or test Lync Server Enterprise Voice.

Remote Call Control

Remote Call Control was the original form of Lync Server PBX integration introduced with Live Communications Server 2005. It enables users to control their legacy desk phone from Lync. Users can click to dial a contact in their buddy list, which actually instructs the desk phone to place the call. It also allows for their presence to be automatically updated to "In a call" when they are using the legacy phone. In this case the media stream and codec negotiation is not handled by Lync Server at all. Instead, Figure 17.9 displays how the traditional desk phone and integrated PBX handles the call.

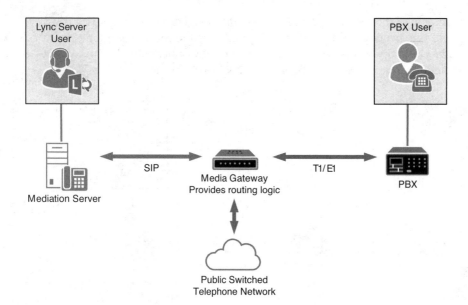

FIGURE 17.8   Media Gateway in front of PBX.

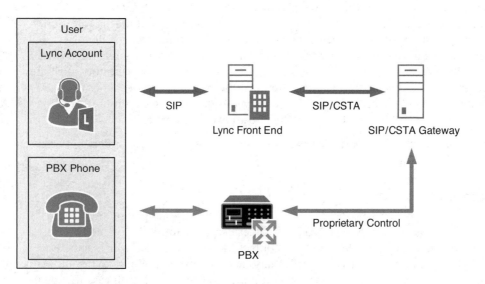

FIGURE 17.9   Remote Call Control with a CSTA gateway.

Be wary of deploying new Remote Call Control setups. Support for new Remote Call Control implementations was originally going to be dropped back when Lync Server 2010 was released, but the product team adjusted that stance and continued support, although some features were not available when a user was enabled for Remote Call Control. When Lync Server 2010 first came out, any user enabled for Remote Call Control could not make or receive a video call. The behavior was fixed in a Cumulative Update delivered 18 months after Lync was released, which might indicate the level of commitment Microsoft has for Remote Call Control deployments.

A Computer Supported Telecommunications Applications (CSTA) Gateway was always required to translate the SIP call signaling between Lync Server and the integrated PBX. These gateways were generally a PBX appliance or an additional server component from the PBX vendor that added complexity and required additional.

Lync Server 2010 added support for the "Get" and "Put" verbs over SIP to control presence, which can negate the need for a CSTA gateway, but many PBXs don't support this feature.

Remote Call Control does not provide users any Enterprise Voice features for controlling calls, assigning delegates, or configuring call forwarding settings. It also does not work remotely, so a user must be on the corporate network, which limits its usefulness for remote workers. Remote Call Control is considered an inferior option and organizations should avoid new deployments of this scenario.

Dual Forking

Dual forking is mentioned here only for clarity, but has not been a supported integration method since Lync Server 2010 was released. The only IP PBX ever qualified for dual forking with Office Communications Server 2007 R2 was the Nortel CS 1000. Dual forking enabled a user to have the same extension exist in both the legacy PBX and Lync Server, and incoming calls would always ring both systems. Calls would gracefully be terminated regardless of which system answered. It was pitched as the ultimate integration scenario, but proved to be a complicated setup and limited some features native to Lync.

17

It is still technically possible with some PBX vendors to maintain the same extension in both systems, but there is no native support for this configuration. It requires extremely complex translation patterns and dialing tricks in both systems, and leads to some strange caveats and end-user experiences. It is generally much simpler to use two different extensions for testing during a migration or coexistence period.

SIP Provider Trunking

The final integration method isn't so much integration with an existing PBX as it is a way to provide voice services between the end users without one of the other methods.

SIP provider trunking uses an ITSP (Internet Telephony Service Provider) to deliver voice services across IP to an organization with Lync Server 2013, similar to how a service provider provisions Internet access.

The advantages to SIP trunking come in the form of flexibility, redundancy, and capacity. Failover of Direct Inward Dial (DID) numbers between geographic regions using TDM infrastructure is usually impossible or incredibly expensive, but because SIP trunks are simply an IP connection, they can point at multiple locations for primary and backup delivery points. Depending on the provider, the trunk capacity can also be adjusted very quickly without having to install or remove a physical circuit connection. This helps to cut down on the lead time to deploy new services.

If integration with an existing PBX is not possible with any of the other means, or if an organization wants to move away from the legacy PBX, an ITSP can replace those services. In this situation Enterprise Voice users can communicate with users still hosted on the PBX, but only by traversing the PSTN. Figure 17.10 shows how this is not an optimal call path for users who might be physically sitting next to each other on different systems, but does provide a connectivity option if no others exist. After users are migrated to Lync, an organization's PBX and existing TDM contracts can be deactivated, allowing for all voice services to be delivered via the ITSP.

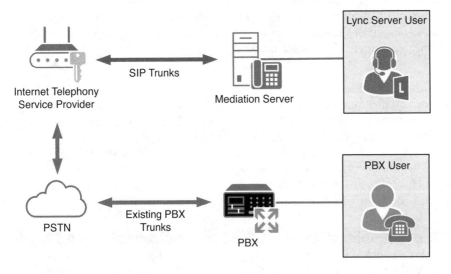

FIGURE 17.10   SIP trunking.

SIP trunks can be delivered to an organization via a few different methods:

▶ **Internet**—Organizations create the SIP trunk between the ITSP's public IP address and a public IP address owned by them. This generally requires a firewall that is SIP aware and can modify the content inside the incoming and outgoing SIP messages dynamically. A traditional firewall NAT is not sufficient for SIP trunking. The primary disadvantage of this method is that traffic is subject to the Internet, which has no Quality of Service and which a business has no control over. Audio packets also might not be encrypted, which could allow an attacker to capture and replay a sensitive phone conversation, or collect transmitted signaling information such as account numbers.

▶ **Site-to-Site VPN**—Instead of using an unencrypted connection across the Internet, this method relies on a site-to-site VPN tunnel between the ITSP and a business. This can help secure the calls through encryption, but adds additional overhead to each packet and does nothing to solve the Quality of Service issue.

▶ **MPLS**—The most reliable method for an ITSP connection is to connect to the provider's MPLS network. In this scenario the SIP trunk appears as a logical connection across a private WAN circuit. Quality of Service can be enabled on the connection and there is no need for firewall traversal and NAT inspection for SIP. This is the best of both worlds, but also usually comes at the highest price. Organizations should strive to leverage this method for the least complex and highest quality connection.

Session Border Controllers

Anytime SIP trunking is discussed, the question about Session Border Controllers (SBCs) appears. An SBC is in the same vein as a media gateway, and in many cases the gateways qualified for Lync can also act as an SBC, but their purposes are very different. The difference with an SBC is that it's exclusively used for SIP-to-SIP connections as opposed to interacting with a TDM infrastructure. These devices are used by the ITSP, but it is entirely optional for an organization to deploy its own SBC. When an SBC is being deployed, there will be a SIP trunk between the ITSP and the SBC, and another between the SBC and the Lync Server environment. There are several advantages to using an SBC, but the necessity of using one will depend on the situation.

▶ **Flexibility**—Microsoft supports a number of ITSPs with Direct SIP connections to the Mediation Server role through a qualification process. In some cases a business might want or need to use an ITSP that isn't directly qualified with Lync. This doesn't mean the service won't work, but using an SBC between the ITSP and Lync will usually allow remediation for any differences between the two sides. Manipulations or conversions in the SIP messaging can be performed at the SBC to allow for the service to function properly.

▶ **Security**—SBCs can perform the NAT and SIP message inspection for firewalls that cannot handle the conversion themselves. This allows an organization to hide any internal server names or IP addresses from being sent to the ITSP.

▶ **Transcoding**—In some cases a provider cannot deliver a G.711 audio stream to the business, or a different codec mighty be desired for bandwidth reasons. An SBC can act similarly to the Mediation Server role and transcode audio streams between differing codecs.

▶ **Authentication**—Some ITSPs offer the capability for authentication on the SIP trunk in the form of a username/password or shared secret. The Mediation Server role cannot perform this function so an SBC can used for terminating the SIP trunk and authenticating the business.

End-User Scenarios

This section discusses the different types of PBX integrations from the perspective of an end user. Organizations can deploy a mix of these scenarios to meet the needs of different users and don't have to pick just one path. For example, some users might be completely migrated to Enterprise Voice, but others might want to retain a legacy phone for use with audio conferencing. While users transition to Enterprise Voice they might even configure call forwarding settings to simultaneously ring their legacy PBX phone. Presenting more options to end users makes managing the solution more difficult, but might be necessary during a coexistence period. What scenarios are possible is very dependent on the integration methods referenced earlier.

Enterprise Voice

In this scenario end users have full Enterprise Voice functionality and use only Lync endpoints as their phones. These endpoints can be a mix of Lync PC or Mac clients, Lync Phone Edition devices, and Lync mobile applications. Enterprise Voice for all users is the long-term goal for voice deployments and also provides the most flexibility to the end users. This is the state Enterprise Voice users are in for a brand-new deployment with no existing PBX, or when a migration has been completed.

Enterprise Voice with Legacy Phone

In this scenario end users have full Enterprise Voice functionality, but also retain a legacy PBX phone on their desks like shown in Figure 17.11. This scenario is typical for migrations from a legacy PBX in which a period of coexistence is required while users become accustomed to the new Lync endpoints. Users have the choice of which system to use when placing or receiving calls through the use of simultaneous ringing. As the users grow more familiar Lync, they will rely less and less on the legacy phone until it becomes unnecessary and can be removed. As the migration ends and legacy devices are retired, the organization actually ends in the pure Enterprise Voice state. Although the idea of simultaneous ringing sounds attractive and it generally works well for basic calls, it's important to work through all the possible use cases required to maintain two systems. For example, consider boss/admin scenarios, voice mail forwarding features, and any directory search attendants.

Most implementations require a user to have two extensions during this period of coexistence. One extension is the user's primary, or publicly known, extension that other users dial and that is associated with the user's Lync account. The other is a secondary, or unpublished, extension that is associated only with the legacy phone.

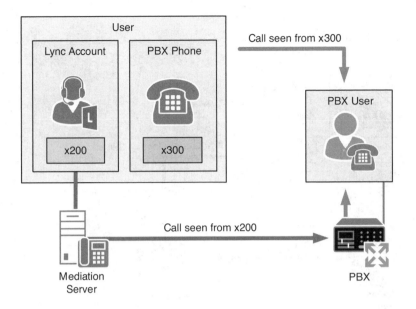

FIGURE 17.11   Enterprise Voice with a legacy phone.

When placing calls, users can choose whether to use Lync or the legacy phone. One caveat shown here in Figure 17.12 is that, when calling from Lync, the callees will see the call from the user's primary, published number in the organization, but calls coming from the legacy phone will show as coming from the unpublished number. This can be mitigated slightly with PBXs that support sending a display name, but the extension might still appear as unrecognized to the callee. Again, as users begin to leverage Lync more and more, this becomes less of an issue.

Receiving calls on both devices in this scenario can be accomplished by the users configuring simultaneous ringing within Lync. Inbound calls will be routed first to the Lync account, which determines what should happen to the call. Users generally set their Lync call forwarding options to simultaneously ring the secondary extension associated with their legacy PBX phone. This allows them to answer incoming calls either with a Lync endpoint or on the legacy phone without the caller's noticing where the call was picked up. As the migration period goes on, users can adjust their simultaneous ringing to stop ringing the legacy phone altogether. The downside to this approach is that users won't be able to use simultaneous ringing with a mobile number since Lync allows only a single number to be targeted for simultaneous ring.

Something to keep in mind is that depending on the current PBX, the simultaneous ringing might not scale well. Consider when a media gateway device is used to bridge a legacy PBX and Lync Server 2013. If inbound calls still flow through the PBX initially, and then are directed through the media gateway to Lync Server, each call requires one channel on the media gateway. If a user configures simultaneous ringing to a legacy phone, yet another channel is required on the media gateway and PBX to support the call.

17

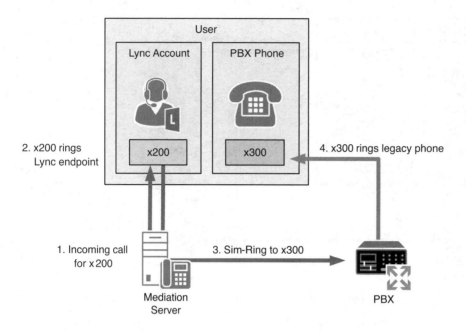

2. x200 rings
   Lync endpoint

4. x300 rings legacy phone

1. Incoming call
   for x200

3. Sim-Ring to x300

Mediation
Server

PBX

FIGURE 17.12   Simultaneous ringing.

NOTE

Analyze peak capacity of the PBX and media gateways when planning for simultaneous ringing. As an example, a media gateway with two T1s configured to a legacy PBX might support an initial pilot integration with Lync Server. Now when users start all using simultaneous ringing, it might be necessary to use up to twice the number of channels, so four T1s might be required to support the coexistence. The simultaneous-ring feature is intended to be used with a mobile or alternate phone number instead of for migration purposes.

Legacy Phone for Conferencing

Another scenario that can be attractive to organizations not looking to fully implement Enterprise Voice features or replace existing handsets is to leverage the conferencing features of Lync Server with their existing investments. This allows an organization to migrate away from a legacy or hosted conferencing system without changing the fundamental way users function. Organizations can save a significant amount of monthly fees for hosted conferencing services just by switching to Lync Server 2013 as the dial-in conferencing solution with existing handsets.

Users in this scenario have full access to the rich conference-scheduling controls within Outlook and Lync, but instead of using a Lync endpoint to participate in audio conferences, they can use their legacy desk phone. This is accomplished through the use of the Join Audio Conferences From setting within Lync. Users can elect to be called at a number published within Active Directory or can enter a number manually. Figure 17.13 shows an example of this configuration so that when a user is joining a conference with audio through Lync, the user's desk phone will ring automatically, so all the user needs to do is answer the phone to join the audio conference. Since the user has already authenticated to the Lync client, there is no need to enter any participant codes or conference IDs.

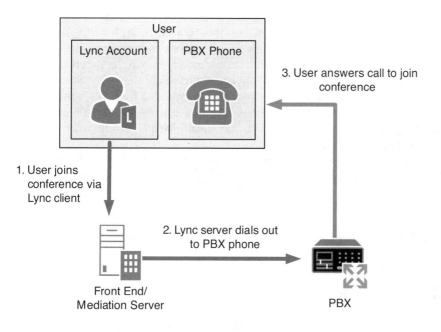

FIGURE 17.13   Legacy phone for conferencing.

Legacy Phone Presence and Click-to-Call

A more limited set of features can be deployed to users that gives the "click-to-call," or Remote Call Control functionality. This allows the end users to click a user within their Lync contact list and have that user's number dialed from their legacy PBX phone. Additionally, presence messages are integrated so that when a user places a call from the legacy phone, the user's presence in Lync automatically updates to "In a Call."

This is one of the most basic integration options; it really does not provide a significant amount of flexibility or features to the end user. In this state call forwarding settings, delegation of calls, and advanced call control features are not available. The click-to-call features also don't work well for remote users because even if they try to initiate a call, it would be placed from a desk phone inside the office, attached to the local PBX.

This is really a legacy feature set that has limped along with minimal updates and attention from Microsoft since the days of Live Communications Server 2005. The inclusion of the feature again is geared toward supporting existing customers that heavily invested in this approach earlier and have not completed a migration to Enterprise Voice yet. New deployments should not consider this approach.

PBX Software Plugin

The final end-user scenario is one in which the PBX vendor uses the Lync client APIs to develop add-on software for the desktop to integrate with Lync. Examples of this are Cisco's UC Integration for Microsoft Lync (CUCILYNC) and Avaya's Application Enablement Server (AES) products, which must be installed and managed separately from the Lync client.

These solutions might seem appealing to organizations with an existing investment in telephony platforms that offer these options, but these plugins can introduce a layer of complexity in troubleshooting any voice issues. These actually remove the Enterprise Voice functionality and instead use their own software shims to control the voice features. Call signaling flows through the PBX and the client's audio or video traffic uses the PBX's configuration and not Lync's dynamic media stack, like shown in Figure 17.14. Instead of seeing the native call controls provided by Lync, users will see a UI developed by the PBX vendor, which could be a point of confusion for end users. These solutions also don't work through the Lync Edge server and require a user to connect a VPN client before signing in through Lync remotely.

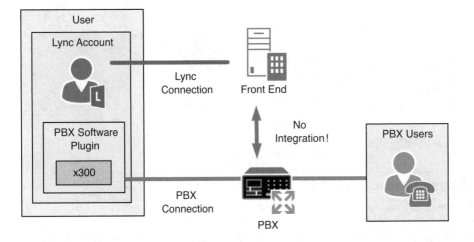

FIGURE 17.14   Lync software plugin traffic flow.

The main difference with these solutions over Remote Call Control is that the presence and phone control features are client-side as opposed to server-side. Instead of Lync Server integrating with a PBX for presence updates and phone control, the software plugin handles the call control and updating the user's presence, meaning no CSTA gateway is required. The confusing end-user experience is the biggest downside, but keep in mind that organizations using this approach are now at the mercy of a PBX vendor for approving any upgrades to both Lync clients and the plugin software. The last point here is to consider how many resources and how much time a PBX vendor really wants to invest in working on improving integration with a competitor's product.

Analog Devices

Support for analog device connectivity, a feature added in Lync Server 2010, remains largely unchanged in Lync Server 2013. Since Lync Server is entirely IP-based, FXS/FXO ports must be provided by some kind of media gateway, similar to how connectivity to digital T1/E1 trunks is achieved. This kind of setup allows Lync to support analog phones, fax machines, paging systems, door buzzers, or any other kind of analog telephony device.

The Lync configuration for an analog device consists of creating a contact object via the New-CsAnalogDevice cmdlet, and assigning a Line URI, dial plan, and voice policy just as with a user account. The main difference with an analog device contact is that it also specifies a gateway parameter so Lync knows exactly which gateway to route the call toward in order to reach the analog device.

> **NOTE**
>
> Any trunk configuration manipulations still apply to calls destined for analog devices through the gateway. Be sure that the gateway configuration of the analog endpoint number accounts for this change.

Inbound Routing

Calls destined for an analog device from a Lync endpoint are sent straight to the gateway specified on the contact object. In this case the Lync user experience is that the call looks like it was placed to a PSTN number. The trickier part is how calls from a caller outside of Lync Server 2013 will reach the analog device. The call flow resembles the following sequence and is depicted in Figure 17.15:

1. The PSTN or PBX caller dials the analog device DID.

2. The call is routed through the media gateway and to Lync Server.

3. Lync determines that the DID belongs to an analog device.

4. Lync places a new, outbound call to the analog device with the calling party set to the PSTN or PBX phone number.

5. The call is routed to the media gateway associated with the analog device.

6. Gateway configuration associates the destination number with a specific analog port, and rings the device.

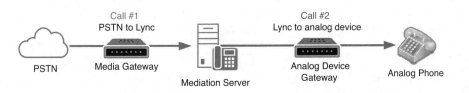

FIGURE 17.15   Inbound call to an analog device.

The takeaway here is that there are really two legs to this call. The first is between the PSTN or PBX caller and the Lync Server, and the second is between the Lync Server and the analog device.

Outbound Routing

Calls placed from an analog device follow a process similar to that for inbound routing, but in a reverse order. Additionally, the dial plan and voice policy assigned to the analog device are applied at the server before the call is placed. This is the process:

1. The analog device dials a DID.

2. Gateway configuration routes all calls from the associated analog device port to Lync Server.

3. Lync determines that the call is from a specific analog device based on the calling party ID matching the Line URI configured on the analog device contact object.

4. Lync Server applies the dial plan assigned to the analog device contact.

5. The call is routed to a media gateway based on the voice policy assigned to the analog device contact.

6. The call routes through the media gateway and rings the PSTN or PBX user.

Fax Machines

Fax machines are supported in a similar manner to other analog devices in Lync, but require a bit more planning and configuration. Specifically, there is a parameter on the New-CsAnalogDevice cmdlet called `AnalogFax` that must be set to `$true` for any fax machines. The reason for this is to ensure that the media for a fax call is never routed through Lync.

For an analog phone it's not a big problem if the media stream runs through Lync. The Mediation Server can transcode G.711 audio from a gateway to RTAudio and back again if needed, but the issue is that the Mediation Server cannot handle the T.38 fax tones properly. So the point of identifying fax machines is to indicate to Lync Server that it must remain out of the media path and allow the analog device to leverage media bypass.

The media problem isn't an issue if the fax machine is connected to the same media gateway from which the call came in, but in order to support calls from one gateway reaching a fax machine attached to a second gateway, the two gateways must be configured to route calls between one other. Assuming a call comes in through a media gateway and the fax machine is connected to a device referred to as the fax machine gateway, the call flow resembles the following process shown in Figure 17.16:

1. The PSTN or PBX caller dials a fax machine.

2. The call is routed through the media gateway and to Lync Server.

3. Lync determines that the DID belongs to an analog fax device.

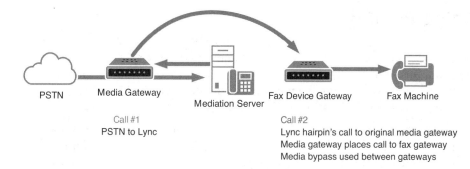

PSTN   Media Gateway   Mediation Server   Fax Device Gateway   Fax Machine

Call #1
PSTN to Lync

Call #2
Lync hairpin's call to original media gateway
Media gateway places call to fax gateway
Media bypass used between gateways

FIGURE 17.16   Fax call.

4. Lync places a new, outbound call to the analog device with the calling party set to the PSTN or PBX phone number. The call is always sent directly back to the same gateway that originally sent the call, not the fax machine gateway.

5. Media gateway is now responsible for routing the new call from the Lync Server to the fax machine gateway.

6. The call is placed from the media gateway to the fax machine gateway, and media bypass is enabled.

7. The two gateways use the G.711 codec between them for the fax transmission.

The takeaway in this scenario is that the Mediation Server is out of the media path and a fax machine behaves like a Lync media bypass client. The difference is that the fax machine gateway is taking the place of the Lync client, but the concept is the same. This requires media bypass to be enabled on the trunk configuration for both gateways. It is also possible for a single physical gateway to have both T1 and FXS ports so that a dedicated analog gateway is not required.

The Routing Choice

Although analog device support exists in Lync Server 2013, it's all done via the media gateways and there is a fair bit of configuration involved, especially when fax machines are included. An alternative method is to simply configure the analog device routing directly on the gateways and bypass the Lync configuration. In this scenario the gateways hold the routing logic of where to send calls destined for analog phones or fax machines, which can help simplify the deployment. It might even reduce the overhead costs involved since many gateway vendors charge extra for IP-to-IP connectivity between two gateways required for fax machines. The biggest disadvantage to this method is the loss of call detail record (CDR) data. Lync creates CDR reports for all calls to or from analog devices which can be tracked through the Monitoring Server reports, but this data is lost when the routing is being configured directly on gateways. Organizations can make these decisions on a case-by-case basis to determine whether CDR data for analog devices is a requirement.

Lync Voice Routing

Configuration of voice routing in Lync involves a combination of what Microsoft refers to as dial plans, voice policies, PSTN usages, routes, and trunks. This section covers the fundamental concepts of these objects and how they all interact so that users can make phone calls from Lync. Any Lync voice administrator should have a solid understanding of these items in order to properly configure Lync Enterprise Voice.

All voice routing in Lync is based on the international standard E.164 format for phone numbers. E.164-formatted numbers start with a + sign and are followed by a country code, and the remainder of the number varies depending on the country. For example, an E.164-formatted number in the United States consists of the + sign followed by the North American prefix, 1, a three-digit area code, and seven additional digits. A fictional sample number usually written as (234) 567-8901 within the United States formatted for E.164 is written as +12345678901.

Lync dial plans, routes, and trunk translation rules use regular expression patterns to offer a degree of flexibility rarely found in PBX systems. Regular expressions, or regex for short, are a special text syntax that can be used to identify a pattern. There are entire books on regular expressions, but for Lync's purpose it allows admins to easily identify specific number patterns. Lync voice administrators should become familiar with basic regular expression syntax before configuring Enterprise Voice.

Dial Plans

The dial-plan object in Lync is responsible for normalization of numbers, which is the process of taking a set of numbers that a user enters and converting the numbers to some other format. The dial plan does not control what numbers a user can call or dictate where a call is sent. Each user enabled for Enterprise Voice is assigned a dial plan, which contains an ordered list of normalization rules that are processed from top to bottom looking for a matching rule.

The first step in placing a Lync call is to normalize the digits a user has entered to the E.164 format. Since regions and countries all dial numbers differently, this ensures that all numbers are in an equivalent format before any decisions on how the call is to be routed are attempted. Lync dial plans must contain rules to normalize the different types of calls users will make. For example, users in the United States are used to dialing seven-digit numbers for local calls from legacy systems, so the dial plan needs logic to convert the seven digits a user enters to E.164 by prepending the + sign, the North America region code, and an appropriate three-digit area code.

Each normalization rule in a dial plan consists of a pattern to match, and a translation pattern. The pattern to match is a regular expression pattern that searches against the number a user entered. If the dialed number matches the pattern, the rule is selected and the corresponding translation pattern applied. The translation pattern uses some part or all of the dialed number and manipulates it to the point where it matches the E.164 format. In the previous example the pattern to match would look for seven dialed digits, and the translation pattern would add the +1 and a three-digit area code. The originally dialed seven digits would be placed at the end of the string.

NOTE

Lync users can bypass the normalization rules by entering a + sign in front of any number. Lync assumes that any number prefixed with a + has already been normalized to the E.164 format.

United States users also dial 10 digits for national calls, but can optionally dial 11 digits when including the North America region code, so the dial plan needs to allow for both of these options. Dialing an international number in North America is done by entering the digits 011 followed by the country code and the remainder of the number. In this case a normalization rule needs to add the + sign and then remove the 011 prefix in order to convert the number to the E.164 format. These examples are specific to the United States, but each country or region has its own standards or habits that normalization rules should accommodate. The end result is that any number a user dials should be converted to E.164 through the dial plan.

Organizations migrating to Lync Enterprise Voice will also need to configure rules for PBX extensions within the Lync dial plan. For example, many businesses use some shortened form of internal dialing such as three- to six-digit extensions that identify each user. This cuts down on the number of digits users need to dial when calling each other, and even allows users to memorize the extensions for each other.

This form of shortened dialing can be accommodated in Lync through the use of normalization rules within the dial plans. Just as with local, national, or international calls, the rules should search for a matching pattern and apply a translation pattern. For example, one rule might search for four digits and then apply a translation to prepend the + sign, a 1, a three-digit area code, and the three-digit local exchange. In this case a four-digit number entered by a user has been converted to a full E.164-formatted number. It's very common for different internal extension ranges to correspond to different direct inward dial ranges as well, so the pattern 5xxx might need to normalize differently from the pattern 6xxx. Two separate normalization rules are required to handle the differing translation patterns for those scenarios. The number of normalization rules required in each dial plan will be driven by the number of DID ranges a company owns.

The preceding section described how to configure normalization for DID numbers, but some organizations do not allow DID calls, and instead use extensions that are not reachable directly from the PSTN. Outside callers typically route through a single main listed number, which goes to a receptionist or an automated attendant that can transfer callers to the internal user. Lync can accommodate these scenarios as well, by use of a format within the translation rule that specifies an extension. The translation pattern prepends an E.164-formatted main-line number, followed by the string ";ext=" and the user's extension. For example, assuming that the main line is +12345678900, the normalization rule would convert the extension 5555 to +12345678900;ext=5555. The Lync client displays the number in a much cleaner format to the users, so to them the dialed number appears as +1 (234) 567-8900 (X5555).

17

> **NOTE**
>
> Be careful when basing the Line URIs and normalization rules around a published main line or attendant number. This generally prevents Lync users from calling the main line without the use of additional normalization rules. It might be easier to select a new "main" number for the Lync internal-only extensions.

Service Codes

The E.164 format is intended to provide a standard for calls between multiple countries, but each country will usually have its own form of service codes such as directory assistance, emergency services, or automated systems that simply speak the date and time. These systems are not dialed internationally, but still need support within Lync for users within those regions. It is acceptable for these services to provide only normalization rules that simply prepend a + sign and no additional information. For example, dial plans within the United States will have a normalization rule that looks for any digit in the range 2 through 9 followed by two 1s, and prepends only the + sign. This covers services such as 411, 611, and 911. At this point Lync considers the number normalized and it can be included within the voice routes.

Voice Policies

The voice policy in Lync is used to control class of service, or calling capabilities, and is the only other voice routing object assigned directly to users. Voice policies have two pieces of configuration. The first is a set of true or false values indicating which features a user has available. This includes capabilities such as call forwarding, simultaneous ringing, PSTN reroute, or delegate access. The second facet of the voice policy dictates which numbers a user can call, and what route the call should use.

Voice policies are discussed in more detail after PSTN usages and routes are covered. It is important to know the purpose of all three of these objects in order to understand how they work together to place a call. For right now, know that the voice policy holds an ordered list of PSTN usages.

PSTN Usages

The PSTN usage object in Lync Server often seems confusing because it has no settings or configuration options other than a name. There are no user options or policies configured on a usage and it cannot even be created by itself. PSTN usages can be considered the glue between a voice policy and a route in Lync.

PSTN usages are usually named based on a particular type of call and a destination, or an egress point. For example, a usage called US-CA-SFO-National might be used to identify national calls leaving through a gateway in the San Francisco, California, office. Another example could be a usage called US-IL-CHI-Local, which identifies calls considered local to a gateway in the Chicago, Illinois, office.

Remember, though, a PSTN usage is simply a name. Nothing more, nothing less. It is, however, associated with both a voice policy and a route, which is why it is considered the glue between the two.

> **NOTE**
>
> The obvious question here is why bother with PSTN usages if all they do is tie two other objects together? Wouldn't it make more sense to just put routes inside a voice policy? The answer is because a single usage can be associated with multiple routes.

Routes

Routes in Lync consist of a pattern to match and a list of trunks to use, which ultimately determines which gateway or SIP trunk is used to place a call. The patterns on routes again use regular expressions to search for a match against the E.164-formatted number after it has been processed by the dial plan. There are no translation rules on routes—the pattern is only evaluated to see whether a match exists. If the pattern matches, the route can be used and the call will be sent to one of the trunks listed on the route.

Each route is also associated with one or many PSTN usages. The fact that the associated PSTN usages are included in a voice policy is what allows a particular route to be used for a call. The specific pattern a route is searching for is typically described by the name of both the PSTN usage and the route.

Voice Policies Redux

After covering the voice policies, PSTN usages, and routes separately, it's now possible to understand how they all work together. The starting point is the E.164-formatted number that has been normalized by a user's dial plan. The next step is to review the user's voice policy to see whether the user is allowed to call the number.

The first PSTN usage in the voice policy is selected, and any routes associated with that PSTN usage are reviewed. The normalized number is compared to the match patterns on each returned route. If there is a match, the route is selected and the call is placed through one of the trunks.

If there is no match pattern for any of the associated routes, the process repeats. The next PSTN usage in the voice policy is selected, and any routes associated with that usage are reviewed for a possible match. Again, if there is a match, the route is selected and the call is placed through one of the trunks.

This process continues as each PSTN usage and associated routes in the voice policy are reviewed. If the end of the list is reached and no match has been made, it is determined that the user is unable to place that call. Figure 17.7 depicts a simplified version of the call routing logic.

17

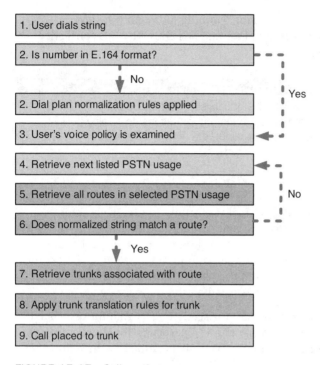

FIGURE 17.17   Call routing process.

For example, assume that a user's voice policy contains only two PSTN usages, such as US-CA-SFO-Local and US-CA-SFO-National. The Local PSTN usage is associated with a route that has a pattern matching a +1 followed by area codes local to San Francisco such as 415, 510, or 650. The National PSTN usage is associated with a route with a pattern that matches a +1 followed by 10 digits.

If the user dials a number matching either of those patterns, the call will route successfully. But if the user tries to dial a hotel in England that starts with the country code +44, the call will fail. In that example the +44 is first compared against the US-CA-SFO-Local PSTN usage and any associated routes. There is no match, so the next PSTN usage, US-CA-SFO-National, is evaluated. Again, there is no match. Since there are no more PSTN usages to evaluate, the call fails and the user is informed that they are not allowed to dial that particular number.

Trunks

Trunks are just a logical representation between Lync and some form of PSTN or PBX connectivity. The end of a trunk might be a media gateway, another PBX, or an ITSP providing a SIP trunk. A Lync trunk consists of an IP/PSTN gateway name or IP, a listening port on the IP/PSTN gateway, a Mediation Server, and a listening port on the Mediation Server. Routes include a list of trunks that can be used to place a call after a route is selected.

Trunk configuration in Lync is used to apply additional logic to a call after a voice route and trunk have been selected. At this point the server knows which trunk the call will be sent to, but trunks can all have different settings. This allows Lync to accommodate many gateway vendors and PBX integrations with different support for features like media bypass, SIP refer messages, and the Real-Time Control Protocol (RTCP).

The other main use for trunk configuration settings is to provide manipulation for the called and calling party numbers. While numbers and routing decisions within Lync are based on E.164, the majority of PBXs and telephony providers don't support the format. The trunk configuration allows Lync to manipulate the numbers into a format that will be supported on the other end of the trunk immediately before delivering the call.

Each trunk configuration contains an ordered list of trunk translation rules that evaluated in a top-to-bottom order. These trunk translation rules are very similar to dial plan rules in that they are composed of a pattern to match and a translation rule. This allows Lync administrators to search for specific patterns on numbers and manipulate the format before sending the call to a PBX or gateway. If there are no trunk translation rules, or if the number dialed does not match any patterns, then the call is placed in the E.164 format.

An example of a trunk translation rule might be to prepend a leading external-access prefix used by the PBX such as a 9 to PSTN calls. Another example would be to prepend the 011 string to any international calls.

New to Lync Server 2013 is the capability to manipulate the calling party (caller's) number. Lync Server 2010 allowed manipulation of the called party (dialed) number, but any source-number manipulation had to be done at the PBX or gateway. The addition of the calling party manipulation per trunk is a great addition that should make life much easier on Lync administrators.

Summary

Lync Server 2013 provides a strong platform that organizations can use to provide highly reliable and resilient voice services. The platform is also extremely flexible and offers various integration methods so that businesses can quickly establish coexistence, and work toward migrating users incrementally if needed.

The voice routing engine composed also offers a high degree of customization and granularity over any call decisions. This allows administrators to provide various classes of service depending on the user, while accommodating all local dialing habits.

Best Practices

The following are best practices from this chapter:

- ▶ Identify whether an existing IP PBX supports SIP for a Direct SIP integration path.

- ▶ Evaluate the media gateway vendors and devices to find a feature set that meets the needs of the organization.

▶ Ensure that media gateways have enough channels to handle peak capacity, especially when using simultaneous ringing.

▶ Identify which features end users will be provisioned with before determining hardware requirements.

▶ Spend time training users on the integration and how to use the systems during a period of coexistence.

▶ Avoid new deployments involving Remote Call Control or PBX software plugins.

CHAPTER 18

Advanced Lync Voice Configuration

Lync Server 2013 is no longer being questioned about whether it can serve as an organization's Private Branch Exchange (PBX); it offers an exceptional amount of flexibility and control, and becomes a very attractive telephony platform for nearly any business.

With each release, Microsoft has made great strides to address shortcomings of previous versions and improve the overall stability of the product. Lync Server 2013 is no different and builds on an already solid foundation by providing new features such as inter-trunk routing and M:N trunk associations.

This chapter discusses the configuration of Enterprise Voice components found in Lync Server 2013 from dial plans to trunk configurations, and on to more advanced concepts such as Call Admission Control and E911. It also covers the supporting features like dial-in conferencing, Response Groups, and how to configure analog devices.

> **TIP**
>
> This chapter focuses on the administrative steps required to configure each of the voice features. For a more detailed discussion about planning for each of these scenarios, see Chapter 32, "Planning for Voice Deployment."

Building the Lync Topology

The necessary components such as Mediation pools, Survivable Branch Appliances or Servers, PSTN gateways, and trunks in the Lync topology must be created and published before any voice routing is configured.

Defining Mediation Pools

The easiest way to deploy a Mediation pool is to simply collocate the Mediation Server role on a Front End pool. Perform the steps outlined in Chapter 5, "Microsoft Lync Server 2013 Front End Server," and simply check the box Collocate Mediation Server on the Select Collocated Server Roles page while defining the Front End pool, as shown in Figure 18.1. This approach is recommended when Media Bypass can be used because minimal load is placed on the Mediation Servers.

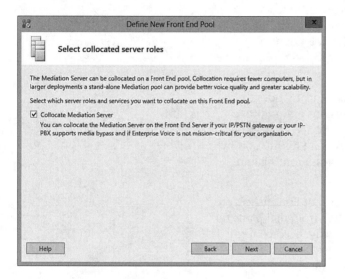

FIGURE 18.1 Collocating the Mediation Server role.

Alternatively, it is still possible to create a dedicated Mediation pool. Within Topology Builder follow these steps:

1. Right-click on Mediation Pools and select New Mediation Pool.

2. Enter a Pool FQDN, select either Multiple Computer Pool or Single Computer Pool, and click Next.

3. If deploying a multiple computer pool, enter the Computer FQDN of each server and click Add. Click Next when all servers have been added, and click Next.

4. Select a Front End pool as the Next Hop Pool for the Mediation pool, and click Next.

5. If necessary, select an Edge Pool to be used for media traversal by the Mediation pool, and click Next.

6. Click Finish.

If the Mediation pool needs to listen for unsecured TCP SIP connections, follow these additional steps:

1. Right-click the pool and select Edit Properties.

2. Select Enable TCP Port and enter a TCP port range.

3. Click OK.

Defining PSTN Gateways

Each media gateway, IP PBX, or ITSP SIP trunk must be defined as a PSTN gateway within the Lync topology so that it can be referenced by a trunk.

Follow these steps within Topology Builder to define the PSTN gateways and trunks:

1. Expand Shared Components, right-click on PSTN Gateways, and select New IP/PSTN Gateway.

2. Enter the FQDN or IP address for the PSTN gateway and click Next.

3. Select whether to Enable IPv4 or IPv6 for communications to the gateway, and click Next.

4. Enter a Trunk Name, which represents the connection between a Mediation pool and a gateway with a unique port combination.

5. Enter a Listening Port on the IP/PSTN Gateway where calls will be sent.

6. Select whether to use TCP or TLS as the SIP Transport Protocol.

7. Select an Associated Mediation Server pool for the trunk.

8. Select an Associated Mediation Server Port to use to receive calls.

9. Click Finish when complete.

Repeat these steps for any additional PSTN gateways in the environment.

Defining Additional Trunk Associations

A single trunk is created when a new PSTN gateway is being defined, but administrators can always create additional trunks to the same PSTN gateway later with the new M:N trunk routing support. To create a new trunk to an existing PSTN gateway, follow these steps within Topology Builder:

1. Expand Shared Components, right-click on Trunks, and select New Trunk.

2. Enter a Trunk Name, which represents the connection between a Mediation pool and a gateway with a unique port combination.

3. Select an Associated PSTN Gateway.

4. Enter a Listening Port on the IP/PSTN Gateway where calls will be sent.

18

5. Select whether to use TCP or TLS as the SIP Transport Protocol.

6. Select an Associated Mediation Server pool for the trunk.

7. Select an Associated Mediation Server Port to use to receive calls.

8. Click OK when complete.

A sample configuration is shown in Figure 18.2.

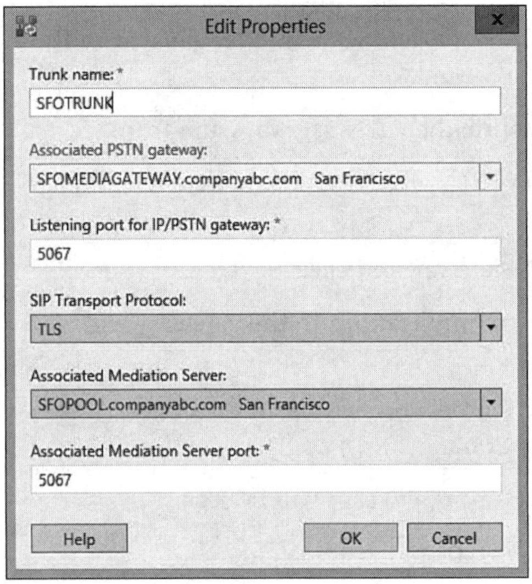

FIGURE 18.2   Defining a trunk.

Repeat these steps for any additional trunks that need to be created.

Defining Branch Sites

The first step, whether deploying a Survivable Branch Appliance or a Survivable Branch Server, is to define each branch site within the Lync Server topology. Within Topology Builder follow these steps:

1. Right-click Branch Sites and select New Branch Site.

2. Enter a Name for the site and, optionally, a Description.

3. Click Next.

4. Enter the City where the site is located.

5. Enter a State/Region where the site is located.

6. Enter a two-digit Country Code where the site is located.

7. Click Next.

8. Clear the check box Open the New Survivable Wizard When This Wizard Closes, and then click Finish.

A Survivable Branch Appliance or Server can be added to the site later.

Defining Survivable Branch Appliances and Servers

After defining each of the branch sites, the Survivable Branch Appliances or Servers must be added to the topology. The processes of defining them are identical:

1. Expand the branch site, right-click Survivable Branch Appliances, and then select New Survivable Branch Appliance.

2. Enter the FQDN of the Survivable Branch Appliance or Server, and then click Next.

3. Select the Front End Pool associated with the Survivable Branch Appliance or Server and click Next.

4. Select the Edge Pool associated with the branch site for media traversal and click Next.

5. Enter the FQDN of the IP/PSTN gateway associated with the Survivable Branch Appliance or Server.

6. Enter a Define Root Trunk Name, which will be the primary trunk used with the IP/PSTN gateway. An additional trunk to a Front End pool for redundancy can be created later.

7. Click Gateway FQDN or IP Address and enter the name or IP address of the gateway used for routing inbound and outbound calls with the branch site.

8. Enter a Listening Port for the IP/PSTN Gateway.

9. Select either TCP or TLS for the SIP Transport Protocol.

10. Click Listening Port and enter the correct port.

11. Click Finish.

Be sure to publish the topology after all Mediation pools, PSTN gateways, branch sites, and Survivable Branch Appliances or Servers have been defined.

Deploying a Survivable Branch Appliance

The exact procedures for each Survivable Branch Appliance will vary depending on the vendor, but there are generally some steps common to each deployment that are outlined in the following sections.

18

> **NOTE**
>
> Use the same procedures as a Front End Server when deploying a Survivable Branch Server to prepare the local configuration store, install server components, and issue certificates. The following sections are specific to Survivable Branch Appliances and should not be performed for Survivable Branch Servers.

Adding the Survivable Branch Appliance to Active Directory

Each Survivable Branch Appliance deployed needs to have a computer account in Active Directory defined before being placed in operation. The intent of this step is that the technician in a branch site will not have rights to join a server to the Active Directory domain.

Follow these when deploying only a Survivable Branch Appliance:

1. Log on to a computer with the Active Directory Domain Services role administration tools installed.

2. Open Active Directory Users and Computers.

3. Right-click an organizational unit, select New, and select Computer.

4. Enter a Computer Name for the Survivable Branch Appliance. This is just the hostname, not the fully qualified domain name.

5. Under User or Group, click the Change button.

6. Enter `RTCUniversalSBATechnicians`, and then click OK.

7. Click OK.

Defining the Service Principal Name

After a computer account has been staged for the Survivable Branch Appliance, a service principal name (SPN) must be added to the computer account.

Follow these steps to add the SPN:

1. Open ADSI Edit.

2. Right-click the ADSI Edit root node and select Connect To.

3. Leave the default options selected and click OK.

4. Expand the Default Naming Context and locate the Survivable Branch Appliance computer account.

5. Right-click the account and select Properties.

6. Highlight `servicePrincipalName` and click Edit.

7. Enter `HOST/<Survivable Branch Appliance FQDN>` and click Add.

8. Click OK twice.

NOTE

Normally, using the SETSPN command is the preferred way to manage SPNs associated with domain accounts. Because the Survivable Branch Appliance has not joined the domain yet, the SETSPN commands do not work properly. Instead, use ADSI Edit to configure the appropriate SPN.

Installing a Survivable Branch Appliance

Installation and configuration varies widely depending on the Survivable Branch Appliance vendor and software. Most of the installations include the following tasks:

1. Physically cable the Survivable Branch Appliance.

2. Configure an IP address.

3. Join the domain.

4. Enable replica of configuration.

5. Request and assign certificates.

6. Start services.

7. Test connectivity.

8. Move user accounts.

NOTE

The user account used to join the Survivable Branch Appliance to the domain must be a member of the RTCUniversalSBATechnicians group. This is the group selected to join the computer to the domain when the computer account is created in Active Directory.

Voice Routing

Voice routing in Lync Server 2013 is determined by the association of various components such as policies, routes, and trunks. A quick overview of the key pieces is given here:

▶ **Dial Plan**—Dial plans are the equivalent of location profiles for those migrating from Office Communications Server. A dial plan contains a set of normalization rules to convert digits entered by a user into a routable format.

▶ **Normalization Rules**—Normalization rules are associated with a dial plan and converts the digits a user might dial in to a standard, expected format like E.164.

▶ **Voice Policies**—Voice policies determine what voice features users are allowed to use, such as call forwarding, simultaneous ringing, and call transfer. It also defines which PSTN usages can be accessed by a user.

▶ **PSTN Usages**—Usages are a class of call that is then associated with voice policies. If a user's voice policy does not contain a specific PSTN usage, the user is not allowed to place the call.

▶ **Routes**—Routes are used in Lync Server to direct calls through a specified trunk or set of trunks.

▶ **Trunks**—Routes deliver calls to specified trunks, which can be a media gateway or a direct SIP trunk.

▶ **Trunk Configuration**—Each trunk might require unique settings or translation rules, so a trunk configuration defines those parameters per trunk.

▶ **Translation Rules**—Translation rules associated with a trunk configuration to manipulate dial strings before being delivered to the trunk. These rules can manipulate the dial string sent across the trunk if the opposite end is not capable of handling E.164 numbers.

Configuring a Dial Plan

A dial plan in Lync Server 20103 is associated with users and contains a set of normalization rules. Normalization rules are used to convert dial strings entered by users into a format routable by Lync. Dial plans can differ based on region or site depending on how users are used to dialing digits. Additional dial plans are usually created to accommodate different dialing habits based on sites or users. A dial plan can be scoped to apply at the site level, to a specific pool, or even just to a specific set of users.

TIP

Global, site, or pool dial plans cut down on administrative steps when enabling users, but tagged, or user, dial plans offer the most flexibility because they can be assigned directly to individual users.

Lync Server dial plans have the following options available:

▶ **Simple Name**—A name used by the system for the dial plan that includes no spaces or special characters. Leaving the default, suggested Simple Name is usually sufficient.

▶ **Dial-In Conferencing Region**—The dial-in region name associated to users assigned this dial plan. This name appears in Online Meeting invitations.

▶ **External Access Prefix**—A leading digit used to indicate that a call is trying to dial an external number. Many organizations use the digits 8 or 9 for this functionality.

▶ **Associated Normalization Rules**—An ordered list of normalization rules that will be applied to calls coming from users assigned to this dial plan.

To create a new dial plan, follow these steps:

1. Open the Lync Server 2013 Control Panel.

2. Click Voice Routing.

3. Click Dial Plan.

4. Click New, and then select Site dial plan, Pool dial plan, or User dial plan.

5. Leave the suggested Simple Name for the dial plan.

6. Enter a Description for the dial plan.

7. If the dial plan is associated with a dial-in conferencing region, enter the name of that region.

8. Enter an External Access Prefix if used.

9. Select any Normalization Rules to be included in the dial plan.

10. Click OK to save the dial plan.

Alternatively, the `New-CsDialPlan` cmdlet can be used to create a new dial plan using the Lync Server Management Shell. One parameter is not available in the Lync Server Control Panel Interface:

▶ `OptimizeDeviceDialing`—A `true` or `false` value that determines whether the External Access Prefix will be applied for calls placed to numbers external to the company.

Creating Normalization Rules

Normalization rules are associated with a dial plan and provide a way for administrators to translate dial strings that users enter into full E.164 format. For instance, a country code and local area code might be automatically appended when a user tries to dial only seven digits. Many organizations use four- or five-digit internal extensions, and normalization rules can convert those dial patterns to a full E.164 number.

Administrators can define the normalization rules either using regular expressions or using the Normalization Rule tool. To create a new normalization rule, follow these steps:

1. On the Edit Dial Plan screen, click the New button in the Associated Normalization Rules section.

2. Provide a name for the rule and a description for the rule.

18

NOTE

This example uses the Normalization Rule tool, but for more advanced pattern matching, click the Edit button at the bottom of the screen to manually enter the matching pattern and translation rule using regular expressions.

3. In the Starting Digits field, enter the beginning digits of the string to be matched.

4. Specify a Length of the string to be matched. Options include matching at least a specific number of digits, exactly a certain number of digits, or any number of digits.

5. Specify a number of Digits to Remove after a string matches the starting digits and length. These digits will be removed from the left side of the number.

6. Specify Digits to Add after the selected number of digits have been removed.

7. If the pattern matches numbers that are internal to the organization, check the box Internal Extension.

8. Click OK to save the translation rule and click OK again to save the trunk configuration.

NOTE

The internal extension check box works in conjunction with the external access prefix specified on the dial plan and is specific to off-hook dialing from Lync Phone Edition (LPE) clients. Off-hook dialing refers to when a user either lifts the receiver or presses the speakerphone button before dialing. If an LPE client enters the external access prefix as the first digit during an off-hook dial, the client will skip all the rules flagged as an internal extension. This helps ensure that the user does not accidentally dial an internal extension because they entered digits too slowly.

The `New-CsVoiceNormalizationRule` cmdlet can also be used to create rules using the Lync Server Management Shell.

Configuring Voice Policies

Voice policies in Lync Server 2010 are a way of controlling features and calling abilities of users. Voice policies are assigned to user accounts through a global, site, or direct method. The following options are available when a voice policy is being created:

▶ **Enable Call Forwarding**—Enables users to forward calls to other users or devices.

▶ **Enable Delegation**—Enables users to specify other users to answer and place calls on their behalf, or schedule Online Meetings for another user.

▶ **Enable Call Transfer**—Enables users to transfer calls to another user.

▶ **Enable Call Park**—Enables users to place a call on hold and pick it up from another phone or location by dialing a call park orbit number.

▶ **Enable Simultaneous Ringing of Phones**—Enables users to simultaneously ring another user or phone number such as a mobile phone.

▶ **Enable Team Call**—Enables users to answer calls on behalf of another team member.

▶ **Enable PSTN Reroute**—Enables users to place calls to be rerouted to the PSTN network when the wide area network (WAN) is congested or unavailable.

▶ **Enable Bandwidth Policy Override**—Enables users to avoid limitations imposed by Call Admission Control policies. This applies only for inbound calls to a user.

▶ **Enable Malicious Call Tracing**—Enables users to report malicious calls, which are viewable in the Lync monitoring reports.

▶ **Associated PSTN Usages**—Allows specific PSTN usage to be accessed by users assigned to this voice policy.

▶ **Call Forwarding and Simultaneous Ringing PSTN Usages**—Defines which PSTN usages can be accessed during a call-forwarding or simultaneous-ringing situation. Administrators can enforce calls only to internal users, or a custom set of PSTN usages.

To create a new voice policy, complete the following steps:

1. Open the Lync Server 2013 Control Panel.

2. Click Voice Routing.

3. Click Voice Policy.

4. A voice policy can be scoped to apply at the site level or pool level. Click New and then select either Site Policy or User Policy.

5. Enter a Name and Description for the policy.

6. Select or deselect the various Calling Features discussed previously.

7. Click Select to choose any PSTN usages that should be associated with the voice policy. Highlight any desired PSTN usages and click OK.

8. In the Call Forwarding and Simultaneous Ringing PSTN Usages selection, either leave the default option to use the voice policy's PSTN usages, or else choose to route to internal Lync users only, or Route using custom PSTN usages. After selecting Route Using Custom PSTN Usages, click Select again to choose any PSTN usages that should be associated with the voice policy for forwarding. Highlight any desired PSTN usages and click OK.

9. Click OK to save the voice policy. Figure 18.3 shows an example of a voice policy.

Alternatively, the Lync Server Management Shell can be used to create a new voice policy through the `New-CsVoicePolicy` cmdlet. Several parameters are not available in the Lync Server Control Panel Interface:

▶ `EnableVoicemailEscapeTimer`—Has a `true` or `false` value that helps ensure that calls to a mobile device that is turned off or out of cellular service do not end up in the mobile device's voice mail.

18

▶ **PSTNVoicemailEscapeTimer**—Specifies the amount of time in milliseconds that a call was answered too quickly and is assumed to be the mobile device voice mail.

▶ **PreventPSTNTollBypass**—Forces calls between branch sites to leverage the PSTN network instead of WAN connections.

▶ **VoiceDeploymentMode**—Indicates that the voice policy is for OnPrem, Online, OnlineBasic, or OnPremOnlineHybrid.

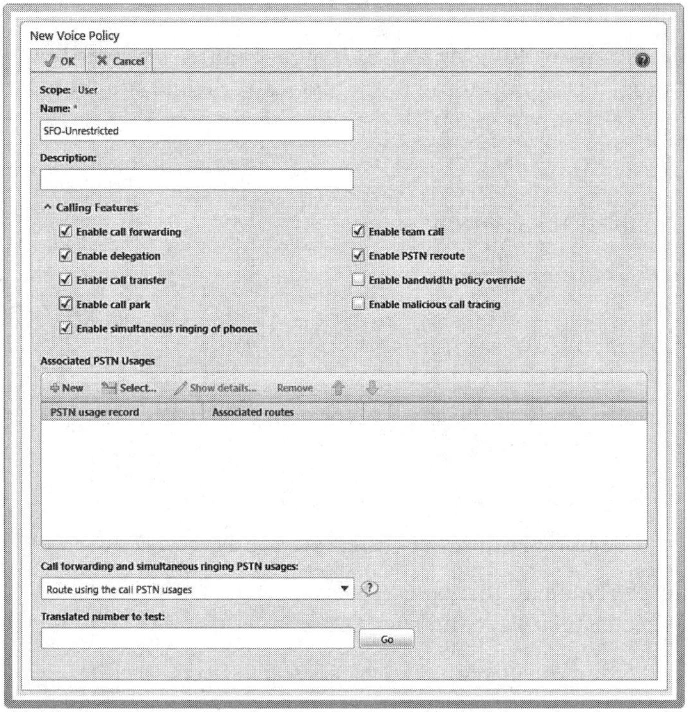

FIGURE 18.3   Voice policy options.

Creating Voice Routes

Routes are used in Lync Server to direct calls through a specified gateway or a set of gateways. Routes are processed after numbers are normalized based on a dial plan, and they determine which gateway will place a call. Creating a new route has the following options:

▶ **Starting Digits for Numbers That You Want to Allow**—Routes are based only on a matching pattern. Enter the beginning of the digit string, including the + symbol.

▶ **Exceptions**—In some cases, using route priority might be difficult or some patterns should be excluded from traversing a specific trunk. The Exceptions option enables an administrator to exclude strings that would otherwise match the route pattern.

▶ **Suppress Caller ID**—This option enables an administrator to prevent the caller's actual caller ID from being passed along on the route. An alternative caller ID must be entered that is typically a main or generic phone number. A limitation here is that this cannot be variable based on the calling party ID. Instead, only a single phone number displayed for all outbound calls can be used.

▶ **Associated Trunks**—A list of trunks that calls matching this route can use. Calls will be placed in a round-robin fashion if multiple trunks are associated.

▶ **Associated PSTN Usages**—This specifies the PSTN usages allowed to use this route. Usages are associated with users through voice policies.

To create a new route, follow these steps:

1. Open the Lync Server 2013 Control Panel.

2. Click Voice Routing.

3. Click Route.

4. Click New to create a new route.

5. Enter a Name for the route.

6. Enter a Description for the route.

7. In the Starting Digits for Numbers That You Want to allow field, enter the beginning digits that this route should match, and then click Add.

8. Repeat this step for any additional patterns this route should handle.

9. If any numbers that might match this pattern should be excluded, click the Exceptions button and enter those numbers.

10. If the outbound caller ID should be altered for this route, check the box Suppress Caller ID and enter an Alternate Caller ID.

11. In the Associated Trunks section, click the Add button, select the outbound trunks, and click OK.

12. In the Associated PSTN Usages field, click Select, choose any PSTN usages, and click OK.

13. Click OK to save the route.

The Lync Server Management Shell can also be used to create new voice routes via the `New-CsVoiceRoute` cmdlet. A Priority parameter is available that can be used to order the listing of voice routes *displayed*, but it should not be used to try to control the order of route *selection*. That should instead be done by ordering PSTN usages within the voice policies.

18

Creating PSTN Usages

PSTN usage records are associated with routes and voice policies to provide a way to control which users are allowed to use specific routes. Voice policies are applied to users, containing a list of PSTN usages. If a user dials a number that matches a route with one of those PSTN usages, the call is placed. If not, the user is unable to make the call.

To create a new PSTN usage record, follow these steps:

1. On the Edit Voice Policy screen, click the New button in the Associated PSTN Usages section.

2. Enter a Name for the PSTN usage.

3. Click the Select button in the Associated Routes section to associate the usage with an existing route. Alternatively, click New to create a new route for the usage.

4. Select a route and click OK.

5. Click OK to save the PSTN usage record.

Creating a Trunk Configuration

A trunk is a logical connection between the Mediation Server role and a PBX, PSTN gateway, or Internet telephony service provider. Trunk configurations can be scoped so that they apply globally, to a Lync Server site, or to a specific trunk. If these settings vary across devices connected via trunks, a new trunk configuration might be required.

> **NOTE**
>
> These settings are specific to the signaling and features available across a SIP trunk. Use Topology Builder to create the actual SIP trunk definitions.

A new trunk configuration has the following options:

▶ **Maximum Early Dialogs Supported**—This is the number of forked responses the device on the opposite side of the trunk can support for a single SIP invite that is sent to the Mediation Server.

▶ **Encryption Support Level**—Required means that Secure Real-Time Transport Protocol (SRTP) must be used to encrypt the media traffic on the trunk, Optional means that the Mediation Server attempts to use encryption if the gateway supports it, and Not Supported means that the media traffic is not encrypted on the trunk.

▶ **Refer Support**—This indicates whether the trunk supports Lync sending the SIP refer method for call transfers. Third-party call control (3pcc support) on the trunk is another available choice that can be useful for E911 or operator-based SIP services.

▶ **Enable Media Bypass**—Use this option if Lync endpoints should be allowed to send G.711 streams to the opposite side of the trunk. This configuration is highly recommended to reduce processing on the Mediation Server.

▶ **Centralized Media Processing**—Use this option if the signaling and media traffic for this trunk terminate at the same IP address. If Media Bypass is enabled, this option must also be selected.

▶ **Enable RTP Latching**—RTP latching is an alternative option used to support NAT traversal on a SIP trunk when an SBC or a firewall is incapable of properly fixing the SDP messages for specifying the media IP address.

▶ **Enable Forward Call History**—Use this to include any forwarded call history across the trunk. This might be required by SIP trunk providers in forwarding or simultaneous ring situations to validate that the call was originally destined to a number associated with the organization.

▶ **Enable Forward P-Asserted-Identity Data**—Use this if the P-Asserted-Identity (PAI) SIP header should be forwarded across the SIP trunk.

▶ **Enable Outbound Routing Failover Timer**—This flag places a 10-second limit on responses from the opposite end of the trunk. If the trunk device takes longer than 10 seconds to respond, Lync will try the next available route, or end the call if no more routes are available.

▶ **Associated PSTN Usages**—This is used for inter-trunk routing in Lync Server 2013. This parameter specifies which usages are allowed to be called through this trunk.

▶ **Calling Number Translation Rules**—New to Lync Server 2013, this is used to manipulate the calling party of numbers dialed through this trunk.

▶ **Called Number Translation Rules**—This is used to manipulate the called party of numbers dialed through this trunk.

To create a new trunk, complete the following steps:

1. Open the Lync Server 2013 Control Panel.

2. Click Voice Routing.

3. Click Trunk Configuration.

4. Click New, and then select either Site or Pool scope.

5. Enter a value for the Maximum Early Dialogs Supported field.

6. Select an Encryption Support Level.

7. Select an option for Refer Support.

8. Optionally, check the box for Enable Media Bypass.

9. Optionally, check the box for Centralized Media Processing.

10. Optionally, check the box for Enable RTP Latching.

11. Optionally, check the box for Enable Forward Call History.

12. Optionally, check the box for Enable Forward P-Asserted-Identity Data.

18

13. Optionally, check the box for Enable Outbound Routing Failover Timer.

14. Click Select and choose any PSTN usages that can be accessed through this trunk via inter-trunk routing.

15. Select any Calling Number Translation Rules and Called Number Translation Rules to be associated with the trunk.

16. Click OK to save the trunk configuration.

Alternatively, the Lync Server Management Shell can be used to create a trunk configuration via the `New-CsTrunkConfiguration` cmdlet. Several parameters are available only through the Lync Server Management Shell:

▶ **EnableMobileTrunkSupport**—A `true` or `false` value to indicate whether the trunk is a mobile carrier.

▶ **EnableSessionTimer**—A `true` or `false` value to indicate whether each session is timed to determine whether it is currently active. Calls exceeding the session timer without a keep-alive response are dropped.

▶ **EnableSignalBoost**—A `true` or `false` value to indicate whether the opposite end of the SIP trunk should boost the audio volume of packets sent to Lync. This works only if the opposite end of the SIP trunk supports the feature.

▶ **RemovePlusFromUri**—A `true` or `false` value to indicate whether the Lync Server should remove the plus prefix (+) from any URIs before sending them across this SIP trunk.

▶ **RTCPActiveCalls**—A `true` or `false` value to indicate whether the trunk sends RTP Control Protocol packets for active calls.

▶ **RTCPCallsOnHold**—A `true` or `false` value to indicate whether the trunk sends RTP Control Protocol packets for calls placed on hold.

▶ **EnableOnlineVoice**—A `true` or `false` value to indicate whether the trunk supports Office 365 hosted voice mail for on-premises Lync users.

▶ **EnablePIDFLOSupport**—A `true` or `false` value to indicate whether the trunk supports the PIDF-LO location information sent by a Lync client for E911 purposes.

Configuring Inter-Trunk Routing

Inter-trunk routing is a feature new to Lync Server 2013 that allows calls to route through Lync. This enables administrators to place Lync "in front of" a PBX or another system, and still be able to route calls to the downstream, legacy PBX.

Inter-trunk routing is configured by assigning a collection of PSTN usages to a specific trunk configuration. As calls come in to Lync through that trunk, they will be evaluated against the PSTN usage list and potentially routed out another trunk. From an outbound routing perspective, treat the trunk the call was received on as the Lync voice user. Similar to how a user's voice policy processes PSTN usages to select an outbound route, the PSTN usages assigned to that trunk will be processed and look for a matching route.

Creating Translation Rules

Translation rules are a powerful new feature first introduced in Lync Server 2010 that enables digit manipulation to a PBX or media gateway. Lync Server recommends that all numbers be in the E.164 format, but a PBX or gateway might be configured for local dialing or might require special access codes before accepting dial strings. Lync Server 2013 has expanded on the initial functionality and now includes the capability to manipulate the calling party of numbers on a trunk.

Trunk translation rules are assigned to trunk configurations and behave identically to dial plan normalization rules. Administrators can define the translation rules either by using regular expressions or by using the Translation Rule tool.

To create a new translation rule, complete the following steps:

1. On the Edit Trunk Configuration screen, click the New button in the Associated Translation Rules section.

2. Provide a Name for the rule and a Description for the rule.

> **NOTE**
>
> This example uses the Translation Rule tool, but for more advanced pattern matching, click the Edit button at the bottom of the screen to manually enter the matching pattern and translation rule using regular expressions.

3. In the Starting Digits field, enter the beginning digits of the string to be matched.

4. Specify a Length of the string to be matched. Options include matching at least a specific number of digits, matching exactly a certain number of digits, or matching any number of digits.

5. Specify a number of Digits to Remove after a string matches the starting digits and length.

6. Specify Digits to Add after the selected number of digits have been removed.

7. Click OK to save the translation rule and click OK again to save the trunk configuration.

> **TIP**
>
> The Trunk Configuration page now includes a Phone Number to Test field, similar to the Dial Plan page. Use this to validate calling and called number manipulations without resorting to SIP traces.

The `New-CsOutboundCallingNumberTranslationRule` and `New-CsOutboundTranslationRule` cmdlets can also be used to create new rules through the Lync Server Management Shell.

Publishing Voice Configuration Changes

Changes made through the Lync Server Control Panel are always entered in a pending state and are not actually actively used until the changes are committed. This enables administrators to fully configure all aspects of voice routing before pushing a single change to the end users.

To publish the uncommitted changes, follow these steps:

1. Open the Lync Server 2013 Control Panel.

2. Click Voice Routing.

3. From any submenu, click the Commit button, and then select Commit All.

4. The uncommitted changes are displayed again on this screen. Review the modifications and then click Commit to save the changes.

> **NOTE**
>
> Navigating away from the Voice Routing page before committing changes will cause pending changes to be lost.

Export and Import Voice Configuration

Lync Server 2013 enables administrators to easily export and import the entire voice-routing configuration.

> **TIP**
>
> Always export the voice configuration before making any modifications. This enables an administrator to easily roll back any changes that might have introduced an issue to the environment. This is especially important in organizations with multiple voice administrators because the last administrator to commit a change will overwrite any previous ones.

To export a configuration, follow these steps:

1. Open the Lync Server 2013 Control Panel.

2. Click Voice Routing.

3. From any of the submenu selections, click Actions, and then click Export Configuration.

4. Select a location and filename for the configuration file, and then click Save.

To import a previously saved configuration file, follow these steps:

1. Open the Lync Server 2013 Control Panel.
2. Click Voice Routing.
3. From any of the submenu selections, click Actions and then click Import Configuration.
4. Locate the configuration file and click Open.
5. Commit the changes using the steps discussed previously.

Creating Test Cases

Test cases enable administrators to verify that the voice configuration works as expected without resorting to testing using a client or SIP traces. Within each test case an administrator can define a source dialed number, a dial plan, a voice policy, and the expected number translation, PSTN usage, and route. To create a new voice routing test case, follow these steps:

1. Open the Lync Server 2013 Control Panel.
2. Click Voice Routing.
3. Click Test Voice Routing.
4. Click the New button to create a new test case.
5. Enter a Name for the case.
6. Enter a Dialed Number to Test. This is the number a user enters into the Lync client and is normalized based on the dial plan selected next.
7. Select a Dial Plan.
8. Select a Voice Policy.
9. Enter an Expected Translation. This is the string that the dialed-number-to-test string is expected to be translated to, including the leading + sign. If a normalization rule in the dial plan does not convert the dialed number to this string, the test is recorded as a failure.
10. Select an Expected PSTN Usage for the test case. This field is optional. If the test case matches a PSTN usage other than the one selected here, the test is recorded as a failure.
11. Select an Expected Route for the test case. This field is optional. If the voice test matches a route other than the one selected here, the test is recorded as a failure.
12. Click the Run button to begin the test, as shown in Figure 18.4.
13. To save the test case, click the OK button.

18

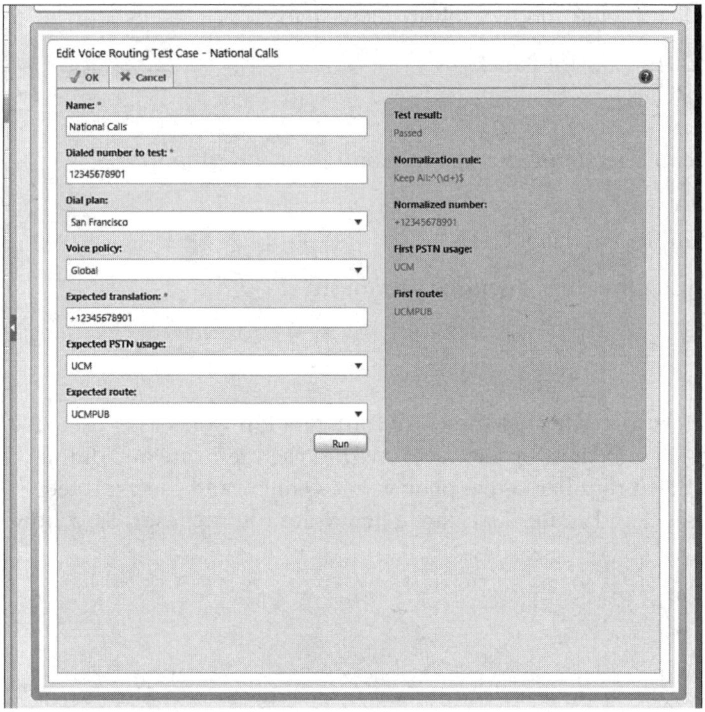

FIGURE 18.4   Creating a voice routing test case.

After each voice routing change, the test cases can be run to ensure that call routing is still working as expected. The test cases do have some limitations because it will not account for failover routing, but it does provide a simple way to validate basic functionality.

Voice Features

The voice-features section of Lync Server 2013 contains two additions carried over from Lync Server 2010 that were not possible in Office Communications Server 2007 R2. The first feature, Call Park, enables users to place a call on hold and pick it up from another extension or endpoint. The second feature, Unassigned Numbers, enables the organization to route calls to numbers not associated with a specific user to some other location. Configuration of analog devices is also covered in this section.

Call Park

The Call Park service, first introduced in Lync Server 2010, enables users to place a call on hold and then pick up that same call at another location or extension. To enable a call park, administrators must first configure a call park orbit table or a group of extensions to be used for parking calls. As users park calls, an extension is randomly selected from these orbit tables and assigned to the call.

To create a new range for parking calls, follow these steps:

1. Open the Lync Server 2013 Control Panel.

2. Click Voice Features.

3. Click Call Park.

4. Click New to create a new number range.

5. Enter a descriptive Name for the range.

6. Enter a beginning and ending number for the Number Range. The range can use up to nine total digits and can begin with a # or * so as not to overlap with existing extensions.

7. Select a FQDN of Destination Server from the selection box. Calls parked to the specified extension range are handled by the specified Front End pool.

> **TIP**
>
> Numbers in the call park orbit ranges should not be manipulated by normalization rules, or the number might not route to the call park service. An advantage to using the # or * prefix is that it won't overlap with any existing extensions or normalization rules.

Alternatively, the Lync Server Management Shell can be used to configure a new call park orbit through the `New-CsCallParkOrbit` cmdlet.

Configuration of the following additional call park settings can be performed only in the Lync Server Management Shell through the `Set-CsCpsConfiguration` cmdlet:

- ► `CallPickupTimeoutThreshold`—The amount of time a call that has been parked waits without answer before it rings back to the endpoint that originally answered. This is to ensure that a call is not parked and then forgotten.

- ► `EnableMusicOnHold`—A `true` or `false` value that determines whether on-hold music is played to the caller while parked.

- ► `MaxCallPickupAttempts`—The number of times a call rings back to the phone that originally answered before it times out and is forwarded to a specified SIP URI.

- ► `OnTimeoutURI`—A SIP URI where calls that are not picked up are forwarded. This is typically an operator or a main line.

Configuring Call Park Music on Hold

Whether on-hold music is played is determined by the `EnableMusicOnHold` parameter, but the actual music on-hold file is configured using the `Set-CsCallParkMusicOnHoldFile` cmdlet.

18

First, the `CsCallParkMusicOnHoldFile` cmdlet requires the `AudioFile` parameter in byte format. To make the transfer easy, store the file in a variable, and then pass that variable to the `Content` parameter. Storing the audio file correctly looks like the following example:

```
$AudioFile = Get-Content -ReadCount 0 -Encoding byte <Path and File Name>
```

Then use the `Set-CsCallParkMusicOnHoldFile` cmdlet to assign the audio file:

```
Set-CsCallParkMusicOnHoldFile -Service ApplicationServer:<FQDN of
➥ Front End Pool with music file> -Content <Byte[]>
```

Unassigned Numbers

Similar to Call Park, the Unassigned Numbers feature was first introduced in Lync Server 2010 and will be a welcome addition for organizations migrating from Office Communications Server 2007 R2. The Unassigned Numbers range enables companies to send calls that don't match a user to an operator or attendant instead of returning a user-not-found message to the caller.

> **NOTE**
>
> The ranges defined for unassigned numbers can actually contain numbers that *are* assigned to users. Lync prioritizes a user matching the number over the unassigned number range so that it does not interfere with call routing. A best practice is to include each number range used by an organization.

Calls that match an unassigned number range can be routed in only two ways: Either an announcement can be played to the caller or the caller can be transferred to an Exchange Unified Messaging Auto Attendant extension.

To create a new unassigned number range, follow these steps:

1. Open the Lync Server 2013 Control Panel.

2. Click Voice Features.

3. Click Unassigned Number.

4. Click New.

5. Enter a Name identifying this range of numbers.

6. In the first Number Range field, enter the first number in the range.

7. In the second Number Range field, enter the last number in the range.

8. In the Announcement Service field, select either Announcement or Exchange UM. Refer to the appropriate section for each option in the following text to continue the necessary steps.

Playing an Announcement

Before you can use a prerecorded audio file as an announcement, it must be imported using the Lync Server Management Shell. To import a file, first store the content in a temporary variable:

```
$MyAudioFile = Get-Content <File path and name> -ReadCount 0 -Encoding Byte
```

Then import the announcement file to the file share using the variable:

```
Import-CsAnnouncementFile -Parent service:ApplicationServer:<Front End
➥FQDN> -Content $MyAudioFile
```

Finally, complete the remaining steps:

1. Click Announcement Service.

2. Click Select.

3. Choose an application server in the organization with an audio announcement configured and then click OK.

4. Select an Announcement to be played and then click OK.

5. Click OK again to save the range definition.

Transferring to an Exchange UM Auto Attendant

1. Click the Auto Attendant phone number.

2. Click Select.

3. Choose a phone number to transfer callers to and then click OK.

4. Click OK again to save the range definition.

> **TIP**
>
> These two options are mutually exclusive within the Unassigned Number configuration, but keep in mind you can always use the custom greetings on an Exchange Unified Messaging Auto Attendant to also play an announcement for callers.

18

Configuring Analog Devices

Analog devices in Lync Server are configured using only the Lync Server Management Shell, and are represented as an Active Directory Contact object that is SIP enabled. Each contact is explicitly assigned a gateway parameter so Lync will route all calls destined for that analog device to the gateway it is physically attached to.

To create a new analog device and contact object, use the `New-CsAnalogDevice` cmdlet:

```
New-CsAnalogDevice -Gateway <FQDN or IP of IP/PSTN Gateway>
➥-LineUri <String> -OU <Organizational Unit>
➥-RegistrarPool <FQDN of Primary Registrar> -DisplayName
➥<Active Directory Contact Display Name>
➥-DisplayNumber "<Phone Number Display Format>" -AnalogFax <$True | $False>
```

The only difference when configuring a fax device is to set the `AnalogFax` parameter to `$true`. This ensures the media for calls to those devices will never traverse a Lync Mediation Server. Set the `AnalogFax` parameter to `$false` for all other types of analog devices.

Dial plans and voice policies will not be applied locally by an analog device, but can still be assigned so that the server will enforce these policies.

To grant a dial plan to an analog device, use the `Grant-CsDialPlan` cmdlet:

```
Grant-CsDialPlan -Identity <Analog Device Account Name>
➥-PolicyName <Dial Plan Policy Name>
```

To grant a voice policy to an analog device, use the `Grant-CsVoicePolicy` cmdlet.

```
Grant-CsVoicePolicy -Identity <Analog Device Account Name>
➥-PolicyName <Voice Policy Name>
```

Advanced Enterprise Voice Features

This section covers topics that might not be applicable to all deployments, and are considered more advanced configuration options. These features include Call Admission Control, Media Bypass, and E911.

Defining the Network Configuration

The first step in configuring the three advanced Enterprise Voice features, Call Admission Control, Media Bypass, and E911, is to define the network configuration. Each of these features relies on the network configuration to work correctly. The following section explains how to create the necessary network objects before configuring any of the advanced features.

Creating Network Regions

A network region in Lync Server 2013 is generally a large area that encompasses a number of network sites. These are the hubs or backbones of the network. Each region is associated with a central site where a Lync Server 2013 Front End pool exists.

> **TIP**
>
> For a typical MPLS WAN architecture, define the network region as the MPLS cloud, and create a network site for each site with an MPLS connection.

A primary driver for creating multiple network regions is to have multiple Policy Decision Points (PDPs) so that the failure of a central site in one region does not impact the capability of a central site in another region to enforce Call Admission Control locally.

Follow these steps to create a new network region:

1. Open the Lync Server 2013 Control Panel.

2. Click Network Configuration.

3. Click Region.

4. Click the New button.

5. Enter a Name for the region.

6. Select a Central Site for the region. This is a site in the topology containing Lync Servers.

7. Select Enable Audio Alternate Path if this region allows audio traffic to use alternative routes. This must be selected for calls to Internet users to succeed.

8. Select Enable Video Alternate Path if this region allows video traffic to use alternative routes. This must be selected for calls to Internet users to succeed.

9. Click Commit. Network sites can be associated later.

Alternatively, a new network region can be created with the Lync Server Management Shell through the `New-CsNetworkRegion` cmdlet.

Creating Network Sites

A network site represents a particular office location that can be a main headquarters, a branch office, or a collection of buildings in a campus. Although not required, network sites typically have similar bandwidth, and each site is then associated with a network region. The network site serving as the central site defined for the region must also be created because it is not done automatically.

Follow these steps to create a new network site:

1. Open the Lync Server 2013 Control Panel.

2. Click Network Configuration.

3. Click Site.

4. Click the New button.

5. Enter a Name for the site.

6. Enter a Description for the site.

7. Select a Region to associate the site with from the drop-down menu.

18

8. Bandwidth Policy, Location Policy, and Associated Subnets can be added later after those objects exist.

9. Click the Commit button.

Alternatively, a new network site can be created with the Lync Server Management Shell through the `New-CsNetworkSite` cmdlet.

Creating Network Subnets

Network subnets in Lync Server 2013 are the glue that binds a client connection to a specific network site and region. When a Lync client signs in, its network address is delivered to the server, which then associates the client to a network site and region based on the subnet.

Follow these steps to create a new network site:

1. Open the Lync Server 2013 Control Panel.

2. Click Network Configuration.

3. Click Subnet.

4. Click the New button.

5. Enter a Subnet ID that is the actual network IP address.

6. Enter a Mask for the subnet. This value is the number of bits used for the subnet mask. For example, if the subnet uses a 255.255.255.0 mask, enter 24 for this value.

7. Select a Network Site ID to associate with the subnet.

8. Enter a Description for the subnet.

9. Click Commit.

Alternatively, a new network site can be created with the Lync Server Management Shell through the `New-CsNetworkSubnet` cmdlet.

TIP

Do not summarize network subnets in this section. Instead, enter the network address for each individual subnet at a particular site. Call Admission Control supports summarization, but Media Bypass does not. To support both features, the Subnet ID entered on this screen should always be the network address of the subnet. This is because the Lync client will apply its own local subnet mask to its IP address before sending its network address to the server.

Configuring Call Admission Control

After network regions, sites, and subnets have been created, Call Admission Control can be configured and enabled. Be sure to create all the necessary objects before proceeding with the Call Admission Control configuration. Call Admission Control enables clients to determine whether an audio or video call can actually be established based on available network bandwidth.

Defining Bandwidth Policy

After the required network objects have been created, the next step in configuring Call Admission Control is to create bandwidth policies. Each bandwidth policy defines the total bandwidth limit for a site or region, and the bandwidth limit per session for both audio and video. The per-session limits refer to one-way traffic.

Follow these steps to create a new bandwidth policy profile:

1. Open the Lync Server 2013 Control Panel.

2. Click Network Configuration.

3. Click Policy Profile.

4. Click the New button.

5. Enter a Name for the profile. Usually this is indicative of the link speed of the network to which it is applied, or matches a network site name.

6. Enter an Audio Limit in kbps. This is the collective limit of all audio sessions.

7. Enter an Audio Session Limit in kbps. This is the limit applied to an individual audio session.

8. Enter a Video Limit in kbps. This is the collective limit of all video sessions.

9. Enter a Video Session Limit in kbps. This is the limit applied to an individual video session.

10. Enter a Description for the bandwidth policy profile.

11. Click Commit.

Alternatively, a new bandwidth policy profile can be created using the Lync Server Management Shell with the `New-CsBandwidthPolicyProfile` cmdlet.

Associate Bandwidth Policy Profile

The next step is to associate the bandwidth policies to network sites. To use the Lync Server Control Panel to perform this task, follow these steps:

1. Open the Lync Server 2013 Control Panel.

2. Click Network Configuration.

3. Click Site.

4. Highlight an existing site, click the Edit button, and select Show Details.

5. Select a Bandwidth Policy from the selection box.

6. Click Commit, as shown in Figure 18.5.

7. Repeat these steps to associate each site with a bandwidth policy profile.

18

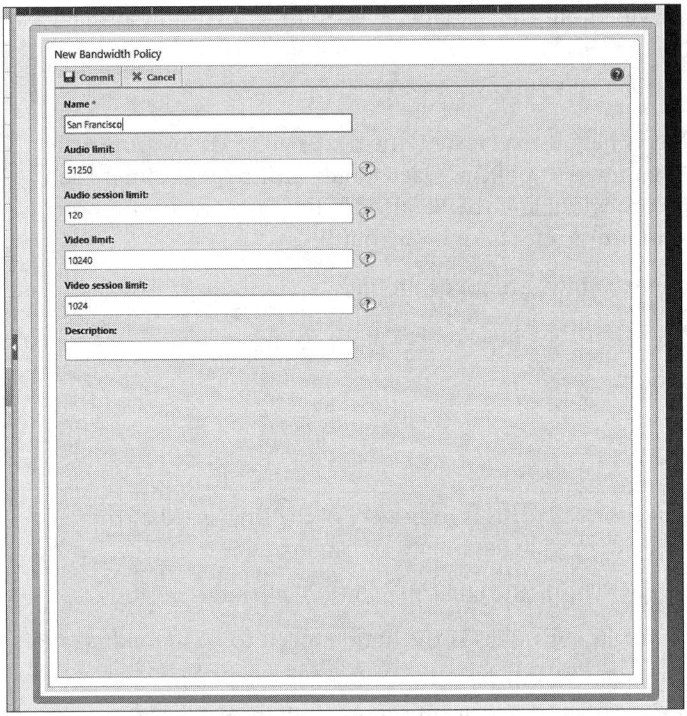

FIGURE 18.5   Creating a bandwidth policy.

Alternatively, to use the Lync Server Management Shell to associate a bandwidth policy profile with a site, use the Set-CsNetworkSite cmdlet.

> **TIP**
>
> If a deployment has a single central site, there is no need to define the network region links or network region routes discussed next. Skip to the "Creating Network Inter-Site Policies" section.

Network Region Links

Network region links in Lync Server represent a bandwidth constraint between two network regions or central sites. Because network regions are generally geographically large, these links apply to a number of sites when communicating across regions. For example, a region link might be defined between North America and Europe for an organization. Region links are created between only two regions and can have a bandwidth policy profile associated. The bandwidth policy can be an existing policy or an administrator can create a new policy specifically for the region link.

To create a new network region link, follow these steps:

1. Open the Lync Server 2013 Control Panel.

2. Click Network Configuration.

3. Click Region Link.

4. Click the New button.

5. Enter a Name for the link.

6. Choose a Network Region #1 from the selection menu.

7. Choose a Network Region #2 from the selection menu.

8. Choose an existing Bandwidth Policy.

9. Click Commit.

Alternatively, to use the Lync Server Management Shell to create a network region link, use the New-CsNetworkRegionLink cmdlet.

Creating Network Region Routes

A network region route object represents the network path between two regions. This might sound similar to a network region link. However, whereas a region link defines bandwidth on a direct link, a route defines only the network path between regions.

In many cases, such as a direct connection, there is a 1:1 ratio between region links and region routes, but this might differ when direct links between regions do not exist. For example, consider a scenario in which North America and Europe have direct connectivity, and Europe and Asia also have direct connectivity, each with network region links defined. Since North America and Asia do not have directory connectivity, a Network Region Route must be created to indicate that calls between those two regions must traverse through Europe.

In simple terms, a region route is a list of the region links traversed when communication is taking place between two regions. When a call traverses multiple region links, the bandwidth policy of each link is applied.

To create a new network region route, follow these steps:

1. Open the Lync Server 2013 Control Panel.

2. Click Network Configuration.

3. Click Region Route.

4. Click the New button.

5. Enter a Name for the route.

6. Choose a Network Region #1 from the selection menu.

18

7. Choose a Network Region #2 from the selection menu.

8. Click the Add button, select a region link, and click OK.

9. Repeat for any additional region links that will be traversed by this path.

10. Click Commit.

Alternatively, to use the Lync Server Management Shell to create a network region route, use the `New-CsNetworkInterRegionRoute` cmdlet.

Creating Network Inter-Site Policies

Network inter-site policies are used to define a bandwidth policy between two sites that are connected to the same region, but that also have a direct link to each other. In some cases this link might have additional WAN bandwidth that can be leveraged for calls, or that might even be preferred over a call traversing through the central site. Similar to a region link, two sites are defined and a bandwidth policy profile is associated with the link. It's very possible that no network inter-site policies need to be created. Network inter-site policies can be created only using the Lync Server Management Shell.

For each inter-site policy required, use the following syntax:

```
New-CSNetworkInterSitePolicy -InterNetworkSitePolicyID <Inter-Site Policy Name>
➡-NetworkSiteID1 <Network Site 1 ID> -NetworkSiteID2 <Network Site 2 ID>
➡-BWPolicyProfileID <Bandwidth Policy Profile ID>
```

Enabling Call Admission Control

After all the required objects and links are configured, the final step in the process is to actually enable Call Admission Control.

To enable the feature, follow these steps:

1. Open the Lync Server 2013 Control Panel.

2. Click Network Configuration.

3. Click Global.

4. Highlight the global policy, click Edit, and then select Show Details.

5. Check the box Enable Call Admission Control.

6. Click Commit.

Alternatively, the Lync Server Management Shell cmdlet `Set-CsNetworkConfiguration` can be used to enable Call Admission Control.

Media Bypass

Media Bypass is a feature that allows Lync endpoints to send a G.711 audio stream directly to a device on the opposite side of a trunk, as opposed to sending the media through a Mediation Server. For Media Bypass to work, the following requirements must be met:

▶ Media Bypass must be enabled on the SIP trunk configuration. The centralized media processing option must also be enabled on the trunk.

▶ Media Bypass must be enabled at a global level.

Enabling Media Bypass

Media Bypass must be enabled at a global level before clients attempt to use the bypass features. An administrator has two options to choose from when enabling Media Bypass:

▶ **Always Bypass**—This choice instructs clients to always bypass the Mediation Server role, but works only if a trunk configuration also has the Enable Media Bypass option selected. All Lync clients must have good network connectivity to the other end of every single SIP trunk for this option to be effective. This option might make sense in very small deployments.

▶ **Use Sites and Region Configuration**—This choice is a better option when Lync endpoints might not have good network connectivity to each SIP trunk; it enables the network region and site configuration to limit when Media Bypass is actually used. Enable Bypass for Non-Mapped Sites can be selected only if Use Sites and Region Configuration is selected first. This allows for sites and subnets not explicitly configured to still use Media Bypass.

NOTE

If Call Admission Control is enabled, the only available option for Media Bypass is to use the network site and region configuration.

To select a choice in enabling Media Bypass, follow these steps:

1. Open the Lync Server 2013 Control Panel.
2. Click Network Configuration.
3. Click Global.
4. Highlight the global policy, click Edit, and then select Show Details.
5. Check the box Enable Media Bypass.
6. Select either Always Bypass or Use Sites and Region Configuration.
7. If selecting the Use Sites and Region Configuration, optionally check the box Enable Bypass for Non-Mapped Sites.
8. Click Commit.

Creating Bypass IDs

All Lync network sites have a Bypass ID parameter assigned that is used to determine whether a client can use Media Bypass between itself and a trunk. This determination is based on comparing the Bypass ID of the trunk with the Bypass ID of the Lync endpoint.

In a new environment all network sites share the same Bypass ID, which means Media Bypass can be used between any site. After a site has a bandwidth policy applied, it is assigned a unique Bypass ID, but the other sites all retain the same, shared Bypass ID.

Media Bypass is blocked only if there is a bandwidth constraint between the two sites, so to prevent Media Bypass from being used between two sites, an administrator must associate a bandwidth policy to either network site. The actual values of the bandwidth policy don't matter, but as long as a bandwidth policy is applied, a unique Bypass ID is generated for the site.

If the Bypass IDs of the client and trunk match, Media Bypass can be used. If they are different, Lync assumes that there is bandwidth constraint between the sites and will not use Media Bypass for the call to help preserve bandwidth.

Configuring E911

Enhanced 911 (E911) is a feature first introduced in Lync Server 2010 and provides the caller's telephone number and street address to a dispatcher automatically. This is an advantage over a very basic 911 service that requires the caller to provide an address where assistance is required.

Lync Server 2013 maintains a Location Information Service (LIS) database for an organization that associates specific gateways, subnets, and wireless SSIDs with physical location addresses. Lync Server 2013 supports E911 with support from a certified emergency services provider or through an ELIN certified media gateway. Emergency calls are routed through these options to the emergency services provider.

Configuring Site Locations

Lync Server 2013 enables clients to detect their locations on a network automatically, but a database of locations in the organization must be defined in advance for this automation to work correctly. Lync can match clients to a street address location based on the following network objects:

- ▶ **Wireless Access Point**—Matches a wireless access point based on the Basic Service Set Identifier (BSSID) of the wireless access point.

- ▶ **Subnet**—Matches a site based on the subnet network address of the Lync endpoint.

- ▶ **Switch and Port**—Matches a unique port on a switch based on the switch's MAC address and the port ID. This requires the switch to support LLDP-MED and works only with Lync Phone Edition devices.

- ▶ **Switch**—Matches a switch based on the chassis ID MAC address. The Lync endpoint sends its own IP and MAC address to the Lync Server, which then leverages a third-party service to perform a lookup and determine which switch that device is attached to. The MAC address of the switch in the response is then matched to the MAC defined for a specific switch and location in the LIS.

When defining each of the previous objects, they can be associated with an address. The address parameters configurable are listed here:

▶ `City`—The location city, for example, `San Francisco`.

▶ `CompanyName`—The name of the company at this location, for example, `Company ABC`.

▶ `Country`—The two-character location country, for example, `US`.

▶ `HouseNumber`—The location address number, for example, `123`.

▶ `HouseNumberSuffix`—Additional information after the address number, for example, `B`.

▶ `Location`—A more detailed location after the street number, such as a suite or specific floor, for example, `Suite 456`.

▶ `PostalCode`—The location postal code, for example, `12345`.

▶ `PostDirectional`—Any directional information after the street address, for example, `NE`.

▶ `PreDirectional`—Any directional information before the street address, for example, `SW`.

▶ `State`—The location state, for example, `CA`.

▶ `StreetName`—The location street name, for example, `Market`.

▶ `StreetSuffix`—The location street suffix, for example, `Street` or `Avenue`.

TIP

The Lync client displays the text for a matching Location and City in the Location field. Using the previous example, a client would show that its own location is "Suite 456 San Francisco."

All the location information must be entered through the Lync Server Management Shell. Creating each object is done through the following cmdlets:

▶ `Set-CsLisWirelessAccessPoint`

▶ `Set-CsLisSubnet`

▶ `Set-CsLisPort`

▶ `Set-CsLisSwitch`

For example, to create a new subnet and location definition, use this:

```
Set-CsLisSubnet -Subnet 192.168.22.0 -Description "Client Subnet"
➥-CompanyName "Company ABC" -HouseNumber 123 -Location "
➥Suite 456" -StreetName "Fake" -StreetSuffix "Avenue"
➥-City "San Francisco" -State CA -PostalCode 12345 -Country US
```

18

Because importing every single wireless access point, subnet, port, or switch manually would be a tedious effort, defining all the required objects in advance through a CSV file can help speed up the process of building the LIS database. The CSV file can then be used with the Lync Server Management Shell for a bulk-import process.

After all the Location Information Service objects have been created, the configuration must be published before becoming active. To publish the location database, run the following cmdlet from the Lync Server Management Shell:

```
Publish-CsLisConfiguration
```

Validating Civic Addresses

Lync Server 2013 cannot route emergency calls with location information directly by itself and instead relies on an E911 service provider to route the calls appropriately. To bypass the step of an E911 operator validating an address, all address information can be validated in advance. This validation is done through a web service URL supplied by the service provider.

To configure a service provider, use the following cmdlet:

```
Set-CsLisServiceProvider -ServiceProviderName <Name> -ValidationServiceUrl
➥<URL from Provider> -CertFileName <Certificate path and filename issued
➥by provider> -Password <Password issued by provider>
```

After a provider has been provisioned, each address in the location database should be validated with the provider. To run a test against all existing addresses, use the following cmdlet:

```
Get-CsLisCivicAddress | Test-CsLisCivicAddress -UpdateValidationStatus
```

UpdateValidationStatus also stamps each address with an attribute indicating that it has been verified successfully.

Create Location Policy

For Lync to support location information objects, users must be associated with a location policy that allows these features. Location policies can exist at the global, site, or user level. When creating a location policy, an administrator has the following options:

▶ **Enable Enhanced Emergency Services**—This setting enables the client for E911.

▶ **Location**—This setting takes effect only if emergency services are enabled, and it is used when a Lync client cannot determine a location automatically. Setting this value to No means the user is not prompted for a location. A value of Yes means the user sees a visible red error in the location field, so he enters the information. Disclaimer means the user is prompted for a location and cannot dismiss the prompt until a location is entered. Users cannot place any calls except to emergency services unless entering a location with this setting.

▶ **Use Location for Emergency Services Only**—Location information gathered from Lync clients can also be shared with team members. Selecting this option prevents Lync from sharing location information between users.

▶ **PSTN Usage**—This is the PSTN usage associated with placing emergency calls. This determines which voice routes are used for emergency calls associated with this location policy. This usage must already exist, so be sure to define a new emergency services usage before configuring a location policy.

▶ **Emergency Dial Number**—This is the number sent by Lync to match a route within the emergency services PSTN usage. Do not include the leading + sign.

▶ **Emergency Dial Mask**—This is a list of semicolon-separated dial strings that users might use to dial emergency services. This can include an external access prefix, or additional codes sometimes used to call emergency services.

▶ **Notification URI**—This is the SIP URI that receives an instant message notification when an emergency call is placed. Should contain the "sip:" prefix. This can be useful for security teams to receive notification that a user has called emergency services.

▶ **Conference URI**—This is the SIP URI that should be conferenced into the call when an emergency call is placed. Should contain the "sip:" prefix and can also be a phone number.

▶ **Conference Mode**—This specifies whether the conference URI contact can be included in the call using one-way or two-way communication. One-way means the conference URI can only listen to the call as it occurs and two-way means the contact can participate.

To create a new location policy, follow these steps:

1. Open the Lync Server 2013 Control Panel.

2. Click Network Configuration.

3. Click Location Policy.

4. Click New and select either Site Policy or User Policy.

5. Check the box Enable Enhanced Emergency Services to enable the feature.

6. Select a Location specification requirement policy.

7. Select whether to Use Location for Emergency Services Only.

8. Enter an Emergency Dial Number.

9. Enter any Emergency Dial Masks, separated by semicolons.

10. Enter a Notification URI, if necessary.

11. Enter a Conference URI, if necessary.

18

12. Select a Conference Mode.

13. Click Commit as shown in Figure 18.6.

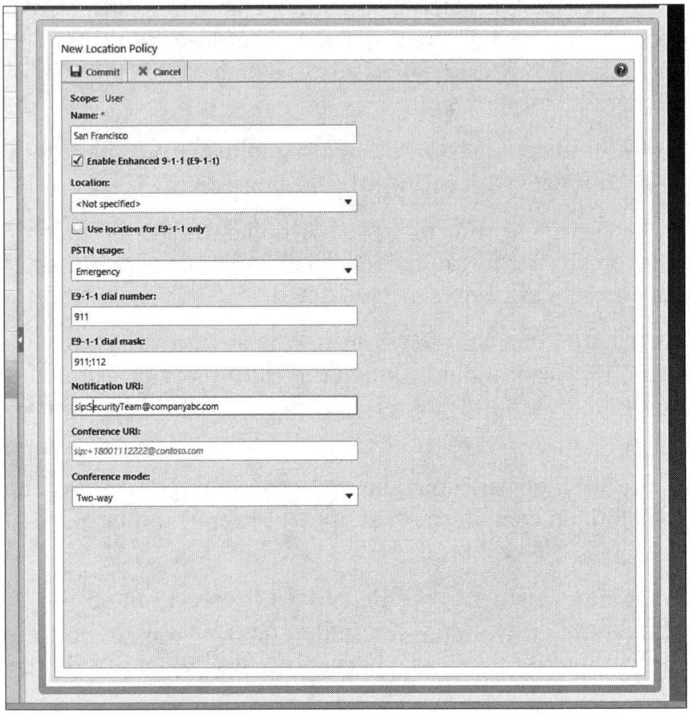

FIGURE 18.6   Creating a location policy.

Alternatively, the Lync Server Management Shell can be used to create a location policy through the New-CsLocationPolicy cmdlet.

Dial-In Conferencing

Leveraging the Lync Server 2013 dial-in conferencing features depends greatly on the voice routing and trunk configuration already in place. The actual steps for adding dial-in conferencing to a functional voice infrastructure are not difficult and can be provisioned quickly. This section covers the different aspects of the configuration process.

Creating Dial-In Conferencing Regions

Each dial plan created can be associated with a dial-in conferencing region, which is what determines the access numbers displayed for Online Meeting invitations. Despite the identical and overused terminology, regions are not actually tied to the network region definitions used for the Call Admission Control and Media Bypass features. Dial-in conferencing regions can be defined and created only through a dial plan object in the voice routing section, as described earlier in this chapter.

Creating Dial-In Access Numbers

Dial-in access numbers are the phone numbers users dial to reach the audio conferencing service. For each access number, a SIP-enabled contact object is created within Active Directory.

Each dial-in access number has a dial-in conferencing region associated that ties it to a particular dial plan. The following options are available when you are creating a dial-in access number:

- ▶ **Display Number**—The text format of the number as it is displayed to users in the Online Meeting invitation.

- ▶ **Display Name**—The name of the Active Directory contact created for the access number.

- ▶ **Line URI**—The phone number assigned to the dial-in access contact. This should be specified in E.164 format with the "tel:" prefix.

- ▶ **SIP URI**—The SIP URI assigned to the contact object. It must be unique within the organization and use a "sip:" prefix.

- ▶ **Pool**—The pool where the contact object is homed.

- ▶ **Primary Language**—The primary language used to make conferencing announcements.

- ▶ **Secondary Languages**—Any secondary language choices for conferencing announcements. Up to four secondary languages can be specified.

- ▶ **Associated Regions**—Dial plan regions that are associated with the dial-in access number. Multiple regions can be associated to a single number, or a region can be associated to multiple dial-in access numbers.

Perform the following steps to create a new dial-in access number:

1. Open the Lync Server 2013 Control Panel.

2. Click Conferencing.

3. Click Dial-In Access Number.

4. Click New.

5. Enter a Display Number for the contact.

6. Enter a Display Name for the contact.

7. Enter a Line URI in E.164 format using a "tel:" prefix.

18

8. Enter a SIP URI using a "sip:" prefix and select a SIP domain internal to the organization.

9. Select a Pool where the object will be homed.

10. Select a Primary Language for the conference announcements.

11. Click the Add button and select up to four Secondary Languages.

12. Click the Add button and select Associated Regions for the dial-in access number.

13. Click Commit when finished.

To use the Lync Server Management Shell to create the dial-in access number, use the `New-CsDialInConferencingAccessNumber` cmdlet.

Modifying a Conferencing Policy

After a dial-in access number is configured, it does not appear in Online Meeting invitations unless the conference organizer's conferencing policy allows PSTN dial-in. The key settings in the conferencing policy that should be reviewed include the following:

▶ **Allow Participants to Invite Anonymous Users**—Controls whether anonymous, unauthenticated users from outside the organization can participate in conferences. Although this setting is not required to be enabled, if it is not selected, it limits the use of audio conferencing to only users inside the organization.

▶ **Enable PSTN Dial-in Conferencing**—Must be enabled for dial-in conferencing to function. It controls whether dial-in conferencing is allowed for meetings scheduled by users assigned this policy.

▶ **Allow Anonymous Participants to Dial Out**—Controls whether anonymous, unauthenticated users from outside the organization can join an audio conference and be called at a PSTN number by the conferencing service. Users may still dial in to the conferencing service if this option is not selected, but may not request the conferencing service call them.

▶ **Allow Participants Not Enabled for Enterprise Voice to Dial Out**—Controls whether authenticated users without Enterprise Voice can request that the conferencing service call them to join the conference.

To verify that these settings are configured correctly, perform the following steps:

1. Open the Lync Server 2013 Control Panel.

2. Click Conferencing.

3. Click Conferencing Policy.

4. Highlight an existing conferencing policy, click Edit, and select Show Details.

5. Verify that the Allow Participants to Invite Anonymous Users option is set.

6. Verify that the Enable PSTN Dial-In Conferencing option is set.

7. Verify that the Allow Anonymous Users to Dial Out option is set.

8. Verify that the Allow Participants Not Enabled for Enterprise Voice to Dial Out option is set.

9. Click Commit.

The Lync Server Management Shell can also be used to configure these settings with the `Set-CsConferencingPolicy` cmdlet.

Modifying PIN Policies

Lync Server 2010 enables users to join audio conferences either through a Lync client or by simply dialing in from a phone. When dialing from a phone, the users are unauthenticated until they enter an extension and matching PIN. This is required because when joining conferences from a Lync client, users are already authenticated after passing Active Directory credentials to log in to Lync. When dialing in from a phone, the PIN and extension provide a method for Lync to still validate the user as internal to the organization. Administrators can define PIN policies that apply globally to all users, only to a specific site, or to assigned user accounts.

> **NOTE**
>
> The PIN policy discussed here is separate from an organization's PIN for Exchange Unified Messaging. The PINs between the two systems are not synchronized in any way, and users must maintain them separately. For that reason, strong end-user communication is encouraged so that the users understand the difference and the need to change PINs in both locations. Future versions of Lync Server and Exchange Server will hopefully introduce synchronization of PINs and PIN policies.

When configuring a PIN policy, administrators have the following options:

▶ **Minimum PIN Length**—The minimum number of digits a user may use for a PIN. Only a minimum value can be specified, so users may choose any number of digits for their PIN equal to or more than this value.

▶ **Maximum Logon Attempts**—The number of times a user may attempt to authenticate with a PIN before the PIN is locked out and must be reset by an administrator. If a user successfully authenticates with a PIN, this counter is reset to zero.

▶ **PIN Expiration**—A setting that determines whether a PIN will expire. The PIN expiration value is set in days. Using a value of 0 for PIN expiration means the user PINs will never expire.

▶ **PIN History Count**—The number of PINs the system remembers before a user is allowed to reuse a PIN.

▶ **Allow Common Patterns**—A setting that determines whether commonly used patterns are allowed for a PIN. Examples of common patterns are repeating digits, four consecutive digits, and PINs that match a user's phone number or extension.

To create a new PIN policy, perform the following steps:

1. Open the Lync Server 2013 Control Panel.

2. Click Conferencing.

3. Click PIN Policy.

4. Click New and select either Site Policy or User Policy.

5. Select a Minimum PIN Length.

6. Select whether to Specify Maximum Logon Attempts and enter a maximum number of attempts.

7. Select whether to enable PIN Expiration and enter a number of days.

8. Select whether to enable Allow Common Patterns.

9. Click Commit when complete.

To create a new PIN policy using the Lync Server Management Shell, use the `New-CsPinPolicy` cmdlet.

Modifying Meeting Configuration

The meeting configuration commands in Lync Server 2013 are provided to give organizations more control over what types of meetings are allowed to occur. When a meeting configuration is being modified, the following options are available:

▶ **PSTN Callers Bypass Lobby**—Controls whether users who dial in to the conference from a PSTN phone are automatically entered into the meeting. If this option is not enabled, a presenter must admit all users in the lobby before they can participate in the conference. This generally is not an obstacle when the presenter is using Lync and can visibly see that users are waiting in a lobby, but consider a scenario in which presenters dial in from a PSTN number and do not have this visual clue. Presenters can use DTMF controls to admit users in the lobby, but not all users know this feature or find it easy to use.

▶ **Designate as Presenter**—Controls which users can be promoted as presenters throughout the meeting. This can be set to no one, people from inside the organization, or everyone.

▶ **Assigned Conference Type by Default**—Controls whether meetings are created with unique meeting IDs. An assigned conference in Lync is a static, persistent URL and conference ID that each user has. If set to `true`, each scheduled meeting has the same ID by default. If set to `false`, each meeting generates a unique ID. Using a unique ID can be helpful so that if a user has back-to-back meetings, attendees from the second meeting do not accidentally join the first meeting.

▶ **Admit Anonymous Users by Default**—Controls whether anonymous, unauthenticated users are admitted into meetings by default.

▶ **Logo URL**—Provides a custom image that is inserted in Online Meeting invitations.

▶ **Help URL**—Provides a custom URL users can access to receive assistance with Online Meetings.

▶ **Legal Text URL**—Provides a custom URL users can access to read legal disclaimer information.

▶ **Custom Footer Text**—Adds text to the end of Online Meeting invitations.

To configure the meeting configuration, perform the following steps:

   1. Open the Lync Server 2013 Control Panel.

   2. Click Conferencing.

   3. Click Meeting Configuration.

   4. Highlight an existing configuration, click Edit, and select Show Details.

   5. Select whether PSTN Callers Bypass Lobby.

   6. Select a group to Designate as Presenter.

   7. Select whether to use Assigned Conference Type by Default.

   8. Select whether to Admit Anonymous Users by Default.

   9. Optionally, enter custom URLs for Logo URL, Help URL, and Legal Text URL.

  10. Optionally, enter any Custom Footer Text.

  11. Click Commit when complete.

Two parameters for the meeting configuration are available only through the `Set-CsMeetingConfiguration` cmdlet:

▶ `RequireRoomSystemsAuthorization`—A `true` or `false` value indicating whether all users must authenticate before joining a meeting using a Lync room system video endpoint.

▶ `EnableAssignedConferenceType`—A `true` or `false` value indicating whether the persistent, static conference IDs are allowed to be used.

18

Modifying Conference Announcements

Conference announcements settings in Lync control what occurs when participants join or leave a meeting. These settings can be configured at a global level or assigned to a specific site.

> **NOTE**
>
> Enabling or disabling the announcements is a default preference that can be passed to users. However, users can change this default as they desire.

When you are configuring conferencing announcements, the following options are available:

▶ **Enable Name Recording**—Controls whether users are prompted to record their name before joining the conference. Internal users are not prompted to record a name, and their name is played through the text-to-speech engine instead.

▶ **Entry and Exit Announcements Type**—Defines the type of announcement played when attendees join or leave the meeting. The options are to use the person's name or to simply play a tone.

▶ **Entry and Exit Announcements Enabled by Default**—Controls whether announcements are enabled or disabled by default for new Lync user accounts. This is simply a default setting passed to users that they might change.

The conference announcement settings can be configured only through the Lync Server Management Shell using the following syntax:

```
Set-CsDialInConferencingConfiguration -Identity <Identity>
➥-EnableNameRecording <$True | $False> -EntryExitAnnouncementsEnabledByDefault
➥<$True | $False> -EntryExitAnnouncementsType <UseNames | ToneOnly >
```

Customizing DTMF Commands

Lync Server 2013 enables attendees to use DTMF commands when in a conference to control certain features normally visible within a Lync client. For example, users can send DTMF tones that might mute their microphone, play an attendee roll call, or lock the conference. Usually these features can be accessed through a Lync client, but without a visible user interface, DTMF tones must be used. By default, a global configuration of the key mappings is assigned to all users. If required, administrators can modify the global configuration or modify the key mappings on a per-site basis.

The following DTMF commands are available to assign to phone keys:

▶ `AdmitAll`—Enables users waiting in the lobby to join the meeting. This key is not enabled by default. Assign a value to enable this feature.

▶ `AudienceMuteCommand`—Mutes all microphones except the presenter. This key is 4 by default.

▶ **CommandCharacter**—Designates the key pressed before entering any other DTMF command digits. This key is * by default.

▶ **EnableDisableAnnouncementsCommand**—Toggles whether entry and exit announcements are played during the meeting. This key is 9 by default.

▶ **HelpCommand**—Plays a summary of the DTMF commands available to a user. This key is 1 by default.

▶ **LockUnlockConferenceCommand**—Toggles whether the audio conference is locked or unlocked to allow new participants to join. This key is 7 by default.

▶ **MuteUnmuteCommand**—Toggles whether the participant's audio microphone is muted or unmuted. This key is 6 by default.

▶ **PrivateRollCallCommand**—Plays a roll call of participants only to the user issuing the command. This key is 3 by default.

To set the DTMF values, an administrator must use the following Lync Server Management Shell syntax:

```
Set-CsDialInConferencingDtmfConfiguration -Identity <Global or site:<Site Name>
➡-AdmitAll <Digit> -AudienceMuteCommand <Digit> -CommandCharacter <Digit>
➡-EnableDisableAnnouncementsCommand <Digit> -HelpCommand <Digit>
➡-LockUnlockConferenceCommand <Digit> -MuteUnmuteCommand <Digit>
➡-PrivateRollCallCommand <Digit>
```

Response Groups

Response Groups are a feature first introduced in Office Communications Server 2007 R2 that were enhanced in Lync Server 2010 and remain largely unchanged in Lync Server 2013. A Response Group is a method to route calls to a specific queue or set of agents. Some consider Response Groups to be on a similar level as hunt groups from traditional telephony, but an administrator typically has much greater control over a Response Group than a PBX hunt group. Many PBXs call this feature Automatic Call Distribution (ACD).

Response Groups in Lync are composed of the following components:

▶ **Agent Groups**—Agent groups contain a specified set of user accounts that belong to a Response Group. How calls are routed in the group and what options a member has are configured at the agent group level.

▶ **Queues**—A queue is an object that holds callers as they dial in to the Response Group. A queue can contain multiple agent groups, or sometimes just a single agent group is included. Settings such as timeouts and call capacity are configured at the queue level.

▶ **Workflows**—Workflows are the glue that ties together the agent groups and the queues. The workflow settings determine how a caller reaches a specific queue depending on question responses, time of day, or holidays.

The following sections explain each of these components in more detail and discuss how to configure a complete Response Group.

Configuring Agent Groups

Agent groups are a collection of users, which can be distribution groups or individual user accounts. The following options are available during creation of an agent group:

▶ **Participation Policy**—Determines whether agents need to sign in or out of the group manually. Selecting Formal here means users have to manually enter and leave the agent group through a web page. Informal means the agents are automatically included in the group as long as they are signed in to Lync.

▶ **Alert Time**—Sets the number of seconds a call rings an agent before attempting to ring the next agent.

▶ **Routing Method**—Specifies how the calls are routed among agents in the group. Options include Longest Idle, Parallel, Round Robin, Serial, and Attendant.

▶ **Agents**—Specifies the user accounts or a distribution group used for the agent group membership. Keep in mind that distribution groups do not recognize nested groups and that only one distribution group can be specified.

> **NOTE**
>
> Response Group agents must be Enterprise Voice users. Users enabled for Lync services but not Enterprise Voice cannot be selected to participate in an agent group.

Understanding Routing Methods in Agent Groups

The routing methods are a key part of defining how agents take calls. These options are separated here for some additional clarity on behavior:

▶ **Longest Idle**—The call is routed to the agent who has had a presence status of Available the longest without taking a call. For example, if three agents are part of the agent group and one agent is Busy while two are Available, the call is routed to the user who has had the Available presence the longest.

▶ **Parallel**—This rings all agents at the same time. The agent who accepts the call first is placed in a conversation with the caller.

▶ **Round Robin**—Call requests are evenly sent to agents. Assuming that three agents exist, the first call goes to Agent A, the second to Agent B, and the third to Agent C. The fourth call rings Agent A again.

▶ **Serial**—Calls are sent to agents in the order defined in the agent list. Assuming that three agents exist, the first call goes to Agent A. The next call again attempts to ring Agent A, and if Agent A is unavailable, the call then goes to Agent B. The difference from round robin distribution is that the next call follows the same order, starting with Agent A again.

▶ **Attendant**—Calls are routed to all agents just as in parallel fashion, but this option includes agents who are busy or currently in a call. Calls are not routed to agents with a status of Do Not Disturb.

Creating an Agent Group

To create a new agent group, follow these steps:

1. Open the Lync Server 2013 Control Panel.

2. Click Response Groups.

3. Click Group.

4. Click New.

5. Select an Application Server and click OK.

6. Enter a Name for the group.

7. Enter a Description for the group.

8. Select a Participation Policy for the agents.

9. Specify the Alert Time (Seconds) for how long a call will ring an agent.

10. Select a Routing Method for the group.

11. If using a distribution list for the agent list, select Use an Existing Email Distribution List and then enter the Distribution List Address.

12. If manually adding agents to the group, select Define a Custom Group of Agents and click the Select button.

13. Enter a search for users and click Find.

14. Highlight the selected user and click OK.

15. Repeat for any additional users who will be part of the agent group.

16. Click Commit after all agents have been added.

Alternatively, the Lync Server Management Shell can be used to create a new agent group through the New-CsRgsAgentGroup cmdlet.

Configuring Queues

A Response Group queue is used to hold calls while waiting for an agent to answer. A queue can contain a single agent group, or administrators can add multiple agent groups to a queue. The following options are available during creation of a queue:

▶ **Groups**—The agent groups that are responsible for answering calls in this queue. The groups can be ordered so that certain groups are attempted before others.

18

▶ **Enable Queue Time-out**—A determination of whether a time limit is enforced when callers wait for an agent.

▶ **Time-out Period**—The number of seconds a caller can remain in the queue before timing out.

▶ **Enable Queue Overflow**—A determination of whether the queue supports a maximum number of calls.

▶ **Maximum Number of Calls**—The number of calls that can be in the queue at any given time.

▶ **Forward the Call**—A determination of whether the call is forwarded when the queue reaches a maximum number of calls. Administrators can choose to forward either the oldest call in the queue or the newest call.

▶ **Call Action**—The action taken when a call reaches the time-out period. The options for call targets are discussed in greater detail later in this section.

In a situation in which either the time period elapses or the maximum number of calls is reached, an administrator has several choices for how to route the call:

▶ **Disconnect**—Drops the call.

▶ **Forward to Voice Mail**—Forwards the call to an Exchange UM voice mail address, which must be a SIP URI.

▶ **Forward to Telephone Number**—Forwards the call to a telephone number in the sip:<number>@<domain> format.

▶ **Forward to SIP Address**—Forwards the call to another user account in the sip:<username>@<domain> format.

▶ **Forward to Another Queue**—Forwards the call to another Response Group queue.

Creating a Queue

To create a new queue, follow these steps:

1. Open the Lync Server 2013 Control Panel.

2. Click Response Groups.

3. Click Queue.

4. Click New.

5. Select an Application Server and click OK.

6. Enter a Name for the queue.

7. Enter a Description for the queue.

8. Click Select to choose existing agent groups that belong to the queue.

9. Highlight any groups to add and click OK.

10. Check the box for Enable Queue Time-out if required.

11. After selecting queue time-out, enter a Time-out Period.

12. After selecting Queue Time-out, select a Call Action and enter an appropriate SIP URI if required.

13. Check the box for Enable Queue Overflow if required.

14. After selecting Enable Queue Overflow, enter a Maximum Number of Calls.

15. After selecting Enable Queue Overflow, click Forward the Call and select an option.

16. After selecting Enable Queue Overflow, select a Call Action and enter an appropriate SIP URI if required.

17. Click Commit when completed.

Alternatively, the Lync Server Management Shell can be used to create a new queue through the `New-CsRgsAgentGroup` and `New-CsRgsCallAction` cmdlets.

Configuring Workflows

The Response Group workflow is what ties together the agent groups and workflows along with how calls should be routed. There are two types of workflows that can be created:

▶ **Hunt Group**—A simple workflow that routes callers to queues based on time of day and agent availability.

▶ **Interactive**—Allows the user to be prompted with questions and is then routed to queues based on the responses.

The two types of workflows share many configuration options, which are discussed in detail in the following:

▶ **Activate the Workflow**—If this is selected, the workflow immediately begins to accept calls. This parameter can be changed later if the workflow should not immediately be active.

▶ **Enable for Federation**—The workflow can be contacted by federated contacts if this option is selected.

▶ **Agent Anonymity**—Selecting this option hides the identity of the agent after the call is established. There are some feature limitations imposed during the call if this is enabled. For example, conferencing, application and desktop sharing, file transfer, and call recording are not available.

▶ **Group Address**—This is the SIP URI assigned to the workflow. This should be a unique URI in the organization.

18

▶ **Display Name**—This is the name visible to clients when calling the workflow.

▶ **Telephone Number**—This is the line URI for the workflow.

▶ **Display Number**—This is the number visible to clients when calling the workflow. This can be in any format.

▶ **Description**—This is a description for the workflow.

▶ **Workflow Type**—This controls if the workflow can be left unmanaged, or managed by designated Response Group managers.

▶ **Language**—This determines the language used for speech recognition or text-to-speech conversion.

▶ **Welcome Message**—A configurable audio message can be played to callers as they enter the workflow. This can be accomplished either through text-to-speech or by uploading an existing audio recording.

▶ **Time Zone**—This is the time zone that the opening and closing times are based around.

▶ **Business Hours Schedule**—The schedule for the workflow can be based on an existing schedule created separately or it can be a custom schedule defined directly within the workflow.

▶ **Outside Business Hours Message**—A configurable audio message can be played to callers if they dial the workflow outside of the defined business hours. This can be done through text-to-speech or by uploading an existing audio recording.

▶ **Outside Business Hours Action**—If callers reach the workflow outside of the defined open hours, the call can be disconnected, forwarded to a voice mail box, forwarded to another SIP URI, or forwarded to a telephone number. This action occurs after the message is played, if it is defined.

▶ **Holiday Lists**—This is a collection of days that are defined as holidays. A separate action can be taken on these days.

▶ **Holidays Message**—A configurable audio message can be played to callers if they dial the workflow on a defined holiday. This can be done through text-to-speech or by uploading an existing audio recording.

▶ **Holidays Action**—If callers reach the workflow during a defined holiday, the call can be disconnected, forwarded to a voice mail box, forwarded to another SIP URI, or forwarded to a telephone number. This action occurs after the message is played, if it is defined.

▶ **Queue**—The queue selected here receives calls for this workflow.

▶ **Music on Hold**—The default music on hold can be selected or administrators can configure a custom music on-hold file.

Creating Workflows

To create a new Response Group workflow, follow these steps:

1. Open the Lync Server 2013 Control Panel.

2. Click Response Groups.

3. Click Workflow.

4. Click Create or Edit a Workflow.

5. Select an Application Server to host the Response Group and click OK.

The Response Group Configuration Tool opens in a web browser. Unlike the rest of the Response Group setup, workflow creation is done using an interface separate from the Lync Server Control Panel. What type of workflow is created depends on the administrator. Steps for creating each type of workflow can be found in the next section.

> **NOTE**
>
> The Response Group Configuration Tool opens in a web browser. Unlike the rest of the Response Group setup, workflow creation is done using an interface separate from the Lync Server Control Panel. What type of workflow is created depends on the administrator. Steps for creating each type of workflow can be found in the next section.

Creating a Hunt Group Workflow

To create a new hunt group workflow, follow these steps after launching the Response Group Configuration Tool:

1. Under Hunt Group, click the Create button.

2. Select whether to Activate the Workflow.

3. Select an option for Enable for Federation.

4. Select an option for Enable Agent Anonymity.

5. Enter a SIP Address for the workflow. The "sip:" prefix is automatically prepended.

6. Enter a Display Name for the workflow.

7. Enter a Telephone Number to associate with the workflow. The "tel:" prefix is automatically included, so just the E.164 format is required with the + sign prefix.

8. Enter a Display Number for the telephone number.

9. Enter a Description for the workflow.

10. Select whether the Workflow Type is Unmanaged or Managed, and specify any Managers.

11. Select a Language.

12. Choose whether to Play a Welcome Message and select the message type.

13. Specify the Time Zone.

14. Select a Business Hours Schedule by choosing Use a Preset Schedule or by choosing Use a Custom Schedule and defining the schedule.

15. Select whether to Play a Message When the Response Group Is Outside of Business Hours, and select a message type.

16. Select an action to take when Outside of Business Hours, Process Call as Follows.

17. Select a Standard Holiday List if one has been created.

18. Select whether to Play a Message During Holidays, and then select a message type.

19. Select an action to take regarding During Holidays, Process Call as Follows.

20. Configure a Queue to receive the calls.

21. Select an option to Configure Music on Hold.

22. Click Deploy to complete the workflow creation.

Creating an Interactive Workflow

To create an interactive workflow, follow these steps after launching the Response Group Configuration Tool:

1. Under Hunt Group, click the Create button.

2. Select whether to Activate the Workflow.

3. Select an option for Enable for Federation.

4. Select an option for Enable Agent Anonymity.

5. Enter a SIP Address for the workflow. The "sip:" prefix is automatically prepended.

6. Enter a Display Name for the workflow.

7. Enter a Telephone Number to associate with the workflow. The "tel:" prefix is automatically included, so just the E.164 format is required with the plus prefix.

8. Enter a Display Number for the telephone number.

9. Enter a Description for the workflow.

10. Select whether the Workflow Type is Unmanaged or Managed, and specify any Managers.

11. Select a Language.

12. Choose whether to Play a Welcome Message and select the message type.

13. Specify the Time Zone.

14. Select a Business Hours Schedule by Use a Preset Schedule or by Use a Custom Schedule, and then define the schedule.

15. Select whether to Play a Message When the Response Group Is Outside of Business Hours, and select a message type.

16. Select an action to take when Outside of Business Hours, Process Call as Follows.

17. Select a Standard Holiday List if one has been created.

18. Select whether to Play a Message During Holidays and select a message type.

19. Select an action to take During Holidays, Process Call as Follows.

20. Select an option to Configure Music on Hold.

21. Select whether to Use Text-to-Speech or Select a Recording to use for the first interactive question.

22. Enter a Voice Response text phrase and select a digit to Assign Keypad Response.

23. Select a Queue the caller is placed in when matching the voice or keypad response.

24. Repeat the previous steps for any additional valid responses or questions that should be asked.

25. Click Deploy to complete the workflow creation.

Configuring Business-Hour Collections

Business-hour schedules can be created in advance, and reused across multiple workflows. Defining business-hour collections is a task that can be performed only via the Lync Server Management Shell. Use the `New-CsRgsTimeRange` cmdlet to create each unique new time range, and store it in a variable that can be passed to a business-hours collection object later. Times should be defined using a 24-hour format.

```
$Weekdays = New-CsRgsTimeRange -Name <Name of Time Range> -OpenTime
➥<Time when business hours start> -CloseTime <Time when business hours end>
```

After a unique variable has been created for each different set of hours, the business hours collection object can be created with the `New-CsRgsHoursOfBusiness` cmdlet:

```
New-CsRgsHoursOfBusiness -Parent ApplicationServer:<Front End Pool FQDN> -Name
➥<Business Hours Collection Name> -MondayHours1 <Time Range Object>
➥-TuesdayHours1 <Time Range Object> -WednesdayHours1 <Time Range Object>
➥-ThursdayHours1 <Time Range Object> -FridayHours1 <Time Range Object>
➥-SaturdayHours1 <Time Range Object> -SundayHours1 <Time Range Object>
```

This cmdlet accepts two values for each day of the week. If the business hours stay open with no break, only `Hours1` parameters need to be specified. If the business hours include a break, such as from 12:00 to 13:00, the `Hours1` parameter should be from business open to 12:00, and the `Hours2` parameter should be from 13:00 to business close.

18

Configuring Holiday Sets

Much as with business-hour collections, Lync administrators can create a holiday set to define the appropriate holiday schedule for a business. A holiday set can also be created only using the Lync Server Management Shell.

The first step in defining a holiday set is to create a unique variable for each holiday, which defines a name, a start date, and an end date. After all the holidays are stored in a variable, they can be added to a holiday set. To create a holiday and store it in a variable, follow this syntax:

```
$Christmas = New-CsRgsHoliday -Name <Holiday Name> -StartDate <Date formatted as
➥dd/mm/yyyy> -EndDate <Date formatted as dd/mm/yyyy>
```

After repeating the previous step to create each of the holiday objects, use the following syntax to create the holiday object. Naming the object based on the year usually makes the most sense because some holidays might fall on different days depending on the year. To configure a new holiday set, use the following cmdlet:

```
New-CsRgsHolidaySet -Parent ApplicationServer:<Front End Pool FQDN> -Name
➥<Holiday Set Name> -HolidayList (<Comma-separated list of each variable
➥representing a holiday>)
```

Creating Workflows Using the Lync Server Management Shell

Creating a Response Group workflow entirely in the Lync Server Management Shell gives some added flexibility to configuration. Specifically, interactive workflows have no limit to the number of questions or responses, unlike the Response Group Configuration Tool, which limits both items.

TIP

Take care to not make interactive workflows with too many menu levels because callers can quickly become frustrated and end the call if they have to navigate through too many levels.

NOTE

Much of the Response Group configuration done using the Management Shell relies heavily on storing objects as variables. Being descriptive with variable names can reduce the complexity involved when trying to tie all the pieces together.

A basic hunt group workflow can be created easily. All workflows need a default action defined, so the first step in creating a workflow within the Management Shell is to store a default action in a variable. The New-CsRgsCallAction cmdlet creates an action stored in memory that can be used in another command. A simple example that stores the action and sends calls to a specific queue is displayed here:

```
$TransferToCustomerServiceQueue = New-CsRgsCallAction -Action TransferToQueue
➥-QueueID CustomerService
```

After an action has been created, a workflow object can be created. The actual workflow setup is flexible and can become extremely complicated. Building off the previous example and stored $TransferToCustomerService variable, a simple hunt group workflow example is presented as follows:

```
New-CsRgsWorkflow -Name MyWorkflow -Parent
➥service:ApplicationServer:lyncpool.companyabc.com -PrimaryUri
➥CustomerService@companyabc.com -DefaultAction $TransferToCustomerServiceQueue
➥-Description "Routes callers dialing customer support" -DisplayNumber "
➥+1 (234) 456-7890" -LineURI "tel:+1234567890"
```

> **NOTE**
>
> An interactive workflow requires more upfront preparation and object configuration before creation of the workflow object. Each prompt, question, and answer object must be defined in advance of the Response Group configuration since much of using the Management Shell relies heavily on storing objects as variables. Being descriptive with variable names can reduce the complexity involved when trying to tie all the pieces together.

To get started, a new prompt must be created and saved using the New-CsRgsPrompt cmdlet. The New-CsRgsPrompt cmdlet accepts an audio file as input if one has been stored in a separate variable; the alternative is to enter a text string that reads as text-to-speech. For example, to store the prompt in a variable using an audio file saved earlier as $MyAudioFile, use the following:

```
$PromptDoYouNeedHelp= New-CsRgsPrompt -AudioFilePrompt $MyAudioFile
```

After creating a prompt to be played to calls, a question must be posed in an interactive workflow. What might seem a little backward is that an answer list must be formed before a question can be created when the shell is used. For example, to store an answer option if the caller says yes or presses 1 on the keypad, use this:

```
$AnswerYesMaybe = New-CsRgsAnswer -Action $TransferToCustomerServiceQueue
➥-DtmfResponse 1 -VoiceResponseList "Yes"
```

Because there is more than one option, assume that another Response Group Answer object exists called $AnswerNo and that it disconnects the call if the user says no or presses 2 on the keypad.

After all the possible answers have been defined, a Response Group Question object can be created. Continuing the previous example, assume that the custom prompt asks the caller if she actually needs help. So far, a response of yes has an action that transfers the caller to the Customer Service queue. If the user says no, the call ends. The following example ties the two responses into a question and stores it in yet another variable:

```
$DoesCustomerNeedHelpQuestion = New-CsRgsQuestion -Prompt $DoYouNeedHelp -AnswerList
➥$YesMaybe,$No -Name "Do you need help" -NoAnswerPrompt $AreYouStillThere
```

18

This example shows creating just one question with only two responses. Be sure to thoroughly plan a workflow before continuing with the setup because it does require quite a bit of scripting. Repeat the previous steps for any additional prompts, questions, and answers that will be part of the workflow.

Before the workflow can be created, the initial prompt must be assigned to a default action object:

```
$AskIfHelpNeeded = New-CsRgsCallAction -Action TransferToQuestion -Question
➥$DoesCustomerNeedHelpQuestion
```

Now that a question and call action have been created, an entire interactive workflow can be initiated. To finish the example, the following commands create the workflow that asks the caller whether he needs help:

```
New-CsRgsWorkflow -Name "Customer Service Workflow" -Parent
➥service:ApplicationServer:lyncpool.companyabc.com –PrimaryUri
➥CustomerService@companyabc.com - -DefaultAction $AskIfHelpNeeded
➥-Description "Asks user if they need help and routes to Customer Service if yes"
➥-DisplayNumber "+1 (234) 456-7890" -LineURI "tel:+1234567890"
```

Best Practices

The following are best practices from this chapter:

- ▶ Collocate Mediation Servers with a Front End Server when possible to reduce the hardware requirements for each deployment.

- ▶ Create multiple trunk associations between different pools to the same gateway for additional resiliency.

- ▶ Carefully follow the steps provided by a Survivable Branch Appliance vendor before placing the SBA in service.

- ▶ Use a unique dial plan for each location that has different dialing habits.

- ▶ Use translation rules on a trunk configuration only if the opposite end of the trunk is not manipulating digits.

- ▶ Configure the required network objects before attempting Call Admission Control, Media Bypass, or E911 setup.

- ▶ Use test cases to verify an Enterprise Voice configuration before publishing changes.

- ▶ Use a Survivable Branch Appliance or Survivable Branch Server in each remote office without a resilient WAN connection to the central site.

- ▶ Plan a Response Group workflow with diagram tools before attempting to create the workflow.

CHAPTER 19

Lync Native Video and Data Conferencing

Although video and data conferencing technology is not new to Microsoft UC, Lync 2013 introduces many enhancements to this functionality. Lync 2013 allows more endpoints to participate in high-definition video conferences, while at the same time allowing administrators greater control over video conferencing usage. Lync 2013 also expands on the existing application-sharing and desktop-sharing functionality by introducing enhanced PowerPoint presenting capabilities that support animations, transitions, and synchronous video playback from within PowerPoint presentations. All of this functionality is integrated into the Lync 2013 client.

The new functionality introduced with Lync 2013 allows users to have a more immersive UC experience, while at the same time introducing new administrative and planning challenges for IT administrators. This section provides details on what this new functionality is, what is required to implement it, and how to properly manage it.

Lync 2013 Peer-to-Peer Video

Lync 2013 allows users to participate in immersive HD video calls with other Lync users. Peer-to-peer (P2P) video has been available in the Microsoft UC Suite since LCS and has seen many evolutions over the years. In Lync 2013 Microsoft placed a major focus on video. With the introduction of the H.264 SVC codec to the Lync 2013 platform, HD video can now be extended to almost all users. This is great functionality to offer end users, but organizations must plan carefully and make sure that their environment can support HD video. This section outlines what the new video features in Lync 2013 are, including details on the

H.264 codec. This section also covers important bandwidth and hardware requirements for video, and lastly covers common configuration options for P2P video.

New Video Features

Lync Server 2013 introduces key peer-to-peer and conferencing video features. At the core of these changes is a new default video codec, H.264 SVC. The use of this codec allows for higher-quality video, with fewer server and client resources. The following features are new to Lync 2013, and affect P2P video functionality:

▶ **H.264 Video Codec**—The H.264 video codec supports a greater range of resolutions and frame rates, as well as improving video scalability.

▶ **1080p Video**—HD 1080p video is now available in two-party and multiparty conferences.

H.264 Video

The H.264 video codec has been adopted today for everything from video conferencing to Blu-ray. In Lync 2013, Microsoft has introduced H.264 SVC as the default codec for peer-to-peer video calls and conferences. SVC stands for Scalable Video Coding, and this extension to H.264 adds new profiles and scalability capabilities, which provide major advantages for real-time video communications.

The term *scalability* can be used to describe many audio and video codecs in the industry. However, the scalability that H.264 SVC provides is complimentary to one of the goals of Microsoft Lync: To provide end users with full functionality on any device, and on any network connection. H.264 SVC allows Lync Server to provide a rich conferencing experience to all endpoints by allowing users to view different levels of video quality on demand, and it does not require real-time decoding or encoding of video streams by the Multipoint Control Units (MCU) (in the case of Lync, the A/V Conferencing Server). H.264 SVC leverages the endpoints (PCs, tablets, phones, cameras) to perform the processing of the video streams. This allows Lync 2013 endpoints to dynamically send and receive a video resolution and frame rate that best suits them. As a result, the Lync Server 2013 A/V Conferencing Server is now able to act as a simple video relay mechanism, sending video streams to endpoints that they request on demand, and without requiring an increased processing load. The introduction of this functionality is what has allowed Microsoft to include HD resolutions in video conferences and at the same time to remove the need for a dedicated A/V Conferencing Server role.

How Does H.264 SVC Work?

H.264 SVC provides the scalability described previously by building video streams out of individual, complementary layers. This all starts with the base layer, which has the lowest resolution and frame rate that can be displayed. Enhancement layers are then provided as needed, which will provide higher quality to endpoints that request it. Again, these enhancement layers are complementary, so when combined with the base layer, the video resolution and frame rate are increased. This is best described in the form of a diagram, as shown in Figure 19.1.

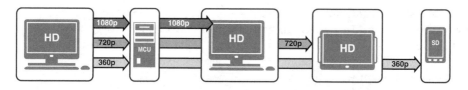

FIGURE 19.1   H.264 SVC layering example.

In this example, a PC endpoint is able to send up to 1080p HD video, and is connected to a conference. That conference is run by an MCU (Lync A/V Conferencing Server), and there are three other participants in the call. In previous versions of Lync, the video resolution would be dropped to the lowest common denominator. For example, if the phone that supported only 360p video joined the video conference, everyone would send and receive 360p video. With Lync 2013 and H.264 SVC that limitation no longer exists.

In this scenario, the base layer is built on 360p video, which is the lowest resolution needed for participants in the conference. The endpoint knows how to build its layers based on what each endpoint asks the MCU for when joining the conference. The sending endpoint then adds additional layers, for additional resolutions all the way up to 1080p, because another participant has asked for that resolution.

The sending endpoint sends all layers to the MCU, and the MCU then sends each layer that is requested to the other participants. Since the mobile phone is limited to 360p, it is sent only the base layer. The tablet, on the other hand, can support 720p video, so it is sent two layers to make up the 720p video stream. The third participant can also support 1080p video, so it is sent all three layers. It is important to remember that these layers are additive, so there is no duplicate data sent, only the delta. Because only the delta data is sent in the enhancement layers, the bandwidth used by H.264 SVC calls is similar to that of other codecs. Another great feature introduced with this codec is that everything is dynamic. Participants in the conference notify the MCU of any changes to its capabilities. A great example of this happening would be if the second PC that is capable of 1080p video did not have the video in full-screen mode. If that user is not requesting to view a 1080p video stream, there is no reason for the other party to encode and transmit a 1080p stream. If that user then decided to expand to full-screen, however, the MCU would dynamically change the stream resolutions. This allows for efficient processing and bandwidth utilization on the MCU and the endpoints.

The largest benefit to this technology is seen by the A/V Conferencing Server. Although this role has never encoded or transcoded media, only with the introduction of H.264 SVC is Lync Server now able to introduce more functionality, without increasing processing requirements. This does, however, increase the processing load on endpoints. Microsoft has always leveraged endpoints for encoding and decoding media streams, for both audio and video. In Lync 2013, this processing load is increased for HD video scenarios, and the details of those requirements are covered in the "Peer-to-Peer Video Endpoint Requirements" section.

19

Microsoft's H.264 SVC Implementation

Now that we have a basic understanding of how H.264 SVC works, let's cover how Microsoft chose to implement H.264. As with all codecs, there are many variations of H.264 SVC, and although it is a "standards based" codec, companies often choose to implement them in different ways.

Microsoft partnered with Polycom, HP, and LifeSize to form the Unified Communications Interoperability Forum (UCIF), which was focused on creating specifications and guidelines for common UC protocols. From this partnership, Microsoft also announced that it would be adopting the H.264 SVC technology that Polycom developed. The version of H.264 SVC that Microsoft has adopted supports many different configuration modes; however, Microsoft has chosen to implement only two of these configuration modes in Lync 2013:

▶ UCConfig Mode 0—Non-Scalable Single Layer AVC BitStream

▶ UCConfig Mode 1—SVC Temporal Scalability with Hierarchical P

The additional modes are these:

▶ UCConfig Mode 2q—SVC Temporal Scalability + Quality/SNR Scalability

▶ UCConfig Mode 2s—SVC Temporal Scalability + Spatial Scalability

▶ UCConfig Mode 3—Full SVC Scalability (Temporal + SNR + Spatial)

With each mode, a new level of scalability is introduced. Each mode is additive, and in the end you are left with Full SVC Scalability.

Mode 0 essentially means that no scalability is supported. This mode should be supported by all systems that support this type of H.264 SVC Codec. This mode will most likely be important in Interop scenarios in the future. This mode does allow for multiple streams to be sent, but not multiple frame rates per resolution. Table 19.1 shows an example of the Mode 0 layers that would be available.

TABLE 19.1   H.264 SVC Mode 0 Sample Layers

Stream	Layer
1	1080p 30fps
2	720p 30fps
3	360p 30fps

Mode 1 introduces temporal scaling. This level of scalability starts to introduce some of the "cool" stuff that H.264 SVC can do. With Mode 1, the endpoint can send a single video stream per resolution for multiple frame rates. The receiving endpoint can then decide whether it wants to display that resolution at 30fps, 15fps, or 7.5fps by dropping entire frames of the video sequence. For example, if the highest frame rate sent is

30fps, the receiving endpoint could scale down to 15fps by dropping every other frame it receives. Table 19.2 shows an example of H.264 SVC Mode 1 Layers.

TABLE 19.2   H.264 SVC Mode 1 Sample Layers

Stream	Layers		
1	1080p 30fps	1080p 15fps	1080p 7.5fps
2	720p 30fps	720p 15fps	720p 7.5fps
3	360p 30fps	360p 15fps	360p 7.5fps

Lync 2013 leverages H.264 SVC UCConfig Mode 1 for video conferencing functionality. There are three more UCConfig Modes that are included in the spec published by Microsoft and Polycom; one would assume that this functionality will be introduced in later releases.

In addition to the flexibility that H.264 SVC provides, Microsoft has also added dynamic Forward Error Correction (FEC). If you are not familiar with FEC, in short, it allows for media streams to be dynamically rebuilt in packet-loss scenarios. This functionality, combined with H.264 SVC, provides room for impressive video quality on any type of network connection.

As you can see, H.264 SVC introduces the flexibility required for many of the new features in Lync 2013. H.264 SVC allows Lync 2013 to enhance the video conferencing quality, and functionality, without increasing the load on the A/V Conferencing Server. By introducing H.264 SVC as the default video codec in Lync Server 2013, Microsoft has also opened the door for many new interoperability scenarios. Because H.264 is the base for many standard video codecs, integration with systems that use a compatible version of H.264 will allow for higher quality and simplified video interoperability scenarios.

Peer-to-Peer Video Bandwidth Requirements

As mentioned before, the new functionality in Lync 2013 does not come without a price. Let's be honest—many organizations are not even using HD video today because of the network impact. Many organizations are moving toward adopting and supporting this technology, but for the majority of organizations it is not widely deployed yet. Table 19.3 lists some bandwidth examples for Lync 2013 that are provided by Microsoft.

TABLE 19.3   Lync 2013 Bandwidth Requirements

Quality	P2P or Single View	
	Bandwidth (Max)	Resolution
Minimum	100Kbps	160×90
Okay	250Kbps	424×240
Good	1,500Kbps	1280×720
Optimum	4,000Kbps	1920×1080

When comparing the bandwidth numbers to those for Lync 2010, you can see that there is not much of a difference. There is essentially the introduction of 1080p video, which, as you can see, comes with a much larger bandwidth utilization. For organizations currently exploring 1080p video on other platforms, these numbers should be similar to those in the rest of the industry.

One area that Microsoft can improve on is to introduce more bandwidth compression. The H.264 codec does allow for more compression than Microsoft is currently using, with bandwidth reductions up to 50% of what is displayed in Table 19.3. When and whether Microsoft will choose to introduce this technology is unknown. A major caveat of introducing that bandwidth reduction is an even greater processing load on the endpoints.

When organizations are planning for peer-to-peer bandwidth, it is recommended that they consider the max possible bandwidth used in a media stream, which is what is shown in Table 19.3. However, there is the concept of an average bandwidth usage to be considered as well. In video calls, only data that is changed is sent. For example, less bandwidth is used with less movement. If I am sitting still in my office chair, and none of my background is changing, technically less data is being transmitted, and you will see a reduced bandwidth utilization. Additionally, the capability to dynamically reduce the frame rate allows for less bandwidth utilization as well.

Peer-to-Peer Video Endpoint Requirements

In the "H.264 Video" section, it was mentioned that Lync 2013 video requires more processing power on the endpoints for HD video. Although this is true, Microsoft has also introduced the capability for hardware-accelerated encoding and decoding. Hardware acceleration is the use of a graphical processing unit (GPU) for encoding and decoding of video. Rather than using the software and the primary CPU, this processing load can be offloaded to the GPU chip. Hardware-accelerated video encoding and decoding is available on many modern platforms. This can be included in processors, graphics cards, and even USB webcams. Microsoft supports the following types of hardware acceleration in Lync 2013:

▶ H.264 Encoding, with support for Intel HD Graphics accelerating processing units (APUs) on second- or third-generation SandyBridge and IvyBridge CPUs

▶ Second-Generation Advanced Micro Devices (ARM) fusion APUs

▶ H.264 HW Encoding based on USB Video Class v1.5 Standard

Because of hardware acceleration, Lync 2013 now supports HD video on endpoints with dual-core CPUs, removing the previous requirement for quad-core CPUs. Table 19.4 outlines the hardware requirements that are provided from Microsoft for video. It is important to note, in addition to CPU requirements, Microsoft is also leveraging WinSAT scores to determine capabilities. For encoding, VideEncodeScore is leveraged and for decoding GraphicsScore is used. Hardware accelerated decoding is also available using DirectX Video Acceleration (DXVA).

TABLE 19.4   Lync 2013 Video Endpoint Requirements

Capable Encode Resolution	Capable Decode Resolution	Requirement	Notes
424x240	424x240	1 core and VideoEncodeScore >4.0	No DXVA and No Hardware Acceleration
640x360	640x360	2 Cores and VideoEncodeScore >4.5	
640x360	1280x720	2 Cores and VideoEncodeScore >4.5	
640x360	1920x1080	4 Cores and VideoEncodeScore >4.5	
1280x720	1280x720	4 Cores and VideoEncodeScore >7.3	
1280x720	1920x1080	4 Cores and VideoEncodeScore >7.3	
1920x1080	1920x1080	N/A	
424x240	1920x1080	1 Core and VIdeoEncodeScore >3.0	DXVA but no Hardware Acceleration
640x360	1920x1080	2 Core and VIdeoEncodeScore >4.5	
960x540	1920x1080	2 Core and VIdeoEncodeScore >6.0	
1280x720	1920x1080	4 Cores and VideoEncodeScore >6.7	
1920x1080	1920x1080	4 Cores and VideoEncodeScore >8.2	
1280x720	1920x1080	All 2nd and 3rd Generation Intel HD Graphics	DXVA and Intel HD Graphics Hardware Acceleration
1920x1080	1920x1080	All 2nd and 3rd Generation Intel HD Graphics and GraphicsScore>5.0	

NOTE

Windows 7 has a maximum WinSAT score of 7.9. Therefore, the encoding capability without hardware acceleration can only be achieved on Windows 8 where the maximum WinSAT score is 9.9.

The adoption of H.264 SVC in Lync 2013 expands the endpoints that can participate in HD video conferences. Now even ARM-powered tablet devices will be able to encode and decode HD H.264 video. Also, much like other popular video platforms, USB camera options are available that provide HD video by leveraging an onboard processor for encoding and decoding the media stream.

Organizations deploying Lync 2013 should carefully consider the impact that video will have on existing machines. Even with Lync 2010, some customers would experience issues in which older PCs would be negatively impacted by the Lync client during audio and video calls. This can not only cause a poor user experience for Lync, but also impact other business applications. Before you upgrade to Lync 2013, it is important to perform an audit on the PCs that will be used by end users. If it is known that machines are not capable of supporting high-quality video, the video quality should be restricted using in-band provisioning.

The next section outlines common configuration tasks for peer-to-peer video in Lync 2013.

19

Configuring Peer-to-Peer Video Options

Not only did Microsoft introduce enhanced video functionality in Lync Server 2013, but in Lync Server 2013 administrators are able to have greater control over Lync video functionality through in-band provisioning.

In Lync 2010 video bandwidth could be controlled through two key policies: the conferencing policy assigned to users, and the media configuration. In addition to these policies, Call Admission Control (CAC) could be used to control video bandwidth across sites.

In Lync 2013 the conferencing policy and CAC configurations remain, but the media configuration policy is no longer used by Lync 2013 servers and users.

> **NOTE**
>
> Lync 2010 clients will still use the media configuration value `MaxVideoRateAllowed`. This should be considered in coexistence scenarios where Lync 2010 clients may be connecting to Lync 2013 Servers.

Although it is called a conferencing policy, in Lync 2013 the conferencing policy still is the place where administrators will control video bandwidth for peer-to-peer and conference calls. The Lync Server 2013 conferencing policy includes new attributes that relate to peer-to-peer video and conferencing calls. These settings can be managed using the following:

- ▶ `Get-CSConferencingPolicy`

- ▶ `Set-CSConferencingPolicy`

- ▶ `New-CSConferencingPolicy`

The new attributes introduced with Lync 2013 are as listed here:

- ▶ **`VideoBitRateKb`**—This setting specifies the maximum video bit rate in Kbps for video that is sent by a user.

- ▶ **`TotalReceiveVideoBitRateKb`**—This setting specifies the maximum allowed bit rate in Kbps for all the video streams that the client receives. It specifies a combined total of all video streams, except for any panoramic video streams.

> **NOTE**
>
> If you enable Gallery View video in Lync conferences, `TotalReceiveVideoBitRateKb` must not be set below 420Kbps, or Gallery View will not work.

- ▶ **`MaxVideoConferencingResolution`**—This setting is for legacy clients only, but it does apply to Lync 2013 conferences. In scenarios with coexistence with Lync 2010 or older clients, administrators should consider configuring this setting as well.

The listed features are used in parallel with CAC, if both are deployed. The conferencing policy will specify how much bandwidth can be used for video irrespective of the path, while CAC will set a bandwidth limit specifically on the media path. For example:

▶ If the `VideoBitRateKb` is set to 500Kbps, and the CAC policy for the media path is set to 250Kbps, the limit will be set to 250Kbps.

▶ If the `VideoBitRateKb` is set to 250Kbps, and the CAC policy for the media path is set to 500Kbps, the limit will bet set to 250Kbps.

The preceding examples are pretty straightforward; the lowest limit will always take effect, which should be the desired behavior. It is important to carefully plan your conferencing policies and CAC configuration together.

A common question asked is how Lync enforces the bandwidth limits for media streams. Lync does not buffer packets because it can cause issues with the real-time media stream. However, Lync does dynamically adjust attributes of the codec to keep in line with the bandwidth rate that is enforced. This can also happen irrespective of any policies or CAC configuration. With video, there are much fewer tweaks that can happen when compared to audio streams; however, it is common for the frame rate and resolution of a video stream to dynamically adjust to respect policy enforcement, or real-time bandwidth congestion.

The "Lync Server 2013 Video Conferencing" section explains how these policies can impact conferencing scenarios.

Lync Server 2013 Video Conferencing

Lync Server 2013 video conferencing sees the greatest benefit from the introduction of the H.264 SVC codec. This codec allows for more video capabilities in conferences, with much fewer server resources. This section covers what the new features introduced in Lync 2013 are, as well as some key requirements for these features.

New Video Conferencing Features

Lync Server 2013 introduces the capability to have HD video in conferences, as well as the capability to view up to five active speaker video streams. However, there are other new features in Lync Server 2013 that should be called out:

▶ **Gallery View**—In video conferences, users can see video of up to five participants at once. If the conference has more than five users, video of the most active five users is shown, and a photo appears for the rest of the users.

▶ **HD Video**—In video conferences, users can now send and receive HD video streams.

▶ **Face Detection**—In video conferences, Lync 2013 automatically tracks and frames the participants' faces. This helps users stay focused on the center of the video stream being sent by other users. Additionally, these framed video streams are used in the Gallery View to provide a consistent video experience in conferences.

▶ **Split Audio and Video**—With Lync 2013, participants can add their video stream to a conference but join audio through another endpoint.

▶ **Video Spotlight**—Presenters are able to "pin" the video spotlight on a participant during a conference. When this is done, every participant sees that video stream in the main window, and this stream will be a full frame and resolution of the video stream, up to HD quality.

Gallery View

A great feature in many video conferencing systems is the capability to view multiple active speaker video streams at once. Some people have referred to this as the "Brady Bunch" view or "Hollywood Squares." Many video conferencing systems provide the capability to view multiple squares of live video from participants. If you think back to the two classic TV shows just mentioned, this reference should be clear.

Before Lync 2013, this was a major feature that Microsoft lacked. With the introduction of H.264 SVC, Microsoft has now enabled this functionality in Lync Server 2013. The new video codec allows the Lync Server 2013 A/V Conferencing Server to provide multiple video streams with very little processing power. If you remember from the earlier sections, H.264 SVC has intelligence that allows for the MCU to act as a simple video switch, while leveraging the endpoints to facilitate which level of video quality it is capable of sending and receiving. Some traditional video conferencing systems leverage very powerful MCUs to actively build the multiple video-stream view and deliver that view to endpoints as a single video stream. This approach requires much more processing power in the central MCU, and this would not work well in a Lync Server environment.

This functionality definitely brings video conferencing in Lync Server 2013 to a whole new level. As you can see in Figure 19.2, Microsoft has implemented this functionality in an extremely elegant way, always focusing on end user experience.

FIGURE 19.2   Lync 2013 Gallery View.

How Does Gallery View Work?

Lync Server 2013 Gallery View works great, and looks great on the client side, but how does it work? The addition of this functionality has introduced another level of intelligence to the Lync Server A/V Conferencing Server. The A/V Conferencing Server in Lync 2010 would actively manage all video streams from participants, but it still was just a video switch and would not encode or decode media. The easiest way to think of this was in the form of a simple on or off switch. Lync 2010 was limited to a single active speaker, and there were only two active video streams in a conference at one time. The current active speaker video stream would be sent to all participants in the video conference, and the previous active speaker video stream would be sent to the new active speaker. Although all participants were sharing their video, they would not be actively sending a video stream until they were designated the active speaker. This helped to reduce the bandwidth requirements and processing load on the A/V Conferencing Server. This is also why there was a slight delay in the video switching to the active speaker.

In Lync 2013 the intelligence is increased to include not only up to five different video streams, but also multiple resolutions and frame rates. The H.264 SVC codec handles most of this functionality. Each video endpoint is responsible for providing the A/V Conferencing Server what it is capable of sending and receiving for video streams. The A/V Conferencing Server is capable of dynamic optimization during a conference, including the following situations:

▶ **New Participants Joining**—When a new participant joins the conference, the A/V Conferencing Server will automatically adjust video streams that are sent and received based on participants who enter and leave the meeting.

▶ **Bandwidth Changes**—For each participant, if the network conditions change at all, the A/V Conferencing Server dynamically adjusts video streams to accommodate.

▶ **Video Window Size Changes**—Each participant has the capability to view video streams in different sizes. The A/V Conferencing Server dynamically adjusts the video streams that are sent and received by each participant however they want to see it. For example, if Randy has his video full-screen, but Alex has his video smaller as part of the presentation window, Tom's video stream will be sent to the A/V Conferencing Server as a full-screen (HD) stream, but Alex will receive only the reduced video size. If Randy was to shrink his video window and HD video was no longer needed from Tom, then Tom would stop sending HD video to the Conferencing Server.

▶ **Forward Error Correction**—Forward Error Correction is built into the Lync Server and Lync Client media codecs. This is the capability to rebuild media streams in packet-loss scenarios. Essentially, if packet loss is detected, FEC will kick in and endpoints will start sending redundant packets. The receiving endpoint then has the intelligence to rebuild the media stream with the packets it receives. The A/V Conferencing Server is also able to use FEC for video conferencing scenarios.

Lync Server 2013 video conferencing utilizes much of the same intelligence described previously for non–Gallery View conferences. The only difference between regular video conferences and Gallery View conferences is that there are more than two streams to manage for a conference; other than that, the way the A/V Conferencing Server functions is the same.

19

Server Requirements for Video Conferencing

In Lync Server 2013 the dedicated A/V Conferencing Server role that was introduced with Lync Server 2010 has been removed. This might come as a shock, especially considering the introduction of 1080p video to Lync video conferences. However, it shows how powerful the H.264 SVC codec is, and how much it really has allowed Microsoft to expand on video conferencing technology with little processing requirement on the servers.

With that said, the A/V Conferencing Server role will always live in a Lync Front End server. This can be part of an Enterprise Edition Pool, or a Standard Edition Server. Table 19.5 outlines the requirements for each.

TABLE 19.5   Lync 2013 Video Conferencing Server Requirements

Server Role	CPU	Memory	Disk	Network
Enterprise Edition	Dual processor, quad core 2.0 GHz or higher OR Quad processor, dual core 2.0GHz or higher	16GB	2 or more 10KRPM disks with at least 72GB disk space	1Gbps or higher; 2 NICs recommended for redundancy
Standard Edition	Dual processor, quad core 2.0 GHz or higher OR Quad processor, dual core 2.0GHz or higher	16GB	4 or more 10KRPM disks with at least 72GB disk space	1Gbps or higher; 2 NICs recommended for redundancy

As you can see, this information is the same as the requirements for any Lync Front End server. It is more important to understand that the A/V Conferencing Server role is now always collocated with the Lync Front End server.

Video Conferencing Bandwidth Requirements

Many organizations that look to deploy video conferencing might be worried about the bandwidth requirements, and this is a perfectly reasonable concern. In Lync 2013, the introduction of up to five active video streams can have a major impact on the network. Additionally, the support for 1080p video in conferences must carefully be planned for. When planning for conferences without Gallery View, organizations should reference Table 19.3, which is valid for conferencing scenarios without Gallery View. Table 19.6 outlines the bandwidth requirements for Lync 2013 video conferencing with Gallery View.

TABLE 19.6   Lync Server 2013 Bandwidth Requirements

Quality	Five Gallery View Streams	
	Bandwidth (Max)	Resolution
Minimum	420Kbps	90×90
Okay	1,000Kbps	240×240

Quality		Five Gallery View Streams
Good	2,500Kbps	360×360
Optimum	4,000Kbps up to 8,000Kbps	540×540 or two 1080×1080

Although five Gallery View video streams can require a large amount of bandwidth, it is probably not as much as many people would originally estimate. The reason for this is that it is not possible for a single endpoint to receive multiple high-resolution video streams. Screen real estate will always be limited, and therefore it is not possible for a single endpoint to receive five 1280×720 video streams (which would require 7500Kbps of bandwidth). If you consider a modern PC display that could handle a 1920×1280 resolution, it would be possible to fit only a single full 1280×720 video stream and then one-half of a second video stream at that same resolution.

Instead of attempting to send five full-resolution video streams to conferencing participants, Lync Server 2013 sends smaller, square versions of the original video stream. It is because of this functionality that Gallery View in Lync Server 2013 does not exponentially increase bandwidth utilization as video streams are added.

Configuring Video Conferencing Options

Many of the configuration policies used for peer-to-peer video sessions are also used for video conferences in Lync Server 2013. This is where the use of the conferencing policy actually makes sense, in conferencing scenarios. Administrators can manage video conferencing settings and bandwidth through conferencing policies in addition to Call Admission Control. These settings can be managed using the following:

▶ Get-CSConferencingPolicy

▶ Set-CSConferencingPolicy

▶ New-CSConferencingPolicy

As a reminder, the new attributes introduced with Lync 2013 are as shown here:

▶ VideoBitRateKb—This setting specifies the maximum video bit rate in Kbps for video that is sent by a user.

▶ TotalReceiveVideoBitRateKb—This setting specifies the maximum allowed bit rate in Kbps for all the video streams that the client receives. It specifies a combined total of all video streams, except for any panoramic video streams. This is important for conferencing scenarios, specifically with Gallery View.

▶ AllowMultiView—This setting specifies whether users can schedule conferences that allow the Lync 2013 Gallery View, showing up to five active video streams. This setting applies to the organizer of the conference, not to the attendees.

19

▶ **EnableMultiViewJoin**—This setting specifies whether users can join conferences that allow the Lync 2013 Gallery View. This setting is applied at the per-user level, meaning you could have a conference with users who can see the Gallery View, and users who are not allowed to see the Gallery View.

> **NOTE**
>
> If you enable Gallery View video in Lync conferences, `TotalReceiveVideoBitRateKb` must not be set below 420Kbps, or Gallery View will not work.

▶ **MaxVideoConferencingResolution**—This setting is for legacy clients only, but it does apply to Lync 2013 conferences. In scenarios with coexistence with Lync 2010 or older clients, administrators should consider configuring this setting as well.

For more details on how these configuration options coexist with Call Admission Control, see the earlier section "Configuring-Peer to-Peer Video Options."

Lync Server 2013 Data Conferencing

The term *data conferencing* is a generic term used to describe sessions among two or more participants that involve sharing computer data in real time. In the UC world this is often referred to as web conferencing and can include the sharing of applications, desktops, and other content through a UC desktop application or a web browser. Web conferencing is at the core of enhanced collaboration across organizations. In Lync Server 2010, Microsoft collapsed all web conferencing functionality into the Lync 2010 client, providing enhanced conferencing functionality all in a single UI. With Lync 2013, Microsoft has added new features and fine-tuned existing features to provide an even greater web conferencing experience for users.

New Data Conferencing Features

Lync Server 2013 introduces key new features that make Lync Server 2013 a best-in-class conferencing solution for organizations of all types. This includes the following features:

▶ **Join Launcher**—When a client of any type attempts to join a meeting, the web service will validate each meeting before launching a client. This allows for a better user experience if there is an error contacting the meeting. In Lync 2010, meeting join failures on mobile and desktop clients were not very informative for end users. The new Join Launcher helps to provide users with more information on the meeting join process. Additionally, this consolidates the meeting join functionality for all clients on computers and mobile devices.

▶ **PowerPoint Sharing with Office Web Apps**—Lync Server 2013 now requires Office Web Apps Server to handle PowerPoint presentations. The use of this server allows for higher-resolution display of PowerPoint presentations and better support for enhanced PowerPoint capabilities.

▶ **Archiving Updates**—When organizations configure integrated archiving with Exchange Server 2013, any documents that are shared in meetings will also be placed into the Exchange Archiving Store. This includes PowerPoint presentations, attachments, whiteboards, and polls.

In addition to adding this functionality, Microsoft has spent a significant amount of time fine-tuning the media codecs used for desktop and application sharing. This provides a greater experience when sharing applications with high-end graphics and real-time media.

Lync Server 2013 data conferencing is made up of three content sharing types: desktop sharing, collaboration content, and PowerPoint sharing. These next few sections outline exactly what functionality is included in each content sharing type, and provide a technical overview of how Lync Server 2013 makes all of this work.

Desktop Sharing

Desktop sharing in Lync 2013 is the capability to broadcast a Lync user's desktop to another Lync client in peer-to-peer and conferencing scenarios. Lync Server 2013 utilizes the Remote Desktop Protocol (RDP) over RTP to deliver the desktop media stream between Lync users. Presenters can share any number of monitors that are used on the PC, as well as specify a single application to be shared.

Lync Server 2013 introduces performance tuning to the RDP codec used for desktop sharing in the Lync client. Specifically, Lync 2013 increases application sharing performance for applications with media. This can include CAD, and other applications that might include animations or high-quality graphics.

How Does Desktop Sharing Work?

In Lync Server 2013 the Application Sharing Conferencing Server service is responsible for desktop and application sharing in conferences. This role is installed on all Lync Front End servers, and is one of the many MCUs in Lync Server 2013. Because each Lync Server handles all conferencing modalities, the boundaries for each MCU are often mixed up. The following list describes the MCUs in Lync Server 2013, and what they are used for:

▶ **Web Conferencing**—Manages conferencing data collaboration (see the section "Collaboration Content" for more information).

▶ **A/V Conferencing**—Manages audio and video media streams in conferences.

▶ **IM Conferencing**—Manages Instant Messaging conferencing in conferences.

▶ **Application Sharing Conferencing**—Manages desktop and application sharing media streams in conferences.

19

> **NOTE**
>
> In Lync Server 2010 a Legacy Web Conferencing MCU was installed on each Front End server, providing access to legacy conferencing scenarios involving the Live Meeting 2007 client. This role is not included in Lync Server 2013, which must be considered for migration scenarios from OCS 2007 R2 to Lync Server 2013.

The App Sharing MCU was introduced in Lync Server 2010, and in Lync Server 2013 the functionality remains the same. The key functionality that this MCU allows for is the capability to present and share control of specific applications. This MCU uses the following protocols:

▶ **C3P/HTTP**—The C3P protocol is used to communicate conferencing control commands. C3P over HTTP is used by the conferencing servers to communicate with each other.

▶ **C3P/SIP**—Lync clients also communicate with the conferencing server using C3P to create conferences and to communicate changes to the conference. For Lync clients this is done securely over SIP.

▶ **SIP/SDP**—Application and desktop sharing traffic is delivered over RTP, and because of this, Session Description Protocol (SDP) is used to establish the RDP over RTP media stream. Lync clients communicate with the App Sharing MCU over SIP to perform this negotiation and establish a media stream.

▶ **RDP/RTP**—Lastly, the desktop and application sharing media stream uses the RDP codec, and it is delivered over an RTP media stream.

Application and desktop sharing is also available in peer-to-peer sessions between two users. These sessions do not interact with the App Sharing Conferencing Server, because they are only between two participants. These sessions do use the same protocols and the functionality is very much the same as in conferences.

It is important not to overlook the bandwidth requirements for desktop sharing. The Microsoft RDP codec can provide very high-quality desktop sharing capabilities; however, this can come at a huge cost in bandwidth utilization. Bandwidth utilization for desktop sharing is dynamic, and can fluctuate depending on many variables such as these:

▶ Resolution of the shared desktop

▶ Application that is shared

▶ Amount of movement in shared desktop

▶ Number of monitors shared

These factors can cause Lync Server 2013 desktop sharing to use up to 10Mbps of bandwidth. On average, desktop sharing in peer-to-peer and conferencing scenarios use between 70Kbps and 2Mbps. Administrators should consider controlling this functionality, while still considering the end-user experience. Limiting the bandwidth available for desktop sharing will limit the quality of the sharing experience. Lync Server 2013 allows administrators to control the bandwidth used by application sharing in the Lync conferencing policy. See the "Configuring Data Conferencing Options" section for more information on how to configure these polices. When you are controlling the bandwidth used by Lync desktop sharing, it is important to understand that reducing the bandwidth used will only degrade the sharing frame rate. At this time, it is not possible to adjust color depth, resolution, or other quality factors in Lync Server 2013. If bandwidth is limited for Lync desktop sharing, users will have a negative experience, but this might be required to maintain network capacity in certain scenarios.

Although Lync 2013 application and desktop sharing can use up to 10Mbps of bandwidth, more realistic numbers are provided in Table 19.7. These numbers are provided by Microsoft as guidance for network scaling, assuming common usage scenarios.

TABLE 19.7   Lync Server 2013 Desktop Sharing Bandwidth Requirements

Modality	Bandwidth	
	Average (Kbps)	Max (Kbps)
Application sharing using RDP	434 sent per sharer	938 sent per sharer

It is best practice for organizations to use the bandwidth estimates referenced in Table 19.6 when planning to implement Lync Server 2013 desktop sharing.

Collaboration Content

Lync Server 2013 allows users to collaborate in real time during conferences by sharing whiteboards and polls. Virtual whiteboard functionality was introduced in Lync Server 2010 and is one of the most commonly used collaboration features in Lync Server. Whiteboards allow users in a Lync conference to collaborate in real time on drawings, pictures, tables, and more. Polling functionality is often used in web conferences to collect participant feedback. Many presenters utilize this functionality to either understand the audience they have in front of them, or collect feedback after a presentation. The polling functionality in Lync Server 2013 allows presenters to collect feedback that can be kept private, or shared with the audience. Additionally, the results of the polls can be exported by the presenter.

How Does Collaboration Content Sharing Work?

The Web Conferencing Conference Service is responsible for managing collaboration content sharing in conferences. This service is installed on all Lync Front End servers. When whiteboards and polls are shared during a meeting, the content is created and stored in the Lync Server File Store defined for the pool of the conference organizer. This content is then distributed to conference participants over HTTPS. Internal and external users connect to the web service URLs defined in topology. For external users, this traffic travels through the reverse proxy solution deployed.

19

When a presenter decides to share a whiteboard or poll, the presenter uploads the content to the conference using the Persistent Shared Object Model (PSOM) protocol. This protocol is a Microsoft proprietary protocol that has been used in web conferencing since OCS 2007 and the Live Meeting products. In addition to the initial content upload, any modifications of a whiteboard are submitted using the PSOM protocol. See the diagram in Figure 19.3 for the content upload and download process in a web conferencing scenario.

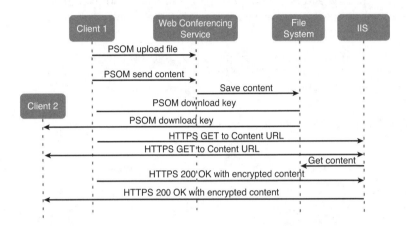

FIGURE 19.3   Content upload over PSOM and download over HTTPS.

In Figure 19.3, client 1 is a presenter in the conference who is sharing a whiteboard. The details of the whiteboard sharing process are described below:

1. Client 1 sends a PSOM upload request to the web conferencing service.

2. After the conferencing service validates the request, the client sends the actual whiteboard content to the service.

3. The Web Conferencing Service saves the content to the Lync file store defined for that pool. This content is created in a subfolder specific to the organizer and the conference.

4. The Web Conferencing Service then sends the presenter and participants a download URL and key to be used when making the HTTPS download request. This request is sent to the Lync clients over PSOM.

5. Each client then sends an HTTPS request to the Lync Web Services for the content.

6. The Lync Web Services requests the content from the file store, and delivers this to each user over HTTPS.

In Lync Server 2013, if archiving is enabled, any content including whiteboards and polls that are uploaded to a meeting will be archived. If Exchange Server integration is enabled, this content will be archived in to the Exchange Server data store.

Lync Server 2013 collaboration content sharing does not have a major network bandwidth impact on many organizations. The data that is sent and received during meetings is often very small. However, organizations that are expecting a heavy usage of this functionality should consider the read and write impact on the file servers that will be maintaining the Lync file store. Table 19.8 is provided by Microsoft for file activity capacity planning for Content Collaboration sessions.

TABLE 19.8   Lync Server 2013 Content Collaboration Upload and Download Rates

Modality	Usage in Bytes per 10,000 Users	
	Average Usage	Max Usage
Web Conferencing Service content upload and download	Received: 706,655 bytes Sent: 860,224 bytes	Received: 17,803,480 bytes Sent: 19,668,079 bytes

PowerPoint Sharing with Office Web Apps

Lync Server 2013 introduces a complete overhaul to the PowerPoint sharing experience in conferences. In Lync Server 2010 PowerPoint content was delivered using the Web Conferencing Service. Although this worked, it provided limited functionality. PowerPoint presentations were often delivered at low quality, and given the Silverlight requirements in Lync 2010, the content was not viewable on a wide range of devices. In Lync Server 2013, Office Web Apps Server is used to provided PowerPoint sharing in conferences.

Office Web Apps Server is a product designed to deliver browser-based versions of Microsoft Office applications. This server is required in any Lync deployment using conferencing. Without this server role, users will not be able to share PowerPoint presentations.

Using Office Web Apps Server for PowerPoint sharing in Lync Server 2013 has the following benefits:

▶ **Support for more devices**—Because Office Web Apps Server is designed to work with products that support the Web Application Open Platform Interface protocol (WOPI), nearly any device with a web browser can now view PowerPoint sharing in Lync Server 2013. Additionally, with the introduction of the HTML5-based Lync Web App, this functionality is natively integrated to that experience, and allows for conferencing support on many endpoints.

▶ **More PowerPoint Functionality**—Lync Server 2013 allows users to share high-resolution PowerPoint presentations that include slide transitions and animations. In Lync 2013, the transitions and animations play during the presentation; this functionality was not available in previous versions of Lync. In Lync Server 2013 conferences, users with appropriate privileges are able to scroll through a PowerPoint presentation independent of the presentation itself. Additionally, if videos are embedded in a PowerPoint presentation, Lync conferences support synchronous playback of videos to participants.

The Office Web Apps Server or Server Farm used by Lync Server 2013 does not have to be a dedicated deployment. Organizations can leverage a shared infrastructure to support their SharePoint, Exchange, and Lync deployments that require Office Web Apps.

Supported Office Web Apps Server Topologies

The actual process of integrating Office Web Apps Server and Lync Server 2013 is covered in Chapter 11, "Dependent Services and SQL." This section provides a brief overview of how to plan for integration of your Office Web Apps Server installation with Lync Server 2013.

Option 1: Office Web Apps Server Installed On-premises in the Same Network Zone as Lync Server 2013   In this configuration, the Office Web Apps Server farm is installed on the organization's network and ideally in the same network zone as the Lync Server. It is not a requirement for the server to be installed in the same network zone; however, this does reduce the administration overhead of configuring firewall rules and routing. With this topology, internal Lync clients connect to the Office Web Apps Server using an internally defined URL, and any external clients connect through the reverse proxy solution to an externally defined URL. This topology works best for organizations that are deploying a dedicated Office Web Apps Server farm for Lync Server 2013. Figure 19.4 shows how the topology would look.

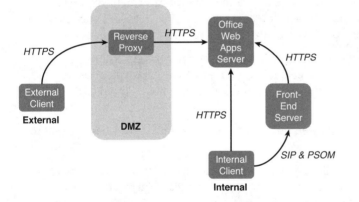

FIGURE 19.4   Office Web Apps Server on-premises on an internal network.

Option 2: Office Web Apps Server Installed On-premises in the DMZ   Because Office Web Apps Server is able to provide services to Lync, Exchange, and SharePoint, some organizations might also choose to deploy this server in the DMZ. In this configuration both internal and external clients are routed through the reverse proxy server to access the Office Web Apps Server. This topology is ideal for organizations that are looking to deploy a shared Office Web Apps Server Farm for multiple server technologies. Figure 19.5 shows how this topology would look.

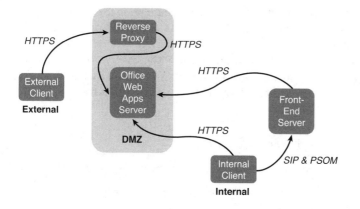

FIGURE 19.5   Office Web Apps Server on-premises in the DMZ.

Option 3: Office Web Apps Server as a Hosted Service Outside the Internal Network   Office Web Apps Server can also be provided as a third-party hosted service. In this topology, Lync Server 2013 is deployed on-premises but uses an externally hosted Office Web Apps Server. Figure 19.6 shows how this topology would look.

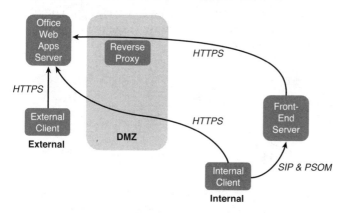

FIGURE 19.6   Office Web Apps Server hosted on an external network.

Firewall requirements for all of these scenarios are outlined in Chapter 12, "Firewall and Security Requirements." However, it is important for organizations that are planning an Office Web Apps Server deployment to take note that not only the Lync clients but also the Lync Front End server must be able to communicate with the Office Web Apps Server farm.

Topology Impacts
Each Lync Front End Pool will establish connections with the configured Office Web Apps Server farm in order to establish PowerPoint sharing sessions for conferences. The

PowerPoint file is stored with Lync Server, but the delivery mechanism is the Office Web Apps Server. The Lync Front End server acts as a facilitator for all conferencing modalities; it is responsible for establishing a session with the Office Web Apps Server and then providing each Lync 2013 client with a URL to view and modify the content on the Office Web Apps Server. The URL that is provided depends on the location of the user, and the topology defined. Table 19.9 outlines the content URL that is used based on the topology and client location.

TABLE 19.9   Lync Server 2013 Office Web Apps Content URLs

Web Apps Server Configuration	Lync Client Location	Content Download URL
Internal	Internal	Internal URL
Internal	External	External URL
External	Internal	External URL
External	External	External URL

Configuring Data Conferencing Options

As with Lync video conferencing, administrators can control data conferencing functionality through a set of policies that are delivered in-band by the Lync Server. Lync conferencing policies are used to control data conferencing functionality. These policies are managed using the following PowerShell commands:

▶ Get-CSConferencingPolicy

▶ Set-CSConferencingPolicy

▶ New-CSConferencingPolicy

This section explains common conferencing policy attributes that are used for Lync Server 2013 data conferencing.

▶ **AllowAnnotations**—This setting will indicate whether or not annotations will be allowed on any content shared during a meeting. Additionally, this setting determines whether or not whiteboard sharing is allowed in a conference. This setting applies to the organizer of the conference.

▶ **AllowParticipantControl**—This setting will control whether or not meeting participants are able to take control of desktops or applications that are shared during a meeting. This setting applies to the organizer of the conference.

▶ **AllowPolls**—This setting will control whether or not users are allowed to create polls during online meetings. This is also a setting applied based on the organizer of the conference.

▶ **AppSharingBitRateKb**—This setting can be used to define the maximum bit rate in kilobits that can be used for application sharing. Administrators should use this to control the bandwidth used by each application and desktop sharing session. This setting will apply to peer-to-peer and conferencing sessions.

▶ `AllowUserToScheduleMeetingsWithAppSharing`—This setting specifies whether an organizer can schedule a meeting with application and desktop sharing. This setting applies to the organizer of the conference. If this is set to false, any conference the organizer schedules will not allow app sharing of any type. If this is set to true, and administrators wish to limit what certain users can share in meetings, they should set the `EnableAppDesktopSharing` attribute.

▶ `EnableAppDesktopSharing`—This setting controls what type of applications are able to be shared in a conference. Administrators can specify the following options:

> `Desktop`—Users are able to share their entire desktop.

> `SingleApplication`—Users are allowed to share only a single application.

> `None`—Users are not allowed to share any applications or their desktop.

This setting is enforced at the per-user level. For example, some users in the conference might be allowed to share their desktop, some might be allowed to share an application, and some might be allowed to share nothing.

▶ `EnableDataCollaboration`—This setting controls whether users can organize meetings that allow the sharing of whiteboards and annotations.

▶ `DisablePowerPointAnnotations`—This setting applies specifically to PowerPoint sharing in Lync Server 2013. If this is set to `true`, users cannot annotate PowerPoint presentations. However, if `AllowAnnotations` is set to `true`, users have access to whiteboard functionality.

Lync Server 2013 provides administrators with the ability to enable or disable functionality for data conferencing scenarios at the organizer, and the participant level. This is important because some participants may require restrictions on content that they can share, but they should be able to join meetings that include application or desktop sharing sessions.

Summary

Lync Server 2013 provides video and data conferencing functionality that empowers users to efficiently collaborate from anywhere. Lync Server 2013 was released with an emphasis on providing high-definition video to as many endpoints as possible, and in conferencing scenarios. Lync Server 2013 also introduced the capability for conference participants to share high-quality, interactive PowerPoint presentations.

The combination of new video conferencing functionality and data conferencing functionality in Lync Server 2013 enables organizations to collaborate through Unified Communications without any sacrifices. The Lync Server 2013 platform is also extremely flexible, allowing organizations to configure policies that adapt Lync Server 2013 functionality to their technical and business requirements.

19

CHAPTER 20

Video Integration with Third-Party Products and Services

Microsoft Lync Server has been capable of integrating with third-party video systems for some time now, but the coexistence story has been murky, with a multitude of vendors and different forms of integrations available, each with its own set of caveats or restrictions. The interoperability has also been hampered by Microsoft's use of a proprietary codec, RTVideo, for any kind of high-quality video.

Starting with Lync 2013, Microsoft has moved to using the industry-standard H.264 codec, which will likely improve the integrations available. This does not mean that all H.264 equipment is suddenly compatible with Lync, because there are still differences in the signaling layers and profiles used within the codec. In fact, as of this writing, no third-party integrations qualified or supported with Lync 2013.

This change will allow Lync endpoints and the third-party endpoints to negotiate HD resolutions up to 1080p, which will certainly improve the desktop user experience, and open many new possibilities in conference rooms, but those integrations are not available yet. This chapter focuses on how third-party video conferencing was integrated in Lync Server 2010 and should serve as a foundation for those looking to integrate in Lync Server 2013. Many of the concepts and methods described in this chapter are still relevant, although the codec, video quality, and features available in each case might change slightly.

Signaling Gateways

The first type of video integration that ever existed between Lync, or OCS, and third-party systems was achieved using a signaling gateway. In this scenario, a SIP trunk exists between a Lync pool and the third-party system's control unit. This is not the same type of SIP trunk used with Mediation Servers for voice calls, nor is it defined and managed the same way. A Mediation Server does not proxy video as part of its back-to-back user agent (B2BUA) model, so video calls to other systems must be managed differently.

Trusted Applications

Integration with a signaling gateway is achieved by first defining the third-party systems as trusted applications within the Lync Topology. The definition as a trusted application is what allows the Lync systems to establish a connection to other servers or endpoints that are not actually Lync systems.

Before a trusted application can be created, administrators must first define a trusted application pool in the topology. After the trusted application pool is created, the trusted application representing the third-party system can be created.

Static Routes

Next, a static route must be created for a particular matching SIP URI, and then pointed to the trusted application pool as a next hop. This URI is typically a separate SIP namespace, but there is nothing that prevents an organization from using the same SIP URI as used for Lync.

Figure 20.1 demonstrates the logical structure of this integration.

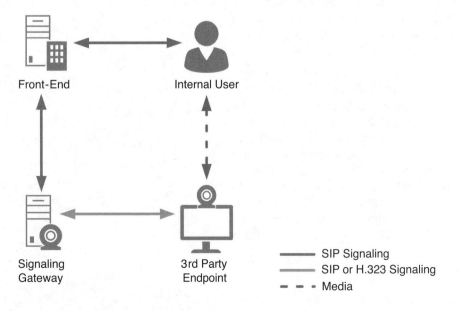

FIGURE 20.1   Trusted application.

Lync operates similarly to Exchange's Internal Relay method for an accepted domain with respect to a shared SIP domain. It first attempts to resolve a URI internally, and only if no match is found does it route the call to the third-party system.

> **NOTE**
>
> The concept of sharing the same domain was not possible in Office Communications Server 2007 R2 and was only first introduced in Lync Server 2010.

The end result is that Lync will send audio or video calls for a matching URI to the trusted application pool as a next hop, which is the third-party system.

The overall process can be simplified with this logical summary and is depicted in Figure 20.2.

1. Lync user `tom@companyabc.com` places a video call to `randy@video.companyabc.com`.

2. Lync determines `video.companyabc.com` is not an internally supported SIP domain.

3. Lync locates the static route for `video.companyabc.com`, which points to a next hop defined as `videogateway.companyabc.com`.

4. Lync forwards the SIP Invite message to `videogateway.companyabc.com`.

5. The `videogateway.companyabc.com` device determines that it is authoritative for the video and rings endpoint registered as `randy@video.companyabc.com`.

6. The third-party user `randy@video.companyabc.com` receives the incoming video call.

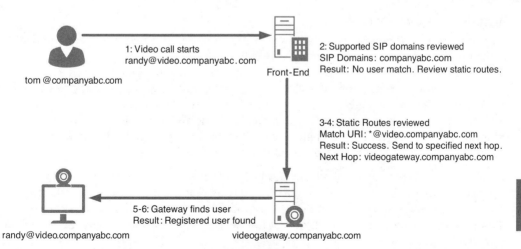

FIGURE 20.2 Static route to a third-party system.

The third-party endpoint can be registered to the signaling gateway via SIP or H.323, depending on the product. The signaling gateway might even accept a mixture of the two protocols among endpoints.

Codec Support

This form of integration is very basic, and ultimately relies on the fact that both video endpoints support the same video codec. The signaling gateway and Lync Front End pool communicate via SIP to provide the signaling traffic, but the Lync user's endpoint and the third-party system's user endpoint must have direct IP connectivity to send the media stream between each other. For many years this kind of integration was limited to H.263 CIF quality video using a 352×288 resolution, which was entirely due to the fact that the third-party endpoints did not support Microsoft's RTVideo codec at any resolution. Without any RTVideo support, the only available option was to fall back to H.263 CIF.

The fact that the integration is limited to such a low-quality resolution generally limits the use case to desktop video. For traditional video systems placed in conference rooms and connected to a high-definition television, this low-resolution quality looks especially terrible on a large screen.

> **NOTE**
>
> The Lync 2013 client no longer supports H.263 CIF video, and it will not be offered as an available codec during the media negotiation process. Keep this in mind when planning the client upgrade strategy if there is any existing interoperability with third-party video systems.

Integration Limitations

This form of integration historically provided a very limited feature set between the two systems. The capability to make and receive calls works well, but little or no presence information is shared between Lync users and the other system. Lync users can add the third-party endpoints to a contact list, but the presence will always appear as "Presence Unknown." This is not a great experience for the end users because there is no way to tell whether the user on the other end is actually online and available. Even worse, if the third-party endpoint is in a conference room, there is not a way to determine whether someone else has a meeting in progress at that time.

There is also no capability to share any kind of content between the two systems in this scenario. Calls are purely an audio and/or video conversation, and information shared by one side is not visible to the other. The protocols Lync uses for sharing desktops, PowerPoint, whiteboards, and polls do not follow the standards traditionally used in video conferencing systems.

This type of integration typically does not support media encryption, or remote user connectivity, and becomes a single point of failure between the two systems. If the signaling gateway is unavailable, there is no way for the third-party endpoints to contact the

Lync endpoints and vice versa. Most signaling gateways support some form of high-availability with redundant pairs in an active/active or active/passive configuration.

Namespace Considerations

With any signaling-gateway integration, it is very important to spend time planning the namespaces and to determine whether any overlap exists. With Lync 2013 it is possible to use the same SIP namespace within Lync and the third-party system, but there is no requirement to do so. Many organizations use separate domains or subdomains for the video infrastructure to logically separate components such as using companyabc.com for Lync users and video.companyabc.com for video endpoints.

Using the same namespace presents a unified appearance to external partners, but can introduce additional challenges. Lync clients have historically used specific SRV records for remote sign-in, but Cisco clients can have overlap with some of these records.

Additionally, a large amount of SIP traffic will be passed between the two systems when sharing a SIP domain. This is because each system must first attempt to resolve a user internally whenever a presence request is made, and then forward that request to the opposite system if there is no internal match. The large amount of unnecessary traffic being passed back and forth can cause issues depending on the signaling gateway's hardware specifications.

If separate namespaces are used, presence requests will be forwarded only for contacts belonging to the opposite system's namespace. It also helps uniquely identify where the traffic will ultimately terminate.

> **NOTE**
>
> Even if a separate namespace is used for the video endpoints, it might still be of some value to configure the additional namespace support within Lync. It should not be assigned to any users as a SIP domain, but this will allow federation requests to flow through the Lync infrastructure and reach the video endpoints.

Gateways

In Polycom's infrastructure the signaling gateway product used to achieve this type of integration is called the Distributed Media Application (DMA). The previously described configuration with a static route is still valid for integration with a Polycom DMA. Organizations can even have multiple DMAs in a single location for redundancy, or place DMAs in separate geographical locations with different static routes pointing to each DMA.

When a DMA is used, there is a signaling connection between the Front End pool and DMA, but all media traffic is directly between the Lync endpoint and the Polycom endpoint.

The Cisco equivalent of Polycom's DMA is called Video Communication Server (VCS). Both of these products do much, much more in traditional video communication than the Lync integration discussed here, but they do provide this base level of interoperability.

NOTE

The static route methodology discussed previously applied to Cisco VCS versions prior to 7.x. The back-to-back user agent (B2BUA) was introduced in version 7 and provides some additional functionality.

Back-to-Back User Agent

Cisco introduced the back-to-back user agent starting in version 7 of the VCS platform, which provides a simplified configuration for Lync integration. To start with, the static route is completely gone from the equation and should actually be removed as part of the upgrade process if it previously existed.

The B2BUA serves a similar role for video as the Lync Mediation Server does for audio calls, and it terminates two independent calls. The difference from a static route configuration is that the endpoints no longer relay media directly to each other. Instead, the Cisco video endpoint sends a stream to the B2BUA, and the Lync endpoint does the same on the opposite side. The B2BUA does not do any kind of media transcoding or scaling, so the two endpoints still need to support the same codec as if they were still relaying traffic directly.

Although this approach simplifies the integration, it does introduce a bottleneck in the deployment because all video between the two systems must now pass through the B2BUA. This can be an issue for calls between two internal systems that must now traverse the WAN to pass through the B2BUA.

The B2BUA also enables a feature called FindMe by Cisco, which enables the B2BUA to synchronize Lync presence with a user's Cisco endpoint and fork calls between the systems. The idea here is that if a user receives a call on his Cisco endpoint, his Lync client will ring and be answered at either endpoint. The same is true for calls to the user's Lync endpoint.

Edge Traversal

The DMA does not support Lync Edge Server connectivity, so calls between remote Lync clients and DMA endpoints must be performed on the internal network.

The B2BUA works only for calls within the internal network by default, but can be configured to communicate with the Lync Edge Server in order to relay traffic for remote users. This capability works only with the B2BUA mode, and requires an OCS Enhanced Collaboration key to be loaded on the VCS control system.

The Edge traversal is achieved by providing a username and password that is already provisioned for Lync, or specifically provisioned to provide Edge connectivity in to VCS. This username will register to Lync, receive Media Relay Authentication Service (MRAS) credentials, and then be used to support calls between Lync users and internal or remote endpoints registered to VCS.

Native Registration

Another type of integration used by third-party systems is native registration to Lync Front End pools where the third-party system's video endpoint registers to Lync just like any other endpoint. In many cases, the third-party endpoint supports dual-registration so that it can maintain a connection to its traditional control system, and simultaneously stay registered to Lync, as depicted in Figure 20.3.

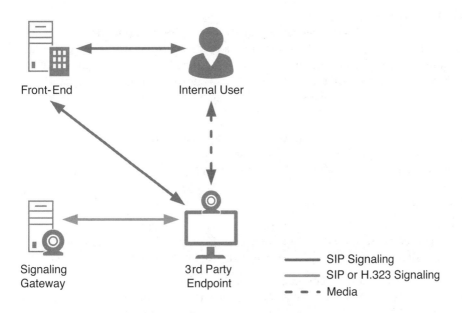

Front-End

Internal User

Signaling
Gateway

3rd Party
Endpoint

SIP Signaling

SIP or H.323 Signaling

Media

FIGURE 20.3   Native Lync registration.

The process for this is usually much more straightforward and involves minimal server configuration. A user account is created to represent the third-party endpoint, and the endpoint is then configured with those credentials. The process will vary slightly depending on the vendor, but it generally requires a server name, SIP address, username, and password. The endpoint then uses NTLM authentication to authenticate to the Front End pool, and then behaves like another Lync user.

20

> **NOTE**
>
> The fact that NTLM authentication is required is an important point. If an organization disables NTLM authentication for security reasons, third-party endpoints will be unable to register to the Lync server.

The advantage to this method is that it provides presence for the endpoint so that other Lync users can tell whether it is available or currently in a call. This solves a number of problems, and results in a much more refined user experience. Seeing "Presence Unknown" for every third-party endpoint is confusing to end users because there is no notification that this is expected, so it appears there is an error with Lync. Having the presence reflected even unidirectionally is a big step forward.

Video Codec Support

Just as is the case with using a signaling gateway, this form of integration relies on the third-party endpoint and the Lync endpoint sharing a common codec within their media stack. This common codec was also traditionally H.263 CIF quality, so even with native registration the video quality with a Lync 2010 client was not very clear on large screens. Even if the codec supported native registration and Lync presence, the video quality was still limited to 352×288.

Polycom was the only vendor to add native support for RTVideo, which was introduced as an RTVideo license key for their HDX codec series. This change enabled a regular Lync client to conduct a CIF, VGA, or 720p-quality peer-to-peer video call using RTVideo.

Conferencing

The same Polycom feature key for RTV also enabled CCCP (C3P) support in Microsoft Lync organized conferences, so a Polycom HDX could participate in a Lync conference. Users were able to drag and drop an HDX into an existing Lync conference.

Although the HDX can join a Lync conference with the RTV feature key, it does not provide interoperability for all features. Specifically, the sharing modalities for desktop sharing, PowerPoint, whiteboards, and polls do not function for an HDX in a Lync meeting.

However, the fact that Polycom supported this functionality is a significant advantage over competing solutions. LifeSize endpoints can join a Lync conference if the UVC Video Engine is in place, but it does not actually support CCCP like Polycom. All the other vendors can only use multiparty conferencing with Lync endpoints by leveraging a multi-point Control Unit (MCU), discussed later in this chapter.

Edge Traversal and More

Native registration to Lync also allows for additional features to be used, such as STUN/TURN and secure RTP media encryption. The signaling gateway scenario usually only allows for calls to work within the internal network. Since the signaling gateway does not register to a Lync Edge Server, no remote or relay candidates are presented during the media negotiation phase, and the calls will fail if a remote Lync user has not connected a VPN before calling a third-party system.

With native registration the third-party endpoint will receive MRAS credentials from the Lync Edge Server and present remote and relay candidates when participating in Lync calls, enabling remote users to seamlessly connect without VPN.

Additionally, native registration will support secure RTP transport of the media stream. The signaling gateway method provides an unencrypted media stream between Lync endpoints and the third-party systems.

Polycom endpoints also support Lync Enterprise Voice features, so they can be enabled for inbound and outbound voice calls. The dial-plan normalization rules are applied by the Lync server, but dial plans, voice policies, and conferencing policies can all be assigned to an HDX account. Another advantage to this native registration is that Polycom supports Lync Call Admission Control policies. No other vendor supports this functionality today.

Media Transcoding Gateways

Another approach to integrating with Lync is to use a media transcoding gateway. This gateway typically works in conjunction with a signaling gateway to provide additional capabilities, such as the capability to transcode different codecs between two endpoints. For example, a third-party endpoint can send 720p H.264 video to the media transcoding gateway while a Lync endpoint can send 720p RTVideo to the same gateway. The media transcoding device then transcodes, or converts, the streams to the appropriate formats for each endpoint. The endpoints do not communicate directly in this scenario, so the third-party endpoints maintain an H.264 peer-to-peer conversation with the gateway, and the Lync client maintains an RTVideo peer-to-peer conversation with the gateway.

Figure 20.4 shows an example of the traffic flow in this scenario.

This approach works around the limitation of Lync and the third-party endpoint only supporting H.263 CIF as a common codec, and allows for higher-resolution video to take place between the two systems. The disadvantage here is that just as with a signaling gateway, the media transcoding gateway becomes a single point of failure.

Hardware Versus Software

Media transcoding gateways can be either hardware- or software-based, which generally determines the price point. The Cisco Advanced Media Gateway is an example of a hardware-based transcoding device that is typically deployed to provide HD video integration with legacy Cisco/Tandberg systems. This system comes at a fairly significant price point that puts it out of reach for many organizations.

LifeSize, on the other hand, provides a software-based media transcoding device as part of the UVC platform. The UVC platform can be deployed on a virtual infrastructure, so it is limited by the hardware an organization runs it on rather than what a vendor bundles and ships.

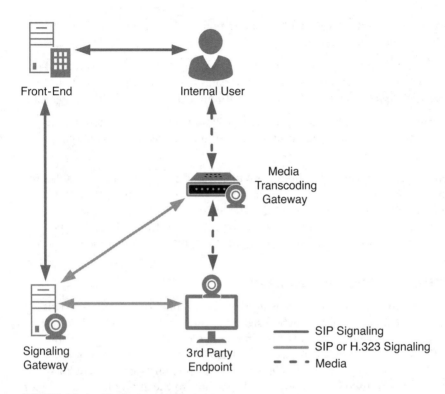

Front-End

Internal User

Media Transcoding Gateway

Signaling Gateway

3rd Party Endpoint

——— SIP Signaling

——— SIP or H.323 Signaling

- - - Media

FIGURE 20.4   Media transcoding gateway.

Any kind of transcoding gateway requires a significant amount of processing power, so these types of products generally can handle only a handful of simultaneous calls.

Media Flow

It is important to understand that all media must pass through this gateway to be converted when using a media transcoding gateway. This is not an issue for SIP signaling traffic, but it can have a significant impact on the user experience when the media transcoding gateway is located across a WAN connection.

Consider a scenario in which a Lync endpoint and third-party endpoint are in the same office, but the media transcoding device is in a datacenter geographically far from the office. Instead of relaying the traffic between the two endpoints in a peer-to-peer sense, both endpoints must submit their media stream across the WAN connection to the media transcoding gateway, as shown in Figure 20.5. The voice and video quality might suffer depending on the latency between the office and the datacenter.

Considerations When Using Media Transcoding

When vendors support interoperability with Lync 2013 endpoints using H.264 video, the media transcoding gateways will become largely irrelevant, and, unfortunately for the companies that invested in one, not of much use. As of this writing, it is hard to recommend that any organization invest in a media transcoding gateway unless there is a plan to support Lync 2010 endpoints for a long time.

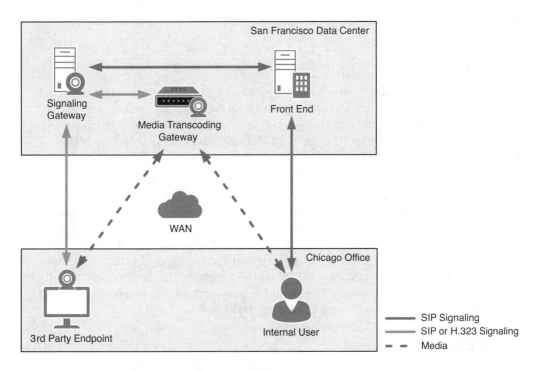

FIGURE 20.5   Media transcoding gateway WAN.

Cisco also requires the OCS Enhanced Collaboration key to support SRTP media encryption when making calls with the Advanced Media Gateway, which comes at an additional cost.

LifeSize has an interesting approach with the UVC Video Engine for Microsoft Lync product. A UVC Video Engine server is typically deployed in each branch on a virtual host in order to minimize WAN usage or the hairpin behavior introduced by the Cisco AMG. The other notable feature is that the media transcoding gateway is used only when available, so it does not become a single point of failure within the network. If the LifeSize product is offline or unavailable when a user tries to make a call, the call is simply made in standard definition rather than failing.

Multipoint Control Units

Multipoint Control Units, or MCUs as they are more commonly called, allow for multiple participants to interact in a conference. The MCU is in control of the conference and determines what codecs are used, who is a presenter, and which video to show, and it mixes the audio. It is a complicated and critical component in conferences.

The Lync A/V MCU service is a software-based MCU that provides this functionality for Lync endpoints, but traditional video conferencing has used a hardware-based MCU. Polycom has a product called the RMX, and Cisco has their own MCU, previously called the Codian devices while under the Tandberg name. The shortcoming of a hardware-based MCU is that it has a fixed hardware specification and can handle a limited number of total participants.

Layout Control

Traditional MCUs, however, have previously provided features that Lync did not include. Until Lync Server 2013, only active-speaker switching for video was available in conferences, which meant that only one video stream could be seen at a time. The only exception was if a participant used a Polycom CX5000 device (previously called the Microsoft Roundtable), and then a panoramic room view would be shown in addition to the active speaker.

Third-party MCUs are capable of showing multiple video streams in a single conference, which is referred to as continuous presence. Many products also include the capability to customize the layout of the video streams in a conference, or overlay text to identify specific users or locations. Lync Server 2013 does allow for up to five concurrent video streams to be displayed and has the capability to pin specific video streams for viewing, but still falls short of the flexibility provided by third-party MCUs. For the vast majority of use cases, the native Lync functionality should be sufficient, but there might be cases in which it's still advantageous to use a third-party MCU.

Interoperability

One specific use case that Lync does not solve on its own is the capability to conduct a conference using many types of endpoints. The Lync MCU can host a meeting with Lync endpoints and third-party endpoints using native Lync registration, but there is no support for any other third-party systems or partners to join a Lync meeting using traditional video endpoints.

Using a third-party MCU for hosting a meeting can allow both Lync endpoints and traditional video endpoints to participate in a single meeting. These meetings typically are limited to audio and video only because the protocols used for content sharing differ, but there are some workarounds that have been implemented, such as sending the content share as a video stream to Lync endpoints.

Cisco endpoints are unable to join any Lync Meetings because they do not register to the Lync server at all. The B2BUA signaling gateway provides presence updates for the Cisco endpoints, but does not facilitate any kind of conferencing or C3P support, so calls between VCS endpoints and Lync are limited to two-party connectivity.

The only form of conferencing available between Cisco and Lync endpoints must occur on a Cisco MCU or more advanced codecs that include a built-in MCU that Cisco refers to as Multiway. Lync endpoints can be joined into a Multiway conference, which is hosted on the Cisco endpoint rather than a dedicated MCU. These built-in Multiway bridges typically scale up to about four calls, which actually covers a good majority of ad hoc or smaller conferences.

Virtual Meeting Rooms

Integration with a Polycom RMX was traditionally done as a signaling gateway, but Polycom has expanded on the native registration concept by allowing RMX-hosted Virtual Meeting Rooms (VMRs) to also register to Lync. A VMR is a virtual conference that exists on an RMX either persistently or for a period of time, but is a configured meeting space where conferences can be conducted and third-party endpoints or Lync endpoints can join the conference at any time.

Polycom's RMX has the capability to register the VMRs as a Lync endpoint and provide presence to other users, enabling them to see whether a VMR is currently occupied. Organizations can create multiple VMRs that users can leverage as huddle spaces, or virtual conference rooms for meetings.

This integration is accomplished by defining the RMX as a trusted application within a trusted application pool. A Lync-enabled Active Directory account is then provisioned for each VMR with a username that matches the name of the VMR. The password is irrelevant because the RMX will act on behalf of the VMR user accounts through the trusted application definition, and register the users with Lync to provide presence updates.

Edge Traversal

Yet another advantage of the Polycom RMX MCU is its capability to register with the Lync Edge Server and receive MRAS credentials. This enables any RMX VMR to provide remote and relay candidates for media relay during the ICE negotiation process, so remote Lync users can seamlessly join meetings hosted on the RMX.

Cisco's MCUs are not directly capable of this Edge registration, so users must be on the internal network or VPN to connect to a Cisco MCU-hosted conference.

> **NOTE**
>
> Keep in mind that the Edge traversal discussed here is specific to enabling remote Lync endpoints to join a conference and that remote third-party endpoints are not capable of joining the meeting through a Lync Edge Server. Third-party vendors usually provide a similar border element to facilitate remote standards-based endpoints joining a meeting such as Polycom Video Border Proxy (VBP) or Cisco's VCS Expressway (VCSe).

If an organization has deployed the B2BUA with Edge registration, it might be possible to connect a remote user to a Cisco MCU, but that feature is dependent on the OCS Enhanced Collaboration license key.

Cloud MCUs

An emerging trend in the video conferencing industry is the move from an on-premise hardware- or software-based MCU to a cloud-hosted MCU. Companies such as Blue Jeans and Polycom have already started to introduce services with these features. The advantage to this approach is that an organization can limit the on-premise investment in MCUs, which was sometimes very cost-prohibitive in the case of a hardware-based MCU. Software-based MCUs generally came at a lower price point, but a hosted subscription model in the cloud is becoming a very popular concept.

The shift to these cloud MCUs has also sparked new possibilities for interoperability that were previously not considered with traditional MCUs. For example, Blue Jeans supports nearly any type of endpoint all joining the same meeting through their service including Lync, Skype, Google, Polycom, Cisco, LifeSize, traditional H.323 systems, or even clients through a web browser. The frustrating days of trying to configure a meeting between two partners using different video vendors are addressed by using a cloud service that supports nearly any type of system.

Cloud MCUs might sound very attractive, and they certainly do have their advantages, but there is a level of control that is lost, as is the case with any cloud service. There are options to customize and control meetings, but a traditional on-premise MCU typically has many more options available to administrators.

The other consideration with a cloud MCU is that all video traffic is going out to the Internet and back, even for calls that only involve the organization, as shown in Figure 20.6. A call that might have typically traversed the WAN or stayed on the internal network now requires a significant amount of Internet bandwidth. The cloud MCU might or might not make sense depending on an organization's network architecture and Internet service.

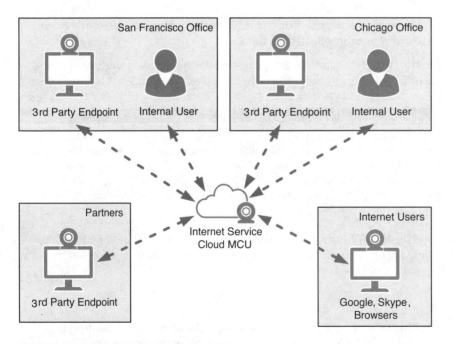

FIGURE 20.6   Cloud MCU interoperability.

Software Plugins

Some organizations are providing video interoperability to Lync through the use of a software plugin on the desktop clients. These plugins effectively replace the capability to make Lync video calls using Lync, and instead are a shim for placing the call through the plugin, but still presented on the user's desktop as if the user made a Lync call. Examples of this include Cisco's CUCILYNC plugin and Avaya's Aura product. The pitch with these products is generally along the lines of selling the organization on managing the video in a single system the business has already invested heavily in. The disadvantage is that these products typically require additional licensing, limit the great features within Lync, and result in a really poor, and confusing, end-user experience.

End-User and Client Confusion

These products bolt onto the Lync user interface and provide contextual menus for launching a video call using their backend system rather than Lync video. It's important for IT administrators to carefully plan the deployment and ensure that the appropriate Lync options are disabled so that users don't see two different video call options, which of each might work differently.

Edge Traversal

These products also don't work seamlessly without VPN like the Lync client. Consider a basic scenario in which a remote Lync user signs in without VPN, but then has to manually establish the VPN connection before placing an audio or video call. It is technically possible to implement the system this way, but user adoption typically suffers and the response to the deployment will probably not be favorable.

Software Updates

Organizations deploying these software plugins become dependent on the plugin vendor to certify and approve all updates to Lync servers and clients going forward. It's conceivable that a future update will change how the plugin interacts with the Lync client, or even break some other functionality. Businesses might end up being unable to upgrade servers or clients to fix one issue just because the software plugin is no longer compatible.

Summary and Comparison

This section covers some specific examples of products developed by vendors that fit into each of the categories discussed in this chapter. This is not meant to be an exhaustive list of every product available, but is meant to provide an overview of typical solutions used.

Signaling Gateway Vendor Examples

This list highlights the vendors that support native registration to a Lync server:

▶ **Polycom DMA**—The Polycom DMA provides a connection point for standards-based video endpoints and flexible routing rules.

▶ **Cisco VCS**—Cisco VCS is a very similar product to the Polycom DMA and also provides standards-based integration and registration among H.323, SIP, and ISDN systems.

▶ **Radvision SCOPIA Video Gateway**—The Radvision product provides signaling integration between Lync endpoints and their H.323 gatekeeper product. It does not provide registration for H.323 devices by itself like a Polycom DMA or Cisco VCS, but it does double as a media transcoding device.

Native Registration Vendor Examples

This list highlights the vendors that support native registration to a Lync server:

▶ **Polycom HDX**—The Polycom HDX codec series supports native Lync registration out-of-the-box. The RTV license key can be added to any of these devices.

▶ **LifeSize Team and Passport**—The Team 220, Unity Series, and LifeSize Passport all support native Lync registration, SRTP for media encryption, and Edge Server traversal.

Media Transcoding Gateway Vendor Examples

This list highlights the vendors that handle media transcoding between Lync and third-party endpoints:

▶ **Cisco Advanced Media Gateway**—The Cisco AMG is an expensive, hardware-based transcoding device.

▶ **LifeSize UVC**—The LifeSize UVC platform is considered a media quality "helper" more than a gateway. The UVC virtual platform is not a single point of failure and enables the call to continue even if it is not available.

▶ **Radvision**—The SCOPIA Video Gateway includes the ability to transcode between H.264 and RTVideo codecs. Multiple gateways can be placed together to add capacity as needed.

Hardware MCU Vendor Examples

The following devices support conferencing for Lync endpoints:

▶ **Cisco MCU**—Cisco's MCUs provide advanced layout and overlay controls for conferences involving standards-based endpoints.

▶ **Polycom RMX**—The Polycom RMX platform is a scalable system that also provides advanced conferencing services for standards-based endpoints.

▶ **Radvision MCU**—The Radvision MCU allows for layout flexibility and virtual rooms. A SCOPIA Video Gateway must be used to connect Lync endpoints to these MCUs.

Codec with Built-in MCU Vendor Examples

The following codecs or endpoints include a built-in MCU that can be joined by Lync endpoints through either native registration or a signaling gateway:

▶ **Cisco C Series and EX Series**—Conferences hosted on a Cisco endpoint must be joined through the VCS signaling gateway.

▶ **Polycom HDX with Multipoint**—Multipoint conferences on an HDX endpoint can be joined through native registration or through Lync.

▶ **LifeSize Team 220 and Room 220**—Conferences hosted on a LifeSize endpoint are joined via Lync native registration.

Cloud MCU Vendor Examples

The following cloud-based video services support some form of Lync integration:

▶ **Blue Jeans**—Currently supports the highest number of video platforms, including Lync, Skype, Google, H.323, and browsers.

▶ **Polycom CloudAXIS**—Integrates with other systems for address-book functionality and allows browser-based conferencing.

Software Plugin Vendor Examples

The following products can be considered a software plugin method for providing third-party video:

▶ **Cisco UC Integration for Microsoft Lync (CUCILYNC)**—Cisco's product that integrates with VCS and Cisco Unified Communications Manager. All the media is done through Cisco's plugin rather than the Lync client.

▶ **Avaya Microsoft Lync Integration**—Previously called Microsoft ACE, this product behaves similarly to CUCILYNC and ensures that all the media occurs within Avaya infrastructure.

The video integration story is constantly changing, and always improving as vendors find new methods for providing interoperability. As video vendors begin to support integration with Lync Server 2013, the codec changes will conceivably allow for high-definition conferences to occur between Lync and third-party endpoints as vendors. Microsoft has certainly opened the door to more possibilities with the media stack changes introduced in Lync Server 2013.

20

PART VII

Integration with Other Applications

IN THIS PART

CHAPTER 21

Exchange and SharePoint Integration

Previous versions of Lync have featured some useful integrations with Microsoft Exchange and SharePoint, and these have proven to extend the value of all three of the products. With Lync 2013, Microsoft continues to support these same hooks into Exchange and SharePoint, and is introducing some additional integrations that are available with the 2013 versions of these applications. This chapter focuses on the details behind these integration features that will no doubt provide additional value for many organizations that deploy these applications together.

Server-to-Server Authentication

To allow Lync 2013, Exchange 2013, and SharePoint 2013 systems to communicate securely with each other, the OAuth (OpenAuthentication) protocol is used. OAuth certificates allow the exchange of security tokens that grant access to resources for a time. Server-to-server authentication and authorization using OAuth is required for any of the integration features described in this chapter. For a full description of the process used to request and install an OAuth certificate for Lync Server 2013, see Chapter 11, "Dependent Services and SQL."

After an OAuth certificate is installed on the first Lync 2013 Front End Server in the environment, the certificate is automatically replicated to other Lync Servers via Central Management Store replication, thereby establishing the required trust relationship between Lync servers. Similarly, Exchange 2013 and SharePoint 2013 use certificates to establish trust with other servers running the same software. However, for Lync 2013 to establish trust with Exchange 2013 and SharePoint 2013, the certificates on both sides must first be exchanged, and then the applications must also be configured as partner applications on both sides. A partner application is any application that Lync 2013 can exchange security tokens with directly, without the need for a third-party security token server.

To facilitate the certificate exchange between systems, each application features an authentication metadata document, which contains the certificates and other authentication information required to establish trust. The metadata documents are then exposed to the other application using a web service, as described in the sections that follow.

Exchange 2013 Autodiscover Configuration

An initial prerequisite that must be met to allow integration between Lync, Exchange, and SharePoint is the configuration of the Exchange 2013 Autodiscover service. The Exchange 2013 Autodiscover service is used by both Lync and SharePoint to find and read the Exchange authentication metadata document; therefore, Autodiscover must be configured and operational before these applications are configured as partner applications for Exchange. In mixed Exchange environments that include both Exchange 2010 and Exchange 2013, Lync and SharePoint should be configured to connect to the Exchange 2013 Autodiscover service.

Exchange Autodiscover can be configured using the `Set-ClientAccessServer` cmdlet, for example,

```
Set-ClientAccessServer -Identity ex2k13.companyabc.com
➥-AutoDiscoverServiceInternalUri https://autodiscover.companyabc.com/autodiscover/
➥ autodiscover.xml
```

Additional tasks that are required for Autodiscover to function include the configuration of a DNS host record for the service, as well as the installation of a server certificate assigned to IIS that includes the Autodiscover name as a subject alternative name.

TIP

As part of the Exchange 2013 installation, a self-signed certificate named Microsoft Exchange Server Auth Certificate is created and placed in the local certificate store of each system. This default server authentication certificate is automatically associated with the server authentication configuration, and is suitable for this purpose. On Client Access Server systems, however, an additional self-signed certificate is created and assigned to IIS and other Exchange services; this certificate must be replaced with a server certificate from an internal or third-party certificate authority before integration with Lync is established. The reason for this is that Lync will attempt to connect to the Exchange 2013 Autodiscover service hosted on IIS to read the Exchange authentication metadata document, and the certificate must be trusted for this connection to succeed. At a minimum, the certificate must include the Autodiscover FQDN as a subject alternative name to enable Lync to successfully connect to the Exchange authentication metadata document.

The following sections provide details on the procedures required to establish server-to-server authentication between these systems.

Configuring Lync and Exchange as Partner Applications

After Autodiscover is configured, Lync and Exchange can be configured as partner applications by exchanging certificates using the authentication metadata documents exposed on each side. On the Exchange 2013 side, a PowerShell script named `Configure-EnterprisePartnerApplication.ps1` is provided, and is used to connect to the URL of the Lync 2013 metadata document and retrieve the required information from it. The default URL for the Lync authentication metadata document is https://<LyncFqdn>/metadata/json/1, where <LyncFqdn> is the fully qualified domain name of a Lync Front End Server. For example, the following procedure would be used to configure Lync as a partner application for the `companyabc.com` Exchange 2013 deployment:

1. Log on to a system where the Exchange 2013 administrative tools are installed using an account that has administrative rights to Exchange.

2. Open the Exchange Management Shell, and navigate to the Exchange scripts directory, which is by default `C:\Program Files\Microsoft\Exchange Server\V15\Scripts`.

3. Execute the following command:

   ```
   .\Configure-EnterprisePartnerApplication.ps1 -AuthMetadataUrl
   ➥https://lyncse1.companyabc.com/metadata/json/1 -ApplicationType Lync
   ```

4. If the command is successful, the script creates a disabled user account linked to the partner application, and assigns several Exchange management roles to the account to grant the required permissions, as shown in Figure 21.1.

FIGURE 21.1   Configuring Lync as a partner application in Exchange.

5. To prepare the system for new OAuth connections, execute the `iisreset` command on both the Client Access and the Mailbox Servers in the site.

On the Lync 2013 side, the `New-CsPartnerApplication` cmdlet is used to configure Exchange 2013 as a partner application for Lync. The default URL for the Exchange authentication metadata document is https://autodiscover.<domain>/autodiscover/metadata/json/1, where <domain> is the DNS domain of the Exchange systems. For example, follow these steps to configure Exchange as a partner application for the `companyabc.com` Lync deployment:

1. Log on to a system where the Lync administrative tools are installed using an account that is a member of the `CsAdministrator` group, and has administrative rights on the local system.

2. Open the Lync Server Management Shell, and execute the following command:

   ```
   New-CsPartnerApplication -Identity exchange -ApplicationTrustLevel full
   ➥-MetadataUrl https://autodiscover.companyabc.com/autodiscover/metadata/json/1
   ```

3. If the command is successful, the properties of the new partner application are displayed, as shown in Figure 21.2.

FIGURE 21.2   Configuring Exchange as a partner application in Lync.

After Lync and Exchange have been configured as partner applications, server-to-server authentication between the systems can be tested by using the Lync Server Management Shell to execute a synthetic transaction. The `Test-CsExStorageConnectivity` cmdlet has been provided for this purpose. This synthetic transaction uses OAuth to write an item into the conversation history folder of an Exchange 2013 mailbox, and then optionally deletes the item. For example, the following command is used to test server-to-server authentication between Lync and Exchange for `companyabc.com`, specifying the SIP URI of a Lync user who has an Exchange 2013 mailbox:

```
Test-CsExStorageConnectivity -SipUri jrico@companyabc.com -Binding NetTCP
➥-DeleteItem -HostNameStorageService lyncse1.companyabc.com
```

Configuring Lync and SharePoint as Partner Applications

Before Lync and SharePoint are configured as partner applications, certificates must be installed for each application. For Lync, server authentication certificates are installed as part of the Lync deployment process. For SharePoint, certificates are not installed by default as part of the deployment process; therefore, at least one server certificate must be installed and mapped to a SharePoint site before server-to-server authentication with Lync is configured.

After the certificates are installed on both sides, Lync and SharePoint can be configured as partner applications by exchanging the certificates using the authentication metadata documents exposed on each side. On the SharePoint 2013 side, the `New-SPTrustedSecurityTokenIssuer` cmdlet is used to connect to the URL of the Lync 2013 metadata document and retrieve the required information from it. The default URL for the Lync authentication metadata document is https://<LyncFqdn>/metadata/json/1, where <LyncFqdn> is the fully qualified domain name of a Lync Front End Server. For example, the following procedure would be used to configure Lync as a partner application for the `companyabc.com` SharePoint 2013 deployment:

1. Log on to a system where the SharePoint 2013 administrative tools are installed using an account with local administrative rights on the system, and that has been assigned the `securityadmin` fixed server role on the SharePoint SQL instance, as well as the `db_owner` fixed database role on the SharePoint SQL databases.

2. Open the SharePoint Management Shell, and execute the following command:

```
New-SPTrustedSecurityTokenIssuer -MetadataEndpoint
https://lyncse1.companyabc.com/metadata/json/1 -IsTrustBroker
➥-Name "Lync trust"
```

3. If the command is successful, the Management Shell displays details regarding the Lync certificate and the new partner relationship.

On the Lync 2013 side, the `New-CsPartnerApplication` cmdlet is used to configure SharePoint 2013 as a partner application for Lync. The default URL for the SharePoint authentication metadata document is https://<SPfqdn>/_layouts/15/metadata/json/1, where <SPfqdn> is the fully qualified domain name of any SSL-enabled web application on the SharePoint 2013 farm. For example, the following procedure would be used to configure SharePoint as a partner application for the `companyabc.com` Lync deployment:

1. Log on to a system where the Lync administrative tools are installed using an account that is a member of the `CsAdministrator` group, and has administrative rights on the local system.

2. Open the Lync Server Management Shell, and execute the following command:

```
New-CsPartnerApplication -Identity sharepoint -ApplicationTrustLevel full
➥-MetadataUrl https://abcsite.companyabc.com/_layouts/15/metadata/json/1.
```

3. If the command is successful, the properties of the new partner application are displayed, as shown in Figure 21.3.

FIGURE 21.3 Configuring SharePoint as a partner application in Lync.

Configuring SharePoint and Exchange as Partner Applications

To enable SharePoint eDiscovery of Lync archive data, SharePoint 2013 must be configured as a partner application to Exchange 2013 as opposed to Lync 2013. The reason for this is that Lync 2013 must first be configured to archive content to Exchange 2013 before SharePoint eDiscovery can be used to search that data. Similar to the configuration of Lync and Exchange as partner applications, the Exchange 2013 Autodiscover service must be configured and operational as a prerequisite before SharePoint and Exchange can be configured as partner applications.

After Autodiscover is configured, SharePoint and Exchange can be configured as partner applications by exchanging the certificates using the authentication metadata documents exposed on each side. On the Exchange 2013 side, a PowerShell script named `Configure-EnterprisePartnerApplication.ps1` is provided, and is used to connect to the URL of the SharePoint 2013 metadata document and retrieve the required information from it. The default URL for the SharePoint authentication metadata document is https://<SPfqdn>/_layouts/15/metadata/json/1, where <SPfqdn> is the fully qualified domain name of any SSL-enabled web application on the SharePoint 2013 farm. For example, the following procedure would be used to configure SharePoint as a partner application for the `companyabc.com` Exchange 2013 deployment:

1. Log on to a system where the Exchange 2013 administrative tools are installed using an account that has administrative rights to Exchange.

2. Open the Exchange Management Shell, and navigate to the Exchange scripts directory, which is by default `C:\Program Files\Microsoft\Exchange Server\V15\Scripts`.

3. Execute the following command:

   ```
   .\Configure-EnterprisePartnerApplication.ps1 -AuthMetadataUrl
   ➥https://abcsite.companyabc.com/_layouts/15/metadata/json/1
   ➥-ApplicationType sharepoint.
   ```

4. If the command is successful, the script creates a disabled user account linked to the partner application, and assigns several Exchange management roles to the account to grant the required permissions.

On the SharePoint 2013 side, the Exchange Web Services Managed API V2.0 must first be installed, and then the `New-SPTrustedSecurityTokenIssuer` cmdlet is used to configure Exchange 2013 as a partner application for SharePoint. The default URL for the Exchange authentication metadata document is https://autodiscover.<domain>/autodiscover/metadata/json/1, where <domain> is the DNS domain of the Exchange systems. For example, the following procedure would be used to configure Exchange as a partner application for the `companyabc.com` SharePoint deployment:

1. Log on to a system where the SharePoint administrative tools are installed using an account that has SharePoint administrative rights.

2. Download Exchange Web Services Managed API V2.0 from the Microsoft Download Center, and install the software using the default installation options.

3. Open the SharePoint Management Shell, and execute the following series of commands:

```
New-SPTrustedSecurityTokenIssuer -name "Exchange" -MetadataEndPoint
➥https://autodiscover.companyabc.com/autodiscover/metadata/json/1
$sts=Get-SPSecurityTokenServiceConfig
$sts.HybridStsSelectionEnabled = $true
$sts.AllowMetadataOverHttp = $false
$sts.AllowOAuthOverHttp = $false
$sts.Update()
$exchange=Get-SPTrustedSecurityTokenIssuer "Exchange"
$app=Get-SPAppPrincipal -Site https://abcsite.companyabc.com
➥-NameIdentifier $exchange.NameId
$site=Get-SPSite https://abcsite.companyabc.com
Set-SPAppPrincipalPermission -AppPrincipal $app -Site $site.RootWeb
➥-Scope sitesubscription -Right fullcontrol -EnableAppOnlyPolicy
```

Exchange Integration Features

With Lync Server 2013, the integrations with Exchange that existed in previous versions will continue to be featured, and several additional integrations are introduced as well. Lync 2013 integrations for Exchange include the following:

▶ Unified contact store (new)

▶ Lync archiving integration (new)

▶ High-resolution photo storage (new)

▶ Outlook Web App integration

▶ Unified Messaging voice mail integration

NOTE

The new Exchange integration features previously listed require both Lync 2013 and Exchange 2013. Therefore, an organization must upgrade both products to the newest versions in order to take advantage of all the Exchange integration features built into Lync 2013.

Unified Contact Store

A brand-new integration feature that is available with Lync 2013 and Exchange 2013 is the unified contact store, which presents a common repository for user contacts that is shared between the Lync and Outlook clients. When it's enabled, the Lync client connects to Exchange Web Services (EWS) to read and maintain contacts instead of using SIP to connect the Lync Front End server for contacts, as in previous versions.

Migrating Users to Unified Contact Store

There are no adjustments to the Lync topology that are required to enable the unified contact store. After the prerequisites for Lync and Exchange integration have been met, the unified contact store is automatically enabled. There are three conditions that must be met for a user's contacts to be migrated to unified contact store:

▶ The user is assigned a user services policy where the UcsAllowed property is set to True (the default).

▶ The user is provisioned with an Exchange 2013 mailbox, and has logged in to that mailbox at least once.

▶ The user logs in to Lync using the Lync 2013 client.

If these three conditions are met, the user's contacts are automatically migrated from the Lync Server database to Exchange 2013. The user can then manage their contacts using Lync 2013, Outlook 2013, or Outlook Web App.

TIP

If a user logs in to Lync using the Lync 2010 or earlier client, and the user's contacts have not already been migrated to unified contact store, the user services policy applied to the user will have no effect, and the user's Lync contacts will remain stored in the Lync Server database. This is also true if the user is not provisioned with an Exchange 2013 mailbox, or has never logged on to the mailbox. If a user logs in to Lync using the Lync 2010 or earlier client after the user's contacts have been migrated to the unified contact store, the contacts will be available and up to date. However, the user will not be able to manage those contacts using the legacy client.

The first time the user logs in to Lync after being enabled for unified contact store, in-band provisioning will cause the user's contacts to be migrated to a new folder in the Exchange 2013 mailbox named Lync Contacts. After the migration is complete, the user is prompted to sign out of Lync and sign back in to access his contacts, as shown in Figure 21.4.

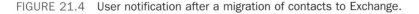

FIGURE 21.4   User notification after a migration of contacts to Exchange.

There are several ways to determine whether a user's contacts have been successfully migrated to unified contact store. From the client computer, the Lync client configuration settings can be viewed to determine the source of the user's contacts. To access the Lync client configuration settings, hold down the Ctrl key and right-click on the Lync system tray icon in the lower-right corner of the desktop, and then select Configuration Information from the menu. Included in the resulting Lync Configuration Information screen is the Contact List Provider, which displays either Lync Server, if the contacts have not been migrated, or UCS, if the contacts have been migrated, as shown in Figure 21.5.

Another way to determine whether the contacts have been migrated from the client side is the following registry key: HKEY_CURRENT_USER\Software\Microsoft\Office\15.0\ Lync\<SIP URL>\UCS, where <SIP URL> is the user's SIP address. If the user's contacts have been migrated, this key will contain a property named InUCSMode, and the value of the property will be 2165. From the Lync Server side, the Lync Server Management Shell can be used to determine whether a user's contacts have been migrated to unified contact store using the TestCsUnifiedContactStore cmdlet. The user's credentials must first be supplied as a parameter, and these are obtained via the Get-Credential cmdlet. The following example shows the commands used to determine the contact migration status for a user:

```
$cred = Get-Credential "companyabc\jrico"
Test-CsUnifiedContactStore -TargetFqdn lyncse1.companyabc.com
➥-UserSipAddress sip:jrico@companyabc.com -UserCredential $cred
```

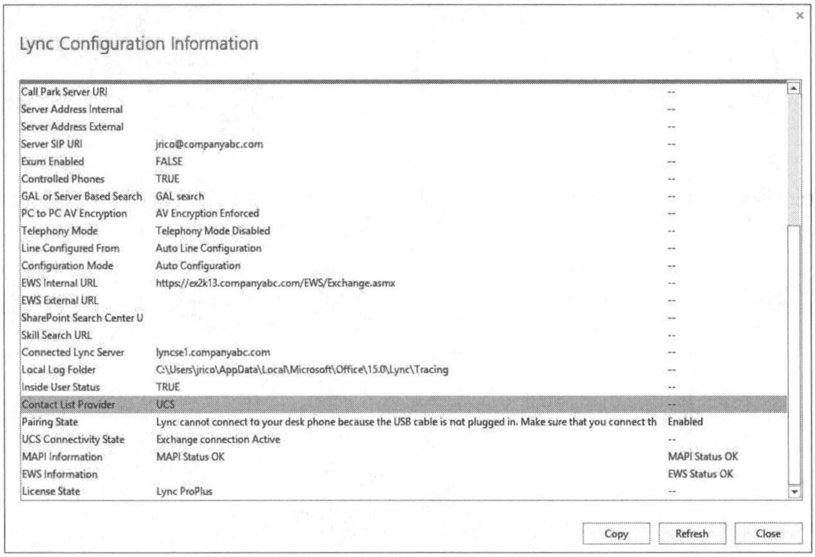

Lync Configuration Information

Call Park Server URI		--
Server Address Internal		--
Server Address External		--
Server SIP URI	jrico@companyabc.com	--
Exum Enabled	FALSE	--
Controlled Phones	TRUE	--
GAL or Server Based Search	GAL search	--
PC to PC AV Encryption	AV Encryption Enforced	--
Telephony Mode	Telephony Mode Disabled	--
Line Configured From	Auto Line Configuration	--
Configuration Mode	Auto Configuration	--
EWS Internal URL	https://ex2k13.companyabc.com/EWS/Exchange.asmx	--
EWS External URL		--
SharePoint Search Center U		--
Skill Search URL		--
Connected Lync Server	lyncse1.companyabc.com	--
Local Log Folder	C:\Users\jrico\AppData\Local\Microsoft\Office\15.0\Lync\Tracing	--
Inside User Status	TRUE	--
Contact List Provider	UCS	--
Pairing State	Lync cannot connect to your desk phone because the USB cable is not plugged in. Make sure that you connect th	Enabled
UCS Connectivity State	Exchange connection Active	--
MAPI Information	MAPI Status OK	MAPI Status OK
EWS Information		EWS Status OK
License State	Lync ProPlus	--

Copy   Refresh   Close

FIGURE 21.5   Using the Lync Client to view the unified contact store status for a user.

The first command causes an interactive prompt for the password user. After the credentials are entered, they are stored in the variable that is referenced in the second command. The end result is then displayed as success or failure. If a failure occurs, error messages can also be displayed to facilitate troubleshooting the issue further.

Selectively Enabling Users for Unified Contact Store

As noted previously, unified contact store automatically becomes available and is enabled when the environmental and systems prerequisites are met. However, in some network envrironments it might be advantageous for a Lync administrator to selectively enable users for unified contact store. This can be accomplished using several Lync Server Management Shell cmdlets that were created for this purpose. Using these cmdlets, users can be enabled globally, by site, by individual user, or by distribution group.

Since unified contact store is enabled by default, if selectivity will be used it is first necessary to disable the feature globally. The following procedure would be used to globally disable the users for unified contact store using the Lync Server Management Shell:

1. Log on to a system where the Lync administrative tools are installed using an account that is a member of the CsAdministrator group, and has administrative rights on the local system.

2. Open the Lync Server Management Shell, and execute the following cmdlet to disable unified contact store for all users:

```
Set-CsUserServicesPolicy -Identity global -UcsAllowed $False
```

After unified contact store has been disabled globally, it can be enabled selectively. For example, the following command would be used to enable the feature for a specific site, in this example, the site named SF:

```
New-CsUserServicesPolicy -Identity SF -UcsAllowed $True
```

To selectively enable individual users for unified contact store, the user policy must first be created, and then applied to the user accounts. For example, the following two commands would be used to first create a policy for enabling the users, and then apply the policy to an individual user:

```
New-CsUserServicesPolicy -Identity "Enable Users for UCS" -UcsAllowed $True
Grant-CsUserServicesPolicy -Identity "John Rico" -PolicyName "Enable Users for UCS"
```

Unified Contact Store Rollback Procedure

At times, it might be necessary to roll back a user's contacts from Exchange to Lync. For example, in a mixed environment if the user's mailbox is moved from Exchange 2013 back to Exchange 2010, or if the user account is moved from a Lync 2013 pool back to Lync 2010, the user's contacts will first need to be rolled back to Lync. This can be accommodated using the `Invoke-CsUcsRollback` cmdlet.

The `Invoke-CsUcsRollback` cmdlet can be executed against a single user by simply including the identity of the user in the command. However, at times it might be necessary to roll back a group of users, for example, an entire pool. This can be accomplished by using the `Get-CsUser` cmdlet to retrieve a specific list of users filtered by the required criteria, and then piping the output to the `Invoke-CsUcsRollback` command. For example, the following command could be used to roll back contacts for an entire pool of users:

```
Get-CsUser -Filter {RegistrarPool -eq "lyncse1.companyabc.com"} |
➥Invoke-CsUcsRollback -Confirm:$False
```

> **TIP**
>
> If a user's contacts are rolled back from Exchange to Lync because the user's mailbox will be moved to Exchange 2010, and then the user's mailbox is subsequently moved back to Exchange 2013, the user's contacts will migrate back to Exchange in 7 days. This behavior is due to the user services policy remaining enabled for unified contact store. If the intention is to prevent the user's contacts from being moved to unified contact store for whatever reason, the user services policy must be adjusted to prevent this.

Lync Archiving Integration

Another new integration feature introduced with Lync 2013 and Exchange 2013 is Lync archiving integration. With Lync archiving integration, Lync archive data is written to a user's Exchange 2013 mailbox instead of the Lync archiving database. The end result is a common repository of archival data that simplifies compliance and eDiscovery tasks across the two communications platforms. Coexistence between the archiving platforms is also supported, such that archive data for some users can be maintained in Lync, while archive data for other users is stored in Exchange. This is particularly beneficial for mixed environments that include both Exchange 2010 and 2013. For example, if an organization is gradually transitioning mailboxes from Exchange 2010 to Exchange 2013, archiving to Exchange is supported for the users with Exchange 2013 mailboxes, and archiving to the Lync Archiving Server can be used for users with Exchange 2010 mailboxes.

When Lync archiving integration is enabled for a user, the archive data is written to the Purges folder in the user's mailbox. This folder is hidden from the user's normal view but is indexed by the Exchange 2013 search engine, and can therefore be viewed using either the MailboxSearch function or SharePoint 2013 Discovery Center. This same folder is also used as the target for the Exchange 2013 in-place hold feature; therefore, all user archive data becomes searchable using a single centralized location.

Archiving Policies in Lync and Exchange

There are several levels of polices that come into play to determine whether Lync archiving integration will be enabled for a user. First, there is the Lync archiving configuration, which can be used to enable or disable archiving integration at the global, site, and pool levels. If archiving to Exchange is enabled at one of these levels, several other policies come into play at an individual user level, depending on whether Lync and Exchange are installed in the same Active Directory forest or in separate forests.

When Lync and Exchange are installed in the same forest, and archiving to Exchange has been enabled within Lync, Exchange 2013 in-place hold policies determine whether archive data will be stored in Exchange. In-place hold policies are used to preserve mailbox items indefinitely, for a specific period, or based on a match of query parameters. Authorized users can place a mailbox user on an in-place hold to allow eDiscovery searches to be performed, either to satisfy litigation requirements or for other purposes. When archiving to Exchange is enabled within Lync, and an in-place hold has been placed on a user's mailbox, the Lync Server 2013 User Replicator will detect this and will enable the user for archiving to Exchange.

When Lync and Exchange are installed in separate forests, and archiving to Exchange has been enabled within Lync, the ExchangeArchivingPolicy parameter applied to the Lync user determines whether archiving to Exchange will be enabled. Four possible values can be configured for the ExchangeArchivingPolicy parameter:

▶ **Uninitialized**—Allows the Exchange 2013 in-place hold settings to determine whether archiving to Exchange is enabled.

▶ **UseLyncArchivingPolicy**—Specifies that archiving to Lync Server should be used rather than Exchange.

▶ **NoArchiving**—Disables archiving for the user, overriding any Lync Server archiving polices assigned to the user.

▶ **ArchivingToExchange**—Enables archiving to Exchange 2013, regardless of whether in-place hold settings are assigned to the user's mailbox.

Archiving Configuration

The first step in configuring Lync archiving integration is enabling this feature using a Lync archiving configuration at the global, site, or pool level. This is accomplished via the Lync Server Control Panel, or the Management Shell using the `Set-CsArchiving Configuration` cmdlet. There is only one global archiving configuration, which is automatically created when Lync is deployed, and is simply named Global. This Global archiving configuration contains default settings that can be changed as needed, but the Global configuration itself cannot be deleted. If additional archiving configurations are created at the pool or site level, these override the same settings that are configured at the global level for the affected users.

In addition to enabling archiving for Exchange, the archiving configuration is used to determine the type of content to archive: IM sessions, web conference sessions, or both. For example, the following procedure is used to enable archiving of IM and web conference sessions to Exchange on a global level, and to purge all archiving data after 120 days:

1. Log on to a system where the Lync administrative tools are installed using an account that is a member of the `CsAdministrator` group, and open the Lync Server Control Panel.

2. In the left pane, select Monitoring and Archiving, and then click the Archiving Configuration tab at the top.

3. Select the Global archiving policy, and then from the Edit drop-down menu, select Show Details.

4. At the Edit Archiving Setting–Global screen, use the drop-down menu under the Archiving setting to select Archive IM and Web Conferencing Sessions.

5. Select the options for Exchange Server Integration and Enable Purging of Archiving Data.

6. Keep the default radio button option of Purge Exported Archiving Data and Stored Archiving Data After Maximum Duration (Days), and then change the number of days to 120.

7. When finished, the configuration should appear as shown in Figure 21.6. Click Commit to save the changes to the Global archiving configuration.

After archiving is enabled within Lync, the next step is dependent on whether the Lync and Exchange systems are installed in the same Active Directory forest, or separate forests. If Lync and Exchange are part of the same forest, Exchange in-place hold polices can be configured against user mailboxes to enable the archiving of Lync data to Exchange. For example, the following command is used in the Exchange Management Shell to create a mailbox search with in-place hold against a user with an Exchange 2013 mailbox:

```
New-MailboxSearch -Description "dross in-place hold" -Name dross
➥-InPlaceHoldEnabled $true -SourceMailboxes dross
```

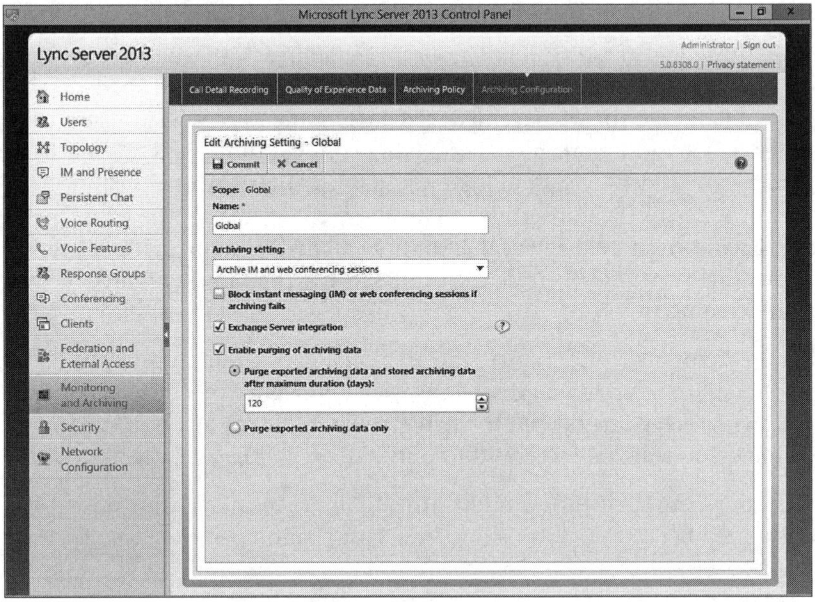

FIGURE 21.6   Archiving to Exchange enabled at a Global level.

After this command is executed, within a few minutes the Lync 2013 User Replicator detects this change and configures Lync to begin archiving to the user's mailbox.

If Lync and Exchange are in separate forests, the ArchivingToExchange parameter can be configured for each Lync user to determine whether archiving to Exchange will be enabled. The ArchivingToExchange parameter can be configured only from the Management Shell, using the Set-CsUser cmdlet. The following example shows the command that is used to configure a user for archiving all data to Exchange:

```
Set-CsUser dross -ExchangeArchivingPolicy ArchivingToExchange
```

After this is executed, all Lync archive data is stored in the user's Exchange 2013 mailbox.

High-Resolution Photos

The capability to use photos with Lync contacts was introduced in Lync 2010, with the source of those photos limited to either the Active Directory user object (using the thumbnailPhoto attribute) or a URL reference to a public website. Although Active

Directory was naturally the better choice for organizations seeking to standardize this feature, many Lync administrators held back from implementing photos in Lync due to concerns with how Active Directory replication would be impacted. For this very reason, limitations were also placed on the resolution of photos that could be used with Lync 2010.

In an effort to circumvent these limitations, Lync 2013 offers additional options for the use of photos by way of integration with Exchange 2013. Although the storage of limited-resolution photos (up to 48×48) using the Active Directory `thumbnailPhoto` attribute is still supported, for organizations that use both Lync and Exchange the use of high-resolution photos stored in Exchange is a much more attractive option. When Lync 2013 and Exchange 2013 are configured for integration, photos of up to 648×648 resolution can be stored as a hidden item at the root of a user's Exchange 2013 mailbox. The photos can be uploaded to the mailbox by the user using Outlook Web App, or by an Exchange administrator using the `Set-UserPhoto` cmdlet in the Exchange Management Shell.

An additional benefit of this new feature is that the upload process stores the photo in an internal format that supports different resolutions for different platforms. For example, uploading a high-resolution photo using the Exchange Management Shell automatically updates the `thumbnailPhoto` attribute of the user's Active Directory account with a 48×48 version of the photo.

> **NOTE**
>
> Only the newer methods of uploading photos into Exchange result in an update to the Active Directory `thumbnailPhoto` attribute. If any other method is used to update the AD `thumbnailPhoto` attribute directly, this does not cause the photo in the Exchange 2013 mailbox to be updated.

Uploading Photos Using the Exchange Management Shell

To upload a photo using the Exchange Management Shell, place a copy of the photo in a local subdirectory that is accessible to the Management Shell. The filename of the photo can then be referenced in a variable within the shell and used to apply the photo to the user account. For example, the following series of Exchange Management Shell commands would be used to upload a photo with a filename of `dross.jpg` to the corresponding user account:

```
$photostring = "c:\temp\dross.jpg"
$pic=([Byte[]] $(Get-Content -Path $photostring -Encoding Byte -ReadCount 0))
Set-UserPhoto -Identity dross -PictureData $pic -confirm:$false
Set-UserPhoto -Identity dross -save -confirm:$false
```

Uploading Photos Using Outlook Web App

To upload photos as a user, Outlook Web App (OWA) is used. The following procedure would be used by the end user to upload the same photo to the mailbox using OWA:

1. Open a web browser and connect to the OWA URL, which by default is the fully qualified name of the Exchange 2013 Client Access Server, followed by /owa, for example, https://ex2k13.companyabc.com/owa.

2. At the Outlook Web App screen, enter the credentials for the user whose photo will be uploaded, and click Sign In.

3. If this is the first time the user is logging on to OWA on this system, an additional screen is presented allowing preferred display language and home time zone settings to be changed. Make any changes if necessary, and click Save.

4. When the mailbox is displayed, click on the user's name in the upper-right section of the OWA window. The first item that appears in the resulting drop-down menu is the photo section; click the Change link.

5. At the Change Photo screen, click Browse, and then navigate to the location of the photo for the user. After the photo is selected, click Open.

6. The photo is now uploaded to the mailbox and is displayed in the Change Photo screen, as shown in Figure 21.7. Click Save.

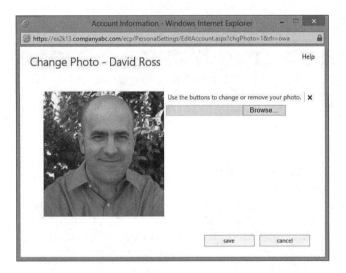

FIGURE 21.7   Uploading a photo using OWA.

Outlook Web App Integration

Outlook Web App integration is a feature that provides a nice convenience for Lync users who frequently use OWA to connect to their Exchange mailbox. Lync integration with OWA allows presence and IM capabilities to be extended to an OWA session, and also includes the following useful features:

▶ Presence for internal and federated Lync Server contacts

▶ The capability to start and maintain chat sessions directly from OWA

▶ Lync Server contact list integration, including adding and removing contacts and groups

▶ The capability to control Lync presence states from OWA

> **NOTE**
>
> OWA integration is possible using either Exchange 2010 or 2013. However, depending on the version of Exchange and the topology, it may be necessary to configure OWA as a trusted application within Lync 2013. Also, if Exchange 2013 is used, then the Unified Communications Managed API 4.0 Runtime must be installed on the Exchange Backend server.

Depending on whether Exchange UM is configured, the systems running OWA may need to be added to the list of known servers within Lync, which can be accomplished using the `New-CsTrustedApplicationPool` cmdlet. After Exchange is trusted by Lync, the OWA integration can be performed by adjusting the properties of the OWA virtual directories. For example, the following commands would be used in the Exchange Management Shell to configure the OWA virtual directories for Lync integration, with a combination Front End/Backend Exchange 2013 server named `ex2k13` and the Lync pool named `lyncse1. companyabc.com`:

1. Log on to a system where the Exchange 2013 administrative tools are installed using an account that has administrative rights to Exchange.

2. Open the Exchange Management Shell, and execute the following command to view the certificates that are available to be used with Exchange:

   ```
   Get-ExchangeCertificate
   ```

3. From the list of certificates presented, identify the certificate that has been assigned to IIS, which will be the first certificate listed where the letter W appears in the Services column. Then, copy the thumbprint for this certificate to the Windows Clipboard and use it to add the following two lines to the <AppSettings> section of the Web.config file in the c:\Program Files\Microsoft\Exchange Server\V15\ ClientAccess\Owa directory:

   ```
   <add key="IMCertificateThumbprint"
   ➥value="03554BB4BF96AC1081BDA4878997C7FE52D43127"/>
   <add key="IMServerName" value="lyncse1.companyabc.com"/>
   ```

4. Using a single command, execute the `Get-OwaVirtualDirectory` cmdlet to retrieve the OWA virtual directory, and then pipe the results to the `Set-OwaVirtualDirectory` cmdlet to adjust the properties of the OWA virtual

directory. For example, the following command would be used to enable OWA integration for a server named ex2k13:

```
Get-OwaVirtualDirectory | Set-OwaVirtualDirectory
➥-InstantMessagingEnabled $True -InstantMessagingType OCS
```

5. Execute the following command to enable Lync integration for the default OWA mailbox policy:

```
Set-OwaMailboxPolicy -Identity Default
➥-InstantMessagingEnabled $true -InstantMessagingType OCS
```

After OWA integration has been enabled, the users will see the results the next time they log in to OWA. The first indication that OWA integration has been enabled is that the presence states are listed in the drop-down menu that appears when a user clicks on the display name in the upper-right section of the OWA window, as shown in Figure 21.8.

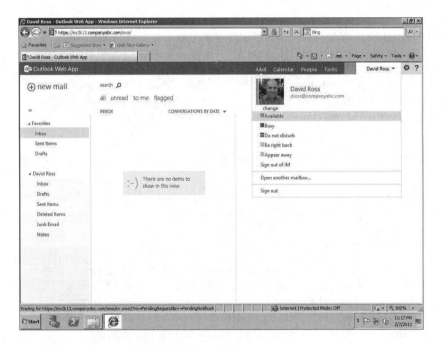

FIGURE 21.8   Lync presence states within OWA.

Unified Messaging Voice Mail Integration

Exchange Unified Messaging (UM) is an optional Exchange 2013 component that serves as an integrated voice mail system for Exchange mailbox users. Exchange UM allows voice mail, email, and fax messages to be consolidated into a user's inbox, and provides additional features to enhance the UC experience, such as Outlook Voice Access and automated attendants. Although Exchange UM certainly adds to the UC experience for users of Microsoft Exchange, it provides even more value when configured for integration with Lync. The integration of Lync with Exchange UM enables users to view and manage voice mails directly from the Lync client, providing additional flexibility and efficiency in terms of how the various forms of communication are handled.

> **NOTE**
>
> Microsoft has made several architectural changes to Unified Messaging in Exchange 2013. With previous versions of the product, UM was a unique server role requiring dedicated hardware. With Exchange 2013, the UM components are split between the Client Access Server and the Mailbox Server roles. Essentially, the Client Access Server acts as a proxy for incoming calls using the Unified Messaging Call Router service, whereas the Mailbox Server handles the majority of the voice load by way of the Unified Messaging service. However, these server roles can also be collocated, such that both the front-end and backend UM services are hosted on a single system.

Exchange UM Components

The deployment of Exchange Unified Messaging involves the configuration of several internal components, and these must be configured in a specific way to allow for integration with Lync. This section includes a description of these components to provide background on Exchange UM, as well as an explanation as to how the Exchange UM components fit into the picture with Lync and Exchange UM integration.

Following are the components included in an Exchange 2013 UM deployment:

▶ **UM Dial Plan**—UM dial plans are the central component of the Exchange unified messaging architecture. A UM dial plan logically corresponds to the set of extensions that are planned and assigned using a PBX. Some additional important purposes of the UM dial plan are that it associates the extension for subscriber access, and it establishes a common set of policies for a group of users, such as number of digits in an extension. Even in an environment where Lync is used for Enterprise Voice and is therefore used to establish the dial plan for the organization, one UM dial plan is still required for Lync to integrate with Exchange UM.

▶ **UM Mailbox Policy**—Unified Messaging mailbox policies are used to apply and standardize configuration settings for UM-enabled users. Some of the more important policy settings applied by a Unified Messaging mailbox policy include PIN policies, dialing restrictions, and maximum greeting duration. By default, a single UM mailbox policy is created every time a UM dial plan is created, and is named after the dial plan. The new UM mailbox policy is also automatically associated with the UM dial plan. Although only a single UM mailbox policy is required to enable users for Unified Messaging, additional UM mailbox policies can be created in order to apply a common set of mailbox policy settings for groups of users. The mailbox of each UM-enabled user must be linked to a single UM mailbox policy when the mailbox is enabled for Unified Messaging.

▶ **UM IP Gateway**—A Unified Messaging IP gateway object is a container object that logically represents a physical IP gateway hardware device, an IP-PBX, or another SIP server that can interoperate with Exchange Unified Messaging. Before the IP gateway can be used to process UM calls, it must be represented by an object in Active Directory. The combination of the IP Gateway object and a UM hunt group object establishes a logical link between an IP gateway hardware device and a UM dial plan. There can be only one UM IP gateway for each physical IP/VoIP gateway, and this is enforced through IP addresses.

▶ **UM Hunt Group**—With Exchange UM, hunt groups are used to act as a link between the UM IP gateway and the UM dial plan. UM hunt groups are used to locate the PBX hunt group from which the incoming call was received. A pilot number that is defined for a hunt group in the PBX must also be defined within the UM Hunt group, and is used to match the information presented for incoming calls through the SIP signaling information on the message. The pilot number enables the Unified Messaging service to interpret the call together with the correct dial plan so that the call can be routed correctly.

▶ **UM Auto Attendant**—Unified Messaging auto attendants are used to help internal and external callers locate users or departments that exist in an organization and transfer calls to them. The UM auto attendant is a series of voice prompts or `.wav` files that callers hear when dialing the organization.

Exchange UM Configuration for Lync

Since the Exchange UM components are included in the Client Access Server and Mailbox Server roles with Exchange 2013, the installation of Exchange UM is much more streamlined than with previous versions. However, the configuration of Exchange UM involves several steps, and these need to be completed before integration between Lync and Exchange UM can be configured. Although the full details of the planning and deployment process for Exchange UM are outside the scope of this chapter, the steps required to configure Exchange UM in preparation for Lync integration are included in the text that follows. This will serve to provide a background on the Exchange UM configuration process, as well as the details on how the Exchange UM configuration is affected when integration with Lync is planned.

Following is a summary of the steps involved in configuring Unified Messaging for integration with Lync:

▶ **Create the UM Dial Plan**—The UM dial plan is created manually using either the Exchange Administrative Center or the Exchange Management Shell. For integration with Lync, the number of digits configured for the UM dial plan should match the number of digits used in the PBX or Lync dial plan. Additional important choices include the URI type, which should be specified as SipName to cause the calling and called party information from Lync to use the standard SIP addressing format. The VOIP security mode chosen must also be compatible with the encryption level configured for the Lync client; setting the VOIP security mode to Secured will cause SIP signaling and media traffic to be encrypted as a requirement. Following is a sample command that would be used to create a UM dial plan using the Exchange Management Shell:

```
New-UMDialPlan -Name "SF_UM_Dial_Plan" -VoIPSecurity secured
➥-NumberOfDigitsInExtension 3 -URIType sipname -countryorregioncode 1
```

▶ **Assign a Subscriber Access Number**—A subscriber access number is used to specify the extension that is used by subscribers to access the voice mail system. When the UM dial plan is created, no subscriber access number is assigned, and therefore it must be assigned manually using the Exchange Management Shell. For example, the following command would be used to assign a three-digit extension as the subscriber access number for an existing UM dial plan: :

```
Set-UMDialPlan –Identity "SF_UM_Dial_Plan" –AccessTelephoneNumbers 123
```

▶ **Configure the UM Mailbox Policy (Optional)**—A UM mailbox policy is automatically created whenever a UM dial plan is created. However, the default settings in the policy might need to be adjusted to meet the requirements of the organization. If desired, additional UM mailbox policies can also be manually created using the Exchange Administrative Center or the Exchange Management Shell, and assigned to individual users when they are enabled for UM as needed. The following sample Management Shell command would be used to adjust an existing UM mailbox policy to change the minimum pin length to 4:

```
Set-UMMailboxPolicy -Identity "SF_UM_Dial_Plan Default Policy" -MinPINLength 4
```

▶ **Create the UM IP Gateway and UM Hunt Group**—For integration with Lync, a UM IP gateway and UM hunt group are automatically created to represent the Lync pool by executing the `exchucutil.ps1` PowerShell script, which is located in the `Scripts` subdirectory on an Exchange 2010 or 2013 server. In addition to creating the UM IP gateway and IP hunt group objects, the script grants permissions to Lync to read the required UM-related objects in Active Directory. The name applied to the gateway object is by default the same as the name of the Lync pool. Figure 21.9 shows an example of a UM IP gateway object that is automatically created as a result of the `exchucutil.ps1` script being run.

▶ **Create Auto Attendants (Optional)**—If Exchange UM will be used to handle incoming calls and direct these to the appropriate mailbox, one or more auto attendants need to be configured. Each auto attendant is created as part of a UM dial plan, and is assigned a unique access number that will be used to handle incoming calls. Auto attendants can be created as part of the UM dial plan configuration in the Exchange Administrative Center, or using the Exchange Management Shell. The following sample Management Shell command would be used to create an auto attendant, assign it to a dial plan, and assign a pilot number to handle inbound calls:

```
New-UMAutoAttendant -Name "SF_AutoAttendant" -UMDialPlan "SF_UM_Dial_Plan"
➥-Status Enabled -SpeechEnabled $true -PilotIdentifierList +14151234567
```

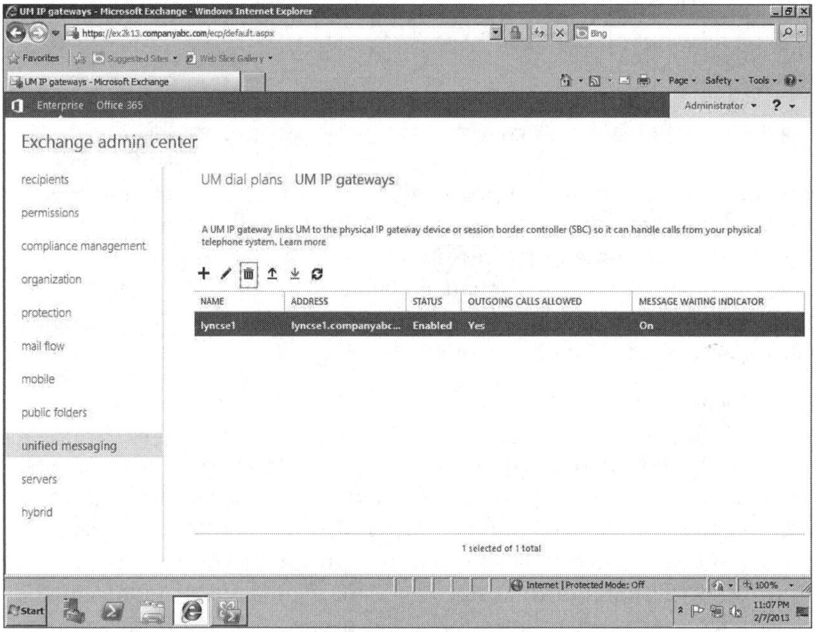

FIGURE 21.9   Exchange UM IP gateway automatically created for the Lync pool.

▶ **Change the UM Service Startup Mode**—By default, the UM service is configured to start up in TCP mode, which is not compatible if encryption is being used. The startup mode of the UM service must therefore be changed to dual mode to support encryption that is required for Lync integration. The following sample Management Shell command would be used to add the dial plan to the server and change the UM startup mode to dual:

```
Set-UmService -Identity ex2k13 -Dial Plans "SF_UM_Dial_Plan" -UMStartupMode
➥dual
```

▶ **Assign a Certificate to the Unified Messaging Service**—By default, no certificates are assigned to the Unified Messaging service within the Exchange configuration. To allow Exchange UM to communicate securely with clients and with Lync, a server certificate must be assigned to the service. This can be accomplished using either the Exchange Administrative Center or the Exchange Management Shell. The following sample Management Shell commands would be used to assign an existing certificate to the Unified Messaging service, and then restart the service:

```
Enable-ExchangeCertificate -Thumbprint 03554BB4BF96AC1081BDA4878997C7FE52D43127
➥-Services UM
Stop-service MsExchangeUM
Start-service MsExchangeUM
```

▶ **Enable Mailboxes for UM**—Each user must also be associated with a UM mailbox policy at the time that the user is enabled for UM. Users can be enabled for UM using the Exchange Administrative Center or the Exchange Management Shell. The following sample Management Shell command would be used to enable a user for UM and assign a mailbox policy:

```
Enable-UMMailbox -Identity dross@companyabc.com
➥-UMMailboxPolicy "SF_UM_Dial_Plan Default Policy" -Extensions 8122 -PIN 13579
➥-SIPResourceIdentifier "dross@companyabc.com" -PINExpired $true
```

▶ **Integrate the UM Call Router with Lync**—The Exchange UM Call Router must be prepared for integration with Lync, which requires several Exchange Management Shell commands. The following sample Management Shell commands would be used to prepare an Exchange 2013 Client Access Server named ex2k13 and a dial plan named SF_DP for integration with Lync, followed by a restart of the UM Call Router service:

```
Set-UmCallRouterSettings -UMStartupMode dual -DialPlans SF_DP -server ex2k13
Enable-ExchangeCertificate -server ex2k13 -Thumbprint
➥ 03554BB4BF96AC1081BDA4878997C7FE52D43127 -Services iis,umcallrouter
Stop-service MsExchangeUMCR
Start-service MsExchangeUMCR
```

Lync Configuration for Exchange UM

With the Exchange UM configuration in place, Lync can be configured to integrate with Exchange UM as the final step in the process. If Lync dial plans have not already been configured at this point, the dial plans would need to be configured to allow call routing between the various components. For details on the process for configuring Lync dial plans and voice routing, see Chapter 17, "Lync Telephony and Voice Integration." After a dial plan is in place, the remaining task is to create the AD contact objects that are required to resolve and locate the Exchange UM subscriber access and auto-attendant services. To facilitate creating these contact objects, Microsoft provides the Exchange UM Integration Utility, which has an executable filename of OcsUmUtil.exe, and is located in the subdirectory C:\Program Files\Common Files\Microsoft Lync Server 2013\ Support on each Lync Front End Server. The following procedure is used to configure the subscriber access and auto-attendant contact objects using the Exchange UM Integration Utility:

1. Log on to the Lync Front End Server using an account with permissions to create Active Directory objects in the domain, and then use Windows Explorer to navigate to the C:\Program Files\Common Files\Microsoft Lync Server 2013\Support directory, and click on OcsUmUtil.exe.

2. The Exchange UM Integration Utility dialog box appears. Click Load Data, which causes the Exchange UM Dial Plan Forest field to automatically populate the AD forest name, as shown in Figure 21.10. Any UM Dial Plans that have been created in Exchange also appear in the SIP Dial Plans column.

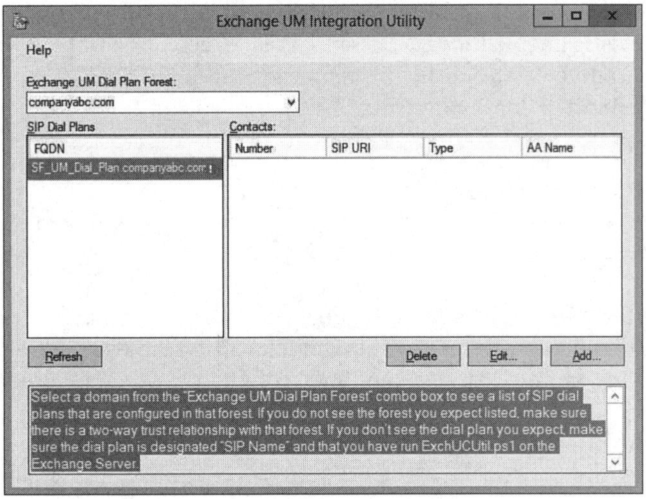

FIGURE 21.10   Exchange UM integration utility.

3. Click Add, and then at the Contact dialog box click Browse. Use the OU Picker to browse Active Directory and select the organizational unit that will be used as the location for the contact objects. It is also possible to create a new OU for this purpose by clicking the Make New OU button. After the OU has been specified, click OK to return to the Contact dialog box.

4. Review the default setting and make adjustments where necessary. For example, default values are displayed for the contact name and SIP address, but these can be edited if necessary. In the Phone Number section, verify that the phone extension specified as the subscriber access number in Exchange UM is automatically populated, as shown in Figure 21.11.

5. Keep the default Contact Type of Subscriber Access, and then click OK to create the subscriber access contact object.

6. To create an auto-attendant object, click Add; then at the Contact dialog box, in the Contact Type section select Auto-Attendant.

7. If several auto attendants have been created in Exchange UM, use the drop-down menu at the bottom of the dialog box to select the auto attendant for which a contact object will be created.

8. Review the remainder of the fields that are automatically populated for accuracy, and make any adjustments if necessary. When finished, click OK to create the auto-attendant object.

9. If additional auto-attendant contact objects are needed, repeat steps 6 to 8 to create additional contact objects for these.

10. When finished, exit the Exchange UM Integration Utility.

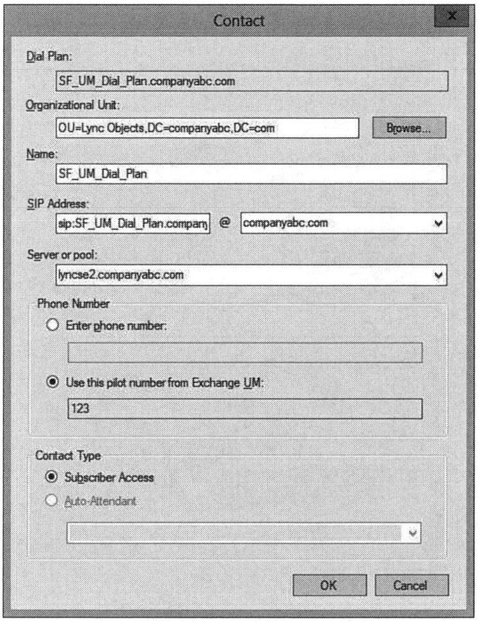

FIGURE 21.11   Creating a subscriber access contact object.

Testing the UM Integration

Microsoft provides two synthetic transactions that can be used to test the UM integration feature. The `Test-CsExUmConnectivity` cmdlet tests whether Lync 2013 can connect to Exchange 2013 UM for a given user, and the `Test-CsExUmVoiceMail` cmdlet deposits a voice mail into the user's inbox.

The following Lync Management Shell commands would be used to test the Exchange UM integration for a user:

```
$credential=Get-Credential -UserName companyabc\dross
Test-CsExUMConnectivity -TargetFqdn lyncse1.companyabc.com
➡-UserSipAddress dross@companyabc.com -UserCredential $credential
```

The following series of commands would be used to deposit a voice mail for the same user, using a sample .wma file that is included as part of the Lync Audio Test Service:

```
$credential=Get-Credential -UserName companyabc\dross
Test-CsExUMVoiceMail -SenderSipAddress dross@companyabc.com
➡-ReceiverSipAddress jrico@companyabc.com -SenderCredential $credential -WaveFile
➡"C:\Program Files\Microsoft Lync Server 2013\Application Host\Applications
➡\Audio Test Service\Media\en-US\Welcome.wma"
```

After Lync has been successfully configured for Exchange UM integration, and the user has been enabled for UM, a voice mail icon will automatically appear within the Lync client, as shown in Figure 21.12.

FIGURE 21.12   Exchange UM Voice Mail in the Lync Client.

SharePoint Integration Features

With Lync Server 2013, the integrations with SharePoint that existed in previous versions will continue to be supported, and some added integration features are introduced as well. Lync 2013 integrations for SharePoint include the following:

▶ eDiscovery of Lync archive data (new)

▶ IM and presence integration

▶ Skill search

eDiscovery of Lync Archive Data

A new integration feature with Lync 2013 and SharePoint 2013 is the use of SharePoint eDiscovery to search Lync archive data. eDiscovery describes the process of searching through electronic content, which could include documents, websites, email messages, and other electronic sources, and then collecting and acting on the content that meets a particular criteria, such as that which might be needed for a legal case. Typically, eDiscovery is a task that is performed by records managers and litigators, and SharePoint 2013 facilitates the eDiscovery process for content that is stored in SharePoint through the use of eDiscovery Centers. An eDiscovery Center is a central SharePoint site that is used to manage perseveration, search, and export of content stored in SharePoint and Exchange across multiple servers and server farms. For example, the in-place hold feature can be used to preserve data within SharePoint sites or Exchange mailboxes, but still allow users to continue editing and deleting preserved content.

Although eDiscovery of Lync archive data can correctly be called an integration feature for Lync 2013 and SharePoint 2013, in reality this feature involves integration of both products with Exchange 2013 as well. The reason for this is that Lync 2013 must first be configured to archive content to Exchange 2013 before SharePoint eDiscovery can be used to search that data. In reality then, the first task involved in configuring eDiscovery of Lync archive data is the integration of Lync archiving to Exchange, as detailed in the "Lync Archiving Integration" section earlier in this chapter.

> **NOTE**
>
> To enable discovery of Lync content through SharePoint, all three of the products involved must be running the 2013 version of the software: Lync 2013, Exchange 2013, and SharePoint 2013.

After Lync 2013, Exchange 2013, and SharePoint 2013 have been configured as partner applications as described in the "Server-to-Server Authentication" section earlier in this chapter, and after Lync archiving integration has also been configured, SharePoint eDiscovery can be configured to search Lync data that has been archived to Exchange. The following example shows the steps involved in using SharePoint eDiscovery to search Lync archive data:

1. To begin the eDiscovery process, the user that will be performing the discovery must be assigned to the Discovery Management role group in Exchange. The following Exchange Management Shell command would be used to assign a user to the role:

   ```
   Add-RoleGroupMember "Discovery Management" -member cbennett
   ```

2. The next step is to create an eDiscovery site. For example, the following two commands would be used in the SharePoint Management Shell to create an eDiscovery site under an existing SharePoint site named abcsite.companyabc.com, with the user who will be performing the discovery being specified as the owner:

   ```
   $template=Get-SPWebTemplate | where-object {$_.title -eq "eDiscovery Center"}
   New-SPSite -Url http://abcsite.companyabc.com/sites/Discovery
   ➥-OwnerAlias cbennett -Template $template -name "Discovery Center"
   ```

3. To generate Lync archive data to be searched using eDiscovery, the Lync archiving policy needs to be enabled for archiving to Exchange for at least one user. For a detailed description of the Lync archiving integration feature, see the "Lync Archiving Integration" section earlier in this chapter. The following sample command would be used to enable archiving to Exchange for an individual user:

   ```
   Set-CsUser dross -ExchangeArchivingPolicy ArchivingToExchange
   ```

4. After Lync data has been archived to Exchange, Exchange 2013 needs to be added as a content source in SharePoint. The SharePoint 2013 Central Administration site can be used for this. Start by selecting Search Service Application from the Manage Service Applications menu.

5. Add a new result source named Exchange, with the protocol also specified as Exchange. For Exchange Source URL, enter https://<ExchangeFQDN>/ews/exchange. asmx, with <ExchangeFQDN> being the fully qualified domain name of the target Exchange 2013 server, as shown in Figure 21.13. Also, ensure that Autodiscover is not selected.

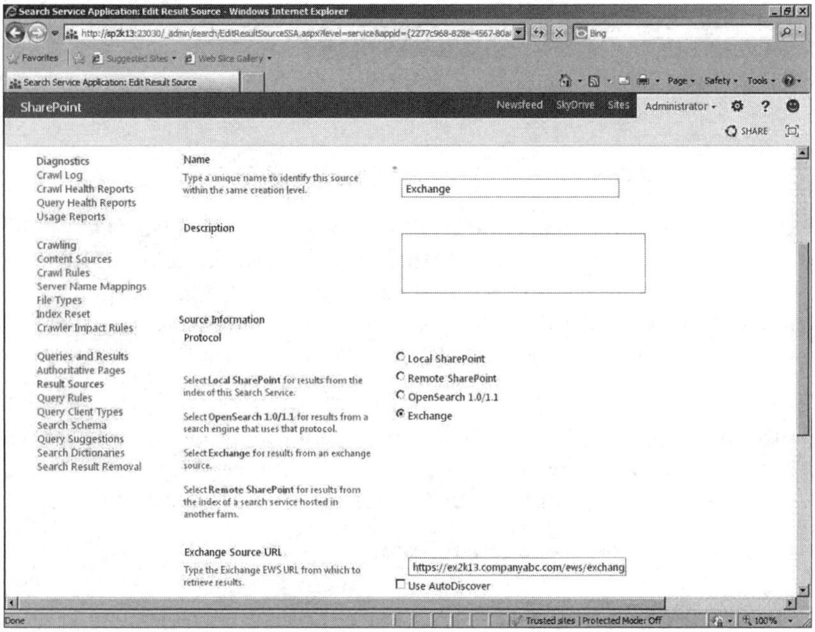

FIGURE 21.13   Exchange configured as a content source in SharePoint.

6. The user who has been granted Discovery Management rights now logs on to the Discovery site created previously, and uses it to create an eDiscovery case. The URL to connect to is https://<SharePointSite>/sites/discovery, or for this example http:// abcsite.companyabc.com/sites/discovery. When a title and website address are specified for the case, these should be named in a descriptive manner so that the case can be easily found; for example, the name of the user whose mailbox will be searched can be included in both.

7. After the case has been created, the final task is to create an eDiscovery set using the eDiscovery case created in the preceding step. Within the properties of the eDiscovery set, specify the user who has been configured for archiving to Exchange. Start and end dates for the discovery can also be specified, and in-place hold can be enabled as well.

8. SharePoint now initiates a search against the specified mailbox and displays the results in a preview window. The eDiscovery can be saved at this point so that the same discovery criteria can be used later.

IM and Presence Integration

After Lync 2013 and SharePoint 2013 are configured as partner applications, SharePoint is automatically able to take advantage of presence information from Lync. From a user's perspective, Lync integration with SharePoint becomes the most noticeable when the user is browsing documents in a SharePoint document store. When documents are being viewed, the name of the person who posted the document is displayed in SharePoint. With Lync integration, the presence information for each of those users is also displayed. This integration feature can be quite a convenience; for example, if there is a question about a particular document posted in SharePoint, the viewer is immediately made aware of whether that person is available. The SharePoint user can then quickly determine whether it makes more sense to send an IM, initiate a call, or perhaps create a conference that enables the parties to collaborate on the document.

Presence within SharePoint does not require any additional modifications to either SharePoint or Lync. Presence is displayed via an ActiveX control and Lync APIs. On the client side, the only requirement is that a version of Microsoft Office be installed on the client computer where presence will be displayed.

Skill Search

An interesting integration feature that was introduced with Lync 2010 and continues to be supported with Lync 2013 is skill search. Skill search enables Lync users to search skills, expertise, and organizational information from SharePoint My Sites. If users populate expertise information into fields in their SharePoint My Site, Lync users will be able to discover this information based on the content of these fields. For example, an IT Manager user might have a need to track down an internal resource with skills in a particular development platform. To find someone with these skills, the manager simply enters the search criteria in Lync, and a list of internal contacts who have flagged themselves as experts in that development language are listed. This integration feature can therefore result in a real-time savings, especially for a large organization, because it is no longer necessary to manually build a list of whom to contact for specific subjects. Users can instead build a dynamic searchable database of skills and organizational information right from the Lync client, which makes it much easier to find the right personnel to collaborate with.

To enable skill search, users must have a SharePoint deployment that includes My Sites. The full version of SharePoint must also be used, because Windows SharePoint Services is not compatible with skill search. The SharePoint search center URL is made available to Lync clients through in-band provisioning, which also means that SharePoint must be published to the Internet for remote users to take advantage of this feature.

To configure skill search, a Lync client policy must be configured and applied to the Lync clients specifying the SharePoint URLs. A single policy can be used to configure both the `SPSearchInternalURL` and the `SPSearchExternalURL` values. Using the Lync Server Management Shell, the following two commands are used, where `<SPserver>` is the name of the SharePoint Server:

```
Set-CSClientPolicy -SPSearchInternalURL http://<SPserver>/_vti_bin/search.asmx
Set-CSClientPolicy -SPSearchExternalURL http://<SPserver>/_vti_bin/search.asmx
```

Optionally, the Search Center URL can also be configured to display at the bottom of the search results when users run a skill search query. To configure the URL to be displayed, the following two additional Management Shell commands would be used:

```
Set-CSClientPolicy -SPSearchCenterInternalURL
http://<SPserver>/SearchCenter/Pages/PeopleResults.aspx
Set-CSClientPolicy -SPSearchCenterExternalURL
➥http://<SPserver>/SearchCenter/Pages/PeopleResults.aspx
```

After these commands are run, a Lync client will pick up the change through in-band provisioning the next time the client is started. There are two ways to determine whether the skill search settings have been applied. First, as shown in Figure 21.14, when a user is searching a contact in the Lync client, two additional options are now listed: Name and Skill.

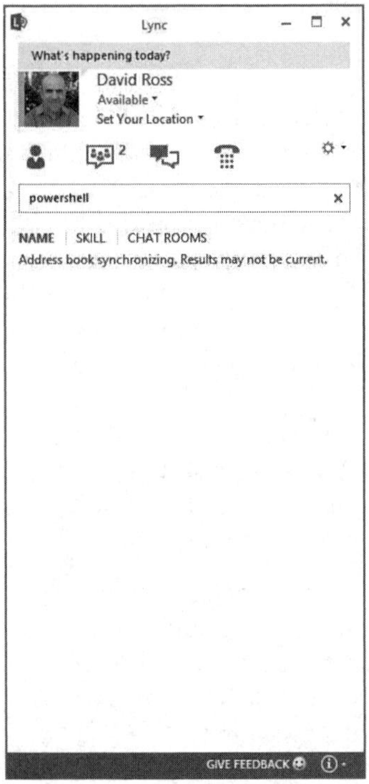

FIGURE 21.14   Skill search options in the Lync client.

The other way to determine whether skill search has been applied is by viewing the Lync client configuration settings. To access the Lync client configuration settings, hold down the Ctrl key and right-click on the Lync system tray icon in the lower-right corner of the desktop; then select Configuration Information from the menu. Included in the resulting Lync Configuration Information screen is the skill search URL, as shown in Figure 21.15.

Lync Configuration Information		
URL Internal From Server	https://lyncse1.companyabc.com:443/abs/handler	--
URL External From Server	https://lyncse1.companyabc.com:443/abs/handler	--
Voice mail URI	sip:dross@companyabc.com;opaque=app:voicemail	--
Exum URL	EUM:dross@companyabc.com;phone-context=SF UM Dial Plan.companyabc.com	--
MRAS Server		
GAL Status	https://lyncse1.companyabc.com:443/abs/handler	--
Focus Factory	sip:dross@companyabc.com;gruu;opaque=app:conf:focusfactory	--
Line		--
Location Profile		--
Call Park Server URI		--
Server Address Internal		--
Server Address External		--
Server SIP URI	dross@companyabc.com	--
Exum Enabled	TRUE	--
Controlled Phones	TRUE	--
GAL or Server Based Search	GAL search	--
PC to PC AV Encryption	AV Encryption Enforced	--
Telephony Mode	Telephony Mode Disabled	--
Line Configured From	Auto Line Configuration	--
Configuration Mode	Auto Configuration	--
EWS Internal URL		--
EWS External URL		--
SharePoint Search Center U	http://sp2k13.companyabc.com/SearchCenter/Pages/PeopleResults.aspx	--
Skill Search URL	http://sp2k13.companyabc.com/_vti_bin/search.asmx	--

Copy   Refresh   Close

FIGURE 21.15   Skill search URL in the Lync client configuration settings.

If results are found, at the bottom of the client an option is presented to view the results in SharePoint. This connects the user to the full SharePoint interface to display more detailed information about the results.

Summary

As with previous versions, Microsoft continues to put significant development efforts into the integration features of Lync, Exchange, and SharePoint. With the 2013 versions of these applications, there are more ways than ever for organizations to leverage features across these three applications. The integrations that became popular with previous versions continue to be supported, and newer integrations such as unified contact store and eDiscovery of Lync archive data allow even greater efficiencies and cost savings for organizations that deploy these products together.

PART VIII

Office 365 and Lync Online

IN THIS PART

Lync Online and Hybrid Deployments

In an effort to keep pace with the movement toward cloud-based IT services, in recent years Microsoft has been heavily focused on developing the online versions of popular Microsoft applications, including Lync. With the initial release of Lync Online, for the first time organizations had a choice between implementing Lync 2010 on-premise, and using the online version of the product, either as a standalone service or as part of the Office 365 online suite. With the 2013 release of Lync, Microsoft is continuing to develop the online version as well, and has rolled out an update to Lync Online along with the rest of the Office 365 applications, which is based on the 2013 version of the products. This new online release not only improves the features that are offered, but also gives organizations an additional Lync topology choice: the hybrid Lync deployment. This chapter provides a description of the updated version of Lync Online, along with the deployment steps for both cloud-only and hybrid installations.

Overview of Lync Online and Office 365

Lync Online is a service offering that can be purchased either separately or as part of Office 365 Enterprise, Microsoft's cloud collaboration and productivity suite, which also includes Exchange Online, SharePoint Online, Office Professional Plus, and Office Web Apps. Lync Online offers features that are very similar to Lync Server 2013, including IM and presence, sharing and collaboration, peer-to-peer voice and video calls, and online meetings. With the purchase of third-party services from an approved

Microsoft partner, hosted voice and dial-in conferencing are also included as part of the feature set.

With the updated release of Office 365, Microsoft is seeking to close the gap by offering additional features, as well as support for hybrid deployments involving both on-premise and cloud services for the same SIP domain. Microsoft offers a standard set of features for all cloud services, including Lync Online. Following is a summary of the standard Microsoft cloud service features:

▶ **Secure Access**—All traffic is secured using 128-bit SSL or TLS encryption.

▶ **Intrusion Monitoring**—Microsoft continuously monitors all online systems for unusual or suspicious activity, and notifies customers of issues as needed.

▶ **Security Audits**—Microsoft regularly assesses the infrastructure of online systems to ensure that antivirus signatures are updated and security updates are installed.

▶ **High Availability**—There is a 99.9% scheduled uptime for online systems, with SLA guarantees in place.

▶ **Service Continuity**—Redundant systems are located in geographically dispersed data centers to handle unscheduled service outages.

▶ **Directory Synchronization**—Synchronization of directory information between the local Active Directory and Office 365 is made available using the free Directory Synchronization tool.

▶ **Single Sign-on**—Single sign-on is achieved by deploying an instance of Active Directory Federated Services on-premise, and using it to federate with the cloud tenant.

System Requirements

As a cloud service, there are not many system requirements that need to be met to use Lync Online. However, there are some prerequisites that need to be met to ensure compatibility, or in the very least to allow for the best user experience. The following sections provide details on the specific requirements.

Operating System and Browser Requirements

Lync Online and Office 365 are compatible with specific combinations of operating systems and web browsers, as shown in Table 22.1.

TABLE 22.1   Operating System and Browser Requirements for Lync Online

Operating System	Supported Browsers
Windows 7 (32-bit)	Internet Explorer 8 and later Firefox 3 and later Chrome 6 and later

Operating System	Supported Browsers
Windows 7 (64-bit)	Internet Explorer 8 and later
	Firefox 3 and later
	Chrome 6 and later
Windows Vista with SP2 (32-bit)	Internet Explorer 7 and later
	Firefox 3 and later
	Chrome 6 and later
Windows Vista with SP2 (64-bit)	Internet Explorer 8
	Internet Explorer 7
	Firefox 5
Windows XP with SP3 (32-bit)	Internet Explorer 7 and later
	Firefox 3 and later
	Chrome 6 and later
Windows XP with SP2 (64-bit)	Internet Explorer 8
	Internet Explorer 7
	Firefox 5
Windows Server 2008 and Windows Server 2008 R2	Internet Explorer 7 and later
	Firefox 3 and later
	Chrome 6 and later
Mac OS X 10.5 or Mac OS X 10.6	Firefox 3 and later
	Safari 4 and later

22

Software Requirements

To use Lync Online, either the Lync 2010 client with cumulative update 2 or higher or the Lync 2013 client is supported. An additional requirement is the Microsoft Online Services Sign In Assistant, which is used to allow Lync to authenticate to Microsoft Online Services. The following are some additional software requirements, depending on the client operating system:

▶ Microsoft .NET Framework 3.0 (for Windows XP)

▶ Java client 1.4.2 (for Mac OS X)

Office Desktop Setup

To simplify the installation and maintenance of components and updates that are required for the functionality of Lync Online and Office 365, Microsoft provides a free piece of software named Office Desktop Setup. The Office Desktop Setup software includes the following features:

▶ Automatically detects required updates and components, and installs these upon approval or silently from a command line

▶ Automatically configures the Lync client for use with Lync Online

▶ Uninstalls itself automatically from the client system after running

Experiencing Lync Online

Lync Online offers many, but not all, of the features that are included in an on-premise deployment. The following sections provide a summary of the features that are available to a Lync Online user compared with those that are available only with an on-premise Lync deployment.

Lync Online Clients

The same Lync 2010 and 2013 client software is used for Lync Online and Lync on-premise. All the basic features of Lync are available to Lync Online users, including IM and Presence, peer-to-peer and multiparty audio and video calls, online meetings (both scheduled and ad hoc), and content sharing. In addition to the Lync client software, Lync Web App Client software is available for external users for attending online meetings. Lync Phone Edition devices are supported for use with the Lync-to-phone feature. The mobile device clients that are supported for use with Lync on-premise are also supported for use with Lync Online, including Windows Phone 7, iPhone, Android, and iPad.

> **NOTE**
>
> Although multiparty video is supported, Lync Online does not support interoperability with third-party, room-based conferencing systems.

Lync Web Scheduler

For users that do not have Outlook installed on their client system, and therefore cannot benefit from the Online Meeting Add-in that enables meetings to be scheduled from within Outlook, the Lync Web Scheduler is provided. The Lync Web Scheduler, accessed using the URL https://sched.lync.com, provides Lync Online users with a simple web interface for managing meetings, as shown in Figure 22.1. After meetings have been created, they can be exported from the Web Scheduler as an iCalendar event, and then sent to meeting attendees.

Integration Features

Lync Online offers client software integration features that are similar to Lync on-premise. Lync Presence information is embedded into other applications that are included in Office 2007 and above. Single-click scheduling of online meetings is available in Outlook. If Exchange Online is also used, Presence status is automatically updated based on Exchange calendar information, and IM and Presence are made available from Outlook Web App. If SharePoint Online is also used, presence indicators are also displayed in SharePoint. However, the Lync Skill Search feature is not available with Lync Online.

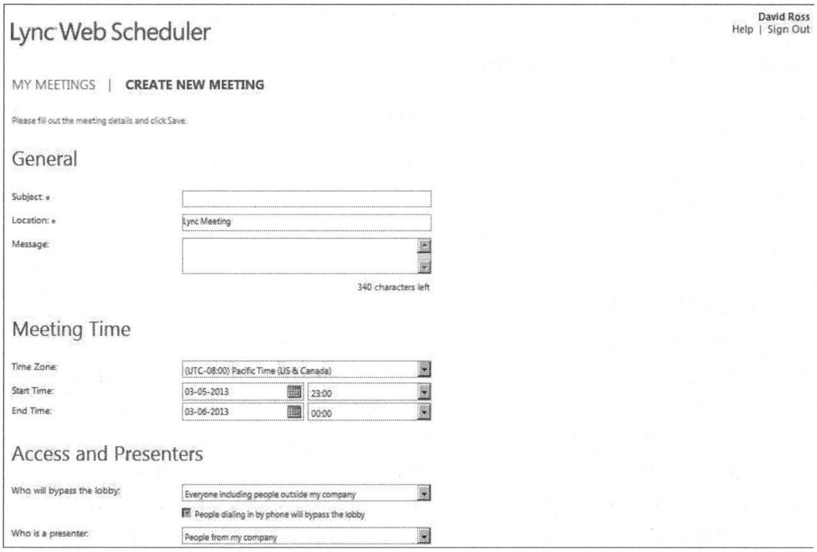

FIGURE 22.1   Lync Web Scheduler.

> **NOTE**
>
> Lync Online also supports interoperability with on-premise deployments of Exchange (2007 and above) and SharePoint. Lync Presence indicators in SharePoint Online and Outlook are available only on systems where the Lync client is installed.

Lync-to-Phone

Lync-to-phone is a feature that provides a "single work number" experience for Lync Online users, and is available with licensing for Lync Online Plan 3. To enable Lync-to-phone, a separate calling service from a qualified Office 365 partner is required, and enables connectivity to the PSTN from Lync Online. After the service is purchased and configured, the following features are available with Lync-to-phone:

▶ Capability for PSTN phone calls to be made and received using the Lync client on multiple devices, using a single phone number provided by the calling service. Laptops, smartphones, and tablet devices with the Lync client are all supported.

▶ Click-to-call functionality from Outlook and other office applications.

▶ Simultaneous ring to a mobile phone.

▶ Initiating calls using a smartphone or tablet with the Lync work number displayed to outside parties.

▶ Mid-call transfer from a PC to a mobile phone or to another number.

▶ Drag-and-drop of contacts into an existing Lync call or meeting.

▶ Delegation, enabling an assistant to make or receive calls on a user's behalf.

▶ Team call, in which several users can be grouped to pick up incoming calls.

▶ Voice mail and auto attendant (also requires licensing for Exchange Online Plan 2).

Lync Federation and Public IM

Lync Online supports federation with other organizations that use either Lync Online or Lync on-premise. Federated contacts can see each other's presence, and can use IM, peer-to-peer audio, and video to communicate. As with an on-premise deployment, federation needs to be configured by both parties, and public DNS configuration is required. Whitelists and blacklists are also available to control which domains are available for federation. One difference between the federation features of Lync Online and Lync on-premise is that file transfer is not available with Lync Online federated connections.

In addition to Lync federation, Lync Online users can communicate with contacts that use Skype. However, federation with AOL and Yahoo!, as well as federation with XMPP networks, is not available for Lync Online.

> **NOTE**
>
> Federation with Skype is disabled by default, but can be enabled by a Lync Online service administrator.

Dial-in Audio Conferencing

Although Lync Online does not natively provide dial-in audio conferencing capability, Plan 2 licensing does allow interoperability with third-party audio conferencing services. The service also allows for scheduling and joining a Lync meeting from any phone, and initiating a call to an external number from within a Lync meeting. Microsoft maintains an up-to-date list of approved audio conferencing partners that can be used for this service on the Office 365 Marketplace site.

Deploying Lync Online

There are several steps involved in starting a new deployment of Lync Online for an organization. After a subscription to Lync Online has been purchased, the following sections provide details on the procedures required to get Lync Online up and running.

Adding Domains to Lync Online/Office 365

The first task involved in getting Lync Online up and running is adding the SIP domains that will be used with the service. When you are signing up for a Lync Online or Office 365 subscription, a single DNS domain is assigned. This initial domain is referred to as the tenant domain, and always has a suffix of `.onmicrosoft.com`. This tenant domain is meant only for administration of the Lync Online organization, and is not intended to be used as a SIP domain.

To add a new domain to Lync Online/Office 365, follow these steps:

1. Log on to the Office 365 Portal.

2. On the left side of the main page, click Domains.

3. At the Domains page, click the link for Add a domain.

4. At the Add a domain to Office 365 page, click the link for Specify a domain name and confirm ownership.

5. At the Provide domain name page, enter the fully qualified name of the domain owned by the organization that will be used for Lync Online, and click Next.

6. At the Confirm ownership page, read the instructions presented regarding the requirement for adding a DNS record to verify ownership of the domain. The drop-down menu offers a choice of common DNS providers; select one of these to view instructions for adding the required DNS record using that DNS provider. If the DNS registrar for the SIP domain being added does not appear in this drop-down list, select General Instructions to view the generic steps for adding the required DNS record, as shown in Figure 22.2.

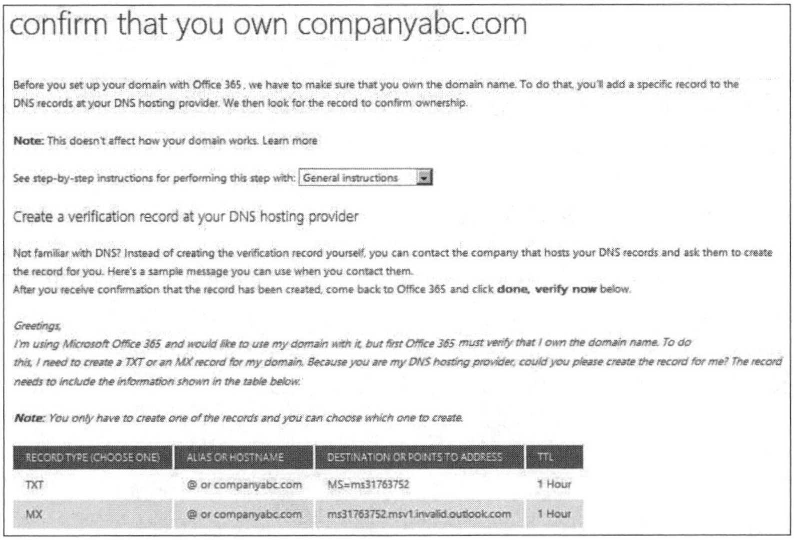

FIGURE 22.2   Office 365 domain verification instructions.

7. Follow through with the instructions to add either the TXT or the MX record to the public DNS zone, and then wait for the change to take effect. The amount of time required will depend on DNS propagation delay, as well as the DNS provider being used.

NOTE

Although either the TXT or the MX record can be used for validation with Office 365, the TXT record is the preferred method of validation. The reason for this is that the MX record required for validation specifies an address value ending in `.invalid`, and not all DNS providers support this record. The TXT record, on the other hand, is much more commonly supported.

---

8. Click the Done, go check button to complete the verification process. If the domain verification is not successful, it might be necessary to wait some additional time and continue clicking this button until the verification succeeds.

9. After the verification is successful, the next screen confirms that the domain has now been added to the account. Click Finish to return to the Add a domain to Office 365 page.

10. If new users will be added to the domain right away, click the link for Add users and assign licenses, and then follow the instructions in the "Adding Lync Online User Accounts" section later in this chapter to add the new users. Once the new users have been added, return to the Add a domain to Office 365 page and click the link for Set the domain purpose and configure DNS.

11. At the Set domain purpose page, select the check box for Lync Online. If the domain will also be used with Exchange Online or SharePoint Online as part of an Office 365 subscription, these can be selected as well. When finished, click Next.

12. At the Add DNS records page, the online portal displays a list of DNS records required for the domain, based on the services that were selected on the previous page. If the DNS records required for Lync Online have not already been configured based on the information in Chapter 28, "Planning for Lync Online and Hybrid Deployments", then these DNS records will need to be added.

13. Once the DNS records are in place, click the Done, go check button to complete the DNS record verification process. If the domain verification is not successful, it might be necessary to wait some additional time and continue clicking this button until the verification succeeds.

14. After the DNS record verification is successful, the next screen confirms that the required DNS records were found. Click Finish to complete the procedure. The new domain now appears in the list of verified domains, as shown in Figure 22.3.

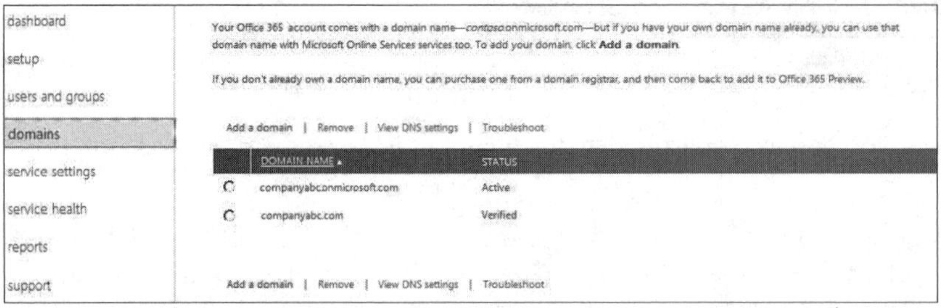

FIGURE 22.3   Newly verified domain listed in the Office 365 portal.

Adding Lync Online User Accounts

There are several methods that can be used to add user accounts to Lync Online/Office 365. User accounts can be added manually using either the online portal, or Windows PowerShell. It is also possible to create user accounts in bulk using an import process. User accounts can also be automatically created using directory synchronization, which is described in detail in the "Configuring Directory Synchronization" section later in this chapter.

Adding User Accounts Using the Online Portal

Use the following procedure for creating a new user account using the Online Portal:

1. Log on to the Office 365 Portal.

2. On the left side of the main page, click Users and Groups.

3. At the Users and Groups page, click on the plus symbol just above the user list.

4. At the Details page, mandatory fields for the new account are displayed, as shown in Figure 22.4. Enter the first name, last name, and username for the new user account. The display name is automatically derived from the First name and Last name fields but can also be edited manually if necessary.

FIGURE 22.4   Creating a new user account using the Office 365 Portal.

5. Use the drop-down menu at the end of the User name field to select from among the available domains for this user account. This list is automatically populated with domains that have already been verified for this Lync Online/Office 365 account.

6. Click on Additional details to display a number of optional fields that can be filled out, including job title, department, phone numbers, and addressing information. Fill out any fields that are desired, and then click Next.

7. At the Settings screen, if the user will be assigned administrative permissions to the Lync Online/Office 365 tenant, click Yes under the Assign role section, and use the drop-down menu to select the administrative role for the user. Also, enter the alternate email address of the user, which will be used to allow reset of the user's password if it becomes lost or forgotten.

8. Under the Set User Location section, use the drop-down menu to select the user's location, and then click Next.

TIP

Although it might not seem evident, the user location setting is actually quite important, because certain Lync Online/Office 365 services are not available in some locations. After the user location is configured, the following page will allow licensing to be applied only for services that are available in that location.

---

9. At the Assign licenses screen, select the check box for the Lync Online plan that the user will be licensed for, along with any other Office 365 services and plans that the organization has a subscription for.

10. At the Send results in email page, keep the default selection of Send email if the username and temporary password for the new account should be sent to an administrator via email, and then enter up to five recipient email addresses separated by semicolons. When finished, click Create.

11. At the Results page, verify that the user account has been successfully created, and make note of the temporary password automatically generated. Click Finish to complete the procedure and return to the Users and Groups page, or click the link for Create another user to add another user account.

Adding User Accounts Using PowerShell

User accounts can be added to Lync Online/Office 365 using Windows PowerShell in conjunction with the Microsoft Online Services Module. The installation steps and system requirements for the Microsoft Online Services Module are detailed later in this chapter in the section "Establishing Trust with Office 365 for SSO." After the Microsoft Online Services Module is installed on a system with PowerShell, use the following steps to create a new user account using PowerShell:

1. Log on to the system where Windows PowerShell and the Microsoft Online Services Module are installed.

2. Open Windows PowerShell and import the Microsoft Online Services Module using the command `Import-Module MSOnline`.

3. Execute the command `$cred=Get-Credential`, and then at the prompt enter the credentials of an Office 365 administrative account.

4. Execute the command `Connect-MsolService -Credential $cred`, which creates a connection to Office 365, as required to run the remaining cmdlets.

5. Execute the `New-MsolUser` cmdlet to create the new user account. For example, the following command would be used to create a new account named Lois Victoria in the `companyabc.onmicrosoft.com` organization:

```
New-MsolUser -UserPrincipalName "LoisV.companyabc.onmicrosoft.com"
➥-DisplayName "Lois Victoria" -FirstName "Lois" -LastName "Victoria"
```

6. If the command completes successfully, the new user account properties will display, including the temporary password assigned to the account.

TIP

The `New-MsolUser` command creates the user account; however, it does not apply licensing to the user. The licenses can be assigned after the user account is created using the online portal.

Adding User Accounts in Bulk

User accounts can be added to Lync Online/Office 365 using a comma-separated values (CSV) file. The CSV file must be specifically formatted with the correct column headings to be successfully imported. To facilitate this process, Microsoft provides a sample CSV file with the appropriate column headings that can be downloaded from the Online Portal and then adjusted using a text editor.

The following steps describe the process for downloading the sample CSV file, editing the file, and then importing it into Lync Online/Office 365:

1. Log on to the Office 365 Portal.

2. On the left side of the main page, click Users and Groups.

3. At the Users and Groups page, click on the Bulk add symbol, which is just to the right of the plus symbol above the user list.

4. At the Select a CSV file page, click on Download a sample CSV file.

5. At the File Download prompt, click Save and then choose a local subdirectory to save the file to.

6. Use Excel or a text editor such as Notepad to navigate to the location where the file was saved, and open the file named `Import_User_Sample_en.csv`.

7. Edit the file, replacing the sample entries with actual user accounts that will be imported into Lync Online.

8. When finished, save the file, and return to the select a CSV file page in the Online Portal. Click Browse, navigate to and select the import file, and then click Next.

9. At the Verification results screen, the results of the import process are displayed. If there are errors, click on the View link to display the log file and determine the cause of the errors. For example, in Figure 22.5 the log file reveals a spelling error in

the domain name of one of the user accounts, whereas the other accounts were verified. At this point, it is possible to correct any errors in the CSV file, click the Back button, and then reimport the file.

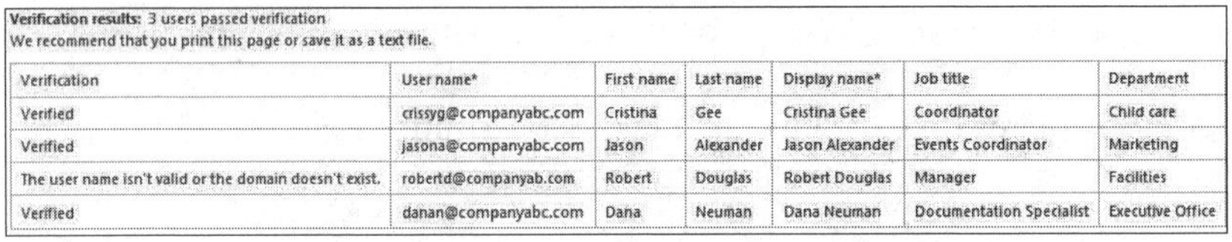

Verification	User name*	First name	Last name	Display name*	Job title	Department
Verified	crissyg@companyabc.com	Cristina	Gee	Cristina Gee	Coordinator	Child care
Verified	jasona@companyabc.com	Jason	Alexander	Jason Alexander	Events Coordinator	Marketing
The user name isn't valid or the domain doesn't exist.	robertd@companyab.com	Robert	Douglas	Robert Douglas	Manager	Facilities
Verified	danan@companyabc.com	Dana	Neuman	Dana Neuman	Documentation Specialist	Executive Office

Verification results: 3 users passed verification
We recommend that you print this page or save it as a text file.

FIGURE 22.5   Log file from the bulk user import process.

10. After all user accounts have been verified, at the Verification results screen click Next.

11. At the Settings screen, under Set sign-in status select either Allowed or Blocked to set the initial status of the users when the accounts are created.

12. In the Set user location section, use the drop-down menu to select the user's location, and then click Next.

13. At the Assign licenses screen, select the check box for the Lync Online plan that the user will be licensed for, along with any other Office 365 services and plans that the organization has a subscription for.

14. At the Send results in email page, keep the default selection of Send email if the username and temporary password for the new account should be sent to an administrator via email, and then enter up to five recipient email addresses separated by semicolons. When finished, click Create.

15. At the Results page, verify that the user accounts have been successfully created, and make note of the temporary passwords automatically generated. Click Close to complete the procedure.

Preparing Client Systems for Lync Online

The preparation of client systems for Lync Online is largely a matter of installing the Lync client on each system. However, there are several additional requirements for client systems to be compatible with Office 365:

▶ The Microsoft Online Services Sign In Assistant must be installed to enable Lync to authenticate to Microsoft Online Services. Much like the Lync client, this software is provided in the form of a Windows Installer file, and it can therefore be installed using any of the standard deployment methods.

▶ Although not an absolute requirement, it is highly recommended to run the Microsoft Office 365 Desktop Setup utility on each client system, because the tool automatically detects and installs required updates and components.

Configuring Federation and Public IM

For each new instance of Lync Online, federation with other organizations and with public IM providers is by default disabled for the organization. The following steps are used to enable federation and public IM:

1. Log on to the Office 365 Portal.

2. On the main page, click the Admin tab at the top, and then select Lync from the drop-down menu to open the Lync Admin Center.

3. On the left side, click Organization, and then click on the link for External communications at the top.

4. At the External communications page, under External access, use the drop-down menu to select the domain federation option that meets the organization's policy for communication with external organizations. If the organization will manage a blacklist of SIP domains for which communication is not allowed, select the option for On except for blocked domains. If the organization will instead manage a whitelist of SIP domains for which communication is allowed, select the option for On only for allowed Domains.

5. To enable communication with public IM providers, click the check box under Public IM connectivity.

6. Depending on the domain federation mode option chosen in the previous step, the SIP domain list displayed under the Blocked or allowed domains section will be used as either a whitelist or a blacklist. To add a SIP domain to the list, click the plus symbol that appears above the list.

7. At the Add a domain box, enter the name of the domain that will be allowed or blocked in the Domain name field, and then click Add to save the setting. The domain is then listed as an allowed or blocked domain, as shown in Figure 22.6.

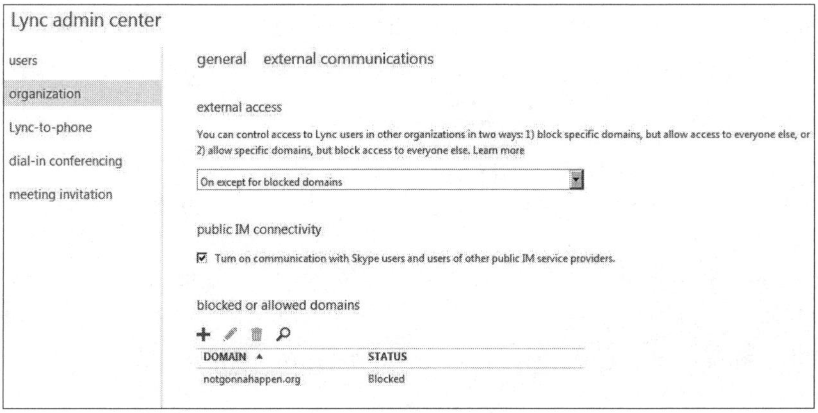

FIGURE 22.6   Federation and public IM settings in the online portal.

8. Repeat steps 6 and 7 to add any additional SIP domains that will be blocked or allowed as needed.

TIP

Turning on federation or public IM for a Lync Online organization, along with the configuration of a SIP domain whitelist or blacklist, can require up to a day to activate due to replication requirements within the Microsoft data center infrastructure. With that in mind, it is recommended to enable these features and immediately configure the whitelist or blacklist at least several days before the users need to begin communicating with external organizations.

Configuring Dial-in Conferencing

If a dial-in conferencing service has been purchased from an approved Microsoft partner, dial-in conferencing can be enabled for each user by configuration of the dial-in conferencing properties of the user accounts. Although this can be performed manually, if there are many accounts to be configured, then this would require a lot of administrative effort. To ease this process, it is possible to import a file supplied by the audio conferencing provider containing the phone numbers and passcodes for the user accounts. To start the process, a file containing the list of users to be enabled for dial-in conferencing must be exported using the online portal. This list is then used by the provider to generate a file that can be used to import the settings for the user accounts.

The following steps are used to configure dial-in conferencing for Lync Online users in bulk using the export and import method:

1. Log on to the Office 365 Portal.

2. On the main page, click the Admin tab at the top, and then select Lync from the drop-down menu to open the Lync Admin Center.

3. On the left side, click Dial-in conferencing, and then click on Provider at the top.

4. Under Import and Export users, click the link for Export wizard.

5. At the Export Users Wizard Getting Started screen, click Next.

6. At the Select Users screen, click the Ctrl key, select each of the users in the list that will be enabled for dial-in conferencing, and then click Add. When finished, click Next.

7. At the File Download prompt, click Save and then choose a local subdirectory to save the file to.

8. Click Finish to complete the Export Users Wizard and return to the Dial-in Conferencing Provider page.

9. Send the downloaded file, named `AcpUsers.csv`, to the audio conferencing provider so that the appropriate dial-in conferencing properties can be filled in.

10. After the file has been returned by the audio conferencing provider, save the file to a local subdirectory, and return to the Dial-in conferencing Provider page in the Lync Admin Center.

11. Under Import and Export users, click the link for Import wizard.

12. At the Import Users Wizard Getting started screen, click Next.

13. At the Select File screen, click Browse. Then navigate to and select the import file that was sent by the audio conferencing provider, and click Next.

14. At the Results screen, the results of the import process are displayed. If the import was successful, click Finish to complete the Import Wizard. If errors are contained in the file, the option to download the error log file is automatically selected. If this is the case, click Finish; then at the File Download prompt, click Save and choose a local subdirectory to save the error log file to.

15. If necessary, send the downloaded error log file named `ErrorUsers.csv` to the audio provider to make any needed corrections.

16. After the adjusted file has been returned, repeat steps 12 to 15 to import the adjusted file and confirm that the import is now successful.

17. After the file from the audio provider is successfully imported, click on Dial-in users in the Lync Admin Center to view the newly applied conferencing properties for the users, as shown in Figure 22.7.

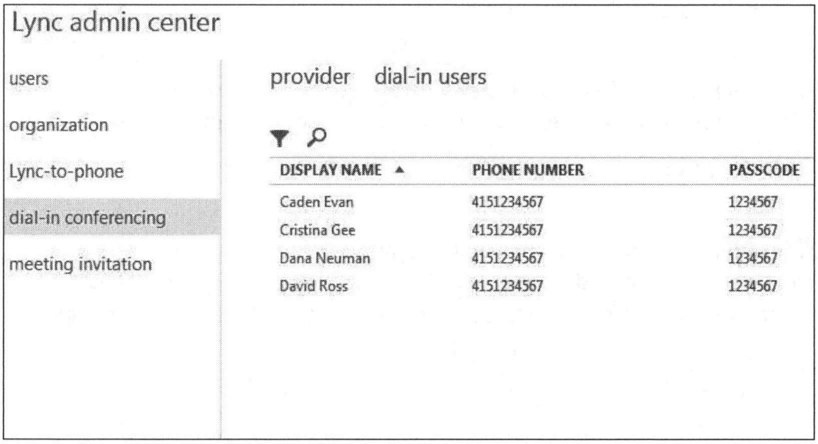

Lync admin center

	provider dial-in users		
users			
organization	▼ 🔍		
Lync-to-phone	**DISPLAY NAME** ▲	**PHONE NUMBER**	**PASSCODE**
dial-in conferencing	Caden Evan	4151234567	1234567
	Cristina Gee	4151234567	1234567
meeting invitation	Dana Neuman	4151234567	1234567
	David Ross	4151234567	1234567

FIGURE 22.7   Dial-in conferencing properties applied to Lync Online user accounts.

Configuring Lync Properties for User Accounts

After user accounts have been added to Lync Online, the Lync properties of the user accounts can be configured using the Online Portal. Use the following procedure to adjust the Lync properties for a user:

1. Log on to the Office 365 Portal.

2. On the left side of the main page, click Users and Groups.

3. At the Users and Groups page, select the check box for the user account to be edited; then, under Quick Steps on the right side of the screen, click on Edit Lync Properties.

4. At the Options screen, options are presented for various basic Lync features, as shown in Figure 22.8. Select or deselect the check boxes to enable or disable individual features.

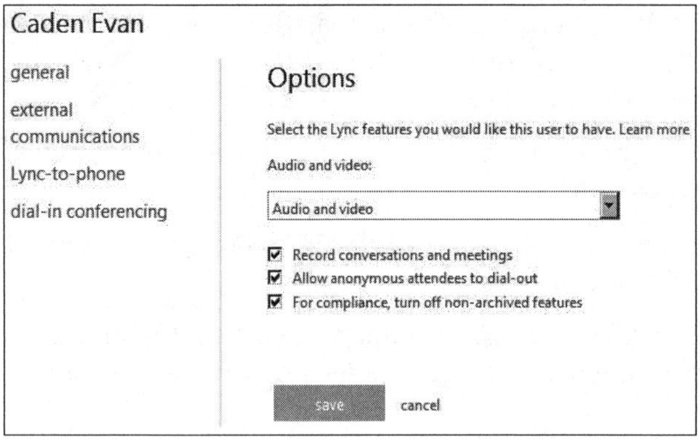

FIGURE 22.8   Editing the Lync properties of a user account.

5. On the left side, click External communications to view options for federation and public IM. Select or deselect the check boxes to enable or disable individual features.

6. On the left side, click Lync-to-phone. If a Lync-to-phone service has been purchased, the service can be selected from the drop-down menu.

7. On the left side, click Dial-in conferencing. If a dial-in conferencing service has been purchased, select the provider from the drop-down menu. The values for toll number, toll-free number, and passcode can then be assigned using the appropriate fields.

8. When finished, click Save.

TIP

The values for dial-in conferencing can also be applied to user accounts in bulk, instead of configuring each user account manually. For details, see the "Configuring Dial-in Conferencing" section of this chapter.

Configuring Lync-to-Phone

If a hosted voice service has been purchased from an approved Microsoft partner, you can enable the service for each user by configuring the Lync-to-phone provider for the user account, and then adding the user's phone number to the Office number field.

Use the following steps to enable a user for Lync-to-phone using the online portal:

1. Log on to the Office 365 Portal.

2. On the left side of the main page, click Users and Groups.

3. At the Users and Groups page, click on the name of the user to be enabled for Lync-to-phone to open the account properties.

4. On the left side, click Details, and then click Additional details to display the optional user properties.

5. Enter the phone number that will be used with the user's Lync-to-phone service in the Office phone field, and then click Save to return to the Users and Groups page.

6. Select the check box for the user account to be edited; then, under Quick steps on the right side of the screen, click on Edit Lync properties.

7. On the left side, click Lync-to-phone.

8. Under Properties, use the drop-down menu to select the Lync-to-phone provider, as shown in Figure 22.9.

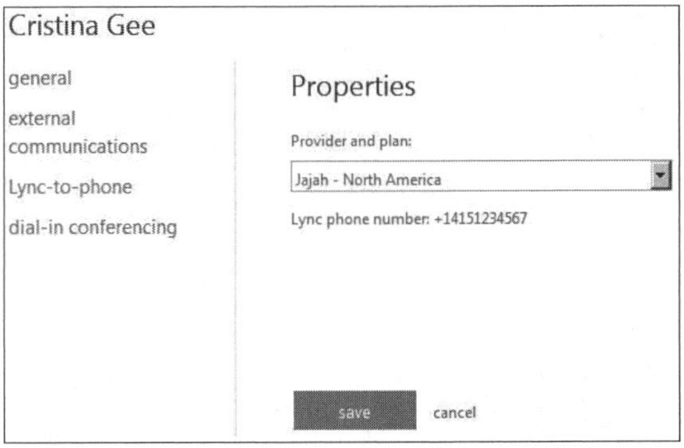

Cristina Gee	
general	**Properties**
external communications	Provider and plan:
Lync-to-phone	Jajah - North America
dial-in conferencing	Lync phone number: +14151234567
	save cancel

FIGURE 22.9   Assigning a Lync-to-phone provider to a user account.

9. Click Save to complete the Lync-to-phone configuration.

Configuring Exchange UM Integration

If Lync-to-Phone has been purchased and configured as part of the Lync Online subscription, and Exchange Online Plan 2 and above has also been purchased, then Exchange UM can be configured to provide voice mail for Lync clients. The following sections provide details on the deployment of features that are available with the integration of Exchange UM and Lync Online.

Creating a SIP URI Dial Plan

The following procedure is used to configure a SIP URI dial plan required for integration between Lync Online and Exchange Online UM:

1. Log on to the Office 365 Portal.

2. On the main page, click the Admin tab at the top, and then select Exchange from the drop-down menu to open the Exchange Admin Center.

3. On the left side, click Unified messaging, and then click on UM dial plans at the top.

4. At the UM dial plans page, click on the plus symbol.

5. The New UM dial plan window appears, as shown in Figure 22.10. Enter the name of the new dial plan, and the number of digits that will be used.

FIGURE 22.10   Creating a new SIP URI dial plan.

TIP

Lync-to-phone supports dialing using full E.164 phone numbers only; abbreviated dialing using office extensions is not available with this service. For example, 415-123-4567 is a valid number to dial, but 4567 is not. This means that the number of digits specified for the SIP URI dial plan should include the area code and prefix, which would be 10 digits in this example.

6. Use the drop-down menu to select a Dial plan type of SIP URI, and select the Audio language that will be used for the service.

7. Enter the Country/Region code for the dial plan to enable domestic and international dialing; for example, the correct region code for the United States is 1.

8. When finished, click Save.

If necessary, after the SIP URI dial plan is created, you can edit additional properties by selecting the dial plan in the UM dial plans page of the Exchange Admin Center, and clicking the Edit icon. For example, additional properties of the SIP URI dial plan that can be configured include minimum PIN length, limits on personal greetings, Outlook Voice Access settings, and much more.

Enabling Users for Exchange UM

Use the following procedure to enable a Lync Online user for Exchange UM:

1. Log on to the Office 365 Portal.

2. On the left side of the main page, click Users and Groups.

3. At the Users and Groups page, select the check box for the user account to be enabled for Exchange UM; then, under Quick steps on the right side of the screen, click on Edit Exchange properties.

4. On the left side, click Mailbox features.

5. Under Phone and Voice Features, click the Enable link under Unified Messaging: Disabled.

6. At the Enable UM mailbox screen, click Browse, and then select the SIP URI dial plan previously created. Click OK, and click Next.

7. In the Extension Number field, enter the full phone number for the user, which should match the number of digits specified for the dial plan, as shown in Figure 22.11.

8. Under PIN Settings, either keep the default setting of Automatically generate a PIN, or select the option to Type a PIN and manually enter the initial PIN number, using the minimum number of digits specified for the dial plan.

9. Determine whether users will need to reset their PIN the first time they sign in by selecting or deselecting the check box, and then click Finish to complete the Exchange UM configuration for the user and return to the Mailbox features page.

10. At the bottom of the screen, click Save.

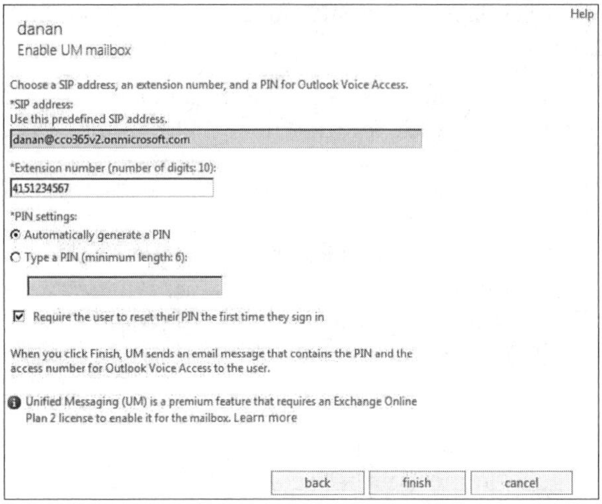

FIGURE 22.11   Enabling Exchange UM for a user account.

Configuring an Auto Attendant Number

If the auto attendant feature of Exchange UM will be used with Lync Online, each auto attendant number used must be added to the Exchange UM dial plan, and also must be configured as an access number within Lync Online. The following procedure is used to configure a new auto attendant number using the online portal:

1. Log on to the Office 365 Portal.

2. On the main page, click the Admin tab at the top, and then select Exchange from the drop-down menu to open the Exchange Admin Center.

3. On the left side, click Unified messaging, and then click UM dial plans at the top.

4. At the UM dial plans page, select the SIP URI dial plan previously created from the list, and click the Edit icon.

5. At the Dial plan properties page, under UM Auto Attendants, click the plus symbol.

6. The New UM auto attendant page appears, as shown in Figure 22.12. Enter a name for the auto attendant in the Name field, and select the check box for Create this auto attendant as enabled. If desired, also select the option for Set the auto attendant to respond to voice commands.

7. Under Access numbers, enter the phone number that users will dial to reach the UM auto attendant, using the full E.164 number format (for example, +14151112222). The number of digits entered should also match the number of digits associated with the dial plan. After the number is entered, click the plus symbol to add the number to the list of access numbers. This step can then be repeated as many times as necessary to associate additional numbers with this same auto attendant if desired.

8. When finished, click Save to return to the Dial plan properties page.

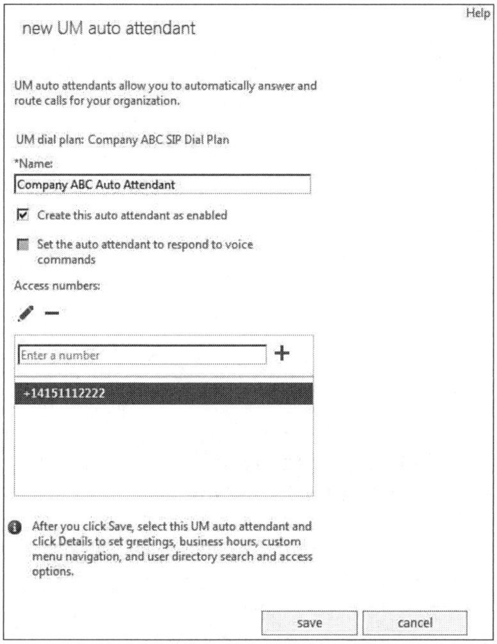

new UM auto attendant   Help

UM auto attendants allow you to automatically answer and
route calls for your organization.

UM dial plan: Company ABC SIP Dial Plan

*Name:

Company ABC Auto Attendant

☑ Create this auto attendant as enabled

☐ Set the auto attendant to respond to voice
    commands

Access numbers:

Enter a number   +

+14151112222

ℹ️ After you click Save, select this UM auto attendant and
    click Details to set greetings, business hours, custom
    menu navigation, and user directory search and access
    options.

                          save   cancel

FIGURE 22.12   Creating a new Exchange UM auto attendant.

9. The new auto attendant now is displayed under the UM Auto Attendants section of the dial plan properties. If necessary, additional settings can be configured for the auto attendant by selecting it from the list and clicking the Edit icon. For example, custom greetings can be configured, along with business hours, menu navigation settings, and more. After the configuration of the auto attendant is complete, click Close at the Dial Plan Properties page to return to the Exchange Admin Center.

10. Click the Admin tab at the top, and then select Lync from the drop-down menu to open the Lync Admin Center.

11. On the left side, click Lync-to-phone, and then click on access numbers at the top.

12. At the Access numbers page, click on the plus symbol.

13. The Access numbers properties page appears, as shown in Figure 22.13. Enter the same phone number that was configured for the auto attendant in step 7, again using the full E.164 numbering format.

14. Under Address, enter a unique prefix for the SIP address that will be associated with the auto attendant, such as CompanyABC_Main_AA, and then use the drop-down menu to select the SIP domain that will be associated with this auto attendant.

15. If desired, enter a description to clarify the purpose of this auto attendant in the Description field.

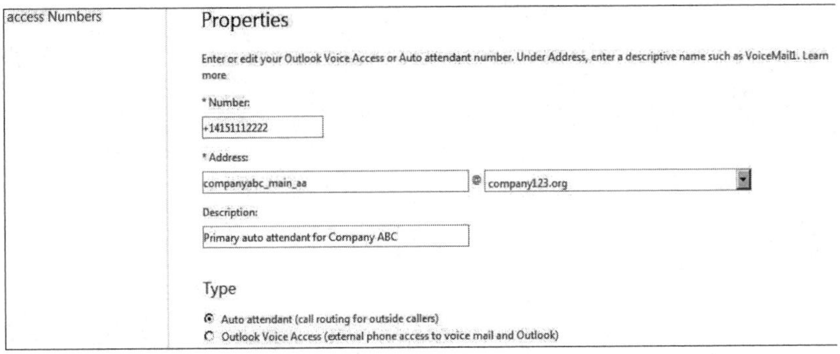

610 CHAPTER 22 Lync Online and Hybrid Deployments

<grep>FIGURE 22.13 Creating an auto attendant for Lync Online.</grep>

16. Under Type, select Auto attendant, and then click Save. The new auto attendant is now displayed in the list of access numbers configured for Lync Online.

Configuring a Subscriber Access Number

If the Outlook Voice Access feature of Exchange UM will be used with Lync Online, each subscriber access number used must be added to the Exchange UM dial plan, and also must be configured as an access number within Lync Online. Use the following procedure to configure a new subscriber number for the Outlook Voice Access feature using the online portal:

1. Log on to the Office 365 Portal.

2. On the main page, click the Admin tab at the top, and then select Exchange from the drop-down menu to open the Exchange Admin Center.

3. On the left side, click Unified messaging, and then click on UM dial plans at the top.

4. At the UM dial plans page, select the SIP URI dial plan previously created from the list, and click the Edit icon.

5. At the Dial plan properties page, under UM Dial Plan, click Configure.

6. On the left side, click Outlook Voice Access.

7. At the Outlook Voice Access page, under Outlook Voice Access numbers, enter the phone number that users will dial to sign in to their mailboxes, using the full E.164 numbering format (for example, +14151113333). The number of digits entered should also match the number of digits associated with the dial plan. After the number is entered, click the plus symbol to add the number to the list of Outlook Voice Access numbers. This step can then be repeated as many times as necessary to associate additional numbers with this same dial plan if desired.

8. When finished, click Save, and then click Close at the Dial plan properties page to return to the Exchange Admin Center.

9. Click the Admin tab at the top, and then select Lync from the drop-down menu to open the Lync Admin Center.

10. On the left side, click Lync-to-phone, and then click on Access numbers at the top.

11. At the Access numbers page, click on the plus symbol.

12. The Access numbers properties page appears, as shown earlier in Figure 22.13. Enter the same phone number that was configured for Outlook Voice Access in step 7, again using the full E.164 numbering format.

13. Under Address, enter a unique prefix for the SIP address that will be associated with the subscriber access number, such as `CompanyABC_SubscriberAccess`, and then use the drop-down menu to select the SIP domain that will be associated with this subscriber access number.

14. If desired, enter a description to clarify the purpose of this auto attendant in the Description field.

15. Under Type, select Outlook Voice Access, and then click Save. The new subscriber access number, along with any auto attendant numbers previously configured, are displayed in the list of access numbers configured for Lync Online, as shown in Figure 22.14.

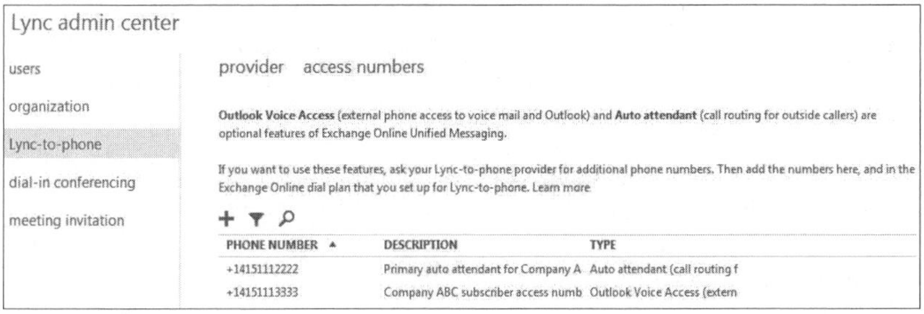

FIGURE 22.14   Access numbers configured for Lync Online.

AD FS Deployment for SSO

After Lync Online is up and running, Active Directory Federated Services (AD FS) can be deployed to enable single sign-on (SSO) functionality. For an introduction on using AD FS to achieve SSO with Office 365, as well as detailed information on systems requirements for the AD FS deployment, see Chapter 28. The following sections provide details on the AD FS software deployment and subsequent configuration for use with Lync Online.

Preparing Systems for AD FS

Systems that are planned for the federation server role should be fully patched and joined to the domain before AD FS installation. Systems that are planned for the federation server proxy role should be patched and then connected to a DMZ subnet as a workgroup member. If multiple servers will be used for resiliency, the load-balancing configuration should also be completed before AD FS installation on both federation server and federation server proxy systems. Although any load-balancing solution can be used with AD FS, this section provides guidelines for the configuration of Windows NLB for use with AD FS, since this is a very common solution.

Following are some guidelines regarding the installation of NLB in preparation for AD FS:

▶ The NLB feature is integrated with both the Standard and Enterprise Editions of Windows Server 2008 and Windows Server 2008 R2; therefore, it simply needs to be installed from the list of available Windows features, and typically Standard Edition is fine for this purpose.

▶ Two network adapters are typically recommended for each NLB node, although this is not required. The second adapter allows for one adapter to be dedicated for NLB functions, while the other adapter can be used for other network functions.

▶ NLB is not supported for use with DHCP; therefore, a static IP address must be applied to a system before NLB is installed.

▶ A cluster IP address must be selected as the virtual IP that is shared by every member of the NLB cluster. The IP address must be unique within the environment, and will be used to receive traffic destined for the federation service.

▶ The cluster operation mode can be specified as either unicast or multicast. While either mode can work, multicast is often recommended when NLB is installed on virtual machines, because it tends to reduce the complexity involved in ensuring that traffic flows properly through the virtualization environment.

▶ The default port rules configuration specifies load balancing for all ports. For a federation server cluster, the default port rule can be modified to configure load balancing for only ports 80 and 443, because these are the only ports that will be used by the federation service. For a federation server proxy cluster, only port 443 is required.

An additional requirement before running the AD FS Configuration Wizard is the installation of the SSL certificate that will be used as the Server Authentication Certificate. The certificate must be purchased from a public CA that is trusted by all the client systems that will be connecting to AD FS, and must use the federation service FQDN as the subject name. After the certificate is installed into the local certificate store on a federation server system, it must then be applied to the Default Web Site within IIS. After the certificate has been applied to the Default Web Site, it will automatically be discovered by the AD FS 2.0 Federation Server Configuration Wizard.

> **TIP**
>
> If a Lync hybrid deployment is planned, the subject name of the server authentication certificate will instead need to be `sts.<SIPdomain>`, where `<SIPdomain>` is the DNS domain that will be split across the Lync Online and Lync on-premise deployments. For details, see Chapter 28.

Preparing the Network for AD FS

After the NLB cluster has been created, several DNS records need to be manually created, and several firewall ports might need to be opened, depending on whether AD FS will be available externally. For specifics on which DNS records and firewall port openings are required for a given scenario, see Chapter 28.

If a dedicated service account will be used for AD FS, as required for a multiple-server deployment, the account must be created before the initial configuration of AD FS. The service account does not require any particular rights to the AD domain; however, it must be a member of the local Administrators group on each federation server.

Installing AD FS Software

The AD FS 2.0 software can be downloaded from the Microsoft download site, and is used for both the federation server and the federation server proxy systems. Installation of the AD FS 2.0 software can be performed either via the setup wizard or via the command line. Use the following procedure to install the AD FS 2.0 software using the setup wizard:

1. Log on to the server using an account with local administrator rights.

2. Use Windows Explorer to navigate to the location where the AD FS 2.0 installation file was saved, and double-click on the AdfsSetup.exe setup file.

3. At the Welcome to the AD FS 2.0 Setup Wizard page, click Next.

4. At the End User License Agreement page, read the license terms; then, if you agree to the license terms, select the I Accept the Terms in the License Agreement check box, and click Next.

5. At the Server Role page, select the role that this system will be used for, either Federation Server or Federation Server Proxy. Click Next.

6. At the Install Prerequisite Software page, click Next to begin the software installation.

7. After all software prerequisites have been installed, the Completed the AD FS 2.0 Setup Wizard page appears. Verify that the Restart Now check box is selected, and then click Finish to restart the computer and complete the installation.

After the system is back online, the Federation Server Configuration Wizard automatically starts, as described in the next section. The latest hotfixes for AD FS should also be downloaded and installed at this point. Similar to other Microsoft products, update rollups are periodically released to consolidate a number of individual hotfixes into one installation package. The most recent update rollup for AD FS 2.0 should be installed on each system.

Configuring the First Federation Server in the Farm

By default, when a system restarts after being targeted as a federation server during the AD FS 2.0 software installation, the AD FS 2.0 Federation Server Configuration Wizard automatically starts. The wizard can then be used to configure the first federation server in a farm, using the following procedure:

1. At the Welcome page, verify that Create a New Federation Service is selected, and then click Next.

2. At the Select Stand-Alone or Farm Deployment page, select New Federation Server Farm, and then click Next.

3. At the Specify the Federation Service Name page, verify that the SSL certificate displayed matches the name of the certificate that was previously imported into the Default Web Site in IIS. If the certificate displayed is incorrect, select the appropriate certificate from the SSL certificate list.

4. At the Specify a Service Account page, click Browse. In the Browse dialog box, locate the domain account that will be used as the dedicated service account for the federation server farm, and then click OK. Enter the password for this account, confirm it, and click Next.

5. At the Ready to Apply Settings page, review the details. If the settings appear correct, click Next to begin configuring the AD FS instance with these settings.

6. At the Configuration Results page, review the results. After all the configuration steps have completed, click Close to exit the wizard and complete the configuration.

> **TIP**
>
> After the configuration of the first federation server is complete, the AD FS 2.0 Management snap-in automatically opens and a message appears, indicating that the configuration is incomplete and that a trusted relying party should be added. This message can safely be disregarded, since the relying party trust for Lync Online/Office 365 will be added during a later step.

Adding Federation Servers to the Farm

After the first federation server has been configured, the AD FS 2.0 software can be installed to additional servers. The same SSL certificate installed on the primary federation server should be imported to any additional servers, and applied to the IIS Default Web Site before AD FS is configured. By default, when a system restarts after being targeted as a federation server during the AD FS 2.0 software installation, the AD FS 2.0 Federation Server Configuration Wizard automatically starts. To add an additional server to the federation service farm, use the following procedure:

1. At the Welcome page, verify that Add a Federation Server to an Existing Federation Service is selected, and then click Next.

2. At the Specify the Primary Federation Server and Service Account page, under Primary Federation Server Name, enter the name of the primary federation server and click Browse. In the Browse dialog box, locate the domain account of the dedicated service account for the federation server farm, and then click OK. Enter the password for this account, confirm it, and click Next.

3. At the Ready to Apply Settings page, review the details. If the settings appear correct, click Next to begin configuring the AD FS instance with these settings.

4. At the Configuration Results page, review the results. After all the configuration steps have completed, click Close to exit the wizard and complete the configuration.

Verifying That the Federation Service Is Operational

After the federation service has been configured, there are two methods that can be used to verify that the service is operational:

▶ On a client computer that is a member of the same AD forest as the federation service, open a web browser and connect to the following URL, where <fedservFQDN> is the fully qualified domain name of the federation service: https://<fedservFQDN>/FederationMetadata/2007-06/FederationMetadata.xml.

At the certificate warning prompt, click Continue to This Website. If the connection is successful, the expected output is a federation service description document in XML format.

▶ On a server where the federation service role has been installed, open the Event Viewer. Under Applications and Service Logs, expand AD FS 2.0 Eventing, and then click on Admin. In the Event ID column, search for an event with ID 100. If event ID 100 is shown, this indicates that the federation server was able to successfully communicate with the federation service.

Federation Server Proxy Configuration

After the federation service is up and running, the AD FS configuration can be performed on the systems that will be used as federation proxies. The same SSL certificate installed on the federation servers should be imported to each server that will be used as a federation server proxy, and applied to the IIS Default Web Site before configuring AD FS. By default, after a system restarts after being targeted as a federation server proxy during the AD FS 2.0 software installation, the AD FS 2.0 Federation Server Proxy Configuration Wizard automatically starts. To configure the federation server proxy role, use the following procedure:

1. At the Welcome page, click Next.

2. At the Specify Federation Service Name page, under Federation Service Name, enter the fully qualified domain name of the federation service.

3. If an HTTP proxy server is required to forward requests to the federation service, select the Use an HTTP Proxy Server When Sending Requests to This Federation Service check box; then, under HTTP Proxy Server Address, type the address of the proxy server, and click Test Connection to verify connectivity. When finished, click Next.

4. At the prompt, enter the credentials of the dedicated AD FS service account that was specified during the configuration of the federation service. This account is used to establish trust between the federation server proxy and the federation service.

5. At the Ready to Apply Settings page, review the details. If the settings appear correct, click Next to begin configuring the federation server proxy settings.

6. At the Configuration Results page, review the results. After all the configuration steps have completed, click Close to exit the wizard and complete the configuration.

Verifying That the Federation Proxy Is Operational

After the federation proxy service has been configured, use the following procedure to verify that the service is operational:

1. Log on to the federation server proxy system using an account with local administrator rights.

2. Open the Event Viewer; then, under Applications and Service Logs, expand AD FS 2.0 Eventing, and click on Admin.

3. In the Event ID column, search for an event with ID 198. If event ID 198 is shown, this indicates that the federation server proxy service was started successfully and is now online.

Establishing Trust with Office 365 for SSO

After the federation service is fully operational, the next step is to configure the trust between AD FS and Office 365. This is accomplished using the Microsoft Online Services Module for Windows PowerShell, which installs a set of Windows PowerShell cmdlets that can be used to configure the trust and enable SSO for a domain, as described in the following sections.

Installing the Microsoft Online Services Module

The Microsoft Online Services Module can be downloaded directly from the Office 365 site, and is available in both 32-bit and 64-bit versions. Following are the requirements for a system to run the Microsoft Online Services Module:

▶ Supported operating systems are Windows 7 or Windows Server 2008 R2.

▶ .NET Framework 3.5 SP1 must be enabled as a Windows feature.

▶ Office 365 software updates should be downloaded and installed from the Office 365 portal to ensure that the appropriate versions of all software are used.

The Microsoft Online Services Module also requires administrative access to AD FS 2.0 for the cmdlets to execute successfully. If the module will not be installed and run directly on a federation server, remote access to AD FS must be enabled. You can accomplish this by opening Windows PowerShell as an administrator on the federation server and executing the cmdlet `enable-psremoting`.

Adding or Converting a Domain for SSO

Each domain that will be used for SSO with Lync Online/Office 365 must either be added as an SSO domain or be converted from a standard domain to SSO. The Microsoft Online

Services Module is used to add or convert the domain, which sets up a trust between the internal AD FS deployment and Office 365.

Use the following procedure to add a new domain for SSO:

1. Open the Microsoft Online Services Module.

2. Execute the command $cred=Get-Credential, and then at the prompt enter the credentials of an Office 365 administrative account.

3. Execute the command Connect-MsolService -Credential $cred, which creates a connection to Office 365, as required to run the remaining cmdlets.

4. Execute the command Set-MsolAdfscontext -Computer <ADFSprimary>, where <ADFSprimary> is the fully qualified domain name of the primary federation server. This cmdlet creates a connection to the internal federation service.

> **NOTE**
>
> If the Microsoft Online Services Module is installed on the federation server, the Set-MsolAdfscontext cmdlet is not required.

5. Execute the command New-MsolFederatedDomain -DomainName <Domain>, where <Domain> is the domain to be added and enabled for SSO.

6. The results of the New-MsolFederatedDomain cmdlet include information that must be used to verify ownership of the new domain. Specifically, a new DNS record (either a TXT record or an MX record) must be created within the zone that will be enabled for SSO, and this DNS record is used by Office 365 to confirm domain ownership. Follow through with the instructions to add either the TXT or the MX record to the public DNS zone, and then wait for the change to take effect. The amount of time required will depend on DNS propagation delay, as well as the DNS provider being used.

> **NOTE**
>
> While either the TXT or the MX record can be tested for validation for Office 365, the TXT record is the preferred method of validation. The reason for this is that the MX record required for validation specifies an address value ending in .invalid, and not all DNS providers support this record. The TXT record, on the other hand, is much more commonly supported.

7. After the DNS verification record has propagated, the New-MsolFederatedDomain cmdlet is executed a second time, specifying the same domain name to finalize the addition of the new SSO domain.

The following procedure would be used to convert a domain that has already been added to Office 365 from a standard domain to SSO:

1. Open the Microsoft Online Services Module.

2. Execute the command `$cred=Get-Credential`, and then at the prompt enter the credentials of an Office 365 administrative account.

3. Execute the command `Connect-MsolService -Credential $cred`, which creates a connection to Office 365, as required to run the remaining cmdlets.

4. Execute the command `Set-MsolAdfscontext -Computer <ADFSprimary>`, where `<ADFSprimary>` is the fully qualified domain name of the primary federation server. This cmdlet creates a connection to the internal federation service.

> **NOTE**
>
> If the Microsoft Online Services Module is installed on the federation server, the `Set-MsolAdfscontext` cmdlet is not required.

5. Execute the command `Convert-MsolDomainToFederated -DomainName <Domain>`, where `<Domain>` is the domain to be converted to SSO.

> **NOTE**
>
> When a domain that has already been added to Office 365 is converted to SSO, every licensed user automatically becomes federated for SSO.

Configuring Directory Synchronization

For most organizations that deploy SSO, directory synchronization is the next step, because the combination of SSO and directory synchronization offers a seamless experience for Lync Online users. The first step with directory synchronization is to validate that the Active Directory environment has been prepared for synchronization, with the help of the Microsoft Office 365 Deployment Readiness Tool. For details on preparing AD for directory synchronization with the use of this tool, see Chapter 28. After the environment has been fully prepared, the information in the following sections can be used to configure synchronization with Active Directory.

Activating Directory Synchronization

Before installing the Directory Synchronization tool, you must first activate the feature using the Office 365 Portal. Use the following procedure to activate directory synchronization using the online portal:

1. Log on to the Office 365 Portal.

2. On the left side of the main page, click Users and groups.

3. At the top of the Users and Groups page, click on the Set up link next to Active Directory synchronization.

4. At the Set Up and manage single sign-on page, under Activate Active Directory synchronization, click the Activate button.

5. At the prompt, click Activate. A notification that Active Directory synchronization is being activated should appear, as shown in Figure 22.15.

Set up and manage single sign-on

ⓘ Active Directory synchronization is being activated. This process may take up to 24 hours to complete.

When you set up single sign-on (also known as identity federation), your users can sign in with their corporate credentials to access the services in Microsoft Office 365 for enterprises. As part of setting up single sign-on, you must also set up directory synchronization. Together, these features integrate your on-premises and cloud directories.

1 **Prepare for single sign-on**
Learn about the benefits of single sign-on and make sure you meet the requirements before you set it up.
Learn how to prepare for single sign-on

2 **Plan for and deploy Active Directory Federation Services 2.0**
Work through the in-depth documentation to deploy and configure AD FS 2.0.
Follow instructions for planning and deploying AD FS 2.0 for single sign-on

3 **Install the Windows Azure Active Directory Module for Windows PowerShell**
Download the Windows Azure Active Directory Module for Windows PowerShell, which includes cmdlets to establish the trust relationship between your AD FS 2.0 server and Office 365 for each of your domains that use single sign-on.
Learn about installing and configuring the Windows Azure Active Directory Module for Windows PowerShell

    ⦿ Windows 32-bit version
    ○ Windows 64-bit version

    [download]

FIGURE 22.15   Activating the AD synchronization feature in the online portal.

NOTE

The activation process can require up to 24 hours to complete. After the activation is complete, the notification displayed in Figure 22.15 will no longer be displayed. Lync Online administrators should plan ahead and activate AD synchronization several days before the AD user accounts need to be populated into the online directory.

Installing the Directory Synchronization Tool

The Microsoft Online Services Directory Synchronization tool can be downloaded directly from the Office 365 Portal. Several sets of administrative permissions are required for the user account that runs the tool:

▶ Local administrator permissions on the system where the Directory Synchronization tool will be installed

▶ Enterprise Administrator permissions in the Active Directory forest of which the system running the Directory Synchronization tool is a member

▶ Administrative permissions to the Lync Online/Office 365 tenant

Use the following procedure to download and install the Directory Synchronization tool on a system that has been prepared for this purpose:

1. Log on to the system using an account with local administrator permissions.

2. Open a web browser, and log on to the Office 365 Portal.

3. On the left side of the main page, click Users and groups.

4. At the top of the Users and Groups page, click on the Set Up link next to Active Directory synchronization.

5. At the Set up and manage Single sign-on page, under Install and configure the Directory Sync tool, click the Download button.

6. At the prompt, click Save, and then choose a local subdirectory to save the file to.

7. After the file has been downloaded, double-click on the `dirsync.exe` file to begin the installation.

8. At the Welcome screen, click Next.

9. At the Microsoft Software License Terms screen, read the license terms; then if you agree to the license terms, select the I Accept radio button and click Next.

10. At the Select Installation Folder screen, either keep the default installation folder path or specify an alternative path if desired, and then click Next.

11. After the installation is complete, click Next.

12. At the Finish screen, if the directory synchronization configuration will be performed right away, select the check box for Start Configuration Wizard Now. If the configuration will be performed later, deselect this check box. Click Finish to complete the installation.

Synchronizing the Directories

After the Directory Synchronization tool has been installed, it can be used to synchronize the directories for the first time. For the first synchronization, a copy of the local users and groups is written to the Office 365 directory. From there forward, the Directory Synchronization tool checks for any changes to the local AD objects and updates the Office 365 directory with the changes.

If the default option was selected on the final page when the Directory Synchronization tool was installed, the Microsoft Online Directory Services Synchronization Configuration

Wizard starts automatically. If not, you can invoke the wizard by logging on to the system where the tool is installed, and, from the Start menu, selecting All Programs, Microsoft Online Services, Directory Synchronization, Directory Sync Configuration. Use the wizard to configure directory synchronization, as detailed here:

1. At the Welcome screen, click Next.

2. At the Microsoft Online Services Credentials screen, enter the credentials of an Office 365 administrator account, and click Next. The wizard verifies that directory synchronization has been activated in the online tenant. If a configuration error message appears, the activation of the feature might not be complete within Office 365, which can be verified using the online portal. After activation is verified, the wizard continues.

3. At the Active Directory Credentials page, enter the credentials of an Enterprise Admin account, and click Next.

4. At the Exchange Hybrid Deployment page, click Next to continue.

5. When the configuration is complete, click Next.

6. At the Finished page, verify that the Synchronize Directories Now check box is selected, and click Finish.

NOTE

When configured, the directory synchronization service automatically creates a service account named MSOL_AD_SYNC in the Users container at the root of Active Directory, and applies a randomly generated password that never expires. This service account is used by the Directory Synchronization tool to read the local Active Directory and write to Office 365, using the credentials provided in the Microsoft Online Services Credentials page of the Configuration Wizard. This service account should never be moved or removed, and the password on the account should never be manually reset; otherwise, synchronization failures will occur.

After directory synchronization has been configured, it will run every three hours automatically. If there are changes that need to be synchronized more urgently, there are two methods that can be used to force synchronization. The first method is to run the Directory Services Synchronization Configuration Wizard, following the same procedure already described. To force directory synchronization, the Synchronize Directories Now check box should be selected on the final page of the wizard. Though simple, this method of forcing synchronization does require the appropriate credentials to be entered each time the wizard is run. To force directory synchronization without the need to enter credentials, Windows PowerShell can be used. Use the following procedure to force directory synchronization using a Windows PowerShell cmdlet:

1. Log on to the system where the Directory Synchronization tool is installed using an account with local administrator permissions.

22

2. Use Windows Explorer to navigate to the directory where the Directory Synchronization tool is installed (by default, `%programfiles%\Microsoft Online Directory Sync`), and double-click on the `DirSyncConfigShell.psc1` file, which opens a Windows PowerShell window with the directory synchronization cmdlets loaded.

3. Execute the cmdlet `Start-OnlineCoexistenceSync` to force directory synchronization.

Activating Synchronized Users

After the initial synchronization is complete, AD users and groups will appear in the Lync Online/Office 365 directory with a status of "Synced with active directory," as shown in Figure 22.16. Although the users are now part of the directory, they are not enabled for Lync Online until they are activated. To activate newly synchronized user accounts, use the following procedure:

1. Log on to the Office 365 Portal.

2. On the left side of the main page, click Users and groups.

3. At the top of the users list, click the Filter icon, which has the funnel symbol.

4. Use the drop-down menu to select Unlicensed users.

5. From the list of unlicensed users, either click the check box next to individual user accounts, or click the check box at the top of the list to select all user accounts.

6. From the Quick steps menu at the right, click on Activate synced users.

7. At the Assign licenses screen, select the check box for the Lync Online plan that the user will be licensed for, along with any other Office 365 services and plans that the organization has a subscription for.

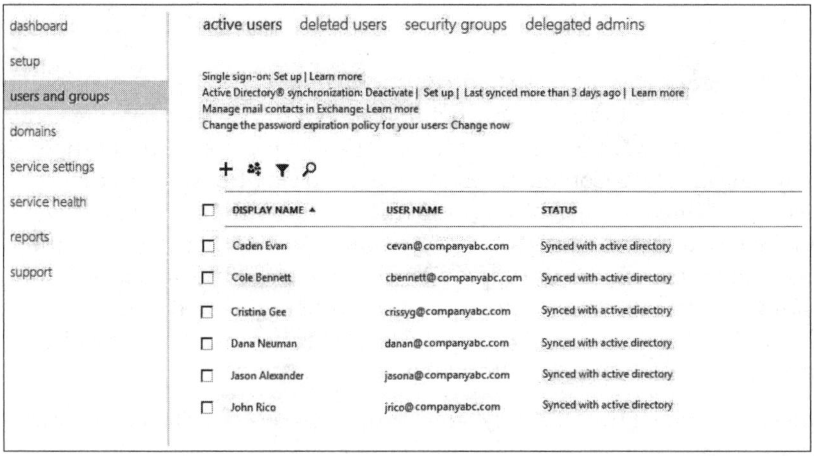

FIGURE 22.16   Newly synchronized users in the Lync Online/Office 365 directory.

8. At the Send results in email page, keep the default selection of Send email if the username and temporary password for the new account should be sent to an administrator via email, and then enter up to five recipient email addresses separated by semicolons. When finished, click Activate.

9. At the Results page, verify that the user account has been successfully activated, and make note of the temporary password automatically generated. Click Finish to complete the procedure.

Lync Hybrid Deployment

The procedures for building a Lync hybrid deployment can be significant, depending on whether there is an existing Lync or OCS installation in place, or whether the entire environment will be built from scratch. Many of the tasks involved in building a hybrid deployment are found either in other sections of this chapter or in other chapters of this publication. Although these other sections will be referred to for the appropriate guidance, there are also some deployment tasks that are specific to the hybrid environment, and these are detailed in the following sections.

Installing the On-Premise Systems

A Lync hybrid deployment starts with the installation of the on-premise Lync infrastructure, if there is no existing Lync environment in place. At a minimum, the on-premise deployment requires one Front End pool and one Edge pool, with the Edge pool enabled for federation. Although a Lync 2010 Front End pool and Edge pool can be used for this, at least one Lync 2013 Front End Server needs to be installed to support advanced voice features. For further details on the on-premise topology options supported for a hybrid deployment, see Chapter 28. Although it's not required, consideration should be given to building high-availability into the solution, leveraging the built-in resilience features of Lync 2013. For details regarding the planning process for the Lync on-premise systems, see Chapters 29 to 32.

After the Lync on-premise installation is in place and functional, and the Lync Online or Office 365 subscription is active, the next steps are required to prepare the on-premise systems for a hybrid deployment:

▶ If it has not already been added, the SIP domain that will be split between the on-premise and cloud deployment will need to be added to Lync Online/Office 365, with the ownership verified. For details on this procedure, see the "Adding Domains to Lync Online/Office 365" section of this chapter.

▶ Install Active Directory Federated Services to enable SSO for the hybrid deployment, using a minimum of one federation server. If users will be connecting remotely, at least one AD FS proxy should also be included, and should be installed in a DMZ subnet. As part of the deployment, request an SSL certificate from a public certificate authority with the `sts.<SIPdomain>` name specified as the subject name, and apply the certificate to the Default Web Site on both the federation server and the federation proxy server systems.

▶ After the internal federation service is operational, a trust relationship must be established with the Lync Online/Office 365 deployment. For details on planning AD FS
for use with Lync Online, see Chapter 28. For details on installing AD FS and configuring it for SSO with Lync Online, see the "AD FS Deployment for SSO" section of
this chapter.

▶ Activate the online tenant for AD synchronization; then configure directory
synchronization between the on-premise Active Directory and the Lync Online/
Office 365 directory, and synchronize the on-premise users and groups to Lync
Online. For details on planning directory synchronization between AD and Lync
Online/Office 365, see Chapter 28. For details on installing and configuring directory synchronization, see the "Configuring Directory Synchronization" section of
this chapter.

Preparing the Network for a Lync Hybrid Deployment

The network requirements for a Lync hybrid deployment are similar to the requirements
for a cloud-only deployment. However, there are several additional firewall port requirements compared to a cloud-only deployment, and there is at least one additional DNS
requirement for the hybrid deployment, depending on the configuration. For specifics
on which DNS records and firewall port openings are required for a given scenario, see
Chapter 28.

Configuring Federation with Lync Online

To establish interoperability between the on-premise deployment and Lync Online, the
on-premise Edge pool must be configured for federation with the Lync Online tenant. The
following steps are used to configure federation between an on-premise Edge pool and a
Lync Online tenant:

1. Log on to a system where the Lync Server management tools are installed, and open
the Lync Server Management Shell.

2. Execute the following command to enable federation and set basic parameters:

```
Set-CSAccessEdgeConfiguration -AllowOutsideUsers 1
➥-AllowFederatedUsers 1 -UseDnsSrvRouting
```

3. Execute the following command to establish federation with Lync Online:

```
New-CSHostingProvider -Identity LyncOnline -ProxyFqdn
"sipfed-tip.online.lync.com" -Enabled $true -EnabledSharedAddressSpace $true
➥-HostsOCSUsers $true -VerificationLevel UseSourceVerification -IsLocal $false
```

Moving Users Between Lync On-Premise and Lync Online

After both environments have been fully deployed and the relationship between them
has been established, users can be moved from an on-premise pool to the Lync Online
tenant using a PowerShell cmdlet. Before moving users to Lync Online, the pool FQDN of

the Lync Online tenant must first be determined, since it must be entered as one of the parameters for the PowerShell cmdlet. The following steps can be used to determine the pool FQDN of the Lync Online tenant:

1. Log on to the Office 365 Portal.

2. On the main page, click the Admin tab at the top, and then select Lync from the drop-down menu to open the Lync Admin Center.

3. In the browser address bar, copy the first portion of the address listed, up to the `lync.com` string. For example, a typical Lync Online pool FQDN would be `https://admin.online.lync.com`. Then, append the following string to the URL just copied: `/HostedMigration/hostedmigrationservice.svc`. These two strings combine to form the `HostedMigrationOverrideUrl` value, which will be specified in the PowerShell cmdlet used to move users to the online tenant. Using the preceding example, the resulting URL value would be `https://admin.online.lync.com/HostedMigration/hostedmigrationservice.svc`.

After the `HostedMigrationOverrideUrl` value is identified, use PowerShell to move an on-premise user to the online tenant, using the following steps:

1. Log on to a system where the Lync Server management tools are installed, and open the Lync Server Management Shell.

2. Execute the following command to establish credentials for the session:

   ```
   $cred=Get-Credentials
   ```

3. At the prompt, enter the credentials of a Lync Online/Office 365 administrative account.

4. Execute the following command to move the user to the online tenant, where `<SIPaddress>` is the SIP URI of the user account, and `<URL>` is the value previously identified as the `HostedMigrationOverrideUrl` for the online tenant:

   ```
   Move-CsUser -Identity <SIPaddress> -Target sipfed.lync.online.com
   ➡-Credentials $cred -HostedMigrationOverrideUrl <URL>
   ```

To move a user from the online tenant back to an on-premise Lync pool, use the following procedure:

1. Log on to a system where the Lync Server management tools are installed, and open the Lync Server Management Shell.

2. Execute the following command to establish credentials for the session:

   ```
   $cred=Get-Credentials
   ```

3. At the prompt, enter the credentials of a Lync Online/Office 365 administrative account.

4. Execute the following command to move the user to the on-premise Lync pool, where `<SIPaddress>` is the SIP URI of the user account, and `<PoolFQDN>` is the fully qualified domain name of the on-premise Lync pool:

```
Move-CsUser -Identity <SIPaddress> -Target <PoolFQDN> -Credentials $cred
```

Summary

As Microsoft continues to develop their portfolio of cloud services, Lync Online will no doubt continue to gain momentum, because it provides an attractive alternative for rolling out UC features at a reasonable cost. The addition of a hybrid Lync deployment option will provide unprecedented flexibility for meeting the varied UC needs of many organizations. There are several unique steps involved in the deployment of any Lync Online solution, whether cloud-only or hybrid. In addition to providing an overview of Lync Online and a description of the user experience, this chapter includes detailed guidance on the steps involved in provisioning Lync Online for all topology options, and serves as a comprehensive build reference for any Lync Online initiative.

PART IX

Lync Server 2013 Clients

IN THIS PART

CHAPTER 23
Mac Client

Although Lync Server 2013 is an impressive platform, most users will experience Lync Server 2013 through only one, maybe two if you count mobile, of its many clients. Microsoft has gone out of its way to provide clients for most of the larger platforms. Microsoft Lync:Mac 2011 is the Mac-based client that enables users to access the client-side functionality of Lync Server 2013. The client was first released midstream for Lync Server 2010 and is updated for Lync 2013. The client includes the following functions:

▶ Instant messaging

▶ Presence

▶ PC-to-PC calls

▶ Enterprise Voice functions

▶ Video conferencing

▶ Web conferencing

▶ Desktop and sharing

As such, this chapter covers the more commonly used functions of the Microsoft Lync:Mac client and should act as the basis of end-user training that most administrators want to provide to their user community to ensure success-ful adoption of Lync Server 2010 among Mac users.

The Lync:Mac client has finally nearly reached parity with the Windows client, but there are still a few key features missing. We intend to cover the good, but we'll also review the bad, providing an honest analysis of Microsoft's Lync for Mac solution.

It's important to point out that the Microsoft Lync:Mac client isn't the same as the Microsoft Messenger client that installs as part of Office 2011. Microsoft Messenger cannot connect to Lync and is meant for the pubic IM services provided by Microsoft. Microsoft Lync:Mac is an add-on to Office 2011 that allows for connectivity to Lync 2010 and Lync 2103 and offers the additional integration into Office 2011 applications.

Installing the Client

Although the Microsoft Communicator client for Macintosh integrates into the Office 2011 suite, it is actually a separate install. Given that most clients want to integrate the functions, we're starting with the steps for installing Office 2011 itself and then the Communicator client. To install Office 2011, perform the following steps:

1. Download the Lync:Mac 2011 installer. This is likely in the form of a .DMG file.

2. Double-click the .DMG file.

3. Double-click the Lync Installer icon, shown in Figure 23.1.

FIGURE 23.1   Running the Lync Installer.

4. The installer offers to guide you through the install. Click Continue.

5. Read the licensing agreement and click Continue.

6. Click Agree to accept the license agreement.

7. The installer tells you which hard drive will be used for the installation. Click Change Install Location if you want to change installation locations, or click Install to accept the recommended location.

8. When prompted, enter your password to authorize the installation. Click OK.

9. The installation prepares and a scrolling candy cane appears. Packages are validated and the installation commences.

10. When the installation completes successfully, click Close.

There is now a big blue L icon in the Chooser, as shown in Figure 23.2. Click it to launch Lync:Mac.

FIGURE 23.2   Lync:Mac loaded in the Chooser menu.

When the Microsoft Lync:Mac client launches, you are asked to again accept the license agreement. Click Accept. Lync:Mac offers to make itself the default application for the following functions:

▶ Presence

▶ Telephone calls

▶ Conferences

For each offer, check the box marked Do Not Show This Message Again, and click Use Lync.

The Lync:Mac client loads and prompts the user for an email address and provides an option for the user to sign in as a certain status, as shown in Figure 23.3.

> **NOTE**
>
> Unfortunately, the Email Address label on the first field is a bit of a misnomer. What the field is actually asking for is the user's SIP URI. This might or might not match the user's email address, depending on the environment.

After the user is signed in, the client populates with any contacts added to the list and any user-created groups, as shown in Figure 23.4.

FIGURE 23.3   Lync:Mac login screen.

FIGURE 23.4   Lync:Mac contact list.

NOTE

The Lync:Mac client does not support Distribution List expansion. That functionality is available only in the Windows and Mobile Clients.

If the necessary SRV records are not present, the Lync:Mac client has options to manually configure the connection; however, using the correct SRV records is the preferred method and it makes the sign-in process more transparent to the end user. This process is covered in detail in Chapter 11, "Dependent Services and SQL," of this book.

Dealing with Certificates

Unlike PCs, Macintoshes don't automatically trust certificate authorities that are tied to Active Directory. If you have deployed Lync Server with internally generated certificates, they will need to import them into a Keychain on the Macintosh. This is a relatively simple process and can be completed with the following steps:

1. Open Finder.

2. Expand Applications and then Utilities.

3. Drag the Root Certificate Authority certificate to Keychain.

4. Select the System Keychain and click Add.

5. When prompted, type a name and password with local administrator rights and click OK.

Feature Comparison

The new Lync:Mac 2011 client replaces the previous Communicator for Mac client. Lync:Mac improves on many previous features and introduces some new ones as well, as shown in Table 23.1. Also shown is an overall comparison to the feature-complete Windows Lync client.

Feature support is indicated by the following circles in the table:

● Feature is supported

◒ Feature is partially supported

○ Feature is not supported

23

TABLE 23.1   Client Comparison[1]

Unified User Interface	Lync for Mac	Communicator for Mac	Lync for Windows
See photos of contacts for quick identification.	●	○	●
Get easy access to presence, instant messaging, voice, audio, video, and online meeting.	●	●	●
See and monitor the meeting roster for participants who are having difficulty with audio, video, or sharing connections during online meetings.	●	○	●
Join, accept, decline, or redirect the meeting invites, audio/video calls, and instant messages right from the invite alerts.	●	◐	●
Communicate from within Outlook, Word, or PowerPoint.	●	●	●
Communicate from within SharePoint.	○	○	●

Rich Presence and Instant Messaging	Lync for Mac	Communicator for Mac	Lync for Windows
Send instant messages.	●	●	●
Display published phone numbers, job titles, and office information all on contact cards.	●	●	●
Set presence status manually or automatically based on calendar, login status, and more.	●	●	●
Specify access levels for sharing information with different contacts.	○	○	●
Connect with people outside the organization with public instant-messaging connectivity (PIC), such as AOL Instant Messenger (AIM), Yahoo!, and Windows Live Messenger.	●	●	●

Enterprise Voice	Lync for Mac	Communicator for Mac	Lync for Windows
Place a call from the Lync/Communicator contact card.	●	●	●
Receive call notifications on the computer.	●	●	●
Configure call forwarding in Lync/Communicator.	●	○	●

Unified User Interface	Lync for Mac	Communicator for Mac	Lync for Windows
Access voice mail from Lync/Communicator.	○	○	●
Use the Lync/Communicator dial pad to call external numbers.	●	●	●
Add outside phone numbers to your Contact List.	●	○	●

Audio, Video, and Web Conferencing	Lync for Mac	Communicator for Mac	Lync for Windows
Connect using audio calls.	●	●	●
Connect using video calls.	●	●	●
Make audio and video calls to your Windows Live Messenger contacts.	●	○	●
Schedule conferences in Outlook.	●	○	●
Start an impromptu online meeting, with the click of a mouse.	●	○	●
Join conferences scheduled from Outlook.	●	●	●
Join an audio conference call using a regular mobile, desk, or home phone.	●	●	●

Desktop and File Sharing	Lync for Mac	Communicator for Mac	Lync for Windows
Share your desktop with other contacts.	●	●	●
Add audio and video to the desktop sharing session and see participants from around the world at their desks.	●	●	●
Join and control a PowerPoint presentation initiated from a Windows desktop.	●	○	●
Initiate a PowerPoint sharing session from Lync/Communicator.	○	○	●
Collaborate with rich whiteboarding, including the capability to copy and paste images and other content, annotations, and polling.	○	○	●
Conduct polling.	○	○	●
Upload files to share with meeting participants.	●	○	●

[1] Source: http://mac2.microsoft.com/help/office/14/en-us/lyncdeploy/item/49da1cec-2998-4466-9c66-970e6f488b97?category=fb7c71bb-c9bd-4f45-873f-851be7af1489

23

Navigation and Layout

In the Lync:Mac client, many options can be configured. For users not familiar with Mac operating systems, options that are normally found in the client interface on a PC are typically moved to the menus at the top of the screen. Although there is a main GUI that looks like the PC client, there are also context-based menus that appear at the top of the screen depending on which application is currently the focus. In the case of Lync:Mac, these options across the top of the application include the following:

- Lync
- Edit
- View
- Status
- Contact
- Conversation
- Window
- Help

The menus for each of these buttons are explained in the following sections.

Lync

The Lync menu has basic program commands for the Lync:Mac application, including these:

- **About Lync**—Gives version information and a summary of the end-user license agreement.
- **Preferences**—Enables the user to set general application preferences for Lync:Mac. It includes the submenus Appearance, General, Phone Calls, Account, Alerts, History, and Photos.
- **Services**—Doesn't actually have a function of any options for the Lync:Mac client, although it is a standard for Mac applications.
- **Hide Lync**—Hides the Lync:Mac client, as might be obvious.
- **Hide Others**—Hides all other applications besides the Lync:Mac client.
- **Quit Lync**—Quits and exits the Lync:Mac application.

Edit

The Edit menu has the usual suspects one would expect. They are outlined here:

- **Undo**—Undoes the previous action if possible.
- **Cut**—Cuts the selected text.

- **Copy**—Copies the selected text.

- **Paste**—Pastes from the clipboard.

- **Clear**—Clears the selected area.

- **Select all**—Selects all in the active window.

- **Spelling**—Offers, via a submenu, the option to Show Spelling and Grammar.

- **Special Characters**—No, this is not how you insert an image of your favorite sci-fi cameo star into your IM. Instead, this brings up a menu of special ASCII characters for making ASCII art, or for other communication uses.

View

The View menu enables the user to change the way the client appears and how contacts are organized. These are the options:

- **View by Name**—Organizes contacts by name. Note that there is no apparent order to the names; it's not alphabetical.

- **View by Group**—Organizes contacts into user-created groups.

- **Use Compact View**—Removes user photos and displays only the presence icon for users. Also does not show status messages or out-of-office updates.

- **Show Status Text**—Shows user's status in text to the right of the user's name if checked.

- **Show Friendly Name**—Shows the display name if this option is checked; otherwise, shows the SIP URI of the user.

- **Show Offline Contacts**—Includes contacts who are offline in the user's contact list. If this is unselected, offline contacts are hidden from the contact list.

- **Collapse All Groups**—Collapses all expanded groups. Great for cleaning up the user interface in a hurry.

- **Show All Fields**—Shows any currently hidden fields.

- **Show Message Timestamp**—Shows the timestamp when each IM message is sent or received.

Status

The Status menu includes options for changing presence status and a command to sign out. There is no need to review the status options here because they are covered elsewhere; however to summarize, they are Available, Busy, Do Not Disturb, Off Work, Be Right Back, and Appear Away. The other options for this menu are reviewed here:

- **Sign Out**—Signs the user out of the Lync:Mac client.

- **Reset Status**—Resets the user's status to the Outlook integrated setting.

Contact

The Contact menu outlines options and modalities for contacting a user. The action is performed on the selected contact in the user's contact list. The options include these:

- ▶ **Send an Instant Message**—Sends an IM to the selected contact.

- ▶ **Call**—Calls the selected contact. It has a submenu that includes the various options and phone numbers for calling the contact.

- ▶ **Start a Video Call**—Begins a video conference with the selected contact.

- ▶ **Share Desktop**—Starts a desktop sharing session with the selected contact.

- ▶ **Send a File**—Sends a file to the selected contact. When this is selected, the application brings up a Finder window enabling the user to choose a file to share.

- ▶ **Send an Email Message**—Opens the preferred email client and sends an email addressed to the selected contact.

- ▶ **Schedule a Meeting**—Opens a Lync meeting invite and adds the selected user to the To field.

- ▶ **Move Contact To**—Opens a submenu with all the groups a user has created. It enables the user to move the contact to a different group.

- ▶ **Copy Contact To**—Opens a submenu with all the groups a user has created. It enables the user to copy the contact to a different group while also leaving the contact in the current location.

- ▶ **Block**—Prevents all communication to or from the selected contact.

- ▶ **Remove from Group**—Removes the selected contact from the current group but leaves the contact in any other groups.

- ▶ **Remove from Contact List**—Removes the selected contact from all groups and the contact list completely.

- ▶ **Create New Group**—Creates a new contact group in the client. After clicking this option, the user is asked to create a name for the new group.

- ▶ **Rename Group**—Enables the user to rename an existing contact group. Available only when a group is selected.

- ▶ **Delete Group**—Enables the user to delete an existing contact group. Available only when a group is selected.

- ▶ **View Past Conversations**—Shows all previous conversations with the selected contact. Available only if the Save Conversations to Outlook option is also checked.

- ▶ **View Contact Card**—Displays the Office contact card for the selected contact.

> **NOTE**
>
> The Lync:Mac client uses LDAP for retrieving contact information instead of Exchange Web Services like the Windows client. This means that in most environments contact cards are unavailable when outside the corporate network.

Conversation

This menu outlines conversation options. It includes the Meet Now option, which starts an ad hoc meeting.

▶ **Meet Now**—Enables a user to start an ad hoc conference with audio, video, or desktop sharing.

▶ **Join Online Meeting by URL**—Enables a user to join a Lync meeting by typing or pasting a URL.

▶ **Save**—Saves the content of the current conversation.

▶ **Save as Web Page**—Saves the content of the current conversation as HTML.

▶ **Print**—Prints the content of the current conversation.

Window

The Window menu has options for viewing windows and changing their characteristics:

▶ **Minimize**—Minimizes the current window.

▶ **Zoom**—Zooms in on the current window.

▶ **Close**—Closes the current window. Note that this does not exit the client if the main Lync:Mac application is the current window.

▶ **Contact List**—Shows the main Lync:Mac application with the contact list in focus.

▶ **Conversation History**—Shows conversation history. Note that this includes only conversations that have happened on the same Mac. In other words, it's a local store and does not integrate with the conversation history folder in Microsoft Exchange and Outlook.

▶ **Bring All to Front**—Brings all Lync windows to the front.

▶ **Other**—Provides a list of all open Lync:Mac windows. Select one to bring it to the front.

Help

The Help menu offers a search bar and a link to Lync help topics. It also enables the user to manually check for updates from Microsoft.com.

Managing Contacts

Most people have grown accustomed to the behaviors in Outlook in which you can quickly look up a user in the contacts or by starting to type the person's name. Microsoft Lync:Mac follows this model by organizing contacts by groups and by enabling you to quickly search for contacts by typing the person's name.

For example, on the search line (indicated by a magnifying glass), if you type a name, the client suggests names based on the user's personal contacts and the global address list. From here, click and drag the contact to add the contact to a contact group. When this occurs, the person you added receives a notification that you added him and has the option to add you as well. When added, the contacts appear in the group you selected and you are able to see the presence information at any time.

After a contact is added, you can move the contact from one contact group to another by clicking and dragging the contact. By holding the mouse over the name of the contact, you can see the notes he has set in his client, as well as his picture, as shown in Figure 23.5.

FIGURE 23.5   Lync:Mac contact details.

Managing Groups

The Microsoft Lync:Mac client enables users to organize their contacts by placing them inside groups. By default, the group is Other Contacts.

These groups show a status of how many contacts there are in that group and how many are currently online. For example, you might see Other Contacts (4/5) to indicate that four of the five contacts in that group are online. You can expand the group by clicking the hollow triangle to the left of the name to populate the full list of contacts.

A convenient use of groups is to organize members of a project or department. By right-clicking the group name, you can choose to launch a conference call that will invite all members of that group. Similar functionality can be achieved by selecting multiple contacts by Control-clicking them and then right-clicking to choose Start a Conference Call. This call can use Lync's PC-to-PC call features, through the PSTN or an attached PBX.

IM Features

For most environments, the most commonly used feature in the Microsoft Lync:Mac client is Instant Messaging. This function enables users to stop cluttering mailboxes with "where do you want to go for lunch?" types of messages and enables users to limit their messages to only people who are likely to respond quickly. This also is where accurate presence information comes in handy.

Starting an IM conversation is as simple as double-clicking a contact. Doing so launches the IM window, which defaults to the IM tab, as shown in Figure 23.6.

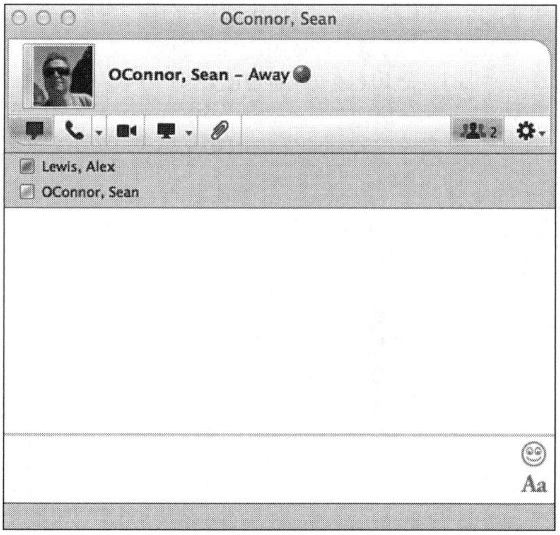

FIGURE 23.6   IM conversation.

The Lync:Mac IM client works much like any other IM client. You can see the status information for the person with whom you are communicating, and there are two areas in the window: one in which to type and one in which to display the conversation. Users have access to the usual features such as altering the font, color, and size of the text, as well as a menu of emoticons.

Audio/Video Calls and Conferencing

One of the more interesting features in the Microsoft Lync:Mac client is the capability to participate in audio or video conferences with other users of the Lync Server 2013 environment. Before the first participation in either an audio conference or a video conference, users should configure their audio and video devices in the audio and video device preferences section. After these devices are configured, a user is ready to start the first conference.

For purposes of this section, view a call and a conference as essentially the same event, with the only difference being the number of parties involved. If two parties are involved, it's a call. If more than two parties are involved, it's a conference. Generally, the steps are identical for initiating and managing both. Whenever the steps vary, they are called out as such.

Making an Audio Call

Initiating an audio call is as simple as clicking a contact and selecting the call option, which is a retro microphone icon as shown in Figure 23.7 After this is done, the contact receives a pop-up and an audio notification and has the option to answer, decline, or redirect. Answer and decline are obvious in what they do. Redirect gives the option to reply through IM or to set one's status to Do Not Disturb. Accepting the call updates both users' status to In a Call.

FIGURE 23.7   Initiating a call.

If you're already in an IM conversation, you can add audio by clicking the telephone icon and choosing how you'd like to reach the person—either via Lync call or over the PSTN. A call connecting is shown in Figure 23.8.

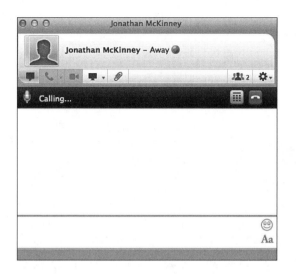

FIGURE 23.8   Calling a Lync contact.

Making a Video Call

Initiating a video call is as simple as clicking a contact and then selecting start a video call. Much as with the audio call, the recipient has the option to accept, decline, or redirect. Redirect gives the option to reply with an IM as well.

When the call is accepted, the usual client window opens in the Video view. The recipient initially sees the caller but the caller won't see the recipient until she clicks Start My Video in the window. By default, each participant in a two-way call sees herself in a picture-in-picture window inside the main video window. The picture-in-picture can be moved anywhere within the video window and will not block access to the following buttons. You can modify the picture-in-picture, also called the preview, by right-clicking it. This gives the options to hide or resize the preview.

Inside the video window are several buttons, including the following:

▶ End Video Call

▶ Put Video Call on Hold

▶ Enter Full Screen

▶ Mute Microphone

▶ Adjust Volume or Mute Speakers

▶ Network Quality

▶ Time in the Call

Enter Full Screen expands the video windows to encompass the entire screen. The option at the upper-right corner becomes Exit Full Screen.

Clicking End Video Call ends the call and downgrades to a simple IM conversation.

Web Conferencing

Probably the biggest driving force behind companies implementing Lync Server 2013 is replacing outsourced web conferencing services. Many companies spend hundreds of thousands of dollars a month on services such as WebEx or GoToMeeting. Although there might be situations in which a company running Lync Server 2013 needs to create a conference so large that its infrastructure isn't sufficient, the other 95% of the time it can use a platform it owns rather than paying an external company for the services. In many environments, Lync 2010 implementations paid for themselves in three to six months for this reason. Lync Server 2013 looks to offer similar to faster return on investment for companies in need of web conferencing.

Whereas the Mac Communicator client did not support web conferencing, the Lync:Mac client does! It offers an almost complete experience as compared to the Windows client; see the comparison in Table 23.1 for more details.

Joining a Conference

Most invitations to a web conference arrive through email. This is to say that in most corporate environments invites to web conferences are part of an Exchange meeting invite. It appears as a web link inside the meeting invite, as shown in Figure 23.9.

Clicking the web link results in the default web browser launching. If pop-up blockers are turned on, the Lync Server warns the user. He can opt to disable the pop-up blocker for this site and refresh, or he can click a link to Join with Pop-up Blocker Turned On, although that might interfere with screen sharing. It is recommended to disable the pop-up blocker and refresh the connection.

Client Integrations with Other Applications

As is typical with many Microsoft back-office applications, one of its key value propositions is its integration with other Microsoft applications. Microsoft always touts its concept of "better together" when selling its products, and Lync Server 2013 is no different. After the client is installed, there are hooks into several other Microsoft applications, which are discussed in the following sections.

Integration with Outlook

One of the strongest areas of integration for Lync:Mac is with Outlook. When Lync:Mac is installed, it adds hooks into the Outlook view that integrate into contact information. For example, when an email is received in Outlook, you can immediately see presence information for any Lync Server users who are listed in any of the To, CC, or From fields. This immediately tells the recipient whether these people are available. By placing the mouse over a name with presence information, you receive information about the users and are presented an interface that contains many of the Communicator buttons, as shown in Figure 23.10.

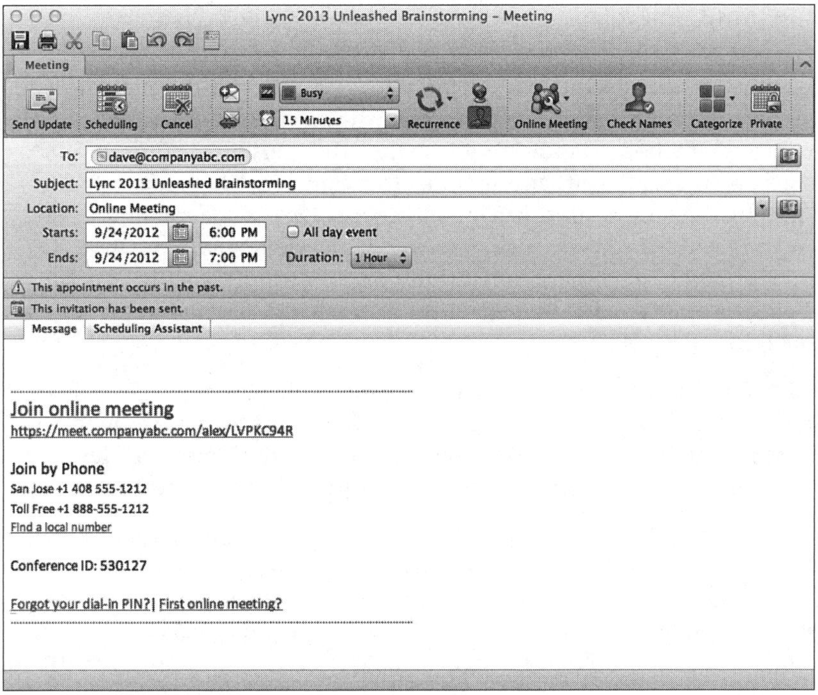

FIGURE 23.9 Invitation to Join a Lync web conference.

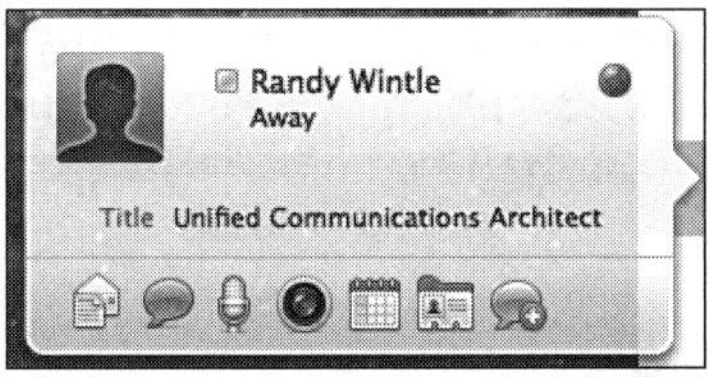

FIGURE 23.10 Office contact card.

Visible in the initial pop-up is the display name of the user, the current status, calendar information, and the status message. The available options include the following:

- Send Mail
- Send an Instant Message
- Call Contact

▶ Start a Video Call

▶ Schedule a Meeting

▶ Open Outlook Contact

▶ Add Contact to Lync Contact List

Focusing on the options that are specific to the Lync:Mac client integration, clicking Send an Instant Message spawns the typical IM window from within Lync:Mac. Sending an IM results in the contact getting a pop-up indicating that the other person is requesting an IM conversation. This pop-up can be either responded to or ignored. This process is effectively identical to finding the contact in the Communicator client and launching an IM conversation, but with the added convenience of having done it directly from Outlook. In this manner, you get additional choices in terms of how you will interact with another user. Rather than being forced to reply to an email through email, you can choose to communicate through instant messages.

Clicking Call Contact results in the contact getting a pop-up indicating that the other person is requesting an audio call. Accepting the call connects the two users through an audio conference that is hosted by Lync Server. This is a useful option to avoid a lengthy email reply or if a conversation is of a sensitive nature and shouldn't be stored in email.

Clicking Start a Video Call results in the contact getting a pop-up indicating that the other person is requesting a video connection. Assuming that the user has a camera, she is able to join a video call with the other person. As with any video call, the person who receives the call needs to start the video if she has a camera and wants the other person to see her. Similarly, video calls include audio so that the two are able to easily communicate with each other.

Clicking Add Contact to Instant Messenger Contact List adds contacts that don't yet exist in the Lync:Mac contact list.

The Lync:Mac client also accesses your calendar if you are hosted on Exchange. From this connection, it is able to see calendar availability and can automatically change your status based on the calendar. For example, if you are in a meeting, your status automatically changes to Busy (In a Meeting).

Tuning Hardware for the Lync:Mac Client

The Lync:Mac client enables users to communicate with each other through both audio and video. As such, it's a good idea to tune the audio and video subsystems of the Macintosh that is running the client in order to optimize the experience for the user.

For those who might not be familiar with the Macintosh operating system, items such as audio and video are managed through System Preferences. This can be accessed either through the Dock (the icons displayed on the bottom of the screen) or by clicking the Apple logo at the upper-left corner of the screen and choosing System Preferences. When looking for System Preferences in the Dock, look for a grey square with a large gear and two smaller gears.

Tuning the Display

The System Preferences interface is broken up into five rows, including Personal, Hardware, Internet & Wireless, System, and Other. Clicking the Displays icon, located in the Hardware row, opens a new menu. From this menu, you can select screen resolutions. In general, for the best visual results, pick the native resolution of the screen. This is especially important when using an LCD, or liquid-crystal display. Although displays can generally run in multiple resolutions, they are optimized for one particular resolution. As Wikipedia describes it, "While CRT monitors can usually display images at various resolutions, an LCD monitor has to rely on interpolation (scaling of the image), which causes a loss of image quality. An LCD has to scale up a smaller image to fit into the area of the native resolution. This is the same principle as taking a smaller image in an image editing program and enlarging it; the smaller image loses its sharpness when it is expanded." Thus, you are when using an external LCD or the built-in LCD display on a Macintosh laptop, it is important to ensure that it's running at its native resolution. Typically, a monitor can inform a computer of its native resolution through extended display identification data (EDID). If a monitor doesn't support this standard, search online for the native resolution. If it can't be found, experiment with various resolutions. Generally, it is obvious when you select the native resolution because the text will look significantly crisper.

Another feature that is available on the Macintosh laptops is support for automatically adjusting brightness as ambient light changes. This enables the laptop screen to adjust to the conditions of the room and is helpful when users move their laptop back and forth between well-lit and poorly lit locations.

Clicking the Color button offers additional options for managing the display profiles. Picking a profile that matches the output monitor can result in a more accurate representation of colors, which means people will look more natural when in a video call.

Tuning the Audio

In the Hardware row of the System Preferences page is an icon for sound. Clicking this icon opens a screen with three tabs, which include Sound Effects, Output, and Input. Sound effects are used by various notifications within the Communicator client and their relative volume can be managed here.

Clicking the Output tab enables you to control overall volume of the output and gives you control over basic audio features such as left/right balance.

Clicking Input enables you to modify the sensitivity of the microphone. This is probably the most critical step in optimizing the experience in audio calls. If the microphone is too sensitive, it can clip or send a distorted signal. If sensitivity is too low, other users will have a difficult time hearing the person speaking into the microphone. One excellent feature offered on the Macintosh is native noise reduction. If the box labeled Use Ambient Noise Reduction is used, less distracting background noise will be sent over the microphone and this will benefit anyone in the audio conference.

Troubleshooting

The Lync:Mac client is a huge upgrade and generally easy to use, but there are a few things that might go wrong in a large deployment:

▶ If the client doesn't connect, try setting the client to a manual configuration and list the pool name. If this results in the client connecting, your service records in DNS are not configured properly.

▶ If a manual connection still doesn't work, try pinging the pool name. If it fails to resolve, there might be an issue with DNS. Try pinging the DNS server as well; it's possible you're having other network issues.

▶ If you're getting audio feedback when conferencing, your sound card might not support noise cancelation. Having a good sound card results in a better overall experience. Another possible fix is to run the configuration utilities for your sound card. This enables you to correctly set levels for the speakers and the microphone. This can prevent clipping of the signal that can result in a distorted voice.

▶ If you aren't getting presence information or if the client complains about Outlook integration, it's possible that you activated an account for Lync Server 2010 and created a SIP name for the user that doesn't match the email address. These need to match for everything to work perfectly.

▶ If you are using certificates from your own CA and external users are having issues connecting, they might not trust your root CA. The public certificate from the Root CA needs to be imported into the Trusted Root store in Keychain. If external systems trust the Root CA but aren't able to reach the Certificate Revocation List for the CA, they will fail to connect.

▶ An excellent way to check on network connection to Lync Server 2010 is the `netstat` command. If a connection on TCP 5061 is in a `Syn_sent` state, it means the Lync Server is unavailable. If the connection is sitting at `Time_Wait`, odds are that the application is having issues. It means that the connection was acknowledged, but the application isn't sending data.

Best Practices

By following a few best practices, you can optimize the Microsoft Lync:Mac experience for your users. Employing little tricks to ensure that things work the first time and configure automatically simplifies the deployment of the Microsoft Lync:Mac client:

▶ Whenever possible, use a certificate from a public CA to ensure that clients will automatically trust the CA and that the CRL will be readily available.

▶ A quality Lync certified headset will do wonders for audio quality.

▶ If you plan to do video conferencing, spend a couple of bucks and get a nice webcam. Pan-and-tilt support is a great feature for keeping people well centered in the view.

▶ Always properly calibrate cameras and microphones to give users the best possible experience with the Lync:Mac client.

▶ Always be sure to configure the Lync client to use the microphone you want. It's common for webcams to have a built-in microphone and Lync might default to this, even though the user is playing sound through the headset. This typically manifests itself in the person's voice being faint. Or, in some cases, it might be distorted because the user might have turned up the sensitivity all the way thinking that the problem was with the headset microphone.

▶ Be sure to end your meetings when they are over. Otherwise, you needlessly tie up resources on the back-end servers.

▶ Although this is a good idea for any type of meeting, avoid having side conversations during a conference. Not only does it cause background noise that can distract others, but you potentially take focus from the presenter if it is a video conference.

▶ Make sure you don't have anything non-business-related on your screen if you are doing a full desktop share. The potential here for embarrassment is significant.

▶ If you are inviting meeting attendees from outside your company, set the meeting options to first place these guests into the waiting room so that you can verify their identity before allowing them into the meeting.

▶ Finish your meetings with the Remove Everyone and End the Meeting function from the People menu.

▶ Consider using Managed Preferences to block specific features or functions of the Lync:Mac client.

23

Mobile Clients

In an increasingly mobile world, a Unified Communications solution must be able to provide a seamless user experience across all devices, including mobile endpoints. In recent years it is common for users to be outside of the office more than they are inside the office. Mobile workers typically rely on cellphones for communication, and with the recent influx of tablet devices, getting work done when mobile is an everyday experience. Microsoft introduced mobile client experience with Office Communications Server on the Windows Mobile Platform. In Lync Server 2010 this mobile experience was enhanced and introduced to all major cellphone platforms. This includes Windows Phone, Android, Apple iOS, and Nokia Symbian. Additionally, Blackberry devices have always had a mobile experience provided through Blackberry Enterprise Server (BES) integration with OCS and Lync.

This chapter provides an overview of the Lync Server 2013 mobile experience, including a feature comparison across versions and platforms. Additionally, a technical review of the Mobility architecture, including critical services and protocol flows, is covered. Lastly, steps to deploy and maintain Lync Server 2013 Mobile Services are explained.

Mobile Clients Overview

The Lync Server 2010 mobile experience introduced IM/ Presence and Enterprise Voice functionality to end users. Additionally, iPad devices are capable of consuming PowerPoint content in Web Conferences. With Lync Server 2013, Microsoft plans to expand this functionality to include Voice and Video over IP connections (Wi-Fi, 3G, 4G, and LTE), as well as include conferencing functionality on tablet devices. As of the writing of this book, this functionality will be delivered in a service pack to Lync Server 2013. However, the functionality, architecture, and requirements have all been released by Microsoft and are explained here. Figure 24.1 provides an overview of each interface across the major mobile platforms.

| Windows Phone | Android | iPhone | iPad |

FIGURE 24.1   Mobile client experience overview.

When Lync 2010 mobile clients were introduced, the focus was on the core functionality user experience. This included the following features:

▶ Managing a user's presence

▶ Managing a user's contact list

▶ Instant messaging

▶ Single-click conference join

▶ Enterprise Voice through Call-Via-Work

▶ Managing Enterprise Voice settings such as call forwarding

Lync Server 2013 will have a primary goal of expanding Voice and Video over IP functionality, as well as introducing more collaboration features to tablet devices.

Features Available to Lync Mobile Clients

Table 24.1 provides an overview of the features available to all Lync Mobile Client versions in Lync Server 2010 and at the launch of Lync Server 2013.

TABLE 24.1   Lync Mobile Client Comparison

Feature	Windows Phone 7.5+	Nokia Symbian	iPhone (iOS 4+)	iPad (iOS 4+)	Android 2.3+
Instant messaging	✓	✓	✓	✓	✓
Presence colors and status	✓	✓	✓	✓	✓
Photos	✓	✓	✓	✓	✓
View Lync Contact list	✓	✓	✓	✓	✓
Search corporate directory	✓	✓	✓	✓	✓
View Contact Card	✓	✓	✓	✓	✓
Multipart IM	✓	✓	✓	✓	✓
Distribution list expansion	✓	✓	✓	✓	✓
Send Bing map location data via IM	X	X	✓	✓	X
Contact management	X	✓	X	X	X
Join Conference	✓	✓	✓	✓	✓
Conference callback	✓	✓	✓	✓	✓
Conference Calendar information	✓	✓	X	X	X
URL-based join	X	X	X	X	✓
Meeting pane join	X	X	✓	✓	X
Single Number Reach	✓	✓	✓	X	✓
Dial pad	✓	✓	✓	X	✓
Call from Contact Card	✓	✓	✓	X	✓
Call from conversation window	✓	✓	✓	X	✓
Call via Work	✓	✓	✓	X	✓
Call forwarding control	✓	✓	✓	✓	✓
Visual Voicemail	X	X	✓	✓	X

24

Lync Server 2013 will introduce an expanded feature set with a later cumulative update. This release will focus on the following functionality:

▶ Voice and Video over IP (3G, 4G, LTE, Wi-Fi) on all smartphones and tablet platforms

▶ Conferencing attendee experience (consume not share) on tablet devices

▶ Maintenance of feature parity across all platforms

Lync Server 2013 Mobility Technical Review

When the mobile clients were introduced in Lync 2010, a new client architecture was also introduced. Lync desktop clients communicate with Front End and Edge Servers using the SIP protocol. To provide a better user experience on mobile devices, Microsoft introduced a new communication method for mobile devices. Lync mobile clients communicate over HTTPS to send XML messages that are then translated into SIP messages on the server. This allows for a lighter-weight protocol to be used on the devices, which results in greater battery life, a seamless experience across device platforms, and the capability to maintain connection state on mobile devices. Additionally, a new server discovery mechanism was required for mobile devices. Before Lync mobile, autodiscovery of Lync services was done through DNS SRV records. However, DNS SRV records would point directly to SIP services on Lync Servers; a new method was required to direct mobile clients to the HTTPS web service for mobility. Figure 24.2 provides an overview of the architecture for Lync 2013 Mobility.

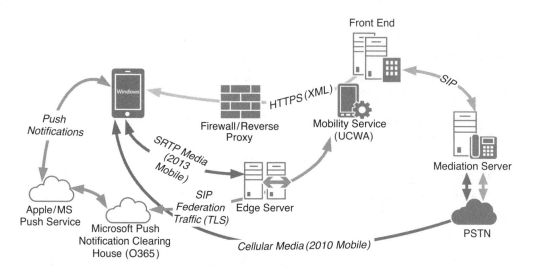

FIGURE 24.2   Lync Mobile architecture overview.

This section outlines the architecture and new services introduced with Lync Mobility.

Understanding the LyncDiscover Service

The LyncDiscover service was introduced in Lync Server 2010 to provide autodiscovery of Lync services to Lync mobile clients. In Lync Server 2013, this service will also provide autodiscovery of services to the Lync 2013 desktop and tablet clients. The LyncDiscover service can be compared to the Exchange Server Autodiscover Service. The simple principle is that users will connect to a web address, authenticate, and then request the next server to connect to for appropriate services. In Lync Server 2013, the LyncDiscover service will provide web URLs for mobility as well as SIP servers for clients such as Front End and

Edge Servers. This enables organizations to simplify the deployment of Lync clients of all types.

The LyncDiscover service runs as a web service on all Lync Front End and Director Servers. When mobility is enabled in a 2010 environment, or on all 2013 environments, the LyncDiscover IIS directory will be created. The goal of the LyncDiscover service is to provide Lync clients with a valid home server to register against. Requests to LyncDiscover are authenticated before delivering service information using WebTicket authentication. When a sign-in request is started by a client, the client will end the requesting user's SIP URI in the request. When the LyncDiscover receives the HTTPS request from the client and validates the WebTicket provided by the client, it will identify the home server of the requesting user and then deliver critical information for client registration to the client. This will include the following:

▶ Web service URL to connect to Mobility Services

▶ Front End Server FQDN for SIP client connectivity

▶ FQDN and port of the Access Edge Service associated with the Front End Server pool for remote SIP client connectivity

The LyncDiscover service operates on a static DNS entry. All clients will try to connect to `LyncDiscover.<sipdomain>` and `LyncDiscoverinternal.<sipdomain>`. For a user in the `companyabc.com` SIP domain, this FQDN would be `LyncDiscover.companyabc.com`. Whereas the Lync 2013 desktop client will fail back to DNS SRV record lookup for discovery, the mobile and tablet clients, including Windows 8, will only look for LyncDiscover. This service is absolutely critical for any Lync deployments for client sign-in.

The "Putting It All together: Protocol Flow" section provides details on the messages exchanged between the client and the server for LyncDiscover.

CAUTION

Mobile devices and desktops clients located on the internal corporate network can connect to the `LyncDiscoverinternal` URL for server discovery. Because of this, it is important to identify a certificate strategy for those clients that might not trust a private certificate authority by default, such as smartphones. The "Certificate and DNS Requirements" section covers this topic in greater detail.

Understanding the Mobility Service

To enable Lync 2010 mobile clients to communicate with Lync servers, a new service was introduced in Lync Server 2010. Mobile clients communicate over HTTPS with XML messages. A service was introduced to translate traffic and allow these clients to communicate with the Lync Server infrastructure that operates on SIP. The MCX Service is the service responsible for translating mobile communications into SIP communications that Lync Servers can understand. In Lync Server 2013, a new service is introduced, the Unified Communications Web API (UCWA); it is used to facilitate communications from all

HTTPS-based clients. This service is open to developers, and is also responsible for providing Lync Web App connectivity. Lync 2013 mobile clients will connect to the UCWA service, and Lync 2010 clients will continue connecting to the MCX service for legacy compatibility.

SIP traffic is often referred to as chatty—chatty traffic can consume a lot of bandwidth and power. When a mobile client is being deployed, it is critical that this client does not decrease the increasingly precious battery life of mobile devices. By implementing an HTTPS/XML-based client, Microsoft is able to achieve the following:

▶ Standardize and simplify the clients across multiple platforms

▶ Decrease the frequency and size of traffic used when compared with SIP

▶ Decrease the battery drain of the mobile clients

▶ Increase session resiliency and session recovery time for mobile clients, which are often changing connection state frequently

The Lync Mobility Services act under a simple concept: translate mobile XML messages to SIP messages that Lync Servers can understand. This service acts much like a back-to-back user agent (B2BUA), receiving a request from a mobile device and then initiating another request over SIP and maintaining the state of the two separate connections. The Mobility Services will perform functionality such as updating presence, initiating calls, and issuing push notification requests.

The Lync UCWA and MCX services are deployed on all Front End Servers in the environment, and details on the actual messages exchanged between clients and servers will be shown in the "Putting It All Together: Protocol Flow" section.

Push Notifications

Apple and Windows mobile operating systems have restrictions on which applications can run in the background of the operating system. With this restriction in place, both Apple and Microsoft provide a hosted service that enables developers to deliver push notifications to devices. These notifications are used to notify users of application activity even when the application is not open, such as receiving an instant message (IM). The latest versions of Microsoft and Apple mobile operating systems enable VoIP applications to run in the background for the purpose of receiving calls. For the Lync 2013 clients that will be delivered after the initial release of Lync Server 2013, it is assumed that these clients will take advantage of that functionality and the Push Notification Service will still be used for instant messaging notifications.

In Lync Server 2010 and 2013, push notifications are delivered to mobile devices through a federated connection to the Microsoft Push Notification Clearing House. This service lives in the Office 365 cloud service, and acts as an intermediary between a Lync Server deployment and the Apple and Microsoft Push Notification Services for mobile devices. Organizations that want to enable push notifications will federate with the Office 365 service specifically for push notifications, and the MCX service will deliver push notification requests to that service.

When a mobile client registers and push notifications are enabled, the MCX service also registers a push notification identity for that user. The state of that user is maintained in the MCX service, and when a message is sent to that user, the MCX service initiates a request to the unique push notification ID, ultimately ending up at mobile endpoint as a notification. The details of this process are outlined in the following section.

Putting It All Together: Protocol Flow

Understanding how Mobility Services function in detail will help with deploying and troubleshooting Lync Mobile. Administrators should be familiar with the expected behavior in common scenarios. This section covers the most common scenarios in Lync Mobile.

Sign-In

The sign-in process is a very involved process, especially with the new LyncDiscover and Mobility Services. The following list provides each step of the LyncDiscover process. Figure 24.3 provides an overview of the LyncDiscover process.

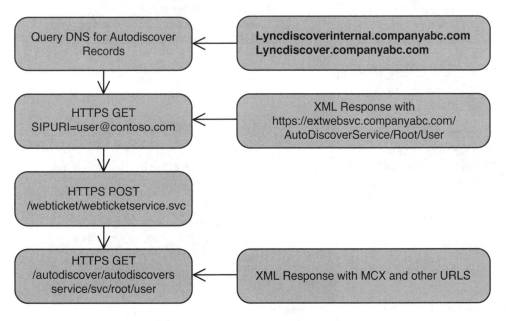

FIGURE 24.3   LyncDiscover process.

1. The client first queries the DNS records for LyncDiscoverinternal and then LyncDiscover.

2. The client connects to the appropriate URL, including the SIP URI of the user as part of the URL.

3. The LyncDiscover service responds with the full LyncDiscover service URL and web ticket service URL for users to request server information.

4. The LyncDiscover service requires the client to authenticate and receive a valid web ticket. The client performs authentication with the web ticket service before attempting to interact with the LyncDiscover service again.

5. When the client has a valid web ticket, it sends a full request to the LyncDiscover service. If the message is valid, the LyncDiscover service returns connectivity information for that client and user.

At this stage, a client will have authenticated with the web ticket service, essentially authenticating with Active Directory. Also, the client will have received the Mobility Service URL and the FQDN for a Front End Server and associated Edge Server for SIP connectivity. Next, the mobile client must register against the Mobility Service URL. Figure 24.4 outlines the registration process for a Lync 2010 mobile client to the MCX service.

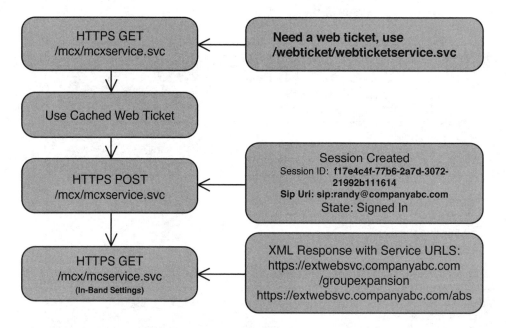

FIGURE 24.4   Lync 2010 Mobile Client Registration Process.

The following list outlines the Lync 2010 Mobile Client registration process:

1. The mobile client initiates a registration request to the MCX service. The MCX service requests a valid web ticket.

2. The mobile client sends another registration request with the web ticket authentication. At this stage a session is created on the Front End Server for this mobile device and user. A unique ID is created to specifically identify the endpoint.

3. The client begins receiving in-band settings from the server. This includes services such as the address book service, group expansion, and policy settings that apply to the mobile endpoint.

4. The client starts to process the contact list for that user. This includes downloading the contact list objects, subscribing to presence, and downloading photos. These requests are all similar to the Lync desktop client; however, the requests are made in XML messages over HTTPS to the MCX service.

At this stage the Lync mobile client will act much like any other Lync client. The key difference is the format in which messages are delivered to clients.

Push Notifications

The push notification process involves many Lync Server components. Figure 24.5 provides an overview of the push notification process when an internal Lync user sends an instant message to a user on a mobile device.

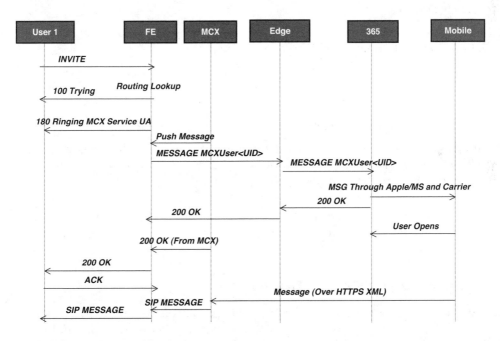

FIGURE 24.5   Push notification process.

The following list outlines the Push notification process:

1. The user (user 1) sends a SIP INVITE to the Front End Server that is destined for the mobile user.

2. The Front End Server performs a routing lookup and identifies a registered endpoint for the user. The Front End Server identifies the endpoint registered as a mobile endpoint and starts communicating with the MCX service.

3. The SIP 180 ringing message that is returned to user 1 contains the MCX user agent header for that user. See the example that follows. This shows the user Randy Wintle being connected on a Windows Phone device.

    P-ASSERTED-IDENTITY: "Randy Wintle"<sip:rwintle@companyabc.com>

    SERVER: RTCC/4.0.0.0 McxService/4.0.0.0 WPLync/4.1.7947.0 (Microsoft Windows CE 7.10.7720; SAMSUNG SGH-i937 2103.11.10.1)

4. The MCX service generates a push notification SIP message that is sent to the unique ID for that endpoint. This message is sent to the user push@push.lync.com and is sent to the Front End Server for routing.

5. The Front End Server routes this federated request to the outbound federation route for that site. This traffic is sent to the Microsoft Push Notification Clearing House, shown as 365 Figure 24.5.

6. The Microsoft Clearing House service securely communicates with the Apple or Microsoft Push Notification Service. The details of this communication are not publicly available.

7. The Apple or Microsoft Push service securely delivers the push notification to the mobile endpoint through a mobile carrier connection.

8. When the user receives the push notification on his device, a 200 OK message is delivered to the MCX service and ultimately the Front End Service on the federation channel.

9. The 200 OK message is relayed to user1.

10. At this stage, a SIP session is active between the two endpoints. All messages will follow the same path as described previously, and the MCX service will facilitate communications to the mobile endpoint over HTTPS.

Federation plays a critical role in delivering push notifications to users. The push notification process should outline the protocol flow for all SIP signaling messages in Lync 2010 mobile.

Deploying Lync 2013 Mobility

Lync Mobility relies on various services and must be carefully planned for to ensure a successful deployment. The LyncDiscover, UCWA, and MCX services are all installed by default on all Front End Servers. No additional configuration is required to install these services. However, configuration is required for DNS, Certificates, Reverse Proxy, Hardware Load Balancers, and Mobile policies. This section outlines the steps to deploy Lync Mobile Services.

Certificate and DNS Requirements

The LyncDiscover service requires a static DNS entry that is dedicated to this service. The DNS requirements for Lync mobile are given in Table 24.2.

TABLE 24.2   LyncDiscover DNS Requirements

DNS Record	Points To
LyncDiscoverinternal.companyabc.com	Internal IP address of the Front End Server or Front End Web Services VIP
LyncDiscover.companyabc.com	External IP address of the reverse proxy for external web services

The LyncDiscover service will be used by Mobile devices and Lync 2013 desktop clients. To properly support devices that are connected to either the internal corporate network or a public network, both the LyncDiscoverinternal and the LyncDiscover records must be created, and must point to the appropriate IP addresses.

DNS Requirements for Push Notifications

As described earlier, push notifications require federation with the Microsoft Push Notification Clearing House. For this service to function properly, the appropriate DNS records must be deployed to support inbound federation to the organization. This includes the DNS SRV records for federation autodiscovery. The Microsoft Push Notification Clearing House does not have the capability for manually defining a Lync Access Edge Server for federation; therefore, when push notification communicating is happening, the service must validate the federation connection using the DNS SRV records.

For push notifications to work, be sure to deploy the _sipfederationtls._tcp. <sipDomain> DNS SRV record, and point this record to the Access Edge Server used for federation.

Certificate Requirements for LyncDiscover

The certificate implications for the previous requirements become increasingly important in Lync Server 2013. In the past a single, privately issued certificate was common for all Front End Services. When certificates are being configured for a Lync Front End Server, there is an option to assign a certificate for Default, Internal Web Services, and External Web Services. This essentially enables administrators to assign a certificate for each of the web service directories, and then all other Lync services. With Lync Mobile, the possibility of devices that would not automatically trust the privately issued certificate connecting to the LyncDiscoverinternal service will require either the configuration of a public certificate for the web services, or the manual installation of root certificates on mobile devices.

Table 24.3 outlines a possible certificate configuration to provide Autodiscover Services to all endpoints.

TABLE 24.3   LyncDiscover Certificate Requirements

Friendly Name	Lync Server Cert	Lync Web Services Cert
Issued By	Private CA	Public CA
Usages	Server default	Web server internal
		Web server external

Friendly Name	Lync Server Cert	Lync Web Services Cert
Common Name	Nypool.companyabc.local	Nypoolwebsvc.companyabc.com
	Sip.companyabc.local	Nypoolwebsvc.companyabc.com
		Nypoolwebsvcexternal.companyabc.com
		LyncDiscoverinternal.companyabc.com
		LyncDiscover.companyabc.com
		Meet.companyabc.com
		Dialin.companyabc.com

In the configuration outlined in Table 24.3, the web services certificate could be applied to the Front End Server web services, as well as the public reverse proxy interface. This would allow for internal clients that are connecting to the internal LyncDiscover service to connect seamlessly, as well as external clients.

The preceding example is just one way to work with the certificate requirements for LyncDiscover. There are many ways to meet the requirements of an organization. The key is that the LyncDiscover records must be present on a certificate, and the clients must trust that certificate.

Federation Requirements for Push Notifications

Federation must be configured with the Microsoft Push Notification Clearing House to deliver push notifications to Apple and Microsoft mobile users. In Lync Server 2013, this is done by adding a new hosting provider configuration. Perform these steps to enable the hosting provider for push notifications:

1. Open the Lync Server Management Shell (PowerShell).

2. Run the following command to add the hosting provider:

```
New-CsHostingProvider -Identity <Lync Online hosting provider>
➥-Enabled $True
➥-ProxyFqdn <FQDN for the Access Server used by the hosting provider>
➥-VerificationLevel UseSourceVerification
```

   The following example shows the command that would be used for `companyabc` with an the Push Notification Clearing House identity being `sipfed.online.lync.com`:

```
New-CsHostingProvider -Identity LyncPush -Enabled $True
➥-ProxyFqdn sipfed.online.lync.com -VerificationLevel UseSourceVerification
```

3. Add `push.lync.com` as an allowed SIP domain by running the following command:

```
New-CSAllowedDomain -Identity push.lync.com
```

At this point, the federation configuration is complete for push notifications. Follow the steps in the section "Steps to Enable Mobility" to enable Mobile access and push notifications for those clients.

Reverse Proxy and Hardware Load Balancer Considerations for Mobility

All Lync mobile traffic will go through a reverse proxy regardless of the client location. Given the roaming nature of mobile clients, connection affinity is better controlled when the client connects through the same service. In the case of Lync Mobile, that service will always be the external web services directory, which is published through a reverse proxy solution. When external Lync services are being deployed, a reverse proxy must be configured to publish the Front End Pool Web Services to the Internet. The Mobility Service will run on the same URL as the Front End Pool Web Services, and under a subdirectory for the appropriate Mobile Service. However, the LyncDiscover service, although it will point to the same Front End Server Web Service, will require a unique FQDN defined, and the reverse proxy will require an entry to support that FQDN.

Reverse Proxy Certificate Requirements

When Mobility is being deployed as part of a new deployment or this functionality is being added to an existing environment, the key change to the reverse proxy solution is certificates. When the LyncDiscover service is being deployed through a reverse proxy, there are two possible solutions:

▶ Include `LyncDiscover.<sipdomain>` as a subject alternative name (SAN) entry on the web services public certificate. This can become costly when there are many SIP domains supported in the environment.

▶ Publish the LyncDiscover service over HTTP. When the service allows connections on port 80, the initial request will not be over TLS; clients are then redirected to the external web services FQDN for the Front End Server pool, resulting in no requirement for a LyncDiscover entry on the certificate.

Initial requests to the LyncDiscover service, whether they are over HTTPS or HTTP, are not authenticated; as such, there is not a great security risk with publishing this service over HTTP. The initial connection will simply be used to identify the full URL to connect to for the LyncDiscover service, and this information is given to connecting clients whether they connect over HTTP or HTTPS.

For details on configuring a reverse proxy for Lync Server 2013, see Chapter 12, "Firewall and Security Requirements."

Hardware Load Balancer Requirements

Enterprise Edition Lync Front End Server pools will require a Hardware Load Balancer (HLB) to be deployed to provide high-availability to the web services for that pool. In Lync Server 2010, introducing Lync Mobile to the environment required cookie-based persistence to be configured on the HLB to provide session affinity to Lync mobile users. Because the session for each connected client was maintained only on the Front End Server they connected to, the client would always be required to connect to that same server. As such, cookie-based persistence was required to provide this affinity. In Lync Server 2013, the requirements for cookie-based persistence have been removed, including for Lync 2010 Mobile clients connecting to Lync Server 2013 servers. Lync Server 2013

Front End Servers will maintain session affinity for mobile clients; as such, source address affinity should be configured on the HLB instead of cookie-based persistence.

Network and Security Considerations for Mobility

Given the requirements to direct all mobile users to the external web services through a reverse proxy, even for internal clients, a unique hairpin situation is created. In some environments, hair pinning is not allowed. This scenario can arise when the internal traffic is egressing an interface and attempting to immediately ingress on the same interface.

This functionality must be allowed for the Mobility Services to work. A potential workaround for this issue is to deploy the reverse proxy solution separately from the firewall (that is, do not allow RP traffic to traverse the corporate firewall to prevent issues with hair-pinning). In that configuration, the traffic will egress the reverse proxy interface, and then ingress the reverse proxy interface. In the event that the traffic must still pass through the external firewall, it is important to work with the firewall administrators to provide an exception to the hairpin rule for this traffic.

Firewall Rules Required for Lync Mobile

Lync mobile clients connect through the external web services connection, which should be published on port 443 TCP. This requirement should be fairly standard and should be implemented with all Lync deployments involving external users. Apple iOS devices that are connected to the internal infrastructure will require a unique firewall rule for push notification connectivity. When an Apple iOS device attempts to connect to the Apple Push Notification Service, the device initiates an outbound connection on port 5223 TCP. It is important to ensure that this connectivity is allowed outbound from the corporate network for these devices to functional properly.

Steps to Enable Mobility

Deploying Mobility Services in Lync Server 2013 is relatively simple. Following the guidance in previous sections, follow the high-level steps that follow to enable Mobility in a Lync Server 2013 environment.

DNS Configuration for the LyncDiscover Service

DNS records will be required for the LyncDiscover service for both internal and external users.

Create an internal DNS A record for `LyncDiscoverinternal.<sipdomain>` that points to the internal web services IP address or VIP of the Hardware Load Balancer.

Create an external DNS A record for `LyncDiscover.<sipdomain>` that points to the external reverse proxy interface for the external web services.

Configurations for Proper Certificate Configuration

If LyncDiscover services are being deployed over HTTPS, a SAN must be created on all web service certificates for the appropriate LyncDiscover URLs.

Configurations for Push Notifications

Follow the steps in the earlier section "Federation Requirements for Push Notifications" to enable push notifications in the environment. After the federation connection has been established, use the `Set-CSPushNotificationConfiguration` cmdlet to enable this functionality. An example is provided here:

```
Set-CsPushNotificationConfiguration -EnableApplePushNotificationService $True
➥-EnableMicrosoftPushNotificationService $True
```

To test the push notification configuration, use the cmdlet `Test-CSMCXPushNotification`. An example is provided here:

```
Test-CSMCXPushNotification -AccessEdgeFQDN InternalEdgeName.Companyabc.com
```

Enable Mobility for Users

Lastly, enable users for mobility functionality by running the `Set-CSMobilityPolicy` cmdlet. An example is provided here:

```
Set-CSMobilityPolicy -EnableMobility $True -EnableOutsideVoice $True
```

Controlling Functionality with Mobility Policies

Lync Mobile functionality can be controlled using various polices. These policies include configurations targeted at user and server configuration. The user policies are basic, and are used to describe what a user is allowed to do from a mobile device. The server policies give administrators more granular control over server settings related to Lync Mobility Services.

User Policies for Lync Mobile

The user-related policies for Lync mobile users are provided in Table 24.4.

TABLE 24.4   Policies to Control Mobile User Features

Policy Name	Cmdlet to Configure	Scopes Available	Syntax Description
PushNotification Configuration	New-CSPushNotification Configuration	Site Only	Use this cmdlet to enable or disable push notifications on a per-site basis.
MobilityPolicy	New-CSMobilityPolicy	Global, Site, User	Use this cmdlet to enable or disable mobile access, and to enable or disable call via work functionality.

Some examples of how to configure mobile policies for user functionality are provided here:

Example 1

Example 1 shows enabling push notifications for the NewYork site only:

```
New-CSPushNotificationConfiguration -Identity site:newyork
➥-EnableApplePushNotificationService $True -EnableMicrosoftPushNotificationService
➥-$True
```

Example 2

Example 2 shows creating a mobile policy for users that will be assigned to each user with mobile enabled. Also shown is the command to disable mobility at the global level.

```
New-CSMobilityPolicy -identity tag:MobileUsers -EnableMobility $True
➥-EnableOutsideVoice $True
Set-CSMobilityPolicy -Identity Global -EnableMobility $False
➥-EnableOutsideVoice $false
```

Server Policies for Lync Mobile

The server configuration policies for Lync Mobile are shown in Table 24.5.

TABLE 24.5   Lync Mobile Server Policies

Policy Name	Cmdlet to Configure	Scopes Available	Syntax Description
CSWebLink	New-CSWebLink	Site Only	Use this cmdlet to specify LyncDiscover URLs on a site-by-site basis.
AutoDiscover Configuration	New-CSAutoDiscover Configuration	Site Only	Use this cmdlet to specify a list of web links for the LyncDiscover service in a site.
MCXConfiguration	New-CSMCX Configuration	Global, Site, Server (service)	Use this cmdlet to specify configurations such as the expiration timers for mobile clients.

Some examples of common server configurations are provided here:

Example 1

Example 1 shows configuring the MCX service on the NewYork site to expire Android and Nokia phone sessions after 1 day. The default setting is 3 days, which means that Android and Nokia devices would maintain an active connection for up to 3 days before being disconnected.

```
New-CSMCXConfiguration -Identity Site:NewYork -SessionShortExpirationInterval 86400
```

Example 2

Example 2 shows configuring the autodiscover URLs for the NewYork site to be https://LyncDiscover.companyabc.com and https://LyncDiscoverinternal.companyabc.com:

```
$Link1 = New-CsWebLink -Token "CompanyABC"
➥-Href "http://LyncDiscover.companyabc.com"
$Link2 = New-CsWebLink -Token "CompanyABC"
➥-Href "http://LyncDiscoverInternal.CompanyABC.com"

New-CsAutoDiscoverConfiguration -Identity "site:NewYork"
➥-WebLinks @{Add=$Link1,$Link2}
```

Summary

Mobile functionality is key to providing a true Unified Communications Solution. Lync Server 2013 provides users mobile access across all platforms with a consistent and intuitive user experience. New services have been designed to support mobile devices, including the MCX service for Lync 2010 clients, and the Unified Communications Web API service for Lync 2013 clients. These services act as critical intermediary points between the Lync mobile clients that communicate in XML messages over the HTTPS protocol, and the Lync Server Services that communicate in SIP over the TLS protocol. Providing a simple experience for end users on a mobile device is also critical. The LyncDiscover service enables mobile devices to automatically discover critical Lync services, resulting in a seamless automatic configuration of clients.

Deploying Lync Mobility to a Lync Server 2013 deployment introduces unique DNS and certificate requirements, and must be carefully planned for. After these requirements have been identified and met, the actual deployment of the services is a relatively simple process. Also, controlling the Lync Mobile Services and functionality available to end users is available in a few key policies, all controllable through the Lync Server Management Shell and the Lync Control Panel.

Windows Client

Although Lync Server 2013 is an impressive application by itself, most users experience Lync Server 2013 only through one of its many clients. The most common client is likely Lync 2013 in most environments. Lync 2013 is the Windows-based client that enables users to access the client-side functionality of Lync Server 2013. This includes functions such as the following:

▶ Instant messaging

▶ Presence

▶ PC-to-PC calls

▶ Enterprise Voice functions

▶ Video conferencing

▶ Web conferencing

▶ Desktop and application sharing

This chapter covers the more commonly used functions of the Lync 2013 client and should act as the basis of end-user training that most administrators want to provide to their user community to ensure successful adoption of Lync Server 2013.

NOTE

For those upgrading from Office Communications Server 2007 R2, Lync 2013 is a single installation package, so there is no longer a need to install Communicator, Live Meeting, and the Conferencing Plug-In separately.

In older versions of Office Communications Server, there were multiple clients for instant messaging, web conferencing, and group chat. Lync 2013 combines all these features into a single client to make it even more seamless for users to participate in multiple types of collaborative communications.

Installing the Client

The Lync 2013 client for Windows now comes as part of the Microsoft Office 2013 setup package, which enables organizations to leverage familiar deployment tools such as the Office Customization Tool (OCT) when deploying Lync clients to users.

It's certainly still possible to install just the Lync 2013 application by following these steps:

1. Launch the Office 2013 installation package.

2. Accept the licensing terms and click Continue.

3. Click Customize.

4. Click on each product and select Not Available, as shown in Figure 25.1.

5. Click Microsoft Lync and select Run from My Computer.

6. Click Continue.

7. Click Close to exit the installer and then launch the Lync 2013 client.

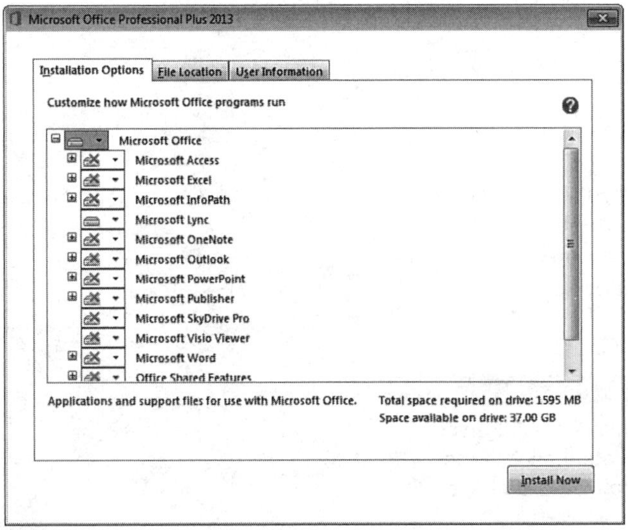

FIGURE 25.1   Lync client installation.

NOTE

The Lync 2013 client can actually coexist on the same system with Communicator 2007 R2 or Lync 2010. The legacy versions are not automatically removed during the installation.

Signing In

After the client is installed, a user can try to sign in. In a typical corporate environment the user's SIP address is automatically detected from Active Directory and credentials are passed to Lync transparently, so no action is required.

In some cases the user might need to enter a SIP address and password. If the user's SIP address is not the same as the user principal name (UPN) within Active Directory, the user will also be challenged for the NetBIOS domain name and username.

If automatic sign-in cannot be used, the server settings can be manually configured through the Lync options. Click the Options icon on the right side of the screen, click Personal, and then click the Advanced button. Select Manual configuration and then enter an internal and external server name. The format for these entries should be `<Lync Pool FQDN>:<Port Number>`. The internal server port will typically be 5061 while the external server port is usually 443.

Navigating in the Client

The Lync 2013 client is broken into a few sections, as shown in Figure 25.2, starting with the user's personal area at the very top. This is where a user can enter a status update in the What's Happening Today? field, change his presence, or define a location they are currently working from.

The next section of the client is a tabbed navigation area that enables the user to jump between her contact list, Persistent Chat rooms, conversation history, and telephony features.

Continuing toward the bottom is a search field where users can enter names or phone numbers when trying to locate a contact. This search happens across the user's Lync contact list and personal Outlook contacts by default.

The main area of the client is next. It displays content for each of the tabbed areas discussed previously, so it will switch between the user's contact list, Persistent Chat rooms, previous conversations, and telephony features.

The final area of the client is displayed at the very bottom and enables the user to easily switch a preferred audio device or manage his call forwarding settings.

FIGURE 25.2   The Lync 2013 client interface.

Configuring Basic Options

You can reach the personal options by clicking on the gear icon at the far right of the navigation tabs. In the Options windows, the options are broken up into multiple categories. These categories are organized in the left pane for easy access and include the following:

▶ **General**—This is where users can turn on or off emoticons, modify background colors for messages, turn logging on or off, and configure tabbed conversations.

▶ **Personal**—This is where users can alter their logon information, determine Lync's startup behavior, opt to integrate presence information with Exchange or Outlook, configure Lync conversation archiving to Outlook, and opt to show photos for contacts.

▶ **Contacts List**—This is where users can adjust how contacts are displayed, how they are ordered, and how much information is shown.

▶ **Status**—This section contains options for how presence is automatically updated and viewable.

▶ **My Picture**—This is where users can determine whether to present a photo with their contact information.

▶ **Phones**—This is where users can modify phone number information, as well as opt to integrate Lync client with the phone system, enable functions such as TTY, or configure behavior for joining conference calls.

▶ **Alerts**—This is where users can choose to be notified if someone else adds them to the contact list or to configure the behavior of their Do Not Disturb status.

▶ **Persistent Chat**—This is where users can customize alerts and sounds for Persistent Chat rooms.

▶ **Ringtones and Sounds**—This is where the user can choose the incoming-call ringtone or configure sounds on specific events.

▶ **Audio Device**—This is where users can choose which audio devices will be used by the Lync client. They can also change the volume associated with the speakers and ringer, as well as modify the microphone sensitivity. These settings are useful for optimizing the user experience. When adjusting the microphone, simply slide the bar all the way to the right and then speak into the microphone a bit louder than normal. If the resulting signal is deemed too high, the slider automatically moves left after you finish speaking.

▶ **Video Device**—This is where users can choose the video source and access that device's settings. These settings include exposure, focus, brightness, contrast, hue, sharpness, gamma, and backlight compensation. The user can also access advanced and extended settings to include zoom, white balance, and even face tracking, if the device supports it.

▶ **Call Forwarding**—This is where users can view and change call forwarding, simultaneous ring, and voice mail settings. Team-call group and delegate members can also be defined on this screen.

▶ **File Saving**—This is where users determine where file transfers and Lync recordings will be saved.

Managing Contacts

Most people are accustomed to the behaviors in Outlook, where you can quickly look up a user in the contacts or find the user by starting to type that person's name. The Lync 2013 client follows this model by organizing contacts by groups and by enabling users to quickly search for contacts by simply typing the person's name.

For example, on the Find Someone or a Room, or Dial a Number line, if you type a name, the client suggests names based on the contacts. From here, right-click on the contact, select Add to Contacts List, and select a group for the user. When this occurs, the person you added receives a notification of the addition and has the option to add you as well. After being added, the contacts appear in the group you selected and you are able to see their presence information at any time.

NOTE

The Lync 2013 client downloads the address book on a random interval after the first sign-in. It might take up to an hour before corporate search results appear. Creating a DWORD called GalDownloadInitialDelay with a value of 0 in the Windows registry at HKCU\Software\Policies\Microsoft\Office\15.0\Lync will force the address book to download immediately.

After a contact is added, you can move the contact from one contact group to another by simply left-clicking and dragging the contact from one group to another. You can also right-click and select Move to another group.

Managing Groups

The Lync 2013 client enables users to organize their contacts by placing them inside groups. The first tab in the Lync 2013 defaults to a view where contacts are organized by groups. By default, these are the groups:

▶ Favorites

▶ All Contacts

The Favorites group is automatically populated by the client based on how often particular contacts are used, or the user can manually pin certain contacts to the group. The All Contacts group becomes the Other Contacts group as soon as a user creates the first custom group. Groups can be deleted or renamed by way of the right-click function.

NOTE

Contacts can exist within multiple groups at a time. Right-click on any contact and select Copy Contact To in order to create a duplicate contact entry within another group.

A convenient use of groups is to organize members of a project or department. By right-clicking the group name, you can choose to launch a conference call that invites all members of that group. You can achieve similar functionality by selecting multiple contacts by Ctrl-clicking them and then right-clicking to choose Start a Conference Call. This call can use Lync's PC-to-PC call features or the PSTN/PBX gateway.

You can organize groups within the client either by using the right-click-accessed Move Group Up and Move Group Down functions or by simply dragging them from one position to another. Right-click on any existing group and select Create New Group to manually build a new group.

Status View

The default view of the contact list is to organize the user's contacts by groups, but users can also sort based on the current status of each contact. In this view, their group membership is irrelevant and only their current status affects where their contact appears. Statuses include these:

▶ Online

▶ Away

▶ Unknown

▶ Unavailable

The status view is a quick and easy way to determine which of your contacts are available at any time.

Relationship View

The third view available in the Lync 2013 client is the relationship view. This view is a bit more interesting because the relationships actually enforce behaviors on the contacts that are members of them. The relationships include the following:

▶ **Friends and Family**—Contacts in this relationship can view all your contact information except meeting details.

▶ **Workgroup**—Contacts in this relationship can view all your contact information except Home and Other Phone; they can interrupt the Do Not Disturb status.

▶ **Colleagues**—Contacts in this relationship can view all your contact information except Home, Other Phone and Mobile Phone, and meeting details.

▶ **External Contacts**—Contacts in this relationship can view only your name, title, email address, company, and picture.

▶ **Blocked Contacts**—Contacts in this relationship can view only your name, email address, office, and picture; they can't reach you through Lync.

Beyond these permissions, the relationship view operates the same way as the other two views in terms of initiating IMs with contacts.

Recent Conversations

The third tab displayed in the client shows conversation history. All instant message conversations, phone calls, and Lync meetings are displayed in this section for reference. Users can also filter for conversations that include audio or by missed conversations within the navigation filters at the top of the screen. Right-click on any conversation and select Continue Conversation to rejoin.

Telephony

The fourth and final tab visible in the Lync client is specific to telephony features and is displayed only when a user is enabled for Enterprise Voice. A dial pad is displayed, and a button to initiate an audio quality test call is available. The user's voice mail is also displayed on this page and can be played back or managed via the Lync client. This helps users' productivity because they don't have to jump between Lync and Outlook to manage voice mail messages. The voice mail options on the right side of the client provide entry hooks to call voice mail, change personal greetings, or run through the initial voice mail setup.

Useful Lync Client Shortcuts

Microsoft has gone out of its way to improve functionality and accessibility in the Lync client, and one of the ways is to create hotkeys for commonly used tasks. This sort of information makes a great cheat sheet for new users of the Lync client because it not only simplifies accessing certain functions, but also serves to highlight what functions are available. Some of those commonly used tasks are highlighted in Tables 25.1, 25.2, and 25.3.

TABLE 25.1   Global Hotkeys

Shortcut Key	Description
Windows key+A	Accept incoming toast invitation
Windows key+Esc	Decline toast invitation
Windows key+Y	Bring Lync main window to foreground
Windows key+F4	Mute or unmute audio
Windows key+F5	Turn camera on or off
Ctrl+Shift+spacebar	Focus on application-sharing toolbar
Ctrl+Alt+spacebar	Take back control during screen sharing
Ctrl+Shift+S	Stop screen sharing

TABLE 25.2   Main Window Shortcuts

Shortcut Key	Description
Ctrl+1	Go to the Contact List tab
Ctrl+2	Go to the Persistent Chat tab
Ctrl+3	Go to the Conversation List tab
Ctrl+4	Go to the Phone tab

TABLE 25.3   Conversation Window Shortcuts

Shortcut Key	Description
Escape	Exit full-screen view if present, or close the conversation window only if it has no audio, video, or sharing
Alt+C	Accept invite notifications
Alt+F4	Close the conversation window

Shortcut Key	Description
Alt+I	Ignore invite notifications
Alt+R	Rejoin audio
Alt+S	Open the Save As dialog box
Alt+V	Invite a contact to a conversation
Ctrl+S	Save conversation to IM history
Ctrl+W	Show/hide IM area
Ctrl+F	Send a file
Ctrl+N	Take notes using OneNote
Ctrl+R	Show/hide participant list
Ctrl+Shift+Enter	Add or end video
Ctrl+Shift+H	Hold or resume an ongoing audio conversation
Ctrl+Shift+I	Mark a conversation as high importance
Ctrl+Shift+Y	Show or hide the sharing stage
Ctrl+Shift+P	Use Compact View
Ctrl+Shift+K	Use the content-only view
Ctrl+Enter	Add or end audio

25

Peer-to-Peer Conversations

Many of the conversations performed within Lync are between only two users in a peer-to-peer fashion. This section covers the different modalities available for two-party interactions. This can include instant messaging, audio or video calls, and content sharing.

Instant Messaging

For most environments, the most commonly used feature in the Lync 2013 client is instant messaging. This function enables users to stop cluttering mailboxes with messages such as "Where do you want to go for lunch," and enables users to limit their messages to only people who are likely to respond quickly. This is where accurate presence information really comes in handy.

Starting an IM conversation is as simple as double-clicking a contact. Doing so launches the IM window that defaults to the IM.

The IM client works like any other IM client. You can see the status information for the person with whom you are communicating, and there are two areas in the window: one to type in and one to display the conversation. Users have access to the usual features such as altering the font, color, and size of the text, as well as a menu of emoticons. You can access emoticons with the usual combinations of characters.

Using Tabbed Conversations

New to the Lync 2013 client is the capability to use tabbed conversations, which is enabled by default. After starting one IM, simply double-click another contact to start a separate conversation and the windows will be automatically grouped together with tabs, as shown in Figure 25.3.

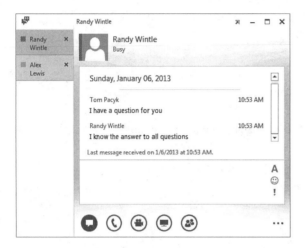

FIGURE 25.3   Tabbed conversations.

> **NOTE**
>
> Tabbed windows apply only to IM or Persistent Chat conversations. When a user makes an audio call or joins a meeting, that conversation is opened in a separate window.

Users can adjust the order of the conversations by left-clicking on a conversation and dragging the tab up or down. Tabbed conversations can also be closed with a click of the X that appears on the right side of each tab.

Users can manually pop out a tab by right-clicking on it and selecting Pop Out Conversation. This can be useful when the user needs to separate the windows for reference.

Archiving IM Conversations

IM conversations can be archived in two ways. One way is for an administrator to implement an archiving policy on an archiving server, but this data is not accessible by the users. The other way is to archive messages into Outlook so that users can reference previous conversations easily. For a review on implementing archiving policies on an archiving server, refer to Chapter 7, "Microsoft Lync Server 2013 Monitoring and Archiving."

In the Options area, under the Personal tab, is the option to Save Instant Message Conversations in My Email Conversation History folder. This is enabled by default, and it ensures that each conversation is saved into this email folder at the time the IM window is closed. This is a useful way to access old conversations, and this folder's contents are indexed for easy searches.

Audio and Video Calls

One of the most interesting features in the Lync 2013 client is the capability to participate in audio or video conferences with other users in the Lync Server 2013 environment. Before their first participation in an audio or video conference, users should configure their audio and video devices as described in the "Configuring Basic Options" section earlier in this chapter. After these devices are configured, users are ready to start their first conference.

Making Audio Calls

Initiating an audio call is as simple as right-clicking a contact, choosing Call, and specifying that it should be a Lync call. Then, the contact receives a pop-up and an audio notification and has the option to answer, decline, or redirect. Answer and decline should be fairly obvious as to what they do. Redirect gives the option to reply through IM or to set one's status to Do Not Disturb. Accepting the call updates both users' status to In a Call.

Users can easily escalate an existing IM conversation to audio by clicking the phone icon at the bottom of the conversation window. This pops the conversation out into its own window, similar to what happens when a brand-new call is placed.

When the call connects, a new window displays that looks similar to the IM window. In fact, it is the same window, but now has the audio portion joined.

The call window enables the user to easily mute the device by clicking the phone icon once more, which shows a microphone during an active call. Muting the microphone alters the icon on the client that muted his microphone. A connection signal strength and call timer are displayed in the upper-left corner of the conversation.

Users can access additional call-management options by hovering over the phone icon. After that, the following options are displayed:

▶ **Dial Pad**—Used to enter DTMF tones when in a call. Users can also start pressing digits on the keyboard without first using the mouse to expose this menu.

▶ **Mute**—Mutes the user's local microphone. The phone icon changes to indicate that the user is muted and cannot be heard by the other party.

▶ **Hold**—Places the call on hold. A notification bar appears with a Resume button to pick up the call again.

▶ **Devices**—Allows the user to fine-tune the speaker volume, or switch to another audio device while in a call.

▶ **Transfer**—Enables the user to transfer the call to a mobile device, or to someone else. The call can also be parked through this option if the Call Park feature is enabled.

The call can be ended with a click of the red phone icon in the upper-right corner of the conversation window. This ends only the audio portion of the call, and keeps the conversation active if IM or sharing is being used. Clicking the standard Windows close icon would end the entire conversation.

If Conversation History is enabled, the call is logged in the user's Outlook folder. The call itself is neither recorded nor stored, but the list of participants and the duration of the call are captured.

Network Connectivity Icon

One of the other icons visible in the window is a Network Connectivity status, which is displayed in the upper-left corner of the call. This indicates the quality of the network connection and is useful in troubleshooting issues with voice quality on a call.

Making Video Calls

Initiating a video call is as simple as right-clicking a contact and choosing Start a Video Call. Much as with the audio call, the recipient has the option to accept, decline, or redirect. Redirect gives the option to reply with an IM or to mark the recipient as Do Not Disturb.

When the call is accepted, the usual client window opens and is located on the Video tab. The recipient initially sees the caller, but the caller doesn't see the recipient until after he clicks Start My Video in the window.

While in an active conversation, users can leverage the new Video Preview feature to check what their video will look like before initiating the call. Hover over the video icon to see a preview, and then click Start My Video to initiate the call.

By default, participants in a two-way call see themselves in a picture-in-picture window inside the main video window. You can hide this preview by hovering over the video and clicking the downward-facing arrow. Click the upward-facing arrow to restore the video preview.

The same audio controls for mute, hold, and devices discussed previously are still available within a video call. Clicking the video icon again stops the user from sending video, and another click resumes it once again.

Users can also detach the video content from the conversation window by hovering over the main video and clicking the arrow in the upper-right corner. This can be useful for users with multiple monitors, enabling them to maximize the video on one screen while continuing to use the other monitor for another purpose.

TIP

If you expect widespread adoption of video conferencing and calls in your environment, don't skimp on the video cameras. Modern webcams have rather nice lenses, and modern processors can easily keep up with the load of high-definition video conferencing.

Sharing Content

Using Lync to collaborate is a favorite feature of end users because of how simple it is to quickly share a desktop or an application. While in an active conversation, move the mouse over the presenter icon, which looks like a monitor, as shown in Figure 25.4. From here a user can share the following types of content:

▶ **All Monitors**—Shares all the screens currently connected. Depending on the resolution of each user, the other end might need to zoom and pan to be able to read the content.

▶ **Specific Monitor**—Shares only a specific screen if multiple monitors are attached. As the user hovers over the monitor options, a yellow border is displayed on the monitor about to be shared. This way a user knows exactly what content will be shown to the other user.

▶ **Program**—Shares only a specific application. This is usually the best experience for users because it is more efficient and uses less bandwidth. It can also be useful for keeping private information hidden from the opposite party.

▶ **PowerPoint**—Escalates the conversation to a Lync meeting and begins sharing a PowerPoint deck. The user is prompted to select a PowerPoint file to present.

FIGURE 25.4   Lync content sharing.

▶ **Whiteboard**—Escalates the conversation to a Lync meeting and begins sharing a new whiteboard.

▶ **Poll**—Escalates the conversation to a Lync meeting and presents a poll for the other person to select. The poll can be given a name, a question, and up to seven possible choices.

Sending and Receiving Files

The IM interface enables one person to send a file to the other participant of the IM conversation. The easiest way to send a file is to just drag it from the desktop onto the current conversation window.

Alternatively, at the bottom of the conversation window is an icon with a monitor in it for sharing. Hover the mouse over that icon and then click Attachments at the top. Clicking Add Attachment launches a window that enables the user to select a file to transfer.

The person set to receive the file receives a notification and has the option to Accept, Save As, or Decline the file. Accepting the file triggers a warning window to warn the user that the file might contain harmful malware and that she should accept files from only someone she knows. After it is accepted, it downloads and a link displays to access the file. The sender of the file receives a notification that the transfer was successful.

Conferencing

Probably the biggest driving force behind companies implementing Lync Server 2013 is replacing outsourced web conferencing services. Many companies spend tens of thousands of dollars a month on services, such as WebEx or GoToMeeting. Although there might be situations in which a company running Lync Server 2013 needs to create a conference so large that its infrastructure isn't sufficient, the other 95% of the time it can use a platform it owns rather than pay an external company for these services.

Conferences in Lync 2013 can be generated in a few ways, but the meeting experience is identical in each case. The most dynamic way to create a meeting is by presenting a PowerPoint, a whiteboard, or a poll within an existing peer-to-peer conversation. Sharing any of those items immediately escalates the conversation to a conference. Similarly, adding a third participant by simply dragging another contact into an existing conversation escalates it to a conference.

> **NOTE**
>
> There is no distinction within Lync about what is an IM conference versus a video conference versus a PowerPoint sharing session. From the client's perspective a conference exists, and any of the modalities are available within that conference.

Using the Meet Now Function

Users sometimes think they need to schedule a conference or reserve resources because of how they interacted with a legacy system. The Lync client can dynamically generate a conference if the user clicks the drop-down arrow next to the Options icon and selects Meet Now. This is equivalent to dragging participants into an existing conversation, but it creates an empty conference that the organizer can then set up before inviting participants.

Hover over the participants icon at the bottom of the window and select Invite More People to see the contact list and add participants. The organizer can also just drag and drop contacts from the main Lync contact list window into the meeting window to add participants.

When contacts are being invited by name or phone number, Lync displays the existing contacts to simplify adding an attendee who is already known to the meeting organizer. Highlighting the contact and clicking OK sends an invite to the contact. The person is notified by a pop-up box and can opt to either join the conference or ignore the invitation.

Controlling a Meeting

Presenter can sometimes find it useful to have a bit more control over the meeting experience. Lync 2013 offers meeting organizers some excellent tools for managing a meeting. For example, right-click on attendees to mute their audio, remove them from the conference, or modify their meeting privileges as presenter or attendee. The mute tool is especially useful when a participant is making a lot of background noise that is impacting the meeting experience.

Hovering over the participants icon while in a conference reveals a number of additional controls:

▶ **Mute Audience**—Mutes the entire audience, which can be useful in presentation mode.

▶ **No Attendee Video**—Prevents attendees from sending any video to the meeting. Again, this is useful in a presentation or broadcast mode in which only presenter video should be shown.

▶ **Hide Names**—Hides names of participants on their photos or video stream.

▶ **Everyone an Attendee**—Forces all meeting participants to be an attendee. This helps ensure that only specified presenters can share content or control the meeting.

▶ **Invite by Email**—Generates an email invitation with the meeting information. This can be sent to participants who should join the conference.

Managing Meeting Content

With the web conference up and running, participants who were allowed to become presenters based on the meeting options can use the Share tab in the Lync client to add resources to the conference. These options include the same features discussed in the "Sharing Content" section earlier in this chapter.

Sharing a whiteboard reveals several tools on the far-right side so users can collaborate easily. There are pointers, text, shapes, pens, highlighters, erasers, stamps, line art, and a tool for inserting an existing image. The three-horizontal-dots icon reveals a few additional options, including the capability to save to OneNote or an image file.

PowerPoint decks can also be uploaded and shared out, and optionally made available for download. After the deck is uploaded, presenters can click on Thumbnails or Notes to view the slide previews and any presenter notes. These features are not available to meeting attendees. The upper-right corner displays a pen icon that offers the use of the same whiteboard markup tools.

> **TIP**
>
> Always use the PowerPoint feature instead of doing a desktop or application share. This ensures that the slides are scaled and formatted to fit the various-size screens that might be viewing the presentation.

After a poll is created, the presenters can choose to show the results to attendees or hide them from attendees, open or close the polls, clear the votes, or save the poll for reference later.

After content has been shared, it stays available within the meeting for reuse or distribution. Hovering over the content icon and selecting Manage Presentable Content displays all the shared content. Presenters can switch between different pieces of content, assign permissions to each piece so that attendees can download it, or remove a component from the meeting.

Changing the Layout

Within each conference is a Layout icon, which is the second icon from the right in the lower corner. This enables the users to modify their view of the meeting experience. Depending on the meeting, one of the following layout options might make more sense than others:

▶ **Gallery View**—This view uses a mixture of video or photos along the top of the screen, and then shows the shared content below.

▶ **Speaker View**—This view focuses on the active speaker. The current speaker's video is displayed next to the shared content.

▶ **Presentation View**—This view removes the video from the display and focuses on only the shared content.

▶ **Compact View**—This view hides the video and shared content. The user can hear audio and see the participant list.

While in the Gallery View, right-click any user's photo video feed and select Pin to Gallery to always show that content. The Gallery View is displayed in Figure 25.5.

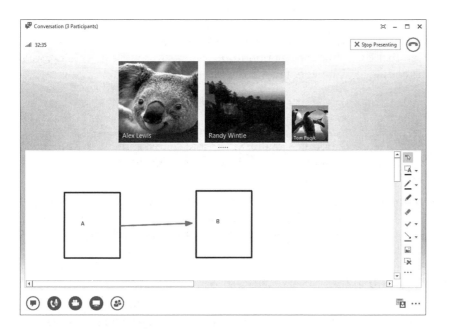

FIGURE 25.5 Lync 2013 Gallery View.

Customizing Meeting Options

Within any existing Lync meeting is the capability for organizers to adjust the meeting settings. Clicking the three-horizontal-dots icon at the lower-right corner of the conversation window and selecting Lync Meeting Options reveals the various options available:

▶ **Lobby**—Controls who gets access to the meeting automatically. This can be set to Anyone (no restrictions), Anyone from My Organization, People I Invite, or Only The Meeting Organizer. PSTN callers can optionally bypass the lobby.

▶ **Announcements**—Controls whether an announcement is played as users enter and exit the meetings. Whether names or tones are used is controlled by a server policy. Users cannot customize that choice.

▶ **Presenters**—Controls who is allowed to share content and let participants into the meeting.

▶ **Annotations**—Dictates who can mark up and annotate PowerPoint presentations.

▶ **Content Viewing**—Controls who can view content at their own pace, such as flipping between different PowerPoint slides without affecting the presenter's view.

Meeting Information

While in a meeting, there can sometimes be a need for participants to view the meeting URL or conference ID so that it can be distributed to someone else. Clicking the three-horizontal-dots icon at the lower-right corner of the conversation window and selecting Meeting Entry Info displays details about the current meeting. There is a Copy All Info button on this screen that copies the information to the Clipboard so that it can be pasted into an email or instant message, or stored in personal notes.

Recording

If administrators have enabled recordings for conferences or peer-to-peer conversations, users will be able to save conversation IMs, audio, video, and shared content. Within an active conversation click the three-horizontal-dots icon and select Start Recording. This alerts all participants that a recording has started so that they are not caught off guard.

The recorder sees controls to pause or stop the recording at any time. After the recording has stopped, the Lync Recording Manager application begins converting the recorded content and stores it as a saved MP4 video file. This file can then be distributed to users who might have missed a meeting or training session.

Scheduling a Meeting

Dynamically creating an ad hoc meeting has been discussed previously in this chapter, but many users will need to schedule Lync meetings in advance. This can be done through Outlook with the plugin that's installed with the Lync client.

> **NOTE**
>
> Users must be signed in to Lync in order to schedule Lync Meetings through Outlook.

Within Outlook, click the New Items menu and select Lync Meeting. The meeting URL and dial-in bridge information are automatically populated into the meeting notes section. Proceed with adding attendees the same way any other Outlook meeting would be created.

The Lync Meeting button also appears within the ribbon when a regular Outlook meeting is being scheduled. Users can then just click the Lync Meeting button to populate the notes field with the meeting URL and dial-in information, as shown in Figure 25.6.

The Meeting Options button also appears within the Outlook ribbon so an organizer can customize the meeting experience before the invitation is sent to users. Clicking the Meeting Options button reveals the screen where an organizer can use the dedicated meeting space, or create a new space for the meeting with a unique conference ID, as shown in Figure 25.7. The PSTN dial-in numbers displayed can also be changed through the Phone section within the Meeting Options.

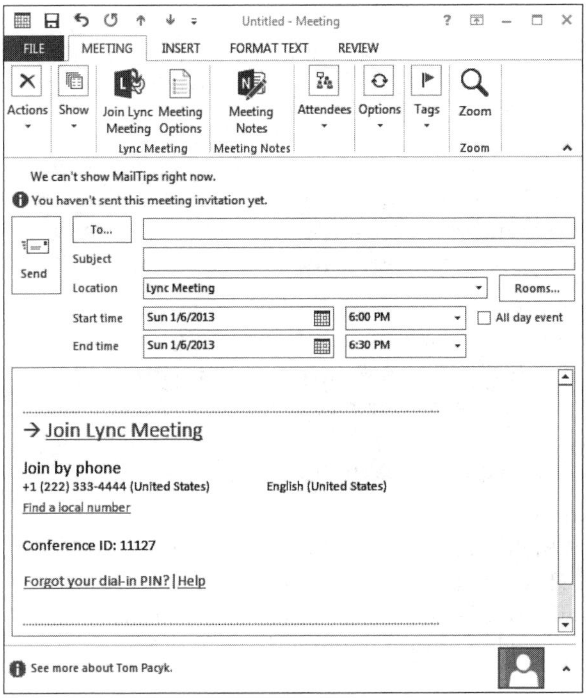

FIGURE 25.6   Lync meeting invitation.

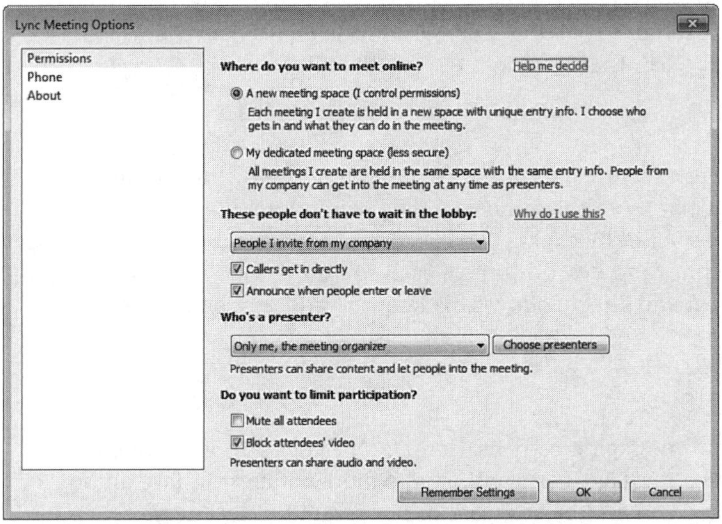

FIGURE 25.7   Lync meeting options.

Joining Meetings

Joining meetings with the Lync client is a simple experience for users. Clicking the Join Lync Meeting hyperlink found within any Lync Meeting automatically launches the conference.

The other easy way to join Lync Meetings is to leverage the Outlook meeting reminder that pops up before a meeting. When Outlook detects that the meeting is a Lync Meeting, it displays a Join Online button to the user. The user does not even need to open the calendar invite, but can instead click the Join Online button and immediately enter the meeting.

Users can also dial in to the conference bridge through the Lync client, or have another participant drag them into an existing meeting. This can sometimes be faster than trying to hunt for a calendar invite, especially if Outlook is not already open. There is also no requirement to use both the web conferencing and dial-in bridge. The web conferencing components can be used even if no audio is required in a meeting.

By default, Lync joins the user's PC audio to a conference, but if a user has selected the option Before I Join Meetings, Ask Me Which Audio Device I Want to Use, they are prompted by Lync for an audio source. This enables the user to not join audio at all, which can be useful on a PC with no audio device. Users can also specify a number, such as a mobile phone, for Lync to call them at when they're joining the conference.

Persistent Chat

New to the Lync 2013 client is the Persistent Chat feature, which was previously an entirely separate application called Group Chat. The two products are now tightly integrated, with Persistent Chat rooms becoming a tab within the main Lync client. If a user is not enabled for Persistent Chat, that user does not see the tab.

Following Rooms

The concept of a joining a Persistent Chat room is referred to as following a room. Users can search for a Persistent Chat room the same way they search for a user, or they can see which rooms they are a member of by clicking the Persistent Chat tab, and then clicking Member Of. A list of the names and descriptions of each room the user belongs to is then displayed. Right-click a room and select Follow This Room to add the room to the user's Followed list.

Using Rooms

Similar to starting an instant messaging conversation, double-click a room to open the contents and begin sending a message. Persistent Chat windows appear in tabs among a user's other IM windows, and can also be arranged or popped out if necessary.

Type a message and press Enter to deliver the text. The difference with Persistent Chat is that the message will still be there the next time the user or any other user visits the room.

Persistent chats sometimes involve longer posts, referred to as stories. To enter a large portion of text that doesn't cause the room to scroll very far, right-click in the text window and select Post as a Long Message. Then enter a message title and post the longer text. Other users see the longer message as a collapsible hyperlink that helps keep the room organized.

Users within the same room are displayed along the top in a Gallery View, but for larger rooms it can be useful to see a bigger roster. Click the participants icon at the bottom of the room to view an expanded roster.

Using Topic Feeds

Topic feeds in Persistent Chat can be used to receive notifications when a particular keyword is posted in a room. This feature is useful for monitoring specific phrases such as a customer, project, or product name and then being alerted to the discussion in real time.

To create a new topic feed, click the + sign in the upper-right corner of the Persistent Chat section and select Create a New Topic Feed. Enter a name for the feed, select people whom the feed pertains to, and enter keywords to search on. A user can also override the default Persistent Chat settings for a particular feed.

Ego Feed

A single topic feed called the Ego Feed is enabled for all users when they first sign in, which alerts them if their name is mentioned by anyone. This feed can be deleted by an end user and is intended to just provide a feed example.

Searching Group Chat Rooms

Users can also conduct searches against rooms they follow. Each room presents a search button at the bottom of the conversation window that enables searching that specific room for content. Users can also create a new search across all rooms by clicking the + sign in the upper-right corner of the Persistent Chat section and selecting Search Room History. This enables the user to search across any rooms they follow or belong to, and specify specific date ranges or users that should be searched.

Managing Rooms

Management of Persistent Chat rooms is actually done through a web interface. There are various integration points for Persistent Chat moderators to be redirected to that web interface when they're trying to create or modify an existing room. The steps for creating and managing rooms are covered in much more detail in Chapter 10, "Persistent Chat."

Integration with Other Applications

As is typical with many Microsoft back-office applications, one of its key value propositions is integration with other Microsoft applications. Microsoft touts its concept of "better together" when selling its products, and Lync Server 2013 is no different. After the client is installed, there are hooks into several other Microsoft applications, which are discussed in this section.

25

Outlook

One of the strongest areas of integration for the Lync client is with Outlook. When the Lync client is installed, it adds several buttons to the Respond area of the Outlook toolbar with the capability to reply via IM or initiate a call.

Instead of being locked into responding to an email with another email, you can choose to start up an IM conversation, initiate a voice call, or initiate a web conference. This offers tremendous flexibility in how to collaborate with co-workers.

This integration extends to the contacts managed by Outlook. By looking at an email received from a co-worker and double-clicking that person's name, you can see the integrated Lync functionality on the contact card. Figure 25.8 shows how you can trigger an IM or a call, or immediately start a shared desktop conference, with the other user. You can also see the presence information for the other user, which often influences how you respond.

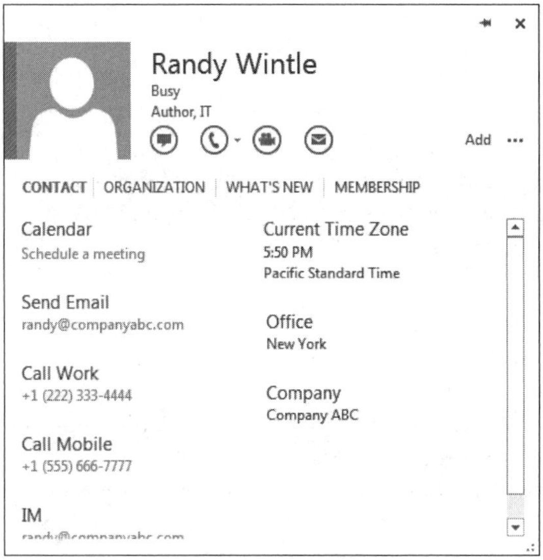

FIGURE 25.8   Outlook contact card.

The last area of integration is presence information. When looking at email messages from other Lync Server 2013 users, you can see their current status. Hovering the mouse over the presence icon gives additional information and exposes the menus to enable you to immediately send an IM, place an audio or video call, schedule a meeting, or start sharing resources.

One Note

Lync 2013 has a new level of integration with OneNote for taking notes during Lync Meetings. Just as in previous versions of the product, users can initiate a new note from an existing conversation. Click the Presentation icon, select OneNote, and select My Notes.

This prompts the user to select a notebook for the note, and then automatically populates the subject, date, time, and participants.

New to Lync 2013 is the capability to select Shared Notes, which again prompts the user for a notebook to store the notes in. The difference with Shared Notes is that all meeting participants can simultaneously edit the notes, which helps ensure that no information is missed. This feature is dependent on all meeting participants having access to a shared notebook on SharePoint or Windows SkyDrive. Lync provides the integration point, but does not provision or provide access to the shared notebook. This functionality can be tested in advance of a meeting to ensure it works properly.

Office Applications

Lync offers some integration with Microsoft Office that can make it easier to collaborate with other users. For example, in Microsoft Word, you can go into the File area of the ribbon and look at the info page. The name of the person who authored the file and the name of the person who last edited the file are located on the far right. Notice that the presence "jelly bean" is shown next to each of the names with accurate presence information. If you have a question about the last set of edits made to a document, simply hover over the Last Modified By name to get the option to IM or call that person through Lync. This level of integration makes collaborative communications easy, and they quickly become second nature for most users.

Lync integration with Office also adds two share options in the Review ribbon.

You can send the document to a contact through the Send by IM button, or you can click Share Now and choose a contact to open a screen-sharing session with that user. This enables two people to share the document and make changes to it collaboratively.

Summary

In this chapter we've covered the primary clients for Windows users to connect to Microsoft Lync Server 2013. We've seen what features are available in terms of IM, audio/video conferencing, and application sharing. As users become more and more familiar with the application, this chapter will serve as a guide for how users access various functions within the system and should help ease the transition to this application.

Administrators should take advantage of the troubleshooting and best practices offered in this chapter to try to provide for the best end-user experience possible. Ultimately, the success of a Microsoft Lync Server 2013 deployment will be measured by the end users, and taking advantage of the information in this chapter will help increase the odds of having happy end users.

It is useful for administrators to understand the limitations of the various clients users can be trained and informed about the different features available. This can be especially useful when external users who attach via the web-based clients are involved. By knowing when to use various client options, administrators and help desk staff can guide users toward the best decisions on how to meet their needs.

CHAPTER 26

Browser Client

Lync Server 2013 introduces enhanced cross-platform support for all communication modalities. Lync Server 2013 Web App enables users to join conferences from a browser and participate in full-featured conferencing without the need to install a client. This chapter provides an overview of the browser capabilities across all operating systems, as well as a technical review of how Lync Web App is deployed and provides services to users. Lastly, the requirements to deploy Lync 2013 browser capabilities are reviewed.

Lync 2013 Browser Capabilities

Lync Server 2010 introduced basic browser capabilities. Users who joined meetings through a web browser were able to view and present content, as well as initiate a dial-out to a PSTN phone number to join through audio. Lync Server 2013 introduces a new experience for users in the web browser. Lync Web App provides web-based conferencing functionality to users, including audio and video, without a requirement for a Lync client to be installed. Refer to Table 26.1 for Lync Web App capabilities.

TABLE 26.1   Lync Web App Browser Capabilities

OS	Meeting Join	View Content	Full Audio and Video
Windows 7 SP1	X	X	X
Windows Server 2008 R2 SP1	X	X	X
Windows 8	X	X	X
Mac OS-X	X	X	X
Windows XP SP3	X	X	
Windows Vista SP2	X	X	
Windows Server 2008 SP2	X	X	
Linux			

Microsoft's goal was to enable a seamless experience between Lync Web App and the Lync 2013 client. Short of a few supportability gaps in older operating systems or web browsers, users can experience full functionality in the browser.

Joining Meetings from the Browser Client

Lync Web App enables Guests and Authenticated Lync Users to join Lync meetings with a single click. To join with audio and video, a plugin is required. This plugin is designed to be a rapid install with user-level dependencies, and Silverlight is no longer required.

Content Collaboration

Lync Web App users are able to participate in a full collaboration experience. This includes Desktop Sharing, Application Sharing, control of desktop, real-time note taking, PowerPoint sharing, Whiteboard, and Poll.

Voice and Video

Lync Web App users that install the browser plugin are able to participate in IP audio and video. Multiparty HD video is also available to users who join through Lync Web App. Additionally, dial-out functionality is still available to users who want to join from a PSTN device.

Meeting Management

Lync Web App users also can manage the meeting from the browser. Meeting presenters can manage the participant list and basic meeting control. However, meeting options such as allowed functionality or locking of the meeting cannot be adjusted in Lync Web App.

Figure 26.1 provides an example of Lync Web App being used to present video in a Lync meeting.

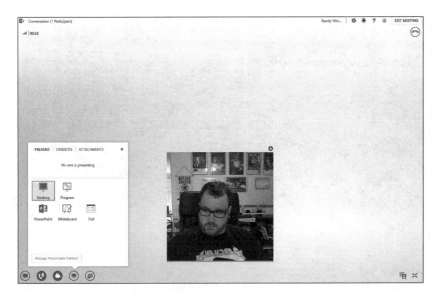

FIGURE 26.1   Lync Web App functionality.

Lync Server 2013 Web App Technical Review

26

Lync Server 2013 Web App is an HTML-based user interface. This is a drastic change from previous versions that leveraged Silverlight for client rendering. Understanding this new architecture will go a long way in deploying and troubleshooting conferencing deployments with Lync Web App functionality.

Architecture Overview

Lync Web App is built around two core components:

▶ **JavaScript-Powered HTML User Interface**—This interface is responsible for rendering most of the UI. It was designed to work on many platforms.

▶ **Native UI**—The Native UI is responsible for rendering audio, video, and screen sharing during meetings.

Figure 26.2 outlines the logical separation of these components.

Lync Web App communicates directly with Unified Communications Web API (UCWA), which is a new API introduced with Lync Server 2013 enabling applications to leverage Lync functionality in a web browser. UCWA will communicate to the Lync Conferencing Servers to establish signaling sessions. The Lync Native UI, which is the plugin-based UI, will talk to the media stack on the Lync Servers for audio, video, and application/desktop-sharing functionality.

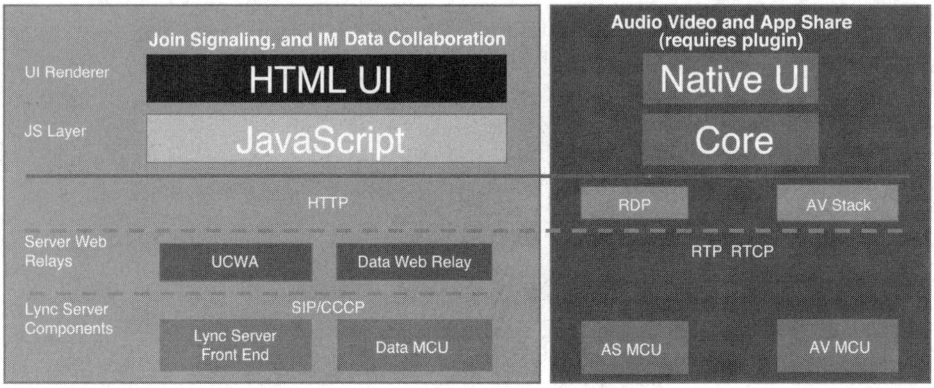

FIGURE 26.2   Lync Mobile Architecture.

Lync Web App Websites

Lync Web App is provided through internal and external websites. Similar to all Lync Web Services, Lync Web App is deployed on each Front End Server; the logical separation of internal and external web directories provides additional security, while enabling internal users to have a seamless join experience.

Authentication Methods Supported

Lync Web App supports standard authentication methods. On-premise users are able to authenticate through forms-based authentication, through Integrated Windows Authentication, or through multifactor authentication that is powered by ADFS. For Lync Online users, OrgID authentication is supported, which is the primary authentication method for all Microsoft Online services. Lastly, guests or unauthenticated users can join if the conferencing policy permits.

Lync Web App Proxy Support

Lync Web App enables users who are configured with an HTTP proxy to use Lync Web App for all functionality. If an HTTP proxy is configured for Basic Authentication, Media traffic does not work. For media to pass through the HTTP proxy, the proxy must be configured for Kerberos, NTLM, or Digest authentication.

Lync Web App Port Requirements

Lync Web App is a web application that communicates over HTTPS. By default, this traffic is over port 443 TCP and is secured with certificates. Administrators can adjust this port if desired.

TIP

Although Lync Web App communicates only over 443 TCP for web traffic, the A/V plugin communicates directly with the Conferencing Server or Edge Server using standard media ports. Keep this in mind when planning your Lync Web App deployment.

Lync Web App Join Process

This section provides an overview of the join process in Lync Web App. Understanding how clients connect to these services will greatly help in deploying and troubleshooting Lync Server 2013 conferencing. Figure 26.3 and the list that follows outlines the join process.

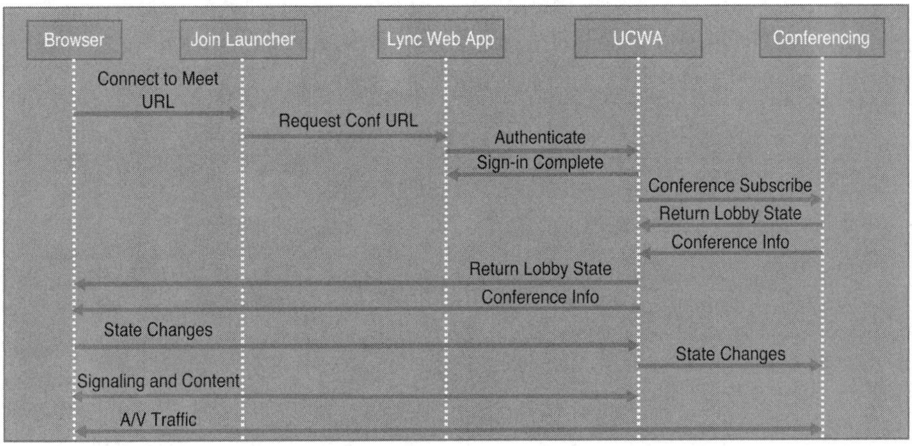

FIGURE 26.3   Lync Web App join process.

26

1. When a client clicks the meeting URL in the meeting invite, they are connected to the Lync Web Services. The Join Launcher component identifies the client type that is connecting and either launches the installed Lync client or launches Lync Web App.

2. The Join Launcher connects to Lync Web App and requests the conferencing URLs to be used.

3. Lync Web App communicates with UCWA to authenticate the user. This can happen over various methods, but ultimately the connecting user must be issued a web ticket to securely connect to Lync Web App and UCWA.

4. When initiated, UCWA initiates requests to the Conference Focus to join the user to the conference.

5. The user is placed in the meeting lobby and joins when admitted.

6. Going forward, all communications with the conferencing focus happen through UCWA. These communications include state changes for the user and the conference.

7. The user receives conference join information in-band to connect to the A/V portions of the conference. Going forward, the browser client communicates directly with the Conferencing Server for media, or through the Edge Server if they are remote.

For those familiar with the conference join process in Lync Server 2013, you will notice that the join process for Lync Web App users is very similar. An important note: UCWA will always be involved to facilitate signaling for browser-based users.

Components and Protocols for Lync Web App Collaboration

This next section briefly describes the components a Lync Web App client interacts with during a collaboration session through the browser. As described in earlier sections, the Lync Web App Client facilitates all signaling through the Unified Communications Web API service running on the Lync Front End Services. However, the Web App Client will also communicate directly with conferencing components for media traffic. Figure 26.4 outlines the protocol flow for Lync Web App collaboration sessions.

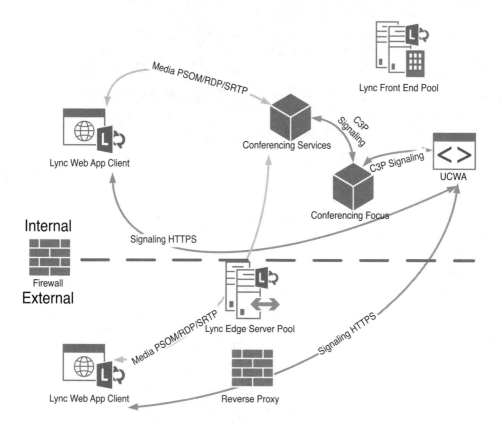

FIGURE 26.4   Lync Web App protocol flow.

The following information is outlined in Figure 26.4:

▶ The Conferencing Services and Conferencing Focus are logical services located on Lync Front End Servers. The Conferencing Focus is responsible for coordinating conferencing resources and the conferencing join process for clients. The

Conferencing Services would include the Audio/Video Conferencing Service, Application Sharing Conferencing Service, Data Conferencing Service, and IM Conferencing Service. The services have been combined in the diagram for simplicity.

▶ Lync Web App clients send all signaling traffic to the Front End Pool and through the UCWA service. If the user is external (see the bottom of the diagram), this traffic must be securely published through a reverse proxy solution.

▶ Lync Web App clients send media traffic through the appropriate conferencing service. If the user is external, the traffic is securely relayed through the Lync Edge Server.

Summary of the Browser Client Architecture and Components

In Lync Server 2013 the browser-based capabilities have received a major overhaul. With the major change in functionality, a new architecture was introduced. At the core of the new architecture is the Unified Communications Web API. This API enables web-based clients to communicate over open standards and perform full Lync functionality. The UCWA service acts as a communication proxy between web-based clients and the other Lync services. UCWA is also at the core of mobility scenarios, and is an API that can be developed on to enhance Lync functionality even further.

After the Lync Web App client has connected to the UCWA service for signaling, it acts much like any other Lync client for collaboration scenarios. The Lync Web App client communicates over HTTPS to receive collaboration content such as PowerPoint presentations and whiteboards, while the ActiveX plugin enables the client to communicate with the media conferencing services over secure RTP.

Requirements to Deploy Lync 2013 Browser Functionality

Deploying Lync 2013 Web App is a relatively simple process. However, this section outlines the client and server requirements for a successful implementation.

Installing Lync Web App Server

Lync Web App functionality is installed on all Front End Servers in the environment. No extra steps are required to install these services. When Lync Front End Servers are configured, all services, certificate, and DNS requirements for Lync Web App Server are completed as well.

Configuring Lync Web App

Although Lync Web App components are installed by default, there are several common configurations to control Lync Web App functionality and access.

Enabling Lync Web App Access for Anonymous Users

For anonymous users (users not enabled for Lync) to join meetings through Lync Web App, you must configure the web service configuration for your Lync topology to allow this. This is done using the `Set-CSWebServiceConfiguration` PowerShell cmdlet. An example of how to perform this configuration is shown here:

1. Open the Lync Server Management Shell.

2. Run the following command to see the existing web service configuration:

   ```
   Get-CSWebServiceConfiguration
   ```

   Here is the sample output:

   ```
   Identity                                 : Global
   TrustedCACerts                           : {}
   MaxGroupSizeToExpand                     : 100
   EnableGroupExpansion                     : True
   UseWindowsAuth                           : Negotiate
   UseCertificateAuth                       : True
   UsePinAuth                               : True
   AllowAnonymousAccessToLWAConference      : False
   EnableCertChainDownload                  : True
   InferCertChainFromSSL                    : True
   CASigningKeyLength                       : 2048
   MaxCSRKeySize                            : 16384
   MinCSRKeySize                            : 1024
   MaxValidityPeriodHours                   : 8760
   MinValidityPeriodHours                   : 8
   DefaultValidityPeriodHours               : 4320
   MACResolverUrl                           :
   SecondaryLocationSourceUrl               :
   ShowJoinUsingLegacyClientLink            : True
   ShowDownloadCommunicatorAttendeeLink     : True
   AutoLaunchLyncWebAccess                  : True
   ShowAlternateJoinOptionsExpanded         : False
   UseWsFedPassiveAuth                      : False
   WsFedPassiveMetadataUri                  :
   AllowExternalAuthentication              : True
   ```

   By default, there is only a Global web service configuration. However, if you have previously configured site- or pool-specific configurations, you can access them through the following command:

   ```
   Get-CSWebServiceConfiguration -Identity <XDS Identity>
   ```

   `<XDS Identity>` refers to the name of the service; for a site this is `site:<site name>`.

3. If `AllowAnonymousAccesstoLWAConference` is set to `false`, run the following command to enable this functionality:

```
Set-CSWebServiceConfiguration -AllowAnonymousAccesstoLWAConference $true
```

4. Running `Get-CSWebServiceConfiguration` again should return the following results:

```
Identity                                : Global
TrustedCACerts                          : {}
MaxGroupSizeToExpand                     : 100
EnableGroupExpansion                    : True
UseWindowsAuth                          : Negotiate
UseCertificateAuth                      : True
UsePinAuth                              : True
AllowAnonymousAccessToLWAConference     : True
EnableCertChainDownload                 : True
InferCertChainFromSSL                   : True
CASigningKeyLength                      : 2048
MaxCSRKeySize                           : 16384
MinCSRKeySize                           : 1024
MaxValidityPeriodHours                  : 8760
MinValidityPeriodHours                  : 8
DefaultValidityPeriodHours              : 4320
MACResolverUrl                          :
SecondaryLocationSourceUrl              :
ShowJoinUsingLegacyClientLink           : True
ShowDownloadCommunicatorAttendeeLink    : True
AutoLaunchLyncWebAccess                 : True
ShowAlternateJoinOptionsExpanded        : False
UseWsFedPassiveAuth                     : False
WsFedPassiveMetadataUri                 :
AllowExternalAuthentication             : True
```

Lync Web App Conferencing Policies

Users who join a conference through Lync Web App will honor all conferencing policies associated with that conference, and their own conferencing policy if applicable. It is important to treat the Lync Web App Client as another Lync client; if conferencing functionality is enabled for regular Lync users, it is also available in the Lync Web App client.

Publishing Lync Web App Service to External Clients

External users access Lync Web App through the Lync Web Services. Lync Web Services are published for several critical Lync client services including Meeting Join, Dial-in Conferencing information page, Address Book Service, Collaboration Services, and Lync Web App. Lync Web Services, and as a result, Lync Web App, must be securely published through a reverse-proxy solution to provide access to external users. For information on deploying Lync Web Services through a reverse proxy, see Chapter 12, "Firewall and Security Requirements."

Operating System Requirements for Lync 2013 Web App Client

The following operating systems are supported for the Lync 2013 Web App client:

- ▶ Windows 8 (Intel-based)
- ▶ Windows 7 with SP1
- ▶ Windows Vista with SP2
- ▶ Windows XP with SP3
- ▶ Windows Server 2008 R2 with SP1
- ▶ Windows Server 2008 R1 with SP2
- ▶ Mac OS-X (Intel-based)

Windows 8, Windows 7, Windows 2008 R2, and Mac OS-X systems that meet the preceding requirements are able to perform full collaboration sessions including audio and video through the web browser. Windows XP, Windows Vista, and Windows Server 2008 R1 systems that meet the requirements do not have audio and video available; these clients can still perform application viewing and sharing through Lync Web App.

Browser Requirements for Lync 2013 Web App Client

The following web browsers are supported for the Lync 2013 Web App Client:

- ▶ 32-bit Internet Explorer 10
- ▶ 64-bit Internet Explorer 10
- ▶ 32-bit Internet Explorer 9
- ▶ 64-bit Internet Explorer 9
- ▶ 32-bit Internet Explorer 8
- ▶ 64-bit Internet Explorer 8
- ▶ 32-bit Firefox 12.x
- ▶ 64-bit Safari 5.x
- ▶ 32-bit Chrome 18.x

A Microsoft ActiveX browser plugin is required for participating in audio and video sessions through the web browser. Refer to Table 26.2 for a full matrix of browser and operating system support combinations.

TABLE 26.2   Supported Operating Systems and Web Browsers for Lync Web App

OS	32-Bit IE10	64-Bit IE10	32-Bit IE9	64-Bit IE9	32-Bit IE8	64-Bit IE8	32-Bit Firefox	64-Bit Safari	32-Bit Chrome
Windows 8	Yes	Yes	N/A	N/A	N/A	N/A	Yes	N/A	Yes
Windows 7	Yes	Yes	Yes	Yes	Yes	Yes	Yes	No	Yes
Windows Vista	Yes	No	Yes	No	Yes	No	Yes	No	Yes
Windows XP	N/A	N/A	N/A	N/A	Yes	No	Yes	No	Yes
Server 2008 R2	Yes	Yes	Yes	Yes	Yes	Yes	Yes	No	Yes
Server 2008 R1	Yes	No	Yes	No	Yes	No	Yes	No	Yes
Mac OS-X	N/A	N/A	N/A	N/A	N/A	N/A	Yes	Yes	Yes

Summary

Lync 2013 enables browser-based users to experience full-featured conferencing functionality. This service can be provided across both Windows and Macintosh operating systems, and through various popular web browsers. The architecture changes introduced to the server platform to support this functionality are built-in standard applications and codecs. Understanding the components and architecture for Lync Web App will enable an administrator to deploy and support Lync Web App functionality with confidence.

26

CHAPTER 27

Lync and VDI

In recent years, server virtualization has revolutionized IT, to the degree that many organizations have adopted a "virtualize first" approach for all server deployment projects. With the benefits of server virtualization being well understood and widely adopted, many organizations are turning their attention to VDI, or Virtual Desktop Infrastructure, as a technology that can provide similar benefits for the deployment and management of desktops. With VDI gaining so much attention, it is no surprise that Microsoft has focused efforts on improving the perfor- mance of the Lync client in the VDI environment. The end result of these efforts is the Lync VDI plugin, which is being offered for the first time with Lync Server 2013. This chapter provides some background on VDI technology, and then presents details on the Lync plugin that Microsoft has developed to optimize the performance of Lync for VDI.

> **NOTE**
>
> Although Microsoft does also support installation of the Lync 2010 client in a virtualized environment, there are several limitations and potential complications that come into play. For example, IM and Presence is supported in Lync 2010 as a virtualized workload, but audio is supported only with the use of a Lync-qualified desk phone using USB redirection, and video is not supported at all. With the introduction of the Lync VDI plugin for Lync 2013, Microsoft's goal is to overcome all these limitations and allow a full UC experience within the VDI environment, essentially the same as running Lync on a local desktop.

VDI Basics

Although there are certainly different approaches used and different technologies implemented by VDI vendors, the idea behind VDI is consistent. It is a technology that enables users to connect remotely to a desktop environment that is stored, executed, and managed centrally, with the presentation of the desktop being delivered to the user via a remote desktop protocol. VDI is also powered by virtualization technology in the datacenter, which enables the desktop to be separated from the underlying hardware. The end result is a flexible desktop environment that increases management control compared to the physical desktop environment, which can potentially decrease desktop costs. There are also potential security benefits with VDI, because it can be used to gain tighter control of corporate resources that are typically distributed on desktop systems throughout an organization, sometimes in a rather haphazard manner.

Following are the components that are commonly included in the majority of the VDI solutions on the market:

▶ **Hypervisor**—The software layer used to manage the hardware allocation of a server host, and handle the creation and management of virtual desktops on that host.

▶ **Connection Broker**—Software used to handle the provisioning of virtual desktops to users, typically based on user credentials.

▶ **Application Presentation**—A system that centrally manages the distribution of applications to the virtual desktop environment, typically allowing a centralized repository of standard applications and on-demand delivery.

▶ **Virtual Desktop**—The virtual machine that is accessed remotely by the user, providing an isolated desktop environment that can be either customizable or restricted.

▶ **Remote Desktop Presentation Protocol**—A technology used to present the desktop interface to the client device, which can either be installed as client software or integrated with the client hardware. The most common remote desktop presentation protocols are Remote Desktop Protocol (RDP), Independent Computing Architecture (ICA), and PC-over-IP (PCoIP).

▶ **Endpoint Device (or Access Device)**—The hardware device used to access the virtual desktop.

VDI Vendors

As the interest in VDI has increased, so has the number of vendors providing VDI solutions. Although many firms offer VDI products, two vendors stand out in the crowd as providing enterprise-ready end-to-end VDI solutions: Citrix, with the XenDesktop product, and VMware, which offers View. Microsoft has also invested heavily in VDI technology and includes a VDI offering with the Windows operating system as part of the Remote Desktop Services portfolio. However, for enterprise-level VDI, Microsoft has largely partnered with Citrix to offer a complete solution. There are numerous other players in the VDI market as well, some offering alternatives to the mainstream VDI approach, and others marketing a specific part of the solution, such as application packaging and deployment or performance monitoring for the VDI environment.

Challenges to VDI Adoption

Even with the benefits noted previously, VDI is still a relatively new technology, and with practically any new technology there are challenges to overcome before widespread adoption can be achieved. One of the primary challenges for VDI has been that, although many applications are very well suited for the VDI environment, some applications do not function nearly as well with VDI as they do in a native desktop environment. Most often this is due to performance characteristics of the application or hardware dependencies. With Microsoft Lync and other unified communications software, performance-related challenges come into play when real-time media workloads are virtualized. Because of this, with Lync 2013 Microsoft has focused on directly addressing these issues in an effort to allow near-native performance for the Lync client when running in the VDI environment. The end result of Microsoft's efforts is the Lync VDI plugin, which is explored in detail in the following sections.

Introducing the Lync VDI Plugin

The Lync VDI plugin is a brand-new component for Lync 2013, and was created to provide an audio and video experience for a Lync client in a VDI session that matches the experience of a locally installed client. To support this, the VDI plugin uses media redirection, in which the encoding and decoding of media are offloaded from the datacenter and handled directly by the thin client or access device, using the client's local resources. Other nonmedia features of Lync, such as IM, Presence, and desktop sharing, are still executed from within the virtual desktop.

Prior versions of the software, such as Lync 2010, had several inherent limitations that were presented when the Lync media workloads were virtualized. For example, note the peer-to-peer audio communication scenario depicted in Figure 27.1, in which one user is running Lync 2010 locally on a desktop, and the second user is running Lync 2010 within a VDI client. Unlike in a standard peer-to-peer audio session using two locally installed clients, the media stream for the VDI desktop user is sent and received from the datacenter, as opposed to the user's location. This results in higher bandwidth usage at the datacenter, limits audio and video conferencing capabilities, reduces the scalability of the server, and frequently results in a poor media experience for the user.

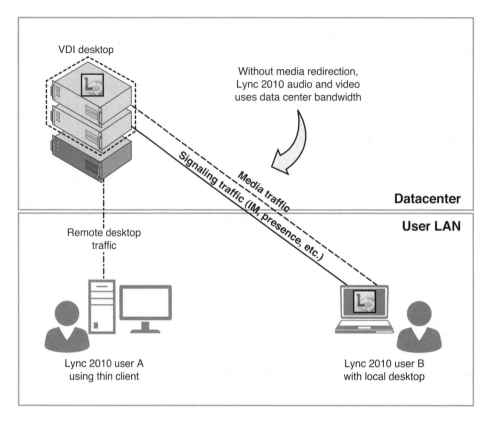

FIGURE 27.1 Peer-to-peer communication with VDI using Lync 2010.

In contrast, Figure 27.2 shows the same peer-to-peer communication, but this time using Lync 2013 along with the VDI plugin. With this set of components, audio and video originate and terminate at the plugin running on the thin client, while the signaling traffic continues to use the VDI desktop in the datacenter. This results in minimal bandwidth consumption between the end device and the datacenter, enables all conferencing capabilities, and provides a significantly better media experience for the user. An additional benefit that results from this media redirection is that Lync server scalability improves, as the CPU-intensive media processing is offloaded to the client for each VDI user.

Lync VDI Plugin Device Support

For use with the VDI plugin, Microsoft supports any audio and video devices that are qualified for Lync, such as headsets and cameras. The following features are supported when these devices are used in combination with the VDI plugin:

▶ Call controls from a device

▶ Presence integration on a device

▶ Multiple HID (human interface device) support

▶ Location and emergency services support

▶ Support for all Lync modalities, including IM, audio, video, desktop and application sharing, file transfer, and so on

▶ Audio and video support for peer-to-peer and conference calls

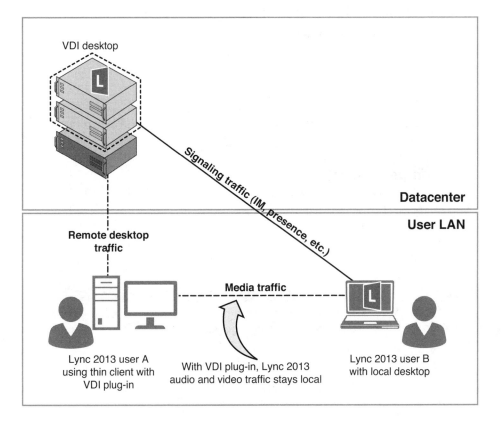

FIGURE 27.2   Peer-to-peer communication with VDI using Lync 2013 and the VDI plugin.

NOTE

Use of a Lync Phone Edition device is not supported in combination with the VDI plugin.

Lync VDI Plugin Limitations

Although the majority of the functionality included in a standard Lync client deployment is also available in a VDI session, there are some features that are not supported. Following are the known limitations for using Lync in a VDI environment:

▶ Integrated audio and video device tuning pages are not available (device selection and tuning can be adjusted using the access device).

▶ Multiview video is not supported.

▶ Recording of conversations is not supported.

▶ Joining meetings anonymously (specifically, meetings hosted by an organization that is not federated) is not supported.

▶ Customized ringtones and music on-hold features are not supported.

▶ The Call Delegation and Response Group Agent Anonymization features are not supported.

▶ Lync Phone Edition devices are not supported in combination with the VDI plugin.

▶ Call continuity in the event of a network outage is not supported.

▶ The Lync VDI plugin is not supported for use with an Office 365/Lync Online environment.

Lync VDI Plugin Deployment

The Lync VDI plugin is a standalone application that is available in 32-bit and 64-bit versions, and can be freely downloaded from the Microsoft download site. The plugin must then be installed on the endpoint device that will be used to access the VDI desktop, which is typically a repurposed desktop or a thin client device. To use the plugin, there are systems prerequisites that must first be met, as detailed in the following section.

> **TIP**
>
> The full Lync client does not need to be installed on the endpoint device used to access the VDI desktop; only the Lync plugin software is required.

System Requirements

Before the VDI plugin is used, there are prerequisites that must be met for both the virtual machine and the access device used for the VDI session:

▶ The VDI desktop must be running one of the following operating systems: Windows 7, Windows 8, or Windows Server 2008 R2 with the latest service pack.

▶ The access device must be running one of the following operating systems: Windows Embedded Standard 7 with SP1, Windows 7 with SP1, or Windows 8.

▶ Minimum hardware specs for installing the VDI plugin on an access device include a 1.5GHz processor, 2GB RAM, and either 700MB hard drive space (for the 32-bit plugin) or 900MB hard drive space (for the 64-bit plugin).

▶ If Remote Desktop Services will be used to host the virtual desktops, the bitness of the Lync VDI plugin must match the bitness of the OS on the access device, either 32-bit or 64-bit accordingly. However, the bitness of the OS on the access device does not need to match the bitness of the OS on the virtual machine. If a different virtualization solution is used to host the VDI desktops, different bitness requirements might apply and will depend on the virtualization solution used.

▶ If Remote Desktop Services will be used to host the virtual desktops, and the access device is running Windows 7 with SP1 or Windows Server 2008 R2, the Windows 8 version of the Remote Desktop Services client should be installed. Before the Windows 8 version of the Remote Desktop Services client is installed, the Windows update described in Microsoft Knowledge Base article #2574819 must first be installed as a prerequisite. After the prerequisite update is installed, the following link can be used to download the Remote Desktop Protocol update for Windows 7 SP1 and Windows Server 2008 R2 SP1: http://support.microsoft.com/kb/2592687.

Remote Desktop Connection Settings

If Remote Desktop Services will be used to host the virtual desktops, the remote desktop client settings must be configured so that audio plays on the local system, and remote recording must be disabled. The following procedure is used to configure the Remote Desktop Connections settings on the local system in preparation for the deploying the Lync VDI plugin:

1. Log on to the local system, and open the Remote Desktop Services client by selecting Start, All Programs, Accessories, Remote Desktop Connection.

2. Click on Options to expand the dialog box, and then select the Local Resources tab.

3. In the Remote Audio section, click Settings to display the remote audio settings, as shown in Figure 27.3.

FIGURE 27.3   Remote audio settings used with the Lync VDI plugin.

4. Under Remote Audio Playback, select Play on This Computer.

5. Under Remote Audio Recording, select Do Not Record, and then click OK.

6. Select the Experience tab.

7. In the Performance section, clear the option for Persistent Bitmap Caching.

8. Select the General tab and then click Save As, and at the Save As dialog box choose a location where the RDP file will be saved.

Lync Client Policy Configuration for VDI

Lync client policies are used to determine the features of Lync Server that are made available to users. Client policies can be configured at the global, site, and user level; a policy at the user level has the highest priority, and a policy configured at the site level overrides the policy at the global level for any users in that site. For Lync 2013, a client policy is automatically created at the global level, and is simply named Global.

TIP

It is easy to confuse client policy with client version policy based on the similar names, but these two policies have very different purposes in Lync. Client version policy is used to control the specific applications that can be used to log on to Lync Server. Client policy, on the other hand, is used to control the specific Lync features that will be available to users.

For Lync Server 2013, a new client policy setting was created to allow Lync administrators to be selective regarding which users are enabled for the media redirection feature. By default, media redirection is disabled within the default client policy at the global level. This means that before users can leverage the Lync VDI plugin, either media redirection must be enabled in the global client policy, or a new client policy must be created with the setting enabled, and then applied at either the site or the user level. To create a new Lync client policy, or to adjust an existing one, the Lync Server Management Shell is used.

The following example outlines the procedure for using the Lync Server Management Shell to create a new client policy named VDI_Policy with media redirection enabled, and then apply the policy to all users in the IT department:

1. Log on to a system where the Lync administrative tools are installed using an account that is a member of the CsAdministrator or CsServerAdministrator groups in AD, and that has administrative rights on the local system.

2. Open the Lync Server Management Shell, and execute the following command to create a new client policy named VDI_policy with media redirection enabled:

   ```
   New-CsClientPolicy -Identity VDI_Policy -EnableMediaRedirection $true
   ```

3. If the command is successful, the client policy is created and the properties of the policy are displayed, as shown in Figure 27.4.

4. Execute the following command to apply the new client policy to each user in the IT department:

   ```
   Get-CsUser -LDAPFilter "Department=IT" | Grant-CsClientPolicy
   ➡-PolicyName VDI_Policy
   ```

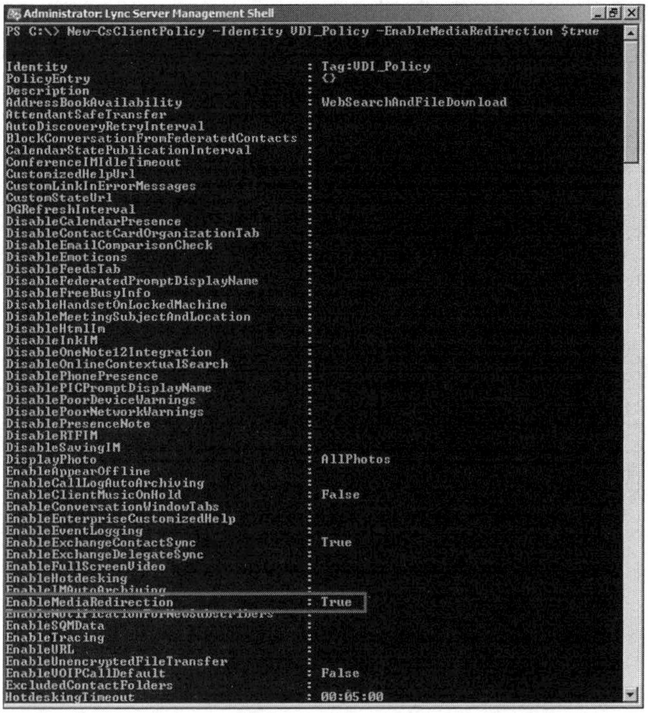

FIGURE 27.4   Creating a new client policy with media redirection enabled.

In the first portion of the PowerShell command executed previously in step 4, the Get-CsUser cmdlet is used with an LDAP filter to return a collection of users whose Department attribute in Active Directory is configured as IT. The results are then pipelined to the second portion of the command, where the Grant-CsClientPolicy cmdlet is used to apply the client policy to the IT users. There are many combinations of these cmdlets that can be used to selectively apply client policies to users across the organization, granting the ability to use media redirection along with a host of other features, many of which are displayed in Figure 27.4. After the client policy has been applied, the Get-CsUser cmdlet can be used to verify that the client policy has been correctly applied to the user, as shown in Figure 27.5.

TIP

The only policy settings that are displayed when the Get-CsUser cmdlet is used are those that are applied at the user level. However, for each Lync policy, a user-, site-, or global-level policy setting is applied for each user. If some policy values display as null with the Get-CsUser cmdlet (such as shown in Figure 27.5), this means that either a site-level policy is applied (if it exists) or a global policy is applied. You can verify this by first retrieving the user's site identity and then determining whether a particular policy is applied at the site level. If not, the global policy settings are applied to the user for that particular policy.

27

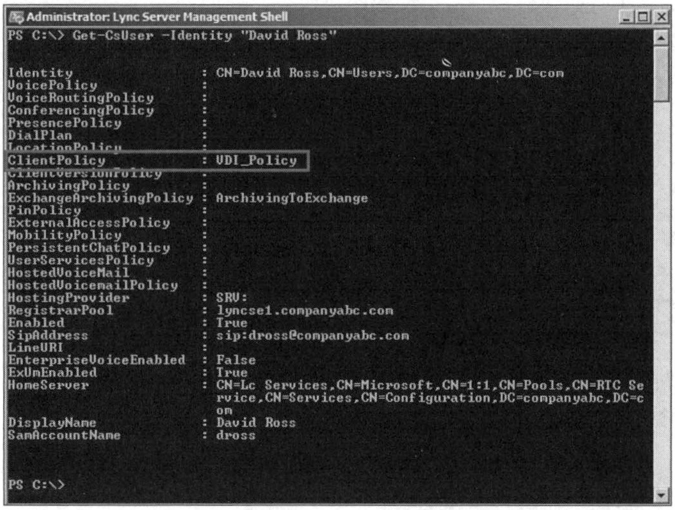

FIGURE 27.5   Verifying the client policy setting for a user in the Management Shell.

Lync VDI Plugin Installation

The Lync VDI plugin can be downloaded from the Microsoft download site, and is available in 32-bit and 64-bit versions. Use the following procedure to install the VDI plugin on a system that will be used to access VDI desktop sessions with Lync 2013:

1. Log on to the system where the plugin will be installed using an account with local administrator rights.

2. From the Microsoft download site, download the version of the VDI plugin that matches the local hardware, either 32-bit or 64-bit, and save the file to a local subdirectory on the system.

3. Double-click on the downloaded file, named Lyncvdi.exe.

4. At the Read the Microsoft Software License Terms screen, read the software license terms, then click the I Accept the Terms of This Agreement option if you agree to the terms, and click Continue.

5. At the Choose the Installation You Want screen, either click Install Now to install the software using the default settings, or click Customize to choose specific installation options.

6. If you chose to customize the installation in the preceding step, three tabs offering several options for customization are displayed, as shown in Figure 27.6. If there are specific features that will not be installed, this can be configured on the Installation Options tab; click the drop-down menu next to the feature and select Not Available. If a customized installation path for the plugin files is needed, this can be configured on the File Location tab; enter the new path or browse to the desired location. If the

user information needs to be adjusted from the default values, this can be configured on the User Information tab. When finished, click Install Now.

7. After the software is installed, click Close.

8. If prompted, click Yes to reboot the system and complete the installation.

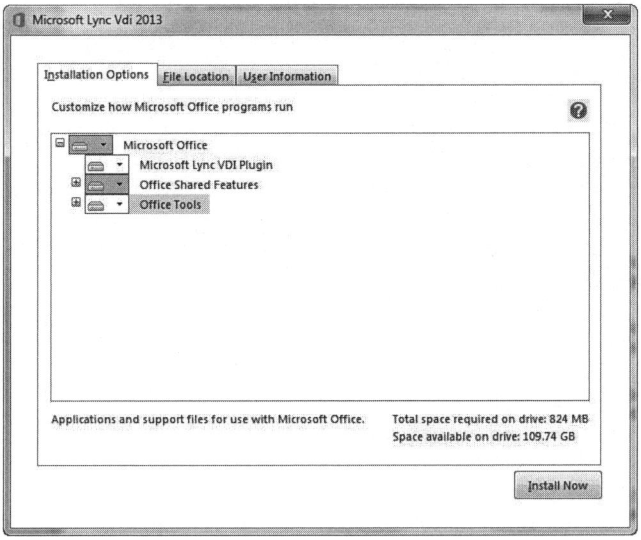

FIGURE 27.6   Customization options for the Lync VDI plugin.

TIP

After the plugin is installed, two files named `LyncVdiPlugin.dll` and `UcVdi.dll` should be present in the `C:\Program Files (x86)\Microsoft Office\Office15` directory (for 32-bit installations) or the `C:\Program Files\Microsoft Office\Office15` directory (for 64-bit installations).

User Experience with the Lync VDI Plugin

As noted previously, the primary goal for developing the VDI plugin is for Lync 2013 users to have the same experience, regardless of whether Lync is running on a physical desktop or as part of a VDI session. As such, there is practically no noticeable difference in the user experience between a local Lync installation and a VDI installation, with the exception of the initial login process. When the user signs in to the Lync client from a VDI desktop, the client detects the presence of the plugin. At that point, the user is prompted to reenter credentials, as shown in Figure 27.7. This additional credential prompt is necessary to confirm the pairing of the plugin with the client, since the plugin is installed only on the local hardware. After the Lync client and the plugin have been paired, the user is not prompted again during the session, and the Lync client looks and performs exactly the same as it would on a local desktop. Additionally, the user can select the Save My Password check box displayed in Figure 27.7 to prevent being prompted to reenter credentials when signing in to Lync from the VDI desktop in the future.

FIGURE 27.7   User prompted for credentials to confirm pairing of the Lync client with the VDI plugin.

There are also visual cues that appear within the VDI session that indicate the status of the Lync plugin. While the Lync client is in the process of pairing with the plugin, the status bar at the bottom of the Lync client displays two icons. As shown in Figure 27.8, the icon on the left indicates that no audio devices are yet available, and the icon on the right blinks to indicate that the VDI pairing is in progress.

FIGURE 27.8   Lync client status bar indicating that pairing with the VDI plugin is in progress.

After the pairing process is complete, the left icon indicates which audio device will be used for Lync calls, and the right icon indicates that pairing with the VDI plugin is complete, as shown in Figure 27.9. The user can now answer and place calls using the audio device shown, and presence will be displayed on all compatible devices.

FIGURE 27.9   Lync client status bar indicating that pairing with the VDI plugin is successful.

Protocol Partner Solutions for the Lync VDI Plugin

Out of the package, the downloadable Lync VDI plugin software supports only a native Windows environment, using Remote Desktop Protocol. However, Microsoft also has a goal of achieving platform independence with this new technology. To allow for this, the plugin was built to leverage Dynamic Virtual Channels (DVCs), which is a standard set of APIs that are platform independent. Other Remote Desktop Protocol vendors can then take advantage of DVCs to deliver their own solutions, which combine the Lync VDI plugin with their own software. VDI vendors that are developing solutions with Microsoft based on the Lync VDI plugin are referred to as protocol partners.

> **NOTE**
>
> The Dynamic Virtual Channel APIs have already been implemented in Microsoft Remote Desktop Protocol version 8, which is the reason that RDP is natively supported with the Lync VDI plugin.

For the initial release of the VDI plugin, Microsoft has been working with two of the leading VDI vendors to develop third-party solutions based on the VDI plugin: Citrix and VMware. The following sections provide a description of the Lync VDI solutions that are planned for each of these partners. It should be noted that the information in this section is based on the prerelease versions of this technology, and is therefore subject to change before the partner solutions are officially released.

Citrix Receiver with Integrated Lync VDI Plugin

Citrix has been a steady player in the virtualization business for many years, starting with the XenApp product line, which has long been used to extend the application presentation functionality of Microsoft's Terminal Services and Remote Desktop Services components. In more recent years, Citrix has developed the XenDesktop product line into one of the most popular VDI products on the market. XenApp and XenDesktop are often used together as complimentary products to create a comprehensive VDI solution, with Citrix Receiver used as the client component to provide access to the VDI desktop. Citrix has developed versions of Citrix Receiver for Windows, Mac, Linux, and more, making it a truly multiplatform VDI solution.

To optimize Lync 2010 with XenApp and XenDesktop solutions, Citrix released the Citrix HDX Optimization Pack for Lync 2010. The concept behind the Citrix HDX Optimization Pack for Lync 2010 was very similar to that of the VDI plugin developed by Microsoft for Lync 2013, in which the media processing bypasses the Citrix server environment and is instead handled by the client device. It is no surprise, then, that Microsoft and Citrix

27

are working together to provide the same optimized architecture for running Lync 2013 in a XenDesktop VDI environment. The end result of this effort will be an update to the Citrix Receiver that includes the Lync VDI plugin functionality. The same presentation protocol used with most all XenApp and XenDesktop solutions, Independent Computing Architecture, will be used to present the desktop interface to the user.

After the Lync VDI plugin functionality is included in Citrix Receiver, XenDesktop users will be able to use USB-connected audio and video devices that are certified for Lync within a VDI session, along with other standard features of Citrix Receiver. For the initial release of the Lync-optimized version of Citrix Receiver, support is planned for Windows, Mac, and Linux. Use of the VDI plugin with Citrix Receiver and ICA therefore provides an advantage over Microsoft Remote Desktop Services and RDP, because this allows non-Windows endpoints to be used to connect to XenDesktop for VDI, and then use Lync with excellent performance.

The end goal is to provide a seamless Lync experience for two common remote desktop scenarios: with Lync 2013 installed as an application within a XenDesktop VDI instance, or with Lync being published as an application using XenApp. In either scenario, the Lync user experience will be optimized if the appropriate version of Receiver with integrated VDI plugin technology is used for the connection.

VMware View with Lync VDI Plugin

VMware is widely considered to be the market leader in virtualization technology, primarily due to the popularity of the vSphere product line for server virtualization. VMware has also been able to capitalize on their market share by developing VMware View as one of the more popular enterprise-level VDI products offered. View leverages vSphere to host virtual desktops for a VDI deployment, with the VMware View agent installed as part of the virtual desktop build to allow connections from client systems. The VMware View client is then installed on user desktops or thin client systems to connect to the View VDI desktops.

The presentation protocol used by VMware View is PC-over-IP, more commonly referred to as PCoIP. PCoIP compresses, encrypts, and encodes the user desktop experience at a datacenter and transmits the associated pixels to a VMware View client, with PCoIP integrated.

VMware View 5.0 went through validation testing for Lync 2010, and is therefore already a Microsoft-supported client virtualization product for use with Lync 2010. However, VMware is developing a PCoIP version that will leverage the Lync VDI plugin for use with Lync 2013. This updated PCoIP software will be required to leverage the media redirection capabilities of Lync 2013, resulting in an optimized Lync client experience for users of VMware View. Although the details behind the new PCoIP software along with any related systems requirements are not yet available, no doubt these updated components will result in significant improvements for users who run Lync from a View desktop.

Thin Client Hardware Optimized for Lync 2013

Since a large percentage of VDI implementations make use of thin client hardware as an endpoint device, Microsoft has worked with some of the leading thin client manufacturers to test and validate the functionality of the Lync VDI plugin on thin client devices. Although the opportunity to test and validate endpoint devices for Lync 2013 optimization is available to any thin client OEM partner, for the initial release of the plugin, Microsoft has chosen to partner with two market leaders in this area: Dell Wyse and HP.

Both Wyse and HP have been leading manufacturers of thin client devices for several years, including units that are specifically designed to work with Microsoft and Citrix VDI environments. Wyse was recently acquired by Dell, giving Dell a significant footprint in the desktop virtualization space, which includes not only the thin client hardware portfolio, but also enterprise device management and cloud computing software.

There is a rich diversity among the thin client hardware products in the Dell Wyse and HP portfolios. For example, there are low-cost "zero client" models with no operating system, flexible thin clients that provide expansion options, and mobile thin clients that resemble laptop systems, with built-in LED screens and keyboards.

Partnering with Dell Wyse and HP results in the Lync VDI plugin being used to enable media redirection and other optimizations for VDI sessions that use Dell Wyse and HP thin clients. With certain models, the Lync VDI plugin is being combined with additional VDI optimization technologies, such as Microsoft RemoteFX, to further enhance the UC experience when these devices are used. With any of the Dell Wyse or HP thin clients that are validated for Lync 2013, any Lync-certified USB audio and video devices can be connected to the device and accessed from the VDI session, with the media being redirected locally.

> **NOTE**
>
> For organizations that routinely deploy thin clients, it is a standard practice to develop an image that administrators can use to deploy the devices quickly with all required software and configuration settings, because this reduces the amount of management required and helps ensure consistency for the builds. If Lync 2013 will be among the standard applications accessed using thin clients, it is important for administrators to include the Lync VDI plugin as part of the packaged image.

For the initial testing and validation of the Lync VDI plugin with Dell Wyse hardware, the following thin client models were validated:

- **Z90D7**—Thin client device with dual-core AMD processor running Windows Embedded Standard 7.

- **R90LE7**—Thin client device with AMD Sempron processor running Windows Embedded Standard 7.

- **X90m7**—Mobile thin client device with dual-core AMD processor and built-in LED backlit display, running Windows Embedded Standard 7 (see Figure 27.10).

27

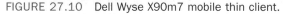

FIGURE 27.10   Dell Wyse X90m7 mobile thin client.

For the initial testing and validation of the Lync VDI plugin with HP hardware, the following thin client models were validated:

▶ **t610**—Thin client device offering flexible configuration options, with dual-core AMD processor running HP ThinPro, Windows 7e Embedded, or Windows Embedded Standard 2009 (see Figure 27.11).

▶ **t5740e**—Thin client device with Intel Atom processor running Windows Embedded Standard 7.

FIGURE 27.11   HP t610 thin client.

Additional Dell Wyse and HP thin client models are being tested and validated with the goal of providing customers with additional VDI endpoint options that are optimized for use with Lync 2013.

Summary

As VDI continues to gain popularity in the enterprise, the importance of ensuring a quality UC experience for VDI users will also increase. Although many efforts have already been made by different vendors to improve the media experience for VDI, developing the Lync VDI plugin was an important step in the right direction for Microsoft. Not only does the VDI plugin enable Lync to be optimized for Microsoft native remote desktop technologies, but it was developed as an extensible solution, such that other VDI vendors can leverage the plugin to develop their own Lync optimized VDI solutions. As a result, the Lync 2013 user experience can be virtually the same whether a local desktop or a remote VDI desktop is used, with various Remote Desktop Protocols and endpoint devices to choose from.

27

PART X

Planning for Deployment

IN THIS PART

CHAPTER 28

Planning for Lync Online and Hybrid Deployments

Whether Lync Online was purchased as a separate service or as part of the Office 365 suite, the planning process for a Lync Online deployment is very different from that of an on-premise deployment, and includes some unique requirements. Microsoft has recently released an update to the Office 365 online suite which is based on the 2013 versions of the products, including Lync Online. With this new version of Lync Online/Office 365, hybrid deployments that blend the Lync cloud offering with an on-premise deployment have become an option for the first time. A hybrid deployment will have its own unique requirements, and will involve additional upfront planning to ensure a seamless unified communications experience for Lync users. This chapter provides a preview of the steps involved in planning for both cloud-only and hybrid installations.

Comparing Topologies

One of the biggest planning considerations with regard to Lync Online is whether a cloud-based Lync deployment is the right choice, and if so, which cloud deployment option best meets the needs of the business. Now that the updated Lync Online/Office 365 platform is available, there are three Lync topology options to choose from: cloud-only topology, on-premise topology, and hybrid topology. The following sections present some comparisons and considerations that can be used to help an organization determine which Lync topology best meets the requirements of the business.

Lync Online Versus Lync On-Premise

Lync Online offers many, but not all, of the features that are included with an on-premise deployment. This means that although a cloud-based UC platform will provide a cost savings for many organizations, an on-premise deployment might still be a more appropriate solution for some organizations, depending on which UC features are critical to deploy. As part of the overall Lync planning process, it is therefore important to consider the feature differences between the two platforms. The following list summarizes the features that are available with an on-premise Lync deployment but are not included in any of the Lync Online service plans:

▶ Lync-to-Lync high-definition video

▶ Lync Skill Search in SharePoint

▶ Persistent Chat

▶ Privacy mode

▶ Federation with AOL and XMPP networks

▶ Interoperability with on-premise video conferencing systems

▶ Outgoing direct inward dialing (DID) manipulation

▶ E-911 (standard 911 service provided with purchase of hosted voice from third-party Microsoft partner)

▶ Dial plans and policies

▶ Resilient branch office appliance

▶ Call Admission Control (CAC)

▶ Support for analog devices (such as fax)

▶ Network QoS (using DSCP)

▶ Response groups

▶ Call park

▶ Private line

▶ Interoperability with third-party PBX or trunks

▶ Malicious call trace

▶ Unassigned number

▶ Media path optimization

▶ CDR and billing reporting

▶ Integration with call-center solutions

▶ Lync 2010 Attendant client

▶ CDR and QoE reporting

If none of these features is considered a requirement, a cloud-only Lync Online deployment is a valid option. However, many of the features that are not included with a cloud-only topology, particularly the voice features, are available with a hybrid topology. With that in mind, if voice features are important, a hybrid topology should be considered, and the following sections provide some background to help guide this decision.

From a cost perspective, it is important to note that each Lync Online subscription includes the Client Access Licenses (CALs) that are required to use the features included with that subscription. Therefore, any budgeting exercise that compares the cost of a cloud topology with that of an on-premise topology should take into account the cost of both licensing and hardware that would be required for an on-premise deployment. The planning topics outlined in this chapter should also be compared with the information in Chapters 29 through 32 to determine the true cost of an on-premise deployment versus that of a Lync Online deployment. This comparison will allow an organization take into account not only the feature sets included with each topology option, but also the hardware, software, licensing requirements, and effort involved in building and maintaining each type of deployment.

Lync Hybrid Deployment Considerations

With the next update to Lync Online and Office 365, Microsoft will for the first time support a Lync hybrid topology option. A Lync hybrid deployment involves an on-premise deployment of Lync Server, which is federated with a Lync Online organization, enabling the same SIP domain to be applied to both on-premise and online users. The end result is that Lync users within an organization can be moved between the on-premise deployment and the cloud, and can use the Lync on-premise infrastructure, including PSTN connectivity, regardless of the location of their account.

> **NOTE**
>
> With the first release of Office 365 and Lync Online, it was possible for an organization to deploy Lync Server 2010 for some users on-premise, and simultaneously provision the Lync Online cloud-based service for other users, with Lync federation configured between the two deployments. However, this configuration required separate SIP domains to be used for the on-premise Lync organization versus the cloud-based Lync organization. Due to this restriction, very few organizations deployed Lync Online in tandem with Lync on-premise with the first version of the cloud service. With the new version of Office 365/ Lync Online, this is likely to change, as the Lync hybrid deployment will allow more organizations to test-drive the cloud-based Lync services before making a full commitment to Lync Online.

The value proposition for Lync hybrid depends on the overall UC goals for an organization. For example, some organizations have a goal of moving all enterprise services to the cloud, but are forced to do so in a gradual fashion due to business or technical constraints. The Lync hybrid deployment would allow such an organization to perform a phased transition of UC services to the cloud, and continue to provide a full UC feature set and a seamless experience for users throughout the transition period. For other organizations, moving to a cloud UC service has good potential, but a period of time is needed to test-drive the Lync Online offering and compare it to the Lync on-premise deployment. The Lync hybrid deployment provides the opportunity to test out Lync Online functionality without making a full commitment. Finally, still other organizations might desire to provide different levels of UC service for various types of users, and this might include having certain user profiles hosted in the cloud, with other user profiles hosted on-premise. For example, this enables an organization to continue to leverage existing investments in an on-premise PBX and other dedicated telephony systems for the users who require these services, yet provide a more basic set of functionality for cloud users who do not require it. The Lync hybrid deployment easily allows for such a configuration and makes it easy to move user accounts back and forth as needed.

Comparing Voice Options Between Topologies

For many organizations, enterprise voice capabilities have the largest impact on the choice of which platform to use. Microsoft of course recognizes this, and as a result has moved quickly to ensure that there are several voice options to choose from within the available Lync topologies. For organizations that rely heavily on voice, it is important to understand the differences between the voice features offered with the various platforms. With that in mind, Table 28.1 presents a list of important Lync voice features, and shows which of these features are offered across the three Lync topologies. After the specific voice requirements of an organization are well understood, these requirements can be compared with the information in Table 28.1 to determine which platform presents the right voice feature set.

TABLE 28.1   Lync Voice Options Per Topology

Lync Voice Features	On-Premise Enterprise Voice	Lync Online Hosted Voice (Lync-to-Phone)	Lync Hybrid Voice
Call Hold/Retrieve	X	X	X
Call Transfer	X	X	X
Call Forwarding	X	X	X
Voice Mail (Exchange UM)	X	X	X
USB peripherals	X	X	X
Outside voice—mobile	X	X	X
Delegation, Team Call	X	X	X
Integration with on-premise PBX	X		X
Remote Call Control (RCC)	X		
Private line	X		X
Voice resiliency	X		X
Enhanced 911	X		X
Unified Communications (UC) devices	X	X	X

Lync Voice Features	On-Premise Enterprise Voice	Lync Online Hosted Voice (Lync-to-Phone)	Lync Hybrid Voice
Response Group Service (RGS)/Call Park Service (CPS)	X		X
Analog devices, Common Area Phones	X		X
Integration with on-premise call-center solutions	X		
Media bypass	X	N/A	X

Lync Online and Office 365 Subscription Plans

An important part of the initial planning for Lync Online is determining which of the subscription plans represents the best fit for an organization. Lync Online can be purchased as a standalone service, or it can be included as part of a more comprehensive Office 365 subscription. The details on each of these options are provided in the following sections.

Lync Online Subscription Plans

Lync Online offers three separate plans and pricing tiers, with each successive plan offering additional Lync services. The lowest tier is Plan 1, which is the least expensive and offers the following basic set of Lync features:

▶ User authentication

▶ IM and Presence

▶ Online meeting attendance

▶ PC-to-PC audio and video calling

▶ Federation with other organizations that use Lync

The next tier is Plan 2, which offers all the features included with Plan 1, and adds the following:

▶ Initiation of online meetings with up to 250 attendees, both ad hoc and scheduled

▶ Initiation of multiparty audio/video sessions

▶ File transfer using the Lync client

▶ Content sharing within online presentations (screen sharing, whiteboard, PowerPoint upload)

▶ Interoperability with certified partners for dial-in audio conferencing

▶ Client-side API support

28

The third tier is Plan 3, which offers all the features of the first two plans and adds the following:

► PSTN dialing through interoperability with partners that provide calling services

► Interoperability with Exchange Online voice mail (also requires an Exchange Online plan that includes voice mail)

► User call controls (call transfer, simultaneous ring, and so on)

> **NOTE**
>
> Each Lync Online subscription plan includes the rights to Lync Server Client Access Licenses with the plan. Plan 1 includes a Lync Standard CAL for each user, Plan 2 includes the Enterprise CAL, and Plan 3 includes the Enterprise and Plus CAL.

Office 365 Subscription Plans

It is also possible to purchase Lync Online by way of a more comprehensive Office 365 Suite subscription plan. Several of the Office 365 "E" plans include Lync Online Plan 2, and the highest-level subscription plan (E4) also includes Lync Online Plan 3. With the licensing included in Plan E4, an organization also has the option of applying Lync Plus CALs to users of an on-premise Lync deployment, while granting those same users access to the other Office 365 applications in the cloud. For some organizations, this may be a cost-effective way to provide users with full Enterprise Voice features via an on-premise Lync deployment, but use the cloud for the other Office 365 applications. Table 28.2 shows the components that are included in the Office 365 "E" subscription plans at the time of writing.

TABLE 28.2   Office 365 Subscription Plans

Office 365 Plan E1	Office 365 Plan E2	Office 365 Plan E3	Office 365 Plan E4
Exchange Online (Plan 1)	Exchange Online (Plan 1)	Exchange Online (Plan 2)	Exchange Online (Plan 2)
SharePoint Online (Plan 1)	SharePoint Online (Plan 1)	SharePoint Online (Plan 2)	SharePoint Online (Plan 2)
Lync Online (Plan 2)	Lync Online (Plan 2)	Lync Online (Plan 2)	Lync Online (Plan 2)
	Office Web Apps	Office Web Apps	Office Web Apps
		Office Professional Plus	Office Professional Plus
			Lync Online (Plan 3)

Deciding on a Subscription Plan

In terms of whether to pursue a standalone Lync Online subscription or a full Office 365 subscription, this is of course dependent on whether cloud services are desired for the other Office applications outside of Lync. Also, as shown in Table 28.2, Lync Online Plan 1 is available only as a standalone subscription, because it is not included in any of the Office 365 subscription plans. This means that for organizations that are looking for only the most basic UC functionality, and are not pursuing cloud services for Exchange, SharePoint, or Office, Lync Online Plan 1 is likely the right option. Following are some additional key points that can be taken into account in comparing the three Lync Online subscription plans:

▶ For organizations seeking to supplement an existing VOIP system with additional functionality such as IM and Presence, Lync Online Plan 1 would be a good option and would be the lowest cost. Currently, Plan 1 is priced at $2 per user per month.

▶ If online meetings are a requirement but PSTN connectivity is not, Lync Online Plan 2 would be a good fit. Interoperability with third-party dial-in conferencing partners is also included in Plan 2, and can be used to extend conferencing to PSTN users. Currently, Plan 2 is priced at $5.50 per user per month standalone, or it can be purchased as part of Office 365 Plans E1 to E4.

▶ If all the features offered with Lync Online need to be leveraged, including the capability to use a third-party partner for PSTN services, then Lync Online Plan 3 is needed. Currently, Plan 3 is priced at $9.50 per user per month standalone, or it can be purchased as part of Office 365 Plan E4.

> **NOTE**
>
> The dial-in conferencing and hosted voice options included in Lync Online subscription Plans 2 and 3 require these services to be purchased separately from an approved Microsoft partner. These additional costs should therefore be taken into account when cost comparisons are made.

Planning for Lync Online

After it has been determined that a cloud UC deployment meets the needs of the business, the planning process for Lync Online can begin. At the start of the planning phase, it is important to identify the business goals that the organization seeks to achieve as a result of the deployment. For example, the desired Lync Online user experience should be defined, and the organization's plan for administering the online tenant should also be well understood. Identifying these business goals will help the organization make the first important decision regarding the Lync Online service: determining which Lync Online identity scenario will allow the organization to achieve these goals.

Lync Online Identity Scenarios

Lync Online and Office 365 offer several identity scenarios that should be evaluated to determine which of these meet the specific business goals of the organization. The following sections describe the characteristics, advantages, and disadvantages of each of these identity scenarios.

Cloud Identity

The cloud identity scenario is ideal for smaller organizations, including those that do not maintain an on-premise Active Directory. Each Lync Online user's identity is maintained only in the cloud, resulting in a simple deployment and minimal management. However, if password-protected systems are maintained on-premise, users will need to manage several sets of credentials. An additional consideration is that cloud identity does not allow for two-factor authentication options. For these reasons, the cloud identity scenario is not likely to be used by organizations that use Active Directory.

Cloud Identity + Directory Synchronization

Cloud identity + directory synchronization is similar to the cloud identity scenario already described, but is a more attractive option for organizations that maintain Active Directory on-premise. The directory synchronization features enable local AD user and group accounts to be synchronized to Lync Online/Office 365, allowing coexistence. However, the passwords are not synchronized between the local and cloud user accounts; therefore, users are still required to maintain two sets of credentials with this scenario, and no two-factor authentication options are available. Some smaller organizations that use AD might find that cloud identity + directory synchronization is a good fit due to the simplicity of the deployment and limited management, because directory synchronization does not require much in the way of administration after it has been deployed. However, medium-to-large organizations will not likely choose this scenario due to the multiple sets of credentials required.

Federated Identity

Federated identity involves the configuration of single sign-on (SSO) using Active Directory Federated Services (AD FS), as well as directory synchronization. The combination of these two technologies creates the most seamless experience for Lync Online users, because only a single set of credentials is required. However, federated identity is clearly the most complex option in terms of both implementation and ongoing management. Federated identity is also the only identity scenario that allows the use of two-factor authentication. Small organizations will likely find federated identity to be too complex, whereas for medium-to-large organizations this will be the most attractive option.

Planning Lync Online Administration

An important aspect of planning for Lync Online is determining how the cloud deployment will be administered. Much like an on-premise Lync deployment, Lync Online and Office 365 follow a role-based access control (RBAC) model, in which permissions and capabilities are defined by management roles. When an organization signs up for a Lync Online or Office 365 subscription, the individual who handles the sign-up process automatically becomes a global administrator, or top-level administrator for the cloud deployment. Additional administrators can then be added as needed to handle various aspects of the online tenant. There are a total of five administrator roles within Office 365, as shown in Table 28.3. Each user account that is added to the cloud organization is automatically assigned the user role, which has no administrative permissions. Individual user accounts can then be assigned to one of the administrative roles to delegate permissions to the online tenant.

TABLE 28.3   Lync Online/Office 365 Administrator Roles

Office 365 Admin Role	Description
global administrator	Includes full permissions to the online organization. This role is assigned to the initial user account created for the subscription, and is used to assign admin permissions to other users.
billing administrator	Includes full permissions for billing tasks only, and read-only permissions for other objects. A user assigned to this role receives notifications for billing events.
password administrator	Includes read-only access to all objects, and has password reset privileges. However, a user assigned to this role cannot reset the password of a global administrator, billing administrator, or user management administrator.
service administrator	Includes read-only access to all objects, but can manage individual services.
user management administrator	Includes read-only access to all objects, and administrator permissions for user accounts. However, a user assigned to this role cannot make changes to the account of a global administrator or billing administrator.

NOTE

For each administrator account added to Lync Online/Office 365, an alternative email address can be assigned to the account, which is used to reset the account password in the event that the password is lost or forgotten.

Planning the SIP Namespace

A key decision in the Lync Online planning process is the SIP namespace that will be used for Lync Online users. The deciding factor in this decision, however, is typically very simple: To provide a seamless UC experience for users, the SIP namespace used for Lync Online must match the primary SMTP namespace used with the organization's messaging system. Since most organizations that sign up for Lync Online already have an established primary SMTP namespace for use with their existing messaging system, this same namespace is also specified as the Lync Online SIP domain. Multiple domains can also be added and used with Lync Online if this is necessary.

TIP

A good example of the importance of matching the namespace between Lync Online and the messaging system is seen in the interaction between the Lync client and the Outlook client when a new online meeting is created. When Lync is installed on a system where

Outlook is installed, the Online Meeting Add-in for Lync is automatically enabled, and is used to allow quick scheduling of online meetings from the Outlook client. When the user creates a new meeting request, the Outlook client attempts to redirect to Lync Online using the user's SMTP address to create the meeting request. If the SMTP address does not match the SIP address, the online meeting request fails. In a circumstance in which it is not possible to match the SIP and SMTP namespaces, users are forced to use the Lync Web Scheduler to create online meetings instead of Outlook.

After the SIP namespace has been determined, the SIP domain name is entered into the Office 365 portal as part of the initial setup process.

Planning the Network for Lync Online

One key area that could easily be overlooked during the planning of a Lync Online deployment is network planning. The following sections provide details on the various network elements that can be affected by a Lync Online deployment so that these can be planned appropriately.

Planning Internet Connection Bandwidth for Lync Online

With Lync Online, the media experience for users is directly tied to the amount of Internet bandwidth available for use with Lync. Particularly if an organization has been using the Internet only for web browsing, consideration needs to be given to adding bandwidth to accommodate the network requirements for Lync audio and video.

To assist organizations with this aspect of planning for Lync Online, Microsoft provides the Transport Reliability IP Probe, or TRIPP. TRIPP is a tool that tests an Internet connection for connectivity to a Lync Online service data center, and helps an organization to determine whether adjustments might need to be made to an Internet connection that will potentially be used for Lync Online. The tool specifically tests for response times, bandwidth, allowed ports, routes, and connection quality with respect to real-time media. The feedback provided by the tool can be quite detailed and useful for proper planning of the network for Lync Online. For example, Figure 28.1 shows the resulting values of a test for jitter and packet loss using TRIPP, which helps identify the expected audio quality of Lync Online audio if used with this Internet circuit. The TRIPP tool is available at several URLs published on the Microsoft support site, which allows the user to select the URL closest to the user's physical location. Java Runtime Environment is a prerequisite for running the tool.

Firewall Port Requirements for Lync Online

Another important consideration with regard to planning the network for Lync Online is firewall port requirements. Lync Online does not have any port requirements for inbound traffic; however, many organizations use outbound filters or proxy servers to control the type of traffic that is permitted outbound. If outbound filtering is used, specific ports need to be opened on the firewall or proxy server to allow Lync outbound traffic, as shown in Table 28.4.

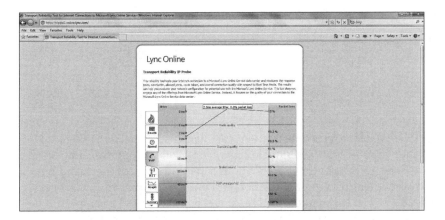

FIGURE 28.1   TRIPP jitter and packet loss results.

TABLE 28.4   Firewall Port Requirements for Lync Online

Port	Protocol	Direction	Usage
443	STUN/TCP	Outbound	Audio, video, and application sharing sessions
443	PSOM/TLS	Outbound	Data sharing sessions
3478	STUN/UDP	Outbound	Audio and video sessions
5223	TCP	Outbound	Lync Mobile push notifications
20000–45000	UDP	Outbound	Lync-to-phone
50000–59999	RTP/UDP	Outbound	Audio and video sessions

TIP

Not all ports listed in Table 28.4 are required for all Lync Online deployments. For example, TCP port 5223 is required only if Lync mobile clients use a corporate Wi-Fi connection for push notifications, and UDP ports 20000 to 45000 are required only if Lync-to-phone will be used with an approved Microsoft voice partner.

As for individual client systems, when the Lync client is installed, the required adjustments are automatically made to the Windows Firewall to enable Lync Online traffic to flow. Therefore, no additional adjustments to the Windows Firewall should be needed.

DNS Requirements for Lync Online

For each DNS domain that will be used with Lync Online, several external DNS CNAME records need to be added to support the client Autodiscover service. Table 28.5 shows the external DNS CNAME records that are needed, where <DomainName> is the external DNS domain that will be used with Lync Online.

28

TABLE 28.5   External DNS CNAME Records Used to Support Autodiscover with Lync Online

Client Type	Host Name	Destination	TTL
Desktop	sip.<DomainName>.com	sipdir.online.lync.com	1 hour
Mobile	lyncdiscover.<DomainName>.com	webdir.online.lync.com	1 hour

In addition to the CNAME records used for authenticated clients, several external SRV records might be required to support additional scenarios. Specifically, one external SRV record is needed to allow Autodiscover for anonymous (unauthenticated) users, and one external SRV record is needed to support federation and public IM connectivity if these will be used. Table 28.6 shows the external SRV records that are required to support these scenarios, where <DomainName> is the external DNS domain that will be used with Lync Online. The first entry would be used to support Autodiscover for anonymous users, whereas the second entry would be used to support federation and public IM.

TABLE 28.6   External DNS SRV Records Used for Anonymous Autodiscover and Federation

Service	Protocol	Port	Weight	Priority	TTL	Name	Target
_sip	_tls	443	1	100	1 hr	<DomainName>.com	sipdir.online.lync.com
_sipfederationtls	_tcp	5061	1	100	1 hr	<DomainName>.com	sipfed.online.lync.com

---

TIP

For most organizations, the DNS records detailed in this section are required for external DNS zones only. Although this approach is not typical, some organizations filter outbound DNS queries using firewalls or Internet proxies. If this is the case, it is necessary to add the same DNS records to internal DNS zones to support these same Lync Online functions from inside the network. If this is not possible, Autodiscover does not function, and the Lync client needs to be manually configured to connect to the following server name for both internal and external connections: sipdir.online.lync.com:443.

Planning for Federation and Public IM

Lync Online enables users to communicate with other users from external organizations that also use Lync or Office Communications Server by way of federation. In addition, Lync Online users can communicate with Skype users via public IM federation. By default, both of these services are turned off for new Lync Online deployments. However, making use of these services is as simple as logging on to the Office 365 portal and enabling the features. Since up to a day or so is required before activation after these services are enabled, Lync Online administrators should plan ahead and enable the services several days before the Lync Online users need to begin using them.

From a planning perspective, one additional consideration is the policy the organization will adopt with regard to communication with external organizations. Lync Online provides support for maintaining either a whitelist of organizations that the users will be allowed to communicate with, or a blacklist of organizations that the users will not be allowed to communicate with. These lists are configured by entering the SIP domains of the organizations that will be either allowed or blocked; therefore, this configuration will dictate the level of maintenance that will be required on the part of the Lync Online administrators to support the federation policy of the organization.

Using a blacklist results in a more open policy that should be adopted by organizations that are less concerned about which external organizations their users are communicating with, and it requires less maintenance for that very reason. On the other hand, organizations that prefer to maintain tight control of communication with external organizations need to use the whitelist approach. This of course results in a higher level of maintenance to uphold the policy, particularly if there are many SIP domains to which the organization would like to communicate. This is because the Lync administrators need to first determine the SIP domain for any organization that will be allowed for federation, and then add each SIP domain to the whitelist. Further, the external organization also needs to be configured for federation with the Lync Online organization, and depending on whether that organization has an open or closed federation policy, it might be necessary for the Lync administrators on both sides to communicate the required information before configuring federation.

NOTE

A Lync Online tenant can federate not only with other Lync Online tenants, but also with organizations that use Lync on-premise. The blacklist or whitelist settings configured in the Office 365 portal apply to either type of Lync organization.

Planning for Dial-in Audio Conferencing

Lync Online Plans 2 and 3 natively support online conferences that can be initiated and attended by any user with one of the Lync conferencing clients (including the full Lync Client and Lync Web App). However, dial-in conferencing, which enables attendees to dial into the audio portion of a Lync meeting, requires purchase of a dial-in audio conferencing service from an approved Microsoft partner. This service therefore requires some planning before it can be made available to Lync Online users.

Microsoft maintains a list of partners that are approved for providing dial-in audio conferencing, in the Lync section of the Office 365 Marketplace site, as shown in Figure 28.2. The first step in the planning process is therefore to visit the site, gather information on the available conferencing providers, and use it to evaluate and determine which service will best meet the conferencing needs of the organization.

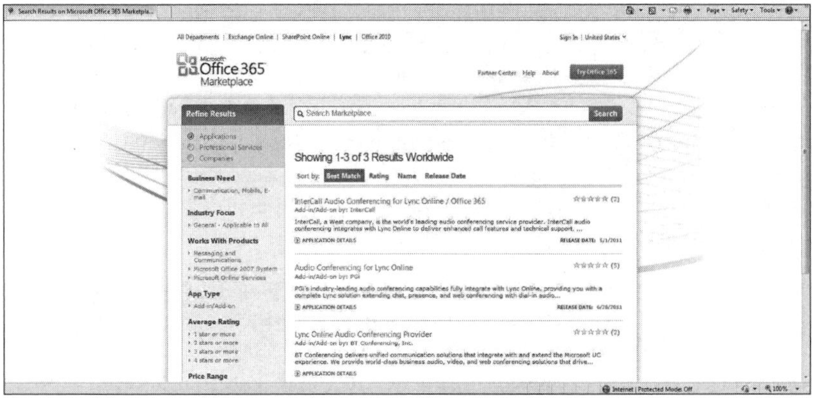

FIGURE 28.2   Approved Lync Online conferencing providers.

NOTE

Organizations that already use dial-in conferencing might be tempted to pursue the use of an existing conferencing provider with Lync Online, even though the service is not from an approved Microsoft partner. However, the use of a nonapproved conferencing service with Lync Online is discouraged for several reasons. For example, the integration of a dial-in conferencing service that has not been approved for Lync Online is complex and trouble-some to set up, because unlike with the approved conferencing services, no preconfigured connection is available for use. Also, if a nonintegrated audio conferencing service is used alongside Lync Online, this results in separate audio streams for the online users versus the dial-in users. This configuration presents additional challenges; for example, the recording of a Lync conference with two separate audio streams will not capture any of the audio that is transmitted using the conferencing provider.

After a dial-in conferencing provider has been selected and the service has been purchased, the organization is assigned a block of toll-free numbers and passcodes for use with the service. These toll-free numbers and passcodes need to then be assigned to the Lync Online users to enable this feature. If there are many users to be enabled for dial-in conferencing, it can be a significant administrative burden to manually configure these values for all of these users. Thankfully, Microsoft provides import/export functions into the Office 365 portal, and these can be used to quickly assign the dial-in conferencing values for the user accounts by direct editing of an XML file.

After the dial-in conferencing values have been configured for a Lync Online user, the phone numbers for dial-in along with passcodes automatically appear on new meeting invites, in much the same fashion as with dial-in conferencing configured for an on-premise Lync deployment.

Planning for Hosted Voice Using Lync-to-Phone

Lync Online Plan 3 supports Lync-to-phone, which is the hosted voice solution for Lync Online. Lync-to-phone requires purchase of a calling service from a qualified Office 365 partner, and therefore some planning is required to make PSTN calling available to Lync Online users.

Similar to dial-in conferencing partners for Lync Online, Microsoft also maintains a list of partners that are approved for hosted voice services in the Lync section of the Office 365 Marketplace site, as shown in Figure 28.3. The first step in the planning process is therefore to visit the site, gather information on the available hosted voice providers, and use it to evaluate and determine which service will best meet the voice requirements of the organization.

FIGURE 28.3   Approved Lync Online hosted voice providers.

The voice partner will also be the provider for 911 service as part of the agreement. If Exchange Online Plan 2 or higher is also purchased, Exchange Unified Messaging can also be used for voice mail, and automatically integrates with the hosted voice platform. The Lync Online administrator can also define Exchange UM auto attendant and subscriber access numbers for use with the hosted voice service.

After a hosted voice provider has been selected and the service has been purchased, a block of DIDs and a routing service are assigned for use with Lync Online. It might also be possible to port existing DIDs to the hosted voice service, and this can be negotiated with the voice partner when the service is provisioned. After the DIDs are provisioned or ported, user accounts are assigned work numbers using the Office 365 portal. After the work numbers are assigned to the user accounts, the appropriate SIP attributes are automatically configured based on these values, enabling hosted voice. Also, if Exchange Online Unified Messaging is licensed and configured, as detailed in the following section, then UM integration is enabled automatically for the user.

28

NOTE

Hosted voice using Lync-to-phone supports dialing using full E.164 phone numbers only; abbreviated dialing using office extensions is not available with this service.

Planning for Exchange UM Integration

In conjunction with the Lync-to-phone feature, Exchange Online Unified Messaging is available as the voice mail solution for Lync Online users. Similar to the integration of Lync and Exchange on-premise, the combination of Lync Online with Lync-to-phone and Exchange Online enables users to access voice mail and receive missed call notifications from either the Outlook or the Lync client. Subscriber access and auto attendant are also optional features that can be enabled with the service.

NOTE

When Lync Online with Lync-to-phone and Exchange Online are integrated, voice mail is delivered directly to a user's email inbox, and is accessible from Lync or Outlook. Subscriber access allows a user to access voice mails from a phone, and is therefore needed only for situations in which a computer or smartphone is not available to access voice mails.

To allow for integration of Lync Online and Exchange Online UM using Lync-to-phone, Exchange Online Plan 2 and above must be purchased. After the licensing is in place, enabling voice mail for Lync-to-phone users is a matter of creating a SIP URI dial plan within Exchange Online, and then enabling each user for Exchange UM. When the user is configured for Lync-to-phone as described previously, integration with Exchange UM occurs automatically.

Aside from the individual phone numbers that will be assigned to users, an additional planning consideration is the minimum number of digits that will be required for PIN access to voice mail, and the procedure that will be used to generate PIN numbers (automatic or manual). The number of minimum digits required for PIN numbers is associated with the SIP URI dial plan, and can be edited as necessary. The user can also be required to change the PIN number at first logon if desired.

If the subscriber access and auto attendant optional features will be used, these features will be applied to calls that originate from outside the organization. One phone number will need to be assigned for each subscriber number and each auto attendant number planned, and therefore this should be taken into account in determining the number of DIDs that are ordered from the Lync-to-phone provider.

Planning for Single Sign-On with AD FS

For organizations that maintain an internal Active Directory deployment, implementing single sign-on (SSO) is typically a high priority, because this provides the most seamless experience for Lync Online users. SSO enables each user to log on to a client system one time with Active Directory credentials, and access both Lync Online and on-premise resources without being prompted for additional credentials. To allow this functionality, Active Directory must first be prepared for SSO, and Active Directory Federated Services must also be installed on-premise and configured for federation with the Lync Online organization.

Specifically, the deployment of SSO for Lync Online requires the following components:

▶ Active Directory must be deployed on-premise using Windows 2003 or higher, with a functional level of either mixed or native mode.

▶ An AD FS 2.0 instance involving at least one federation server must be deployed on-premise, using Windows Server 2008 or higher. If users will be connecting to Lync Online from outside the network, at least one AD FS proxy is also required, and should be installed in a DMZ network.

▶ The Microsoft Online Services Module for Windows PowerShell must be installed and configured to establish a trust with Lync Online.

▶ All required updates for Office 365 must be installed on client systems.

The following sections take a closer look at these requirements as part of the planning process for SSO.

Preparing Active Directory for SSO

Aside from the Active Directory functional level requirements previously mentioned, the user principal name (UPN) configuration might also need to be adjusted in preparation for SSO. Following are the requirements for a UPN to be used with SSO:

▶ The UPN suffix configured for each Lync Online user must be identical to the domain that will be enabled for SSO with Lync Online.

▶ The UPN suffix must be a publicly registered domain.

▶ A UPN used with SSO can contain only letters, numbers, periods, dashes, and underscores.

28

TIP

With many Active Directory deployments, the UPN suffix for users matches the Active Directory DNS domain, and for this reason it is typically a private domain name that registered only on internal DNS servers, such as `companyabc.local`. For SSO to function properly with Lync Online, a publicly registered name must instead be configured for each Lync Online user. Typically, it makes the most sense to use the organization's primary SMTP domain as the UPN value, since this typically is also specified as the SIP domain for Lync Online purposes.

Planning Active Directory Federated Services for SSO

The primary component that drives SSO for Lync Online is Active Directory Federated Services. AD FS is a claims-based authentication platform that runs on Windows, and is used to simplify access to applications and services using secure tokens. In the case of Lync Online, AD FS is used to establish federation between the on-premise Active Directory deployment and the Lync Online tenant. After the appropriate trusts are configured, a secure channel is created over which authentication tokens are passed, allowing users to log on seamlessly to Lync Online using their AD credentials. Although prior versions of AD FS are included with the Windows Server OS, the AD FS version required for Lync Online SSO is version 2.0, which must be downloaded from the Microsoft download site before installation.

> **NOTE**
>
> Although this chapter is focused on Lync Online, SSO is also leveraged with the other applications included in the Office 365 suite. If a full Office 365 subscription is used as opposed to just Lync Online, the same AD FS instance would be sufficient to enable SSO for all applications, and the SSO planning process described in this chapter would also remain the same.

Planning the AD FS Topology

The first consideration in the AD FS planning process is the number of federation servers to be deployed, and the sizing of those servers. In the AD FS section of the TechNet site, Microsoft provides detailed capacity planning guidance along with a sizing calculator that can be used to determine how many federation servers are needed, along with the sizing recommendations for each server. However, the reality is that for a new Lync Online deployment, most organizations will not have the data that must be input to make use of the sizing tools provided. For this reason, and also because the resource requirements for a federation server are not significant, Microsoft also provides separate guidance for AD FS deployments that are planned for Office 365. This information can be used to estimate the number of federation servers and federation server proxies that should be deployed based on the number of users who will be accessing Office 365. For example, Table 28.7 provides guidelines on the number of servers recommended based on the Lync Online user count.

TABLE 28.7   Recommended Number of AD FS Servers Based on User Count

Number of Lync Online Users	Minimum Number of Servers to Deploy
Fewer than 1,000 users	Two collocated federation servers (must be Windows Server 2008 or 2008 R2 systems) and one separate NLB server, or two dedicated federation servers with NLB installed
1,000 to 15,000 users	Two dedicated federation servers with NLB installed
15,000 to 60,000 users	Between three and five dedicated federation servers with NLB installed (five servers is the maximum when WID is used as the database platform)

TIP

As shown in Table 28.7, for small environments with fewer than 1,000 users, it is acceptable to install the federation server role on nondedicated systems and still expect good performance. For example, the federation server role can be installed on domain controller systems. However, the federation server software is compatible only with Windows Server 2008 and Windows Server 2008 R2; therefore, with a Windows Server 2003–based Active Directory environment it might still be necessary to use dedicated federation server systems. Also, if the federation server role is installed on domain controller systems, another system needs to be used for the NLB function to provide redundancy.

Note from Table 28.7 that a minimum of two servers is recommended for all scenarios, regardless of user count. The reason for this is that, although a single federation server can handle many user connections, this configuration would represent a single point of failure for a relatively critical service. Two federation servers is therefore the minimum recommendation to allow resiliency for SSO. Connections to multiple federation servers in a farm must be load balanced, which can be accomplished using Microsoft's built-in network load balancing (NLB) feature, or using a hardware load balancer.

Regardless of the number of servers involved, each deployment of AD FS constitutes a single instance of a federation service, and each federation service is represented by a fully qualified domain name that is unique within the organization. If the federation service will provide connections from external systems, a public DNS name is required. If split brain DNS is used, a DNS host record for the federation service needs to be configured for both the internal and the external zones.

One service account is also used to run AD FS across all servers within a federated service instance. With a standalone AD FS deployment, a dedicated service account is not required, and the NETWORK SERVICE account is automatically specified by the AD FS installer to serve this purpose. However, a dedicated service account is still recommended for standalone deployments to reduce the attack surface of the federation server. A user account should therefore be created for this purpose in Active Directory before the installation of AD FS, and then configured as a dedicated service account for AD FS during the initial configuration. The service account does not require any particular rights to the AD domain; however, it must be a member of the local Administrators group on each federation server.

Choosing the AD FS Database Platform

After it is determined how many servers will be needed, the next important consideration is the database platform. The configuration data for AD FS is stored in the AD FS configuration database. For database platforms, AD FS 2.0 supports either a full installation of SQL Server (2005 or newer) or the Windows Internal Database (WID) feature that is included with Windows Server 2008 and Windows Server 2008 R2. From a performance perspective, there is not much difference between the two database platforms, and the AD FS functionality is also nearly equal between the two.

For use with Office 365 or Lync Online, Microsoft recommends using the WID database platform for the AD FS topology, because this provides data resiliency, is simple to deploy, and also saves on licensing costs compared to SQL. When the first federation server is installed, this server becomes the primary federation server, and a read/write copy of the configuration database based on WID is installed locally. Any additional federation servers added to the farm are secondary federation servers, and replicate changes to the configuration database from the primary federation server to a local read-only copy.

> **NOTE**
>
> WID supports a maximum of five federation servers. Each dedicated federation server can support approximately 15,000 user connections; therefore, WID can be used to support very large Lync Online and Office 365 implementations. If more than five federation servers will be needed, SQL Server should be used as the database platform for AD FS.

Planning for External Access to AD FS

External access to the federation service is granted by means of a federation server proxy. A federation server proxy acts as an intermediary proxy service between client systems on the Internet and a federation service that is located behind a firewall on the corporate network. To enable Lync Online users to log on using SSO from outside the corporate network, a minimum of one AD FS proxy server is needed. However, if remote access to Lync Online is considered critical to the organization, then more than one proxy must be installed, and connections to the proxy systems would be load balanced using either a hardware load balancer or the Microsoft NLB feature.

The federation server proxy system (or cluster, if more than one system is used) must be accessible from the Internet using a public IP address. The DNS name assigned to the federation server proxy must also match the DNS name that is assigned to the internal federation server farm. The public server certificate that is applied to the internal federation server systems is also applied to each of the federation server proxy systems. Federation server proxy systems are typically installed in a DMZ subnet, and are configured as members of a workgroup to reduce the firewall port requirements between the federation proxies and the internal federation servers.

Figure 28.4 shows an example of a fully redundant AD FS topology that can be used to support SSO for Lync Online, using a pair of load-balanced federation proxies and a pair of load-balanced federation servers.

Planning AD FS Hardware

Server virtualization platforms are supported for both the federation server and the federation server proxy roles. The hardware and software requirements for federation server and federation server proxy systems are the same. For either type of system, the following hardware minimums apply:

- ▶ Operating systems—Windows Server 2008 or Windows Server 2008 R2
- ▶ CPU speed—single-core 1GHz
- ▶ RAM—1GB
- ▶ Disk space—50MB

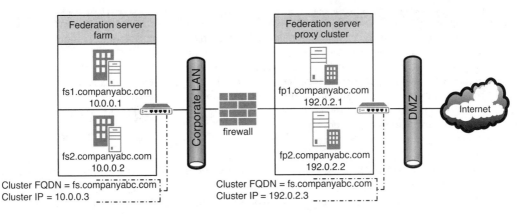

FIGURE 28.4   Example of redundant AD FS topology for Lync Online.

These minimum specifications should be used only as a starting point for resource allocation. To increase capacity, additional RAM and CPU can be added, or the number of servers can be increased. For example, the capacity planning guidelines listed in Table 28.7 are based on the following hardware specifications:

▶ CPU speed—dual quad core 2.27GHz CPU (eight cores total)

▶ RAM—4GB

Planning AD FS Certificates

Several certificates are used with the federation service. The first of these is referred to as the server authentication certificate, which is a standard SSL certificate used to secure communications between federation servers, clients, and federation server proxy computers. The server authentication certificate must be purchased from a public certificate authority using the federation service FQDN as the subject name. The certificate is then applied to each of the federation servers in the AD FS topology.

> **TIP**
>
> If a Lync hybrid deployment is planned, the subject name of the server authentication certificate instead needs to be `sts.<SIPdomain>`, where <SIPdomain> is the DNS domain that will be split across the Lync Online and Lync on-premise deployments. For details, see the "Planning for a Hybrid Deployment" section of this chapter.

The second type of certificate required is the token-signing certificate, which is a standard x.509 certificate used to digitally sign all security tokens that are created. This certificate is not public-facing; however, the public key associated with the cert must be supplied to Lync Online/Office 365 as part of a trust configuration. By default, AD FS automatically generates a self-signed certificate for token-signing every year and automatically rolls it over before the certificate expires.

When the token-signing certificate is rolled over, the online tenant needs to be notified about this change; otherwise, requests to the online tenant will fail. To avoid this situation, Microsoft provides a utility named Microsoft Office 365 Federation Metadata Update Automation Administration Tool, which can be downloaded free. When installed, the tool automatically monitors and updates the Office 365 federation metadata on a regular basis, so that any changes made to the token-signing certificate are replicated to the online tenant automatically, preventing an outage.

The federation server proxy systems also require a standard SSL certificate to secure communications with client systems on the Internet, as well as the internal federation servers. However, as shown in Figure 28.4, the same public FQDN is assigned to both the federation service and the federation proxy cluster. For this reason, the same SSL certificate assigned as the server authentication certificate on the federation servers can also be used on the federation server proxy systems.

Planning the Network for AD FS

Other than standard TCP/IP connectivity, network requirements for AD FS consist of DNS entries that must be configured to direct traffic to the AD FS systems, and firewall ports that need to be opened. Following are the specific DNS requirements for AD FS:

▶ For internal connectivity to AD FS, a single host record can be added to the internal DNS zone, mapping the fully qualified name of the federation service to either the IP address of the federation server (for single-server installations) or the virtual IP address of the load-balancing cluster (for multiple-server installations).

▶ For external connectivity to AD FS, a single host record can be added to the external DNS zone, mapping the fully qualified name of the federation service to either the public IP address assigned to the federation server proxy (for single-server federation proxy installations) or the public virtual IP address of the load-balancing cluster (for multiple-server federation proxy installations).

▶ If the federation server proxy systems in the DMZ are configured to connect to internal DNS servers for DNS resolution, no additional DNS configuration is required to enable the proxy systems to connect to the internal federation servers. However, for security purposes the DMZ servers might not be configured to connect to internal systems for DNS resolution. If there are DNS servers hosted in the DMZ segment for this purpose, a single host record can be added to the DNS zone on the DNS DMZ servers, mapping the fully qualified name of the federation service to either the IP address of the federation server (for single-server installations) or the virtual IP address of the load-balancing cluster (for multiple-server installations). As an alternative, the HOSTS file can instead be edited on each of the federation proxy servers to include the required mapping.

> **TIP**
>
> If a Lync hybrid deployment is planned, additional DNS records will be required to support AD FS with the hybrid configuration. For details, see the "Planning for a Hybrid Deployment" section of this chapter.

Firewall ports that need to be opened for AD FS connectivity include the following:

▶ For external connectivity to the federation server proxy systems in the DMZ, TCP port 443 needs to be opened inbound.

▶ For connectivity between the federation server proxies in the DMZ and the internal federation servers, TCP ports 80 and 443 need to be opened between the systems in both directions.

▶ For connectivity between the internal federation service and Office 365, TCP port 443 needs to be opened outbound.

Planning Browser Support for AD FS

Lync Online and Office 365 are compatible with most modern web browsers, including Internet Explorer, Firefox, Chrome, and Safari. However, by default the use of SSO with Lync Online/Office 365 is dependent on a browser's support for Extended Protection for Authentication, a feature that helps protect against man-in-the-middle attacks. If a browser does not support Extended Protection for Authentication, users will likely receive logon prompts on a regular basis when accessing Lync Online and other Office 365 services.

At the time of writing, several versions of Firefox, Chrome, and Safari did not support Extended Protection for Authentication; therefore, if these browsers are planned for Lync Online, some adjustments to the default configuration might be required. Following are two adjustments that can potentially be used to avoid logon problems for Lync Online users connecting with a browser that does not support Extended Protection for Authentication:

▶ The Extended Protection for Authentication setting can be disabled on AD FS 2.0 systems. To adjust this setting on a federation server, log in using an account with local administrator permissions, open Windows PowerShell, and execute the following command:

```
Set-ADFSProperties -ExtendedProtectionTokenCheck None
```

If multiple federation servers are used, the command must be executed on each federation server in the farm.

▶ The AD FS 2.0 web page on each federation server can be reconfigured to use forms-based authentication instead of integrated Windows authentication. The implications of such a change should be carefully considered before this adjustment is made, because this will affect all Lync Online/Office 365 users, regardless of the browser being used. If it is determined that this change will be made, the AD FS documentation on Technet should be consulted for specific procedures to be used.

28

Planning for Directory Synchronization

Directory synchronization is an important feature for organizations that use Active Directory, because it enables Active Directory user and group accounts to be synchronized to Office 365. For most organizations, it makes sense to use directory synchronization in tandem with SSO, because the combination of SSO and directory synchronization creates a seamless experience for Lync Online users. Although it is possible to configure directory synchronization without SSO, this would result in two sets of credentials to manage, and is therefore recommended only for small organizations.

Directory synchronization with Office 365 is made possible using the Microsoft Online Services Directory Synchronization Tool, which can be used to synchronize up to 50,000 objects. The following sections provide the necessary planning details to ensure that directory synchronization with Lync Online/Office 365 functions smoothly.

> **NOTE**
>
> Directory synchronization with Office 365 should be considered a long-term commitment, particularly since the synchronized objects can be edited only with the on-premise tools.

Activating the AD Synchronization Feature

Before directory synchronization with Lync Online/Office 365 is used, this feature must be activated within the online tenant. Activating the feature is a one-time process and is as simple as clicking on a button within the online portal. However, the activation process can require up to 24 hours to complete. With that in mind, Lync Online administrators should plan ahead and activate AD synchronization several days before the AD user accounts need to be populated into the online directory.

Preparing Active Directory for Synchronization

To ensure that the on-premise Active Directory is prepared for synchronization with the online directory, the Microsoft Office 365 Deployment Readiness Tool is used. The Deployment Readiness Tool inspects the local Active Directory environment, and provides a report that includes a prerequisite check and an attribute assessment, as shown in Figure 28.5. If changes are required, these are listed so that they can be handled before directory synchronization is enabled.

The Deployment Readiness Tool can be downloaded from the Office 365 website, and can be executed on any domain-joined system by any domain user. After the tool is run and the report is generated, any changes that are listed should be made to prepare the environment for directory synchronization. The report can then be rerun as many times as needed to ensure that all required changes have been completed. After the environment is fully prepared, the directory synchronization feature can be enabled by a Lync Online/Office 365 administrator using the online portal.

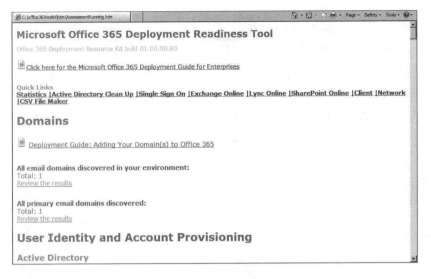

FIGURE 28.5   Report from the Office 365 Deployment Readiness Tool.

Preparing a System for the Directory Synchronization Tool

The Microsoft Online Services Directory Synchronization Tool can be downloaded directly from the Office 365 portal. Before the tool is installed, there are specific requirements for the network as well as the system that will be used to run the tool.

The following requirements apply to the system that will be used to run the Directory Synchronization Tool:

▶ Supported operating systems are Windows Server 2008 and Windows Server 2008 R2.

▶ The system must be a member of an Active Directory domain, and the domain must be within the same forest as the domain that will be synchronized to Lync Online/Office 365.

▶ The system cannot be a domain controller.

▶ The system cannot be running Active Directory Federation Services.

▶ .NET Framework 3.0 or 3.5 must be installed.

▶ Windows PowerShell must be enabled.

28

NOTE

The system that runs directory synchronization contains sensitive information, and therefore from a security perspective it should be afforded the same amount of protection as a domain controller. Only individuals who are granted access to domain controller systems should be granted access to the system that runs directory synchronization.

The performance of the Directory Synchronization Tool is directly dependent on the size and complexity of Active Directory, as well as the hardware used for the system running the tool. Table 28.8 shows the minimum hardware requirements for the system that will be used to run directory synchronization in relation to the number of AD objects. By default, the Directory Synchronization Tool will install an instance of SQL Express to store the directory information. As noted in the table, if there are more than 50,000 Active Directory objects to be synchronized, a full instance of SQL Server 2008 R2 is required.

TABLE 28.8   Minimum Hardware Requirements for the System Running Directory Synchronization

Number of AD objects	CPU	Memory	Hard Disk
Fewer than 50,000	1.6GHz	4GB	70GB
50,000–100,000 Requires full SQL Server	1.6GHz	16GB	100GB
100,000–300,000 Requires full SQL Server	1.6GHz	32GB	300GB
300,000–600,000 Requires full SQL Server	1.6GHz	32GB	450GB
More than 600,000 Requires full SQL Server	1.6GHz	32GB	500GB

Planning for a Hybrid Deployment

Planning for a Lync hybrid deployment involves a blend of planning for Lync Online as described in this chapter, and planning for an on-premise deployment as described in Chapters 29 to 32. Depending on the services that will be included in the hybrid deployment, there are additional requirements and considerations that are unique to a hybrid deployment, and these will be detailed in the following sections.

Using On-Premise Systems with a Hybrid Deployment

The on-premise requirements for a hybrid deployment depend on whether there is an existing Lync or OCS 2007 R2 installation on-premise, as well as whether hybrid voice will be included in the deployment. If there is an existing OCS 2007 R2 pool, a Lync 2013 Front End pool and Edge pool will need to be installed alongside the OCS installation, and users will need to be moved to the Lync 2013 pool before being migrated to Lync Online.

If there is an existing Lync 2010 Front End pool and Edge pool, the Lync 2010 Edge pool can be federated with Lync Online/Office 365 to create a hybrid deployment that offers basic hybrid voice features. Basic hybrid voice features supported with an on-premise Lync 2010 pool include the following:

▶ Call hold/retrieve

▶ Call transfer

▶ Call forwarding

▶ Voice mail

▶ USB peripherals

▶ Outside voice—mobile

▶ Delegation

▶ Team call

▶ Integration with on-premise PBX

▶ Analog devices

▶ Common area phones

Figure 28.6 shows a sample hybrid topology with Lync 2010 on-premise, which can be used to provide basic hybrid voice features for cloud users, and the full Lync voice feature set for on-premise users.

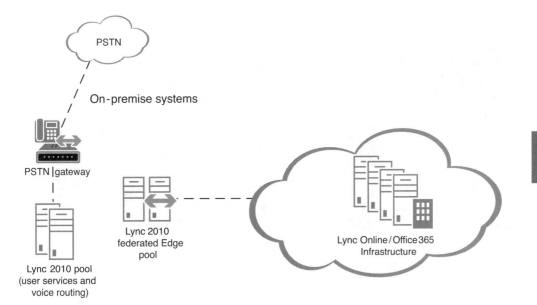

FIGURE 28.6   Hybrid topology with Lync 2010 on-premise, supporting basic hybrid voice features.

If advanced hybrid voice features are required, at least one Lync 2013 Front End server needs to be installed to handle voice routing. In addition, the Lync 2010 deployment must be running cumulative update 5 and above to support this mixed hybrid topology. Advanced hybrid voice features supported only with an on-premise Lync 2013 pool include the following:

▶ Enhanced 911

▶ Response Group Service

▶ Call Park Service

▶ Media bypass

Figure 28.7 shows a sample hybrid topology with both Lync 2010 and Lync 2013 on-premise, which can be used to provide advanced hybrid voice features for cloud users, and the full Lync voice feature set for on-premise users.

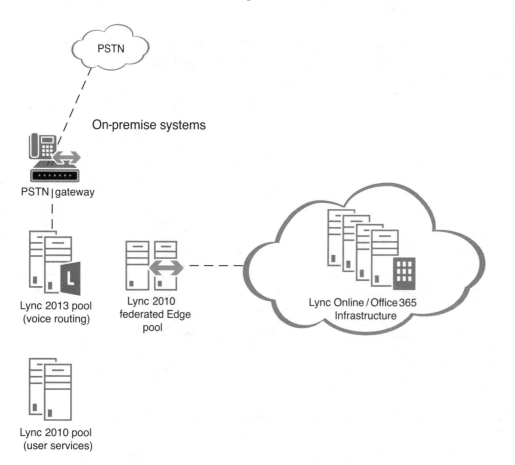

FIGURE 28.7   Hybrid topology with Lync 2010 and Lync 2013 on-premise, supporting advanced hybrid voice features.

For a new on-premise deployment of Lync 2013, one Front End pool is required, using either the Standard or the Enterprise Edition. As would be true of any on-premise deployment, voice functionality requires that the Mediation Server role be installed, along with the PSTN infrastructure. The Mediation Server role can either be collocated with the Front End pool or installed in a separate pool.

With any Lync hybrid deployment, regardless of whether the on-premise installation includes earlier versions of Lync/OCS or just Lync 2013, an Edge pool consisting of at least one Edge Server is required. The Edge pool must also be enabled for federation, including the external DNS records that are required for federation.

> **NOTE**
>
> An Edge pool used with a hybrid deployment takes on additional functions beyond those that are typical for a standard on-premise deployment. In addition to the standard Edge services of remote access and federation, the Lync Edge pool in a hybrid deployment is used for federating with Lync Online/Office 365, routing of SIP signaling traffic between the on-premise deployment and the cloud, and in some circumstances routing of media traffic for Lync Online users who connect via the Internet.

Additional on-premise requirements for a hybrid deployment include the following:

▶ Directory synchronization must be enabled between the on-premise Active Directory and Lync Online/Office 365, as described in the "Planning for Directory Synchronization" section of this chapter.

▶ Active Directory Federated Services must be installed and configured to enable SSO between the on-premise Active Directory and the Lync Online/Office 365 directory, as described in the "Planning for Single Sign-On with AD FS" section of this chapter.

▶ In addition to the standard certificate requirements for the on-premise AD FS deployment, the public SSL certificate used as the server authentication certificate must use a subject name of `sts.<SIPdomain>`, where <SIPdomain> is the primary SIP domain that will be split across the Lync Online and Lync on-premise deployments. If additional, secondary SIP domains will be used, these can also be added as subject alternative names on the certificate.

▶ To access Lync Online, either the Lync 2013 client or the Lync 2010 client running cumulative update 2 and above can be used.

Figure 28.8 shows the components included in a typical Lync hybrid topology with only Lync 2013 on-premise, supporting the full feature set including advanced hybrid voice.

Network Considerations for a Hybrid Deployment

The network planning steps needed for a cloud-only deployment, as described in the "Planning the Network for Lync Online" section of this chapter, are also applicable to a Lync hybrid deployment. This includes bandwidth planning, as well as planning for

28

firewall port and DNS requirements. However, with a hybrid deployment there are several additional firewall port requirements, as well as additional DNS requirements, depending on the configuration, as detailed in the following sections.

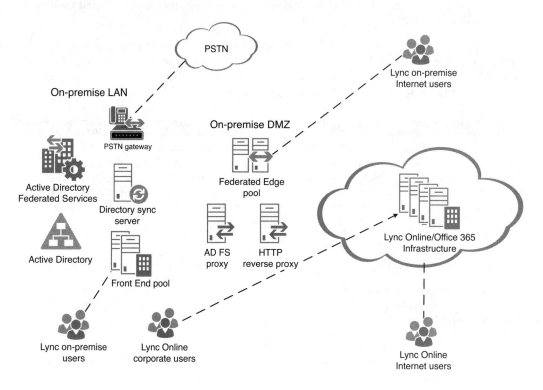

FIGURE 28.8   Components of a typical hybrid topology with Lync 2013 on-premise.

Additional Firewall Port Requirements for a Hybrid Deployment

For a hybrid deployment there are a few additional port requirements for both inbound and outbound traffic, as shown in Table 28.9. Whereas the outbound ports are required only if an organization uses outbound filters or proxy servers to control outbound traffic, the inbound ports are required for all hybrid deployments.

TABLE 28.9   Additional Firewall Port Requirements for a Lync Hybrid Deployment

Port	Protocol	Direction	Usage
443	SSL/TCP	Inbound/Outbound	Between on-premise Edge systems and Lync Online
5061	SIP/TCP	Outbound	Used to connect to Lync Online SIP federation edge

> **NOTE**
>
> The firewall port requirements listed in Table 28.9 are relevant to the communication between on-premise Lync systems and Lync Online/Office 365. However, these are in addition to any firewall port requirements that are relevant to only the Lync on-premise systems. These other port requirements are dependent on the Lync services that are enabled on-premise, and are detailed in Chapter 12, "Firewall and Security Requirements."

Additional DNS Requirements for a Hybrid Deployment

For a hybrid deployment, the external DNS host record that allows outside connectivity to AD FS is different from that of a standard Lync Online deployment. Specifically, this record must use `sts.<SIPdomain>` as the target, where `<SIPdomain>` is the primary SIP domain that will be split across the Lync Online and Lync on-premise deployments. If additional, secondary SIP domains are used, one external DNS host record is also needed for each of these, using the same destination name format of `sts.<SIPdomain>`.

Edge Federation with a Hybrid Deployment

To support a hybrid deployment, the federation configuration for the on-premise Edge pool must match the federation settings configured in the Lync Online tenant. For example, if the on-premise Edge pool is configured for partner discovery, also referred to as open federation, then Lync Online must be configured for open federation as well. If the on-premise Edge pool is configured with an allowed domains list, also known as closed federation, then Lync Online must be configured for closed federation as well. Also, the allowed domains and blocked domains lists configured in the on-premise Edge pool must exactly match the corresponding lists in the Lync Online tenant configuration.

User Management with a Hybrid Deployment

The procedures used to create and manage user accounts with a hybrid deployment are different from a cloud-only deployment in several ways, and should therefore be taken into account when planning the hybrid deployment. After directory synchronization is enabled for a domain, updates and changes to the user accounts must be made using the on-premise tools only. This means that for any new user account that will be a Lync Online user, the account must first be created in the on-premise Active Directory, and then synchronized to Lync Online/Office 365. If a user account is instead created in Lync Online/Office 365 using the online portal, the account will not be synchronized with the on-premise Active Directory. After the account is created, the user can be moved from the on-premise Lync pool to the Lync Online/Office 365 tenant.

The following limitations and considerations should also be taken into account for user accounts that are moved from the on-premise pool to Lync Online:

- ▶ User contact lists, groups, and ACLs are migrated with the user account when an on-premise user is moved to Lync Online. However, the limit for user contacts in Lync Online is 50. When an on-premise user is moved to Lync Online, any contacts beyond 50 are removed from the user's contact list.

28

▶ Conferencing data, meeting content, and scheduled meetings are not migrated with the user account when moved to Lync Online. Users must reschedule meetings after their accounts are migrated to Lync Online.

▶ Users can be enabled for IM, voice, and meetings either on-premise or in Lync Online, but not both simultaneously.

Summary

Cloud-based computing continues to generate much interest in the business world, and this is likely to increase over time. Yet, with this being a relatively new option, the planning aspect of a cloud-based UC deployment is very different from that of an on-premise deployment, and is often not well understood. A hybrid Lync deployment holds promise for nicely bridging the gap between the on-premise and cloud-only options, providing a truly seamless UC environment. However, a hybrid deployment presents even more unique planning considerations that must be taken into account. The information presented in this chapter should be of great assistance to organizations that are considering a cloud-based Lync solution, not only for determining which deployment option meets the needs of the business, but also for ensuring that important details are taken into account ahead of the deployment, ensuring a successful outcome.

CHAPTER 29

Virtualization Support

The majority or organizations today, big and small, take advantage of the cost savings and flexibility of server virtualization in one form or another. Many now operate a "virtualize first" policy for new server deployments and are moving to a "Private Cloud" model for their internal IT. Lync Server 2010 was the first release to support virtualizing every workload, from IM and presence to A/V conferencing to Enterprise Voice. Lync Server 2013 continues to support virtualization of all workloads and adds support for some new virtualization technologies (such as Single-Root I/O Virtualization and support for more than four virtual processors) to enable better performance and scalability in a virtualized environment.

This chapter begins with a basic overview of what virtualization is and of the benefits a company can realize by leveraging virtualization. It also discusses some of the common virtualization platform features and the different names of these features in competing products such as Microsoft Hyper-V and VMware vSphere.

Although virtualization of each role is possible, there are some strict requirements around what is supported and what is not supported when virtual Lync Servers are used. This chapter covers the configuration of Lync virtual servers and virtualization hosts for Lync. This includes processor, memory, disk, and network considerations for each type of server. Sample topologies of some different virtual deployment models are also included. This should give the reader a good understanding of the support boundaries.

Lastly, this chapter covers some notes on client and desktop virtualization followed by overall virtualization best practices.

Virtualization Overview

Virtualization is a technology that has been around for many years in different forms, but has made a significant impact over the past decade. Most organizations already leverage the technology for new flexibility and cost savings. This section covers some of the basic concepts for those unfamiliar with virtualization so that the remainder of the chapter can be understood.

What Is Virtualization?

Virtualization enables a physical piece of hardware to run multiple virtual instances of an operating system. In a traditional physical server deployment, every server had its own dedicated physical hardware, with a single operating system, and the server performed a specific function. When it was time to add a new server to the environment, companies purchased a new piece of hardware, installed the operating system, and then configured any applications or services.

With virtualization, the physical hardware with its resources—such as processing power, memory, and disk space—is referred to as the host. Software called a hypervisor enables the physical host's resources to be shared among many virtual machines. The virtual machine servers are referred to as "guests." Guests have to share the resources from the physical server. For example, if a host machine has 64GB of RAM, only 64GB of RAM is available to be allocated among the virtual machine guests running on that host.

> **NOTE**
>
> Many virtualization products offer the capability to do some form of dynamic memory management so that overallocating or dynamically shifting physical memory between guests is possible, but the bottom line here is that guest machines use the physical resources installed in the host.

With virtualization, companies no longer require new physical hardware for every new server because virtual machines can share a common set of physical resources (typically multiple virtualization host servers).

Hypervisor Types

The key to virtualization is the concept of a hypervisor, which is a software layer that sits between the host physical hardware and the guest virtual machines. The hypervisor facilitates and manages access of the virtual machines to the physical hardware resources.

Virtualization hypervisors come in two distinct flavors. The first, Type 1, enables virtualization to occur directly within existing operating system. Good examples of a Type 1 hypervisor are the Microsoft Virtual PC or VMware Workstation products. These are applications that run in an existing operating system on a workstation or server, and they enable the user to run virtual machines in the operating system. The hypervisor in these instances runs on top of the host operating system, as depicted in Figure 29.1.

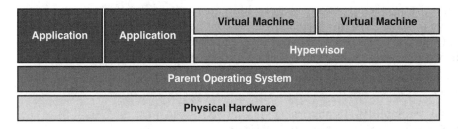

FIGURE 29.1   Type 1 hypervisor.

The second type of hypervisor, Type 2, is far more efficient than Type 1, because it is installed directly onto the physical hardware, as shown in Figure 29.2. This is the type of hypervisor in Microsoft Hyper-V and VMware vSphere products. Type 2 hypervisors are more efficient because there is no need to have the hypervisor first pass through the host operating system before addressing resources for the virtual machine guests.

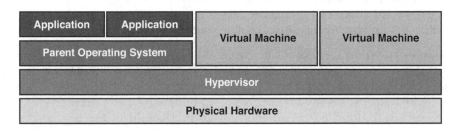

FIGURE 29.2   Type 2 hypervisor.

Benefits of Virtualization

It should be apparent from the previous few pages that virtualization offers companies a new level of flexibility in server deployment and management not possible using only physical hardware. This section summaries some of the benefits that organizations can realize from hardware virtualization:

▶ **Fewer Physical Servers**—By virtualizing servers, an organization requires fewer physical servers. Because modern physical servers support multiple physical processors (with, in some cases, up to 12 cores or more per processor), and up to 384GB or more of RAM, companies can increase their consolidation ratios (ratio of virtual servers to physical servers) by placing more and more virtual machines on the same physical hardware.

▶ **Infrastructure Flexibility**—As physical servers begin to demand hardware upgrades, the traditional model required organizations to purchase new servers, or more memory or processing power. In a virtual environment, administrators can easily shut down a virtual machine and add more virtual memory or processors or even move the virtual machine to a new host with more hardware resources. Some hypervisors and operating systems even allow these configuration changes to happen without shutting down the virtual machine. Additionally, expanding the infrastructure to accommodate new virtual machines can become a simple matter of adding a new physical host to the cluster. This adds an entirely new level of flexibility to managing server resources.

▶ **Increased Availability**—In physical environments, servers were often built to be as redundant as possible with multiple hard drives and power supplies. These additional expenses are still useful for a host server but do not apply to virtual machines. As long as a virtual machine image is made highly available, it can be easily restarted on a different host if a physical host fails. It is still best practice to design the hosts to be fault tolerant, but the additional expense of designing every single server for hardware redundancy becomes unnecessary. Organizations can achieve a higher level of service and availability for servers by abstracting the hardware layer through virtualization.

▶ **Reduced Operating Expenses**—By reducing the number of physical servers in the environment, organizations can also realize decreased operating expenses associated with physical servers, such as rack space, cooling, and power.

▶ **Application Isolation**—A significant challenge in the days of using only physical servers was that each new server required its own physical hardware. Best practice is to isolate each application to a specific server. Typically, this was difficult because of the additional expense involved in purchasing and installing a new dedicated server for each application. To work around budget issues, administrators began to collocate different applications on the same physical server, but because application vendors usually only test and expect their application to have its own dedicated environment, this could cause performance or configuration issues that were difficult to troubleshoot. With virtualization, each application can have its own dedicated server virtual machine.

▶ **Legacy Application Support**—An unfortunate reality for many organizations is a need to support legacy applications that run on only legacy operating systems. As the hardware these systems run on begins to fail or needs replacement, without virtualization, organizations must redeploy these applications on new hardware or operating systems not certified for the product and incur the expense and complexity of redeploying the legacy application. Using virtualization, however, companies can create a new virtual machine running a legacy operating system very easily. They can also perform a physical-to-virtual (P2V) migration of the existing physical server to copy it as-is from a physical to a virtual machine.

Virtualization Vendors

Several vendors produce virtualization technologies today. Some of the most commonly used products are Microsoft Hyper-V, VMware vSphere, and Citrix XenServer. All these vendors offer a fairly similar base feature set with some unique features on top. In relation to Lync Server 2013, Microsoft certifies particular hypervisor products for use in order to be supported. Today, only the Microsoft Windows Server 2008 R2 Hyper-V, Microsoft Windows Server 2012 Hyper-V, and VMware vSphere 5 are certified for use with Lync Server 2013. Additional vendors can work with Microsoft later to achieve certification. This chapter focuses on the Microsoft and VMware hypervisors because they are the two supported platforms at this time.

> **NOTE**
>
> The Hyper-V release in Windows Server 2008 is not supported because it lacks some media support required for Lync Server virtualization. Windows Server 2012 Hyper-V is the recommended hypervisor for Lync Server 2013.

The Microsoft Windows Server 2012 Hyper-V management console is shown in Figure 29.3. You can see the virtual machines, their running state, CPU update, assigned memory, and uptime.

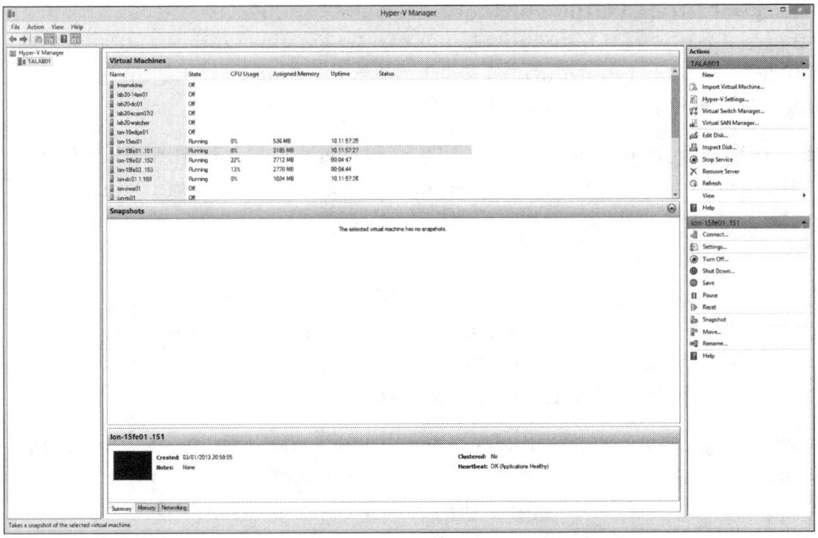

FIGURE 29.3   Microsoft Windows Server 2012 Hyper-V Manager.

Advanced Virtualization Features

As these enterprise-class virtualization products have grown, more features have been added, enabling them to cluster physical host machines, move virtual machines seamlessly between hosts while still online, and manage virtual machines from a single console. Most of these features are similar between VMware and Hyper-V products, but have different names. This section covers those naming differences and describes the different features because they are referenced later and have a direct effect on support in Lync Server 2013.

▶ **Failover Clustering/High-Availability**—This refers to the capability to join multiple physical hosts into a cluster where shared storage from a storage area network (SAN) is provisioned. When running on a clustered set of physical hosts, a virtual machine can be made highly available. If a physical host fails or restarts at some point, the highly available virtual machines running on that host can be automatically restarted on a different host. The virtual machine is also restarted during this process, similar to the power being turned off and then back on.

▶ **Live Migration/vMotion**—This provides the capability to move virtual machines between different hosts in a cluster without any disruption of service or perceived downtime. For example, a virtual machine that is online and running can be migrated to another host while users remain connected to the virtual machine. This is accomplished by the host machines transferring the memory state of the guest over the network and then simultaneously bringing the machine online on the new host while the previous host removes its copy. Both host machines must remain online during this process, and the virtual machine remains available to users during the process.

▶ **SR-IOV (Single-Root Input/Output Virtualization)**—With SR-IOV, the control and management of a physical network adapter can be assigned directly to a virtual machine. This reduces I/O (input/output) overhead and increases performance. SR-IOV is supported in Windows Server 2012 Hyper-V.

▶ **Dynamic Memory/Memory Overcommit**—This involves the capability to dynamically change the level of physical and virtual memory allocated to a virtual machine. This enables the hypervisor to dynamically allocate resources to best meet the guest virtual machines' requirements.

▶ **Quality of Service (QoS)**—QoS at the hypervisor level enables the provisioned virtual network to have an attached Service Level Agreement (SLA), enabling the physical network connection often shared between virtual machines to be configured to ensure that each virtual machine gets appropriate bandwidth.

▶ **System Center Virtual Machine Manager/VMware vCenter**—These two products are Microsoft and VMware's respective centralized management suites. When a single hypervisor is used, management of the host and guest virtual machines can be done individually, but as more hosts and guests are added to an environment, managing each host separately can become tedious. These management products offer a centralized view and configuration store of all the hosts and guests within the virtualization environment.

Lync Server Virtualization Support Guidelines

In Lync Server 2013 all roles are supported in a virtualized environment. The roles and features supported for Lync Server 2013 virtualization are listed here:

▶ **Standard Edition Server**—Supported for all roles (including Presence, IM, Enterprise Voice, A/V, collocated Monitoring and Archiving, XMPP, and conferencing).

▶ **Enterprise Edition Front End Server**—Supported for all roles (including Presence, IM, Enterprise Voice, A/V, collocated Monitoring and Archiving, XMPP, and conferencing).

▶ **Enterprise Edition Backend Server**—Supported for SQL Server and file share server. As with Physical Servers, SQL Mirroring is supported.

▶ **Edge Server**—Supported for all roles (remote access, federation, public IM connectivity, Presence, IM, Enterprise Voice, XMPP, and A/V).

▶ **Director**—Supported for all roles (authentication, routing, and web services).

▶ **Persistent Chat**—Supported for Persistent Chat.

▶ **Survivable Branch Server**—Supported for Registration and Enterprise Voice.

> **NOTE**
>
> In Lync Server 2010, XMPP was a dedicated additional server role that was not supported for virtualization. XMPP is now collocated on the Front End/Edge Server roles and as such is supported in a virtualized environment. In Lync Server 2013, Archiving and Monitoring and A/V Conferencing are always collocated with the Front End/Standard Edition Server role. They cannot be deployed separately so are not called out as specifically supported for virtualization, but are supported as a collocated role on a virtualized guest machine.

The only roles that cannot be virtualized for use in Lync Server 2013 are the IP-PSTN gateways and Survivable Branch Appliances. Considering that most of these appliances require a physical telephony connection (ISDN BRI/PRI, for example) that would be impossible in a virtual environment, this should not be an issue for most organizations. The self-deployed equivalent of a Survivable Branch Appliance, the Survivable Branch Server, is supported in a virtualized environment.

It should be understood that although virtualization of all the Lync Server 2013 roles is supported, there are some very specific support limitations and recommendations:

▶ **Windows Server 2008 R2 Hyper-V, Windows Server 2012 Hyper-V, or VMware vSphere 5**—These are the only supported hypervisors at this time. This includes the Hyper-V 2008 R2 and Hyper-V 2012 standalone free server products and both the ESX and the ESXi products from VMware. This means that older versions such as Microsoft Virtual Sever 2005, Microsoft Windows Server 2008 Hyper-V, and VMware ESX 4.0 are not supported for use with Lync Server 2013.

▶ **No Live Migration**—Live Migration or vMotion of Lync virtual servers is not a supported feature. Because media traffic heavily depends on low latency and CPU processing, moving a Lync VM between hosts can lead to a poor experience for users by either degrading or completely disconnecting a media stream. This means a single Lync Server cannot be considered "high-availability" by virtue of being hosted on a virtualization platform that supports high-availability at the virtualization layer.

▶ **Mixed Virtual and Physical Servers Within the Same Pool Are Not Supported**— There are some additional guidelines when mixing physical and virtual servers for Lync, but the most basic one is that a pool cannot contain a mix of physical and virtual servers. All servers in a single Front End, Edge, Director, or Mediation pool must be either physical or virtual to be supported. Performance of each virtual machine in a pool should be equivalent (users will be balanced over each server equally regardless of each machine's performance characteristics).

▶ **Match Virtual Front End Pools with Supporting Virtual Pools**—To virtualize roles such as the Director or the Edge Server, the associated Enterprise or Standard Edition Front End Server should also be virtualized. This means that if an organization deploys the Front End Servers on physical machines, the Director or Edge Server cannot be virtualized. This negates a common scenario in which it might make sense to use physical hardware for a Front End pool, yet virtualize a less intensive role such as a Director. The opposite case is perfectly valid. Organizations can virtualize the Front End pool but use physical hardware for a Director or an Edge Server.

Virtualizing Servers That Work Alongside Lync Server 2013

This section gives some brief guidance on the supportability of virtualizing server roles that work alongside Lync Server 2013.

Office Web Apps Server 2013

Lync Server 2013 has a dependency on Office Web Apps Server 2013 being available in the environment for PowerPoint sharing. This server is also supported in a virtualized environment. Detailed virtualization requirements are beyond the scope of this chapter; please see the Office Web Apps Server 2013 2013 documentation for detailed requirements.

Exchange Unified Messaging

Exchange Unified Messaging is usually required in a Lync deployment to provide Unified Messaging voice mail and attendant functionality for Lync 2013 users. In Exchange 2010 SP1 and Exchange 2013, Unified Messaging can be virtualized. Detailed virtualization requirements are beyond the scope of this chapter; please see the Exchange documentation for detailed requirements.

Reverse Proxy

An often-overlooked component of a deployment can be the requirement for a reverse proxy server when enabling remote access. Microsoft Thread Management Gateway has been the default position for a reverse proxy, but any product that can support the required functionality will work. The typical requirements for a reverse proxy are not nearly as high as for a Lync Server role but do consume some resources on a host. You should see your specific reverse-proxies documentation for virtualization requirements and support, and remember to include these requirements if you plan to have the reverse proxy on the same host as a Lync Server role.

Hardware and Software Load Balancers

As with Lync Server 2010, in Lync Server 2013 Enterprise pools, HTTP connections require a load balancer. This is typically a physical hardware load balancer, but a number of software load balancers, which can run virtualized, are supported.

At the time of writing, the following software load balancers are supported:

▶ A10 Networks 64-bit AX Series

▶ Citrix Systems Netscaler VPX

▶ KEMP LoadMaster VLM-100, VLM-1000

▶ Riverbed Technology Stingray Traffic Manager

Again, if these virtual appliances are to be collocated on a host with Lync Servers, their virtual hardware requirements should be considered. Be aware of any limitations in scalability of virtual load balancers in comparison to their hardware equivalents.

Understanding the Limits of Virtualization

One of the benefits of virtualization that has led the technology to be so popular is the capability to consolidate many physical servers onto a single virtual host. This is possible because most physical servers rarely utilize all their physical processor, memory and storage capacity, and I/O. So, for example, if you have four physical servers each using around 20% of their CPU, you could consolidate them onto one physical server of the same CPU specification and not expect to impact performance perceivably (assuming that storage, network, and memory are also specified appropriately).

Real-Time Media and Virtualization

It is the hypervisor that shares the physical resources between the virtual servers; if the virtual servers are processing non-time-sensitive data, for example, serving a webpage or forwarding an email, a slight delay in processing might not matter. Lync Server deals with real-time audio and video, and the fact that it is real-time is key. Without consistent performance from the server, audio or video could glitch or freeze. Therefore, a virtual Lync 2013 server must perform consistently.

In Lync Server 2013 the load on the servers increases over Lync Server 2010:

▶ Gallery View now displays video of multiple conference participants simultaneously which impacts processing and network I/O.

▶ The presence database has moved to the Front End Servers and is replicated between Front End Servers, impacting storage I/O and memory utilization.

29

The physical hardware recommendations laid out by Microsoft give us an indication of the processing, memory, storage, and network performance required to deliver good Lync Server 2013 performance. Their hardware recommendations are scaled for 6,600 users per Lync 2013 Front End Server based on their user model data. It is important to understand that virtualization is not going to magically reduce this processing, memory, and storage requirement. In fact, virtualization is actually adding overhead in comparison to deploying directly onto physical hardware. This overhead is estimated at around 10% of performance, assuming that all hardware is specified as per a physical deployment.

There are good reasons for virtualizing Lync Server 2013:

▶ It deploys the Lync deployment onto the existing virtual host infrastructure (often reducing deployment time).

▶ It complies with a strategy of virtualizing all servers, allowing for consistent management and support.

▶ It enables the Lync deployment to be easily migrated to a different physical infrastructure in the future (offline migration).

▶ It can allow virtualization-level backup options.

▶ It reduces the number of physical servers, and associated heat, power, and space costs.

Reducing the amount of hardware required or costs is not a primary goal of virtualizing Lync Server 2013.

Lync Server 2013 Virtual Machine Recommendations

This section details the virtual hardware requirements for Lync Server 2013 virtual guest machines. At the time of writing, Microsoft's guidance for Lync Server 2013 is that virtual hardware should match physical hardware recommendations. All other variables being equal, you can expect around a 10% performance impact (so at least 10% reduction in supported users) on a virtual deployment.

Processor Recommendations

In Lync Server 2010 there was a support limitation of four vCPUs per virtual Lync server, even though eight cores were recommended for a physical Lync 2010 Server. This limitation stemmed from Windows Server 2008 R2 Hyper-V supporting only four vCPUs per guest machine (and therefore Microsoft tested for support only to this level). This was the primary reason for virtualized Lync Server 2010 being specified to support approximately half the number of users of a physical server.

With Windows Server 2012 this Hyper-V limitation is removed (Server 2013 Hyper-V guests can now support up to 64 virtual CPUs), and as such the 4 vCPU supportability limitation on Lync Server 2013 is also removed.

Lync Server 2013 Front End Servers, Backend SQL Servers, Standard Edition Servers, and Persistent Chat Servers are recommended to have six cores. Edge Servers, standalone Mediation Servers, and Directors can have four cores.

The high core count is because processing media requires many CPU cycles. Microsoft recommends dedicating logical cores to each virtual machine, and not overcommitting the cores assigned to Lync Server 2013 Servers. Where possible, use of Media Bypass will reduce the processing load on Front End servers with collocated Mediation Servers.

Memory Recommendations

Lync Server 2013 Front End Servers, Backend SQL Servers, Standard Edition Servers, and Persistent Chat Servers are recommended to have 32GB of RAM. Edge Servers, Standalone Mediation Servers, and Directors are recommended to have 16GB of RAM.

Lync Server 2013 memory requirements do not scale in a linear way. Servers can operate with less RAM, but you are at the risk of falling outside the support boundary.

Storage Recommendations

Disk recommendations for physical servers include using eight or more 10,000 RPM hard disk drives with at least 72GB free disk space, or solid-state drives (SSDs) that provide performance similar to eight 10,000 RPM mechanical disk drives. You are looking to replicate this level of performance, but remember that this is the performance specified per server; so if your host server has four Lync Server virtual machines on, your storage needs to provide this level of performance per virtual machine to reach the suggested user numbers. Capacity sizing recommendations are as per physical deployments.

Virtual Disk Types—Fixed, Dynamic, and Pass-through

When you are creating a virtual machine, options exist to create a hard disk for the VM as a fixed size or dynamically expanding. In VMware, the dynamically expanding disk is referred to as thin provisioning. The difference is that with a fixed-size disk, the space allocated to a virtual machine is immediately accounted for on the host operating system disk volume. For instance, if the host has 500GB of free disk space and a 100GB fixed-size disk is created, the host reflects 400GB of free space. Dynamically expanding disks differ in that a maximum size is specified that the disk can grow to, but the space is not immediately consumed. Continuing the previous example, the virtual machine still believes it has a 100GB hard disk, but space on the host physical disk is consumed only as the virtual machine begins to write data to the disk. The virtual disk is negligible at first, but it might consume 10GB of space after an operating system is installed, and more when applications and data are added.

A third type of option in disk configuration for virtual machines is to use pass-through disks. Pass-through disks present a physical hard disk directly to a virtual machine. This configuration is not as typical for small environments, but where performance must be guaranteed, and resources are not shared with other virtual machines, pass-through disks are an attractive option.

29

For Lync and SQL Servers, Microsoft recommends using either fixed-size disks or pass-through disks, not to use dynamic disks, due to the potential performance overhead in production.

Network Recommendations

Each virtual machine running a Lync Server 2013 role should have at least one virtual network adapter added. Edge Servers require at least two virtual adapters (as with a physical installation). It is recommended that physical adapters be dedicated to the virtual machines, to avoid the impact of sharing network interface cards.

Synthetic Device Drivers

Both the Hyper-V and the VMware virtualization products contain emulated and synthetic device drivers. Emulated drivers were the original approach to virtualization; in this approach each hard disk or network adapter assigned to a virtual machine is emulated in software. The advantage of emulated drivers is that almost all operating systems contain support for these drivers because the network adapter driver emulates a baseline set of capabilities. Synthetic drivers are used to provide an additional level of performance and capabilities within a virtual machine such as jumbo frames or TCP offloading features.

With Lync Server 2013, deployments always use a synthetic network adapter to achieve the best possible performance.

Virtual Machine Queue

Virtual Machine Queue (VMQ) is a network adapter feature that provides some performance benefit in a virtualized environment. VMQ enables the physical network adapter to provide virtual queues for each virtual machine running on the host. This enables the hypervisor to pass external traffic directly to each virtual machine without routing through the management operating system first. This feature should not be confused with Virtual Machine Chimney, which is a separate function that provides TCP offloading features from the guest virtual CPU to the physical network adapter.

If the adapters used on a host machine allow this feature, it should be enabled for optimal performance in Lync Server 2013. Because media traffic is extremely sensitive to latency or delays, any optimizations at the network layer can lead to increased virtual machine performance. Adapters do not support an unlimited number of virtual machine queues, so VMQ should be enabled only for virtual machines that receive a heavy amount of traffic.

> **NOTE**
>
> Early versions of driver software that supported VMQ automatically disabled VMQ if an adapter used for virtual machines was placed in a network team. If you run an older version of the driver, be sure to update to the latest release to enable both teaming and VMQ to function.

SR-IOV

With SR-IOV, the control and management of a physical network adapter can be assigned directly to a virtual machine. This reduces I/O overhead and increases performance. SR-IOV is recommended.

VMware includes a feature called VMDirectPath, which gives a virtual machine direct access to the physical adapters.

Send/Receive Buffers

Microsoft recommends adjusting the send and receive buffers on any network adapter dedicated to virtual machines to be a value of at least 1024. This helps to improve network performance and reduces the number of dropped packets.

MPIO (Multipath I/O)

MPIO provides increased performance and fault tolerance by allowing more than one path between servers and storage. If nondirect attached storage is used, MPIO is recommended.

Guest Virtual Machine Operating System Requirements

Windows Server 2008 R2 and Windows Server 2012 are both supported as the guest operating system for Lync Server 2013 guests. It is strongly recommended to have Windows Server 2012 as the guest operating system, because it has several performance benefits for a virtualized environment.

As with a physical host server, the Lync virtual machines should not run any additional applications or services, because these can impact performance. Any antivirus applications should be configured to exclude the location of any Lync Server 2013 binary files, database files and the Lync service executables.

Host Server Hardware Recommendations

When virtualization of Lync Servers is being planned, the virtual host server hardware and configuration have a direct effect on how well the virtual machine guests can perform. You have seen from the Lync Server 2013 guest specifications that there are some pretty specific requirements in terms of hardware and performance. This section summarizes some of the support requirements and performance recommendations to follow when you are specifying a host server. Most of these requirements are based around treating each Lync virtual machine as if it were a physical server with its own dedicated processor, memory, disk, and network adapter. In many deployments it will make sense to have dedicated hardware for the virtual deployment to meet the specific hardware requirements.

Processor Recommendations

Any host used for Lync virtual machines should have a modern Enterprise-class CPU, which is considered to be 2.26GHz or faster. From a planning perspective, the number of cores on the processor determines the maximum number of virtual machines that can run

29

on the host. To fall within the Lync support boundaries, each virtual machine must have dedicated CPU cores. Therefore, the more cores you have available, the more Lync Servers you can place on a single host.

The number of cores is the important value here, not the number of physical processors. For example, two quad-core processors are equivalent to four dual-core processors. Both yield eight physical cores that can be used by virtual machines. Typically a host will have at least two physical CPUs.

About Hyper-threading

Hyper-threading enables a server to split a single physical core into two logical processors. Again, there is no magic here; this does not double your performance. There is no explicit supportability statement around hyper-threading for Lync, but general guidance is that hyper-threading is not equivalent to dedicated cores.

> **NOTE**
>
> The host server operating systems/virtualization platform is not going to consume many CPU cycles, so for planning purposes in most cases it is acceptable to ignore trying to dedicate a core to the host. If cores for the host were included, everyone would wind up with an odd number of CPU cores.

Memory Recommendations

You can see from the virtual guest requirements that a reasonable amount of RAM is required to meet the needs of the Lync Servers. This memory should be allocated exclusively for each Lync virtual machine. Fortunately, memory is relatively cheap these days. It is recommended to assume that the host OS will occupy around 4GB.

Microsoft does not list a recommended memory for a host machine, but look at your number of cores and virtual machine memory requirements to determine the amount of RAM per host server. The "sweet spot" for amount of RAM for the money is ever changing, but as with all hardware, more is always better; and particularly with database-intensive applications such as Lync, you do not want to be scrimping on memory.

PC3-8500 DDR3 or above speed memory is recommended.

Dynamic Memory/Memory Overcommit

Windows Server 2008 R2 Hyper-V Service Pack 1 and above has a new feature called dynamic memory that allows defining startup and maximum RAM values for a virtual machine. This feature should not be used with Lync Server 2013. Likewise, virtual machines that run on VMware should not be overcommitted on memory. These features cannot be used with Lync and have a negative impact on performance.

Storage Requirements

The actual space consumed by Lync virtual machines varies by role and by business requirements. Typically, 72GB free space is recommended. Lync Back-End database servers hosting a Monitoring or Archiving database are going to consume much more space than a Front End or Edge Server.

Both direct attached storage (DAS) and SAN disks are supported to hold Lync virtual machines. Which option is used depends greatly on the infrastructure that an organization already has in place. SAN provisioning is generally more flexible, but there is a significant upfront cost to these types of systems. DAS storage can be more affordable and yield acceptable performance for virtual machines. Because Lync Server 2013 now uses SQL Mirroring on the backend rather than SQL clustering, there is no shared storage requirement for the backend SQL.

Another consideration for organizations is whether to use a single RAID volume for all virtual machines or to separate each virtual machine disk onto its own physical hard disk. There is no requirement for separate disk spindles, but the best performance is realized if each virtual machine disk can be placed on a dedicated hard disk spindle. The downside to dedicated disks is that unless the disk count is doubled, there is no redundancy at the physical disk level. Many organizations find that placing virtual hard disks on a RAID 1+0 or RAID 5 volume meets the disk requirements of most virtual machines.

Storage I/O performance will be key for virtual hosts. Consider the server roles you have and their combined I/O requirements. The general rule of thumb is that the more spindles there are, and the faster the disks, the better.

> **NOTE**
>
> Separating the disks used for the host operating system can show a performance benefit for both the host and the guest VMs. A common configuration for host machines is to use two hard disks in a RAID 1 mirror set for redundancy, and then provision the remaining number of disks in a RAID 1+0 or RAID 5 configuration for virtual machine storage. This way, the host reads and writes do not compete with the virtual machine hard disk activity.

Network Requirements

Two or more 1GbE or 10GbE adapters are required. Again, consider the combined I/O of your virtual machines; sizing for total throughput is important. Virtual Machine Queue and SR-IOV are recommended.

In Lync Server 2010, there was a fairly strict suggestion from Microsoft that a dedicated network adapter should be used for each Lync virtual machine. As 10GbE network adapters have become more common, it is increasingly challenging to dedicate network cards to specific virtual machines.

In a traditional virtualization environment, most virtual machines share traffic through a single or teamed set of physical network adapters. Virtual machines compete for network bandwidth resources through the same physical links and can be subject to delays or queues when other virtual machines have heavy bursts of traffic. If shared network cards must be used, a level of hypervisor QoS should be utilized to ensure that Lync Server roles are provided with adequate bandwidth at all times.

29

> **CAUTION**
>
> To avoid Lync Servers being affected by these contention issues, Microsoft recommends providing a dedicated physical adapter for each Lync virtual machine. This ensures that each Lync Server has a direct connection to a switch that can help eliminate jitter or delay problems encountered when adapters are being shared.

Hypervisor Requirements

As indicated previously, the only supported hypervisors today are Microsoft Windows Server 2008 R2 Hyper-V, Windows Server 2012 Hyper-V, and VMware vSphere 5. Additional hypervisor support might become available later as vendors certify their platform with Microsoft. For Microsoft, either the full or the core installation of Windows Server 2008 R2 or Windows Server 2012 can be used. The standalone, free product Microsoft Hyper-V R2 and Microsoft Hyper-V 2012 can also be used to virtualize Lync Servers. On the VMware, both the ESX and the ESXi platforms can be used.

> **CAUTION**
>
> Do not run additional applications or services on servers that host the operating system. These applications or services have processing, memory, and network requirements that might have an adverse effect on virtual machines. In addition, ensure that any antivirus application is properly configured, on a virtual host or guest. Antivirus applications can have a serious performance effect on virtual machines.

Lync Server 2013 Sample Virtual Topologies

There are various ways you can deploy a virtual Lync Server 2013 infrastructure. This section attempts to give some sample Lync 2013 Standard Edition and Enterprise Edition deployment topologies for the reader to consider. In each deployment it is assumed that the Office Web Apps Server role is not already deployed and is required as part of the Lync virtual deployment. If there is an existing Office Web Apps server or sever pool, this requirement can be removed.

These topologies do not consider gateways or Session Border Controllers (SBCs) for PSTN access, which are usually physical devices alongside these topologies.

> **TIP**
>
> Proper performance and load testing should be completed with any scenario before the deployment is placed in production.

Single-Host Server Deployment

This topology provides a simple pilot or very small deployment. This topology is primarily geared toward smaller deployments with no need for redundancy or proof-of-concept scenarios in which rapid deployment is a priority. There is no high-availability or backup pool. A single Lync Standard Edition Server and a single SharePoint Office Web Apps server are deployed on a single host as shown in Figure 29.4.

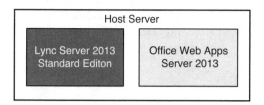

FIGURE 29.4   Single-host server deployment.

There is the potential here to specify the host with enough power (move to dual physical CPU and add RAM) to also run the Lync Edge and Reverse Proxy role, allowing a complete Lync deployment on one physical server, with the inside and outside networks running on different network interface cards. In reality it is rare for organizations to accept that it is secure practice to have a hypervisor as the only barrier between DMZ and internal servers.

If monitoring or archiving are required, a separate Microsoft SQL server would be required to store the data. To summarize, an example host could use the following hardware configuration:

Host Server Configuration

▶ Windows Server 2012 with Hyper-V

▶ 2.26GHz or higher CPU with 10 cores

▶ 48GB RAM

▶ 500GB SAS 10K disks with eight spindles

▶ Four 1Gb network adapters

Guest Configuration

Lync Server 2013 Standard Edition:

▶ Six CPU cores

▶ 32GB RAM

▶ Dedicated 1GB network adapter

Office Web Apps Server 2013:

▶ Four CPU cores

▶ 12GB RAM

▶ Dedicated 1GB network adapter

Small Business Deployment

This topology provides a great value deployment. With Lync Server 2013 pool pairing and resilient Office Web App Servers, you can afford to lose an entire host and quickly recover full functionality. DMZ Host 1 can be physically placed in the DMZ. High-availability of the Edge Server or reverse proxy can be achieved with a second DMZ of the same specification as shown in Figure 29.5.

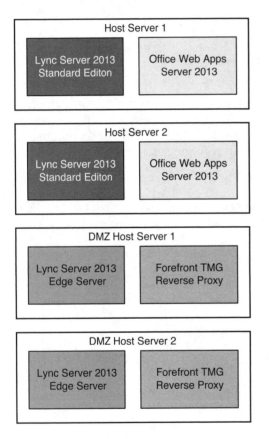

Host Server 1

Lync Server 2013 Standard Editon

Office Web Apps Server 2013

Host Server 2

Lync Server 2013 Standard Editon

Office Web Apps Server 2013

DMZ Host Server 1

Lync Server 2013 Edge Server

Forefront TMG Reverse Proxy

DMZ Host Server 2

Lync Server 2013 Edge Server

Forefront TMG Reverse Proxy

FIGURE 29.5   Small-business deployment.

Although no load balancer is required for Lync Web Services in the Standard Edition model, a load balancer (hardware or software) will be required for the high-availability of the Office Web Apps Server. If the hosts are specified appropriately, a virtual load-balancer appliance could be added to host servers 1 and 2. The requirements on DMZ Host 1 are less so it can be a lower specification physical server. If monitoring or archiving is required, a separate Microsoft SQL server would be required to store the data. A small business deployment could use the following hardware configuration:

Host Servers 1 and 2 Configuration:

- ▶ Windows Server 2012 with Hyper-V
- ▶ 2.26GHz or higher CPU with 10 cores
- ▶ 48GB RAM
- ▶ 500GB SAS 10K disks with eight spindles
- ▶ Four 1GB network adapters

Host Servers 1 and 2, Guest Configuration:

Lync Server 2013 Standard Edition:

- ▶ Six CPU cores
- ▶ 32GB RAM
- ▶ Dedicated 1GB network adapter

Office Web Apps Server 2013:

- ▶ Four CPU cores
- ▶ 12GB RAM
- ▶ Dedicated 1GB network adapter

DMZ Host 1 Configuration:

- ▶ Windows Server 2012 with Hyper-V
- ▶ 2.26GHz or higher CPU with six cores
- ▶ 32GB RAM
- ▶ 500GB SAS 10K disks, eight spindles
- ▶ Four 1Gb network adapters

DMZ Host 1, Guest Configuration:

Lync Server 2013 Edge Server:

- ▶ Four CPU cores
- ▶ 16GB RAM
- ▶ Two dedicated 1GB network adapters

Forefront TMG Reverse Proxy:

▶ Two CPU cores

▶ 8GB RAM

▶ Dedicated 1GB network adapter

DMZ Host 2 Configuration:

▶ Windows Server 2012 with Hyper-V

▶ 2.26GHz or higher CPU with six cores

▶ 32GB RAM

▶ 500GB SAS 10K disks, eight spindles

▶ Four 1Gb network adapters

DMZ Host 2, Guest Configuration:

Lync Server 2013 Edge Server:

▶ Four CPU cores

▶ 16GB RAM

▶ Two dedicated 1GB network adapters

Forefront TMG Reverse Proxy:

▶ Two CPU cores

▶ 8GB RAM

▶ Dedicated 1GB network adapter

Small Highly Available Deployment

This topology moves us to Lync 2013 Enterprise Edition. This means you can scale to a higher number of users, and get true high-availability. You now require a load balancer for both Lync Web Services and Office Web Apps. With Lync Enterprise Edition and Backend SQL Mirroring, you can lose a host and have high-availability for user services with no administrative intervention. With Lync Server 2010 this topology would have required shared storage due to SQL clustering. With SQL Mirroring in Lync Server 2013, this deployment can work with direct attached storage.

DMZ Hosts 1 and 2 can be physically placed in the DMZ. The Lync Edge Servers can be polled and TMG Servers paired to provide high-availability in the event of a DMZ host failure, as shown in Figure 29.6.

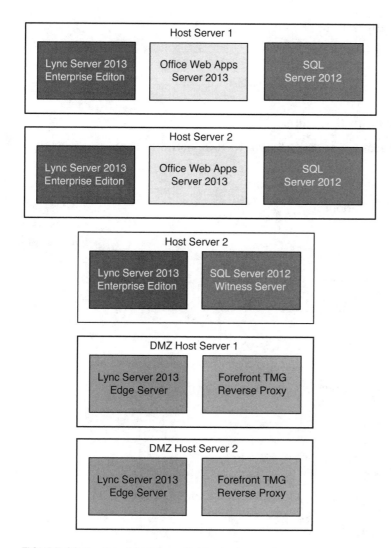

FIGURE 29.6   Small highly available deployment.

There is a fine line between this topology and the dual Standard Edition topology. The Enterprise Edition topology incurs the extra SQL and hardware costs, but is potentially scalable simply with the addition of more Front End Servers.

TIP

It is recommended to have three Front End Servers in a pool in Lync Server 2013, so ideally one of the two hosts would be specified to have two Front End Servers. However, if you lose the host with two Front End Servers, the third server will stop its services due to quorum loss. In this scenario you can use two Front End servers per physical host and the active SQL node will provide the final quorum vote.

29

Host Servers 1 and 2 Configuration:

▶ Windows Server 2012 with Hyper-V

▶ Dual 2.26GHz or higher CPU with 20 cores

▶ 96GB RAM

▶ 500GB SAS 10K disks with 16 spindles

▶ Eight 1Gb network adapters or multiple teamed 10Gb network adapters

Host Servers 1 and 2, Guest Configuration:

Lync Server 2013 Enterprise Edition:

▶ Six CPU cores

▶ 32GB RAM

▶ Dedicated 1GB network adapter or equivalent allocated network bandwidth

Microsoft SQL Server 2012:

▶ Six CPU cores

▶ 32GB RAM

▶ Dedicated 1GB network adapter or equivalent allocated network bandwidth

Office Web Apps Server 2013:

▶ Four CPU cores

▶ 12GB RAM

▶ Dedicated 1GB network adapter equivalent allocated network bandwidth

Host Server 3 Configuration:

▶ Windows Server 2012 with Hyper-V

▶ Dual 2.26GHz or higher CPU with 8 cores

▶ 48GB RAM

▶ 500GB SAS 10K disks with 8 spindles

▶ Four 1Gb network adapters or multiple teamed 10Gb network adapters

Host Server 3, Guest Configuration:

Lync Server 2013 Enterprise Edition:

► Six CPU cores

► 32GB RAM

► Dedicated 1GB network adapter or equivalent allocated network bandwidth

Microsoft SQL Server 2012 Witness Server:

► Two CPU cores

► 4GB RAM

► Dedicated 1GB network adapter or equivalent allocated network bandwidth

DMZ Host 1 and 2 configuration:

► Windows Server 2012 with Hyper-V

► 2.26GHz or higher CPU with eight cores

► 32GB RAM

► 500GB SAS 10K disks with eight spindles

► Four network adapters

DMZ Host 1 and 2, Guest Configuration:

Lync Server 2013 Edge:

► Four CPU cores

► 16GB RAM

► Two dedicated 1GB network adapters

Forefront TMG Reverse Proxy:

► Four CPU cores

► 8GB RAM

► Dedicated 1GB network adapter

Enterprise Deployment

In Lync Server 2013, the architecture of a large Enterprise Edition deployment has become much simpler. There are no Archiving, Monitoring, or A/V Conferencing Servers to deploy because all are now collocated and Director is now officially an optional role. In

29

a large virtualized deployment, you scale to four host servers and split out the SQL for Monitoring and Archiving to a dedicated virtual machine for performance reasons. At this scale it is likely Office Web Apps servers would have their own dedicated infrastructure. Although Directors are optional, they have been included because typically they are required for security reasons at this scale of deployment. This architecture is shown in Figure 29.7.

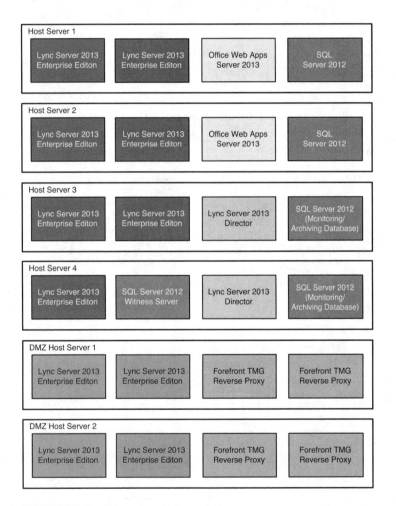

FIGURE 29.7   Enterprise deployment.

Host Servers 1–4 Configuration:

▶ Windows Server 2012 with Hyper-V

▶ Dual 2.26GHz or higher CPU with 24 cores

▶ 128GB RAM

▶ 500GB SAS 15K disks with 16 spindles, or equivalent SAN storage

▶ Eight 1Gb network adapters or multiple teamed 10Gb network adapters

Host Servers 1–3, Guest Configuration:

Lync Server 2013 Enterprise Edition:

▶ Six CPU cores

▶ 32GB RAM

▶ Dedicated 1GB network adapter or equivalent allocated network bandwidth

Lync Server 2013 Director:

▶ Four CPU cores

▶ 16GB RAM

▶ Dedicated 1GB network adapter or equivalent allocated network bandwidth

Microsoft SQL Server 2012:

▶ Six CPU cores

▶ 32GB RAM

▶ Dedicated 1GB network adapter or equivalent allocated network bandwidth

Office Web Apps Server 2013:

▶ Four CPU cores

▶ 12GB RAM

▶ Dedicated 1GB network adapter equivalent allocated network bandwidth

Host Server 4 Configuration:

▶ Windows Server 2012 with Hyper-V

▶ Dual 2.26GHz or higher CPU with 24 cores

▶ 96GB RAM

▶ 500GB SAS 15K disks with 16 spindles, or equivalent SAN storage

▶ Eight 1Gb network adapters or multiple teamed 10Gb network adapters

29

Host Server 4, Guest Configuration:

Lync Server 2013 Enterprise Edition:

▶ Six CPU cores

▶ 32GB RAM

▶ Dedicated 1GB network adapter or equivalent allocated network bandwidth

Lync Server 2013 Director:

▶ Four CPU cores

▶ 16GB RAM

▶ Dedicated 1GB network adapter or equivalent allocated network bandwidth

Microsoft SQL Server 2012 Witness Server:

▶ Two CPU cores

▶ 4GB RAM

▶ Dedicated 1GB network adapter or equivalent allocated network bandwidth

Microsoft SQL Server 2012:

▶ Six CPU cores

▶ 32GB RAM

▶ Dedicated 1GB network adapter or equivalent allocated network bandwidth

DMZ Host Server 1 and 2 Configuration:

▶ Windows Server 2012 with Hyper-V

▶ 2.26GHz or higher CPU with 20 cores

▶ 64GB RAM

▶ 500GB SAS 10K disks with eight spindles

▶ Eight 1Gb network adapters

DMZ Host Server 1 and 2, Guest Configuration:

Lync Server 2013 Edge:

▶ Four CPU cores

▶ 16GB RAM

▶ Two dedicated 1GB network adapters

Forefront TMG Reverse Proxy:

▶ Four CPU cores

▶ 8GB RAM

▶ Dedicated 1GB network adapter

Sample Topology Considerations

These topologies provide some general guidance, but organizations ultimately need to design a virtualized solution that works best for them. These topologies provide a starting point, but should be taken with consideration and adjusted to meet the needs of each organization instead of simply reusing the sample topologies. There are a few key considerations for your virtual topology, and they are discussed in this section.

Guest Placement

It is important to not place all the guests of a specific type on a single host. If you do, a failure of that host could bring down the entire pool, for example, if you located all your Front End Servers on a single host. Also consider the user impact on the loss of a single host. For example, if you have three Front End Servers on one host and one Front End Server on another, the loss of the host with three Front End Servers will cause the entire pool to come down.

Disk Layout and Storage Performance

As you scale the number of hosts on a virtual machine, you must scale storage performance. Understand that different disk types and RAID setups provide different performance profiles. If a single disk in a RAID 0 array fails, the entire array is lost, and all virtual machine disks on that array are unavailable. Using a redundant disk configuration such as RAID 5 or RAID 1+0 for most host servers offers some redundancy but with slightly reduced performance.

Collocating DMZ Roles with Internal Roles

It would be normal for Edge Servers and reverse proxies to be on a dedicated DMZ host. This is because the Edge Server is designed to sit in a perimeter network surrounded by firewalls on both sides.

In reality, some smaller organizations will probably deploy Edge Servers on the same host as other virtual machines. With the capability to tag individual virtual machine adapters with a specific VLAN, the perimeter network traffic can be directed to only the adapters assigned to Edge Servers. Of course, this means the perimeter network traffic passes through the host hypervisor at some level. Of course, the proper firewall rules should be in place to protect both the host and the guest operating systems. However, it continues to be best practice to have a dedicated DMZ host or hosts.

Testing and Measuring Performance

With all deployments, but particularly virtual deployments, performance testing should be done before deployment to ensure that the infrastructure meets the performance objectives. Due to potential changes in the environment (additional servers being added to hosts, or to backend storage, for example), performance should continue to be monitored in production. In particular, paying attention to the following performance counters is valuable:

▶ Processor; % Processor Time (_Total)

▶ Process; % Processor Time (RtcSrv)

▶ Process; % Processor Time (IMMcuSvc)

▶ Memory; Pages/sec ---

▶ Network Interface; Bytes Total/sec ([your network adapter])

Further details of Lync Server role-specific performance monitoring counters can be found in TechNet documentation.

Client and Desktop Virtualization

A popular shift in desktop deployment has been the concept of virtual desktops or using host servers to provide virtual machines for desktop users (virtual desktop infrastructure), which are accessed through some kind of thin client.

There are many different products and technologies to achieve this client virtualization. The issue with many of these deployments is a lack of media support. In Lync 2010 there was no option supported by Microsoft that allowed audio or video in a virtual client deployment. With Lync 2013 there is now an option of virtual desktop support with an API to enable all virtual desktop vendors to support audio and video in Lync within a virtual desktop. This involves running a plugin on the thin terminal, which must be running Windows 7 Embedded or above. Audio and video are then streamed directly from the client, while the user controls the client from within the virtual desktop.

The Lync 2013 Virtual Desktop plugin is explained in more detail in Chapter 27, "Lync and VDI."

Summary

There is little doubt that virtualized deployments will continue to be popular with Lync Server 2013. However, it is important to remember that Lync Server is dealing with real-time traffic and some intense workloads and should be carefully architected to ensure good performance. It should also be remembered that just because virtualization is currently popular, and supported by Lync Server 2013, does not automatically mean it is the correct deployment model. Requirements such as dedicated logical processors and network adapters are not typical in virtual environments, so companies might find themselves having to deploy new hardware specifically for Lync Server 2013 even in a virtual deployment.

Although there are some restrictions and many considerations, using the information in this chapter should enable an organization to effectively plan for and successfully deploy Lync Server 2013 in a virtualized topology.

Best Practices

The following are best practices from this chapter:

▶ Use a supported hypervisor for Lync Server 2013 virtual machines such as Windows Server 2012 Hyper-V or VMware vSphere 5.0.

▶ Use Windows Server 2012 as the guest operating system for any Lync Server 2013 virtual machine.

▶ Allocate dedicated cores, memory, and physical network adapter(s) for each Lync Server virtual machine.

▶ Stress test the virtual environment and monitor the Lync performance counters before placing the system in production.

▶ Do not use Live Migration or vMotion/DRS for Lync Server virtual machines.

▶ Use the VMQ feature if available.

▶ Use Single-Root I/O Virtualization if available.

▶ Continue to monitor performance when in production.

29

Planning for Basic Lync Services

W hen you are deploying a potentially complex application like Microsoft's Lync Server 2013, it is critical to plan the deployment before the build in order to optimize the chances for a successful deployment. By planning the features to deploy and by determining the capacity needed and what hardware and software are necessary to support that capacity, you can avoid the pitfalls of deploying off the cuff and potentially having to make major changes to the architecture midway through a build or, worse yet, midway through a deployment to the users.

Before reading this chapter, you should be familiar with the various roles and tools involved in Lync Server 2013. You should understand the basics of Lync Server topologies, sites, and server pools. If you are not yet familiar with these items, review those sections of this book before proceeding with the upcoming planning chapters.

Determining the Scope of the Deployment

Lync Server 2013 contains such a wealth of features that planning a deployment, even a limited one, can seem quite daunting at first. This section provides some guidance to assist with the process and assist administrators in creating a well-thought-out and well-structured implementation plan.

Rather than forging ahead with no plan or goals and simply building new servers, loading application software, and inserting them into an existing network environment, you should implement a more organized process to control the risks involved and define in detail what the end state will look like.

The first steps involve getting a better sense of the scope of the project—in essence, writing the executive summary of the design document. The scope should define from a high level what the project consists of and why the organization is devoting time, energy, and resources to its completion.

Creating this scope of work requires an understanding of the different goals of the organization, as well as the pieces of the puzzle that need to fit together to meet the company's stated goals for the project. For Lync Server 2013, this means understanding how the various parts of the business will use the new functionality to improve collaboration and real-time communication. Different groups will focus on different aspects, such as IM with federated partners, or on leveraging video conferencing for departmental meetings. Understanding the needs of the various groups is key to a successful deployment.

Identifying the Business Goals and Objectives to Implement Lync Server 2013

It is important to establish a thorough understanding of the goals and objectives of a company that guide and direct the efforts of the different components of the organization, to help ensure the success of the Lync Server 2013 project.

> **NOTE**
>
> It might seem counterintuitive to start at such a high level and keep away from the bits-and-bytes-level details; however, time spent in this area will clarify the purposes of the project and start to generate productive discussions.

As an example of the value of setting high-level business goals and objectives, an organization can identify the desire for zero downtime on IM and conferencing services. Starting with the broad goals and objectives creates an outline for a technical solution that will meet all the organization's criteria, at a lower cost and with a more easily managed solution.

In every organization, various goals and objectives need to be identified and met for a project to be considered successful. These goals and objectives represent a snapshot of the end state that the company or organization is seeking to create. For a smaller company, this process might be completed in a few brainstorming sessions, whereas larger companies might require more extensive discussions and assistance from external resources or firms.

High-Level Business Goals

To start the organizational process, it is helpful to break up business goals and objectives into different levels, or vantage points. Most organizations have high-level business goals, often referred to as the vision of the company, which is typically shaped by the key decision makers in the organization (the CEO, CFO, CIO, and so on); these goals are commonly called the 50,000-foot view. Business unit or departmental goals, or the 10,000-foot view, are typically shaped by the key executives and managers in the organization (the VP of sales, Director of Human Resources, site facilities manager, and so on).

Most organizations also have well-defined 1,000-foot-view goals that typically are tactical in nature and are implemented by IT staff and technical specialists.

It is well worth the time to perform research and ask the right questions to help ensure that the Lync Server 2013 implementation will be successful. To get specific information and clarification of the objectives of the different business units, make sure that the goals of a technology implementation or upgrade are in line with the business goals.

Although most organizations have stated company visions and goals, and a quick visit to the company's website or intranet can provide this information, it is worth taking the time to gather more information on what the key stakeholders feel to be their primary objectives. Often, this task starts with asking the right questions of the right people and then opening discussion groups on the topic. Of course, it also matters who asks the questions because the answers will vary accordingly, and employees might be more forthcoming when speaking with external consultants as opposed to co-workers. Often, the publicly stated vision and goals are the tip of the iceberg and might even be in contrast to internal company goals, ambitions, or initiatives.

High-level business goals and visions can vary greatly among different organizations, but generally they bracket and guide the goals of the units that make up the company. For example, a corporation might be interested in offering the best product in its class, and this requires corresponding goals for the sales, engineering, marketing, finance, and manufacturing departments. Additional concepts include whether the highest-level goals embrace change and new ideas and processes or want to refine the existing practices and methods.

High-level business goals of a company can also change rapidly, whether in response to changing economic conditions or as affected by a new key stakeholder or leader in the company. So it is also important to get a sense of the timeline involved for meeting these high-level goals.

> **NOTE**
>
> Examples of some high-level business goals include a desire to have zero downtime, access to the communications infrastructure from anywhere in the world, and secure communications when accessed inside or outside the office.

Business Unit or Departmental Goals

When the vision or 50,000-foot view is defined, additional discussions should reveal the goals of the different departments and the executives who run them. Theoretically, they should add up to the highest-level goals, but the findings might be surprising. Whatever the case turns out to be, the results will start to reveal the complexity of the organization and the primary concerns of the different stakeholders.

The high-level goals of the organization also paint the picture of which departments carry the most weight in the organization, and will most likely get budgets approved, which will assist in the design process. Logically, the goals of the IT department play an important role in a Lync Server 2013 deployment project, but the other key departments shouldn't be forgotten.

> **NOTE**
>
> As an example of the business unit or departmental goals for an organization, an HR department might typically influence the decision for right-to-privacy access to core personnel records. Or a legal department might typically influence security access on information storage rights and storage retention. These groups will prove invaluable when discussing topics such as archiving and whether to allow integration with public IM infrastructures.
>
> If the department's goals are not aligned with the overall vision of the company, or don't take into account the needs of the key stakeholders, the result of the project might not be appreciated. Technology for technology's sake does not always fulfill the needs of the organization and in the long run is viewed as a wasteful expenditure of organizational funds.

In the process of clarifying the goals, the features of the collaboration system and network applications that are most important to the different departments and executives should be apparent. It is safe to assume that access to collaboration and presentation tools as well as the capability to rapidly communicate with one another will affect the company's ability to meet its various business goals.

The sales department most likely has goals that require a specific type of communication to be supported and will likely push hard for an optimal conferencing experience. The IT department has its key technologies that support the applications in use, store and maintain the company's data, and manage key servers and network devices, and these need to be taken into consideration to ensure that Lync Server 2013 follows practices similar to those of existing systems.

It is also worth looking for the holes in the goals and objectives presented. Some of the less-glamorous objectives, such as a stable network, data-recovery capabilities, and protection from the hostile outside world, are often neglected.

A byproduct of these discussions will ideally be a sense of excitement over the possibilities presented by the new technologies that will be introduced, and will convey to the executives and key stakeholders that they are involved in helping to define and craft a solution that takes into account the varied needs of the company. Many executives look for this high-level strategy, thinking, and discussions to reveal the maturity of the planning and implementation process in action.

> **NOTE**
>
> Examples of some departmental goals include a desire to have an integrated address book that enables them to quickly add contacts for partner companies, the capability to add web-based conferencing to meeting requests, and the capability to participate in video conferences from home.

Determining Your Infrastructure Needs

To build a successful Lync Server 2013 infrastructure to support basic functions such as instant messaging, web conferencing, and group chat, these services need to be built on a stable infrastructure. In other words, the services outside of Lync Server 2013 need to be healthy, available, and of sufficient performance to take on the added load of Lync Server 2013. It is also important to plan the hardware that will be used to support Lync Server 2013 and ensure that it is capable of supporting the new environment.

Planning for Hardware and Software

Although many basic implementations of Lync Server 2013 will be virtualized, both physical and virtual servers used for Lync Server 2013 must meet a few standards. Keep these in mind when planning a Lync Server 2013 deployment.

From a hardware perspective, the following specifications are recommended as a minimum for Lync Server 2013. It is important to note that this specification holds true for all Lync server roles except the backend database.

▶ **CPU**—64-bit, dual quad core, 2.0GHz or higher

▶ **Memory**—16GB

▶ **Disk**—Two or more 10,000 rpm hard disk drives with at least 100GB usable space

▶ **Network**—A 1Gbps network adapter, except for the Edge Server role, for which four 1Gbps network adapters are recommended

From an operating system perspective, plan to use one of the following operating systems to support Lync Server 2013:

▶ Windows Server 2008 R2 with Service Pack 1 (SP1) Standard (required) or latest service pack (recommended)

▶ Windows Server 2008 R2 with SP1 Enterprise (required) or latest service pack (recommended)

▶ Windows Server 2008 R2 with SP1 Datacenter (required) or latest service pack (recommended)

▶ Windows Server 2012 Standard

▶ Windows Server 2012 Enterprise

▶ Windows Server 2012 Datacenter

Note that Lync Server 2013 is *not* supported on the following platforms:

▶ Server Core installation option of Windows Server 2008 R2 or Windows Server 2012

▶ Windows Web Server 2008 R2 operating system or the Windows Web Server 2012 operating system

▶ Windows Server 2008 R2 HPC Edition or Windows Server 2012 HPC Edition

30

Also, plan for a somewhat standardized build for the operating system for Lync Server 2013 systems. By planning what software and features will and won't be present on the system, you'll find it easier to understand the security implication of the systems and they become easier to support because their configuration is well known to the group supporting them.

> **NOTE**
>
> The individual role chapters in this book, which are Chapters 5 through 10, go into detail on which roles need which features and services, and these should be accounted for in the planning of the deployment.

Planning for Network Infrastructure Requirements

When planning a basic Lync Server 2013 deployment, don't forget to take into account the needs you will have of the network. Take into consideration plans for how servers will be logically deployed when planning for their physical deployment. For example, if multiple Front End Servers are load balanced for redundancy, consider placing them into different physical racks and connecting them to independent power circuits.

> **CAUTION**
>
> Placing all the load-balanced systems into a single rack only increases the possibility of a single event taking out all the systems, thus negating the benefits of load balancing for redundancy.

When planning the requirements for the LAN (local area network) or WAN (wide area network), there might be some deviation between predicted loads and actual observed loads. Take this under consideration when evaluating whether existing network connections will handle the added load of Lync Server 2013.

Use the following rules of thumb for Lync Server 2013 when planning network usage:

▶ Plan for 65Kbps per audio stream and 500Kbps per video stream as peak values.

▶ Bidirectional audio and video sessions count as two streams.

▶ Lync Server media endpoints can adapt to varying network conditions and can usually handle oversubscriptions of up to three times. Although an audio stream peaks its usage at 65Kbps, you can typically run three audio streams in the same 65Kbps without users noticing a drop in quality.

▶ If a site lacks the capacity to comfortably run video streams, consider disabling video for that site.

▶ Expect degraded audio and video performance between endpoints separated by more than 150ms of latency.

While Lync supports QoS through DSCP tagging, it is designed to work well in environments without QoS, such as the Internet. By default, Lync assigns a DSCP value of 40 for voice and video traffic.

Planning for Active Directory Dependencies

Like most Microsoft applications, Lync Server 2013 depends heavily on Active Directory to authenticate users, find server pools, and generally keep data flowing. As such, it is critical to account for this when planning a Lync Server 2013 deployment of any kind. Plan to upgrade legacy domain controllers and be aware that Windows Server 2003 mixed mode is not supported by Lync Server 2013.

One of the best things you can do before a large deployment into Active Directory is to perform an Active Directory health check. This involves reviewing event logs, running tools such as DCDiag and NetDiag, and checking replication health to ensure that the directory itself is healthy and operating correctly.

> **CAUTION**
>
> Failure to realize that the directory itself is unstable or unhealthy greatly increases the chances of running into problems during a deployment of an application such as Lync Server 2013.

Although performing an Active Directory health check is beyond the scope of this chapter, many references are available on the Internet. In addition, Sams offers an e-book on this topic, *Performing an Active Directory Health Check* (ISBN: 0768668425).

Planning for Certificates

One of the more difficult decisions when using public key infrastructure (PKI)–enabled applications, such as Lync Server 2013, is the decision to use internal or public certificates. In this context, internal is defined as coming from a Certificate Authority that is not automatically trusted by the operating system, whereas public means one coming from a Certificate Authority that is already present in the trusted root store of operating systems.

Lync Server 2013 uses certificates for the following purposes:

▶ External or remote user access to audio/video sessions, as well as conferencing and application sharing

▶ Remote user access for instant messaging

▶ Federation using automatic DNS discovery of partners

▶ Mutual Transport Layer Security (MTLS) connections between servers

▶ Transport Layer Security (TLS) connections between client and server

30

Regardless of whether internal or public certificates are used, the following requirements must be met:

▶ All server certificates must support server authentication (Server EKU [1.3.6.1.5.5.7.3.1])

▶ All server certificates must contain a valid and reachable Certificate Revocation List (CRL) Distribution Point (CDP)

▶ Key lengths must be either 1024, 2048, or 4096. Note that 1024-bit keys are not considered secure, so using them is not considered a best practice.

▶ All server certificates must use one of the following hashes:

  ▶ ECDH_P256

  ▶ ECDH_P384

  ▶ ECDH_P512

  ▶ RSA

Various Lync Server 2013 roles have specific needs around the names contained in the certificates. Luckily for administrators, the Certificate Wizard builds the certificate request automatically and accounts for pool names, fully qualified domain names of hosts, and simple URLs such as meet or dial-in that are created as a result of roles and features. The Lync Server 2013 administrator should ensure that the Certificate Authority to be used, whether internal or public, supports subject alternate names.

NOTE

In general, subject alternate name (SAN) certificates are more expensive than traditional single-name certificates. Many public certificate providers charge the same price per name as they do a normal single-name certificate. Other providers offer a flat rate for a SAN certificate and allow the purchaser to insert as many names as will fit into the SAN certificate because there is a fixed amount of space available to fit names. The shorter the names, the more will fit. Some providers place arbitrary limits on the number of SAN entries that can go into the certificate.

Planning for Capacity

One of the challenges that faces the new Lync Server 2013 administrator is the eternal question of "How big do I build it?" Luckily, Microsoft offers some guidance, in the following sections, around sizing servers to provide sufficient capacity for various types of deployments. In addition, Lync 2013 offers significant improvement in terms of server collocation allowing for larger scaling with less servers.

General Sizing

Microsoft provides some general sizing guidelines, which are summarized in Table 30.1.

TABLE 30.1   General Sizing of Servers

Server Role	Maximum Number of Users Supported
One Standard Edition server	5,000
Front End pool with eight Front End Servers and one Back End Server	80,000 unique users, plus 50% multiple point of presence (MPOP), for a total of 120,000 endpoints
One A/V Conferencing Server	20,000
One Edge Server	15,000 remote users
One Director	15,000 remote users
One Monitoring Server	250,000 users if not collocated with Archiving Server; 100,000 if collocated
One Archiving Server	500,000 users if not collocated with Monitoring Server; 100,000 if collocated

A dual 2.0GHz, 16GB supports 10,000 users as a Front End Server, whereas a dual 2.0GHz, 32GB supports up to 80,000 users as a Back End Server. That said, it is generally a good idea to account for an n+1 design when populating Front End Servers. If you were to plan for 30,000 users, take that number and divide it by the 10,000 users per Front End Server and add 1 for a total of four Front End Servers. This places a normal load of 7,500 users per server with the capability to redistribute to 10,000 users per server should a Front End Server suffer a failure or should it need to be brought down for maintenance.

If a site has fewer than 10,000 users and a typical audio/video conferencing load, it is generally recommended to collocate the A/V Conferencing Server role with the Front End Server role. Sites with a larger number of users should deploy a dedicated A/V Conferencing Server. In general, an A/V Conferencing Server can support around 1,000 concurrent A/V conference users. So if your users are particularly fond of A/V conferences, you might need to deploy more A/V Conferencing Servers.

For basic deployments that support external users, the typical rule of thumb is one Edge Server for every 15,000 remote users. It is recommended to always deploy at least two Edge Servers to provide for redundancy.

Capacity Planning for Collaboration and Application Sharing

One of the more common uses for Lync Server 2013 conferences is to present a common document or application to multiple users. Sometimes this is a one-sided presentation and other times it might be a collaborative back and forth in which users share control and modify a single document or presentation. As such, it's useful to understand bandwidth and disk usage for application sharing and conferencing collaboration. Microsoft offers the information included in Tables 30.2 through 30.5 to help plan for the impact of this feature.

TABLE 30.2   Application Sharing Capacity Planning

Modality	Average Bandwidth (Kbps)	Maximum Bandwidth (Kbps)
Application sharing using Remote Desktop Protocol (RDP)	434Kbps sent per sharer	938Kbps sent per sharer
Application sharing using compatibility conferencing server	713Kbps sent per sharer 552Kbps received per viewer	566Kbps sent per sharer 730Kbps sent per sharer

TABLE 30.3   Application Sharing Capacity Planning for Persistent Shared Object Model (PSOM) Applications

Application Sharing Usage	Sent and Received (Kbps)	Processor Time	Average Bandwidth Usage per User (Kbps)
15 conferences, 90 users	Received: 1,370 (2,728 peak) Sent: 6,370 (12,315 peak)	Average: 8.5 Peak: 24.4	Sent per sharer: 713.57 Received per viewer: 552.92

TABLE 30.4   Content Collaboration Capacity Planning

Content Type	Average Size	Number of Instances per Conference
PowerPoint	40MB	4
Handouts	10MB	3
Total default share per meeting	250MB	n/a

TABLE 30.5   Content Collaboration Upload and Download Rate

Category	Peak Usage in Bytes per Read and Write, 10,000 Provisioned Users	Average Usage in Bytes per Read and Write, 10,000 Provisioned Users
Data Conferencing Server content upload and download	Received: 17,803,480 bytes/read Sent: 19,668,079 bytes/write	Received: 706,655 bytes/read Sent: 860,224

These values serve as a starting point for administrators and can be scaled up or down if the profile isn't a good match for a specific environment.

Planning for the Address Book

One area that is often overlooked when planning a Lync Server 2013 deployment is the impact of the Address Book on the network. Depending on how well populated the Address Book is and whether all users have pictures in the Address Book, it has the potential to become quite large. Because each user will download the Address Book in its entirety when he first attaches to Lync Server 2013, a wide-scale deployment of clients can have a large impact on bandwidth usage. Microsoft offers the information in Tables 30.6 through 30.8 to estimate space and bandwidth around Address Book planning.

TABLE 30.6   Address Book Bandwidth

Modality	Number of Users	Average Bandwidth (Kbps)	Maximum Bandwidth (Kbps)
Initial Address Book Server download	80,000	99,000	332,000 (fresh deployment with 2,000 users onboarding every hour)
Overall Address Book Web Query service	80,000	40,000	60,000
Bandwidth utilization per query	1	160	240

TABLE 30.7   Storage Rate for Address Book Server Download

Storage	Size for 1 Day	Size for 30 Days
File-share size for Address Book Server, per user	1GB	26GB

TABLE 30.8   Database Storage Rate for Address Book Server and Address Book Web Query Service

Storage	Database Size
Address Book Server database size	3GB

These numbers are based on a large 80,000-user rollout and can be scaled appropriately for smaller deployments.

Planning for IM

Although instant messaging (IM) is one of the simplest features offered by Lync Server 2013, it is nonetheless important to plan for the implications of supporting this feature. Decisions around remote users, public users, and federated users influence how the environment is architected and deployed.

Considerations for Internal Users

When planning a deployment including IM, there are a few items to take into consideration when there will be internal users on the system. Although things such as server capacity are accounted for with the capacity planning of the Front End Server, it is important to consider the following impacts:

▶ Compliance and regulatory requirements

▶ Impacts on supporting systems

▶ End-user training

▶ Appropriate usage policies

When planning a deployment, always be aware of laws and regulations that might affect your users and your implementation. For example, find out whether there are requirements around archiving IM traffic for particular departments such as legal, finance, or executives. If there are, be sure to account for the Archive role in the deployment and determine how much space is required to archive the data for the period specified by company policy or specific applicable regulations.

For general users, determine whether there will be integration between the Lync client and applications such as Outlook. By default, Lync wants to store conversations in Exchange so that they can be recalled later by the user. If this will be enabled, account for the added storage usage in Exchange. If storage quotas are already enforced in Exchange, this might not be an issue, but users should be made aware that their usage within Exchange might increase and that they might end up with a shorter window of messages in their mailbox in order to stay within their quota.

TIP

Consider creating archive rules within Outlook to manage the Conversation History folder.

One area often missed by deployments of enterprisewide applications, such as Lync Server 2013, is the creation of appropriate end-user training. Although administrators spend a lot of their time researching and learning technologies, most end users do not. As such, it is the responsibility of the team deploying the application to develop training for end users. This typically should consist of cheat sheets explaining how to perform basic tasks and, when possible, should include screenshots to make it clear to users where to click and what to do.

The last thing to consider when planning a basic deployment of Lync Server 2013 is the creation of an appropriate use policy. This is where you can set the rules around the usage of IM and define behaviors that are to be avoided. For example, although it might seem common sense to some, set a policy stating that instant messaging is not to be used to send sensitive materials outside the company.

> **TIP**
>
> By setting guidelines ahead of time, you greatly reduce the chances of the new tool being used to circumvent other protective measures that have already been put in place in the enterprise. The main point is to make sure that IM is seen as another potential source for a data leak.

Consideration for Remote Users

One of the big strengths of Lync Server 2013 is the capability to communicate with users that are outside the corporate environment. This might include partner companies or random users on the Internet who need to participate in the occasional conversation and usually includes internal users who are in remote locations. When planning for Lync Server 2013, be mindful of which scenarios need to be supported. Typically, account for the following three major groups of external users:

▶ Remote users

▶ Federated users

▶ Public users

A remote user in this context refers to one who belongs to the organization but needs to connect from outside the organization. This might include situations in which the user travels or otherwise connects to Lync Server 2013 without the need for a Virtual Private Network (VPN) connection into the network.

The primary consideration for remote users includes planning for availability of the Edge Server role to ensure that they can always get a connection into the Lync Server 2013 environment and planning for integration of certificates for Secure Sockets Layer (SSL) connections.

If the Lync Server 2013 deployment uses public certificates, this will likely not be a problem because the major public certificate authorities are already trusted by the operating systems supported by the Lync client and the Communicator client. If, on the other hand, you plan to use an internal Certificate Authority, you should not only plan the deployment of the root certificate into the certificate trust store of the clients, but also ensure that the Certificate Revocation List of the Certificate Authorities involved are reachable by users when they are connecting remotely.

Because most Lync Server 2013 deployments using internal PKI use Active Directory–integrated certificate authorities, typically you can depend on the directory to present the CRL to clients. Because domain controllers are almost never exposed to a demilitarized zone (DMZ) or the Internet, you must depend on the HTTP publishing of the CRL. Because this needs to be reached by remote clients who aren't connected to the internal LAN, the CRL path in the CRL distribution point should reference a web server that is reachable through the Internet. This ensures that systems can access a valid CRL to ensure that the certificates are good and thus enable successful connections over SSL.

30

The other value of an HTTP published CRL is for the support of clients that aren't bound to Active Directory. In many environments, Macintosh computers, which can run the Lync:Mac client to connect to Lync Server 2013, aren't bound to Active Directory. As such, they can't access the CRL through the LDAP path, so they'll end up using the HTTP path for CRL checking.

Federated users refer to those from companies that also run Lync Server 2013 or older versions of Communications Server. Federating is the creation of a formal relationship between the two environments that gives each the capability to share contact lists and presence information with one another. The primary items to plan for are the creation of an external access policy and the establishment of a list of federated domains.

Planning for public users means making a determination of whether the Lync Server 2013 system will integrate with existing public IM services such as AOL, MSN, or Skype. This gives the capability to consolidate all IM traffic into a single client because users would no longer need a secondary client to talk to their public contacts. This can be especially useful in environments that archive IM traffic for regulatory or compliance reasons. It also enables users to potentially use an existing public IM identity through Lync to maintain their original identity in the eyes of Internet public IM users.

Some additional public services can be integrated by using an XMPP gateway. This allows IM-only integration with Google Talk as well as Cisco Jabber.

> **NOTE**
>
> Public IM connectivity with Yahoo! requires a separate license. If you plan to offer public IM connectivity, don't forget to purchase the license and account for the fact that it might take several weeks for these providers to process the SIP routes.

Planning for Conferencing

Conferencing in Lync Server 2013 describes any type of audio or video communication that involves three or more people. Although this chapter focuses on basic deployments of Lync Server 2013, this section also takes into consideration PC-to-PC conferences as part of an audio conference. Because both scheduled conferences and ad hoc conferences can be initiated by users, it is important to take both into account.

> **TIP**
>
> Don't underestimate the popularity of conferencing. After users know it's available, it will become extremely popular. Management will love the potential of reducing costs around external conferencing services, too.

Defining Your Requirements

The first big step in planning a deployment is determining which features you plan to support. This greatly influences the overall design, has a big impact on server roles that are deployed, and affects infrastructure services such as the LAN and the WAN.

If you plan to enable web conferencing, which includes both document and application sharing, account for the following:

► Enable conferencing for the Front End pool in the Topology Builder.

► Account for increased network usage for application sharing. The default throttling is 1.5KB/sec for each session and can be modified as needed.

► Build custom meeting policies if there is a need to enable either application sharing or document collaboration but a desire to prevent the other.

To enable audio and video conferencing, which in this type of deployment includes PC-to-PC calls but not PBX integration, plan for the following tasks:

► Enable conferencing for the Front End pool in the Topology Builder.

► Account for increased network usage, typically 50Kbps for audio and 350Kbps for video. Note that increased bandwidth is required for high-definition (HD) video.

If requirements include supporting external users connecting to internally hosted conferences, consider the following tasks:

► Deploy Edge Servers in the topology.

► Properly protect access to the Edge Servers.

► Properly resolve the meeting URLs externally.

► Be sure users trust the certificates used on the Edge Servers to establish SSL connections.

► Decide whether federation will be supported.

Another decision that must be accounted for is whether it is necessary to support legacy clients on Lync Server 2013. Each time a client connects, its version is checked and compared against policies to determine whether it can be used. Web-based connections attempt to detect a local client and always offer the option of the web-based client. This is an important decision because there are compatibility limitations between various clients and backends. In general, a newer client is not supported talking to an older server version, and it is a best practice to avoid this situation.

Planning Your Conferencing Topology

Conferencing can be deployed in either the Standard Edition of Lync Server 2013 or the Enterprise Edition. New to Lync Server 2013 is that the AV Conferencing role can no longer be split out onto dedicated servers. Due to optimizations in the Microsoft MCUs, scalability is greatly improved, thus removing the need to use dedicated AV Conferencing servers even in large environments. The hardware requirements are the same as noted previously, even now that the AV Conferencing role is collocated with the Front End role.

Note that a new server role is required for conferencing, called the Office Web Apps Server. Although this server is not explicitly part of Lync, Lync Web Conferencing does have a dependency on it. A detailed description of the Office Web Apps Server is covered in Chapter 11, "Dependent Services and SQL."

Planning for Clients and Devices

There are several clients for Lync Server 2013 for which to plan. Administrators have the ability to limit which clients can connect so that users can use only a client that is currently supported. This simplifies troubleshooting because it's possible to prevent unexpected clients from connecting. The current list of clients includes these:

▶ **Lync 2013**—The primary Windows client

▶ **Lync Web App**—The web-based client that provides the primary features

▶ **Lync 2013 Mobile**—The client for smartphones

▶ **Lync 2013 Phone Edition**—The client running on traditional handsets

▶ **Online Meeting Add-in for Lync 2013**—The client that provides integration with Outlook for meeting management

Another item to plan for on the topic of clients is the deployment of clients to end users. The two supported methods are to either deploy the .exe version of the client, or to extract the .msi from the executable and deploy this through Group Policy. It's typically preferred to deploy the executable version through some other application deployment method because the .exe version performs the following tasks that the .msi doesn't:

▶ Automatically performs prerequisite checks

▶ Installs Visual C++ components and Silverlight if missing

▶ Notifies the user about Media Player 11 requirements

▶ Uninstalls legacy OCS and Lync clients

Planning for Archiving

When planning a basic deployment of Lync Server 203, determine whether archiving is required in the environment. Archiving, from the perspective of Lync Server 2013, is the behavior of capturing IM conversations and conference attachments and storing them in a dedicated database for long-term storage. This enables administrators to review IM conversations and to see attachments that were part of conferences. Specifically, the following types of contacts are archived by the Archive server:

▶ Peer-to-peer instant messages

▶ Multiparty IMs

▶ Uploaded conference content

▶ Conference events, such as joining, leaving, and uploading

▶ Audio or video for peer-to-peer IMs and conferences

▶ Application sharing for peer-to-peer IMs and conferences

▶ Conferencing annotations, whiteboard content, and polls

NOTE

Archiving data can also be stored in Exchange 2013, if deployed. For the sake of this example, the assumption is that a dedicated separate SQL database is used.

The primary driver behind archiving in Lync Server 2013 is regulatory compliance. Some industries must archive all communications between users and potentially between internal users and external parties. Lync Server 2013 allows for flexible archiving policies to be deployed to address these needs.

Defining Your Archiving Requirements

The first step in planning for archiving in a Lync Server 2013 deployment is determining the requirements. Start by answering the following questions about the environment:

▶ Which sites and users in the organization require archiving support?

▶ Will archiving be needed for internal communications, external communications, or both?

▶ Should archiving include IM, conferencing, or both?

▶ Is archiving critical enough that IMs and conferences shouldn't be allowed to occur if archiving is unavailable?

▶ How long should archived materials be retained?

Answering these questions enables you to determine how the archiving policies should be created.

Archiving policies are used by Lync Server 2013 to make decisions around what content should be archived, for whom it should be archived, and for how long it should remain in the archive. When planning the archiving policies, keep in mind that there are three types of archiving policies, each with a different intended purpose:

▶ **Global Archiving Policy**—This default policy applies to all users and sites in the deployment. The available options include the archiving of internal communications, external communications, or both. This policy cannot be deleted.

▶ **Site Archiving Policy**—This policy enables or disables archiving for a specific site within Lync Server 2013. Typically when deploying site archiving policies, you should disable archiving in the global policy; otherwise, all sites effectively process the global policy.

▶ **User Archiving Policy**—This policy enables or disables archiving for a specific user within Lync Server 2013, regardless of the sites with which the user is associated. This type of policy is typically used in environments where only a specific class of users requires archiving.

NOTE

If you use Microsoft Exchange 2013 integration to store archived data, your Exchange settings control whether Lync 2103 communications are archived. Controlling archiving for internal or external communications is available only for Lync Policy. For Exchange-integrated archiving, both of them will be either archived or not archived.

In each of the Lync 2103 archiving policies, you can choose to archive IM only, conferences only, or both. If both site and user policies are implemented, user policies will override site policies.

The other decision that must be made when planning archiving policies is whether to implement critical-mode archiving. Critical mode enforces a behavior such that if archiving isn't available, the system prevents IM and conferencing from occurring. Critical mode is configured in the Archiving Configuration tab within the Lync Server 2013 Control Panel.

Finally, when planning the archiving requirements, determine how long archived data should remain in the archive. By default, purging archives is not enabled. The purge period can be set to as low as 1 day or as high as 2,562 days (just over 7 years). You can also choose to purge only exported archiving data. This option purges records that have been exported and marked as safe to delete by the session export tool.

Planning Your Archiving Topology

In Lync Server 2013, archiving consists of two components:

▶ **Unified Data Collection Agents**—These agents are automatically installed on every Front End pool and Standard Edition server. The agent captures messages for archiving and sends them to a local filestore and to the Archiving database.

▶ **Archiving Server Backend Database**—This is the SQL server that stores the archived messages. This database must be on a dedicated instance and is recommended to be on a dedicated server in larger deployments.

There are some common requirements that should be planned. In addition to the normal requirements for Lync Server 2013 in terms of supported versions of Windows, also ensure that a valid version of SQL is used. The Archiving Server is compatible with the following versions of SQL:

▶ Microsoft SQL Server 2008 R2 Enterprise

▶ Microsoft SQL Server 2008 R2 Standard

▶ Microsoft SQL Server 2012 Enterprise

▶ Microsoft SQL Server 2012 Standard

From a scaling perspective, the Archiving Server will easily support all the users supported by the Front End Servers it is running on.

> **TIP**
>
> Be sure not to skimp on disks for Front End Servers when running Lync archiving. The load increase is significant and requires the servers to meet the hardware specification noted earlier in this chapter.

Based on the typical Lync Server 2013 user model, anticipate around 100KB of data per day per user. Based on this, database sizing can be approximated as the following:

DB size = (DB growth per day per user) × (number of users) × (number of days)

For example, with a deployment to 10,000 users that will archive data for 60 days, anticipated database size is the following for a DB size of 60GB:

DB size = (100KB) × (10,000) × (60)

If an organization varies significantly from the average Lync user model, adjust the growth estimate accordingly.

Planning for Management

Lync Server 2013 follows the currently popular model of role-based access control (RBAC). The concept is that one defines a role, typically based around common tasks, and then delegates the performance of these tasks to the role group. Existing security groups or individuals are then populated into that role group to grant them the necessary rights to perform the tasks.

Lync Server 2013 has eleven RBAC groups that cover most of the commonly delegated tasks within Lync Server 2013. These groups and their allowed tasks are as listed here:

▶ **CsAdministrator**—Members of this group can perform all administrative tasks and modify all settings within Lync Server 2013. This includes creating and assigning roles, and modification or creation of new sites, pools, and services.

▶ **CsUserAdministrator**—Members of this group can enable or disable users for Lync Server 2013. They can also move users and assign existing policies to users. They can neither create new policies nor modify existing policies.

▶ **CsVoiceAdministrator**—Members of this group can manage, monitor, and troubleshoot servers and services. They can prevent new connections to servers, apply software updates, and start and stop services. They cannot, however, make changes that affect global configuration.

30

▶ **CsServerAdministrator**—Members of this group can manage and troubleshoot servers and services including preventing new connections, starting and stopping services, and applying software updates.

▶ **CsViewOnlyAdministrator**—Members of this group can view the deployment, including server and user information, in order to monitor deployment health.

▶ **CsHelpDesk**—Members of this group can view the deployment, including users' properties and policies. They can also run specific troubleshooting tasks. They can change neither user properties or policies nor server configuration or services.

▶ **CsArchivingAdministrator**—Members of this group can modify archiving configuration and policies.

▶ **CsResponseGroupAdministrator**—Members of this group can manage the configuration of the Response Group application within a site.

▶ **CsLocationAdministrator**—This group offers the lowest level of rights for Enhanced 911 (E911) management. This includes creating E911 locations and network identifiers and enables associating these with each other. This role is assigned with a global scope as opposed to a site-specific scope.

▶ **CsPersistentChatAdministrator**—Members of this group can manage Persistent Chat features and rooms.

▶ **CsResponseGroupAdministrator**—Members of this group can manage response groups. It can be scoped to specific response groups on a granular level.

To comply with RBAC best practices, do not assign users to roles with global scopes if they are supposed to administer only a limited set of servers or users. This means creating additional role-based groups with similar rights to previous groups, but applied to a more limited scope because all default role groups in Lync Server 2013 have a global scope. That is to say, the rights apply to all users and to servers in all sites.

These scoped role groups can be created through the PowerShell cmdlets provided with Lync Server 2013 by using an existing global group as a template and by assigning the rights to a precreated group in Active Directory. For example:

```
New-CsAdminRole -Identity "Site01 Server Administrators" -Template
➥CsServerAdministrator
-ConfigScopes "site:Site01"
```

This cmdlet gives the Site01 Server Administrators group the same rights as the predefined CsServerAdministrator role, but rather than giving the rights globally, the rights apply only to servers in Site01.

A similar process can be used to create a role that is scoped based on users rather than on sites:

```
New-CsAdminRole -Identity "Finance Users Administrators" -Template
➥CsUserAdministrator
-UserScopes "OU:OU=Finance, OU=Corporate Users, DC=CompanyABC, DC=com"
```

This grants a group called Finance Users Administrators rights similar to the predefined CsUserAdministrator group, but rather than getting the rights across all user objects, they will be limited to user objects in the Finance OU as defined in the cmdlet.

After the necessary role groups have been defined, simply add users or other groups to the role groups through Active Directory Users and Computers.

> **NOTE**
>
> When users are placed into either a new security group or a role group, they need to log out and then log on for the Kerberos ticket to be updated with the new group membership. Without this process, they will not be able to use the new rights that they are granted.

For users who are given any level of administrative rights within Lync Server 2013, carefully consider which tasks they need to perform and then assign them to the roles with the least privilege and scope necessary to perform the tasks.

For administrators interested in what rights are available to each of the predefined groups, Microsoft has published a fairly exhaustive list at the following URL: http://technet. microsoft.com/en-us/library/gg425917(v=ocs.15).aspx.

Documenting the Plan

After all the various requirements have been determined and the options thought out and decided on, put these decisions and requirements into a design document. The complexity of the project affects the size of the document and the effort required to create it. The intention is that this design document summarizes the goals and objectives that were gathered in the initial discovery phase and describes how the project's result will meet them. It should represent a detailed picture of the end state when the new technologies and clients are implemented. The amount of detail can vary, but it should include key design decisions made in the discovery process and collaboration sessions.

The following list gives a sample table of contents and brief description of the design document:

- ▶ **Executive Summary**—Provides a brief discussion of the scope of the Lync Server 2013 implementation. It should also include a high-level overview of the business value.

- ▶ **Goals and Objectives**—Includes the 50,000-foot-view business objectives, down to the 1,000-foot-view staff-level tasks that will be met by the project.

▶ **Background**—Provides a high-level summary of the current state of the network, focusing on problem areas, as clarified in the discovery process, as well as summary decisions made in the collaboration sessions.

▶ **Approach**—Outlines the high-level phases and tasks required to implement the solution (the details of each task are determined in the migration document).

▶ **End State**—Defines the details of the new technology configurations. For example, this section describes the number, placement, and functions of Lync Server 2013.

▶ **Budget Estimate**—Provides an estimate of basic costs involved in the project. Whereas a detailed cost estimate requires the creation of the migration document, experienced estimators can provide order-of-magnitude numbers at this point. Also, it should be clear what software and hardware are needed, so budgetary numbers can be provided.

When developing the document further, one will want to add details in various sections to lay out the costs and benefits, as well as provide a long-term vision to the project. Consider including these details in the various sections of the document:

▶ **Executive Summary**—The executive summary should set the stage and prepare the audience for what the document will contain, and it should be concise. It should outline, at the highest level, the scope of the work. Ideally, the executive summary also positions the document in the decision-making process and clarifies that approvals of the design are required to move forward.

▶ **Goals and Objectives**—The goals and objectives section should cover the high-level goals of the project and include the pertinent departmental goals. It's easy to go too far in the goals and objectives sections and get down to the 1,000-foot-view level, but this can end up becoming confusing; so it might be better to record this information in the migration document and the detailed project plan for the project.

▶ **Background**—The background section should summarize the results of the discovery process and the collaboration sessions, and can list specific design decisions that were made during the collaboration sessions. Additionally, decisions made about what technologies or features not to include can be summarized here. This information should stay at a relatively high level as well, and more details can be provided in the end state section of the design document. This information is useful as a reference later in the project when the infamous question "Who made that decision?" comes up.

▶ **Approach**—The approach section should document the implementation strategy agreed upon to this point, and should also serve to record decisions made in the discovery and design process about the timeline (end to end and for each phase) and the team members participating in the different phases. This section should avoid going into too much detail because in many cases the end design might not yet be approved and might change after review. Also, the migration document should provide the details of the process that will be followed.

▶ **End State**—In the end state section, the specifics of the Lync Server 2013 implementation should be spelled out in detail, and the high-level decisions that were summarized in the background section should be fleshed out. Essentially, the software to be installed on each server and the roles that will be installed on each server are spelled out here, along with the future roles of existing legacy servers. Information on the clients that will be supported, policies that will be enforced, and so on should be in this section. Diagrams and tables can help explain the new concepts and show what the solution will look like, where the key systems will be located, and how the overall topology of the implementation will look. Often, besides a standard physical diagram of what goes where, a logical diagram illustrating how devices communicate is needed.

▶ **Budget Estimate**—The budget section is not exact but should provide order-of-magnitude prices for the different phases of the project. If an outside consulting firm is assisting with this document, it can draw from experience with similar projects of like-sized companies. Because no two projects are ever the same, there needs to be some flexibility in these estimates. Typically, ranges for each phase should be provided. The goal is for the audience of the document to understand what the project will cost and what they are getting for that money. This is also a great place to point out anticipated returns on investment (ROI) because these often act as the primary justification for a Lync Server 2013 implementation. See Chapter 4, "Business Cases for Lync Server 2013," for a full list of business cases and value propositions for Lync Server 2103.

Best Practices

Several items recommended in this chapter should be taken into account when you are planning a basic deployment of Lync Server 2013. By following these recommendations, you can be better prepared for the deployment and can avoid the common pitfalls associated with planning a topology and deployment of a complex technology. The following is a summary of recommended best practices from this chapter:

▶ Start the deployment planning with a comprehensive design document. This ensures that decisions have been made, and it gives an excellent opportunity to shop the design around to other groups to get buy-in and to ensure that other groups know how they'll be affected by the upcoming deployment.

▶ Treat your deployment like a formal project. Produce a project plan that includes anticipated tasks and anticipated durations, and calls out the required resources. This makes it easier to get support from management to dedicate the appropriate resources and time to the deployment.

▶ Make sure that any constraints are understood before the completion of the design. Things such as regulator compliances have a major impact on decisions made in the design.

30

► Make sure that the deployment can handle the anticipated load. Use the Microsoft sizing guidelines to ensure that the design can support the load you expect to place on it.

► If possible, go overboard on RAM and disk speed/spindles. This is where smart administrators will squeeze out the best performance from their Lync deployment.

► Start the deployment with a pilot. This gives an excellent opportunity to validate the impact of users on the system and gives administrators an opportunity to get familiar with the infrastructure while supporting only a limited number of users. Be sure to include users from multiple job functions, not just IT users. This will give the administrator insight into how Lync will be used in their organization.

► Involve the networking group when designing a basic deployment. The new features offered by Lync Server 2013 will greatly impact a WAN, and the networking group will have bandwidth and latency information that might affect the design.

► Make decisions about how external users will be supported early in the process. Designs for internal only versus external support will be significantly different. These decisions affect several other decisions, so the earlier this can be decided, the less impact it has on the overall effort.

► If possible, use public certificates that use subject alternate names. This greatly reduces the impact on end users and on external users because the certificates will already be trusted by the operating system.

► Use modern hardware. Current-generation processors can provide a much larger capacity than processors from only one generation ago. The Microsoft sizing guides are based on current-generation processors. Deviating from that practice renders the sizing guides inaccurate and puts the project at risk of being underpowered. This results in a poor user experience when loads increase.

► Train the end users on how to use the new system. Ensure that the users understand the limitations of various clients because they do not all provide the same features. Consider an online FAQ (frequently asked questions) for users to refer to.

► Define an acceptable use policy for the Lync Server 2013 system. This reduces the exposure of the end users because they will know what behaviors can potentially put them at risk. It also enables administrators to more easily block risky behaviors because there will be a written policy to back up the configuration.

► Make sure that the archive is designed with enough storage to hold the anticipated volume of data.

► Regularly test the recovery of data from the archive. This helps ensure that the data will be available and readable when the time comes that it's needed for something important. Consider a monthly test.

► Plan carefully when using virtualization and understand what other services are provided by the virtualization farm. Most virtualization farms are oversubscribed because virtualization is a popular form of consolidation for servers. Be aware that not having dedicated resources reduces the potential capacity of the systems.

▶ Whenever possible, use a system of role-based access control. Roles should be well defined and administrators should be given only the minimum of rights needed to perform their jobs. If their jobs change, their role-based group memberships should change. Don't forget that this goes both ways: Add them to new groups when they need additional rights, but don't forget to remove them from groups if there are tasks they longer perform.

▶ Don't forget to monitor the Lync Server 2013 environment with an application, such as SCOM, Nagios, or SiteScope, to ensure that the systems are available. Leverage the monitoring software to trend the loads on the system to be able to predict when extra capacity will need to be added to maintain an acceptable load on each server.

By following these best practices, administrators can maximize their chances for a successful Lync Server 2013 deployment and can keep their end users happy and productive.

Summary

As we've seen in this chapter, there's a lot more to preparing for a deployment than merely gathering up the software and installing it. Many of the most important steps are the so-called "soft decisions" and the proper presentation of the project to the decision makers. This includes not only those who make the technical decisions but those who make the financial decisions as well. It's critical to understand the needs of the business and to determine how Lync Server 2013 can address those needs in the best manner. By aligning the technology solutions with the business drivers, one can greatly increase the chances of getting the project approved and of implementing it successfully.

The goal in the preparation phase should be to build an architecture as simple as possible that still meets all the requirements of the environment. By the time the installation occurs, all questions should have already been answered and the answers accepted by all the project stakeholders. In this manner, there won't be any surprises because everyone will already know exactly what to expect from the project.

Always take the opportunity to look beyond the design and implementation and to ask questions such as "Who is going to manage this environment?" or "How will we make sure that the Help Desk can do their jobs without enabling them to break the application?" and plan for those events. When you've accounted for them in the preparation phase, it's easier to avoid situations in which one has to make suboptimal decisions at the last minute. With Lync Server 2013, it's especially true that an ounce of prevention is worth a pound of cure.

30

Planning to Deploy External Services

The Edge Server role is a key part of why Lync Server is such a compelling solution for businesses, but along with that power and flexibility comes a good deal of configuration work and upfront planning. Networking, firewalls, certificates, and load balancing mean the Edge Server touches practically every part of the network and, consequently, almost every team from server administrators to network engineers.

The Edge role has traditionally been the most difficult to configure, and Microsoft has made significant improvements to that process in the latest version. Configuration changes are now pushed out to Edge Servers from a central location instead of individually configuring servers, which cuts down on the chance for human error and ensures consistency among server pool members.

This chapter discusses what details to consider when planning for an Edge Server and how to properly prepare an Edge Server's network adapters. It also details the firewall requirements and different topologies that can be used to support an Edge Server. Certificate requirements and planning guidance for the reverse proxy are also discussed. Lastly, some sample scenarios are presented for various deployment sizes with a full diagram, a list of certificate requirements, and public DNS entries.

Determining Feature Requirements

The first step in planning for Edge services is to determine what the business requirements are, which features need to be deployed, and what kind of topology to use. For instance, a small business that wants to communicate with public IM networks might deploy a single server running the Access Edge Server role, whereas a larger business that wants to replace a hosted virtual conferencing solution might deploy multiple load-balanced Edge Servers with full support for A/V conferencing. This section discusses the different forms of remote access and considerations for each feature.

Providing Remote Access

The primary functionality a Lync Edge Server provides is remote access to the entire Lync environment. One of the most compelling Lync Server features is the fact that a client seamlessly operates identically whether the user is in the office or is working remotely without a VPN, and that functionality is driven by the Edge Server. The Edge Server provides a secure channel for users to sign in remotely, leverage web conferencing, conduct audio/video calls, and even make and receive PSTN phone calls using the Lync client. Deploying an Edge Server to support this functionality is a common part of nearly every Lync server deployment because of the flexibility it provides to an organization's workforce.

Remote access can be configured at a policy level and then granted to specific groups of users if an organization needs to control who can sign in remotely. The sign-in process takes place over an SSL channel on TCP 443 before any credentials are exchanged, and all subsequent traffic is also encrypted.

Using Two-Factor Authentication

Lync Server 2013 does not provide support for any kind of two-factor authentication such as smart cards or security tokens. Instead, remote Lync clients provide NTLM credentials over the secure SSL channel during the initial sign-in, and then use a certificate created by the Lync Front End Servers for any subsequent sign-ins. The certificate is specific to the remote endpoint and is stored locally to expedite the sign-in process for future logins. This also means that any home user with Lync installed on a personal PC can enter her Active Directory credentials to sign in to Lync remotely.

Some organizations have security mandates that require two-factor authentication for any form of remote access, and Lync is unable to meet those mandates. To meet these requirements, a business can still deploy Edge Servers to support federation or PIC but disallow remote access for Lync users through a policy. This forces a user to first establish a VPN connection that requires two-factor authentication, and then Lync can connect to the internal Front End Servers. There are some serious disadvantages to this approach with regard to the media quality discussed later in this chapter.

> **CAUTION**
>
> Although the idea of two-factor authentication or any security enhancement always seems attractive, organizations should consider the complexity of these solutions. Many other applications within the business stack don't support two-factor authentication today, and exploring that option with Lync is not a good place to start. Use remote access policies and advanced system management tools to control access to Lync.

When discussing remote access, organizations should follow these guidelines:

▶ Determine whether remote access will provide additional value to the Lync deployment.

▶ Identify which users should be configured for remote access, and then create appropriate access policies to assign to end users.

▶ Determine whether two-factor authentication is a security requirement, and if so, identify the maturity of the deployed solution and any current issues.

Allowing Anonymous Access

Whether an organization supports anonymous access to Lync Server is a decision the business must make when considering an Edge Server deployment. Allowing anonymous access provides the capability for internal users to invite participants from outside to the organization to web or A/V conferencing sessions. This capability can often replace hosted or subscription-based conferencing services for most users, providing immediate cost savings. For extremely large conferences, it might still make sense to use a hosted service, but the majority of ad hoc or smaller conferences can easily be handled by Lync Server.

Another option is that only specific users, groups, or locations can be allowed to communicate with anonymous users through the use of conferencing policies. This gives administrators the flexibility of allowing all authenticated users to use web conferencing while allowing maybe only a select few to host conferences with anonymous participants. Independent of the remote access for authenticated users, deploying an Edge Server allows for the anonymous users or vendors to participate in an organization's Lync Online Meetings.

When discussing remote access, organizations should follow these guidelines:

▶ Determine whether anonymous access to Lync Online Meetings will be permitted for outside vendors or partners.

▶ Identify which users should be allowed to invite anonymous participants.

▶ Create the appropriate conferencing policies to control anonymous access and features available within meetings containing anonymous participants.

Configuring Federation Types

A consideration for organizations when deploying Lync Server 2013 is to determine whether the federation feature will be used. Federation requires an Edge Server role, so even if remote access will not be allowed for employees, an Edge can still be deployed to provide federation capabilities. Another driver for enabling some degree of federation is the fact that the Lync Mobile clients for Apple iOS and Microsoft Windows Phone receive push notifications through federation with Office 365's push service clearinghouse. So choosing to not deploy an Edge with federation will prevent a business from using push notifications on mobile clients.

Federation allows organizations that have deployed Lync to communicate securely so that not only can users see presence for users within their own organization, but they also can now see presence for partners or vendors they work with frequently. Additionally, all communication modalities are available through federation so users have a consistent experience when escalating an IM to audio, video, or web conferencing.

When deploying Edge Servers, make a decision about whether users are allowed to federate with other organizations that run Lync Server. Making such a decision is the first step, but the second is to determine what type of federation is allowed, because there are a few different levels that can be enabled.

Dynamic Federation

Dynamic federation is a purely automatic feature in which two users in different organizations can simply type in each other's SIP addresses and start communicating immediately. This works well if both organizations have deployed Edge Servers, published the necessary SRV records in public DNS, and used public certificates that are trusted by the opposite party's Edge Server. In many cases this just works and requires no administrator intervention. The user experience is similar to sending an email because users don't have to ask their administrators for permission to contact a third party. Organizations can enable dynamic federation by publishing the necessary SRV records in public DNS and enabling partner domain discovery within the Lync Server Control Panel.

Enhanced Federation

Enhanced federation lifts a security limit imposed within dynamic federation in which an Edge Server will accept only up to 20 SIP messages each second from a partner's Edge Server. This is a reasonable limit for many organizations, and it helps prevent a partner's Edge Server from overwhelming a business's own Edge Server and possibly impacting other services such as remote access.

Enabling enhanced federation for a domain removes this "20 messages per second" limit for the specified partner's SIP domain, but this obviously requires some form of administrator configuration. Organizations should identify partners they will federate with and plan to enable enhanced federation with those partners. Edge Servers will log events indicating which partner SIP domains are using dynamic federation so that Lync administrators can proactively monitor those lists and enable enhanced federation as required. In terms of configuration, enabling enhanced federation for a domain is a matter of simply specifying the partner's SIP domain name but leaving the Access Edge service field empty. Specifying the Access Edge FQDN is required only for direct federation, discussed in the next section. The SRV records published to public DNS for a SIP domain are instead used to locate the partner's Access Edge FQDN.

Direct Federation

The final form of federation is really the legacy version that was introduced back in Live Communications Server 2005. Direct federation requires each partner to specify the SIP domain name *and* the Access Edge service FQDN providing that federation service. Direct federation operates the same way as enhanced federation in that it doesn't allow any more messages per second, and it requires greater administrator overhead. Not only do users need to request federation with a specific partner's SIP domain, but the Lync administrators from both parties must now meet to exchange information about what server names are used.

The main use case for direct federation is when the Edge Server's FQDN does not match the partner's SIP domain. For example, partners trying to reach tom@companyabc.com must locate an Edge Server also in the companyabc.com DNS namespace, or they will drop the connection because the namespace does not match. Direct federation provides an override for that drop, and tells the Edge Server to ignore the name mismatch by connecting to the specified Access Edge service FQDN. The disadvantages to direct federation are in the administration overhead and the fact that this can easily break if one organization changes an Access Edge service FQDN.

A good analogy here when considering whether to enable federation, and allow dynamic discovery, is to think of federation in terms of email. Imagine if email operated like direct federation such that users in different domains could not send mail to each other without an administrator on both sides first manually configuring a connection to the partner domain. If that were the case, email probably would not have become the universal communication modality that it is today. Instead, any user can generally send mail to any domain without administrators making server configuration changes. Dynamic and enhanced federation are the Lync Server equivalent of that capability; users have full access to presence, instant messaging, web conferencing, and A/V conferencing with any other user across the world without any additional configuration. Federation has a leg up on email because it allows for much richer communication methods between partners.

When discussing federation, organizations should follow these guidelines:

▶ Identify whether federation to partners or Office 365 for mobile push notifications is a business requirement.

▶ Discuss whether dynamic federation and partner discovery will be enabled.

▶ Prepare a list of federated partners by involving end users or monitoring existing Lync Edge Server logs, and add those domains for enhanced federation.

▶ Identify which partners will require direct federation and collect the Access Edge service FQDNs.

Enabling Public IM Connectivity (PIC)

Lync Server public IM connectivity (PIC) enables users to communicate with public instant messaging (IM) networks such as MSN, AOL, and Skype. It operates in a similar fashion to federation in that it uses the same ports and topology, but it has a slightly different set of steps to configure. The main difference is that public IM connectivity must be configured through the organization's licensing site with Microsoft. The public IM providers do not use the SRV record for open federation and instead require these manual steps to provision the initial connectivity.

> **NOTE**
>
> Yahoo! Public IM connectivity was previously offered as a per-user subscription license, but the service has been disabled as of December 2012.

Administrators can choose to allow only specific SIP domains to communicate with the public IM providers, and each SIP domain supported for public IM connectivity must be provisioned through the licensing site. After the public IM connectivity is provisioned, it can take up to 30 days before each provider activates the change, and because providers are independent, they can come online at different times.

Public IM connections have a more limited feature set than federation does. The Public IM providers do not support any kind of multiparty IM or conferencing, so all conversations are limited to a maximum of two participants. AOL does not support any audio or video modalities with Lync so conversations with AOL contacts can only include instant messaging.

Public IM providers also do not support any kind of web conferencing or A/V features, even on a two-party basis. The only exceptions to this are the MSN and Windows Live services that actually do allow two-party A/V conversations with Lync Server users. MSN allows for two-party audio and video conversations, and Skype will initially allow for two-party audio calls. In both cases, a Lync administrator must remove the default setting of requiring encryption for all calls because MSN and Skype A/V calls cannot use encryption with Lync users.

When discussing public IM connectivity, organizations should do the following:

▶ Identify whether public IM connectivity to any networks is a business requirement.

▶ Plan to enable PIC within remote access policies only for users that require these features.

▶ Submit the PIC provisioning form early on in the deployment process due to the variable lead time for services to be enabled.

Configuring XMPP Proxy

A new feature in Lync Server 2013 is the XMPP proxy role on the Edge Server, which allows federation with XMPP servers across the Internet such as Google. The XMPP functionality is similar to PIC for AOL in that it is two-party only, and only allows for instant messaging and presence information to be exchanged. There are no audio/video capabilities between Lync and Google or any other XMPP partner today.

When discussing the XMPP proxy, organizations should do the following:

▶ Identify any needs to federate with partners that currently leverage XMPP presence and IM services.

▶ Collect the XMPP partner domains and a proxy FQDN if the DNS SRV records are not published in public DNS.

Planning Edge Server Architecture

When you are planning a Lync Server environment, any remote access or federation features require significant planning to ensure that the features work correctly and to properly secure the infrastructure. Since the Edge Servers and reverse proxy components are typically deployed in a perimeter network, there is an extra level of coordination required between the security teams who manage the firewall, load balancers, or reverse proxy, and the team responsible for deploying Lync.

Organizations might have a dedicated network security team that is different from the team responsible for implementing and managing Lync Server.

Because the deployment planning typically crosses different teams, it is important for all parties to meet early in the planning stages to discuss the deployment requirements. Much of the work and troubleshooting with Edge Server firewall configuration is a collaborative effort between multiple teams to ensure that each component is configured correctly.

The following section discusses the various topologies that can be used for the Lync Edge Server and key considerations for each design.

Edge Server Placement

Edge Server placement is critical in a deployment to optimize media paths. The SIP signaling used for presence and IM is more tolerant of slight delays, but web conferencing and A/V traffic are sensitive to latency, so it is important to properly plan Edge Server placement.

> **TIP**
>
> As a rule of thumb, Edge Servers are generally deployed in any location with a Front End pool that supports remote conferencing or A/V features. This isn't a mandate, and there are many other factors at play, but Edge Servers typically exist near a Front End pool.

For example, consider a small deployment for Company ABC, as shown in Figure 31.1, where a single Front End Server in San Francisco exists. In this deployment, only a single Edge Server is necessary to support all the remote features. Media paths are all local to San Francisco.

Imagine that Company ABC expands with a new office in London with a WAN link back to San Francisco and adds a new Front End pool for the London users. When London users sign in remotely and try to IM with a London user in the office, they will communicate with the Edge Server in San Francisco, which sends traffic to the Front End in San Francisco, which ultimately proxies the SIP traffic to the London user's Front End pool in London, and finally arrives at the London office user. Although this seems like a lot of hops, it's not going to cause an issue for the remote London user. If the user gets a presence update or an IM half a second late, he is not going to notice.

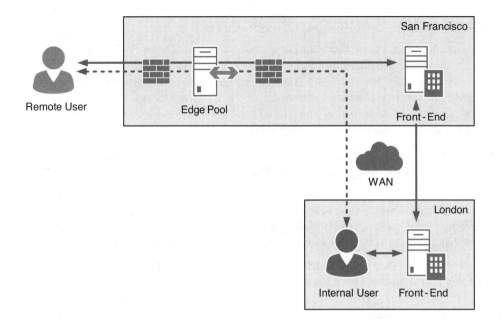

FIGURE 31.1   Single Edge Server with multiple sites.

Now consider if a London user goes home for the day and tries to place an audio call to another London user still in the office. The traffic flow for the audio stream is from the remote user to the San Francisco Edge Server and then straight to the user in the London office. The media stream skips the San Francisco and London Front End hops, but the result is probably still a poor-sounding audio call. Even though the two London users are physically close in proximity, the call is "hairpinning" through the San Francisco Edge Server and possibly creating a lot of latency, or delay, on the call.

The solution in this scenario is to also deploy an Edge Server in London, which would allow for the London office user to have a more direct path to the remote London user. If Company ABC deploys an Edge Server in London, the traffic flow shown in Figure 31.1 changes to the traffic flow shown in Figure 31.2. In this case, the remote users can exchange media traffic with London users directly across the Internet with a lesser amount of latency.

TIP

It isn't necessary to deploy Edge Servers in every location with a Front End pool, but it generally results in an improved experience for the end users. Many deployments try to distribute Edge Servers to service distinct geographical boundaries such as opposite coasts or continents to limit traversing long WAN links. For example, using separate Edge Servers per continent, or on each side of a continent in North America, Europe, and Asia, is a common deployment model.

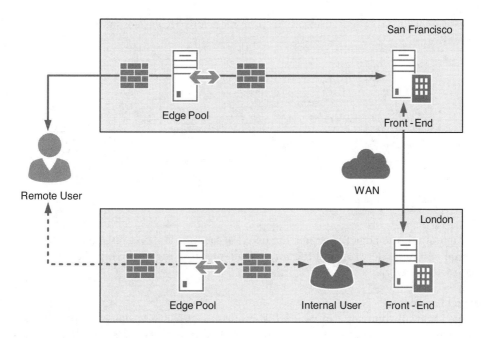

FIGURE 31.2   Multiple Edge Servers.

Perimeter Network Models

A potentially confusing point for organizations trying to deploy Lync Server 2013 is how the Edge Server fits into a network from a logical and physical perspective. Various methods can be used, as discussed in this section.

The key point to keep in mind is that the Edge Server requires two network adapters. One is internal-facing and communicates with the internal Front End Servers, Directors, and clients, and the second adapter is external-facing and communicates with the external traffic from the Internet. The two network adapters must also be in distinct networks, or VLANs (virtual LANs), to be officially supported by Microsoft.

Back-to-Back Firewalls

The ideal approach to any perimeter network or DMZ is to utilize two different security devices such that one provides a layer of defense from the Internet to the perimeter network and the other provides another layer of defense by filtering traffic between the perimeter network and the internal network. The Lync Server Edge Servers are situated between the two firewalls in the perimeter network. This approach is illustrated in Figure 31.3.

This configuration is generally considered the most secure because even if an attack compromises the external firewall, the internal firewall still isolates traffic from the attacker. Organizations might even use different firewall vendors for the two firewalls. This ensures that if a security exploit exists for one firewall, it is unlikely the same exploit can be used against the secondary firewall, keeping malicious attacks contained to the perimeter network.

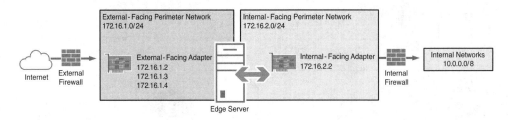

FIGURE 31.3   Back-to-back firewalls.

In this configuration, the Edge Server has the external-facing adapter connected to the more external perimeter network and the internal adapter residing in the internal or more trusted perimeter network.

Three-Legged Firewall

A three-legged firewall approach can be used when it is not feasible to have two physically separate firewall devices separating traffic from the different network segments. Typically, a smaller organization does not have or want to manage a back-to-back firewall, so a single device is used instead to logically construct the same functionality as a back-to-back firewall provides. This single firewall device is generally at least three physical network interfaces or "legs" that are all connected to different networks: one to the public Internet, one to the perimeter network, and one to the internal network.

In this scenario, the Edge Server has two network adapters connected within the perimeter network, but these should still be two separate VLANs. Even though both VLANs exist within the perimeter network zone of the firewall, they are still separate network segments. Figure 31.4 shows the logical layout of a three-legged firewall design.

Firewall rules can still be used to control the flow of traffic between each segment as in a back-to-back scenario, but the primary difference here is that all traffic is run through the same physical device. Whether it is external traffic destined for the perimeter network or perimeter network traffic destined for the internal network, it all flows through the same device.

The primary advantage of a three-legged firewall is that it is generally less expensive because only a single device is required. The disadvantage is that although a three-legged firewall can be used to simulate a back-to-back configuration, the rules can be more difficult to configure, manage, and troubleshoot. It can be easy to mistakenly associate a rule with the wrong source or destination interface.

Another downside compared to a back-to-back firewall design is that if an attacker compromises the firewall, access to all network segments is achieved. Instead of having to infiltrate both firewall devices, simply using one exploit grants access to all networks. That said, a three-legged firewall design is a very popular for small and medium-sized businesses.

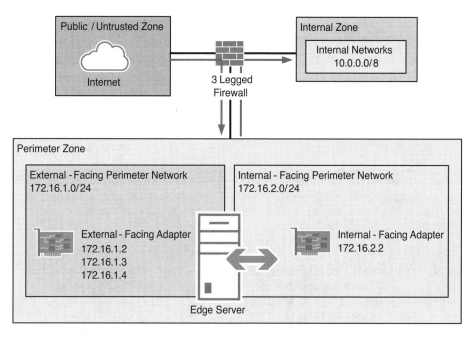

FIGURE 31.4   Three-legged firewall.

Straddling the Internal Firewall

Another firewall topology that, unfortunately, is used too often is where the internal interface of the Edge Server does not pass through any firewall. Instead, it straddles the firewall by being connected directly to the internal network. Administrators still secure the
external adapter in this scenario. However, instead of creating the appropriate rules for the
internal adapter, they just place it on the internal network, as shown in Figure 31.5.

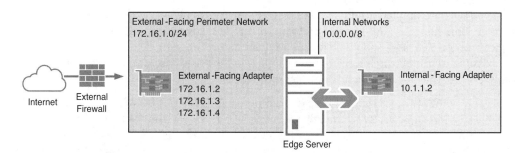

FIGURE 31.5   Lync Server firewall straddling.

There is not much benefit to straddling a firewall with the internal adapter because there
are risks are associated with placing the internal adapter directly on the internal network.
The Edge Server is really designed to be a layer of defense between Internet clients and

internal users, but there is no separation between the Edge and internal network if it can communicate with any client on any port. If the time has been taken to properly secure the external adapter, much of the hard work has already been completed and it shouldn't be difficult to complete the remaining firewall rules to properly secure a server.

Organizations should spend the extra time to properly secure the internal adapter to protect the rest of the Lync Server infrastructure. If a second perimeter network VLAN does not exist, a business should spend time planning to add one to meet the requirements of each Edge adapter being in a separate network.

> **TIP**
>
> Microsoft has designed the Edge Server to be secured properly on both the internal- and the external-facing interfaces. Therefore, always avoid placing the internal adapter directly on the internal network whenever possible.

As a last resort, it is technically possible to place both Edge Server adapters on the same network, but organizations run a risk with this configuration because it is not technically supported. However, some organizations might not allow any device to straddle two perimeter network VLANs, so there might not be another choice. This scenario is a bit more complicated and requires careful planning and configuration of static route commands on each Edge Server.

No Perimeter Network

Organizations without a perimeter network today should take the time to properly plan and design one before deploying Lync Edge services. A Lync Edge Server should never be deployed on an internal network.

Publicly Routable IP Addresses

One consideration when planning for Edge services is that each Lync Edge Server should use three separate publicly routable IP addresses: one for the Access Edge service, one for the Web Conferencing Edge service, and one for the A/V Edge service. All three of these services run on TCP 443, so Lync requires a separate IP address for each unique service. It is possible to run all three services on a single IP address and use non-default ports for some services, but this approach is not recommended.

A decision point for organizations is to determine whether they will assign publicly routable IP addresses directly to the Edge Server adapters, or whether Network Address Translation (NAT) will be used. The deciding factor in that discussion will usually be whether an organization already has a perimeter network segment that uses publicly accessible IP addresses for servers or devices.

Using publicly routable IP addresses on the Edge Server adapter is a perfectly valid design choice, but this suggestion is typically met with a negative reaction from network security teams that are accustomed to using NAT to allow external access to any service. It is important to note that NAT is not a method of security. Instead, it is designed to accommodate a shortage of IPv4 addresses, and although it might mask a server's internal

IP address, as long as the external ports are available NAT does not provide any extra security.

This is not to suggest that an Edge Server external interface should be exposed to the public Internet. Even though publicly routable IP addresses can be bound to the network adapter, the servers are still logically behind a firewall device that limits the ports and protocols allowed to reach the Edge Server. The only difference is that the IP addressing used is part of the public address space instead of a privately addressable space.

> **CAUTION**
>
> Avoid placing the Edge Server's external-facing interface directly on the Internet, even when using publicly routable IP addresses. A firewall should still be used to restrict connections to the Edge Server.

The reason for the publicly routable network requirement is because of how the A/V Edge role uses Interactive Connectivity Establishment (ICE), Session Traversal Utilities for NAT (STUN), and Traversal Using Relay NAT (TURN) to facilitate media traffic between endpoints that might be masked by NAT, such as two users at home behind their own routers. Without delving into too many of the technical details, this requirement comes from the fact that in order for two remote users to communicate, they must be able to send media directly to each other, or both relay their traffic through some common ground such as a Lync Edge Server.

Network Address Translation

The Access Edge and Web Conferencing Edge services have always worked fine with NAT, but when Office Communications Server 2007 was released, it was a requirement to have a publicly routable address space for the external A/V Edge Server interface. In Office Communications Server 2007 R2, support was added for using NAT on the A/V Edge Server interface, but only if a single Edge Server existed in that location. If Edge Server redundancy was required, each A/V Edge interface required a publicly routable address on the adapter.

Lync Server 2010 introduced the capability to use NAT for all three services, including the A/V Edge interface for pools with multiple Edge Servers. Lync Server 2013 continues to support this feature by allowing administrators to specify the public IP address associated with each private A/V Edge address in Topology Builder so that the server will still hand out the correct public IP to clients.

There are some caveats to using NAT, particularly around firewall rules and load balancing.

Hardware Load Balancing

NAT can be used for the Edge Servers only if an organization uses Lync's built-in DNS load-balancing feature. Organizations that prefer to use hardware load balancers for the Edge Servers to support down-level clients or public IM connectivity are still required to use publicly routable IP addresses on the adapters. In this scenario organizations need publicly routable IP addresses for each Edge service, and each hardware load balancer VIP requires a separate public address. The end result is that hardware load balancing requires three additional public IP addresses.

Internal Network NAT

When discussing NAT, the conversation usually centers around the external-facing adapters of an Edge Server. It's important to keep in mind that the internal-facing adapter on the Edge must be *routable* from the internal network. Unlike the external interfaces, it cannot be translated by NAT through a firewall under *any* circumstance. It can be a private address, but it must be completely routable from all server and client subnets without address translation. All clients on the internal network are allowed to communicate directly with an Edge Server's internal-facing interface, and those connections cannot be translated. Using NAT between the internal-facing Edge adapter and the internal network will result in problematic audio/video calls.

The 50,000–59,999 Port Range

The final NAT caveat centers around the TCP/UDP 50,000–59,999 port range that was required to be open to A/V Edge IP addresses in Office Communications Server 2007. This requirement was removed in Office Communications Server 2007 R2, which introduced the capability for Edge Servers to relay media between each other, but since it was not possible to use NAT with multiple Edge Servers back then, it did not cause any issues.

Since Lync Server 2010 and 2013 both support NAT for Edge pools with multiple servers, there is an additional wrinkle to the inbound firewall rules that must be considered. Imagine a scenario in which an organization has two Edge Servers in a single Edge Server pool, both using NAT for the A/V Edge service. If a remote user has media relay IP addresses allocated for them on Edge Server A, and an internal user has media relay IP addresses allocated for them on Edge Server B, the users might be unable to establish a connection.

Normally, in this scenario Edge Server A and Edge Server B would communicate using each other's public IP address, and the connection would work. When the Edge Servers are each hidden by NAT, though, they might be unable to communicate with each other's public IP because of firewall restrictions. Most modern firewalls prevent "hairpinning" shown in Figure 31.6, or the capability for a server in one security zone to reach a public IP that has a NAT to another server in the same zone.

Since the Edge Servers will relay media only through their public IP addresses, the call will fail when the firewall drops the connection due to a hairpinning attempt. There are two possible solutions to this issue if an organization insists on using NAT:

▶ Configure static NAT rules at the firewall to allow the Edge Servers to use hairpinning between each other's A/V Edge public IP address.

▶ Open TCP and UDP 50,000–59,999 inbound to each A/V Edge public IP address.

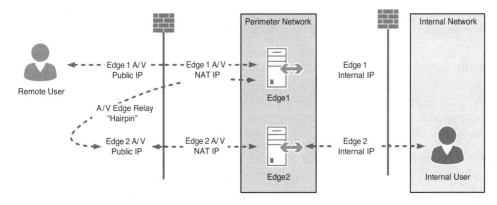

FIGURE 31.6   Edge Server NAT and hairpin.

Planning for High-Availability

When adding high-availability to a Lync Server Edge Server deployment, an organization must make a decision about how it will provide load-balancing features. The only options available for load-balancing Edge Servers are to use Lync's native DNS load-balancing feature or to leverage a hardware load-balancing solution.

> **CAUTION**
>
> Windows Network Load Balancing (NLB) is not supported for load balancing any of the Lync Server roles, including Edge Server features.

DNS load balancing seems like an attractive feature at first because it requires very little configuration, but does have some minor limitations. Organizations should review these limitations and then make a decision about whether a hardware load balancer is required. The main limitation of DNS load balancing is that it does provide automatic failover for some features or legacy endpoints, including these:

▶ Endpoints running previous versions of the Office Communicator client

▶ Federated organizations running Office Communications Server 2007 R2 or previous

▶ Public IM connectivity

▶ Exchange Server 2007 and 2010 Unified Messaging

This doesn't mean these features won't work; it simply means they are not aware of DNS load balancing and the fact that they could leverage a second server if the first DNS record returned is not responding. So in a scenario in which both servers are online there will be no difference, but during an outage these features will not automatically fail over. Administrators might need to manually remove some DNS entries to prevent clients from connecting to a failed server.

Many organizations still elect to use DNS load balancing despite the minor limitations addressed here due to the deployment simplicity and cost savings.

Hardware Load Balancing Requirements

Using a hardware load balancer comes at a greater cost than DNS load balancing, but adds some flexibility and backward compatibility that an organization might require. Configuring the hardware load balancer is typically the most difficult part of an Edge Server deployment simply because of how flexible the load-balancing software generally is.

Some basic guidelines must be followed when using a hardware load balancer for Edge services:

▶ Each external-facing Edge service needs a publicly routable virtual IP address.

▶ Each Edge Server needs three publicly routable IP addresses assigned.

To summarize the requirements, if an organization deploys two Edge Servers with a hardware load balancer, it needs *nine* publicly routable IP addresses: three for the virtual IP addresses and three for each Edge Server. That logical configuration is depicted in Figure 31.7.

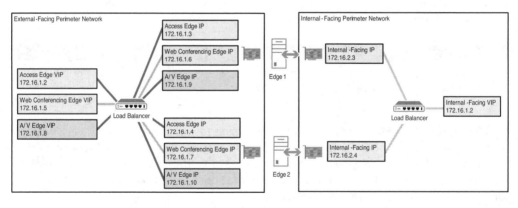

FIGURE 31.7   Hardware load balancer VIPs and Edge Server real IPs.

In addition to the public IP addressing requirements, there are some stipulations about what type of Network Address Translation must be configured on the load balancer. For traffic from the Internet to the server, the hardware load balancer must use Destination Network Address Translation (DNAT).

This means that as a packet is received from the Internet to the virtual IP address, the hardware load balancer rewrites the packet to change the destination IP address to one of the IP addresses actually assigned to an Edge Server network adapter.

> **CAUTION**
>
> The fact that the term NAT is used here does not imply that the Edge Server uses private IP addresses. Even though the Edge Server has a public IP address, the load balancer must somehow still translate requests to the virtual IP address to an IP address actually assigned to an Edge Server.

For traffic from the server to the Internet, the load balancer must be configured for Source Network Address Translation (SNAT). This means that packets sent outbound from the Edge Servers are translated by the load balancer back to the virtual IP address that the external Internet clients expect to communicate with.

Hardware Load-Balancer Configuration

This section discusses the hardware load-balancer configuration for an Edge Server. There are two perspectives to look at for load balancing Edge Servers because the external-facing adapter and the internal-facing adapter have their own requirements. An Edge Server must be load balanced on both sides to function properly, but each side has slightly different requirements as shown in Figure 31.8.

> **CAUTION**
>
> Many load balancers have the option to balance "All Ports" for a given pool. Avoid this configuration, no matter how tempting and easy it seems. Instead, load balance only the ports found in the tables that follow. This allows the load balancer to properly monitor health of a particular service and use different persistence methods for each type of traffic.

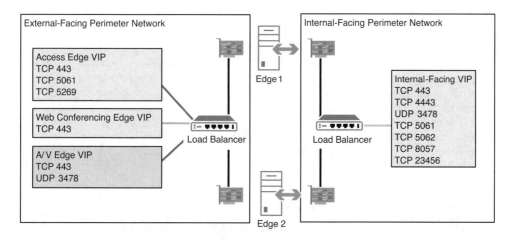

FIGURE 31.8   Edge Server load-balanced ports.

Table 31.1 outlines which ports must be load balanced to each virtual IP address.

TABLE 31.1   External Edge Interface Load Balancing

Virtual IP Address	Port	Function
Access Edge	TCP 443	Remote access
Access Edge	TCP 5061	Federation and Public IM
Access Edge	TCP 5269	XMPP Federation
Web Conferencing Edge	TCP 443	Remote web conferencing
A/V Edge	TCP 443	STUN
A/V Edge	UDP 3478	STUN

After the external interface load balancing has been configured, the internal adapter configuration must be completed. Unlike the external adapter that uses three virtual IP addresses, only a single virtual IP address is required for the internal adapter because each Edge Server has only a single IP address for its internal adapter.

Table 31.2 outlines which ports must be load balanced to each virtual IP address.

TABLE 31.2   Internal Edge Interface Load Balancing

Virtual IP Address	Port	Function
Edge Internal Interface	TCP 5061	Signaling
Edge Internal Interface	TCP 5062	A/V authentication
Edge Internal Interface	TCP 443	STUN
Edge Internal Interface	UDP 3478	STUN

CAUTION

There is no entry here for load balancing the internal Web Conferencing Edge interface. That is not an omission or error; port 8057 on the internal interface should not be load balanced by the hardware load balancer. The Front End pools automatically distribute requests to multiple Web Conferencing Edge Servers if configured. Don't forget to include TCP 8057 in the firewall rules, though, because even though it's not load balanced, the Front End Servers need to be able to reach that port on Edge Servers.

DNS Load Balancing Requirements

If the limitations of DNS load balancing described earlier don't pose any issues to an organization's Lync Server deployment, the organization can proceed with that method instead of purchasing a hardware load balancer. There are actually some advantages to using DNS load balancing, mainly the simplicity involved in configuration that just involves using multiple A records for the same name in public DNS. Table 31.3 shows the DNS records required to achieve DNS load balancing.

TABLE 31.3   DNS Load-Balancing Entries

Host Record	IP Address
sip.companyabc.com	Access Edge Server A IP address
sip.companyabc.com	Access Edge Server B IP address
webconf.companyabc.com	Web Conferencing Edge Server A IP address
webconf.companyabc.com	Web Conferencing Edge Server B IP address
av.companyabc.com	A/V Edge Server A IP address
av.companyabc.com	A/V Edge Server B IP address

When using DNS load balancing, the Edge Server can use private IP addresses that are translated by NAT for all three roles, including the A/V Edge. This is a big advantage for organizations that might not have many public IP addresses available, or an existing perimeter network with publicly routable addresses.

DNS load balancing also requires three fewer IP addresses than a hardware load-balancing solution. Each Edge Server IP still needs to be mapped to a unique public IP address if it is being translated by NAT, but there is no concept of a VIP. Instead, each client has logic built-in to realize that there are multiple servers with separate IP addresses to which it could connect.

Another advantage of DNS load balancing is that the native server-draining feature in Lync Server is available. This enables administrators to prepare a server by maintenance through the Lync Server Control Panel the same way as the other roles.

In some organizations, the team responsible for Lync Server might not be the same team that manages the network and hardware load balancers, which can make it difficult to coordinate preparing a server for maintenance. Instead of the Lync Server administrators quickly draining a server's connections, they might need to submit a request to have the network team drain the load balancer connections for a particular node and then check back later to determine whether the connections have cleared. Sometimes this separation of teams can be just as efficient as one person having complete control, but often it slows down the maintenance process.

NOTE

Although DNS load balancing is available for Edge Servers, keep in mind that the reverse proxy for web component services is a critical piece of remote access. Load balancing for a reverse proxy must be addressed separately and can be done either with a hardware load balancer or possibly through Windows Network Load Balancing (NLB).

Reverse Proxy Planning

A critical piece in planning for Edge services is the reverse proxy. Unfortunately, this tends to be overlooked or considered a secondary task, even though it provides some important functionality to a deployment. Without a reverse proxy the following features will not work:

▶ Lync Mobile clients

▶ Address book download

▶ Distribution group expansion

▶ Web conferencing content such as whiteboards, uploaded presentations, and document sharing

▶ Device updates

▶ Dial-in conferencing page

▶ Simple meet conferencing pages

The first item might be a bit of a surprise, but the mobile clients for Lync use HTTPS web services to encapsulate the SIP signaling information. Organizations that neglect planning for a reverse proxy are effectively preventing their users from using Lync Mobile clients.

The concept of a reverse proxy is simple to understand when considering it as an extra hop or barrier between external clients and an internal resource. What a reverse proxy offers is the capability to inspect the traffic a client sends for any malicious requests, or possibly even pre-authenticates the user before being allowed to reach an internal client. In the overall scheme of external services, the reverse proxy fits in as depicted in Figure 31.9.

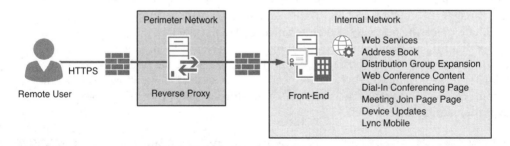

FIGURE 31.9   Reverse proxy for web services.

Reverse Proxy Methodologies

After understanding the functionality of a reverse proxy, it's important to comprehend the different methods a reverse proxy can use to publish internal services. Three main methods are used and not all of them are available depending on the reverse proxy used.

31

SSL Pass-Through

The most basic method is SSL pass-through. This means that the traffic from Internet clients runs through the reverse proxy, but the SSL connection exists from the client all the way to the internal resource as shown in Figure 31.9. This is the most basic form of reverse proxy.

SSL Offloading

Another common methodology in reverse proxy scenarios is to use SSL offloading. In this scenario, the client's SSL tunnel terminates at the reverse proxy, which then initiates a clear-text, HTTP request to the internal resource. Many hardware load balancers offer this functionality and advertise that it can improve performance of servers by "offloading" the SSL encryption and decryption duties from the internal server.

This is a valuable feature when a server is CPU-constrained, but with modern hardware, this is rarely necessary. Any hardware used for Lync Server probably far exceeds the CPU capabilities of most load-balancing devices. Furthermore, Lync Server is designed to operate in a secure manner end-to-end and does not actually support SSL offloading. However, in this scenario the SSL tunnel is terminated at the reverse proxy, which then communicates over port 80 to the Front End pool, leaving an unencrypted component.

SSL Bridging

The final methodology, which is the preferred scenario, is to use SSL Bridging. In this case, the client's SSL tunnels at the reverse proxy as in an offloading scenario, but the reverse proxy then opens a second HTTPS connection back to the internal resource. This ensures that the entire transmission is encrypted from end to end.

There is also some added flexibility in this case, in that a reverse proxy can redirect that second connection to a port other than 443 back on the internal resource without the client's knowledge. As far as the client knows, it still has a connection on port 443 to the internal resource, even though the reverse proxy might bridge this connection to port 4443 on the internal Front End pool. Figure 31.10 shows where the reverse proxy bridges a port 443 connection from the client to port 4443 on the Front End pool, but still secures the traffic.

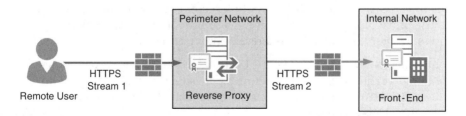

FIGURE 31.10   SSL bridging.

To summarize the options, the preferred method for Lync Server is SSL Bridging to ensure an end-to-end encryption of the traffic with the most flexibility. SSL offloading is not supported, so if bridging is not an option, the reverse proxy deployment should use SSL pass-through.

NOTE

A common question is to ask whether a reverse proxy is actually needed, or whether an organization can simply do a port translation at the firewall to a Front End pool. Though technically possible, this scenario is entirely unsupported by Microsoft and should be avoided. Not using a reverse proxy also means that public certificates might need to be placed on the Front End Servers because they will communicate directly with Internet users.

Placement and Configuration

Placement of the reverse proxy server follows the same concept as the Edge Server, so wherever a Lync Edge Server is deployed, a reverse proxy in that location should be used. This becomes especially important when users leverage web conferencing because the display of content comes through the reverse proxy. As with the Edge Server, optimizing that traffic path results in a better user experience—especially for users joining conferences via Lync Web App.

Setting up the reverse proxy is similar to an Edge Server. Generally the reverse proxy is placed in a perimeter network and has two network adapters: one internal-facing and one external-facing. To reach internal server subnets, route statements must also be configured. Some products also have the ability to use a single network adapter while acting as a reverse proxy.

Microsoft Reverse Proxy Products

Microsoft has had a reverse proxy product of its own since it began providing Microsoft Internet Security and Acceleration (ISA) Server, which eventually became Microsoft Threat Management Gateway (TMG), and was a popular reverse proxy choice for many Microsoft Lync or Exchange deployments. TMG offered an intuitive graphical interface which many users were comfortable using to publish web services. Since Microsoft has made an end-of-life announcement for TMG, customers will have to leverage alternate products for Lync Server 2013 reverse proxy capabilities. Microsoft has also introduced guidance on how to use IIS Application Request Routing (ARR) as a reverse proxy for Lync.

Microsoft is continuing to develop the Microsoft Unified Access Gateway (UAG) product, but does not fully support all the Lync and Exchange publishing scenarios TMG provided. As of this writing, UAG 2010 still has issues with the Lync mobility service and is not recommended for new deployments.

Reverse Proxy Load Balancing

Each reverse proxy product will handle this differently, but planning for redundancy will usually involve using multiple reverse proxy servers and load balancing the services. TMG and UAG allowed for Windows Network Load Balancing, which, although a really poor solution, was leveraged by many organizations because it was free. Depending on the product, a software form of load balancing might be provided, or a hardware load balancer can be used with the reverse proxy to distribute requests to multiple servers. The only port required for load balancing the reverse proxy is TCP 443, but organizations might also want to load balance TCP 80 and redirect that traffic automatically to TCP 443 instead. This ensures that a request is still routed if a user manually types in a friendly URL for meetings or dial-in information but forgets to specify HTTPS.

Cookie Persistence

When Lync Server 2010 was first released, each reverse proxy component required only Layer 4 Source IP persistence for connections. This meant that based on the client's IP address it would continue to be directed to the same real server by a load balancer as long as that server was still responding.

When the Lync Mobile clients were released, this guidance shifted such that cookie-level affinity was required at the load balancers in front of a reverse proxy. Cookie persistence is a small piece of information stored on the client that identifies a particular session on the load balancer. When the client makes a connection request, the load balancer uses the information held in the cookie to route the request to a real server.

The happened because when mobile clients switch between an internal Wi-Fi connection and a cellular data connection, their IP address can change. So after an IP change, when the client made a new request, the load balancer would detect a new source IP address, treat the mobile user as a new connection, and potentially send the user's traffic to a different Front End Server than the previous connection.

This didn't mean that the new connection would fail, but it did create an extra session on the Front End Server; and if a user moved to another Wi-Fi network, yet another session would be opened. When cookie persistence is required for each connection, that same mobile client will always be reconnected to any existing session as it moves between networks. This is because cookie-level affinity only uses the information in the cookie and does not care what IP address the client is using.

The Lync Server 2013 Mobile clients no longer require cookie persistence, and handle the session state within the Front End servers. This greatly simplifies the hardware load balancer and reverse proxy configuration because IP address affinity can again be used.

Pre-Authentication

Pre-authentication is a feature that lets the reverse proxy authenticate a user before completing the SSL bridge back to an internal server. This way, unauthenticated traffic is not allowed to communicate with internal services, which makes the deployment more secure. Without pre-authentication, the SSL traffic is authenticated by the internal pool server. It is still inspected and filtered for malicious code by the reverse proxy, but pass-through authentication requires the internal servers to handle authentication of the requests.

Not all features of Lync Server support pre-authentication, and whether pre-authentication can be leveraged depends greatly on business requirements.

Specifically, if anonymous remote access is required for web conferences or dial-in conferencing, there must still be some form of anonymous access allowed through the reverse proxy without authentication. In those situations, rules at the reverse proxy must be configured to only pre-authenticate traffic destined for specific virtual directories or FQDNs.

Pre-authentication of traffic can add quite a bit of complexity to an environment, so an early step in troubleshooting issues should be to disable this feature if it's enabled.

Exchange Services Publishing

Many components of Lync rely on connections to Exchange Web Services (EWS), a web-based component of Exchange Server since 2007. The Lync client itself is fairly resilient to falling back to MAPI calls to Outlook for information, but clients like Lync Phone Edition or Lync Mobile for Apple's iOS platform are heavily dependent on Exchange Web Services being published remotely.

Exchange Web Services are typically published through the same reverse proxy Lync uses, but in some cases organizations might restrict access to Outlook or Exchange Web Services from remote clients. It's important to discuss Exchange Web Services early on when planning to provide remote Lync services because it can greatly affect the user experience. For example, remote Lync Phone Edition users might be unable to view visual voice mail, access calendar data, or see all call history if EWS is not published. And Lync Mobile for iOS clients cannot view any calendar data or join Online Meetings if EWS is not accessible.

TIP

Advanced scripting engines in some reverse proxy products can be used to restrict Exchange Web Services access to specific application host headers. This can be useful for organizations that want to allow Lync Mobile or Lync Phone Edition clients to access Exchange Web Services, but prevent other applications such as Outlook for PCs and Macs from connecting.

Organizations that rely on products like Good Technology instead of Microsoft ActiveSync for mobile email might also miss out on some features for the Windows Phone and Android mobile platforms in which Lync Mobile integrates with the native calendar and contact applications. The take-away here is that Lync endpoints leverage many components of Exchange, so it is important to ensure that Exchange services are also properly published through a reverse proxy when planning a Lync deployment.

Planning for Certificates

Provisioning certificates for Edge Servers was a sore subject back in the Office Communications Server days, but the process has been greatly simplified by the wizards used since Lync Server 2013. This section discusses the certificate requirements and considerations for organizations deciding between public certificates and privately issued certificates.

An Edge Server requires certificates for three services:

▶ Internal Edge Interface

▶ Access Edge Service

▶ Web Conferencing Edge Service

TIP

Although the A/V Edge Media Relay service also runs on TCP 443, it does not have a certificate assigned. Instead, a key used to encrypt and decrypt the media flowing through this port is first passed through the Access Edge FQDN. There is no need to include the A/V Edge FQDN in any certificate request.

Administrators of Office Communications Server should note that since Lync Server 2010, the certificate requests are commonly broken out more simply to a certificate used for the external-facing Edge interface, and a single certificate is used for the internal-facing Edge interface.

Public Versus Private Certificate Authorities

A common misconception is that all of these certificates should be purchased from a public certificate authority, which is only partly true. Only certificates used for the external-facing Edge interface should come from a public certificate authority. The Edge Server's internal interface certificate can be issued from a private certificate authority that is trusted only by internal servers and clients.

Microsoft has partnered with a few certificate vendors to ensure that the X.509 certificates work with Lync Server. Those vendors are listed here:

▶ Entrust

▶ Comodo

▶ Digicert

▶ GoDaddy

Certificates from other vendors also work if all clients trust the certificate, but Microsoft has not verified those vendors. The vendors listed previously have the best compatibility between different server, desktop, and device platforms.

External Edge Server Interface

This certificate should be issued by a public certificate authority. The specific requirements for subject names and subject alternative names for the certificate on the external interface of an Edge Server pool are outlined next. The same certificate and private key should be exported and installed on each member of the same Edge Server pool.

▶ **Access Edge**—The subject name should match the published name of the Access Edge FQDN in public DNS. If a hardware load balancer is used, this is the name clients resolve to the virtual IP address. The subject alternative name field should contain any supported SIP domains in the `sip.<SIP Domain>` format.

▶ **Web Conferencing Edge**—The subject name should match the published name of the Web Conferencing Edge FQDN in public DNS. If a hardware load balancer is used, this is the name clients resolve to the virtual IP address. No subject alternative names are required.

▶ **A/V Edge**—This service has no certificate associated, but it is included here to provide clarity that the A/V Edge FQDN should *not* be included in a certificate request.

Lync Server 2013 uses subject alternative name (SAN) certificates in many locations, including the external-facing Edge Server certificate. Organizations typically include the Access Edge, Web Conferencing Edge, and any supported SIP domains on a single certificate to reduce maintenance costs and overhead.

Internal Edge Server Interface

This certificate can be issued by an internal, private certificate authority. The specific requirements for subject names and subject alternative names for the certificate on the internal interface of an Edge Server pool are outlined next. The same certificate and private key should be exported and installed on each member of the same Edge Server pool.

▶ **Internal Edge**—The subject name should match the published name of the Edge Server internal pool. If a hardware load balancer is used, this is the name that resolves to the internal virtual IP address. No subject alternative names should be included in this request.

The last certificate required is not actually bound to the Edge Servers and is required for the reverse proxy.

Reverse Proxy Interface

This certificate should be issued by a public certificate authority. The specific requirements for subject names and subject alternative names for the certificate on a reverse proxy are outlined next. The same certificate and private key should be exported and installed on each member of the same Edge Server pool.

▶ **Reverse Proxy**—The subject name should match the published name of the external web services FQDN. The subject alternative name should contain any simple URLs for dial-in, online meetings, and an entry for `lyncdiscover.<SIP Domain>` for each supported SIP domain.

> **TIP**
>
> Organizations can reduce the number of certificates from a public certificate authority by simply including the reverse proxy naming requirements as additional subject alternative names used for the external Edge Server interface. The same public certificate can then be deployed to the Edge Servers and reverse proxy.

Wildcard Certificates

Wildcard certificates in the format of `*.<domain>` have become increasingly popular because they provide a way to secure a large number of websites at a low cost by using only a single certificate. Unfortunately, many functions in Lync Server simply don't work well or at all if a wildcard certificate is used. At this time, the recommendation is to avoid using a wildcard certificate for any Lync Server roles.

Specifically, older Lync or Office Communications Server Phone Edition clients will be unable to access the Device Update Service, and federation with public IM connectivity or down-level partners running Office Communications Server will not work properly. There is a cumulative update available that allows Lync Phone Edition clients to leverage wildcard certificates, but getting this update to the phones still requires a non-wildcard certificate. Additionally, it may be difficult to procure a certificate that includes the wildcard as a subject alternative name, as required by Microsoft.

Network Planning Considerations

Deploying Lync Server 2013 Edge services will always invoke discussions around alternative remote access technologies like VPN, or Microsoft's DirectAccess. There are some additional considerations with network equipment like firewalls or WAN accelerators that should be discussed when any Edge roles are being deployed.

VPN Connectivity to Lync

Virtual Private Network (VPN) is a concept many users and organizations have been familiar with for years. The concept is that a remote user establishes a VPN connection to the office, and has full access to all internal services, which raises the question of why Lync Edge Server is required at all.

VPN works by encapsulating all traffic within a secured tunnel, but that tunnel generally includes a lot of overhead and additional latency. All of Lync's SIP signaling traffic and A/V media traffic is already securely encrypted, so the additional VPN tunnel encapsulating the traffic is really redundant. This isn't a huge problem for SIP signaling, but when two users try to establish an A/V call, that overhead, shown in Figure 31.11, can significantly impact the call quality.

The Lync Edge Server provides the most optimal path for A/V calls for remote users. Any deployment leveraging audio or video features of Lync should not be relying on VPN to provide a way to connect calls for remote users.

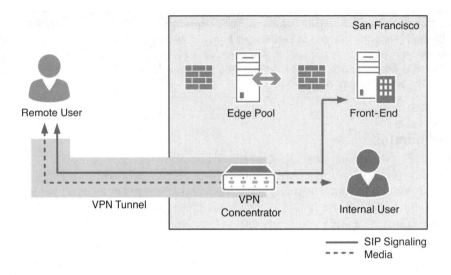

FIGURE 31.11   VPN double encryption.

Blocking Media over VPN

In fact, organizations deploying Lync Edge services should be going out of their way to avoid the possibility of clients connecting a media stream over the VPN tunnel. Lync clients always prefer a direct peer-to-peer connection when negotiating a call, but they don't have any logic to determine whether they are on a VPN connection. So when a user establishes a VPN and then tries to call a user on the internal network, the two clients will think they should connect peer-to-peer instead of relaying their traffic through the Edge Server.

Depending on the VPN technology, organizations can use a combination of defined port ranges, IP address ranges, and source executable names to effectively block Lync clients from connecting over VPN. These blocks need to be put in place between VPN clients and internal network users, and between the VPN users and Lync Front End or Mediation server roles.

After these blocks are established, a user's Lync client will continue to use the Edge Server for all signaling and media, as depicted in Figure 31.12, regardless of whether a user has a VPN connected. This does require split-tunnel access to the Edge server public addresses.

Blocking Media over DirectAccess

Microsoft's DirectAccess technology is another form of remote connectivity that has gained popularity over the past few years. DirectAccess maintains a persistent IPv4 connection to the corporate network's IPv6 resources using tunneling, which then allows remote users to transparently access internal servers. Lync Server 2010 did not support IPv6 at all, but now that Lync Server 2013 does support IPv6, it is technically possible to use DirectAccess to connect a remote Lync user to a Front End pool.

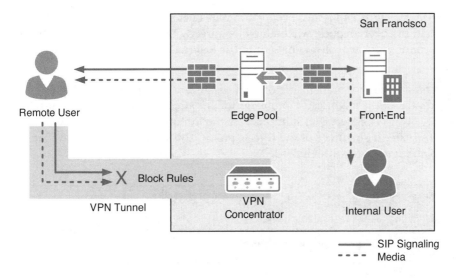

San Francisco

Remote User

Edge Pool

Front-End

X   Block Rules

VPN Tunnel

VPN
Concentrator

Internal User

——— SIP Signaling
- - - - Media

FIGURE 31.12   VPN deny rules.

However, in practice this is still not a good solution for Edge services. DirectAccess suffers the same limitations as any other VPN technology in that it is redundantly encapsulating the media traffic Lync uses for audio or video calls.

Administrators can block remote users from connecting to Lync internal servers over DirectAccess by implementing exceptions in the Name Resolution Policy Table (NRPT) on the DirectAccess servers. DirectAccess is based on FQDNs instead of IP addresses like a traditional VPN technology, so these exclusions prevent remote users from resolving internal Lync resources to their tunneled IPv6 address.

Avoiding WAN Acceleration

Many organizations deploy multiple sites that are separated by wide area network (WAN) connectivity with limited bandwidth, and work to deploy WAN accelerator devices that help optimize the traffic by compressing network traffic. WAN accelerators work only if both sides of a network contain the same device that can compress and then unpack the traffic identically.

Unfortunately, the connections used by Lync servers and clients are completely encrypted, so the accelerator devices are unable to efficiently compress the traffic. WAN accelerators can even negatively affect an audio stream or persistent TLS connections between servers in different sites. A best practice is to exclude all Lync server IP addresses from any form of traffic optimization devices.

Firewall Hairpin for Lync Mobile

The final network device consideration centers around the Lync Mobility service. In Lync Server 2013 all Lync Mobile clients will access the mobility service through the *external* web services FQDN for Front End pools. Even if a mobile device is on an internal Wi-Fi network, the initial discovery request will be handled directly by a Front End server, but any subsequent connections will always be sent to the external interface of the reverse proxy.

This generally isn't an issue for branch sites or if an organization hosts its Lync deployment in a data center, but it might cause problems for an office that has a Lync Front End pool deployed locally, as in Figure 31.13. In this case the internal Wi-Fi clients must be able to contact the external interface of the reverse proxy. This might require additional static NAT configuration rules at the firewall.

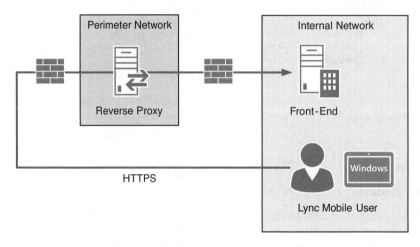

FIGURE 31.13   Lync Mobility firewall hairpin.

Preparing for Edge Servers

A good deal of preparation goes into making an Edge Server ready for deployment, and the actual installation of Lync Server is probably one of the easiest parts after a server is correctly configured. This section discusses some of the configuration requirements and considerations an organization must make when preparing an Edge Server.

Capacity Planning

Organizations should plan for enough Edge Servers in each location to meet the capacity requirements of the environment. Microsoft recommends one Edge server for every 12,000 concurrent remote users based on their standard user model.

Domain Membership Considerations

Edge Servers do not store any directory information or user data, but they should never be joined to an internal Active Directory domain. Edge Servers are typically deployed in workgroup mode, which can create some additional issues, such as security policy enforcement and patching. Administrators must manually account for patching these servers, changing local security policies instead of using Group Policy and Windows Server Update Services (WSUS). By not being part of the domain, these servers can potentially be left unpatched with security vulnerabilities.

There are workarounds to these issues, such as using registry keys to point servers at an internal WSUS server or allowing Edge Servers to automatically update patches. However, organizations might block the ports required for WSUS to a perimeter network or might not want servers to apply patches without being tested first.

Another option is to join Edge Servers to a separate Active Directory forest that has been deployed within the perimeter network. Some businesses deploy a separate forest to work around the management and maintenance issues previously discussed.

If the Edge Server is part of a workgroup configuration, be sure to define a primary DNS suffix for the machine, and use that FQDN within Topology Builder and for any certificates.

Network Adapter Configuration

Setting up IP addresses, DNS servers, and gateways on the Edge Server adapters can be a point of confusion in a deployment because of the requirement for dual network adapters. To begin with, an Edge Server must have two separate network adapters: one that is internal-facing and one that is external- or public-facing.

> **NOTE**
>
> It was possible to use three separate adapters for each external-facing Edge service in Office Communications Server, but Microsoft recommends using a single external-facing adapter with Lync Server 2013. The extra adapters were really unnecessary and complicated the deployment.

The internal adapter should have a single IP address, and the external adapter should have three separate IP addresses associated—one for each Edge service. Using the first entered or primary IP address for the external network adapter as the Access Edge service IP address helps ensure reliable routing.

> **TIP**
>
> It always helps to name the network connections descriptively instead of leaving the "Local Area Connection <Connection Number>" name on the adapter. Naming the interfaces "Internal" and "External" makes a clear distinction about what function each adapter serves.

Default Gateways and Routing

Another point of confusion when one is configuring the network adapters is where to place the default gateway. Many administrators try to place gateways on both network adapters, which causes extremely unreliable traffic flows. It does not matter whether the adapters are all on the same or different subnets; only one adapter should have a default gateway assigned.

For an Edge Server, always place the default gateway on the external-facing network adapter associated with the Access Edge Server IP address. This applies whether a single external adapter is used for all three roles or whether multiple adapters are used. This ensures that all requests the server does not know how to route are passed out through the Access Edge IP address.

The tricky part of configuring an Edge Server is to make sure that it always uses the internal-facing network adapter to communicate with any internal servers or clients. Administrators can accomplish this by creating persistent static routes on each Edge Server. Routing is something generally associated with network devices, but in the case of a multihomed server, an administrator must configure the routing table to act appropriately. For a Lync Server Edge role, the administrator must manually enter route statements to use that internal adapter for internal subnets. Figure 31.14 shows how the external adapter has a default gateway associated, but routing statements for internal networks make use of the internal adapter.

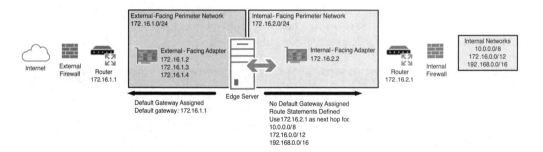

FIGURE 31.14   Edge Server gateways and routing.

It's possible to use the netsh.exe command to add static routes for all of the private IP ranges using the following syntax:

```
netsh interface ipv4 add route 10.0.0.0/8 "<Internal-Facing Interface Name>"
<Internal-Facing Network Gateway>

netsh interface ipv4 add route 172.16.0.0/12 "<Internal-Facing Interface Name>"
<Internal-Facing Network Gateway>

netsh interface ipv4 add route 192.168.0.0/16 "<Internal-Facing Interface Name>"
<Internal-Facing Network Gateway>
```

Be sure to run this command again for any additional publicly routable IP addresses that are part of the internal network.

Summary

Spending a good deal of time planning for Edge services makes any deployment much easier. Admittedly, there are so many moving pieces to an Edge Server deployment that it is easy to miss something, but Microsoft has made great strides to improve the installation and configuration process with Lync Server. Planning the Edge names, IP addressing, routing, and firewall configuration in advance of any installation streamlines the deployment process.

31

CHAPTER 32

Planning for Voice Deployment

Spending time to plan and prepare for a Lync Enterprise Voice deployment is an important step for organizations, and will have a significant impact in determining whether the deployment is a success.

Be sure to review the concepts found in Chapter 17, "Lync Telephony and Voice Integration," before continuing in this chapter. Many of the discussions in this chapter assume that an integration method has been discussed and selected.

This chapter discusses what details to consider when planning for Lync Enterprise Voice, and how those decisions can affect other aspects of the deployment. Dial plans, steering codes, and normalization rules are covered, along with how to apply those concepts to a trunk configuration. Also discussed is how to plan for different classes of service within voice policies, and how least cost routing and tail-end hop off factor into routing.

The different options available for providing voice resiliency are discussed, and the differences between a Survivable Branch Server (SBS) and a Survivable Branch Appliance (SBA) are covered in this chapter. Lastly, planning concepts around Call Admission Control, Media Bypass, E911, and Response Groups is included.

Dial Plan

When beginning a Lync Server 2013 voice deployment, one of the first steps is to determine the dial plan. The dial plan defines how many digits are used in each site, whether site prefixes are used, and any number translations required from site to site. Dial-plan objects in Lync Server

2013 contain a collection of normalization rules that are associated with a site or pool, or that are directly assigned to user accounts.

In many cases an organization's existing dial plan can simply be reused and there is no requirement to assign new telephone numbers to users as they are migrated to Lync. This can be accomplished with some form of PBX integration, either via direct SIP trunk or through a media gateway.

Assigning Telephone URIs

A concept that can seem foreign to traditional voice administrators is that users are assigned a Line URI instead of an extension. These URIs are composed of a Direct Inward Dialing (DID) number, which is unique both internally and across the PSTN, or the URIs can be based on extensions that are unique only to the organization. The point here is that users are not simply an extension attached to a phone; their user account is associated to a Line URI that follows their account and all endpoints.

When assigning URIs to end users, keep in mind that all URIs within the organization must be unique. Typically, organizations with multiple sites have multiple DID ranges per office, or extensions that are unique only within a specific site. To accommodate these scenarios, multiple dial plans and normalization rules can be created to accommodate the expectations of end users. URIs are also assigned in the E.164 format, which resembles tel:+14157773234.

Direct Inward Dialing

The simplest dial plan possible within Lync Server 2010 is when each user in the organization has a direct DID number. DIDs are unique across the PSTN, and therefore unique within the Lync Server deployment. A PSTN caller or an internal user can use the same dial string to reach another user when DIDs are assigned to each user in the organization.

DIDs also typically map to a user's internal extension. For example, at Company ABC's San Francisco office, Alice has a DID of +1 (415) 777-3234, but internal users can simply dial 3234, the last four digits of her extension, to reach Alice. This gives the flexibility of numbers being unique across the site, but with the capability for PSTN callers to reach users directly. Internal users also have a short, four-digit dial string to remember in order to reach Alice.

On the Lync Server 2010 configuration side, Alice's telephone URI field should be entered as tel:+14157773234 to uniquely identify her in the organization. A normalization rule within the San Francisco dial plan converts a four-digit extension starting with the number 3 into the full E.164 URI for users. That rule resembles the following:

Dial Plan: San Francisco

Name: Four-digit San Francisco extensions

Starting Digits: 3

Length: Exactly four digits

Digits to Remove: None

Digits to Add: +1415777

This rule handles the San Francisco DID range, but consider a scenario if Company ABC also has a Chicago office where users have DIDs starting with +1 (312) 444-5xxx. Because all the Chicago extensions start with a 5, any four-digit extension beginning with a 5 can be translated to include the Chicago DID prefix. Chicago users should have a telephone URI assigned resembling tel:+13124445xxx. A second normalization rule can be added to the dial plan to handle this office's DID range:

Dial Plan: San Francisco

Name: Four-digit Chicago extensions

Starting Digits: 5

Length: Exactly four digits

Digits to Remove: None

Digits to Add: +1312444

After this rule is added to the dial plan, San Francisco users can dial by entering just four digits on a keypad or within the Lync client and correctly route to a user in either San Francisco or Chicago.

Internal Extensions

Many times organizations will not offer DID numbers to users, or might assign DIDs to only some users. In this case, the remaining users only have an internal extension defined. This is a completely acceptable deployment option with Lync Server 2010, but there can be some confusion as to how the telephone URI should be assigned to user accounts.

The most common method is to identify a main office, or an automated-attendant phone number, that external users can dial and be transferred to in order to reach users with an internal extension. This type of attendant does not have to exist, but it usually makes sense to leverage this number in the telephone URI. After this number is identified, it should be used as the telephone URI with a ";ext=xxx" suffix. The number of digits in the extension field can vary depending on the organization or even the site.

For example, let's say that Company ABC's San Francisco office does not offer DIDs to users and uses internal extensions only. The main office number is +1 (415) 777-3000 and Alice has extension 234. In this case, Alice's Line URI field should be tel:+14157773000;ext=234, which uniquely identifies her within the organization. Bob might have extension 567 and his Line URI would be tel:+14157773000;ext=567.

TIP

Using extension-based URIs will prevent an organization from assigning that main line URI to a user because Lync considers the numbers ambiguous. Using the previous example, a receptionist cannot have the URI tel:+14157773000 if Alice has an extension URI based on the same number like tel:+14157773000;ext=234. To work around this issue, use tel:+14157773000;ext=3000 for the main line account, and translate calls to the main line into this number.

This extension-based scenario must also be accounted for within a dial plan. The dial plan within San Francisco must include a normalization rule that takes a three-digit dial into this URI, such as the following rule:

Dial Plan: San Francisco

Name: Three digits to San Francisco

Starting Digits: Blank

Length: Exactly three digits

Digits to Remove: 0

Digits to Add: +14157773000;ext=

CAUTION

The Normalization Rule Wizard cannot be used to create this type of rule because the ;ext= component is not a valid number. Instead, define the regular expression matching pattern and translation rule manually. In this example, the matching pattern is ^(\d{3})$ and the translation rule is +14157773000;ext=$1.

Site Prefixes

A common scenario with an organization spread across multiple sites is that extensions are not unique within the organization. Typically, a PBX exists in each site and the same extensions are used across sites. When this occurs, either users can use a full DID to reach users in another site, or a site prefix or steering code might be assigned.

For example, consider a scenario in which Company ABC has offices in San Francisco and Chicago. Alice and Bob both work in the San Francisco office, where Alice has extension 234 and Bob has extension 456. When Bob wants to dial Alice, he can simply dial 234 and be connected immediately. Now assume that Joe works in the Chicago office where a different PBX exists, and also with extension 234. Bob cannot simply dial Joe using 234 because he will connect to Alice instead.

What happens as a workaround is that a site prefix code can be assigned to Bob's dial plan so that he can dial Chicago extensions by prepending an extra digit. In this scenario, assume that 6 is the site prefix for Chicago from San Francisco. This means Bob can dial 6, followed 234, and be connected to Joe, but still dial 234 to reach Alice directly.

The same kind of site prefix is used in this scenario for Chicago users to dial San Francisco users directly. In Company ABC's case, Chicago users can use 7 as a prefix to dial San Francisco. Although Joe and Alice have the same three-digit extension, Joe can contact Alice by dialing 7, followed by 234.

> **TIP**
>
> The number of digits required for site prefixes depends on how many sites with overlapping extensions exist within an organization. If there are only a few sites with overlapping extensions, a single digit can be used to identify each site. If there are many sites with overlapping extensions, it might be necessary to use two or even three digits as a site prefix.

Site prefixes can be potentially confusing for end users because they must remember to dial extra digits for different sites. Often, they have to consult a list of site prefixes or look up a contact phone number when dialing a different location.

Keep in mind that as organizations shift to Lync for voice, the use of site prefixes is reduced because most of the dialing can be done with a simple click on a contact. Unlike with traditional telephony, users will become more and more reliant on click-to-dial features, instead of remembering extensions. Despite the ease of the user experience, administrators will still be tasked with correctly assigning site prefixes to telephone URIs and creating appropriate normalization rules. This can become a complex voice-routing and dial-plan configuration in the end.

> **TIP**
>
> If at all possible, consider using a dial plan with unique extensions across the organization. This might not be possible in all cases, but it greatly simplifies the voice deployment.

Ordering Normalization Rules

Site prefix scenarios directly affect Lync Server telephone URIs and dial-plan normalization rules. In Lync Server 2013, a telephone URI must be unique across the organization for it to be routed correctly. This means that even if Alice and Joe have the same extension within their own offices, their Line URIs must still be unique.

For example, assume that San Francisco users have DID numbers all using the +1 (415) 777-3xxx format. Alice's telephone URI should be assigned as tel:+14157773234. Joe's office has DIDs as well with a +1 (312) 444-5xxx format, and his telephone URI can be assigned as tel:+13124445234.

Now the URIs are unique, but this does not account for the expected user behavior of how to dial three digits in each location to reach local users. For example, users in San Francisco and Chicago both expect to use three-digit dialing, but depending on which office the call originates from, it should route to a different user. Users in San Francisco expect to reach Alice when they dial 234, and users in Chicago expect to reach Joe when they dial 234. This must be handled by using separate dial plans and normalization rules for the two sites.

For each unique site, administrators must create a separate dial plan to be assigned to users. These dial plans also contain different normalization rules depending on the site prefixes assigned.

Continuing the previous example, a San Francisco dial plan is assigned to Alice and Bob, which accommodates three-digit dialing rules that resolve to the local users. A separate rule needs to exist for dialing Chicago extensions which allows callers to reach Joe using 6 as the site prefix.

In this scenario, the San Francisco dial plan should contain rules such as the following:

Dial Plan: San Francisco

Name: Three-digit San Francisco extensions

Starting Digits: Blank

Length: Exactly three digits

Digits to Remove: None

Digits to Add: +14157773

This rule takes three digits and converts them to +14157773xxx so that San Francisco users can use three digits to reach a local user. In addition to this rule, the San Francisco dial plan needs another rule to accommodate dialing a site prefix to Chicago users:

Dial Plan: San Francisco

Name: Four digits to Chicago

Starting Digits: 6

Length: Exactly four digits

Digits to Remove: 1

Digits to Add: +13125554

This rule matches a four-digit string starting with 6, the Chicago site prefix, removes the 6, and then prepends +13125554 to the remaining three digits. Once assigned to the San Francisco users account, Bob can dial 234, which translates to +14157773234 and matches Alice's account. Bob can also dial 6234, which translates to +13125554234 and matches Joe's account in Chicago.

On the opposite site, the Chicago dial plan contains at least two rules to facilitate local three-digit dialing to Chicago users and uses a site prefix of 7 to reach San Francisco users.

Dial Plan: Chicago

Name: Three digits to Chicago

Starting Digits: Blank

Length: Exactly three digits

Digits to Remove: None

Digits to Add: +13125554

Dial Plan: Chicago

Name: Four digits to San Francisco

Starting Digits: 7

Length: Exactly four digits

Digits to Remove: 1

Digits to Add: +14157773

It is easy to see how complex a dial plan can become when multiple overlapping sites are involved. This example uses only two sites, but for an organization with many sites, some significant planning should be performed in advance of the Lync Server 2010 voice deployment. For example, imagine if Company ABC later opens sites in New York and Seattle. Each site will require a unique dial plan, and normalization rules to accommodate extension-based dialing.

When beginning to develop a dial plan use the following tips:

▶ Collect all the existing extensions for a site and the associated DID ranges.

▶ Determine whether sites have overlapping extensions and whether site prefixes will be required.

▶ Order the normalization rules properly within each dial plan. Remember that the rules are processed in a top-down fashion.

▶ Always assign E.164-formatted telephone URIs to user accounts.

Voice Routing

Voice routing in Lync Server 2013 are composed of voice policies, PSTN usages, routes, and trunks. The associations of these items with each other are what determines how a call is eventually routed.

Voice Policies

Voice policies in Lync Server 2013 define what features users might leverage with their Enterprise Voice service. This includes options such as simultaneous ringing, team call, or call forwarding. The other main component of voice policies is that PSTN usages are associated with a policy.

From a planning perspective, examine the various options of a voice policy and make a decision about how many policies are required. Policies can be global, assigned to a site, or directly assigned to user accounts.

Class of Service

Voice policies are typically created at the user level to allow for maximum flexibility when assigning call routes. This enables organizations to have multiple policies that each map to a different "class of service" (in traditional telephony lingo). For example, a policy named "San Francisco—National" can be created and assigned to San Francisco–based users. This policy could include PSTN usages that permit those users to make local, toll-free, and national calls, but prevent international calling. A second policy named "San Francisco—International" can also exist which does include the PSTN usage to permit international calls. Additional policies can be created to offer more flexibility in features and PSTN usage restrictions if necessary, but this enables administrators to easily manage calling capabilities.

> **CAUTION**
>
> Instead of using special dial codes to accommodate long distance or international calling capabilities, like many PBXs, Lync Server 2013 relies on voice policies to enforce dialing restrictions. Voice policies can also be assigned to analog or lobby phones to control outbound calling capabilities.

Least Cost Routing

Voice administrators are commonly asked to implement a feature referred to as least cost routing (LCR). This term is loosely mixed up with tail-end hop off (discussed in the next section). In a traditional telephony environment in which each office or building had a different PBX, this referred to creating "tie-lines" or trunks between the systems so that calls between two internal employees would not traverse the PSTN and incur toll charges. The good news for Lync administrators is that this requires zero configuration in Lync Server 2013. Least cost routing for calls between internal employees is native to the product because all calls route the media in a peer-to-peer scenario.

Tail-End Hop Off

The difference between least cost routing and tail-end hop off (TEHO) is that whereas LCR is geared toward reducing toll charges for calls between employees, TEHO is geared toward reducing costs for calls to the PSTN numbers.

In a simple scenario for Company ABC, the San Francisco users have voice policies that route all calls out the local gateway or trunk, and Chicago users have separate voice policies to route calls out their local gateway trunk. There is nothing wrong with this configuration, and it works just fine. However, if a San Francisco user calls a Chicago-area phone number, it is placed as a long-distance call out the San Francisco gateway and incurs toll charges.

Tail-end hop off can assist here by first routing that call across Company ABC's WAN to the Chicago office, and having the gateway/trunk in the Chicago office place the call. The advantage there is that the call is considered local to the Chicago office and does not incur any toll charges.

This is accomplished with the creation of a PSTN usage and route that matches local Chicago area codes, and the insertion of that usage in the San Francisco voice policy before the usage that allows national calls. As the voice policy is examined, the Chicago usage, route, and gateway/trunk are preferred for those specific area codes.

> **CAUTION**
>
> From a regulatory perspective not all countries allow tail-end hop off to be used. Be sure to review the legal implications of configuring this feature between multiple countries.

Figure 32.1 demonstrates the difference between least cost routing and tail-end hop off.

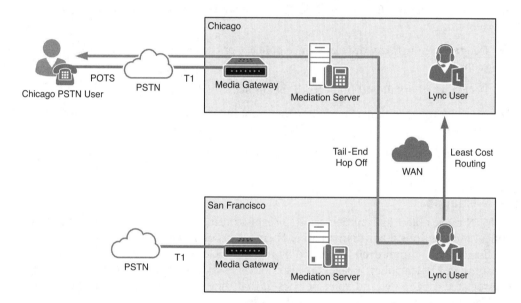

FIGURE 32.1   Least cost routing versus tail-end hop off.

Simultaneous Ring

A consideration in the voice policies is to review the existing or planned PSTN call capacity in each site and make sure it will support the simultaneous ring feature. This is a very popular feature with users because it enables them to answer calls on Lync endpoints or a mobile phone, but it consumes an extra PSTN trunk for each call. In a scenario in which a PSTN caller dials Alice at Company ABC, that call consumes one trunk, and the simultaneous ring to Alice's mobile phone consumes a second. If Alice answers the call on her mobile phone, both trunks are still in use for the duration of the call.

PSTN Reroute

Another feature within the voice policy that requires some additional planning is the PSTN Reroute check box. The idea of this feature is that if the WAN connection between two users is unavailable or constrained by Call Admission Control, the call is placed through the PSTN, even if toll charges are incurred. The configuration step that administrators often miss is that the user's voice policy still controls what numbers can be called. So if a user has a voice policy that does not allow national or international dialing, a PSTN reroute to a number matching those patterns might fail.

The best practice here is to create PSTN usages and routes that match patterns for the organization's own DIDs. This usage can then be inserted in voice policies to allow PSTN reroute to occur, independently of allowing national or international calls to other numbers.

When beginning to plan voice policies, use the following tips:

▶ Review the various features in voice policies and determine which ones will be allowed.

▶ Determine how many different voice policies, or classes of service, are required for each site.

▶ Decide whether tail-end hop off will be implemented in the voice policies.

▶ Consider the trunk capacity if allowing the simultaneous ring feature in voice policies.

▶ Create PSTN usages and routes for internal numbers for PSTN reroute purposes.

PSTN Usages

The PSTN usage object in Lync Server often seems confusing because it has no settings or configuration options other than a name. There are no user options or policies configured on a usage and it cannot even be created by itself. Instead, PSTN usages can be created only through a voice policy. Usages are also not even associated directly with users. They are associated with routes and voice policies so that they can be considered the glue that ties a route to a voice policy associated with a user.

From a planning perspective it's best to strive for a 1:1 ratio between PSTN usages and routes. This will allow for the most flexibility in voice policies and the routing configuration later. Naming the PSTN usages and associated routes identically not only simplifies the deployment, but provides future administrators a clear understanding of how the policies have been configured.

> **TIP**
>
> Remember that the order of PSTN usages within a voice policy is important. Usages and associated routes are examined in a top-down order.

Routes

Routes in Lync Server 2013 are a definition of where to send calls that match a specific dial string. Administrators define a matching pattern and a trunk or multiple trunks associated with the pattern to send a call. Each route is also associated with a PSTN usage, which is then inserted into voice policies to allow users to place calls via that route.

Route Resiliency

Redundancy for a particular voice route can be provided two ways. The easiest is to simply add multiple trunks to the route. If multiple trunks exist on a route, calls will be distributed in a round-robin fashion among all the trunks. Although this is very easy to configure, it can be tough to troubleshoot because each call placed might require logging on a different trunk or gateway. In large environments this configuration is desirable because the calls are load balanced across multiple trunks.

The other option available is to create unique PSTN usages and voice routes for each gateway serving a location, and associate only one gateway to each. Then, add both PSTN usages to voice policies. In this case the calls will always try the gateway in the first listed PSTN usage, but can also use the second gateway in the next PSTN usage if the first is unavailable. This does not load balance calls between gateways, but it does simplify troubleshooting. It can also be useful in scenarios in which organizations want to use one gateway primarily for inbound calls and another for outbound, but allow failover between the two if one is unavailable. Figure 32.2 shows an example of route resiliency.

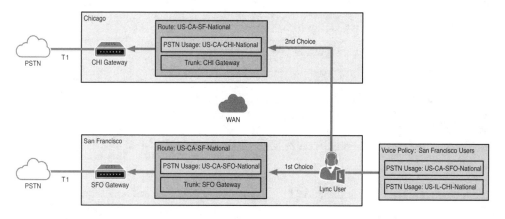

FIGURE 32.2   Route resiliency.

CAUTION

Do not associate multiple routes to a single voice policy and attempt to order them for priority. The results will be unpredictable even though the product allows this configuration. The route selection in that case is based first on the complexity of each route's regular expression pattern.

Sample Routes

It is also advisable to use descriptive names that reference a site name and the destination gateway for voice routes and PSTN usages. A sample set of PSTN usage and route names where round-robin gateway distribution is used for Company ABC's routes is provided here, but these names can be modified for any site or organization's standards. A sample set can look like this:

US-CA-San Francisco-Service Codes-SFGWs

US-CA-San Francisco-Local-SFGWs

US-CA-San Francisco-Toll-Free-SFGWs

US-CA-San Francisco-National-SFGWs

US-CA-San Francisco-International-SFGWs

The advantage to this is that administrators can insert all or some of these usages in various voice policies to control what numbers can be called. Since the names easily identify the type of call, it will be easy to troubleshoot issues that might occur later.

An alternative example in which calls first attempt using SFGW1, and use SFGW2 only if SFGW1 is unavailable, looks like this:

US-CA-San Francisco-Service Codes-SFGW1

US-CA-San Francisco-Service Codes-SFGW2

US-CA-San Francisco-Local-SFGW1

US-CA-San Francisco-Local-SFGW2

US-CA-San Francisco-Toll-Free-SFGW1

US-CA-San Francisco-Toll-Free-SFGW2

US-CA-San Francisco-National-SFGW1

US-CA-San Francisco-National-SFGW2

US-CA-San Francisco-International-SFGW1

US-CA-San Francisco-International-SFGW2

When beginning to plan voice routes, use the following tips:

▶ Identify the area codes considered local to each PSTN gateway.

▶ If using multiple gateways in a site, decide whether outbound calls will be load balanced or distributed in a primary/secondary fashion.

▶ Use the same, descriptive names for PSTN usages and voice routes.

Trunks

The term *trunk* is often overused, and its meaning has slightly changed in Lync Server 2013 now that a single gateway can be associated to multiple Mediation pools. In Lync Server 2013 a trunk consists of an IP/PSTN gateway name or IP, a listening port on the IP/PSTN gateway, a Mediation Server, and a listening port on the Mediation Server. Routes now include a list of trunks, instead of gateways, which can be used to place a call after a route is selected. Figure 32.3 shows how a single media gateway or IP PBX can now be associated with multiple Mediation pools using the new M:N trunk feature.

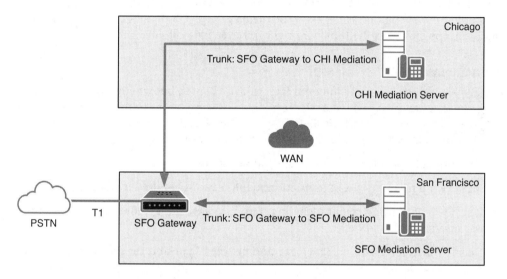

FIGURE 32.3   M:N trunk associations.

In a scenario with a single Mediation Server and gateway, not much has changed. The advantages are seen when multiple Mediation pools exist because each can be paired with the same gateway for redundancy. If one trunk is unavailable because a Mediation pool is offline, the other trunk and Mediation pool can connect to the same gateway. From an inbound perspective, the gateway can deliver calls to either Mediation pool in a round-robin or a primary/secondary configuration done on the gateway itself.

In Lync Server 2010 this same concept was possible, but because it required some DNS tricks with virtual PSTN gateway objects, it was a bit messier.

Trunk Translation Rules

Similar to how dial-plan normalization rules manipulate the digits a user dials, trunk translation rules are used to manipulate how numbers are modified before being delivered to a particular trunk. Often these formats vary by gateway, PBX, or telephony provider. Examples of modifications include adding an external prefix for calls going to a PBX, or prepending the international dialing code for international calls.

It's important to identify all the required rules for each trunk during the planning phases of a deployment.

Encryption

Another decision point in the planning process will be to determine whether the SIP connection and media between the Lync servers and gateway will be encrypted on a particular trunk. If so, the gateways or peer IP PBXs will require certificates trusted by the Lync servers with subject names matching the gateway. This is the preferred approach because it maintains the security of the voice solution, but it can be difficult to manage and troubleshoot encryption issues on some media gateways or IP PBXs. In SIP trunking scenarios it's possible that the provider might not even support encryption.

Media Bypass

Media Bypass is discussed more in depth later in this chapter, but whether it is used with a particular gateway is configured at the trunk level. It's important to review whether the media gateway will support Media Bypass and then ensure that the rest of the Lync network configuration has enabled Media Bypass to function.

When beginning to plan for trunks, use the following tips:

▶ Identify the necessary trunk translation manipulations required by each gateway.

▶ Plan the logical trunk layout including port numbers and IP addresses or names in advance of configuration.

▶ Decide whether SIP and media encryption between Lync and the media gateways is required for each trunk.

▶ Determine whether each gateway supports Media Bypass and ensure that the network subnet for each gateway is entered in the Lync network configuration.

Sizing

How to correctly size an IP/PSTN gateway or SIP trunk for Lync Server 2013 voice services is a common question and, unfortunately, is going to vary greatly depending on the users in each location. Sizing for an IP/PSTN gateway depends on the user's dialing habits as well as whether any simultaneous ringing is configured.

Microsoft offers some planning numbers that can be used to perform a rough analysis. If at all possible, retrieve reporting data from the existing PBX to determine the expected usage requirements for each site. Table 32.1 offers a suggestion on how many PSTN ports to allocate to a site depending on the usage level. For example, in a branch office with 25 users with light usage, only two PSTN ports are suggested, but it is important for each business to determine whether these suggested numbers make sense for their own purpose.

TABLE 32.1   Voice Port Planning Figures

Usage Level	PSTN Calls per Hour	Users per PSTN Port
Light	1	15
Medium	2	10
Heavy	3 or more	5

Voice Resiliency

Resiliency for voice was introduced through Survivable Branch Servers and Appliances starting in Lync Server 2010. This section discusses the various architectures available to organizations planning for voice resiliency.

To revisit the old approach for those performing migrations, back in Office Communications Server 2007 R2 the only way to provide resiliency for a branch site was to leverage dual WAN connections back to the datacenter, or deploy a full redundant set of pool services in the branch. Otherwise, a WAN outage would leave that branch completely offline.

Lync Server 2010 introduced the survivable branch components, which enable a branch to provide a minimal set of services to users in case the connection to the datacenter and main pool became unavailable. Branch components are paired or associated with a particular Front End pool, typically located in a datacenter or primary site.

Providing endpoints with a primary and backup registrar service achieves this redundancy. The registrar service existed in Office Communications Server 2007 R2 as part of the Front End Service, but has been separated into its own role in Lync Server 2010 and Lync Server 2013 to provide failover capabilities for voice features. When Lync endpoints sign in, they are informed through in-band signaling of both a primary and a backup registrar pool associated with their account. The primary registrar pool typically is the Front End pool where the user account is homed, except in branch office scenarios, in which the survivable branch component is the primary registrar and the associated Front End pool is the backup.

> **NOTE**
>
> Refer to Chapter 15, "High-Availability and Disaster Recovery," for a more detailed explanation of the high-availability options between pools and datacenters.

Redundant WAN

The first option is still to leverage redundant WAN connections between a branch site and a datacenter. In this model a media gateway and Mediation server typically are deployed in the branch, and users are homed to a Front End pool that exists in another site, as shown in Figure 32.4. This enables the Mediation Server to locally communicate with the gateway and use RTAudio when interfacing to other Lync servers across the WAN connection.

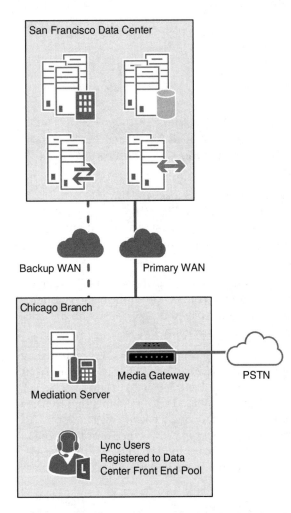

FIGURE 32.4   Offices with redundant WAN connectivity.

Although it is technically possible to not locate a Mediation server in the branch, the local gateway would have to send a G.711 audio stream across the WAN, which is more likely to result in audio quality issues.

This is also a popular model for scenarios with centralized SIP trunking services that are delivered to a datacenter because there is then no local gateway or PSTN connectivity in the branch. In that scenario the only way to ensure that those users can make and receive calls during a WAN outage is to use redundant WAN connectivity.

The disadvantage to this approach comes in the cost of monthly fees for the extra WAN connection, which is not generally used unless there is an outage. Organizations are paying an operational expense to provide redundancy during an outage of the primary WAN circuit. Also, if both WAN circuits are disconnected due to physical issues then users will have no services at all.

Survivable Branch Servers and Appliances

If an organization is already placing a Mediation Server and media gateway in the branch office, a more robust solution is to deploy a Survivable Branch Server or a Survivable Branch Appliance in the office. These solutions provide the same benefits as a local Mediation Server, but also provide local registrar services in the branch. So when the WAN is unavailable, users in the branch stay connected to the survivable branch component and can still make and receive basic phone calls, as shown in Figure 32.5.

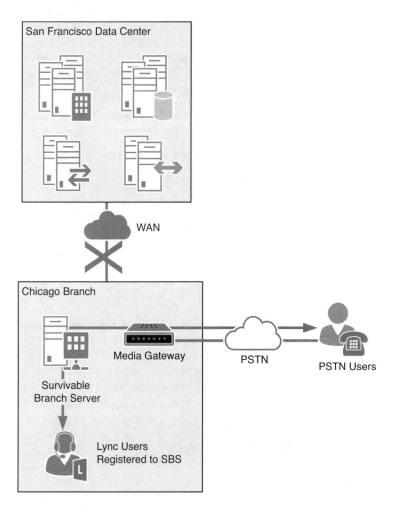

FIGURE 32.5   WAN outage with a Survivable Branch Server.

User accounts are homed to the survivable branch component, but still receive the majority of services from an associated Front End pool in a central site. The survivable branch component is designated as the primary registrar for the users so that when they sign in, they register to a local server.

However, all conferencing and web services exist only on a Front End pool and are still always accessed across a WAN link to the pool associated with the branch site. The survivable branch component is typically paired with a local media gateway to provide branch users with a local route to the PSTN for inbound and outbound calls.

SBA Versus SBS

A Survivable Branch Server is a Lync role that includes a limited Front End service for the registrar functionality, and a Mediation Server. It is installed and deployed like any other Lync role and requires a dedicated physical or virtual server to be created.

A Survivable Branch Appliance is a single piece of hardware that contains a media gateway and a Lync Survivable Branch Server. These appliances are produced by Microsoft partners and are similar to a Survivable Branch Server, but include the Survivable Branch Appliance server and IP/PSTN gateway all in one hardware device. These devices are typically more economical and take up less space than deploying a separate server and IP/PSTN gateway, so it makes sense to leverage these devices in small branch offices.

As with the Survivable Branch Server, users in the branch office use the Survivable Branch Appliance as the primary registrar service.

To recap, an SBA and SBS provide the same features to the end users, but the primary difference is that the SBA is bundled with a media gateway, whereas the SBS and the gateway are separate devices.

The other difference between an SBA and an SBS is scale. SBAs have some scale themselves and come with various amounts of RAM, intended for branch sites of 25 to 1,000 users. For branch sites of 1,000 to 5,000 users, Microsoft recommends using a dedicated Survivable Branch Server, mainly because it can perform better with more RAM and processing power.

Failure Scenarios

In the event of a WAN outage, users in branch sites will have continued voice services through the use of a Survivable Branch Server or Appliance because the primary registrar service is local to the site. The clients will enter "Limited Functionality Mode," in which not all features are available to users while the WAN link is unavailable. Figure 32.5 shows how a branch office user remains connected to the local registrar service when a WAN link is unavailable.

During a WAN outage when branch users cannot contact a Front End pool, the following features are unavailable for users inside the branch:

▶ **Cross-Site Communication**—Any form of communication to other sites is unavailable.

▶ **Conferencing**—All conferencing is unavailable. This applies to instant messaging, meeting, and audio/video conferences involving more than two parties because the multipoint control units (MCUs) exist on the Front End pool and not the survivable branch component.

▶ **Presence-Based Routing**—Because presence data is unavailable, calls to users homed on the inaccessible pool across the WAN link do not have calls routed based on presence. For example, if a user sets the status to Do Not Disturb, instant message and phone calls are still delivered.

▶ **Call Park**—Call Park is provided by the Front End pool, which is inaccessible across the WAN link.

▶ **Response Group Service**—Any workflows and queues associated with the pool across the WAN link are unavailable.

▶ **Modifying Call Forwarding Settings**—Although call forwarding capabilities remain in effect during a failover, users are unable to update or change their call forwarding settings.

The features that are still available for users inside the branch during a WAN outage include these:

▶ **PSTN Calls**—Inbound and outbound calls are possible because the local media gateway is available and not dependent on the WAN link.

▶ **Internal Calls**—Internal voice calls between users within the branch site have no issues. Calls to users in another site must leverage PSTN rerouting out the local media gateway to be completed.

▶ **Call Control**—Users are able to use basic call features such as hold and transfer. Advanced features such as call forwarding, simultaneous ringing, and team call are also available in a failover scenario.

▶ **Instant Messaging**—Instant messaging services are available, but only between two parties within the branch site. No instant messaging conferencing services are available.

▶ **Audio/Video Calls**—Audio and video calls are available between two parties only within the branch site. Audio/video conferencing services are unavailable.

▶ **Call Detail Records**—Call detail records continue to queue on the primary registrar and are delivered after the WAN link is restored.

▶ **Audio Conferencing**—Audio conferencing is possible by the placing of a PSTN call to the dial-in conferencing bridge. Click-to-join for Online Meetings does not function.

▶ **Voice Mail Retrieval**—Assuming that the Exchange infrastructure exists in a primary datacenter, users can still dial the PSTN number for Outlook Voice Access to retrieve voice mail.

▶ **Voice Mail Deposit**—Assuming that the Exchange infrastructure exists in a primary datacenter, Survivable Branch Servers and Appliances can reroute voice mail delivery across the PSTN. This is an Exchange Unified Messaging directory auto attendant that only accepts voice mail and does not allow transfer to users.

In the event of the Survivable Branch Server or Survivable Branch Appliance in the branch site becoming unavailable, users begin to use the backup registrar service on the Front End pool located across the WAN link. In this scenario, users do not experience any loss in functionality. The Front End pool starts servicing the users as if they were homed to it and all features are available. Through the multiple trunk pairing possible in Lync Server 2013, the branch users can also continue to make and receive phone calls using the media gateway in their office.

Front End Pool

A final option for branch sites is to deploy a full Front End pool instead of just a survivable branch component. This approach was historically driven by the need to place conferencing services locally, but had the additional benefit of still providing voice resiliency through backup registrar association in Lync Server 2010. Just like a survivable branch component, Front End pools could be associated with each other for backup registrar services in Lync Server 2010, and there was no limit to the number of associations a single pool could handle.

The change to requiring a 1:1 ratio between paired Front End pools in Lync Server 2013 now prevents administrators from deploying Standard Edition pools in branches and associating all of them to a single Enterprise Edition pool in a datacenter. Additionally, Standard Edition pools are not recommended for pairing with Enterprise Edition pools. Using the old approach, organizations now need to place a paired Standard Edition pool in the datacenter to provide resiliency for any Standard Edition pools deployed in branch sites.

Chapter 15 discusses the key changes in Lync Server 2013 that apply to Front End pools, but the story around the survivable branch components in Lync Server 2013 has not changed much. In fact, there are some trade-offs that are made when users are placed on a survivable branch component instead of a Front End pool. Specifically, the new service that allows replication of all user contact list and conferencing data between pools applies only when the pool is a user's primary registrar. Since the branch component is the primary registrar, any users homed on the branch component do not benefit from the new replication service. Even if an administrator invokes a failover between two paired pools, the users homed to the survivable branch component are still in Limited Functionality mode.

The primary advantage to deploying a Front End pool in a branch is an improved conferencing experience for the local users, since the audio and video mixing happen within the branch. The other improvement with Lync Server 2013 is the capability to provide resiliency for Response Groups through the pool pairings. If a branch relies heavily on Response Groups and needs them available even if the WAN is down, a local Front End pool can still provide the Response Groups, but a survivable branch component cannot.

Considerations

In addition to the architecture choices outlined previously, there are some considerations to factor into decisions on how to provide resiliency for the voice configuration.

PSTN Reroute

The capability to route calls between users in different offices even when the WAN is unavailable is referred to as PSTN reroute. As discussed previously in the "Voice Routing" section, the ability for PSTN reroute to function is based on whether it is enabled in the user's voice policy, and whether a PSTN usage allows calls to the destination number.

When it's enabled, if users in two sites cannot call each other because of a WAN outage, a PSTN call can be placed through a local media gateway, received by a media gateway at the remote site, and still delivered to the user. This happens automatically within the Lync client, and the end user sees a notification that the call is being rerouted and might take longer than usual to connect.

Voice Mail Reroute

Similar to the capability to use PSTN reroute between sites, integration with Exchange Unified Messaging can be achieved through voice mail rerouting configuration. If Exchange Unified Messaging servers do not exist locally, and the WAN is unavailable, Lync servers can place a PSTN call to a specified number when a user tries to access his voice mail. Similarly, if a user diverts an internal or PSTN call to voice mail during a WAN outage, Lync initiates a call to a different PSTN number and transfers the original caller. The caller is presented with an Exchange auto attendant that enables the caller to leave a voice mail message. The original called party information is not transferred in this scenario, so the caller will need to search for the user or enter the user's extension through the attendant before leaving the voice mail message. Figure 32.6 shows how a call normally forwarded to voice mail is rerouted using the PSTN.

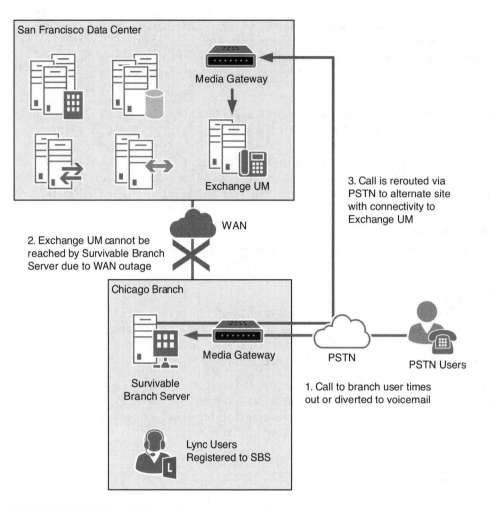

FIGURE 32.6   Voice mail rerouting.

WAN-Dependent Productivity

A final consideration when planning the architecture is whether the users are still productive without a WAN connection. It is possible to design the Lync voice architecture with
a survivable branch component or Front End pool so that voice is unaffected by a WAN
outage, but it might not be worth the trouble if the users still cannot get any work done
because they require WAN access. In this case a better solution might be to tell the users
to go home or to the closest coffee shop to try to work. As Internet users, they can sign in
through the Edge Servers and have full Lync capabilities, except for receiving PSTN calls
through the isolated site. Outbound PSTN calls can be sent out a different media gateway
via additional PSTN usages in the user voice policies. Features such as Enhanced Alternate
Routing (EAR) from a telephony provider can be used to redirect inbound calls to an
auto attendant in the datacenter or a main line in another site. Figure 32.7 displays an

alternative option for businesses, in which workers have remote connectivity to the Lync infrastructure.

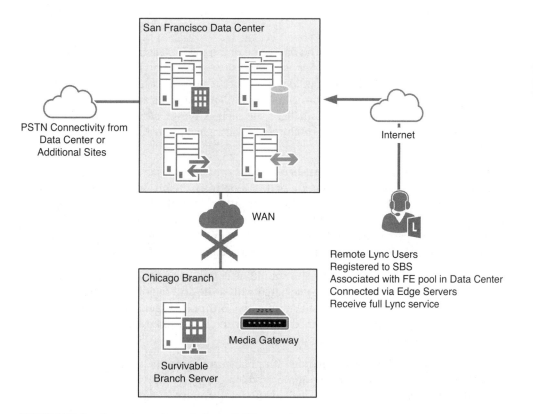

FIGURE 32.7   Remote workers during a WAN outage.

Call Admission Control and Media Bypass

Advanced features such as Call Admission Control and Media Bypass rely on proper configuration of the network components within the Lync configuration. This section discusses those prerequisites and the required planning for Call Admission Control and Media Bypass.

Network Configuration

Call Admission Control, Media Bypass, and E911 are three unique features that are all dependent on the network configuration defined within the Lync topology. Each of these components relies on network regions, sites, and links to be configured correctly before they can be enabled. Defining each region, each site, and all subnets might seem overwhelming at first, but it offers quite a bit of flexibility and control over call routing. The fact that the word *site* is used differently so many places within Lync can also be a point of confusion.

There are a few basic components one must first understand when planning for these services:

▶ **Regions**—Network regions are the backbone of a network. Each network region must be associated with a Lync Server central site (where Lync Front End Servers are deployed) defined within the topology. Network regions are typically a hub where many other network sites are connected. Examples of regions are North America and Europe, or even areas on a smaller scale such as West Coast and East Coast. In a typical MPLS-type mesh WAN architecture, a single region should be created to represent the MPLS cloud.

▶ **Sites**—Each network region consists of at least one site and possibly many more. Sites are offices or locations that are part of a network region. In other words, all the offices or locations that have users homed in the central site for the region should be created as sites. A network site object should also be created for the central site, which might seem redundant, but there is no automatic mapping of a site within the topology to a site in the network configuration.

▶ **Subnets**—Each subnet used at a site should be entered and associated with the correct site. Lync endpoints are associated with a site and region by being matched to a subnet defined here. The Call Admission Control and Media Bypass features rely on matching the subnet of the media gateway to callers, so be sure to include the subnets used for voice hardware.

▶ **Bandwidth Policy Profiles**—Bandwidth policy profiles define a network link speed and the available bandwidth for audio or video calls. The individual, one-way session limit can be specified, as well as the total amount of bandwidth used for audio and video traffic. Bandwidth policy profiles are associated with a site or region link. Sites do not require a bandwidth policy profile to be assigned. In fact, if sites within a region are not bandwidth constrained, no profile should be assigned. Assign bandwidth policy profiles only to sites that require limits on their audio and video WAN usage.

▶ **Region Links**—When multiple regions exist, region links should be defined that identify the amount of bandwidth available between two geographic regions. An example would be a North American region and a European region, each with a central site and multiple branch sites associated. A region link defines the bandwidth available between any North American site and a European site.

▶ **Region Route**—A region route specifies how two regions should be connected. In many cases, a region route mimics a region link and can just be between two different regions. In other cases in which two regions are not directly connected, but share a link to a common region, a region route defines how these regions must traverse the common region to communicate. In that case, two different region links must be crossed, which might each have a different bandwidth policy profile.

▶ **Site Link**—The final component of the network configuration is a site link. In most cases, sites are connected to a network region directly, which acts as a hub for the users. There might be instances in which in addition to a connection to the network region central site, sites have a direct connection to each other that bypasses the central site. Site links are used to create these objects that can then have a bandwidth policy profile associated.

Figure 32.8 shows a logical representation of the different network configuration components.

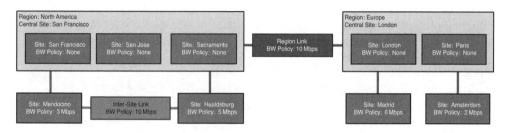

FIGURE 32.8   Logical site and region configuration.

Call Admission Control

Planning to deploy Call Admission Control features in Lync Server 2013 is going to depend greatly on the network configuration discussed in the preceding section. CAC relies on determining an endpoint's site and region through the network subnet. Call Admission Control in Lync Server 2013 applies to both audio and video traffic, but organizations can specify different limits for each type of traffic. Both a session limit (one-way traffic) and a total limit for all sessions can be specified.

The key to successful Call Admission Control deployment is to correctly define and associate the bandwidth policy profiles to sites and links by completing the following steps:

1. Identify the connection speed of each WAN link to sites that are bandwidth constrained.

2. Define the maximum audio and video session and total bandwidth limits to be used by Lync endpoints associated with site and policy. These limits vary based on the desired traffic type and the different audio codecs used.

3. Evaluate the site and make some estimates on the type of audio codecs used to create an appropriate limit. For example, if users make several Lync-to-Lync calls, RTAudio is predominantly used. If most calls are conferences, Siren or G.722 audio might be more prevalent.

It is also important to note that Call Admission Control applies only to Lync Server endpoints traversing a WAN link. Other applications transmitting data on the same WAN link are not affected by Lync Call Admission Control policies. Organizations can define a bandwidth limit for Lync traffic and still see that WAN link become saturated due to other applications. In this scenario, it makes sense to enforce QoS policies on the WAN link to ensure that Lync endpoints can always place calls. These QoS reservations should ideally match the CAC bandwidth limits.

The bandwidth override policy is enforced by the receiving endpoint and not the sender. When a call is placed, the receiving endpoint leverages its subnet information and checks whether the call will exceed the bandwidth policy limit.

The only clients that actually respect Call Admission Control policies are Lync 2010 endpoints. Earlier clients, such as Office Communicator 2007 R2, are not able to perform a bandwidth check when a Lync client calls. However, media calls from Office Communicator 2007 R2 to a Lync endpoint enforce Call Admission Control policies.

Bandwidth Estimates

Table 32.2 defines the various bandwidth estimates for each protocol with all values represented in Kbps. The typical bandwidth usage values can normally be used for planning purposes. Forward Error Correction (FEC) is enabled when Lync clients detect poor network connectivity, and it attempts to provide a more resilient voice connection to compensate for network jitter or latency.

TABLE 32.2   Audio Codec Planning Numbers

Codec	Typical Bandwidth	Maximum Bandwidth without FEC	Maximum Bandwidth with FEC
RTAudio (Narrowband)	29.3	44.8	56.6
RTAudio (Wideband)	39.8	62.0	91.0
G.722	46.1	100.6	164.6
Siren	25.5	52.6	68.6
G.711	64.8	97.0	56.6

CAC Internet Rerouting

When a bandwidth policy limit is exceeded by a user, Call Admission Control kicks in with an attempt to reroute the call. First, the call attempts to be directed over the Internet if both sites have an Edge Server. Instead of using the WAN link, the call traverses the Internet and is relayed between the Edge Servers in each site. If that is not possible or fails, the call can reroute across the PSTN. Whether this is allowed depends on whether the voice policy assigned to the user allows this feature. If neither Internet nor PSTN rerouting is possible, the call attempts to be sent directly to voice mail. Lastly, if voice mail is unavailable, the call simply fails.

> **TIP**
>
> The public IP address of the A/V Edge roles must be entered in the network configuration with a 32-bit mask and associated to the appropriate sites for Edge reroute to work properly.

Figure 32.9 demonstrates how the Internet rerouting feature works between two sites with Edge Servers.

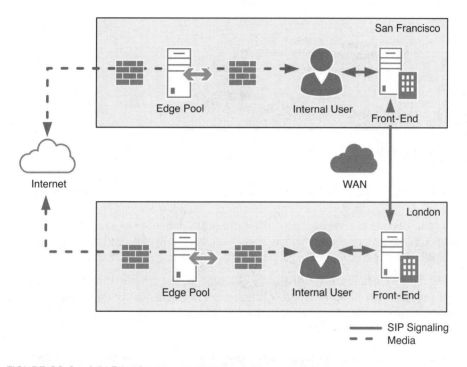

FIGURE 32.9   A/V Edge Internet reroute.

Media Bypass

Planning for Media Bypass is not too complicated because it encompasses only identifying which media gateways in the organization support the feature and then configuring the trunks appropriately to enable the support. The majority of the configuration typically involves defining the previously discussed network topology correctly. Media Bypass enables a Lync endpoint to communicate directly with a media gateway, bypassing the Mediation server role with the G.711 audio stream. Figure 32.10 displays how a user's signaling traffic continues to flow through the server to the media gateway, but the actual audio stream is sent from the user directly to the media gateway.

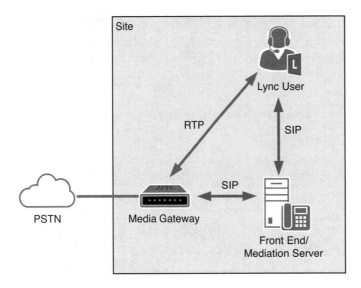

FIGURE 32.10   Media Bypass.

Media Bypass is especially useful in branch office scenarios in which no Mediation server is present, but a local media gateway exists. Without Media Bypass, calls are sent across a WAN link to a Mediation server at the central site, transcoded to G.711, and then sent back across the WAN link to the media gateway. With Media Bypass, endpoints can send the G.711 audio directly to the media gateway without traversing the WAN.

Media Bypass can be enabled in two distinctly different modes. The first mode turns on bypass at all times, and although easy to configure, it can cause quality issues. The second, more preferred approach is to base Media Bypass decisions from the network configuration entered for Call Admission Control.

NOTE

Media Bypass and Call Admission Control can both be enabled, but are mutually exclusive features within a site. For example, a gateway in a site with a bandwidth constraint defined via Call Admission Control does not allow a call from a different site to use bypass. This is because the premise of Media Bypass is that the user and the gateway have no bandwidth restraints between each other, which is the entire point of Call Admission Control.

Bypass IDs

Media Bypass works by assigning a unique bypass ID to each location, and each subnet associated with that location automatically inherits the same bypass ID. When a Lync endpoint attempts a call, the subnet of the endpoint is examined. If the bypass ID of the subnet matches the bypass ID of the subnet where the media gateway resides, Media Bypass will be allowed.

The same concept applies for inbound calls from the PSTN. When the media gateway receives a call and sees an endpoint with a matching bypass ID, the audio flows directly to the Lync client. Using the network configuration example in Figure 32.8, the San Francisco, San Jose, and Sacramento sites share a bypass ID because they are not bandwidth constrained. The Mendocino and Healdsburg sites each receive a unique ID because they have WAN bandwidth limitations.

Keep in mind that a unique bypass ID does not necessarily get assigned to each network region or site. Any network region with sites that have no bandwidth policy profile assigned all share the same bypass ID. This is because without a policy applied, it is assumed that all subnets have sufficient bandwidth between each other and Media Bypass can be used from any endpoint to any media gateway.

If a site does have a bandwidth policy profile assigned because WAN bandwidth is limited, a new bypass ID is generated for the site. Users placing calls from within the bandwidth-constrained site are allowed to use Media Bypass to a local media gateway. When users attempt a call to the same gateway from a subnet with a different bypass ID, Media Bypass is not allowed and the audio flows through a Mediation server. Figure 32.11 shows how a user can leverage Media Bypass in a local office, but be forced to send media through a Mediation server in the Chicago office across a constrained WAN link. This is because the bypass ID of the user's endpoint does not match the bypass ID of the gateway in the Chicago site.

> **NOTE**
>
> Lync Server 2013 creates bypass IDs automatically as bandwidth policy profiles are assigned to a site. These do not need to be created or managed by an administrator.

Emergency Services

How to handle emergency services within Lync can be a tricky topic for organizations to deal with since there are various ways to tackle the issue.

Basic Emergency Calls

From a very basic level there is nothing that prevents an organization from creating a dial plan rule, PSTN usage, and voice route that permit a user to call emergency services. The call follows the same concepts as any other call, and connects just fine, and the caller can provide an address and callback number to the Public Safety Access Point (PSAP). If the user can't provide an address or a phone number, emergency services won't be able to assist. This form of very basic emergency services is rare to run across.

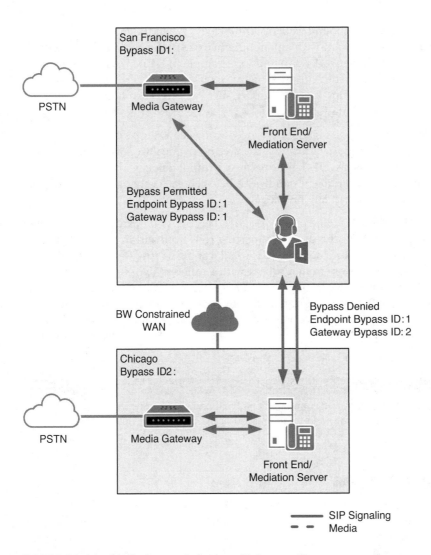

FIGURE 32.11   Media Bypass behavior with bypass IDs.

Enhanced 911

A more common form of emergency service is referred to as Enhanced 911, or E911. The difference with E911 is that the caller's address and phone number are automatically transmitted to the PSAP when the call is placed. This way, the emergency responders can assist the caller even if the caller is unable to provide contact information. The association of address to the call is based on information provided to the telephony provider when the circuit is installed or enabled. This is typically not the user's DID, but a main line or billing phone number associated to an organization.

The disadvantage to using the regular call flow for E911 is that users roaming between offices or signed in via an Edge Server are now placing calls out a media gateway and trunk that are associated to a different physical address. Emergency services might end up responding to the incorrect location.

It's advisable to *not* allow emergency services calls to happen the same way as other calls in Lync because of this scenario. Instead, rules for emergency services should be purposely excluded from the dial plan, and PSTN usages for those calls should be created, but not inserted in voice policies.

Network Site Routing

A workaround for the previous scenario is to base emergency services routing off of the same network location information that might be defined for Call Admission Control and Media Bypass.

After the sites are configured, follow these steps for each site that has an E911 registered phone circuit:

1. Create a PSTN usage and voice route for the emergency call.

2. Create a user location policy with emergency services enabled. Enter the emergency services number and mask.

3. Assign the PSTN usage to the location policy.

4. Assign the location policy to the network site.

The end result is that Lync clients that sign in on network subnets associated to that site automatically receive that PSTN usage, and it is inserted at the top of their voice policy. A normalization rule for the emergency number based on the mask also is inserted. As the users move between offices, a PSTN usage and route for the local gateway are always inserted, ensuring that their emergency calls are sent out the media gateway in the office where they are currently located.

The advantage here is this works *only* for internal Lync clients. The location information is not exchanged for remote users, so users signed in through an Edge Server won't be able to make emergency calls. Organizations should review these options with a legal team, but informing the users that emergency services calls can happen only within the office might be acceptable.

> **TIP**
>
> This method doesn't require an E1 or T1 circuit. For an organization with many small offices, consider a two- or four-port FXO analog gateway in each location that can be used exclusively for emergency calls. All other calls can route to a main gateway with more telephony circuits.

Lync Enhanced 911

All the options discussed previously have been based on the Lync network configuration and are dependent on each building or floor having a unique subnet. This might not always be possible or desirable, so Lync Server 2013 has the capability to provide location information to an Emergency Services Service Provider or an Emergency Location Identification Number (ELIN) gateway through a location information database.

> **NOTE**
>
> Lync E911 is supported only within the United States.

Location Information Database

Lync identifies an endpoint's physical location by examining the network subnet, switch, and wireless access point the client uses. This collection of network objects is referred to as the Location Information Service (LIS) database and must be populated by administrators in advance of enabling E911. The LIS database is completely separate from the Lync network configuration of sites and subnets discussed separately. The LIS database function is only to provide a mapping of network objects to physical addresses that can be sent to the service provider or ELIN gateway.

This database can be populated manually or can be linked to a secondary location information database if one already exists. For Lync Server 2013 to use a secondary location information database, the service must adhere to the Lync Server 2013 Request/Response schema.

If manually populating the location database, start by identifying each of the network access points, switches, and subnets within the organization and the physical location associated with each object. When determining an endpoint's location, Lync Server 2013 first uses the wireless access point, and then the switch ID, and lastly a subnet to determine location. This is because each of these items can potentially span multiple rooms or floors in a building, so none is an exact location.

After the location information database is populated, it should be validated with the Emergency Services Service Provider. This validation process compares the addresses associated to each network object with the database maintained by the provider to ensure that each location entered in Lync Server 2013 can be correctly routed to a PSAP, which can respond to the request. Alternatively, any ELINs must be entered in the telephony provider's Automatic Location Identification (ALI) database.

SIP Trunk Service Provider

The Emergency Services Service Provider is a third-party service that acts as a liaison between a Lync deployment and the PSAP via SIP trunk. It is important to clarify that Lync Server 2013 does not natively contact a Public Safety Access Point directly. Instead, it is the responsibility of the Emergency Services Service Provider to route the emergency calls to the correct PSAP.

Figure 32.12 displays the process that occurs when an emergency call is placed from a Lync endpoint. Lync 2013 provides an endpoint's location to the Emergency Services Service Provider using the PIDF-LO format, which is really an XML blob containing all the detailed address information.

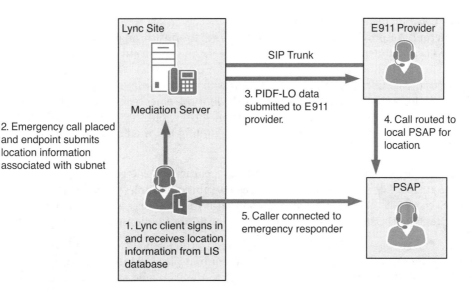

FIGURE 32.12   SIP trunk E911 service provider.

When planning for Enhanced 911 services, an organization must first identify where E911 will be deployed. This might be only within a primary site, in multiple sites, or extended to branch sites. When planning E911 for branch sites, be sure to consider scenarios in which a WAN link is unavailable. It is possible that branch or remote sites will not be able to provide location information or even contact an Emergency Services Service Provider without a resilient WAN link.

The connection to the Emergency Services Service Provider is accomplished through a dedicated SIP trunk. When the SIP trunk is being provisioned, a VPN tunnel to the Emergency Services Service Provider is created using an existing Internet connection, or a dedicated connection can be provisioned to separate and isolate the emergency calls.

An advantage to the service provider method is that it can also serve remote users signed in through an Edge Server. The addresses entered by remote users won't be validated in advance through a master database, but the service provider can answer the call, confirm the address delivered by the Lync client's PIDF-LO data, and then route to an appropriate PSAP for the remote user.

The final consideration with the SIP trunk is to recognize that it does not bypass Call Admission Control policies. If a bandwidth policy is exceeded by an emergency call, the call will not succeed. When planning for E911, be sure to consider the effects of Call Admission Control on where SIP trunks to an Emergency Services Service Provider are placed. For example, in a site where WAN bandwidth is constrained, it might make sense to deploy a local Mediation Server and SIP trunk to a provider to ensure that Call Admission Controls never prevent an emergency call across the WAN link.

Emergency Location Identification Number

Another method for providing detailed address information is through the use of Emergency Location Identification Numbers. Consider an organization that has multiple floors in a single building, and a single PRI circuit for phone calls. When an emergency call is placed, the PSAP can see the physical address for the organization based on the circuit, but no information is passed about which floor the emergency responders should go to. The PSAP has a main number that can be called back, but that number might route to a receptionist who has no idea someone in the building has tried calling emergency services.

An ELIN is a unique phone number that identifies a particular Emergency Response Location (ERL). An ERL could be a floor, a wing, or another arbitrary location within a building. Each ERL is then assigned an ELIN so that if the PSAP sees a call from a particular ELIN, the PSAP should know exactly what area or floor of building has requested help.

Within the LIS database the ELIN is actually entered in the Company field. When the gateway receives the call and the PIDF-LO information, it places a call using the discovered ELIN as the *called* party, which is then routed to the PSAP and answered, as shown in Figure 32.13.

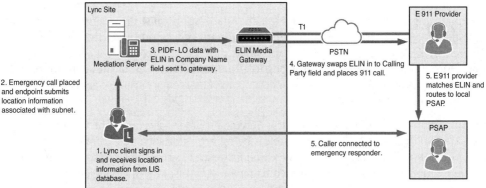

FIGURE 32.13   ELIN E911 routing.

The other feature of ELIN is that it provides a mapping back to the original caller. The PSAP can be connected to the original caller through that ELIN. The media gateways that support ELIN keep a temporary table of callers who dialed each ELIN so that when a call comes back from the PSAP it can be properly routed.

Response Groups

Before configuring Response Groups in Lync Server 2013, an organization should run through a number of planning steps to ensure that the workflow creation is as easy as possible. When a workflow diagram and configuration are created in advance, the actual creation of the workflow in Lync Server 2013 can be completed quickly.

The following steps ease the process of creating workflows:

1. Begin by developing a diagram of the desired workflow. This should include all the possible call flows that a user can be routed through. Also be sure to include scenarios for what happens when a caller becomes unresponsive or does not press a DTMF (Dual-Tone Multi-Frequency) key.

2. Document the exact text that is played to callers so that it is available for text-to-speech translation or to be read for an audio recording.

3. If using audio files, identify a user who is responsible for the recording or hire a professional agency to create the recording.

4. Identify the queues required within the workflow. The queue planning phase should include specifying how many concurrent calls can exist within a queue and what action should be taken when the queue reaches capacity. If sending calls to a voice mail box, be sure that the mailbox is monitored in some way so that callers leaving a message receive a response.

5. Identify the different agent groups that will belong to the queues and the individual agents. Ensure that agents are aware they belong to an agent group and are trained on how to handle calls. If using formal groups, make sure that agents understand how to log in and out of the group to take calls.

6. Identify what business hours and holiday schedules will affect the workflow.

7. After collecting all the required information, proceed with creating the agent groups, queues, and workflow objects.

8. Thoroughly test the Response Group workflow. This should involve traversing every possible option within the workflow to ensure that callers are routed correctly and are never unexpectedly disconnected.

9. Perform any adjustments necessary to the workflow before placing it in production and allowing external callers to reach the workflow.

Additional Considerations

This section discusses other considerations that should be incorporated into Enterprise Voice planning such as end-user devices, PIN policies, and integration with Exchange Unified Messaging.

Devices

After planning the necessary infrastructure components in a Lync Server 2013 deployment, remember to invest some time planning the end-user experience. This includes training around the Lync client, and discussions regarding the devices that end users will be given. The devices deployed alongside the Lync Server 2013 infrastructure have a big impact on how the project is accepted and viewed by an organization.

Handsets and Headsets

Each user enabled for Enterprise Voice services with Lync Server 2013 requires an optimized audio device to ensure a good end-user experience. Enabling Enterprise Voice for users enables them to begin placing and receiving calls using the built-in speakers and microphone, but these calls generally don't sound great and lead to a poor user experience.

Using an optimized device enhances the user experience by ensuring that echo and background noise are reduced to a minimum. Many headset and handset options exist for an organization, and it is likely that many different devices will be selected. Organizations might standardize on a few specific models, but different groups of users might require different feature sets. For example, users primarily in the office and not making many calls generally prefer a stationary handset, whereas customer service representatives on the phone all day might prefer a hands-free headset. Remote or mobile workers also tend to prefer headset devices, which are more portable and enable them to use a high-quality device regardless of location.

After optimized audio devices to end users are distributed, it is important to provide end-user training for how to use these devices effectively. Because most users new to Enterprise Voice are not familiar with these devices, training should include a discussion of the functionality and flexibility available with voice services.

Analog Endpoints

Lync Server 2010 was the first version of Lync to introduce support for analog devices. This helps in scenarios in which it is simply not possible to remove the requirement for analog devices such as with fax machines, PA systems, or elevator phones. These devices are all analog based and there is no equivalent in Lync Server 2013 to replace them.

To support these devices, an Analog Telephone Adapter (ATA) or media gateway with analog ports is required. On the server side, a SIP-enabled contact object is created to represent the analog device. Just as with a user account, a voice policy consisting of allowed PSTN usages can be assigned to the contact object and can control the features that each analog device is allowed to use.

Because analog devices do not register to a Lync Front End pool, the IP/PSTN gateway or Survivable Branch Appliance provides an interface to associate each analog port with a specified Line URI. Outbound calls from the port use the assigned Line URI, and inbound calls to the Line URI are routed to the associated port.

When planning for analog devices, first identify what type and how many analog devices are required for each site. Afterward, determine whether the analog devices should be connected to through the Lync infrastructure. It's possible to keep them separate and use a traditional Plain Old Telephone Systems (POTS) line connected directly to the device.

PIN Policies

The term *PIN* is unfortunately extremely overused within Lync and Exchange server, and leads to some end-user confusion. In an Enterprise Voice scenario a user can have up to three different PINs they need to manage, and they generally won't be able to distinguish where each should be used. First, it's important to identify the different PINs a user can have:

▶ **Lync User PIN**—This PIN is used to sign in to a Lync Phone Edition device using only a PIN and an extension. It is also used for authenticating to the Lync dial-in conferencing bridge.

▶ **Lync Device PIN**—This PIN is created by a user the first time she signs in to a Lync Phone Edition device and locks her personal information such as a contact list and voice mail messages. This PIN is specific only to a single device and cannot be reset by an administrator.

▶ **Exchange Unified Messaging PIN**—This PIN is generated when a user is enabled for Exchange Unified Messaging and it is delivered via email. It does not integrate or sync with Lync at all, and is used only for authentication to Outlook Voice Access.

It's easy to see how a user can become confused by all of these PINs because, from their perspective, they're all just part of the phone system. A way to mitigate this confusion is to make sure the PIN policies for all options are consistent, and to advise users to keep the PINs identical.

> **CAUTION**
>
> The Exchange Unified Messaging PIN allows access to a user's entire mailbox by default, including email, calendar, and contacts. Either disallow access to these items through the Unified Messaging Mailbox Policy, or institute a complex PIN policy that rotates regularly.

Exchange Unified Messaging Integration

Lync Enterprise Voice relies on the Exchange Unified Messaging (UM) role to provide voice mail services. Chapter 21, "Exchange and SharePoint Integration," covers Exchange Unified Messaging configuration in more detail, but this section identifies a few planning considerations.

Dial Plans

Dial plans exist in both Exchange and Lync, but are separate objects and won't always have a 1:1 ratio. Management can be simplified by always creating a matching dial plan in Exchange for each Lync dial plan, but this is not necessarily required. Drivers for creating distinct Unified Messaging dial plans come down to the following considerations:

▶ **Operator Extension**—Each UM dial plan can have only a single operator extension. If users expect to reach different operators by pressing 0 after calling the Subscriber Access number, create a second dial plan.

▶ **Default Language**—Each UM dial plan can support multiple languages, but voice-to-text message preview occurs only for the default language.

▶ **Unique Extensions**—UM dial plans require each user to have a unique extension. Users in two sites can have the same extension through the use of site prefixes or steering codes, but each site requires its own UM dial plan.

SIP Server

Each Exchange Unified Messaging server can target a Lync Edge Server for when it needs to provide media relay to a remote user. By default, each Unified Messaging Server will request MRAS credentials from the first A/V Edge Server that sends it a request, but administrators can optimize this Edge Server selection through the `Set-UMServer` cmdlet. The `SipAccessService` parameter specifies an Edge pool name and A/V Authentication port to use. An example is provided here:

```
Set-UMServer Server1.companyabc.com -SipAccessService EdgePool.companyabc.com:5062
```

Best Practices

The following are best practices from this chapter:

▶ Create a dial plan in advance. Identify all required normalization rules and user dialing habits.

▶ Plan the voice policies, PSTN usages, and routes to match the different levels of service required for each user.

▶ Use existing data to analyze PSTN usage in order to estimate IP/PSTN port requirements.

▶ Assign a backup registrar to pools where voice resiliency is required.

▶ Deploy Survivable Branch Servers or Survivable Branch Appliances in branch offices without resilient WAN links.

▶ Complete the network configuration before attempting to enable Call Admission Control, Media Bypass, or Enhanced 911.

▶ Apply appropriate bandwidth policy limits to sites where WAN bandwidth is constrained.

▶ Use Media Bypass whenever possible to reduce the processing requirements on the Mediation Server role.

▶ Validate all addresses in the location information database before deploying E911.

▶ Train users on the new devices and features they will experience with Enterprise Voice.

▶ Outline Response Group workflows, queues, and agent groups before attempting to create the objects in Lync Server 2010.

Summary

Properly planning and sizing a Lync voice deployment is absolutely critical to a successful rollout. It is important to spend time working through the dial plan and address all extension ranges and anomalies such as main lines, common area phones, or fax machines. Evaluate the voice needs in each office and properly evaluate trunk capacity requirements, and site survivability needs.

Emergency services is another important piece that must be considered. Many states have varying laws on what is required, so be sure to include legal teams and office managers in these discussions.

Lastly, the end user experience is largely what determines how successful a deployment is. Evaluate the handsets, headsets, and peripheral devices which will be used by people on a daily basis. Not all users will like the same device, so offering a variety based on work needs is generally well received.

32

PART XI

Endpoints

IN THIS PART

CHAPTER 33

UC Endpoints

Although many administrators might pass over this chapter in the book, it is likely one of the most important. The concept of "user experience" is an oft-overlooked idea and yet vital to a successful Unified Communications deployment. IT success is often measured by metrics and numbers, but they rarely tell the whole story. UC adoption can be viral, but only if the right tools are in place and end users have a quality experience. The backend infrastructure is certainly important; however, end users never see any of it. What they use everyday is a UC endpoint.

UC endpoints encompass a wide range of devices. Although some people argue that PCs should be included, my personal experience suggests that they provide a poor experience and a dedicated, purpose-built device such as a headset or an IP/USB phone should be used for an optimal experience. For that reason, we'll leave laptops and PCs out of the discussion in this chapter.

Microsoft ensures that specific devices meet set user-experience quality levels through a third-party test and evaluation process. These devices are labeled "Optimized for Microsoft Lync." Without getting into a sales pitch over what's the best, the key point here is to recognize that devices certified to work with Lync are sure to provide a quality end-user experience. In addition, the Lync client will always prefer "Optimized for Microsoft Lync" devices over standard devices. At the writing of this book, Microsoft lists close to 100 optimized devices ranging from wired and wireless headsets to webcams to IP phones to conference devices. Lync optimized devices are literally plug-and-play. The Lync client finds them automatically as soon as they are plugged in and starts using the device immediately. This chapter covers a wide range of devices, including these:

▶ Standalone IP phones

▶ USB headsets, speakerphones and handsets

▶ Webcams

▶ Conferencing devices

Finally, the chapter concludes with best practices for choosing and deploying UC endpoints for various scenarios.

Standalone IP Phones

There are two types of standalone IP phones for Microsoft Lync: "fully featured" phones, which require a user to be signed in all the time, and "basic" or "common area" phones, which can be used without a user credential in public areas or for hot desking with basic functions when a user logs in.

The fully featured phones include the following models and provide a premium experience for users requiring a handset:

▶ Polycom CX700

▶ Polycom CX600

▶ Aastra 6725ip

▶ HP 4120

These phones enable a user to sign in and, if desired, connect the phone to a PC via USB to use it as a USB audio device for Lync Communicator. This is called "USB tethering" or the "better together experience." The phones offer a full-color LCD screen and some models have a touchscreen as well. Per the Microsoft reference design, all phones in this category must also have a speakerphone and support wideband audio or a supported variant of HD voice. They also offer integration features such as calendar view from the on-phone screen.

For common areas or hot desking, there is a different class of phones. This type of phone has become very popular as many enterprises move to a "hotelling" arrangement for seating employees. These phones are generally lower cost and offer functions similar to most standard corporate desk phones available today. Models include these:

▶ Polycom CX500

▶ Aastra 6721ip

▶ HP 4110

Although these phones don't have some of the advanced features of the phones mentioned previously, they offer the capability to be used in common areas and not tied to an actual user. They also have a lower price point comparable to "traditional" PBX phones.

It is important to note that the following Polycom lines also support native integration to Lync although they are not Lync-exclusive phones:

▶ Polycom VVX series

▶ Polycom SoundPoint IP series

▶ Polycom KIRK and SpectraLink wireless phones, with the appropriate controller

USB Headsets, Speakerphones, and Handsets

USB headsets and their bulkier counterparts, handsets, are the most common UC endpoints available, with USB speakerphones having a niche market. The Lync Communicator client functions as a softphone, eliminating the need for a dedicated desk phone for most users.

USB Headsets

The best thing about headsets is they're portable! And they provide a superior experience over a traditional handset in nearly every way...but they do take a little bit of getting used to. A wide variety of headsets are available from various manufacturers. In fact, there are too many individual headset models to discuss all of them here, so the author will highlight a handful of devices, at least one from each category, wired and wireless.

A good example of a USB wired headset is the Plantronics Blackwire 320 as shown in Figure 33.1. This is an affordable solution for desktop users or even mobile users since it comes with a protective case. It provides binaural audio with an adjustable boom microphone.

There are other solutions that include monaural audio, which might be better for some deployments where workers still need to hear the environment around them.

Wireless headsets often have a dongle plugged into the user's PC but need no other connections. The headset enables users to roam freely up to 300 feet (and sometimes farther) from their PC while continuing their conversation. Many also have controls on the headset for redial, answer, hang up, and volume control. Most wireless solutions have docking stations used for recharging, whereas others come with just a USB charging cable. The latter are better for users who travel often or don't have a permanent office. The Plantronics Voyager Legend UC shown in Figure 33.2 is a great example.

FIGURE 33.1   Plantronics Blackwire 320.

FIGURE 33.2   Plantronics Voyager Legend UC.

Then, finally, there are hybrid devices such as the Plantronics Blackwire 720 shown in Figure 33.3. This headset can connect to a PC via USB and to a mobile phone via Bluetooth at the same time. It's truly the best of both worlds. It also supports A2DP for users who want to stream music to their headset while they work.

FIGURE 33.3   Plantronics Blackwire 720.

Speakerphones

Speakerphones become more and more important as "huddle rooms" take the place of classic conference rooms. These devices are great for impromptu meetings or group conversations in locations without a dedicated conferencing device.

The Plantronics Calisto 825, shown in Figure 33.4, in particular has a remote microphone, making it perfect for leading meetings in an auditorium or from across the room from the device.

For pure room-filling power and sleek design, the Jabra Speak 510 can't be beat! It transports in a form-fitting neoprene case and sounds better than most dedicated conference room phones. The Speak 510, shown in Figure 33.5 also has a USB chip enabling it to act as a speakerphone for mobile phones.

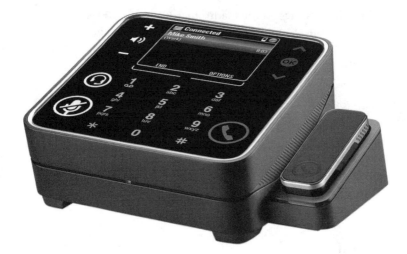

FIGURE 33.4   Plantronics Calisto 825.

FIGURE 33.5   Jabra Speak 510.

USB Handsets

Sometimes there's no need for a desk phone, but a user insists on having a handset form factor. These devices connect to a user's PC via USB but provide the familiar user interface and look and feel of a traditional phone handset. From the PC's perspective, the handset is just another audio device for Lync Communicator. However, for the user, the handset is a familiar tool that works the same way as the legacy phone they're used to. This can be a great tool to begin the process of empowering nontechnical users with UC. The Plantronics Calisto 540 shown in Figure 33.6 is a good example.

FIGURE 33.6   Plantronics Calisto 540.

Webcams

It's hard to say that anything is more revolutionary than desktop video. Even better is high-definition desktop video. Add integration with popular video conferencing solutions from Tandberg and Polycom and you have a complete solution. Adding video to a conversation has a profound impact. Although most newer laptops are equipped with webcams, USB-connected webcams are ideal for users with desktop systems or external monitors. USB webcams also usually offer far superior image quality as compared to webcams built into laptops.

Users with a webcam can share video with one user or multiple users at the same time. The receiving user sees a request bar asking to share video for the current conversation. The Microsoft RT Video codec constantly adapts to network conditions, providing the best quality for the conditions available.

Conferencing Devices

Lync 2013 opens a new world of conferencing devices, especially in the video world, with support for the new H.264 SVC codec.

The Polycom CX3000 conference phone is a true conference room solution. It offers a 3.5-inch QVGA screen with all the Lync integration functions users expect. Most important, it's a standalone device. It just needs power (AC or PoE) and an Ethernet cable; no PC required! It also allows for Outlook contacts search and one-click to join Lync conference calls.

The Polycom HDX room systems natively support the Microsoft RTV and H.264 SVC codecs, making them an easy choice for companies requiring integration between room devices and desktop video conferencing.

LifeSize codecs do not natively support any of the Lync HD video formats; however, they can be integrated through the use of the LifeSize RTV Video Bridge.

Best Practices

▶ Although some users will demand desk phones, in general headsets provide a better and more mobile overall solution.

▶ Replace legacy conferencing devices with Lync-enabled devices such as the Polycom CX3000.

▶ Wherever possible, deploy webcams to users. The addition of video adds a lot of value to communication and collaboration.

▶ Deploy headsets to new employees as part of their laptop/desktop system, and teach them to use the Unified Communications solution during orientation. Training is key, especially for nontechnical users.

▶ Encourage use by letting users choose from various devices depending on their situation.

Index

Numerics

A

A/V Edge Service, 114
    configuring, 127-128
    managing, 138
availability, DAG, 23
avoiding WAN acceleration, 841

B

B2BUA (back-to-back user agents)
    Mediation server role, 164
    third-party integration, 540
backend high availability, SQL servers, 365-368
background section (project design document), 808
backing up SQL database, 279-284
back-to-back firewalls, 821-822
Backup Registrar, 371
bandwidth
    estimating for CAC, 872
    video conferencing requirements, 522
bandwidth policy profiles, 871
baselines, establishing with Performance Monitor, 309-314
    CPU, 311
    disk activity, 312
    memory, 311-312
    network, 312
basic options, configuring for Windows client, 672-673
benefits of virtualization, 759-760
best practices
    Edge Servers, 144-145
    Lync Enterprise Voice deployments, 884
    Lync Server 2013 administration, 359
    Lync Server 2013 deployment, 809-811
    Persistent Chat, 246-247
bidirectional integration, SharePoint and Lync Server 2013, 16
blocking media over DirectAccess, 840-841

branch sites, 460-461
Brick Model, 23
browser client, Lync Web App
    architecture, 695
    authentication, 696
    configuring, 699-701
    content collaboration, 694
    deployment requirements, 699-702
    external user access, 701-702
    installing, 699
    join process, 697-698
    meetings, joining, 694
    port requirements, 696
    protocol flow, 698-699
    system requirements, 702
budget estimate section (project design document), 809
bulk tasks, completing with LSMS, 337
business cases for Lync Server 2013, ROI, 58-63
business goals, identifying
    departmental goals, 789-790
    high-level business goals, 788-789
business-hour collections, configuring, 507

C

CAC (Call Admission Control), 8
    bandwidth estimates, 872
    configuring, 481-486
    Internet rerouting, 872-873
    network inter-site policies, creating, 481
    network region routes, creating, 480-481
    PDP, migrating to Lync Server 2013, 422
    planning for, 869-871
CAL (Client Access List), 8, 13-14
call forwarding, 34-35, 48

D

How can we make this index more useful? Email us at indexes@samspublishing.com

F

G

How can we make this index more useful? Email us at indexes@samspublishing.com

S

How can we make this index more useful? Email us at indexes@samspublishing.com

W

WAN acceleration, avoiding, 841

WAN-dependent productivity, 868-869

watcher nodes (SCOM), 330-332

web conferencing, 6, 44, 55-56

    with Lync:Mac client, 644

    managing on Edge Servers, 137-138

Web Conferencing Edge Service, 113-114

web farm FQDNs, configuring, 299

web publishing rules, configuring for reverse proxy, 299-302

web services FQDN overrides, configuring for Director role, 199-201

webcams, 895

websites for Lync Web App, 696

wildcard certificates, 839

Window menu (Lync:Mac client), 639

Windows 8 mobile client, 29

Windows client

    audio calls, 679-680

    basic options, configuring, 672-673

    conferencing

        layout, changing, 684-685

        Meet Now function, 683

        meeting options, customizing, 685-688

    contacts, managing, 673-674

    conversations, archiving, 678-679

    files, sending and receiving, 682

    groups, managing, 674

    IM, 676

    installing, 670-671

    integration with other applications

        Office applications, 691

        Outlook, 690

    meetings, managing, 683-684

    peer-to-peer conversations, 676-682

persistent chat

    following rooms, 688

    topic feeds, 689

Recent Conversations view, 675

Relationship view, 675

sharing content, 681

shortcuts, 676-677

signing in, 671

Status view, 674-675

tabbed conversations, 678

Telephony view, 675-676

video calls, 680-681

Windows event logs, health monitoring, 318-321

Windows Firewall, 293-295

workflows for response groups, 503-510, 880-881

X-Y-Z

XML (Extensible Markup Language), 9

XMPP Gateway role, 27

XMPP Gateway Service, 114

XMPP proxy, configuring, 818

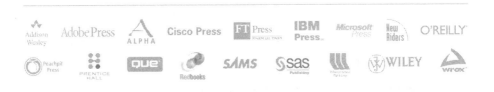

UNLEASHED

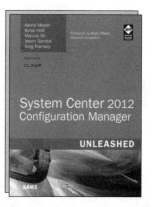

Unleashed takes you beyond the basics, providing an exhaustive, technically sophisticated reference for professionals who need to exploit a technology to its fullest potential. It's the best resource for practical advice from the experts, and the most in-depth coverage of the latest technologies.

informit.com/unleashed

System Center 2012 Configuration Manager (SCCM) Unleashed
ISBN-13: 9780672334375

OTHER UNLEASHED TITLES

System Center 2012 Operations Manager Unleashed
ISBN-13: 9780672335914

Microsoft System Center 2012 Unleashed
ISBN-13: 9780672336126

Microsoft Dynamics CRM 4 Integration Unleashed
ISBN-13: 9780672330544

Windows Phone 7.5 Unleashed
ISBN-13: 9780672333484

Microsoft SQL Server 2008 Reporting Services Unleashed
ISBN-13: 9780672330261

Microsoft SQL Server 2008 Integration Services Unleashed
ISBN-13: 9780672330322

Microsoft SQL Server 2008 Analysis Services Unleashed
ISBN-13: 9780672330018

C# 5.0 Unleashed
ISBN-13: 9780672336904

Windows 8 Apps with HTML5 and JavaScript Unleashed
ISBN-13: 9780672336058

ASP.NET Dynamic Data Unleashed
ISBN-13: 9780672335655

Microsoft Visual Studio 2012 Unleashed
ISBN-13: 9780672336256

WPF 4 Unleashed
ISBN-13: 9780672331190

Visual Basic 2012 Unleashed
ISBN-13: 9780672336317

Windows 8 Apps with XAML and C# Unleashed
ISBN-13: 9780672336010

Microsoft Exchange Server 2013 Unleashed
ISBN-13: 9780672336119

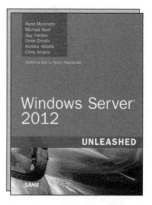

Windows Server 2012 Unleashed
ISBN-13: 9780672336225

SAMS

informit.com/sams

Microsoft®
Lync® Server
2013

UNLEASHED

SAMS

Alex Lewis
Tom Pacyk
David Ross
Randy Wintle

Safari
Books Online

FREE
Online Edition

Your purchase of *Microsoft Lync Server 2013 Unleashed* includes access to a free online edition for 45 days through the **Safari Books Online** subscription service. Nearly every Sams book is available online through **Safari Books Online**, along with thousands of books and videos from publishers such as Addison-Wesley Professional, Cisco Press, Exam Cram, IBM Press, O'Reilly Media, Prentice Hall, Que, and VMware Press.

Safari Books Online is a digital library providing searchable, on-demand access to thousands of technology, digital media, and professional development books and videos from leading publishers. With one monthly or yearly subscription price, you get unlimited access to learning tools and information on topics including mobile app and software development, tips and tricks on using your favorite gadgets, networking, project management, graphic design, and much more.

Activate your FREE Online Edition at
informit.com/safarifree

STEP 1: Enter the coupon code: ELIYKCB.

STEP 2: New Safari users, complete the brief registration form.
Safari subscribers, just log in.

If you have difficulty registering on Safari or accessing the online edition,
please e-mail customer-service@safaribooksonline.com